THE REMINISCENCES OF
Vice Admiral William P. Lawrence
U.S. Navy (Retired)

INTERVIEWED BY
Paul Stillwell

U.S. Naval Institute • Annapolis, Maryland

Copyright © 2011

Preface

The concept that shines throughout this oral history is honor. It was a guiding star in Admiral Lawrence's life. He grew up in Tennessee, part of the mid-American Bible belt, and embodied its values throughout his life. His heroes when he was a youth were Confederate generals from the Civil War. In particular, he admired General Robert E. Lee. Lawrence studied history and biography avidly and used the leadership principles he learned in shaping his own ways of dealing with his fellow human beings.

An early example came when he was the top-ranking midshipman at the Naval Academy. He was bothered by the less-than-ethical practice of fellow midshipmen who shared quiz answers with each other. He joined with other midshipman leaders, including Ross Perot, to develop an honor concept for the Naval Academy. They deemed it both fairer and more pragmatic than the honor code in practice at the Military Academy at West Point. With some modification, Lawrence's honor concept remains in practice at Annapolis to this day.

As a young officer, Lawrence became a naval aviator and joined Fighter Squadron 193, which did pioneering work in night aircraft carrier operations with jets. In the process he developed a close relationship with squadron mate Alan Shepard; within ten years, Shepard became the first American astronaut to fly in space. As a test pilot, Lawrence was the first naval aviator to fly a Navy plane, the F8U-3 Crusader III, at twice the speed of sound. Because of the knowledge and skill he demonstrated as a test pilot, he was assigned in the late 1950s to the staff of Rear Admiral Thomas Moorer, who commanded Carrier Division Six. Lawrence offers a number of insights into the personality and leadership style of Moorer, who later became the Chief of Naval Operations and Chairman of the Joint Chiefs of Staff.

As a pilot, Lawrence helped develop the operational concepts and training for the introduction of the noteworthy F-4 Phantom fighter into the fleet in the early 1960s. But he'd had a few aviation mishaps along the way. Concerned about his wife's peace of mind, he left flying to become navigator of the heavy cruiser *Newport News*. But the pace of surface-ship operations proved too tame for him, and he went back into aviation as a member of Fighter Squadron 14. That tour was cut short when he was yanked out to become senior aide to General Paul D. Adams, a tough Army general who was in the newly created joint-service billet of Commander in Chief Strike Command. Several senior Navy admirals balked at cooperating with this manifestation of jointness. As a result, Lawrence was handpicked because of his diplomatic qualities to serve as a go-between to help forge an alliance between his own service and the Army general. The two men developed a personal bond in the process.

When it came time to go back to the cockpit, Lawrence became the executive officer and then commanding officer of Fighter Squadron 143, better known as the "Pukin' Dogs." His time in command lasted less than a month, because he was shot down over North Vietnam in June 1967 and remained a prisoner of war for five and a half years. In that grim, demanding setting, Lawrence demonstrated extraordinary courage and leadership—asserting command, communicating with his fellow prisoners to keep them going, and enduring horrific torture to avoid being exploited by his captors.

A new trial awaited him when he was released from prison in early 1973. He learned that his wife had divorced him in absentia and married another man. He reluctantly accepted the fait accompli and then worked diligently to provide strong backing for his children to put them on productive paths. Former prisoner John McCain served as matchmaker in getting Lawrence together with Diane Wilcox Rauch, whom he married in 1974.

Fortunately for the released Navy POWs, the service's leadership fostered opportunities for the men to get their careers back on track. After a year at the National War College, Lawrence was selected for flag rank and returned to an operational command, this time as Commander Light Attack Wing Pacific Fleet. That was followed by three years in the head office of naval aviation in the Pentagon.

The Chief of Naval Operations in the late 1970s was Admiral Thomas Hayward, who had known Lawrence since their days as test pilots. He assigned him to serve as superintendent of the Naval Academy. The oral history provides a richly detailed account of Lawrence's three years in Annapolis. He presided when the first class of female midshipmen graduated in 1980 and made it clear by his actions that he strongly supported women's presence and their opportunities for success. He also won praise for his openness in dealing with the news media. When untoward events occurred at the academy, Lawrence made sure the media were informed, rather than letting leaks and attempted cover-ups lead to far more critical coverage.

From 1981 to 1983, as a vice admiral, Lawrence commanded the Third Fleet in the Pacific and led innovative work in developing operational concepts for the new Tomahawk cruise missile. He also pushed for multi-carrier exercises in the North Pacific to test doctrine and to see what sort of reaction he might evoke with operations near the Soviet Union. The reaction was minimal, leading him to conclude that the Soviet Navy did not have aggressive intent.

Admiral Lawrence's final tour of active duty was a trying one. He had many challenges as Chief of Personnel. Among them was that of dealing with the desires of Secretary of the Navy John Lehman in relation to flag selection boards and the assignments to be filled by various flag officers. Lawrence spoke candidly about examples of the ways in which he and two successive Chiefs of Naval Operations felt frustrated in their dealings with Secretary Lehman.

Admiral Lawrence's active career came to a premature ending when he fell into a case of clinical depression in 1985. It seriously affected his ability to do his job and prevented him for moving on to his projected four-star assignment as Vice Chief of Naval Operations. Instead, he retired on disability and spent four years recovering his health, thanks to support provided by Ross Perot, whom he had known since they were midshipmen. In this part of the account, as throughout the entire oral history, Admiral Lawrence was candid. He concluded that he might well have been a victim of his own devotion to fulfilling high standards of service and thus had never taken time off to unwind after being released from prison. The interviews that form this memoir came shortly after the admiral's recovery from his illness. I am grateful for the relationship he and I developed in that time.

In winding up this project, I thank Mary Ripley and Sue Sweeney of the Naval Institute for scheduling its completion to tie in with the advent of the guided missile destroyer *William P. Lawrence*. The ship is due to be commissioned in early June of this year in Mobile, Alabama, and then join the fleet. To that end, I have listened to and compared the 22 tape recorded interviews with the corresponding transcripts and made corrections as necessary. I have also edited the raw transcript with an eye to improving accuracy, clarity, and smoothness while still retaining the conversational flavor of the interviews.

In the process, I have been fortunate to get to know Diane Lawrence, the admiral's gracious and accomplished wife. She also went through the entire edited transcript, did some tweaking of her own, and gave her blessing to the resulting text on behalf of her husband. I inserted dozens of footnotes to provide additional information for the benefit of researchers and other readers. Because a considerable segment of the memoir deals with Admiral Lawrence's time at the Naval Academy, as both star midshipman and later as superintendent, I made heavy use of the academy's Nimitz Library and particularly its special collections branch and archives to look up dates, names, and other information. Jennifer Bryan and David D'Onofrio were especially helpful in finding answers to my questions. Janis Jorgensen of the Naval Institute staff has been a friend of long-standing. It was she who coordinated the printing and binding of the finished history.

In completing this volume, the Naval Institute expresses its gratitude to the Tawani Foundation and the Pritzker Military Library of Chicago for their generous financial support of the oral history program that produced this memoir.

Paul Stillwell
U.S. Naval Institute
April 2011

VICE ADMIRAL WILLIAM PORTER LAWRENCE
UNITED STATES NAVY (RETIRED)

William Porter Lawrence was born in Nashville, Tennessee, on 13 January 1930, the son of Robert L. Lawrence Jr. and Tennie Brewer Lawrence. He entered the U.S. Naval Academy, Annapolis, Maryland, on appointment from his native state in 1947. He graduated with distinction and was commissioned ensign on 1 June 1951.

Following his graduation from the Naval Academy, Ensign Lawrence entered flight training at Naval Air Station, Pensacola, Florida, and on 7 November 1952 was designated a naval aviator. He continued training until February 1953 and the following month became a member of Fighter Squadron 193 (VF-193) as an all-weather fighter pilot. While serving with that squadron, he participated in two Western Pacific deployments on board the aircraft carrier *Oriskany* (CVA-34). During the period from October to December 1955, he attended the Aviation Safety Course at the University of Southern California in Los Angeles, after which he had test pilot training at the Naval Air Test Center, Patuxent River, Maryland. In August 1956 he graduated number one in his class then joined the Test Center staff as a test pilot. He was the first naval aviator to fly Mach II, which he did in the F8U-3 Crusader III.

In June 1959 Lieutenant Lawrence reported as flag lieutenant to Commander Carrier Division Six and in October 1960 joined Fighter Squadron 101 (VF-101) to serve as assistant operations officer. He was navigator on board the heavy cruiser *Newport News* (CA-148) from June 1961 to June 1962, then had duty as maintenance officer of Fighter Squadron 14 (VF-14), which deployed on board the aircraft carrier *Franklin D. Roosevelt* (CVA-42). From February 1964 to January 1966, he served as senior aide to Commander in Chief U.S. Strike Command, General Paul D. Adams, U.S. Army.

Commander Lawrence had prospective executive officer training with Fighter Squadron 121 (VF-121) during the period from February to July 1966, then joined Fighter Squadron 143 (VF-143) as executive officer. He was involved in combat operations in 1966 while deployed on board the aircraft carrier *Ranger* (CVA-61). He assumed command of VF-143 in June 1967 during a break from Vietnam War operations on board the aircraft carrier *Constellation* (CVA-64). While CO, he was shot down over North Vietnam on 28 June and held as a prisoner of war until his release on 4 March 1973. He was awarded the Distinguished Service Medal for his inspirational leadership of fellow prisoners.

After repatriation, Captain Lawrence recuperated at Memphis Naval Hospital, Millington, Tennessee. He reported in August 1973 for duty as a student at the National War College in Washington, D.C., and earned a master's degree in international affairs from George Washington University. Following his promotion to rear admiral in 1974, he spent a year as Commander Light Attack Wing Pacific Fleet, and in 1975 reported to the Pentagon. He served first as Director, Aviation Programs Division on the staff of the Deputy Chief of Naval Operations (Air Warfare), then as Assistant DCNO. From August

1978 to August 1981 he was superintendent of the Naval Academy and from September 1981 to August 1983 he served as Commander Third Fleet, based in Hawaii. His final tour of active duty, from September 1983 to December 1985, was as Chief of Naval Personnel and Deputy Chief of Naval Operations (Manpower, Personnel and Training). He officially retired from active duty on 1 February 1986.

From 1986 to 1991, Vice Admiral Lawrence occupied the Chair of Naval Leadership at the Naval Academy and from 1991 to 1994 served as president of the Association of Naval Aviation. Among his awards are three Distinguished Service Medals, three Silver Star Medas, the Distinguished Flying Cross, the Bronze Star, numerous Air Medals, and two Purple Hearts.

Admiral Lawrence died 2 December 2005 at Crownsville, Maryland. He was survived by Diane Wilcox Lawrence and their children, William Jr., Fritz, Laurie, and Wendy.

Deed of Gift

The U.S. Naval Institute is hereby authorized to make available to individuals, libraries, and other repositories of its choosing the tapes and/or transcripts of 22 oral history interviews concerning the life and naval career of the late Vice Admiral William P. Lawrence. The Naval Institute may also, at its discretion, use the material in electronic/digital format, including posting on the Internet. The interviews were recorded in the period from September 1990 to March 1991 by Admiral Lawrence in collaboration with Paul Stillwell for the U.S. Naval Institute.

The undersigned does hereby release and assign to the U.S. Naval Institute the rights and title to these interviews, with the exception that the undersigned retains the right to use the material for her own purposes, as she sees fit. The copyright in both the oral and transcribed versions shall be the property of the U.S. Naval Institute. The tape recordings of the interviews are and will remain the property of the U.S. Naval Institute.

Signed and sealed this 22nd day of March 2011.

Diane W. Lawrence
on behalf of William P. Lawrence

The United States Naval Institute gratefully acknowledges

Robert S. Madden

for his generous support in underwriting the oral history of

Vice Admiral William P. Lawrence U.S. Navy (Retired)

Interview Number 1 with Vice Admiral William P. Lawrence, U.S. Navy (Retired)
Place: U.S. Naval Institute, Annapolis, Maryland
Date: Monday, 17 September 1990

Paul Stillwell: It's a pleasure to see you here today, Admiral Lawrence. You've been on my target list for some time because of your career and your experiences. We especially try to get the superintendents of the Naval Academy into our collection.

We begin a series, really, at the beginning of an individual's life. You mentioned you want to start even before that with something on your ancestry, please.

Admiral Lawrence: Well, I'm very much a student of my ancestors. I think it's just good for any family to try to keep alive family traditions. So, although I don't know my family tree in the detail I would like, I've studied it at least back through my great-grandfathers.

I basically spring from an Anglo-Saxon heritage. My ancestors principally came from the British Isles, and even though there was an extensive German immigration to the middle Tennessee area where I grew up, I'm not really aware of many Germans in my ancestry. It was principally Scotch-Irish, English, and Welsh. But one thing that I have noted in reading the history of my ancestors is that there is a very strong public service tradition.

My great-grandfather on my mother's side was Sterling Brewer. He was born in North Carolina in 1770 and served in the Revolutionary War—probably as an enlisted man because of his youth. Then he obtained a Revolutionary War grant, which was very common in those days for those who served in the colonial wars. He was given land out of the new territories. So he came into middle Tennessee shortly after Tennessee had become a state in 1796.* He became a very prominent farmer. He ran for public office and became the speaker of the State Senate, who was the person next in succession to the governor. Apparently, in those days they didn't have a lieutenant governor as they do now, so it was the Speaker of the Senate. So he filled that position in addition to being a very prominent farmer. So he was a real public servant in his own way.

---

* On 1 June 1796, Tennessee was admitted to the Union as the 16th state.

Then my great-grandfather, his son, was Sterling Brewer Jr., and he was a Methodist minister and educator. He was a circuit rider, a type of preachers they had back in that time. They traveled by horseback out there in the small farm communities in middle Tennessee.

My grandfather was another Sterling Brewer; his career was as an educator and writer. Although I cannot determine that he obtained a college degree, he was well educated in the schools available at that time. He devoted his whole life to education and did a considerable amount of writing. He and his brother-in-law, Samuel Albert Link, formed a private school in middle Tennessee. He was the brother of Sterling Brewer's wife, formerly Maizie Link. He was listed in *Who's Who in America* back in the late 1800s-early 1900s, because of his reputation as an educator. He was quite well educated, probably holding, at that time, what was comparable to a PhD degree from a small school up in Illinois and the University of Nashville. So I really was aware of that tradition of scholarship and public service from the time I was a young boy.

On my father's side, my great-great-grandfather also came into middle Tennessee in the early 1800s on a Revolutionary War grant and settled on a farm in a place called Beech Grove, Tennessee, about 30 miles southeast of Nashville, the capital of Tennessee. They were principally farmers, although my great-grandfather, born in 1847, William Thomas Lawrence, was very much a public servant. Even when he was in his 30s, he was the deputy sheriff and the justice of the peace for the little community of Beech Grove, Tennessee, a farm community.

As I read a history of that Beech Grove area, I was really impressed with the high level of civilization, so to speak, that existed in those farm communities. People didn't travel very much, because there was no public transportation, and cars were not available. Basically their whole lives were focused on their communities. They developed a very fine educational system, and this was before public education. They had what was called the Beech Grove Academy, which at one time in the history of that community had college-level courses. My great-grandfather spent his whole career as a farmer. After he retired from farming, he moved into Manchester, the county seat of Coffey County. He became a trustee, which is similar to a commissioner of the county. It is an elective office that one had to run for and campaign. His daughter, my Aunt Mary, was primarily his campaign manager and office manager. So he was quite a public servant.

My grandfather chose not to be a farmer; he left the farm and moved to Nashville, which is my home. He was a traveling salesman, but he was very public service oriented.

Paul Stillwell: In what ways?

Admiral Lawrence: Well, he was a Mason, as many Protestant men were, and he did a lot of charitable-type work under the Masons. His main work was in volunteerism, as opposed to public office. As a second career, he volunteered to help the county sheriff run the county jails, because I think he wanted to help rehabilitate people who had been jailed. This was when he was in his 60s. When World War II broke out, he wanted to do something for defense and he went to work in a defense plant in Milan, Tennessee, which was an arsenal for ammunition. So he was very public service oriented.

My father was the first one in the Lawrence line (that we can determine from history) who went to college.* He went to Vanderbilt University in Nashville and was a distinguished engineering graduate in 1925. He also was a very fine athlete; he played baseball and football and was a very fine lineman at Vanderbilt. The teams were ranked nationally in those days.

He went into public service and became the director of the city water works. Then, as the city developed a municipal sewage system, he became the director of water and sewerage services in Nashville, a job he held for about 45 years. He was purely a public servant. So there was that tradition of public service from both sides—my mother's and my father's side—and also my dad's great interest in sports. As a result, I grew up very much a scholar-athlete. I really love sports, and I played sports very actively from the time I was a young boy. I think I played something like 11 years of organized football, counting the time here at the Naval Academy. And it was always equally important to me that I do well in school. Somehow that aspiration was imparted to me at a young age.

---

* His father was Robert Landy Lawrence Jr.

Paul Stillwell: How much of this family tradition was passed down to you at an early age?

Admiral Lawrence: Well, very much. I was quite close to my father and my grandfather. My grandfather was widowed; he lost his wife through the influenza epidemic in 1918.[*] He was a young man, only about 36-37 years old, when he lost his wife, and so he lived with our family. We had a large home in Nashville, and my grandfather had an apartment there. I spent a lot of time with him, and he used to tell me stories about the Civil War, for example. His father was too young to be in the Civil War. I guess he was born in 1847. His older brother went off to be in the war, and my great-grandfather took care of his widowed mother and ran the farm.

My grandfather would tell me about his father's experience from the Civil War, because the federal troops under Grant invaded the Confederacy in 1862, capturing Fort Henry and Fort Donelson on the Tennessee and the Cumberland rivers.[†] After Grant captured those forts, his troops captured Nashville. Middle Tennessee was occupied from mid-1862 through the remainder of the war. My great-grandfather, as a teenage boy, was with his widowed mother on the farm and saw federal troops. In fact, federal troops came and took food from them. So my grandfather had a lot of stories of the Civil War.

He told me about a famous Civil War hero, Sam Davis, who had been hanged by the federal troops as a young scout.[‡] One of his responsibilities was to go behind enemy lines to contact the spies and bring information back out. Of course, they had the law of war to respect in those days, so you had to wear your uniform, or if you didn't and you were caught behind enemy lines, you would be treated as a spy. So Sam Davis wore his uniform as a scout and was captured. The federal troops knew he was making contact with a spy. Sam Davis refused to give the identity of the spy and was hanged. He made a statement before he was hanged that, "If I had a thousand lives to live, I would give

---

[*] In the worldwide influenza epidemic of 1918-19 some 20 million people died, including more than 500,000 in the United States.
[†] Brigadier General Ulysses S. Grant, USA. Later he rose to lieutenant general and commanded all Union armies. The capture of Fort Donelson in February 1862 was the North's first major victory in the war.
[‡] Federal troops captured Private Sam Davis of the First Tennessee Infantry on 20 November 1863 near Minor Hill. He was found to be carrying concealed documents and court-martialed. He was hanged near Pulaski, Tennessee on 27 November 1863, his 21st birthday.

them all before I would betray a friend." My grandfather told me about that at a young age, and so I just had great admiration for Sam Davis. He was one of my early heroes, as was Andrew Jackson.[*]

With my interest in sports, scholarship, and having these heroes from Tennessee history, just seemed to make it natural for me to be inclined towards a military career. And Tennessee has produced some famous naval officers. David Glasgow Farragut was from Knoxville, Tennessee—the first admiral in the Navy.[†] Matthew Fontaine Maury was the first oceanographer in the Navy.[‡] He was from Columbia, Tennessee.

We had two four-star admirals from Tennessee in World War I. Admiral Gleaves was commander of the transport force that took the troops across to Europe.[§] Another four-star admiral was the Commander in Chief of the Pacific Fleet in the World War I period, because the Germans had naval forces out there.[**] He took his forces from the Caribbean area, through the Panama Canal, and out into the Pacific.

Anyway, my father and grandfather would tell me all these stories about both the naval and military tradition. Of course, I was very much caught up in the Civil War, because I grew up in an area where there was quite a bit of Civil War fighting, like the Battle of Nashville, the Battle of Franklin, the Battle of Murfreesboro, Fort Donelson. In those days, in the '30s, Robert E. Lee, was every young boy's hero in the South.[††] In every school in the South you wanted two pictures: George Washington and Robert E. Lee. A school would never have a picture of Abraham Lincoln. It took me many years after I was an adult before I realized that Abraham Lincoln was a great man; we didn't really talk a lot about him.

Paul Stillwell: Would you say there was a legacy of bitterness in that era?

---

[*] Andrew Jackson of Tennessee, a hero of the War of 1812, served as U.S. President, 1829-37.
[†] Farragut was famous for victories on the Mississippi and at Mobile Bay. In July 1862 he was promoted to rear admiral, a first for the U.S. Navy.
[‡] Maury (1806-1873) was born in Virginia but moved to Tennessee as a child. He was the first superintendent of the U.S. Naval Observatory in Washington, D.C., from 1844 to 1861, at which time he was a commander. With the advent of the Civil War he transferred to the Confederate Navy.
[§] In July 1917 Rear Admiral Albert Gleaves became commander of the Navy's Cruiser and Transport Force. He was promoted to vice admiral in December 1918 and to four-star admiral in September 1919, when he became Commander in Chief U.S. Asiatic Fleet.
[**] Admiral William B. Caperton, USN, served as Commander in Chief U.S. Pacific Fleet, 1916 to 1919.
[††] General Robert E. Lee commanded the Confederate Army in the Civil War.

Admiral Lawrence: Well, not really. That had pretty much passed by my father's generation, but it had not for my great-grandfather. My great-grandfather held great bitterness. He recalled the time that the federal troops came to the farm and required his mother to cook for them and give them food. They weren't treated terribly, because there was basically a respect for the laws of warfare. But my great-grandfather, who was a very strong-willed man, refused until his dying day to speak to a neighbor in that area. He felt that this man's family had consorted with the federals, collaborated with the federals, cooperated with the federals. Because there wasn't a uniformity of support for the Confederacy, particularly in Tennessee, which is a border state. In east Tennessee, large segments of people just did not support secession, even at the end of the war.

I remember when I was a boy growing up in a strong Democratic area, my grandfather, great aunts, and so forth, used to say, "There are Republicans over there in east Tennessee."

So I said, "God, that's terrible, to have Republicans."

But one time my great-grandfather was down visiting with us in Nashville. My father, as part of his business, had an engineer colleague from Scranton, Pennsylvania, and my great-grandfather would not come out and meet him. So that was still very strong in his generation. But my father, of course, a college man, didn't share that deep feeling. But it was there. When I was a boy growing up, we displayed the Confederate flag just as much as we displayed the U.S. flag. I had many Confederate heroes: Sam Davis, Nathan Bedford Forrest, Robert E. Lee.[*] I knew more about the Confederate generals than I did about the Northern generals.

Paul Stillwell: Was there a sort of romantic image connected with all this?

Admiral Lawrence: Oh, yes. Of course, Robert E. Lee, to us young boys growing up in the South, epitomized a real leader. We had great reverence toward him. He was the type of individual you wanted to emulate in your life. Then, of course, you'd hear all the stories about Nathan Bedford Forrest, the great cavalry general, who said, "Get there the

---

[*] Forrest entered the Confederate Army in Tennessee as a private and eventually reached the rank of lieutenant general.

fustest with the mostest." Another southern general we knew a lot about was General Hood, who was commanding the Confederate forces in the Battle of Franklin, the Battle of Nashville.* I heard all about these men as a boy growing up. We in the South got good treatment of certain phases of the Civil War in our history as we were growing up.

Paul Stillwell: Probably a relatively one-sided treatment

Admiral Lawrence: Yes, but not as one-sided as you would think. I was fortunate in that my high school principal was a doctor.† He had a PhD in history, and he used to teach a history course. He was a very broad-minded person, well educated, and so he'd try to give a very accurate presentation of history. It wasn't really biased toward the southern point of view.

Then, when I was a midshipman, we had to write a term paper. I chose to write my term paper on the gunboat operations on the western rivers—the Ohio, Tennessee, and the Cumberland—during the Civil War. About eight or ten shallow-draft Navy gunboats supported Grant. The flag officer who headed that group was Andrew Hull Foote, and that was an interesting phase of naval history.

But, even at that time, I developed a great respect for General Grant, because he really made his name out there in the West. He captured Fort Donelson, was in the Battle of Shiloh, and was the one who captured Vicksburg. Then Lincoln brought him in during the final year of the war to command the Army of Northern Virginia because no other general was successful in defeating Lee and capturing Richmond. So as a midshipman, I developed a high degree of respect for U.S. Grant and Sherman. Sherman was working under Grant at Vicksburg and Shiloh, and also in his march to sea after capturing Atlanta.‡

I was really quite a student of history at that young age. As I tell the midshipmen

---

* John Bell Hood was a full general in the Confederate Army; Fort Hood, Texas, is named in his honor. Hood's service is covered in a book written by an individual who entered the Naval Academy a few years after Lawrence graduated. See Commander Thomas B. Buell, USN (Ret.), *The Warrior Generals: Combat Leadership in the Civil War* (New York: Crown, 1997).
† Lawrence attended West End High School in Nashville.
‡ General William Tecumseh Sherman, USA, an individual long reviled in the South for his scorched-earth campaign.

now, I guess nothing has been more value to me during my military career than my knowledge of history. I don't think there's any profession where the lessons of history are so relevant as they are in the military profession. I called on my knowledge of history many, many times in helping me make decisions.

Robert E. Lee was the superintendent at West Point, and I went back and very carefully and read about his experiences at West Point. He had some challenges, some disciplinary challenges, and that was of value to me.

So this was interesting history, which was fostered by my father, my grandfather and my relatives, and by my high school principal. I have carried that with me for the rest of my life. I guess the key point I'm making about it at this point in my life is all those influences from family and teachers, and having grown up as a teenager during World War II, I think really developed this interest in the military profession. I think I had aspired to come to the Naval Academy around the eighth or ninth grade. This was probably about 1943-44, right in the middle of World War II. I'm sure that the influence of World War II was a big factor, but also my father was an engineer, and he always told me that the Naval Academy had a very fine engineering program. I think that was a big factor, because I was very much interested in a scholarship, and I aspired to be an engineer like my father.

Paul Stillwell: Was that what steered you here, rather than to the Military Academy?

Admiral Lawrence: Yes, I think it was my father's perception that the Naval Academy had a high-quality academic program here, particularly in engineering. And I'm sure part of it was just the mystique of the Navy. Those of us who grew up in landlocked areas always seem to be attracted to Navy.

The other factor that attracted me, of course, was athletics. I remember, from the time I was a very young boy, always listening to the Army-Navy football game on the radio. So it was interest in athletics and scholarship and the patriotism of World War

II—great admiration for the military.

I did well in high school. I was a very fine athlete and student; I was all-state in basketball, and I was all-city in football. I was class valedictorian, president of the student body, and commanding officer of the ROTC unit.* So I really, really worked hard to try and do everything I could as well as I could.

Paul Stillwell: What qualities led to your being chosen for these leadership positions?

Admiral Lawrence: I just don't know. I think that from the time I was a young lad, I always seemed to have some inherent leadership qualities. And I see so much that I gained from both of my parents. My father was very strong-willed. He had a high degree of determination, persistence, and he had very strong convictions.

My mother was a lot different from my father.† She was a very strong person, but she was very compassionate. She was not really vocal and strident in any way, but she had a great facility for attracting people as friends. They seemed to respect her for her poise and sense of calm. So I guess I gained a lot of that from my mother, but I can see so much of this determination and strong conviction from my father. A lot of people who know me think I'm basically mild-mannered and easygoing, which I think I get from my mother. They don't realize that beneath that exterior are very strong convictions and feelings. But I just seemed to have a very strong, natural sense of leadership from my early age. I think playing a lot of sports fostered this leadership, because, particularly in that time, inspirational leadership was very much a component of sports. You always respected your captains of your teams; you aspired to be a captain. As I point out to so many young people, I had more heroes growing up than I could keep track of. It saddens me very much that heroes for young people seem to not be part of the lifestyle nowadays.

Paul Stillwell: Well, now the heroes are rock stars and so forth.

---

* ROTC – reserve officers' training corps.
† His mother was Tennie Brewer Lawrence.

Admiral Lawrence: Yes. My heroes were principally fine athletes and principally military men. But I also grew up very much respecting Franklin D. Roosevelt.* We were all Democrats in the South and, of course, Franklin Roosevelt was a Democrat. We all had great reverence for Franklin Roosevelt.

Paul Stillwell: Did the Depression affect your family much?†

Admiral Lawrence: My father was a civil servant, so he was not impacted like those who were not. And we had a car through the Depression; we had a maid. Down in the South you could have maids very inexpensively, and that's another aspect of my makeup. Maybe I inherited this from my mother, who was a very compassionate person—but I have an innate sympathy for the blacks. I just sensed at an early age, "Something's wrong that there's such a different standard of living among the blacks than among the whites." We always had a black maid as I was growing up, and ours for many years was Mary Watkins. She received a dollar a day, plus car fare, and I think her car fare was ten cents a day. We used to have the old streetcars.

Paul Stillwell: Well, I think toting privileges probably were included, weren't they, so she could carry home leftovers?

Admiral Lawrence: Yes. Oh sure. But, as I got older, about ten years old, I felt deep compassion towards Mary Watkins. She was a single mother, as so many black women are. She seemed to have a sense of resignation towards life, that she had been relegated to this situation, and there was just not much hope to improve the situation. I remember she used to take me sometime out to the shanties on the northern side of town, where she lived. I noticed that the blacks used to laugh, and they were very spiritual, and I'd say to myself, "How can these people be so happy when they really don't have so much?"

---

* Franklin D. Roosevelt was President of the United States from 4 March 1933 to 12 April 1945.
† Following the crash of the New York Stock Exchange in late October 1929, the United States was plunged into the Great Depression, from which it did not recover until the nation geared up for World War II at the beginning of the 1940s. The Depression was marked by high unemployment and many business failures.

So at a young age I developed attitudes that have stayed with me for the rest of my life. But I know that I am very unusual for a southerner in my attitudes towards blacks. I've always been one who has worked to improve the status of blacks, push for affirmative action, equal opportunity. In fact, I used to irritate my brothers, because when we moved to a bus system in Nashville, I used to go back and sit with the blacks in the rear of the bus, because I just sensed that it was wrong that they had to sit back there. I wanted to show that I was one white who wanted to be with them. My brothers would say, "Why do you go back there and sit with those blacks?" Something just made me want to do it.

The other thing I sensed at an early age was that things were not equal for women. I think part of it was because I had great admiration and love and respect for my mother more than for my father. I certainly respected my father for all his qualities and his profession, but I had an adoration for my mother; I didn't for my father. My father never mistreated my mother, but he was very much the southern patriarch, that he made all the decisions, and he said, "This was the way it's going to be," and nobody argued. That was very much a southern tradition. His father had been that way, his grandfather, and I saw my mother many times have to go along with his policies, and that bothered me, because of, I guess, my great respect for her.

But my mother was certainly a leader in her own right. She was president of the PTA several times; she was president of the women's club. In her own element, with other women, she was always a leader, but at home she had to be, basically, subservient to my father. My father would never have been seen in the kitchen doing anything. In his 70s, he used to make coffee, and he thought that was a big deal. But you'd never see my father even volunteer to help at all in any of the menial chores in the house. But that also was the southern tradition. I sensed that my mother didn't have it as good as my father in many respects.

So that was another thing I carried with me to adulthood: this compassion for blacks and minorities and for women. I guess that's why I developed a reputation in the Navy as being a woman's advocate. I was here as superintendent when we had the first graduating class with women.* I really fought hard to increase the roles of women. I think it all came from my early years.

When I was in the eighth grade, we had to write a history of the United States, and I developed an outline for it. One of the chapters was called "The Contribution of Women." In the first sentence I said, "Women have never received the recognition that they deserve for their contribution to U.S. history." I had a whole chapter on Florence Nightingale and people like that.† So I developed that feeling at an early age.

Paul Stillwell: That's an unusual degree of sensitivity for a young man.

Admiral Lawrence: Yes, it is. I just don't know now what motivated me to do that.

Paul Stillwell: Did your parents impart values on the question of race?

Admiral Lawrence: Yes. I observed this sense of compassion on the part of my parents. In other words, my father used to really make an effort, as the director of the city water works, to employ blacks and to take care of blacks. One thing that he always fostered in his department was a food basket campaign at Christmas. His department produced a certain number of food baskets that we used to take out to disadvantaged people—principally blacks. He did this even though he was, as I say, a typical southern patriarch, and he had a lot of the vices of a typical southerner.

He also demonstrated his sense of compassion for the blacks, and particularly the way he took care of his black employees and tried to employ blacks. I remember going with him to work sites, where they were laying pipelines or doing some other construction. The black laborers would be there, and he knew all of them by their first names. They would always show great affection towards him. As a young boy, I'd visit with my relatives who had farms. I enjoyed working among the blacks, out doing farm

---

* Vice Admiral Lawrence served as Superintendent of the Naval Academy from August 1978 to August 1981. Women were first admitted to the Naval Academy as midshipmen in the summer of 1976, the same year the other federal service academies admitted women cadets. The first women graduated in 1980.

† Florence Nightingale (1820-1910) was a celebrated British nurse and writer. She became widely known for her pioneering nursing work in the Crimean War in the 1850s. Admiral Lawrence may have been thinking of Clarissa "Clara" Barton, a prominent American nurse who was a contemporary of Nightingale.

work, and I was always amazed. I said, "My gosh, these blacks are happy; how can they be happy?" That was a real personal perplexity in me.

Paul Stillwell: Did you ever come up with an answer?

Admiral Lawrence: I never did.

A black man named Frank Roberts did yard work for us, and he always was happy. Every time he saw us, he'd laugh and say, "Great to see you." But you could see his toes in his shoes, and his clothes were ragged, and he lived over in a shanty in the other part of town.

As I say, I was very close to many blacks as I was growing up.

Paul Stillwell: Well, there's a saying that people are as happy or unhappy as they decide to be.

Admiral Lawrence: Yes.

Paul Stillwell: It depends on what expectations you set.

Admiral Lawrence: But I think those of us who grew up in the South have an inherent sense of respect and compassion towards the blacks, a sense that doesn't exist in other parts of the country, because we really grew up with blacks. I used to play with black children, and we had this black maid whom I was very close to.

I've always been a great proponent of improving the situation for blacks, and in my adult years I get very frustrated when I'll try to do some things and I don't feel that the black leadership is doing all they could. A lot of times people, such as myself, who are really, genuinely, trying to help blacks, would be caught up in these criticisms of racism that you see often.

I remember one time, when I was superintendent, I brought Benjamin Hooks here to be a speaker to the midshipmen. He was the head of the NAACP.* He treated my wife and me very poorly. Here we were trying to be very hospitable, open, lay out the welcome mat, and he treated us with this kind of contempt. That's one thing I've come to realize that you just have to accept in today's world—that the blacks have a deep-rooted resentment towards the whites for the fact that we held them in slavery for 200 years. Then, when we released them from slavery in 1863, through the Emancipation Proclamation by Lincoln, we really didn't do much to help them. So they have this deep-rooted bitterness towards us, and you just simply have to accept that.

Paul Stillwell: Well, you've talked of the things that were handed down in your family; things were undoubtedly handed down in his.

Admiral Lawrence: That's right. So people get all up in arms when they see the Marion Barry, the fact that he was convicted on only a misdemeanor and acquitted on at least ten or so other serious allegations of wrongdoing—felony-type things.† You just have to understand that that deep-rooted bitterness towards the whites overrides every other consideration, even respect for justice and all that. As we work to try to help improve the situation of blacks, we just have to live with that as whites, that they are going to manifest a lot of bitterness towards us. And I think justifiably. Gosh, they were held in bondage for 250 years. We destroyed any sense of tradition, roots, or culture that they had. You just can't expect a race that's been through that to have all of the traditions, customs, and so forth that govern our lives.

Paul Stillwell: Well, even after emancipation, it was a very paternalistic system for many years.

---

* NAACP – National Association for the Advancement of Colored People. Benjamin L. Hooks was executive director of the organization from 1977 to 1993.
† In January 1990, the year of this interview, Mayor Marion S. Barry Jr. of Washington, D.C., was taped smoking crack cocaine. He was convicted of possession and served six months in federal prison.

Admiral Lawrence: Yes, it was paternalistic, but it was very much exploitation—cheap labor. In fact, in some ways, white people in the South had it better after slavery than before, because the blacks worked for us, and yet we didn't have to take care of them. They had to go back out into their little shanty communities and fend for themselves; whereas, when you had slaves, you were responsible for their health and welfare. Fortunately, the strong religious influences that existed down in the South helped bring the blacks to a point they wouldn't have achieved otherwise just by religious traditions. Because there was respect among the slave owners for the importance of family and religious values and so forth. Many of those slaves had a family structure that has largely disappeared today with all the single mothers. They say the endangered species today in our society is the black male. Every indicator—health, education, every well-being statistic, as I call it—is declining for the black male. That's one of the great threats.

Anyway, I dedicate a lot of my personal activity now trying to improve the status of minorities and women. When I was on active duty as the Chief of Naval Personnel and other jobs, I put a great deal of emphasis to improving the status of minorities.[*] As I get into when I talk about my time as Chief of Naval Personnel, one of the most significant achievements I think I made was working with Secretary Hidalgo, who was significantly increasing the Hispanic representation in the Navy.[†]

So those were some of the early influences of my life that stayed with me.

Paul Stillwell: You said your father was strong-willed. Did he try to determine a career path for you?

Admiral Lawrence: No, he really didn't. He greatly concurred in my desire to go to the service academy, but he wanted me to take some responsibility for this. So I had to write

---

[*] Vice Admiral Lawrence served as Chief of Naval Personnel, 28 September 1983 to 31 December 1985.
[†] Edward Hidalgo was Secretary of the Navy from 24 October 1979 to 20 January 1981.

the letter to the congressional representative from our district, a man named Percy Priest.* He wrote back and said that he could give me only an alternate appointment.†

I took the entrance exam for the Naval Academy, which in those days used to be given in the local federal office building. Then my father started exploring other means of getting me an appointment. He found out about Rip Miller, who was the assistant director of athletics here at the academy, and he was also the number-one recruiter.‡ So Rip Miller went to bat to try to get me an appointment.

Also, I found out about how you could apply for an appointment to West Point. West Point had a little bit different appointment provision, and it seemed to me that the superintendent at West Point had somewhat of an appointment authority. I don't remember all of the ramifications of this under the law. But while my father and Rip Miller were searching around for another appointment for me, I got a call from Coach Earl Blaik, who said, "We will offer you an appointment to West Point."§

I said, "Well, that's not my first choice, but I really want to go to a service academy."

Also, I had a scholarship to Yale, because a very prominent Yale graduate was a lawyer in my hometown, and he was always try to get young people there to go to Yale. He had sent my information up to Yale, and the football coach at Yale in those days was Herman Hickman, who had gone to the University of Tennessee.** My scholarship to Yale was based not on athletics; it was on broader scholarship qualities. So I had an appointment to West Point and a scholarship to Yale, but I still wanted to go to the Naval Academy.

---

* James Percy Priest, a Democrat from Tennessee, served in the House of Representatives from 3 January 1941 until his death on 12 October 1956. Prior to entering Congress he was on the editorial staff of the *Nashville Tennessean* from 1926 to 1940.
† First priority for admission would go to the individual who received the congressman's principal appointment for a particular opening at the Naval Academy. Someone with an alternate appointment would get in only if the person with the principal appointment was found to be unqualified or if he decided not to accept the appointment.
‡ Edgar E. "Rip" Miller was a Naval Academy institution. He had played college football at Notre Dame, where in 1924 he was one of the "Seven Mules," the linemen who played in front of the "Four Horsemen" of the backfield. In 1931 to 1933 he was the Naval Academy's head football coach. For many years thereafter he worked as a coach and assistant athletic director.
§ Earl "Red" Blaik was head football coach of the U.S. Military Academy from 1941 through 1958. In his 18 years at West Point, he coached two national champions and six unbeaten teams.
** As Yale University's head football coach from 1948 to 1951, Herman Hickman compiled a record of 16-17-2. Before that he had been an assistant coach at Yale for 13 years.

Then Rip Miller found out that Senator K. D. McKellar had not used all his appointments for the Naval Academy.* When Roosevelt died and Truman had to take over as President, there was no Vice President during the rest of his term.† McKellar became President Pro Tem of the Senate, because he was one of the senior senators at the time. Thanks to Rip Miller, my father got in touch with the publisher of the newspaper in Nashville.‡ He had been a World War II naval officer, Mr. James Stahlman. Mr. Stahlman contacted Senator McKellar and asked him if he would give me an appointment, which he did. So I came in under Senator McKellar. Stahlman was very proud of his service in the Navy; in fact, he had advanced to the rank of captain in the Naval Reserve. After I entered the Navy, he always followed my career with great interest. When I went back to Nashville, I'd always go see him to tell him how I was doing. So it was the publisher of the paper who actually got me the appointment to come into the academy. But, as I say, I almost went to West Point, and I could have gone to Yale. I would have been there with George Bush, because I played baseball.§ We'd have probably played baseball together.

Paul Stillwell: What athletic skills enabled you to be so versatile?

Admiral Lawrence: I don't know. It seemed that my two older brothers and I just had natural affinities for it. So, like our father, we just ate, slept, and breathed sports in our family. And that was very much typical of my friends. Gosh, when I look back at our lives compared to the young people today, it's just amazing. First of all, it was important to all of us who were with me in the public school system in Nashville that we do well. Everybody studied; there was no cynical attitudes that you see today of contempt for study. And we had tough schoolteachers, mostly single ladies, who devoted their lives to education. They really made us work hard. I don't ever remember anybody cursing; I

---

* Kenneth D. McKellar, Democrat from Tennessee, served in the U.S. Senate from 4 March 1917 to 3 January 1953.
† Harry S. Truman became President on 12 April 1945, the day Franklin Roosevelt died. McKellar was president pro tem of the Senate from 1945 to 1947 and was treated by Truman as de facto Vice President.
‡ James G. Stahlman (1893-1976) was publisher of the *Nashville Banner* from 1930 to 1972.
§ George H. W. Bush, who was a naval aviator in World War II, attended Yale following the war and graduated in 1948. He was first baseman and captain of the baseball team. He served as President of the United States from 1989 to 1993.

don't ever remember anybody having any really bad habits. You'd hear about an occasional guy who would go out and have a beer.

We grew up in the Bible Belt tradition. I never saw my parents drink alcohol; it was just very rare that anybody would drink alcohol. We treated our lady friends well. We would have formal dances all the time, where the gals would dress up in evening dresses and men would wear tuxedoes, although I didn't do it. Our family was not well off, but those were the traditions of the old South: this courtliness, this gentlemanly behavior, this chivalry. Our lives were so pure, it just is hard to believe.

I never remember ever locking a locker the whole time I went to school. Never heard about any theft. So it was a wonderful influence. And sports were a big part of it. Every spare moment I had, when I wasn't studying, I was on an athletic field. It was just a natural love and interest I had.

Paul Stillwell: What role did religion play in the life of the family?

Admiral Lawrence: Well, it was important. My father was not really overt in this, but it was strong. Both my mother and my father had been Methodists. My great-grandfather had been a Methodist circuit rider minister. We had the same pew in Belmont Methodist Church for over 40 years. They didn't have formally assigned pews in the church, but just by repetitively going to a certain place, that became your place to sit, and nobody ever would sit there except your family. Gosh, when I went away to the Naval Academy at age 17, I probably missed only three or four times going to church. You always went to Sunday school; you always went to church. You got a lot of valuable education from your Sunday school teachers. I was very knowledgeable, knew all the Bible stories.

There were two rules that were always emphasized to me in Sunday school. One was the Golden Rule: "Do unto others as you would have them do unto you." The other was "Honor thy father and thy mother." Honoring your parents was a very important southern tradition, a wonderful tradition that still exists down there. You revere your parents, and you always ensure that as they get older, they're taken care of.

Paul Stillwell: You have a reputation for honor and integrity and ethics. Where did that input come from?

Admiral Lawrence: Well, I think it was very much of a part of that southern tradition, of living by all those wonderful influences: church, school, and on the athletic field. I had so many wonderful role models as I was growing up. Of course, I grew up in the extended family. My grandfather on my father's side had one brother and five sisters who were living. Those great aunts or great uncles of mine were very important influences in my life. In other words, I felt not only accountable to my father and my mother and my grandfather, but I had about a dozen or more aunts and uncles I felt accountable to.

My Aunt Mary was tough as nails. Boy, she'd come down and she'd say, "What are you doing worthwhile? . . . Give me a report on what you're doing. . . . Boy, you look pretty scruffy." That sense of accountability in this extended family was a big factor for me. Unfortunately, because families move around so much now, you don't have the extended family anymore. But I tell you, one reason I was dissuaded, deterred from doing anything bad was that I knew all these relatives I'd have to account to. My father had just one brother, but he was a very big influence in our lives.

My mother had four brothers and sisters, and I felt accountable to them too. So this extended family concept—which I guess was just all over the country, but it was very pronounced in the South—was a very important influence. We always had reunions in our family. My mother's family had reunions where you had to kind of account for what you were doing with your life. It was a large family, but you carry it back to other generations. My great-grandmother was an Ashley, and the Ashleys were a big family down in that Beech Grove area of middle Tennessee. The Ashleys hosted the family reunions.

Then my teachers were wonderful influences. As I say, in that time, they were mostly maiden ladies, and they were college graduates. I had two very superb English teachers in my high school. They were graduates from Vanderbilt, a very fine private university known as the "Harvard of the South." So these two maiden ladies really taught me the basics of English. Gosh, I remember diagramming sentences, where you'd learn what a participle and a preposition and all those things meant. I really got a thorough foundation in English grammar, and they made us write two or three papers a week in English. These teachers really critiqued your writing style, so I learned to write.

I had a very fine history teacher, who was a PhD and had written a book on history. So I really got a very quality education in the public school system. And, probably 75% of those kids who were in school with me went on to college.

Paul Stillwell: You said you had a somewhat different sense of values from your brothers on the question of race.

Admiral Lawrence: Yes.

Paul Stillwell: Did that extend into other areas as well?

Admiral Lawrence: Well, they just didn't seem to have the same instincts and sense of fairness I did on the issues of race and sex. I don't know how I picked that up, but it just seemed to be part of my makeup that they didn't have. Although they were good, solid, fine guys who did well in school and did well in college, college graduates, professional men. But I just seemed to have some senses that they didn't have. One of them was on the racial situation. I never remember their showing the same degree of compassion towards the blacks that I did.

Paul Stillwell: How much sibling rivalry was there?

Admiral Lawrence: Well, like all kids who were growing up, we used to have fights. My father was smart enough to know it was going to happen, so he got us boxing gloves. We used to box all the time. That's the way my father would let us satisfy this sibling rivalry. But as we got older, we really became very close. We were two years apart, so we played together on athletic teams.

I remember my next oldest brother and I played on the same basketball team, and we won the city championship. We really didn't have any deep-rooted rivalries, and we were just far enough apart in age where we weren't competing for the same things. We were a very, very close, very close-knit family.

Then when I was 13—the third in line—we had another little brother, which was a real surprise to my parents, because my mother was 42 years old. I never really got to spend that much time with him, because when he was four years old, I went off to the Naval Academy. He's been a very successful man and went on to college. He probably could have avoided going to the Vietnam War, but while I was a POW, he went into the Army and became an officer.* He was a platoon commander in the 82nd Airborne Division in Vietnam. He was up in the area northwest of Saigon, where the fighting was pretty tough. He served six months as a platoon commander and then went on to the battalion staff.

So all four of the brothers in my family have become very responsible citizens. The one that was two years older than I, unfortunately, died of a heart ailment.

Paul Stillwell: What were the forms of recreation for the family?

Admiral Lawrence: Well, we didn't do a lot of formal vacations that families seem to do today. We grew up very much in the lifestyle of the Depression, where there were a lot of things you just simply couldn't do. But my father loved to travel, and we would take trips, primarily to see relatives. Many of the Tennesseans, back in the 1800s, went to Texas. That was the practice, like Davy Crockett, Stephen Austin, Sam Houston. Texas was the land of opportunities, so many of my relatives went down there. We would drive down to see a great aunt who lived in Dallas. We had a great uncle in Atlanta whom we'd go down to see. So really our principal mode of recreation was going to see relatives. That was always very much a southern tradition. It was amazing the things that they would do in that time that you wouldn't think of doing now. I've heard my father say, "Well, let's go down to Manchester," without any prior announcement. He'd just drive down and drop in on the relatives.

---

* As related in detail in a later interview, Lawrence was a prisoner in North Vietnam from 1967 to 1973. His younger brother Thomas also served in the Vietnam War.

They'd say, "Oh, great! Great to see you," and produce a big meal. It was just accepted. It wasn't regarded as an imposition at all to drop in on your relatives without any prior notice. Really wonderful love and mutual respect existed among family, and also with friends. I think it was a wonderful thing in what I call the Bible Belt culture. You really were taught the Golden Rule.

Just this past June we had a reunion of basketball teams from our high school, which won the state championship three times in a six-year period. I always played on one of the state basketball teams. This was a reunion of all the basketball players along with our coach from the 1943 to '48 era in Nashville. That same great mutual respect and affection among players were very obvious at that reunion. Almost all of us hadn't seen each other for about 40 years. It was a wonderful tradition to grow up in, frankly. I'm saddened at what I see happening in the world where a lot of that is disappearing. A very strong commitment to excellence was a part of our tradition, as well as this great mutual love and admiration that just don't seem to exist today.

Paul Stillwell: Well, the camaraderie you felt on those sports teams was paralleled, probably, in some of the wardrooms when you were in the Navy.

Admiral Lawrence: Oh, yes, that's so correct. And that's why I'm so much an advocate of sports here at the academy. Sports are so valuable in preparing military officers, because the traditions of sports are very similar to those in the military. I think it's a wonderful influence for young people growing up as well. People, midshipmen and others, would say, "How do you develop courage? What is courage?"

I say, "Well, those qualities that constitute courage really have to be fostered at an early age, within your home. Integrity and courage are so inextricably linked that you really can't separate one from the other in my view." I haven't seen any military leaders who didn't have both courage and integrity, because it's hard to have one without the other. I think you have to have one to have the other.

I always use the quote by Theodore Roosevelt.* He said there was one time in his life when he was very much afraid of bears, gunfighters, and mean horses. He said, "As I got older, I tried to pretend like I wasn't afraid of them, and then later on I found out I wasn't afraid."

I said, "My point is that a young person growing up simply has to be exposed to mean horses, bears, and gunfighters, because that's what develops that courage, that sense of confidence, the ability to deal with the challenges and those things that are onerous and, maybe, where your life is at risk." That's why I'm a great advocate of, as I say, of sports here at the Naval Academy. I think a lot of those qualities that constitute courage can be developed on the athletic field. But there's a very much larger component: that is being committed to a higher purpose in your life. In other words, this love of country and preserving the important values and traditions in your country, give you that courage to go, even though your life is at risk, because you know you're doing it for a higher purpose than just your own life and welfare.

So I feel that a sense of patriotism, where the country is a very important higher component of courage for a military officer. But these other values, including being exposed to challenges from a very early youth, are important.

Paul Stillwell: Well, another big fear is that of the unknown. Sometimes you hesitate to take on a challenge, because you don't know what's there, but once you do, you get some confidence and that gives you more courage.

Admiral Lawrence: That's right. The analogy that I use with the midshipmen is scaling pyramids. There's a very famous quote by Wolfe, the guy who wrote *The Right Stuff*.† He makes the analogy of being trained in military aviation as scaling a pyramid until finally you reach the pinnacle. He says at the apex of the pinnacle is the fighter pilot in combat. He points out that you simply have to do those things that enable you to scale

---

* Theodore Roosevelt was President of the United States from September 1901 to March 1909. He was such a strong advocate of naval power that for many years his birthday, 27 October, was observed in the United States as Navy Day.
† Tom Wolfe, *The Right Stuff* (New York: Farrar, Straus, and Giroux, 1979). The book focuses on test pilots and their contributions to the early part of the space age.

that pyramid and gather all these qualities to be an effective combat aviator. This is the point I make to midshipmen: "You are scaling a pyramid at the academy, and all the things that we make you do are to bring you up that pyramid." I said that it's symbolic that we have you scale Herndon Monument at the end of plebe year.* That's a symbol of what you have done during that year, that you've moved up that pyramid. You have to start people scaling pyramids at a young age.

As I look back, my father was a very shrewd, astute guy, because he always made us meet some challenge. He didn't do it in a really overt way, but he got us on athletic teams early and developed that interest. And he always had the requirement that we were well aware of, "If you don't keep your grades up, you don't play." I didn't have a problem, because I had always that great desire to be a scholar, but my older brother, who did all right, didn't have all that great love for books. My father was telling us, "You're coming off that team if you don't keep those grades up. You'd better understand that right now." So that made him study, because he didn't want to get off the team. But having those types of standards imposed on you from an early age is very important.

I do a lot of volunteer work. Right now I'm on a task force with the governor of Tennessee, Board of Education. I said that the two key factors I look back on my career on why I got a good education is, because, first was parental involvement. I said my parents were very keenly interested in my education, and they set standards they expected us to achieve. The other is the quality of teachers. If the parents are interested and involved and you have good quality teachers, you don't really have to have all that fine a facility. Those were the two key ingredients that I had when I was growing up. Unfortunately, a lot of that has disappeared, because parents are too busy nowadays to be concerned about their kids. Somehow we've let the quality of teachers decline, because of various factors in this country. One is that there is not sufficient pay; the other condition we've allowed it to develop in our country is that being a secondary school teacher or below is not a highly respected position any more. So young people don't

---

* One of the long-standing Naval Academy traditions involves the obelisk-shaped Herndon Monument that stands across the street from the chapel. At the end of their first year, midshipmen join hands around the greased monument, building higher and higher until finally one of the number is able to reach the top and remove a hat that has been glued there. Legend has it that the plebe who grabs the hat will be the first in the class to be selected for admiral.

aspire to that as a profession that they admire. Whereas, when I was growing up, gosh, my teachers were really highly respected in the community. So we've got to do something to increase parental involvement and to enhance the stature of our teachers. I said that if you take care of those two factors, the young kids will get better educations.

A lot of the cost per capita of education today is going into administrators and people like that. It's a situation I call layering, people who don't make any real contributions to the system. They're just paying groups of bureaucrats, and that's the big problem in the D.C. public school system. They put a lot of money in, but it goes a lot to administrative level.[*]

Paul Stillwell: You have to have some of that.

Admiral Lawrence: Well, you have to, certainly; there's no question about it. But when the D.C. government has 48,000 employees, you have to really wonder what all those people do.

Anyway, I was so fortunate in growing up in the influences we had. And I was growing up in a time the South was still recovering from the Civil War.

Paul Stillwell: In what ways?

Admiral Lawrence: Well, the South had really been devastated economically.

Paul Stillwell: The southern states were treated like colonies during the Reconstruction period.

Admiral Lawrence: Yes. So in the 1930s, not only did we have the national Depression, but the South was still trying to recover from the things that had been lost in the Civil War time. Of course, having been largely an agrarian economy down there, some of the things we had were not as sophisticated as they had in the North, like banking systems and all of that. So, in spite of that deficit, I would not give anything for the influences I

---

[*] D.C. – District of Columbia.

had when I was growing up. Of all the bad things about that culture down there—first of all, holding people in slavery, which I think was very bad—there were several mighty good aspects about it.

Paul Stillwell: How much of a social life did you have in Nashville before going to the Naval Academy?

Admiral Lawrence: As I say, it was very much in the traditions of that culture. We had a lot of parties and social activities, and much of what you did was associated with your church and school. We had sweethearts, but nothing at all like it is in the present time. You really were chaperoned a lot. It was very rare at the time I was growing up that you'd go out on a date by yourself. It just was not done. I had sweethearts at various stages in my experience. I think that's just part of the southern tradition. But, even though I had a high school sweetheart when I came to the Naval Academy, that didn't endure very long, because my sweetheart pursued her own interests, and it was obvious to us both that they were divergent. Even so, we're still good friends; we still communicate with each other. We didn't really stay that close, although I did invite her to come up for one June Week at the Naval Academy while I was here.* She and I still write. We see each other now and then.

It was a very active social experience, but much of what we did was under the surveillance and supervision of adults. We had a lot of formal events; we had high school fraternities and sororities. I was a member of a high school fraternity, although I was never really all that serious about it, because I was more interested in sports and schoolwork than getting really actively involved in a fraternity.

It was a very wholesome type of relationship with your friends and with the opposite sex. Being courteous towards members of the opposite sex and respecting them were important. Yet, at the time I always was pretty much of an advocate for women doing significant things, getting good educations, and going into professional careers. I was never one who felt women should be principally educated and trained to be mothers

---

* June Week was the term at the time for the collection of festivities surrounding the graduation and commissioning of the first classmen. Naval Academy classes now graduate in late May during what is known as Commissioning Week.

and homemakers. I really support women who go on to professional careers. I still keep in touch with a large number of my school friends. I had little opportunity to spend much time with them over the years, but I still stay pretty close to them.

Paul Stillwell: Of course, one of the ironies is that as women have become more prominent in the professional field, that's weakened their ability to perform the family role.

Admiral Lawrence: That's right. But I think in a lot of respects it's been an overall benefit to society, because I think many women have managed that dual role very effectively. The other thing that's happened is that the old patriarchal concept is changed, and men now are more readily disposed to helping wives in taking care of the family. And I sensed that as I was a young man coming along. I did far more things than my father would have ever done, in taking care of children and changing diapers, helping in the kitchen, and so forth. I think it's an overall plus to society that women are making a greater contribution professionally. I think it's been a real advantage for the military too. I think, frankly, that the quality of the military has been enhanced by the increased role of women. I'll talk more later about things that I did during my career here to enhance the role of women, because I certainly worked very actively at that in several jobs I had.

Paul Stillwell: How much did you keep up with news events in the wider world?

Admiral Lawrence: Well, I was really very active in that in my younger years. My father was a very avid, prolific reader. He was a real intellectual, and so am I. We always subscribed to many magazines, and he always was reading books. We had a fairly extensive library. He always had at least three different types of encyclopedias, which I used all the time. A magazine that I used to read from cover to cover as a young boy growing up was *Life*. That's how I kept abreast of World War II.

I can remember very vividly the day of the attack on Pearl Harbor.* My family had come back from church, and I remember sitting there in our home. We had the radio on and they announced. That was because of the five- or six-hour time difference between where we were and when the attack occurred at 7:00 o'clock or so out in Pearl Harbor.

I remember other key events. I remember V-E Day, V-J Day, and when Franklin Roosevelt died in April of 1945.† We were out doing spring football practice in our high school, and they came out and announced Franklin Roosevelt died. I remember just the great sadness that all of us felt.

Paul Stillwell: He had been President through all your conscious years up to that point.

Admiral Lawrence: That's right. He'd been President since March of 1933, and I was born in 1930. We had great reverence for Franklin Roosevelt. Of course, I remember the "Day of Infamy" speech he made after the Pearl Harbor attack. I can remember listening to it on the radio. I used to be so impressed with his diction. And, of course, I remember listening to his fireside chats on the radio. Although I didn't understand all of it, I certainly kept abreast of that. So I was quite well aware of things going on in the world.

Of course, when I came to the Naval Academy, I got so busy in my studies and other activities that a void developed in my awareness of world events. That's why in my adult years, I had to go back and do a lot of studying about what really happened from 1947 to 1951, because you very rarely had any time to read a newspaper here at the Naval Academy, when I was going through as a midshipman. You just were so busy. And I was extremely busy. I played three sports. We were just going 90 miles an hour all day long when I was a midshipman.

Paul Stillwell: When you were still in school back in Tennessee with the sports and the

---

* On Sunday, 7 December 1941, Japanese carrier planes attacked and heavily damaged American warships at the naval base at Pearl Harbor, Hawaii. The U.S. Congress declared war on Japan the following day.
† V-E Day – Victory in Europe Day, 8 May 1945, when the German surrender was ratified in Berlin. V-J Day – Victory over Japan Day, marked the end of the war in the Pacific on 15 August 1945. Because of the time difference it was 14 August in the United States when combat ended. Roosevelt died on 12 April.

studies, did you have any time left over for mischief?

Admiral Lawrence: No, not really. I don't remember any of my friends doing something like pranks or vandalism. As I say, we had a very few guys who would go out on a weekend and have a beer. It was really being racy to do something like that. I can't believe how good we were, but I never recall ever seeing anybody cheat or anybody steal. It just wasn't done in those days. It's the old Bible Belt culture. But it wasn't the redneck Bible Belt culture, where a component of it was a lot of prejudice. I didn't see those strong prejudices that you saw in the other parts of the South, because there was a lot of compassion, empathy toward the blacks.

Paul Stillwell: Well, anything else to say about those Tennessee years before we get to the Naval Academy?

Admiral Lawrence: I count my blessings every day that I grew up under those influences with wonderful teachers and members of my family that gave me so much. So I was really well prepared for the academy. In other words, it was just like fish in water coming here to the Naval Academy. I loved every aspect of the Naval Academy.

Plebe year was not really difficult for me, because I had a high degree of personal discipline.* In those days, we seemed to be able to keep our sense of humors. And, of course, my plebe year was unusual, because my first classmen were in the Class of '48B.† The lower half of the class of '48 had to go four years, whereas, the upper half of the class, academically, had three. My upperclassmen were kind of bitter that they had to go that fourth year, so they weren't all that caught up in their duties as first classmen. They probably ignored us more than they bothered us.

But, anyway, I never, really, during my four years at the academy, had to have any external stimulation. I was very much of a self-starter, and I just tried to do as much

---

* A midshipman in his or her first year is called a plebe; second year, youngster or third classman; third year, second classman; fourth year, first classman.
† During World War II the Naval Academy curriculum was shortened to three years. To return to the four-year format after the war, the class of 1948 was divided into A and B sections. A graduated in 1947 and B the following year.

as I could here at the academy. Of course, I never had time, really, to have much of a social life. In those days we were very much inwardly oriented here at the academy. In my four years here, I'll bet I went outside the gate just a handful of times. The main times I went out were on athletic trips. If we had free time, which was very rare, we'd go over and play pickup basketball, or something, at McDonough Hall. I very rarely ever went out in town, and I never dated very much as a midshipman. I didn't have a chance to meet young women, and, usually, when I did date, it was because some midshipman asked me if I wanted to have a blind date. But I thoroughly enjoyed every aspect of the academy experience. It was very interesting. Sports were a big part of it. I remember the friendships I made through sports and the camaraderie. But, also, I really loved the academics, really studied hard, worked hard.

Paul Stillwell: Could you talk about the system that was used in the classes at that time?

Admiral Lawrence: We had what we now refer to as the lock-step curriculum. A lot of people referred to the academy in those days as being a trade school. But I do feel that we had a high-quality offering in humanities. In other words, I felt my English courses were very good; I felt my history courses were, the courses that we had in government. In fact, I remember a very fine course on the Constitution, and another very fine one on the diplomatic history of United States. So I really enjoyed those humanities courses. And I thought that the mathematics and chemistry and physics really gave me a good basic foundation.

But we did have a lot of the typical trade-school-type courses, like ordnance and gunnery, marine engineering, where you learned about boilers and how boilers function. Ordnance and gunnery you learned about the function of weapon systems. Those trade-school-type courses were very much rote memorization, and you were tested every day. A typical question would be, "Sketch and describe a Type A boiler," or something like that. But I learned some of the basics of marine engineering, ordnance and gunnery—enough to build on when I went out in the fleet.

Paul Stillwell: Did you have a pretty good facility for the memory-type work?

Admiral Lawrence: Yes, I always was endowed with a good, natural memory. I have to admit that much of my studying here at the Naval Academy was just memorization of those facts I felt that I had to have to be able to pass the daily quiz. A lot of people say, "Well, then that's really not a very good form of education." But an important thing you must learn when you're growing up is discipline, and that method really imparted a high degree of discipline to me. Every day you knew that you were going to be tested and that you had to get in there and master that assignment and to get the key facts to be able to answer that quiz. I'm sure that people say that to be motivated by passing a quiz is the worst form of motivation, but it's a hell of a lot better than none at all.

Paul Stillwell: It's very effective.

Admiral Lawrence: It sure is. I developed a very high degree of discipline from the academic program here at the Naval Academy. As I tell so many people, the most important form of discipline for the full career is intellectual discipline. The academic program here helps impart that to you. James Webb and I are philosophically at opposite ends of the spectrum.[*] He says the academic program gave him nothing of value at the academy. He only did it because he had to; he went through law school only because that was a credential, but it was of no value. I say that's hogwash.

I think a rigorous academic program is of immense value to what you need in this world. It gives you that intellectual discipline as the most important type of discipline that you need. And when you put that academic program in with the professional and the physical fitness requirements, then I think it's a good balance. I would never, ever try to reduce the academic rigor, or never, ever say that academics here should take a second place to anything else, because this is where we get our undergraduate education. Academic programs should be rigorous and demand a majority of the midshipmen's time, because getting that baccalaureate degree is the principal reason you're here.

---

[*] James H. Webb Jr., Naval Academy class of 1968, was decorated for heroism as a Marine Corps officer in combat in Vietnam. He later became an author, served as Secretary of the Navy from 1 May 1987 to 23 February 1988, and in 2007 a U.S. Senator from Virginia. For details see Robert Timberg, *The Nightingale's Song* (New York: Simon & Schuster, 1995).

Paul Stillwell: Well, it wasn't a system that inspired a great deal of independent thinking.

Admiral Lawrence: No, it really didn't. Not at all. But I don't think it thwarted it; I don't think it inhibited you from going on some day to becoming an independent thinker. I think it gave you a lot of discipline and ability to organize your thinking that you need to be good at conceptualizing and so forth.

As I say, I had to really work in my later years to fill in a void of what went on in the world. I very rarely had time to read a newspaper about the emerging Soviet threat and the formation of NATO, all those things.*

Paul Stillwell: McCarthyism.†

Admiral Lawrence: McCarthyism. Also, I had to do a lot of reading later to fill voids in other areas. For example, about ten or 15 years ago, I realized that there were many aspects of World War II that I didn't know a lot about. I knew the Pacific War in great detail, but I didn't know very much about the China-Burma-India campaigns; I didn't know as much as I'd like to about North African, Italian, European campaigns, so I came to the conclusion that the best way to fill that void was to get the *Time-Life* series on World War II. That really filled in a lot of voids for me. I think that is what education is all about.

I think that your education has to continue for your full life. After you've gotten the real formal part of it, which constitutes the degree-gathering years, then I think a person has to very selectively determine the self-education he looks for. I've done a great deal on this self-education and looking at areas of history and other government affairs and all that before I felt I needed to improve my knowledge, and I'd find these books that would do that. I found that biographies have been the best ways of doing this, because biographies not only tell you about the events that occurred in time, but they teach you

---

* NATO – North Atlantic Treaty Organization, which was established in 1949 as a means of coordinating defense against a potential attack from the Soviet Union.
† As a U.S. senator from Wisconsin in the early 1950s, Joseph R. McCarthy went on an anti-Communist witch-hunt that came to be dubbed by the pejorative term "McCarthyism." The Senate eventually censured him.

some important qualities that leaders should have. So I've read every biography I could get my hands on.

Paul Stillwell: Are there any you especially remember?

Admiral Lawrence: Yes, of course.

Paul Stillwell: *Lee's Lieutenants*?

Admiral Lawrence: *Lee's Lieutenants*, of course, is good.* The biography of Robert E. Lee by Douglas Southall Freeman, the six-volume biography of George Washington is a very valuable piece of work.† Douglas Southall Freeman was commissioned by the Congress to write that, the official biography of George Washington, which our country had never really gotten around to until about 1950. Actually, it took him, I think, almost 20 years to write that. But I think every young person in this country should at least read the first three volumes of George Washington. But, anyway, it was important to read about Lee and Washington.

I've read *Coming Forward in History*. I've read all of the highlights of the biographies of most of our presidents, but I also read a lot about Thomas Jefferson. Andrew Jackson, from my home town, I've read all of his biography in great detail. And then Ulysses S. Grant, John J. Pershing, Douglas MacArthur, Nimitz, King, Eisenhower, Bradley, Spruance, Halsey, Mitscher.‡ And then in more modern times, I'm basically familiar with the biographies of Maxwell Taylor, General Westmoreland.§ But most of my collateral reading has been biographies, because I think, as I say, they have the dual

---

* Douglas Southall Freeman, *Lee's Lieutenants: a Study in Command*, three volumes (New York: Scribner's, 1942-44).
† Douglas Southall Freeman, *George Washington, a Biography*, seven volumes (New York: Scribner's, 1948-57). The seventh volume was completed by J. A. Carroll and M. W. Ashworth after Freeman's death.
‡ General Grant was the chief U.S. Army commander in the Civil War, General Pershing in World War I, and Generals MacArthur, Eisenhower, and Omar Bradley had key roles in World War II. Eisenhower also served as President, 1953-61. Admirals Ernest J. King, Chester W. Nimitz, William F. Halsey Jr., and Raymond A. Spruance were top U.S. Navy commanders in World War II.
§ General Maxwell D. Taylor, USA, served as Chairman of the Joint Chiefs of Staff from 1 October 1962 to 3 July 1964; General William C. Westmoreland, USA, was Commander U.S. Military Assistance Command Vietnam from 1964 to 1968.

advantage of teaching you events that occurred during that time frame; secondly, in teaching you important qualities. That's why when I teach leadership or when I was trying to improve my own leadership qualities, I focus to a large degree on those qualities that I found in common among those great military leaders.

Paul Stillwell: How would you articulate these qualities?

Admiral Lawrence: When I came here as a midshipman and started studying military history and everything, and we had a lecture by Douglas Southall Freeman that I still have a copy of. After searching for several years, I found a classmate that still had it, so I copied it, and I have it in my files.

The thing that perplexed me was the fact that all the great military leaders in our history—even counting George Washington, who was really a citizen-soldier, but he was very much a military man, as well as being our President and all of that—I noticed that all of them had distinctly different personalities and style. In other words, Robert E. Lee was quite different from U.S. Grant. Then if you came up to the World War II era, when there really that great number of great military leaders, they were all distinctly different in personality and style. Eisenhower and MacArthur were different as day and night; Nimitz and King were different as day and night; Halsey and Spruance, who were both fleet commanders, were different as day and night.

This used to perplex me. I said, "Gosh, how do you go about developing leadership qualities when you have all these examples and role models, and they're just so distinctly different?" That was when I just finally came to the realization that the style and the personality are not as important as the basic qualities. Then as I started looking as those qualities that I found that were common to most of those great leaders, and that was when I expanded on Douglas Southall Freeman's approach that he gave us in lectures here. He said that the three important qualities were character, discipline, and knowledge. Then the other thesis that he advances is that a good leader must know his job, be a man, and take care of your men. That's another way of saying discipline, knowledge, and character.

I extended it beyond that and a lot of things I write teaching leadership is that, first of all, I noticed all good leaders have a high degree of loyalty to the organization, to their shipmates. Another is that I've noticed that they all eagerly seek responsibility. They readily accept increased accountability that goes with increased authority and responsibility. That's a very important quality. The other is a great knowledge and concern for people, what I call a strong people-sense, and associated with that is I found most important leaders in their own way have a high degree of compassion; even Ernie King was a compassionate guy. He was tough and demanding, but he, as an officer coming along, always had a very great concern for enlisted personnel. So compassion is an important component of this concern for people, people-sense, the artful use of certain practices in motivating and inspiring people.

Another quality, of course, is discipline. You have to learn how to control yourself before you can control others. An important component of that discipline is intellectual discipline: organizing your thinking and developing courses of action for solving problems. And then, of course, professional confidence and intelligence are important. My definition of intelligence is not just possessing knowledge, but it means the ability to perceive the important. Most great leaders that I've worked with—like Admiral Moorer, whom I used to watch carefully—have this uncanny ability to look at very complex situations and then somehow just pick out the guts.[*] That is the mark that I found of great leaders. When the situation gets very confused, complex, and everybody's going, "What will we do?" they'll just say, "Here, that's what we need to do." And what gives a person that capability? I mean, to me really the essence of intelligence is that ability to perceive the important. But how did you gain that? Well, so many things go into that. One is having this ability through observation of events over the years, personal study, experience, to know the relative importance of events.

So I tell young people that you can enhance your intelligence by making yourself observe very keenly events that go on around you all the time, constantly observing that and then having a program of study in professional areas. At the same time, history is

---

[*] Rear Admiral Thomas H. Moorer, USN, served as Commander Carrier Division Six, 1959-60. As covered in a later interview, Lawrence served as Moorer's flag lieutenant in that tour. As a four-star admiral, Moorer was later Chief of Naval Operations, 1967-70, and Chairman of the Joint Chiefs of Staff, 1970-74.

very valuable to you in enhancing your intelligence, because the study of history is so important in military profession, because the lessons of history are so relevant. In our profession, history repeats itself all the time in terms of the nature of events and challenges that we face are very similar to what had happened in previous history. So if you study history, particularly military campaigns, it helps you so much in the modern era. So I do feel that genius is 95% frustration and 5% inspiration. A guy can enhance his intelligence just through hard work.

Another important quality I found that most good leaders possess is a high degree of stamina, the ability to drive themselves is necessary to get a job done. I really noticed this in reading about Robert E. Lee. He really first became known to the senior leadership in the Army in the Mexican War. He was an engineer officer, a captain, and was put on Winfield Scott's staff. In the battle of Vera Cruz and other military campaigns, he was sent out on the battlefield to do a reconnaissance of the enemy and to determine where our artillery should be placed and everything. He would walk over that battlefield for 18 or 20 hours a day, and Winfield Scott said, "My God, Lee is indefatigable."[*] After that experience with Lee as a young captain, Winfield Scott said, "Robert E. Lee is the best officer I have ever seen on the battlefield." The reason for that was his stamina; the ability to keep going on was important.

George Washington, in his early years, was a guide; he would walk, lead parties from Tidewater, Virginia, through the Allegheny Mountains, and over into the Ohio territory. In the French and Indian War, he was a guide for the British troops when they went into Western Pennsylvania, around Pittsburgh, Fort Pitt.

Douglas MacArthur was renowned in World War I for his trooping the battlefield, visiting his troops when he was assistant division commander, 42nd unit.

But then I really saw how long Admiral Moorer could work when he was a task force commander. Arleigh Burke, when he was a chief of staff to Mitscher, would just go for long hours.[†] Of course, in my own career, I found those times I just had to drive

---

[*] General Winfield Scott commanded the southern of two U.S. armies in the Mexican-American War of 1846-48. General Zachary Taylor, a future President, commanded the northern army.

[†] Captain Arleigh A. Burke, USN, was chief of staff to Vice Admiral Marc A. Mitscher, USN, who commanded the Fast Carrier Task Force in World War II. Burke was later Chief of Naval Operations, 1955-61.

myself. So physical stamina is an important part of good leadership. And then the point I bring out is that there's a very close relationship between the psychological and the physiological in leadership.

I really saw that in combat and the POW experience, in particular. Those guys that just had this determination not to give in, somehow didn't. Because that tremendous positive attitude, that psychological drive, determination, enabled them to keep going physically, so there's a very strong synergistic relationship between the mental and the physical. But the relationship, at the same time, can be mutually degrading if a person neglects his physical fitness and health; that can be accompanied by a commensurate degradation in your mental faculties.

Also, I talk about a sense of humor. That can be a very variable leadership trait, although you can certainly say it's not essential. I never saw much of a sense of humor in Douglas MacArthur. Admiral Rickover certainly had zero, minus ten sense of humor.[*] But, on the other hand, a sense of humor can be very effective in being a leader because, first of all, it conveys to your people that you're human. It helps allay tension, keeps things in a proper perspective. A sense of humor can allay, what I call the main concerns of your subordinates, particularly if they're enlisted personnel. But in combat, it's a concern that you're relying on over intensity and so forth that you'll subject them to needless risk. A sense of humor can help allay a lot of that. Nimitz used his sense of humor very, very effectively. Eisenhower had a good sense of humor. And so did many other great leaders that we know.

And then there are the two characteristics that I call the sine qua non of military leaders. Courage and integrity are the absolutely essential qualities, without which the other qualities are not of any value, and that's courage and integrity. And, as I mentioned before, they're inextricably linked.

Paul Stillwell: Well, this debate goes back and forth on whether leadership is innate or whether it's an acquired skill, and my guess is that it involves some of each.

---

[*] Hyman G. Rickover was considered the father of the nuclear Navy. He ran the U.S. Navy's nuclear-power program for many years, from 1948 until he eventually left active duty in 1982 with the rank of four-star admiral on the retired list. Rickover Hall at the Naval Academy is named in his honor, as is the nuclear-powered attack submarine *Hyman G. Rickover* (SSN-709), which was commissioned 21 July 1984.

Admiral Lawrence: Well, it's some of each, and there are certainly people who have those inherent attributes that make them better leaders. But I contend very much that leadership ability can be improved. My thrust is to learn the important qualities, then concentrate your effort on trying to enhance those qualities in yourself, and always be assessing yourself. As I talk about it in discipline, the sense of responsibility, seeking responsibility, loyalty, stamina, and intelligence in the sense of very efficient study to try to enhance your knowledge by observing events around you.

Like Douglas Southall Freeman really gave a strong emphasis to this, the power of observation, as important to a leader. He gave the example of General Cadmus Wilcox in the Civil War, who was a Confederate general and at the time of the Battle of Fredericksburg. Lee had given him the responsibility to protect one of his flanks. So Cadmus Wilcox got up very early in the morning and he looked across the Tappahannock River, and he noticed that all of the federal sentries that were marching back and forth had full packs. He said, "There's no question that they're going to move." His concern was whether they were going to try a flanking movement. So he immediately woke up his troops and got his artillery people going, and they attacked early in the morning before the federal troops moved, to prevent them from engaging in this flanking movement. Freeman used that as an example of how just observation, this very keen interest in events that are going on around you, was a very important quality of leaders that can enhance your intelligence.

But, anyway, I think, as I say, you can improve your abilities as a leader by concentrating on these important qualities.

Paul Stillwell: Well, and courage, I don't know how you can acquire that, but you also have to draw a distinction between being courageous and foolhardy.

Admiral Lawrence: Well, that's right. And then, once assuming that those are views that you bring in your academies or to your commissioning sources, they have had this foundation that's been laid from their early years. Given the basic foundation of courage, the most important things are training and experience. I mean, in the military, you simply just have to train in the types of things that you're going to do in combat.

I just barely missed the Korean War, so my first combat was in the Vietnam War, but by the time I went in combat, I had all these years of training. So I found that right from the very beginning, I felt very comfortable in combat, because I had such a solid foundation of training. When I saw flak coming up at me, I wasn't fearful, because I had this high degree of confidence that I had developed from that basic foundation of very extensive training. So the training, trying to experience as best you can in peacetime, the situations that you're going to encounter in wartime, is a very important component to giving your troops the ability to go into combat. Of course, as George Washington said, "Discipline is the soul of an army." And you only acquire discipline through effective training, growing, and so forth. So that to me is important, assuming that you pick the right type of people to come into your officer corps.

My big concern today, so I follow the fact that we're practicing flagrant careerism. The officer corps has become very politicized. We've departed from what I call the Ernie King tradition, where he spent 22 years at sea before he was a flag officer.[*] He was, to me, the epitome of the professional officer that looked at everything purely from a very professional perspective—what was right for the Navy, his ability to accomplish his mission. He was about as apolitical as anybody you've ever seen. He got where he did, and his successes were based on his doing what naval officers should do, and that's being at sea. We've kind of departed from that Ernie King position.

Paul Stillwell: One thing that Admiral Dunn especially praised you for when I talked to him was your work in instigating the honor code.[†] Could you talk about that, please?

Admiral Lawrence: Well, I can't take credit for having all this brilliant perception and insight. It was just something where events kind of conspired to make this happen. When I was coming along here at the academy, and being an athlete and spending most

---

[*] Admiral Ernest J. King, USN, served as Chief of Naval Operations from 26 March 1942 to 15 December 1945 and as Commander in Chief U.S. Fleet from 20 December 1941 to 2 September 1945; he was promoted to the rank of fleet admiral in December 1944. See Thomas B. Buell, *Master of Sea Power: A Biography of Admiral Ernest J. King* (Boston: Little, Brown, 1980).
[†] Vice Admiral Robert F. Dunn, USN (Ret.), was a Naval Academy classmate of Lawrence. His oral history is in the Naval Institute collection.

of the year on training tables, I saw a practice going on here at the academy that concerned me and it concerned some of my friends.* It was known as the dope system.

See, in those days, we had the lock-step curriculum, where every midshipman took the same courses as every other midshipman. We didn't have the majors program and electives as we do today. The practice was that one regiment would go to class in the morning, and the other regiment would go in the afternoon. The faculty, just basically assuming that the midshipmen were honest, would give the same quizzes in the afternoon that they gave in the morning. So over the years, I guess there were enough midshipmen saying, "Hey, if you talk to somebody that had a quiz in the morning, you could find out what the quiz questions will be for the afternoon." That was called "passing the dope." It got to be kind of prevalent on the training tables because midshipman of mixed regiments ate together, whereas, on the company tables, you ate with everybody from your same regiment.

I noted that this seemed to increase during my time of midshipman, that fellows from one regiment would ask the other regiment, "Hey, what was the quiz question this morning?" This bothered me, because I knew these were fundamentally honest midshipmen, and that it was immaturity and the lack of judgment on their part that made them fall into this dope system.

But some guys got to be very sophisticated; they would get on maybe the deck phone over in their regiment and call over a guy over there and say, "What was your question this morning?" So several of us talked about it and finally did something in the winter of 1950, my third year. I was the president of the class of '51 and there was Chuck Dobony, who was the winter set brigade commander, and I think he was also the vice president of his class.† Jim Sagerholm was the president of the class of '52.‡, and this was in the winter of 1950. Also, there had been a group of first classmen in the fall of 1949 that had talked about this and said that something had to be done at the academy to get rid of the dope system.

---

* Training tables provided meals to athletes separately from the general mess in which most midshipmen ate. The idea was that their diets could be geared to their nutritional needs in sports.
† Midshipman Charles Dobony, USN, class of 1950. In order to provide opportunities to a greater number of midshipmen, the Naval Academy rotated positions so that there were three different "sets" of leaders in the academic year—autumn, winter, and spring.
‡ Midshipman James A. Sagerholm, USN.

The three of us put our heads together. So Chuck Dobony, the brigade commander in January of 1950; I, as the president of our class; and Jim Sagerholm, the president of his class—we decided that on our own initiative, we would assemble each of our classes. Chuck Dobony would also talk to the plebe classes, as well as the first classmen, and we would ask our classes to vow that we would disestablish or exterminate—whatever you want to call it—the dope system. We would not allow the dope system to exist anymore. So each of us assembled our classes, and we got an overwhelming support to do this.

Then, after the fact, we reported this to the leadership of the academy, the commandant and the superintendent. They were very impressed that we had taken it upon ourselves to do this. So they had us form an executive committee, which was composed of the first class stripers and the class officers of the underclass, to discuss and review ways that we could enhance the overall level of honor in the brigade. We held those discussions but didn't do anything definitive the rest of that 1949-50 year, other than observe and make sure the dope system had, in fact, been eradicated.

When I came back in the fall of 1950, I'd been reelected to be the class president, and now was the brigade commander also. So, being both the class president and the brigade commander, being in charge of this executive committee fell to me. But very early in that academic year, we heard from the deputy commandant, whom we called the executive officer of Bancroft Hall.[*] This was Commander John Chew, out of the class of '31, who made captain while he was here later on retired as a vice admiral.[†] He started referring what we call Class-A offenses to this executive committee for our review and recommendation. So we started doing that type of work. Some of those Class-A offenses involved what we used to call moral turpitude cases. So we would review these and discuss them among ourselves, and then we would go back with a recommendation.

Because I was so busy as the brigade commander and everything, I had to give up playing any varsity sports that year. I had played three sports for three years, and I just didn't play anymore because of my responsibilities in my senior year. But I was not a

---

[*] Bancroft Hall is the large multi-wing dormitory that houses Naval Academy midshipmen. It also contains the offices of members of the executive department, including the commandant, executive officer, and battalion and company officers.
[†] The oral history of Vice Admiral John L. Chew, USN (Ret.), is in the Naval Institute collection.

great star, so it was not a great loss to the teams. But I had been a letterman. Anyway, I really concentrated a lot of my effort in that last year as brigade commander and class president, working on things like the honor concept.

Right after the Army-Navy football game was over, the superintendent, who was Harry W. Hill, decided to assemble the entire brigade over in Dahlgren Hall, the old armory.* One thing that we had come up against just prior to that was that a classmate of mine had engaged in some dishonorable activity; he had erased a muster board. We used to have these old muster boards that you'd fill out with pencil, and then after muster was complete and reported, you'd erase it. He missed a church party muster, and he came into the battalion office and wanted to erase the A after his name. He was caught in the act, and so this situation was referred to our executive committee. He was not a really, totally admirable guy anyway, but because of this, plus his flagrant cheating and dishonorable behavior, we recommended to the superintendent that he be separated. And he was separated. That was the most serious thing that we did in our review of these cases that fall.

Anyway, the superintendent got the entire brigade together and said that he was very interested in upgrading the standard of honor. He admired the fact that it eradicated the dope system, and he said that he was going to take other initiatives. One was to absolutely respect a midshipman's signature. If a midshipman signed his name or initialed something, the leadership of the academy would absolutely respect that. The other thing was that he was going to remove all the proctors from examinations. He said, "I'm manifesting this trust and respect to you, and I expect you to meet your responsibilities and maintain a high standard of honor."

Then I realized that, because of the superintendent's emphasis and what we were doing in reviewing these serious cases and the fact that we'd recommended that a classmate be separated, that we simply had to develop a really, really effective means of reviewing these cases and arriving at recommendations that were based on justice and what was right. My committee by this time had an addition. Besides Jim Sagerholm

---

* Vice Admiral Harry W. Hill, USN, was superintendent of the Naval Academy from April 1950 to August 1952.

being the president '52, now Ross Perot was the president of the class of '53.[*] So Ross Perot and Jim Sagerholm and I really led this effort.

I had developed better-defined procedures for summoning of witnesses, how the hearings were conducted, so that we really fully respected the rights of the individuals at these cases that we were reviewing. So we continued that, but we also had a lot of discussions among ourselves about what we should do to improve the standard of honor at the academy. I did a very thorough analysis of the West Point honor code. There were certain aspects of that that I didn't like based on my discussions with the other cadets. One thing, I didn't like their non-toleration clauses. The honor code at West Point, which Douglas MacArthur had established when he was superintendent there in 1921, said that a cadet would not lie, cheat, or steal, nor tolerate those that do.[†] I would talk to the cadets, and I just felt that this mandatory reporting of every offense was not completely productive, because it's really hard for a cadet or a midshipman to report another classmate.

Classmate loyalty is very strong, and they ran up against this conflict between this loyalty and this mandatory reporting. I sensed that there were cases in which the cadets at West Point were looking the other way, because they didn't want to report a classmate. So I pushed for what I called the counseling option, that a midshipman would be allowed to counsel another midshipman rather than have him reported. I felt that there were going to be a lot of these cases that recurred that I observed because lack of experience and maturity, and there would be relatively minor offenses, just a mild case of telling a white lie. So I didn't think it was necessary to have to have a formal investigation—what I called a public embarrassment, demoralization. I saw cases of good cadets at West Point being separated, because they just felt that once a there was an offense against the system, that there was this absolute obligation to separate the cadet.

---

[*] Midshipman H. Ross Perot, USN. He resigned from the active Navy in 1957 and became a successful businessman. He founded Electronic Data Systems (EDS) in 1962. In 1992 he ran unsuccessfully for President of the United States.

[†] Brigadier General Douglas MacArthur, USA, served as superintendent of the Military Academy from 12 June 1919 to 30 June 1922.

Paul Stillwell: Did you go there and interview people?

Admiral Lawrence: No, I just talked to a lot of them down here on exchange visits. And, of course, I went to West Point several times in athletic events. So that's when I espoused this counseling option, which we have still today.

The other thing that I didn't like about the West Point honor code was that it had a long list of "Thou shalt nots." I felt, gee, we had enough of that in our conduct system. We had a big, thick reg book about what constituted an offense. I said we shouldn't have this list of "Thou shalt nots," because I found the West Point cadets were doing some things that I think were counterproductive to what the honor code stood for. For example, it said the cadet would not have alcohol in a room. So they'd tie a bottle of alcohol on a string and put it outside the window. One year they'd say stuffing your bed was an honor offense; the next year they'd take it off. I said, "That's kind of absurd. Really, honor is an attitudinal, philosophical concept. We should concentrate on what we do here creating an attitude, a way of life." So when I made my report after graduation to the superintendent as to what we had done, I embodied these recommendations. The superintendent bought the counseling options; he bought the attitudinal way of life. And that's what led to the using the term "honor concept" as opposed to honor code. I put an article in the June *Shipmate* magazine that elaborated on all this.[*] I wrote it primarily for the incoming plebe class, but also to explain to the alumni what we had really done, to establish the honor concept at the academy.

As I say, I benefited very much from observing the weaknesses I saw in the West Point honor code and talking to the cadets. So the establishment of the honor concept here was something that just kind of evolved, based on fewer midshipmen receiving separation. It was something that needed to be done, and the leadership at the academy eventually became involved. So it evolved into the honor concept, never realizing when we started out that that was going to be the case.

But I think our honor concept here—which is substantially the same as we just developed it back there in 1950-51—has endured, still is very much the same. Although

---

[*] *Shipmate* is the periodic magazine published by the Naval Academy Alumni Association. See "The Nicest Sense of Personal Honor," June 1990, pages 15-17.

I know I'm biased, I think it's proven to be more relevant than the West Point honor code, because the non-toleration clause and this codification of "Thou shalt nots." I think this has led to their having a few more problems with theirs than we have. But they still refuse to do away with that non-toleration clause. They had another vote with the cadets recently, and the cadets voted to keep it in there. But I know that all sorts of accommodations that go on up there that we don't do here. I know that ours, of course, has imperfections, but I think it would do a pretty good job with the honor concept and the other things that we do, or developing this attitude, way of life here at the academy.

That effort consumed a great part of my first-class year.

Paul Stillwell: What do you recall about your dealings with Admiral Hill and Commander Chew specifically?

Admiral Lawrence: Well, I had three very fine leaders. Admiral Hill was the superintendent, but my first three years it was Admiral James L. Holloway Jr.[*] Of course, as an underclassman, I didn't have any interface with him, but he was a wonderful role model. Then Admiral Hill was the superintendent my last year, and I had a lot of interface with him, as the brigade commander within the fall and the spring.

Then we had a commandant, Captain Robert B. Pirie, who later on became a vice admiral—a very colorful gent.[†]

I think it should be pointed out that a lot of changes were brought into effect when Admiral Hill came in. Now, Admiral Holloway, who later on became a four-star admiral, was the one who formulated the Holloway Plan, which was a very rapid expansion of NROTC program in the Navy.[‡] He was very liberal-minded, and he put in a lot of practices here that I think were sound. He let the first class have every other weekend

---

[*] Rear Admiral James L. Holloway, Jr., USN, was superintendent of the Naval Academy from January 1947 to April 1950.
[†] Captain Robert B. Pirie, USN, served from 1949 to 1952 as the Naval Academy's commandant of midshipmen.
[‡] In 1946, the Holloway Plan was enacted to establish a Naval ROTC program that would pay for the college education of individuals and grant regular, rather than reserve, commissions upon graduation. It was named for Rear Admiral James L. Holloway, Jr., USN, who had much to do with its development. Holloway, who retired as a four-star admiral, wrote two articles about the program for the *U.S. Naval Institute Proceedings*. See "The Holloway Plan—A Summary View and Commentary," November 1947, pages 1293-1303, and "A Gentlemen's Agreement," September 1980, pages 71-77.

off; they could wear civilian clothes when they were away on weekends; keep civilian clothes in our room. First class didn't have to march to class.

Then Admiral Hill came in—the old-school naval officer—and he did away with having every other weekend off. Then I think they got two weekends a semester, and you couldn't keep civilian clothes in your room. The first class had to start marching to class except the three-stripers and above. It was really a tightening up across the board. So my classmates were really very bitter, because they looked forward to all these privileges, and they were taken away just as they became first classmen. So I was really caught up in this as the class president and the brigade commander, trying to maintain this linkage between the administration and my class. It was really a tough line to walk. I had several discussions with Captain Chew, who was my principal interface, but I did have occasional audiences with the commandant, and very infrequent discussions with the superintendent. But it was difficult the first part of first class year, getting my class to settle down and to accept their leadership responsibilities in the brigade, because they were very, very upset about this loss of all these privileges.

Paul Stillwell: Did you make any headway at that?

Admiral Lawrence: Oh, yes. I asked and got a meeting of the first class company representatives and the commandant and the deputy commandant. I had some classmates who weren't very subtle. Boy, they stood up and really blasted the commandant. And Admiral Pirie was a very fiery guy. He had a short fuse, so that was a real shootout session. But, as a result of that, they gave us one privilege back. They let us have late lights; instead of having to go to bed at 10:00, we could stay up till 11:00. We told them we simply couldn't do our leadership responsibilities as first classmen if they didn't give us late light privileges, which traditionally were given to first classmen

That's the only thing we got back. We still had to march to class; we still had very few weekends. But, eventually, our class got settled in and did better as the year went on. But it was a very, very busy year for me, because, literally, three nights a week, instead of studying I was working on that honor concept development, because we had to go through all these board sessions, dealing with cases, and trying to develop a good procedure that respected the rights of the individual, due process and all that. We didn't have any lawyers. We had to do it on our own innate sense of what was right. So we really were plowing a lot of new ground. But we had some remarkable maturity among the people that I dealt with: Jim Sagerholm, who retired later on as a vice admiral; Ross Perot was just a young 19-year-old, but he had remarkable wisdom and perception of the right thing to do.

Paul Stillwell: Could you say more about him, please?

Admiral Lawrence: Well, he showed a lot of the qualities as a third class midshipman that he does today. He had a very strong sense of right and wrong, always tell it like it is, kind of a brashness, very much a Texan in the way he spoke, his approach to things. But I had a great respect for his opinion, because even though he was a third classman, he had some good insights. As I say, we were plowing a lot of new ground, because, we had to draw up procedure on our own as midshipmen. When you brought in a midshipman that had been charged with an offense, how should you question him? How should you give him the opportunity to present his side? We developed a concept of having the midshipmen serve as their counselors. In our own inexperienced state, we had an appreciation for due process and all that. So we had to do a lot of hard work to develop these honor-board-type procedures, which are very formalized today.

Paul Stillwell: Do you remember any of the individual cases that came up?

Admiral Lawrence: Yes, I remember this one case where we had to recommend separation for this classmate of mine in erasing that muster board. That June 1990 *Shipmate* article I wrote describes our work in that area. But one comment I made in this report to the superintendent, I said that a large percentage of the cases that came before us were those situations where midshipmen would lie to avoid being caught for another offense, which was a non-honor-type offense. I said the key message we should impart to midshipmen is: "Don't lie to cover something up; admit that something has happened, take your punishment, and you're going to be far better off in the long run." That is one thing I have recommended from that day forward to everybody I've ever advised.

When I came back here as superintendent, that was the first thing I told the midshipmen, "Look, 75% of the honor cases here are going to be when midshipmen lie to prevent being caught for something else. Don't do it. You'll find that in this career, you simply have to be very forthcoming, very quick in admitting wherever there has been a mistake and error, because you're going to be far better off in the long run if you do that. The longer that you allow a mistake or an improper situation to exist, the worse of a problem it's going to be. If you try to cover up something, and it's revealed, you're going to be far worse off than if you admit it right away. Learn that lesson right here at the academy and carry it with you for the rest of your career." So that's something I perceived back as a young midshipman, and it has just been a key principle to me throughout my career.

Paul Stillwell: Any other observations on Captain Pirie? You mentioned that he was colorful.

Admiral Lawrence: Well, as I say, he was a great leader; he had a very short fuse and almost violent temper. But I had some interesting experiences with him. Most of the times when I went in his office, I was in the "receive" mode. [Laughter] Very few things I got to say. But it was tough for him, because the superintendent was making changes in our privileges that he had to implement.

Another unpopular decision was that we were going back to wearing the traditional midshipman full-dress uniform, which had been done away with during the war, because the three-year classes were just trying to save expense and all that. We did away with some of the traditions. Admiral Hill reinstated the full-dress uniform, so my class had to pay over $100.00 for a uniform. I think we wore it twice, because by the time we got it cleaned, we were in spring. So Captain Pirie had to make some of these changes.

Another interesting thing was that the class of 1950 had lost money on their yearbook, the *Lucky Bag*, through mismanagement. So they had to send letters out to the class of '50 after graduation requesting contributions so they could pay the bills. So he called me up to his office and he said, "This is not going to happen to your class. I'm stipulating right now that every member of your class will get two *Lucky Bag*s. No question, no argument, you're going to get two *Lucky Bag*s." So I had to carry that back to the class. Boy, they were pretty upset about that.

But now, of course, they're probably happy because it meant their parents got a book and they got a book. As a result of that, we graduated with $6,000.00 in our class treasury. I stayed here after graduation to train plebes before going down to aviation. So I was the one, as class president, who had to decide what to do with that money. I got in touch with the midshipman financial adviser, who was a lieutenant commander in the Supply Corps. I said, "Do you have any advice for me as how I could best handle this money? My disposition is to put them into savings bonds, defense bonds."

He said, "Well, I'll just tell you there's a kind of a new type investment that you might want to think about. It's called a mutual fund. One of the original mutual fund companies is the Massachusetts Investment Trust in Boston. I can put you in touch with a man over in Washington who can sign you up for this, and you might want to consider it."

So I said, "Well, probably I'll take your advice. I don't have any financial knowledge at all as a former midshipman." So I took $1,000.00 and I put it into Farmers National Bank, just as a source of ready capital in case our class needed it. Then I put $5,000.00 in this the Massachusetts Investment Trust Second Fund, which is now called the Massachusetts Investment Services, a growth stock fund.

After that I went on out to flight training and then went to sea. I'd get these quarterly statements, and I'd just put them in a file, never really carefully looking at them. Finally, in 1957 our class was back on shore duty when a large group of guys on duty here at the academy decided that we would try to establish a class organization. I was down at Naval Air Test Center Patuxent. So I worked with them on this, and we went to a concept of having a class president over a five-year period and selecting other officers, I guess, on an annual basis. Well, I was elected to be the first president of the class. I had to turn over all these records to the guy who was elected treasurer, so I sat down and for the first time I tried to compute where I was. That $5,000.00 that I had invested in 1951 was worth $14,000.00 by '57. So, gosh, we were one of the wealthiest classes at the Naval Academy with that big slug of money, and we've stayed better off financially. We bought a gate at the new stadium over here when it was built in 1958. We've done a lot of other things with the money.

By that time our former commandant was now Vice Admiral Pirie, who was Commander of the Second Fleet.[*] So I wrote him a letter and said, "Dear Admiral Pirie, when you made that decision back in 1950 that we would each buy two yearbooks, it was very unpopular. But I want to tell you that it turned out to be a very good thing for our class because we have all this money."

So he wrote back. He said, "I want to tell you that it makes me feel good that some of the things that I did back in that time have turned out to be good decisions." Anyway, he and I stayed good friends over the years. When I came back here as superintendent, he was the president of the Naval Academy Foundation, which runs the scholarship program. I saw him a lot. So we were very close to each other in his later years until he died last year.[†] But that was one example of some interface with him.

Also, I remember one time we were having a pep rally out in Tecumseh Court.[‡] The superintendent, Admiral Hill, brought Governor McKeldin of Maryland over with their wives to observe the pep rally.[§] Some midshipmen got the bright idea of throwing rolls of toilet paper out of Bancroft Hall in this pep rally. Apparently, a roll of toilet paper came down and hit Mrs. McKeldin on the head. After it was all over, Captain Pirie, the commandant, mustered the entire brigade out in Tecumseh Court. As punishment we had to pick up all the toilet paper.

Another thing that happened involved the new full-dress uniforms, which were produced by the Jacob Reed's in those days.[**] Jacob Reed's was later taken over by Hart Schaffner Marx. I was the one that had to come up and model the first full-dress uniform. I'll never forget going into Captain Pirie's office and Jacob Reed's tailors were

---

[*] Vice Admiral Robert B. Pirie, USN, commanded the Second Fleet from July 1957 to May 1958.
[†] Admiral Pirie died 9 January 1990.
[‡] Tecumseh is the nickname of an American Indian pictured in a prominent bust near the entrance to Bancroft Hall. It is a prominent Naval Academy landmark, often decorated in different colors to celebrate sporting events.
[§] Theodore R. McKeldin was governor of Maryland from 1951 to 1959.
[**] Jacob Reed's Sons of Philadelphia manufactured uniforms for many years.

all there, deputy commandant and everybody. I was standing there, and he looked at this thing. He put his hand underneath where you have the buttons at the collar and cover the chest. He grabbed that uniform, and he said, "Look at this. Look how badly this thing fits." I remember being thrust back and forth in his office. But, really, he was a great naval officer. He went on to be the Deputy Chief of Naval Operations for Air for about four years, and he really was a great leader of naval aviation.[*] I had great admiration for him. He was colorful, very volatile, short fuse, but one of the old school personalities in the Navy.

Admiral Hill was very, very traditional, surface guy. He'd been an amphibious commander in World War II for the invasions of Okinawa and places like that.

Paul Stillwell: And had great enthusiasm for the sports teams here.

Admiral Lawrence: Yes, that's where I first met him. I was on the baseball team. His wife Mary was from Annapolis. So he would come back and visit with her and her family. And he would always come to the athletic events. I remember meeting him when I was on the baseball team. He'd come down in the dugout and say, "I'm Admiral Hill." Because at that time he, I think, was the commandant of the National War College in Washington.[†]

Paul Stillwell: Yes, he was.

Admiral Lawrence: So I met him before he was superintendent. And then he was very, very good to me when I was a brigade commander. After the parades, the brigade staff would go over, and he would introduce us to the dignitary who reviewed the parade. I remember some very famous people came to review our parades. One was Admiral Sherman, who was our Chief of Naval Operations.[‡] The other was Admiral McCormick,

---

[*] Vice Admiral Pirie served as Deputy Chief of Naval Operations (Air) from 26 May 1958 to 1 November 1962. His oral history is in the Naval Institute collection.
[†] Vice Admiral Hill served as commandant of the National War College from 1946 to 1949.
[‡] Admiral Forrest P. Sherman, USN, served as Chief of Naval Operations from 2 November 1949 until his death on 22 July 1951.

who was later CinCLantFlt.* Then, of course, we always had the Board of Visitors, so I had pretty close interface with him as a brigade commander.

Then during June Week, Admiral Hill invited my parents to stay with them in the superintendent's house, and that was a real great thrill for my parents. But I stayed in touch with him over the years. Of course, he retired from here, and then when I would come back to the academy, I'd try to least say hello to Admiral and Mrs. Hill. When I came back as superintendent, Mrs. Hill was still living, and I really tried to stay in touch with her, although he'd passed on.†

I still stay in touch with Captain Chew. He lives over in Providence.‡ He was really the brains in the executive department, the conceptualizer who really guided us so much in the groundwork that we did as midshipmen on this honor concept. In my time, we didn't use the term "honor concept." That was a name that was developed later. Although, after talking to all my friends, we conceived the approach, this philosophical attitude, as opposed to the strictly codified. So they felt that it was only appropriate to call it a concept as opposed to a code.

Paul Stillwell: What did you call it before you called it the honor concept?

Admiral Lawrence: The honor standards.

Paul Stillwell: Captain Pirie had come here to establish the aviation department in the late '40s and had stayed on. How much was aviation emphasized during your time as a midshipman?

Admiral Lawrence: Well, it wasn't emphasized over anything else. It was just a department here, and we took a course in aviation.

Paul Stillwell: But that was a recognition that it had an increased role in the fleet.

---

* Admiral Lynde D. McCormick, USN, served as Supreme Allied Commander Atlantic, Commander in Chief Atlantic Command, and Commander in Chief Atlantic Fleet from 15 August 1951 to 12 April 1954.
† Admiral Hill died 19 July 1971.
‡ Providence is a residential subdivision across the Severn River from the Naval Academy.

Admiral Lawrence: I didn't really get all that much out of those aviation courses that we took. I didn't think that they were really done all that well. It was a little bit too much nuts and bolts as opposed to strategic. What are the broad strategic ways that aviation was being used? Mostly, it was just the basic mechanical aspects of aviation deployment.

So I wasn't really all that impressed with the courses. But it was interesting to have the interface with the aviators teaching these courses. But the first three years I was here, I was very close to a submariner because of my participation in sports. He was the assistant director of athletics and the exec of the physical education department. This was a guy named Dusty Dornin of the class of '35, a really great submarine hero in World War II.[*]

Paul Stillwell: And also a character.

Admiral Lawrence: A real character. He and his family kind of adopted me, and I used to go over to their house a lot. One time my girlfriend from my hometown came up for two weeks, and she stayed at their house. So we became, probably, closer to that family than any other family while I was here.

K. G. Schacht was a good friend of his.[†] I think they were classmates.

Paul Stillwell: They were, yes.

Admiral Lawrence: And both submariners. K. G. had been a POW in World War II. So I was very impressed about that.

They both left at the end of my youngster year. Then I developed a relationship through Commander Chew, although he was a surface officer. A very close friend of his from down in Vista, Georgia, was Captain MacPherson Williams, an aviator out of the class of '30. So Jack Chew was responsible for my meeting my future wife, who was MacPherson Williams's daughter, Anne Williams. I started dating her the spring of my first-class year, and then we eventually got married a year or so later. So that was the

---
[*] Commander Robert E. Dornin, USN.
[†] Commander Kenneth G. Schacht, USN.

sequence—the fact that Dusty Dornin and K. G. Schacht had left, and then I met the Williams family. I started really getting interested in aviation, because he had quite a record in World War II. He was shot down in the Philippines, and he evaded and stayed with the guerrillas for several months. So my association with Captain Williams got my interest piqued in aviation. Although I'd been, initially, attracted to submarines and all the heroic exploits of submariners, I could see that jet airplanes were coming into aviation. I just sensed that that's where my real future was. I read about all the carrier operations in World War II, what the carriers had done. I read very carefully about the Battle of Midway and Coral Sea and the Battle of the Philippine Sea and the Marianas Turkey Shoot.

Paul Stillwell: Any specific anecdotes about Dornin? Certainly he was a colorful character.

Admiral Lawrence: Well, I can't remember any specific anecdotes about him except that both Dusty and K. G. Schacht, their first wives had divorced them.* K. G.'s had divorced him while he was a POW.

Paul Stillwell: She was a movie actress, named Marjorie Weaver.

Admiral Lawrence: So they both had married younger second wives. Dusty's wife was Ellie Dornin. He had a daughter from his first marriage, and then he had a second family with Ellie Dornin. I remember how he was really like my father; he was the patriarch of the household. I remember how impressed I was that these guys whom I perceived as really being old men were probably only about in their mid-30s to late 30s, and they had these two really young, good-looking wives.†

    I can't remember any real specific anecdotes, except that I really always enjoyed going into Dornin's study and looking at his World War II memorabilia. He had one

---

* Dornin's first wife had died.
† Dornin was born in 1912 and Schacht in 1913.

record, which I forget what it was, but I think he had the highest tonnage sunk of a certain category of tonnage that was sunk in World War II when he was submarine commander.

Also, I was close to another submarine commander, who was Elliot Loughlin. He was officer representative of basketball, and I got to know him through my playing basketball.*

So in my early years, I was very close to the submarine officers here, but I think it was Captain Pirie and Captain Williams, who were both aviators, who swung me toward interest in aviation.

I was never very interested in surface Navy. Admiral Hill tried to get us all interested in amphibs, because he'd been an amphibious commander.

It was a great, wonderful time to be here, because we had so many World War II heroes who came back here—both Navy and Marine Corps. I remember some of our Marine officers here had really been heroes. We had Lieutenant Colonel Antonelli, who was one of the battalion officers, and he used to tell the story that he had jumped into foxholes with two Japanese and grabbed them and banged their heads together. Because every time you'd see him walking down the hall, boy, there'd be all fear and trepidation. When we'd see him, we'd visualize him in the foxhole.

Paul Stillwell: Did your grades suffer any in your first-class year from all this responsibilities you had?

Admiral Lawrence: Yes, I think they did, although my class standing remained high. I think if I had not had those responsibilities, I could perhaps have done better. But it really was no greater than I'd had for the first three years because of playing in those sports teams. In a lot of respects, being in sports was more of a burden than what I did the first class year, in terms of overall physical effort.

But I really got the absolute maximum of productivity out of my system while I was a midshipman. That's one good lesson I'd taught myself in early years of playing sports. I never wasted any time here as a midshipman. I started studying at the

---

* Commander C. Elliott Loughlin, USN. The oral history of Loughlin, who retired as a rear admiral, is in the Naval Institute collection.

beginning of the study hour, and I studied right to the end. Even though I would be very tired physically, I got myself into such a high degree of good physical shape, that I could study hard, as well as do the physical things. But my first class year we were working so much on that honor concept that I had to take advantage of my position as brigade commander just to stay up. The brigade commander had his own special room with a little private commode. No basin or anything like that, but you had a commode. So sometimes just not have a light on in the room, I'd go back into that little room and study. I had to do that many times later on. I could probably have stood higher if I'd just had more time to totally dedicate to my studies, but it really wasn't that important to me. I really wanted to do these other things. But still I stood eighth in my class.

Paul Stillwell: Couldn't have been much higher.

Admiral Lawrence: Right.

Paul Stillwell: Well, with all this effective utilization of time, did you deliberately make opportunities to relax, to keep from getting wound too tight?

Admiral Lawrence: No, I never really seemed to have to do that, although I didn't do a lot of social activity. I had the fun times. I would do some things. But going away on athletic trips was a great source of pleasure to me. Because I was very close to my fellows on the team, we'd always do something when we were away on trips. I would always have these guys who would get me a blind date or something like that.

I'll never forget my great memories in the 1948 Army-Navy football game. I was a youngster, and we tied Army, 18-18. Army was the overwhelming favorite in that game. They had a dinner for us at the Bellevue-Stratford Hotel in Philadelphia after the game. A teammate of mine, a classmate named Bob Renneman, who was killed in the Korean War, got me a blind date.[*] I had never had a drink of alcohol in my life. We walked into this thing, and they had all these pre-mixed drinks on trays. The gal I was dating was kind of sophisticated; she had drunk before. Everybody else was drinking, so

---

[*] Midshipman Robert A. Renneman, USN.

I said, "Well, gosh, I'm going to try it." So I drank some drink; it tasted terrible. It was an Old Fashioned or something like that. Then we sat down and had this beautiful steak dinner, and about 20 minutes into that, I got violently ill; I mean really ill. So Bob Renneman had to take me down to my room where I spent the next hour or so throwing up, lying in my bed. Meanwhile, my lovely date was sitting up there by herself. Needless to say, that didn't blossom into a great romantic relationship. That was the first drink of alcohol I ever had, and that was the last time I had any alcohol for a long time.

Paul Stillwell: What were your duties and responsibilities as the brigade commander, in addition to this honor development?

Admiral Lawrence: Well, the brigade ran itself in terms of military evolutions: the parades and the formations. I was the principal link with the executive department, and we would meet about policies or actions that had to be taken. That was done principally through the brigade organization.

But, also, in those days class presidents were a lot more prominent and influential than they are today. Today it's just purely an honorary administration. In those days the first classmen were the stripers, and they had the responsibility as stripers. But in the lower classes, it was the presidents and the class company representatives who ran their classes. Then as first classmen, you also had these company representatives. So most of my honor concept work was really done as a class president, rather than the brigade commander. But the military evolution through the brigade, basic actions that had to be taken in a military sense were done through the brigade stripe organization.

For example, we had to get everybody prepared to go up for the away football games and how the march-ons would be done and military smartness and all those areas, where you had to handle as a striper. As brigade commander, you were the principal interface with the executive department. But it was never clear to me where my brigade commander responsibilities ended and my class president's responsibilities began.

Paul Stillwell: Why would you say that the role of the class president has diminished since then?

Admiral Lawrence: Well, it's just the nature of young people. They don't seem to accord the respect and the importance to those elective positions like we used to. People pick their class officers based on their popularity and respect. Those types of things don't seem to be as important to young people nowadays.

That's one factor. I think the stripers today do more specific responsibilities than we did in our time. For example, they have now the brigade supply officer, [unclear] officer, and they all have a lot more detailed responsibilities than we seemed to in those days. That might be another factor that some of the things that the class presidents and the class officers handle have been more and more taken over by the striper positions.

But I think it's the philosophical aspect of this: that the young people just don't seem to have this peer respect, peer leaders and so forth.

Of course, the other thing--and it's a very significant change---is that your athletes during my time were your principal leaders. Most of your top stripers in those days were also athletes. Today athletes have become so specialized that it's very rare, for example, if a football player gets to be a striper, because he's off separated doing the athletic stuff, and he has to lift weights. It's just a total commitment of his time, so he doesn't get involved in brigade activities.

But my plebe year, we had two brigade commanders. One was Dick Scott, who was an all-American center; the other was Dick Shimshak, who was a tackle.[*] I think one of the three brigade commanders was not a football player, and that was during the fall when the football players were here. My second year, Pete Williams, who was the football captain, was a six-striper.[†] The second-class year the six-stripers were athletes. And then, of course, I got to be six-striper; I played football.

So the respect of athletes was far greater in those days, usually. I guess you have to say that in some respect the six-striper and the brigade striper positions were more honorary, based on the overall respect, popularity of the individuals in the brigade, than it is today, where the decision is based more on other qualities. But I think there were more inspirational leaders that were the stripers in those days than there are now.

---

[*] Midshipman Richard U. Scott, USN, and Midshipman Richard E. Shimshak, USN, class of 1948.
[†] Midshipman Ralph Pete Williams, USN, class of 1949. The midshipman in the top leadership position within the brigade was designated as the six-striper, indicated by the six narrow stripes he wore around each sleeve of his uniform blouse.

Paul Stillwell: Well, one might argue, though, that with that lock-step curriculum that you've described, that being in athletics would be something that would distinguish a person, and that's why he'd become known.

Admiral Lawrence: Yes, that's right, that's right.

And, of course, the midshipmen were more caught up in the spirit of the athletics in those days than they are now, because you were very much focused inwardly here at the academy. You didn't really think a lot about what went on outside the walls. You didn't have this constant stream of midshipmen going out in the town. The activities were in here, and football was really kind of the preeminent sports activity here. So anybody that played football automatically was respected in the brigade. You didn't have the attitude that I see a lot now that, "Oh, he's a football bum." You never saw that when I was here.

A lot of guys who play football today are not held in high respect by other midshipmen. In fact, that's one of our problems today is that the midshipmen don't really respect the football players.

Paul Stillwell: Might that be because the team doesn't win as much as it used to?

Admiral Lawrence: Yes, that's a good question, but I think they also perceive that they're just distinctly different from the rest of the midshipmen, that they're isolated. When I was a football player, we were just totally integrated with the rest of the midshipmen. We had training tables, but everything else we did was integrated.

Paul Stillwell: Any of your athletic coaches you especially remember from that period?

Admiral Lawrence: Oh, sure. In fact, I still stay very close to our basketball coach, Ben Carnevale.* In fact, back in January this last year we had a 40-year reunion of our 1950 basketball team, and Ben Carnevale, who's still living, came back for that.

---

* Bernard L. "Ben" Carnevale compiled a 257-160 record as the Naval Academy's head basketball coach, 1947-67. He was inducted into the Basketball Hall of Fame in 1970. He died in March 2008 at age 92.

Paul Stillwell: Is he still down at Williamsburg?

Admiral Lawrence: Well, he became the director of athletics at William and Mary, and now he's retired living in Williamsburg. I was very close to him.

Paul Stillwell: George Sauer was the football coach, wasn't he?

Admiral Lawrence: Yes. George Sauer coached for my two years of playing on the varsity.[*] Tom Hamilton coached my first year, and when I was on the plebe team.[†] And then, of course, I was very close to our baseball coach, Max Bishop, who was here for years and years and years.[‡] He'd been second baseman for the Philadelphia Athletics back in the Connie Mack era. I played second base most of my time, although I did play shortstop some. But having a coach who'd been a second baseman on the Philadelphia Athletics, it was very tough to play second base. But we all loved Max Bishop.

Max Bishop and then Carnevale were the coaches that I was closest to. Ray Swartz had been the line coach of our plebe team; he was a wrestling coach.[§] I was pretty close to Ray Swartz.

Paul Stillwell: Anything else specific about Bishop that you recall?

Admiral Lawrence: Well, he was really a very nice person. He was a good role model. When I was on the baseball team, it was the first time that a Naval Academy athletic team flew anyplace. We all went up to Friendship Airport in our baseball season in 1949, and we were going to fly up to New England, where we were going to play Dartmouth, Brown, and Harvard.[**] The first game was going to be at Harvard, so I think we flew up

---

[*] George H. Sauer was the head football coach for the 1948 and 1949 seasons. The team's record in those years was 3-13-2.
[†] Captain Thomas J. Hamilton, USN, was the Naval Academy's head football coach in 1946-47, when the team's two-year record was 2-15-1. He was athletic director from 1946 to 1948, when he retired as a rear admiral. His oral history is in the Naval Institute collection.
[‡] Max F. Bishop was the head baseball coach from 1938 up to the time of his death on 24 February 1962. His overall record in those years was 306-143. The Naval Academy baseball park is named in his honor.
[§] Raymond H. Swartz was head wrestling coach from 1938 to 1960. He was U.S. Olympic wrestling coach in 1952.
[**] The airport now known as Baltimore-Washington International was originally Friendship Airport.

to Hanover, New Hampshire. I could tell when we were getting on the airplane that Max had some trepidation about flying. The flight happened to be bumpy—there were some thunderstorms around—and Max got very sick. In those days they used to have these cylindrical cartons you could throw up into. So we had these cylindrical cartons, but there was a teammate of mine, out of the class of '50, named Bill Hawkins, who was probably the best athlete when I was here.[*] During his four years, because his first year as a plebe, he could play on the varsity. I think he scored something like six or seven touchdowns in football with Army. He was a very fine fullback, and he was a pretty good pitcher on a baseball team. Bill Hawkins thought he could sing like Billy Eckstein. Remember that famous singer Billy Eckstein? We'd always sit together on the airplane, and he would get this cylindrical carton out, and he would sing into it and it would amplify his voice, and he would sound like Billy Eckstein. I remember Bill Hawkins and I were sitting on the airplane, and he was singing in this carton, and here is poor old Max violently ill and throwing up.

Anyway, we landed up there, and Max got out of the airplane and said, "That's the last time I'll ever fly anyplace." So he took the train over to Providence and then on up to Boston and back to Annapolis. The rest of us flew. I remember that about Max. But he was a really wonderful guy, and he taught me an awful lot.

We had a trainer named Doc Snyder, who had been a former hospital corpsman. I became very close to him, because he was always our trainer for baseball and basketball. He was not for the football team. One time in my plebe year, I started really feeling bad; I had an upset stomach and everything. So I went to Doc Snyder and said, "Hey, I'm not feeling very good." He was really an old-timer.

He had this black bag he always carried with him. He opened it up and he had some herb medicine or something he made himself. He said, "Hey, take this; this might help you feel good if you're upset and having constipation.

Well, I went back to my room and about 9:00 o'clock, I just absolutely collapsed, and my roommate had to carry me down to sick bay, and it turned out I had appendicitis. The worst thing you give a person with appendicitis is a laxative. So Doc had contributed to my very severe case of appendicitis.

---

[*] Midshipman William F. Hawkins, USN.

But one time Doc came to me, and I could tell he was a little bit reluctant to talk, but he said, "You know, I've got a good friend over in Washington, whose daughter goes to the University of Maryland, and she really wants to come over and see the Naval Academy."[*] I could tell what he had been commissioned to do was to get a date for this man's daughter. I felt so close to Doc that I would do anything for him.

So I said, "Oh, I'd be delighted to escort her around the academy."

He said, "Well, it so happens that she has a friend, and I understand that her friend's kind of tall. Could you get her a date?"

Kit Carson, 6-foot-4, played end on the football team, T. K. Carson.[†] So I said, "I'll ask Kit Carson if he would do this." These gals were going to come over on a Saturday or Sunday afternoon. We'd show them the academy, and then I think they were going to leave the latter part of the afternoon.

Anyway, the two of us walked out to Doc Snyder's house. He lived just off of West Street, right across from where the old Annapolis *Capital* used to be. So we went to his house and sat down. I noticed that after greeting us, Doc and his wife left. That kind of surprised me, but finally I heard something at the door, and these two women came in. My gal is just as cute as a trick, but this other gal was just unbelievably ugly. They went off into their room to take off their coats. So Kit looked at me, and I looked at him, and I could just see this dejected look, but we both broke out in this rocking laughter, uncontrollable laughter. So when these gals came in, they saw these two midshipmen laughing. Finally, we got our composure. I looked at one side of the room, he looked at the other side of the room, and every time our eyes met, we started laughing. So these gals really thought we were a couple of loonies. We sat there and talked and talked, and I could tell that Kit just didn't want to walk back to the academy, because in those days it was a point of pride that you dated only queens.

Finally, we just had to go to the academy. It was in the wintertime, so we walked out, and I noticed that Kit put his coat up—with those big collars we had on our bridge coats, you just hardly see his face—and we walked into the academy. He immediately wanted to go over to the laundry and Halligan Hall, but he didn't want to go into the main

---

[*] Augustus Kent Snyder was athletic trainer at the Naval Academy for many years.
[†] Midshipman Theo K. Carson, USN, a classmate of Lawrence.

part of the yard. Finally, after we had showed our dates the laundry and the boathouse, I said, "Hey, we've got to go over to Bancroft Hall."

We walked into the old Steerage, which was the only place in those days you could go for a snack. We went in and sat at a table, and Kit said, "Hey, I'm sorry, I've got the watch, and I'm going to have to say goodbye." So he walked off and left me with these two. Finally, I think that we finished up the there and they drove off. But Kit never forgave me, because in those days if a date was what we called a brick—if you bricked one of your friends, I mean, that was terrible. But I never could convince him that it was Doc Snyder who did this, that it wasn't me. But, anyway, it was kind of a funny thing.

Paul Stillwell: Another character in the athletic department whom you've already mentioned was Rip Miller. What about your association with him here?

Admiral Lawrence: Well, as a midshipman, of course, I knew him, and in my plebe year, Rip was still serving as a line coach for the football team. So I got to see him out there in the athletic field. He had this very deep voice, and he was a very dynamic guy. But one thing that he liked to do was to bring the plebe backs up, and then we had a drill where you'd have one yard marker and another yard marker, five yards apart. Then you'd have one lineman with a one-on-one situation, in which you'd throw the ball as plebe back and you'd run against this lineman, and they had five yards you could move into. Rip would stand over on the sidelines, critiquing this. You quickly perceived, as a back, that you couldn't dance around or anything like that. The best thing you had to do was just run at the guy. So I remember, as a young plebe back, going against the Dick Scott, an all-American, Dick Shimshak, all-East—these big, powerful linemen. Rip used to thrive on that drill.

When I came back as superintendent, I was talking to Rip one time, and I said, "You know, I remember this drill you used to put us through."

He said, "Yeah, I call that the 'bloodbath.'" But he was a great guy, and he really was good in recruiting. He established very good rapport with the congressional staffs over there, in helping us get appointments for people and that sort of thing. I had great respect and admiration for Rip.

Paul Stillwell: Well, his bloodbath sounds kind of sadistic.

Admiral Lawrence: Yes. I tell you, I didn't look forward to doing that, because we were really cannon fodder in every sense of the word. He was a good guy; I really liked Rip.

I think I might have to knock off here, Paul, and, maybe, I think I come back again on Wednesday.

Paul Stillwell: Good.

Admiral Lawrence: I have to make two speeches tomorrow.

Paul Stillwell: All right, we'll see each other on Wednesday.

Interview Number 2 with Vice Admiral William P. Lawrence, U.S. Navy (Retired)
Place: U.S. Naval Institute, Annapolis, Maryland
Date: Wednesday, 19 September 1990

Paul Stillwell: Admiral, when we got together a couple of days ago, you were talking about your time in the Naval Academy. One thing we didn't get to in much depth was discussing some of your professors and naval officer instructors.

Admiral Lawrence: Well, we talked about Captain Pirie, the commandant; Captain Chew, who was executive officer of Bancroft Hall; and, of course, Admiral Hill and Admiral Holloway, who were the superintendents. There were several other officers; and, of course, we mentioned Dusty Dornin and K. G. Schacht, whom I knew quite well.

The director of athletics, during most of my time here, was Captain Howard Caldwell.[*] Howard Caldwell was out of the class of '27, and he played fullback on the football team. He had a great day in the 21-21 tie with Army in Soldier Field in Chicago in 1926. I was pretty close to him, having played a lot of sports. As the president of the N Club when I was here, I had some interface with the director of athletics.[†]

Then I remember several of the department heads at that time: Captain Kenneth Craig was the head of the aviation department; later on he became a rear admiral.[‡] Captain Smedberg was head of the electrical engineering department; Captain McCorkle, I see up there a picture of the *New Jersey*, was head of seamanship and navigation; and I remember there was a Captain Rice, who was the head of the English and history department.[§]

Paul Stillwell: Any special memories of any of those individuals?

---

[*] Captain Henry Howard Caldwell, USN, was the Naval Academy athletic director from 1949 to 1951.
[†] The N Club comprises midshipmen who have earned letters in varsity sports.
[‡] Craig's daughter Sally married Charles R. Larson. As a rear admiral, Larson served as superintendent of the Naval Academy from 1983 to 1986. As a four-star admiral he again served as superintendent, 1994-98.
[§] Captain William R. Smedberg III, USN, who retired as a vice admiral; his oral history is in the Naval Institute collection. Captain Francis D. McCorkle, USN, who later commanded the battleship *New Jersey* (BB-62) and retired as a rear admiral. Captain Robert H. Rice, USN, who retired as a vice admiral.

Admiral Lawrence: Well, I remember Captain Craig, because he'd been a star basketball player. He'd come out and watch basketball practice from time to time, and I got to know him in that regard.

Then Captain Caldwell, of course, the director of athletics, used to have some of our football players over to his house for dinner from time to time, and I got to know him and his family pretty well.

I remember one situation that I had with him. We had a guy named Alexander Sinclair, who was a classmate of ours in '51.[*] He'd originally been in the class of '50 and had turned back to '51. He stayed out for football the whole time he was here, but he never quite made the varsity and didn't letter. But he was one of the most loyal guys. As I say, he stayed out and played in the junior varsity team for four years, so we wanted to permit him to come to the N dance, which used to be the big thing during June Week. All the letter winners would go. So I went to see Captain Caldwell and said, "The varsity N Club has voted to invite Al Sinclair [we called him 'Mau']– as our special guest." He refused to let us do it. He had his reasons why he really wanted to hew the line on that, but I felt it was very unreasonable. That was one interface I had with him that I remember quite well.

Paul Stillwell: McCorkle is a fellow Tennessean.

Admiral Lawrence: Oh, is he from Tennessee?

Paul Stillwell: He has been pushing—and successfully it turns out—to get a submarine named USS *Greeneville*.[†] He's sort of a rough-hewn gentleman, but very capable in seamanship and navigation.

Admiral Lawrence: Oh, yes, he was head of seamanship and navigation and a very tall man. I didn't realize he was a Tennessean.

---

[*] Midshipman Alexander M. Sinclair, USN.
[†] USS *Greenville* (SSN-772), a *Los Angeles*-class nuclear-powered attack submarine, was named for Greeneville, Tennessee. The ship was launched on 17 September 1994 and christened by sponsor Tipper Gore, wife of Vice President Al Gore of Tennessee. The submarine was commissioned 16 February 1996.

Paul Stillwell: His nickname is Tiny.

Admiral Lawrence: Is that right? Yes, I remember him quite well.

Some of the civilian members of the faculty I remember—of course, Professor Potter, Professor Jeffries, and Rocco Paone.[*] And I remember Professor Smedley, head of the chemistry department.[†] Those are the principal ones I remember.

Paul Stillwell: How capable would you say the instruction in history was, since that was a special interest of yours?

Admiral Lawrence: I thought it was very good. Also, Professor Pat Mahoney was our plebe basketball coach, and he was a history professor.[‡] I remember one course that he taught us that I really enjoyed. It was called A Diplomatic History of the United States. I really learned a lot in that particular course. I saved the textbook for years and years in my personal possessions. I've always had a very keen interest in history; it's just been a natural interest of mine. So I really enjoyed my history courses.

At the time I was here, in 1947-48, taking those history courses, they were still really defining what happened in a lot of those battles. I remember studying the Battle of Midway with great care, and they were still debating exactly what had happened. People like Samuel Eliot Morison and others were really trying to define just precisely what happened in all those Pacific battles.[§]

Of course, our emphasis was oriented to the Pacific naval campaigns. But I remember, really, deeply studying about Midway, Coral Sea, and the Battle of Leyte Gulf. I don't remember any mention of Halsey running off to the north, and they weren't

---

[*] Professor Elmer B. Potter; Associate Professor William W. Jeffries; Assistant Professor Rocco M. Paone—all three in the department of English, history, and government.
[†] Associate Professor William M. Smedley, electrical engineering.
[‡] Associate Professor Elmer J. Mahoney, department of English, history, and government.
[§] Rear Admiral Samuel Eliot Morison, USNR, was a noted civilian historian at Harvard University. He received a Naval Reserve commission in order to collect material for what eventually became the 15-volume *History of United States Naval Operations in World War II*.

highlighting that in the course.* But I really enjoyed my history, and, as I say, I remember Professor Potter at that time. In fact, he'd been a coauthor of a naval history textbook that we used at that time, and I really enjoyed that textbook.

Paul Stillwell: Was there an attempt to make the history relevant, rather than just history for history's sake?

Admiral Lawrence: Yes, I think so, and I think they did a very good job in that respect. I think most of us who came in in '47 had been very much influenced by World War II. We were inspired by the fact that we had a lot of the World War II heroes here. It was really interesting for me to study about the battles. But, also, I remember the great interest I had in naval history, where we went back to the time of the Greeks and the Romans and Spartans, and reading about the naval battles, and the galleys and so forth. It was quite interesting to me to learn about the Phoenicians, because I'd never been exposed to anything like that in my previous education.

Paul Stillwell: Did the civilian instructors, who, presumably, had a broader knowledge, take a different approach, in general, from the officer instructors? Not just in history, but across the board?

Admiral Lawrence: I don't remember a significant difference.

The officer instructors, of course, were not as self-confident. They were not as experienced, I should say. They seemed to follow a kind of a prescribed pattern of instruction in handing out the quiz question, and that sort of thing. Of course, most of our officer instructors were in the trade school-type subjects, like ordnance and gunnery, engineering, where you learn about boilers and turbines and so on. As I recall, most of

---

* Admiral William F. Halsey, Jr., USN, was Commander Third Fleet from March 1943 to November 1945. On 24-25 October 1944, as part of the wide-ranging Battle of Leyte Gulf, he steamed north with Task Force 38, the fleet's carrier striking force and supporting ships. His objective was to sink a force of Japanese aircraft carriers. He unwittingly left San Bernardino Strait unguarded for a foray by Japanese battleships and cruisers. The Japanese surface ships eventually turned around and went back after encountering a plucky U.S. force of escort carriers and destroyers.

our military people were in the professional areas, where we had civilians in the areas like history, and English and foreign language, chemistry, physics.

Paul Stillwell: Well, the officers would know their subjects well, but wouldn't be as polished as instructors.

Admiral Lawrence: Yes, that's right. It was obvious to me that they were kind of following an outline. Some have even admitted to me that they tried to stay about two lessons ahead of us. But I really always really enjoyed academic study. I really enjoyed my academic work here at the Naval Academy. I kept very busy, but that's why I was here: to do a lot of things. It just didn't bother me at all to have a constrained social life, because I so thoroughly enjoyed my sports and academics.

Paul Stillwell: We haven't talked too much about specific exploits on the athletic fields. What can you say about that?

Admiral Lawrence: Well, there's not much to say. I was never a star. I mean, I was on a squad, and I played. I guess I got a total of seven letters in the three years I played. I really couldn't play in my first-class year. Once I became brigade commander, it just became apparent to me that the demands were so great, and particularly, the honor concept work and everything. I talked it over with the coaches, and if I had been a really consistent regular, I'm sure that we would have gone into some negotiation. [Laughter] But I wasn't really a dyed-in-the-wool regular player. We talked this over. The commandant was involved in some of these discussions, as to what was the best thing to do. It was a mutual decision, that, for the greater good of the academy, so to speak, I wouldn't play sports in my last year. But I'm sure if I'd been a key player, that they would have decided that I should play sports. But the sport I played the most in, in terms of playing time, was basketball. That just seemed to be my better sport here at the academy.

Paul Stillwell: I think it would be illuminating for you to contrast the basketball of that era with today's.

Admiral Lawrence: Well, of course, the big difference in the basketball of that time with this time is the big men that have become prevalent. I think it's been just an evolutionary thing that kids are bigger nowadays. Our tallest guy on the teams I played on was about 6-3; occasionally, I think we had one guy that was 6-4, but he wasn't a real player. Out of the five starters, you'd probably have three who were under six feet. It was pretty standard in those days that the two outside guys, which you called the guards, were usually guys under six feet.

The playing in that time was not all that much different from today, except that, I think that like all sports, that they've become more scientific, more defined patterns of plays and that sort of thing. Because they work at it the year round. And most times, we only came out to the beginning of the season to participate in that sport, and then when it was over, you forgot about it until the next season. I wouldn't see the football coach from the end of the Army game until the beginning of spring practice. I wouldn't even have any contact. We didn't have the degree of sophistication that they do nowadays in terms of offensive plays, defensive plays. And basketball's the same way. But I think in a lot of ways, we had a lot more fun. It wasn't so much of a business. The coach wouldn't impose demands on you that they impose on the kids nowadays. This weightlifting is something in which I have great sympathy for the kids that play now. A football player will play a game on Friday, and he has to come back and lift weights for an hour or so on Sunday afternoon. That to me is a real burden.

Paul Stillwell: Well, I got the impression that when Coach Erdelatz came in 1950, that he began to place more of these demands on the team.[*]

---

[*] Edward J. Erdelatz was head football coach of the Naval Academy from the 1950 season to the 1958 season. In that time he transformed Navy into a national power, compiling a record of 50-26-8, for a winning percentage of .643. The reasons for his departure in early 1959 are covered in the Naval Institute oral history of Captain Slade D. Cutter, USN (Ret.)., the academy's athletic director.

Admiral Lawrence: Oh, yes, he did. Sauer, of course, was very demanding too. Sauer was very frustrated. He was really intensely competitive, a tremendous amount of pride, and it really bothered him that we weren't winning. And I think, as happened later on to Erdelatz, that Sauer got kind of crossways with the administration because of this conflict about how much time demand he could impose on the players, versus what the academy wanted.

See, my first year under Sauer in 1948, he really pushed hard to get some concessions for the football players. One thing that he did was to have us go to special classes and to all live together. I didn't like that. I just didn't want to be regarded as being separate from the rest of the brigade. I just didn't feel comfortable with not being close to my company mates. But for that one football season, we had special classes and the same professors. For the football team they picked the old-timers who were well established. I remember in math we had Professor Jim Bland, who had written the book on how to use the slide rule.[*]

So we went to separate classes and lived together. I lived with my two classmates, one who was also my full-time roommate, Gus Leahy, and then Bob Renneman, who was a tackle at the time.[†] I never was comfortable with that arrangement, because I didn't want to be separate from the rest of the company. But Sauer pushed that through. The next year it was disestablished, because the players weren't happy about it, and the administration wasn't either.

I think Sauer left principally because he was just not happy with the administration; he was very frustrated at not winning. That's almost inevitable here with an intense coach who has a strong desire to win, that he's going to get crossways with the administration, because he simply can't have the control of the team that he would like to have. Fortunately, we got George Welsh here, and he really understood the system and was able to conform to it.[‡] I think that most of the coaches we have now conform to it.

---

[*] Professor James R. Bland.
[†] Midshipman John P. Leahy, USN.
[‡] George T. Welsh was the Naval Academy's head football coach for the 1973 through 1981 seasons. The team's overall record in those years was 55-46-1, a percentage of .544. Welsh understood the system because he played for the Midshipmen and graduated from the Naval Academy in 1956.

Three straight coaches there, Sauer, Erdelatz, and Wayne Hardin—all three of them were at odds with the administration.* I guess Erdelatz was actually fired.

Paul Stillwell: Yes, he was. I interviewed Slade Cutter, who said he was the one who did the firing.† The superintendent was Admiral Melson.‡

We talked about the intensely competitive coaches. Would you describe yourself as a competitive-type athlete?

Admiral Lawrence: Well, yes, I certainly am, but I've always kept athletics in perspective. I have to say that it was always more important to me to do well in my studies than to do well on the athletic field from the time I was a young boy. That's one reason why I didn't do as well here in sports as, perhaps, I did in high school, because I wanted to do well in my studies. I refused to allow my studies to degrade. I know that I didn't give the total thought to sports that I could have. For example, you really have to study football a lot—learn your plays, think about the situations, and so forth. I simply could not afford to take the time away from my studies to really think about football. And, of course, I played three sports, which really kept me busy. I probably could have been better if I'd just concentrated, say, on basketball. But I enjoyed everything, and I wanted to be busy and do everything.

Paul Stillwell: We were talking about basketball. Ironically, the three-point shot has been introduced in recent years to sort of open up the game the way it used to be, instead of being clogged up around the basket.

Admiral Lawrence: That's right. Well, Ben Carnevale was my coach. Of course, he coached here for almost 20 years. He was a wonderful gentleman, and we had a 40-year basketball reunion of our 1950 team back in January, and he's still living. I organized

---

* Wayne Hardin was the Naval Academy's head football coach for the 1959 through 1964 seasons. The team's overall record in those years was 38-22-2, a percentage of .629.
† Captain Slade D. Cutter, USN, was the Naval Academy's athletic director. His oral history is in the Naval Institute collection.
‡ Rear Admiral Charles L. Melson, USN, was superintendent of the Naval Academy from June 1958 to June 1960. The oral history of Melson, who retired as a vice admiral, is in the Naval Institute collection.

that because I wanted to pay tribute to him for what he gave to us. We got, principally, the 1950 team, but the guys that were on the '49 team and the '51 team who were interested came as well. So we had about 18 players there and made it a tribute to Ben Carnevale.

I was short, but I had the speed, and I had a pretty good shot. On the 1950 team, I had the highest field goal percentage, but it was something like 36%. Well, today if a kid isn't shooting 50%, I mean, he's terrible. I read those statistics that we still have over in the athletic association archives, and I said, "My God, that's just a pretty graphic indication of how the skill level of kids today is increased from my time, not only the skill but the size and the speed."

Paul Stillwell: But now those people major in basketball.

Admiral Lawrence: Yes, unfortunately, at most schools it's that way.

Paul Stillwell: Did you have any contact with Spike Webb, the boxing coach?[*] He was an institution.

Admiral Lawrence: Yes. I remember Spike quite well. He used to give us some instruction in boxing. I'd see him around over in MacDonough Hall.

I remember our swimming coach, Coach Henry Ortland.[†] For some reason at that time, they would not allow football players to swim. There was the thought that swimming was not a good exercise for football players because of the effect on your muscles. It was just one of many myths that used to exist in that time—like they wouldn't allow us to drink water at practice, a really gross misconception. But my body configuration just didn't lend itself to my being a good swimmer. I didn't really do a lot of swimming as a young kid growing up, so swimming tests were really tough for me. But, fortunately, playing football, all of that was deferred till the end of the season. So

---

[*] Hamilton W. "Spike" Webb was involved in Naval Academy athletics from 1919 to 1954, including service for more than 20 years as varsity boxing coach. For more on his history, see Jack Sweetman, *The U.S. Naval Academy: An Illustrated History* (Annapolis: Naval Institute Press, 1979), pages 181-182.
[†] Henry Ortland Jr. was the Naval Academy's head swimming coach from 1918 to 1950.

then all the football players would go over to the pool, and Henry Ortland, who was kind of really direct, tell-it-like-it-is guy, would come in.* He realized that many of us were lousy swimmers, so he'd just say, "Get in the pool and do the tests." He'd look the other way, and we'd do anything. Then after about 20 minutes, he'd say, "Okay, get the hell out of here." [Laughter] So if it hadn't been for Henry Ortland, I'd have been on the sub squad all the time.

But I remember he used to walk in in his swimming trunks and these wooden plaques, and you'd hear him walking down. He was one of the real characters along with Ray Swartz, the wrestling coach. Those guys were really wonderful institutions here.

Paul Stillwell: There were a couple of black midshipmen here while you were: Wesley Brown and Lawrence Chambers.† Did you have any contact with them?

Admiral Lawrence: Well, I did. Wes Brown was in my company, and he and I were very close friends. For some reason we just hit it off. I told you about this kind of innate empathy that I had toward blacks, and he just seemed to sense that. My initials are W.P., and he used to call me "Whippy, Whippy." And still to this day, he calls me Whippy. He lives over in Washington. He's a retired lieutenant commander and was in the Civil Engineer Corps. I talk to him on the phone from time to time.

Paul Stillwell: He has a very bubbly, effervescent personality.

Admiral Lawrence: Yes, he was a real good guy. He was very popular in our company.

Larry Chambers is out of '52, and I just never really got to know Larry Chambers until after we were commissioned. But I never saw any indication of any racial prejudice or anything towards Wes Brown in my company. He was well accepted and liked.

---

* Ortland first came to the Naval Academy as a chief boatswain's mate during World War I.
† Midshipman Wesley A. Brown, USN, became the first black graduate of the Naval Academy in 1949. His oral history is in the Naval Institute collection. Midshipman Lawrence C. Chambers, USN, was in the class of 1952. He was the first black graduate to become a flag officer.

Paul Stillwell: Well, he'd experienced some of that before you arrived on the scene and gotten past it.

Admiral Lawrence: Yes, probably did. Of course, I remember reading about the time that a black midshipman was brought in here in the early 1900s, and they ended up putting him out on a buoy or something.* Maybe you heard that story.

Paul Stillwell: No, I hadn't.

Admiral Lawrence: Well, it's kind of fuzzy, but it seems to me that there was a black here in the early 1900s, and some midshipmen took him out and chained him to a buoy or something out here. It kind of sticks in my mind that Mitscher may have been involved in that affair, but I could be completely wrong about that.† Anyway, they had a very bad racial incident, and so many years transpired before they got another black here.

Paul Stillwell: Brown has a great sense of humor. He says he will go up to people at his class reunions and say, "You probably don't remember me but I'm Wes Brown."—knowing darn well, of course, that they do remember him.

Admiral Lawrence: Yes, that's right. He's a real fine guy. I really, really enjoyed my friendship with him.

Paul Stillwell: We haven't talked at all about the summer cruises. What role did they play in your professional training?

Admiral Lawrence: Well, they were valuable. Not that I really learned a lot of technical knowledge, but it was just the fact that you were being introduced to the seagoing

---

* The story is probably a myth. The definitive work on the integration of the Naval Academy is Robert J. Schneller, Jr., *Breaking the Color Barrier: the U.S. Naval Academy's First Black Midshipmen and the Struggle for Racial Equality* (New York: New York University Press, 2005). On page ix in his preface, Dr. Schneller says the story of the midshipman and the buoy was widely told, but he found no documentary evidence to support it.
† Midshipman Marc A. Mitscher, USN, class of 1910.

environment, and that was the main thing—just to develop a little appreciation of life aboard ship.

My first cruise was on the aircraft carrier *Coral Sea*, during the ship's shakedown cruise.* They put all of the football team on the *Coral Sea* in the summer of 1948. I guess this was another Sauer initiative to try to keep the football team together during the summer. We used to practice every day up on the flight deck when we were under way. When we went into port, we practiced. The *Coral Sea* was in those days classified CVB-43, and the CVB meant a large aircraft carrier. And, of course the *Midway* had been the first of that class, which was 41, and the *Franklin D. Roosevelt* was 42. *Coral Sea* was the third. We went from Norfolk to Lisbon and then to Gibraltar, and then went to Golfe du Lion, which is adjacent to Cannes on the Riviera. I guess those were really all the ports that we went into.

Paul Stillwell: That's pretty heady stuff for a guy from Tennessee.

Admiral Lawrence: Yes. Oh, and we practiced football every place we went, but we still had plenty of time for liberty. So I really enjoyed that very much.

I remember in Lisbon we went to a beautiful place called Estoril.† I was taking Portuguese, and so this gave me a good opportunity to practice my Portuguese. I remember practicing football in a beautiful soccer stadium in Lisbon. Then, of course, it was really great to be on the French Riviera. I remember taking a tour and going up into the French Alps. That was quite interesting, and I took a lot of pictures. So that was an awful lot of fun to be on a ship and also to be able to play football and be with the football team.

Then from the Mediterranean, we came back and went to Guantánamo Bay, where some more exercising took place.‡ Then they flew the football team from

---

* USS *Coral Sea* (CVB-43), a *Midway*-class aircraft carrier, was commissioned 1 October 1947. She had a standard displacement of 45,000 tons, was 968 feet long, 113 feet in the beam, and had an extreme width of 136 feet. Her top speed was 33 knots. She had 18 5-inch mounts and could accommodate more than 100 aircraft.
† Estoril is a resort town on the west coast of Portugal.
‡ Guantánamo Bay, on the south coast of Cuba, near the eastern end of the island, for many years provided a fleet anchorage and training area for U.S. Navy ships.

Guantánamo Bay back to Annapolis, so that we could get off on summer leave and get back to practice football.

The commanding officer of *Coral Sea* was one of the famous naval aviators, Captain A. P. Storrs, and he's still living.[*] His nickname was "Putt." I remember going up to the bridge when I was standing messenger watches up there, and, gosh, I thought he was God—to see a commanding officer.

Paul Stillwell: He was in a predecessor organization of the Blue Angels.[†]

Admiral Lawrence: Yes, he was one of the old-time naval aviators. He was a career naval aviator, like Marc Mitscher.

Paul Stillwell: How much did the air group operate during that tour?

Admiral Lawrence: Quite a bit, yes. They operated a fair amount.

Paul Stillwell: Still all propeller planes.

Admiral Lawrence: All propeller. I think they had SB2Cs, TBMs, and F8Fs in that era.[‡]

But it was just fascinating for me to learn about shipboard life. I sensed right away that there were a lot of inherent discomforts on the ships, that you just simply couldn't live on a metal structure like that and have the comfort and everything you do at home. You just had to acclimate yourself to the more austere condition of the ship. It really first became apparent to me that when you were sleeping, you were going to have this continuous shipboard noise and machinery.

---

[*] Captain Aaron P. Storrs III, USN, commanded the aircraft carrier *Coral Sea* (CVB-43) in 1947-48. He was in the Naval Academy class of 1923, eventually became a rear admiral, and died on 5 March 1993 at the age of 92.

[†] The Navy's first aerobatics team, in 1928-29, was known as the Three Seahawks. It members were Lieutenant Daniel W. Tomlinson IV, USN, Lieutenant (junior grade) William V. Davis Jr., USN, and Lieutenant (junior grade) Storrs. For details see Tomlinson's oral history in the Naval Institute collection.

[‡] SB2C was a dive-bomber; TBM a torpedo plane; and F8F a fighter.

Paul Stillwell: How crowded was it?

Admiral Lawrence: Well, the *Midway*-class carrier was designed with the kamikaze experience very much in mind.* So it was extensively compartmented for damage control purposes. You don't have these large open bays that you have on other ships. In fact, the berthing compartments are relatively small and separate and distinct compartments, and I guess it was all based on this damage control rationale.

But we were able to get all of my classmates that were on the football team in this one compartment. I remember it was just down about the third deck. We were all crowded in there. We had, I think, three-tier bunks. It was good for us to experience that; that's the value of that youngster cruise. You really learned right away what it was like to be an enlisted man. That's why I say the youngster cruise is so important, because it helps the midshipmen develop appreciation for the life of the enlisted man.

Paul Stillwell: How did you spend your second class summer?

Admiral Lawrence: Well, the second class summer was the aviation summer, and we made a carrier cruise on a CVL out of Norfolk; I forget the name. We were out for two weeks on that carrier cruise and just really learned about the aviation.†

I'm trying to remember anything else that we did in that second class summer, because the aviation cruise was not as long as a standard summer cruise. I guess we spent some time back here at the academy doing some professional things. It was similar to what they now call ProTraMid, the professional training of midshipmen.

Paul Stillwell: Did you get any exposure to the Marine Corps?

Admiral Lawrence: I don't think we went down to Quantico like the midshipmen do

---

* Kamikazes were Japanese suicide aircraft that began showing up in the Philippines campaign in the autumn of 1944. Besides the compartmentation, the ships of the *Midway* class had armored flight decks.
† CVL was the designation for a light aircraft carrier built on a cruiser hull.

now.* It seems to me that I saw Pax River while I was a midshipman.† But that was the aviation summer; there was a lot of emphasis on teaching midshipmen about that.

I guess maybe I made a submarine cruise during that particular summer. I remember going out on a submarine, and I remember I really didn't enjoy the submarine cruise. I felt too confined; being an athlete and everything, I just felt restricted on that submarine, inability to move around and to exercise and things like that. That was the kind of thing that really started tipping the scales against my going in submarines.

I was really was quite interested in what aviation was able to do. I just sensed, with the advent of jets, that that was going to be the future. But I was always a little bit different from some of my peers in aviation. I studied this over the years and developed an appreciation for the mentality of aviators. There are those who go into aviation, and for them flying is just the ultimate experience. They just absolutely love to fly. It's hard to understand the thrill that some guys get out of flying. I didn't really ever embrace flying like that. I always got a satisfaction out of it from the professional confidence and the skill that you had to have. I really prided myself on the excellence of flying, but it wasn't the end all.

Paul Stillwell: It was the means to the end.

Admiral Lawrence: Yes. It was a professional endeavor. I was the type of guy who tried to put flying in balance with everything else; whereas, I used to see a lot of guys, that was all they wanted to do. Flying just totally consumed them. It's kind of like sailors who want to sail more than anything else. It never really consumed me like that. I think that was to my benefit, because I saw a lot of young aviators who were so totally consumed by flying that they really neglected the other aspects of their professional development. For example, when I was a test pilot, I always put flying in the proper balance, with writing the reports and studying and learning and applying myself in the technical areas.

---

* Quantico, Virginia, which is on the Potomac River south of Washington, D.C., is the site of a Marine Corps base.
† Patuxent River Naval Air Station, Lexington Park, Maryland, site of the Naval Air Test Center, where Lawrence was later stationed when he was a test pilot.

I always knew that I was a little different from the average fighter pilot, whose whole life was flying that airplane.

For example, from being closely associated with guys like Alan Shepard and Wally Schirra, who just were so consumed with flying, I knew I was different.[*] I was more of a studious, analytical-type guy and tried to put flying in the proper balance with all these other activities.

Paul Stillwell: And some aviators run into trouble when they get to be lieutenant commanders and have to exert leadership and management techniques.

Admiral Lawrence: Yes, I was always aware that I had to get balance in my career, and I looked into non-flying areas and taking a staff job. In fact, I took a shipboard job because I wanted to learn something else than just flying airplanes. I sensed early that there was a misconception that you had to stay in the cockpit a lot to be proficient. Because once you mastered the basic aviation skills, you didn't lose that proficiency. You could do these other things and still come back and fly airplanes. Admittedly, if you've been away on a shipboard or staff tour, you lose you edge, and you have to go through a period of getting it back, but it comes back pretty rapidly.

Paul Stillwell: How did you spend the first class summer?

Admiral Lawrence: Well, the first class summer was a really interesting summer, because we went out on the battleship *Missouri*—"Missourah," as they say out in Missouri.[†] It was an interesting time because this was the summer of 1950, and the *Missouri* had gone aground off of Fort Monroe in the winter of 1950.[‡] I was well aware

---

[*] On 5 May 1961 Commander Alan B. Shepard, USN, became the first American astronaut to fly into space. Commander Walter M. Schirra Jr., USN, was another of the original seven Mercury astronauts.
[†] USS *Missouri* (BB-63) was commissioned 11 June 1944. She had a standard displacement of 45,000 tons and full-load displacement of 57,600 tons. She was 887 feet long and 108 feet in the beam. Her top speed was 33 knots. Initially she was armed with nine 16-inch guns, 20 5-inch guns, and 80 40-mm guns in quad mounts, and 49 20-mm guns in single mounts. She was best known as the site of the Japanese surrender in September 1945.
[‡] The *Missouri* ran aground near Norfolk, Virginia, on 17 January 1950. She was not refloated until 1 February. See Dr. Malcolm Muir, Jr., "Hard Aground on Thimble Shoal," *Naval History*, Fall 1991, pages 30-35.

of that because, being on the basketball team, we went down and played Duke. I remember we got kidded by the people in the stands, because we were playing a basketball game just after the *Missouri* had gone aground.

But, anyway, they had a new commanding officer on the *Missouri*; the previous commanding officer was Captain Brown, who had been relieved as a result of that grounding accident.* The new skipper was Captain Irving T. Duke.

Paul Stillwell: Captain Page Smith had been in between those two.†

Admiral Lawrence: Oh, really?

Paul Stillwell: He was an interim skipper. He had commanded the ship before Brown, and he told me the reason he was sent back was to restore the confidence of the wardroom officers. They were so demoralized by this incident that they needed someone in whom they already had confidence, and he brought them back up to speed.

Admiral Lawrence: Yes, well, I guess so. I guess I just missed Page Smith, but Irving T. Duke was the commanding officer.‡ And I tell you that he really had tight control of that ship; you could sense it in the officers. That was the event that led to the Navy's decision to take the navigator out from under the ship's operations officer and make navigation a separate department. I think that was being done around that time.

Paul Stillwell: What manifestations did you see of this control that Duke exerted?

Admiral Lawrence: Well, just on going up on the bridge as first classmen, there were very strict limits on what they would allow us to do. You just sensed a formality on that bridge that I had not seen on other ships to that degree, that Duke really had some of the characteristics of a martinet. I guess he was determined that the ship wouldn't have a

---

* Captain William D. Brown, USN, commanded the *Missouri* from 10 December 1949 to 3 February 1950. The executive officer, Commander George E. Peckham, was acting commanding officer, 3-7 February.
† Captain Harold Page Smith, USN, commanded the *Missouri* from 7 February 1950 to 19 April 1950.
‡ Captain Irving T. Duke, USN, commanded the *Missouri* from 19 April 1950 to 2 March 1951.

repeat of the accident. But you could sense that the officers weren't relaxed, and you could sense the tension up there on the bridge. They allowed us to give just one or two orders to the helm as first classmen. They didn't give us any real ship-handling experience.

Paul Stillwell: So your training was inhibited by this approach.

Admiral Lawrence: Yes. I think so. I think it was all related to that grounding.

Paul Stillwell: Then she got yanked out to go to Korea.

Admiral Lawrence: Yes, I remember we were off-loaded in Norfolk, because the Korean attack cut our cruise short.[*] I think we were going down to Gitmo, and we ended up not going to Gitmo. The first part of the cruise we'd gone up to New York City and to Boston. Those were wonderful in-port experiences. One of our battalion officers went out to be the officer in charge of the midshipman detachment. I think it was Captain Warfield; he was out of the class of '32, and they had just made him captain while they were here.[†]

Then there was a lieutenant commander that was the assistant OIC, and his name escapes me right now. He was a civil engineer officer who was teaching on the faculty, and he was our assistant baseball coach, so I knew him really well. I was the midshipman commander of the summer cruise detachment of the first and third class midshipmen. So I had to interface a lot with the officers, and I had a lot of interface with this lieutenant commander who went out there. That was a good leadership experience for me, because the midshipmen essentially ran the program for the midshipmen.

Paul Stillwell: Was there a syllabus for this training?

---

[*] The Korean War began on 25 June 1950, when six North Korean infantry division and three border constabulary brigades invaded South Korea. The troops were supported by approximately 100 Russian-made T-34 tanks. In New York that same day the United Nations Security Council adopted a resolution condemning the invasion.
[†] Captain Thomas G. Warfield, USN.

Admiral Lawrence: No, and that's the great difference between that time and our time. We didn't have a well-defined syllabus; we were pretty much put in the hands of the ship. If the enlisted men and officers who had the responsibility didn't take an interest, you really kind of fended for yourself. That was the way it was on the *Missouri*. We really ran our own show. I had a lot of the responsibility, because I had to maintain accountability for everybody, and I had to impose standards of dress and all that. But it was a good leadership experience for me, being the senior midshipman in charge of all of that—making things happen. I enjoyed that cruise.

Paul Stillwell: Did you live in an officer's stateroom?

Admiral Lawrence: No, I lived in one of these open-bay compartments.

Paul Stillwell: How would you compare the living conditions there with the *Coral Sea*? Those two ships are essentially contemporaries.

Admiral Lawrence: Well, we stayed on the same type of berth—rack, we used to call it. But there were more open compartments in the *Missouri* than in the *Coral Sea*, because of this compartmented construction in the *Coral Sea* and damage control rationale.

Paul Stillwell: Did you, being from the ship, encounter any of the same kind of ridicule over the grounding that you'd encountered in the basketball team?

Admiral Lawrence: No, no. That was down at Duke, and it happened just within a few days of the grounding. That's why we took the ribbing down there. I didn't really see it anymore after that. As I said, we went into New York City and into Boston, and I didn't see kidding about that there.

Paul Stillwell: That was a substantial embarrassment for the Navy at the time.

Admiral Lawrence: Oh, gosh, yes. I was later the navigator of the USS *Newport News*, and I used to come out of Norfolk all the time.* I'm just perplexed how that happened. I bet you we had 100 buoys marking that place where the *Missouri* went aground. Because as you come out of the pier area, the Elizabeth River comes out into the Hampton Roads. As you come up, you're heading right towards Fort Monroe, and you have to make a sharp 90-degree turn to go down to Thimble Shoals. Apparently, the *Missouri* was just late in making the turn and ran on into the shallow water. But, boy, I tell you now, it's so well marked, you can't believe it.

As I say, being a navigator on a ship out of Norfolk, I really got to see that. Of course, I went back and reviewed the history of the grounding of the *Missouri* and tried to learn all the good, useful lessons from that. And being a navigator of a ship, you can really see how things like that happen. Unless you really have tight control and good organization, it's easy to develop confusion on the bridge of a ship. You have an officer of the deck, who might have the conn; you've got the captain there who may take the conn back from the officer of the deck; and you've got the navigator and his people keeping track of the ship.† He has to make a recommendation for action, and you've got the people in CIC doing their thing.‡ That's why, while I was navigator, I tried to develop a concept for better integration of the activities of the bridge plotting team and the CIC team. And that time I was a navigator, they tended to be independent efforts. You have a CIC doing some navigating and the bridge doing navigating under the navigator. The navigator wouldn't have cognizance and control of the CIC effort, so we've changed that a lot on ships now. It's a very integrated thing; now we do radar and the visual together.

Paul Stillwell: We've pretty well run through the Naval Academy. Any concluding thoughts before we get you through June Week to commissioning?

---

* Lawrence was navigator of the heavy cruiser *Newport News* (CA-148) in 1961-62, discussed later in the oral history.
† The individual with the conn—normally an officer—directs the ship's movements in course and speed.
‡ CIC – combat information center. By using ranges and bearings taken from a radar scope, the CIC team can develop fixes and plot the ship's course, either as a backup to the visual navigation or as a replacement for it.

Admiral Lawrence: No, I can't think of anything other than to say that I really enjoyed my midshipman experience. It was the type of life that just was perfect for me. I enjoyed the intellectual and the physical challenge, but I think the thing that really was of great appeal to me was the great camaraderie, the bonding that takes place here. Friendships have always been very important to me, and I think that was one of the great appeals of the academy experience. You made really good, good, deep genuine friendships here, the type that lasts for a lifetime. I really enjoyed my four years here.

Paul Stillwell: Was there any sense of anticlimax from being the number-one midshipman to one of thousands of ensigns?

Admiral Lawrence: No, that really never bothered me very much. In some ways it was a little bit pleasant to get out of the limelight and to become just another ensign.

Paul Stillwell: What do you recall of graduation and commissioning?

Admiral Lawrence: Well, it was, of course, a real thrill for me to have my parents come here and have them experience June Week. I know they had a great sense of pride that their son was the brigade commander, and that I received some awards at graduation. So that was a real pleasant aspect of it, the enjoyment and the pride that my parents got out of coming here.

I was at that time dating my future wife, Anne Williams, and, of course, spent time with her during the June Week experience. Her father was Captain MacPherson Williams, out of the class of '30. At that time he was the commanding officer of the *Greenwich Bay*, which was the Middle East force flagship.* He was away, but my future wife's mother was living here in Annapolis. So it was pleasant to be with my future wife and get to know her mother better and my parents get to know them.

---

* For many years the U.S. Navy maintained a small Middle East Force in the Persian Gulf as a show-the-flag presence. USS *Greenwich Bay* (AVP-41) was a *Barnegat Bay*-class small seaplane tender. From 1949 to 1966 she served as Middle East Force flagship, mostly in rotation with two sister ships, the *Duxbury Bay* (AVP-38) and the *Valcour* (AVP-55).

So June Week was really a very pleasant time. During that period, the initial segment of the graduating class that was going down to flight training was kept here to train the plebes, so I was involved in the training of the class of '55, which came in in '51. But I did not work down as a member of the plebe detail. I was brought up to be a special assistant to the commandant, principally to write up the results of our work on the honor concept and make recommendations as to the course for the future. I spent the two months that I was here very carefully developing these thoughts in my head.

Captain Pirie was the commandant, and he loved to play golf. During the academic year, he was so busy he never got to play, so during that summer he was off playing golf a lot. I filled in by serving as his executive assistant when his executive assistant went on leave. And I used to do some other things up there in the front office. In those days the plebes came in individually; rather than having them all come in at the same time, as they do now, they just kind of dribbled in. After the initial group came in, I used to be the one who would go up and give the welcome-aboard lecture to the new plebes. I enjoyed doing that, and it was good training for public speaking. So I did a lot of odd jobs up in the front office, but the key thing I was doing was getting all my thoughts together and then writing the report on the honor concept. I quoted from that report in my *Shipmate* article this past June. And, of course, the report that I wrote in August of 1951 is in the archives,

Paul Stillwell: Was it because of that work on the honor concept that you didn't get sent to a ship right away?

Admiral Lawrence: No, it was why I was kept in the front office instead of working down in the plebe detail. They used to send about 25 of the graduating class down to flight training rather than going to ships. Those who stood high in the class were usually the ones that got that choice. The practice was to have us stay here until September training the plebes, and then in September go down to Pensacola. But, as I say, I didn't work down in the plebe detail; I stayed up and was really a special assistant to the commandant. I think they wanted me to sit down and really formalize all that had occurred on the honor concept, because I think that Captain Chew, in particular, saw that we really had essentially established an honor standard. Whether it was going to be another honor code like West Point or just what it was going to do, was yet to be determined. But I was the one who really brought it all together and said, "This is what we've done, and this is how I think it should go in the future." So I spent a considerable amount of time preparing that report. Although it isn't a real long report—it's probably only about two or three pages—it took a lot of time on my part to really think through what we had done and how we should proceed in the future. That was when, as I say, I enunciated these principles of having an attitudinal way of life and the counseling option, as opposed to a very codified type of approach.

Paul Stillwell: Well, then you went to Pensacola. What do you recall about that?

Admiral Lawrence: Well, by the time I went to Pensacola in September of 1951, my future wife and I decided that we were going to get married. Our basic plan was that it would be at Christmas, but it depended upon what happened to her father. He was coming to the end of his tour as the commanding officer of USS *Greenwich Bay*, but he really didn't know where he was going. Things were a little bit in a state of flux, but we had pretty much committed ourselves to each other.

The first thing we went into was what they call the ground school, and I think that lasted about a month or so. They gave us these aviation subjects—navigation, air navigation, that sort of thing—and that was really enjoyable. It was entirely a different pace from the Naval Academy. We had freedom every night. This was in the fall, so I played with the NAS Pensacola football team called the Goshawks.[*] In other words, I had time to do that as well as the ground school. I think I had time to play two or three games with them, and that was fun because I got to meet some other people down there.

In those days they let the instructors play; there were also enlisted men who played. I think I was one of the only students who was playing, because most of officers

---

[*] NAS – naval air station.

were instructors. We played against Keesler Field, and I had some classmates who were on that Air Force team.* We played against each other, so that was a lot of fun.

But, anyway, I enjoyed every aspect of Pensacola. When my father-in-law came back, he had orders to go up to the Chief of the Naval Air Reserve staff at Glenview, Illinois.† My future wife and I and our parents decided that we would get married out there at Christmas at Glenview, which we did. As I recall, I had just soloed at Whiting Field before I went off on Christmas leave to get married.‡ After we were married, my wife and I motored down from Glenview to Pensacola. I remember they had 36 inches of snow up there in Illinois, so I was really happy to get out of there and get down to Pensacola.

Paul Stillwell: What were some of the intermediate steps between ground school and soloing?

Admiral Lawrence: Well, in those days they had South Whiting and North Whiting. You did the real basic stuff down in South Whiting and the more advanced stuff up there at North Whiting.

Paul Stillwell: Was that in the SNJ?

Admiral Lawrence: SNJ, yes.§ Before I was married, I lived in the BOQ out there at Whiting Field.** That was really good, because it was right close to the flight line. After

---

* Keesler Air Force Base, Biloxi, Mississippi, was named in honor of Lieutenant Samuel Reeves Keesler Jr., a Mississippi native who was killed as an Army aviator in France during World War I. Some of Lawrence's Naval Academy classmates were commissioned in the recently established Air Force because the Air Force Academy was not yet established.
† Glenview, in the northern suburbs of Chicago, was the site of a naval air station. Ensign Lawrence and Anne Berrien Williams were married in the air station chapel on 28 December 1951.
‡ Naval Air Station Whiting Field, Milton, Florida. It was named in honor of Captain Kenneth Whiting, USN, a pioneer naval aviator who had a great deal to do with the early development and use of aircraft carriers in the U.S. Navy.
§ The SNJ Texan was a training aircraft manufactured by North American Aviation. The Navy first ordered a version of the airplane in late 1936; the Army designation was AT-6. Versions of the Texan continued in use for Navy training well into the 1950s.
** BOQ – bachelor officers' quarters.

I married at Christmas, I had to commute from Pensacola out there to Milton, Florida. But I enjoyed learning to fly. I had no real difficulty at all.

Paul Stillwell: How did the process work?

Admiral Lawrence: Well, you'd have a half a day in ground school and a half a day flying. Of course, you'd start out with the very basic stuff. The first part was heavily oriented to learning how to land and take off. Once you mastered that basic skill, I think we used to solo after about 18 flights, which was probably about 25 hours. As I say, I enjoyed it. I had no trouble with it. I had the typical troubles of a young guy starting out, just learning how to judge your altitude and do a three-point landing, prevent the airplane from swerving, and all that. But I mastered that fairly quickly.

I sensed that flying was fairly natural to me. There was nothing that really gave me any great difficulty. And there were certain phases of flying that, perhaps, I was a little bit stronger on. I've always been a very good instrument pilot—the ability to look at your instruments and translate your interpretation of what the instruments are saying into what you should do. I've always enjoyed instrument flying as a real challenge, as opposed to the completely visual type of flying, where you do everything by your perception of what you see externally. I've probably been a better instrument pilot than the head-out-of-cockpit pilot. That's why I got, very early in my career, into the night fighter world. Alan Shepard and I and a few others did the real pioneering of the night fighter flying on the old straight-deck carriers.* I think it was because I just had a propensity to fly instruments that led me into that night fighter work.

Paul Stillwell: How demanding a regimen was it?

Admiral Lawrence: Well, flight training was not that demanding for me, because you had a lot of free time, as compared to the academy. You didn't have that much academic

---

* The U.S. Navy began adding angled decks to its aircraft carriers in the 1950s to prevent landing aircraft that missed arresting wires from crashing into planes farther forward on the deck. Gradually the straight-deck carriers were converted to the angled decks, and later new carriers from the *Forrestal* (CVA-59) class forward were built with angled decks.

study. I worked hard at the academic study; I wanted to learn everything and do well, but it was not anywhere near as intensive in academics. And then, because you had several students going through, you couldn't fly as intensively as you liked, so it was really a great life. Every weekend you could go to the beach, and it was just a completely less demanding a pace than the Naval Academy. So that was quite pleasant. I really enjoyed flight training. And, of course, that was a pleasant way to start your married life. My wife had been born in Pensacola and had grown up in a Navy family. Her father was a naval aviator, so she understood all of that. So it was really fun to start your married life with your other classmates who were married. Of course, everybody tended to marry earlier in those days. It's not all bad, I think, for people to wait to get married.

Paul Stillwell: Did the married couples congregate in the off-duty hours?

Admiral Lawrence: Oh, yes, we always got together. It so happened that my neighbor was Fred Gante, who was on the football team. So we did a lot of things together. So both professionally and socially it was really a very pleasant experience.

I went rapidly through Pensacola and the basic phase. Then I went down to Corpus Christi area, and I wanted to fly the F8F, which was the most advanced airplane they had.* Luckily, I did get the F8F, and I went down to Naval Auxiliary Air Station at Kingsville, Texas, to fly it. But the F8F had a 4-G restriction, because they had a wing structural problem. So I couldn't go through the full syllabus in the F8F. I did just basic formation and instruments in the F8F, and then moved back up to Cabaniss Field in Corpus Christi.† That involved flying the F6F in the bombing and gunnery, where you had to pull higher G's.‡

---

* Grumman F8F Bearcat fighters first entered fleet squadrons in 1945. The F8F-1 version was 28 feet long, wingspan of 35 feet, gross weight of 12,947 pounds, and top speed of 421 miles per hour. It was one of the best piston-engine planes ever to serve the U.S. Navy but had a short operational life because of the advent of jet fighters.
† Cabaniss Field at Corpus Christi, Texas, was named in honor of Commander Robert W. Cabaniss, USN, naval aviator number 36, who was killed in a plane crash in 1927.
‡ Grumman F6F Hellcat fighters first entered fleet squadrons in early 1943. The most commonly employed version of the airplane was the F6F-5, which was 34 feet long, wingspan of 43 feet, gross weight of 15,413 pounds, and top speed of 380 miles per hour. It was the principal U.S. carrier fighter in the last two years of World War II.

Paul Stillwell: I'd be interested in your comparing those two airplanes.

Admiral Lawrence: Well, the F8F had a higher performance. It had an R-2800 engine, which is a significantly higher performance than the engine that they had in the F6F.* I forget the designation for the engine in the F6F.† But the F8F, the Bearcat, was really a hotrod. You very rarely ever used full power on the airplane, because on takeoff, you went to full power, and, boy, you were airborne right away. It was a real thrill flying the F8F, because it was so responsive. The F6F was a good, solid airplane, but it was kind of a workhorse compared to the F8F. I did all of my bombing and aerial gunnery and tactics in the F6F.

Then I was selected as one of the few people to come back and go through jet training at Kingsville Field. In those days only a fraction of people went through jet training. The old F-80 was an Air Force airplane that was used in the Korean War. The Navy version of that was called the TV, and we had both single-place and two-place versions.‡ So I went through the jet training and I really, really enjoyed it. I could just see that jets were the wave of the future. So I enjoyed that very much.

Paul Stillwell: I'm not an aviator, but I've heard that the jet was easier to fly, because you didn't have to counteract the torque.

Admiral Lawrence: Yes, a jet's a lot easier to fly, because of the torque effect and less vibration. That's what we really sensed right away in the jet—a much smoother platform, and less vibration.

I'd already gotten my wings before I went to the jet training, but I was the first member of my class to finish the flight syllabus and qualify on a ship and get my landings. I did that because I really pushed myself in flight training. I didn't want to go down and be like a lot of guys who just kind of took an even strain. They didn't go

---

* The F8F-1 had a 2,100-horsepower Pratt & Whitney R-2800-34W radial engine. The Bearcat was smaller and lighter than the Hellcat, so it got higher performance from essentially the same engine.
† The F6F-5 had a 2,000-horsepower Pratt & Whitney R-2800-10W radial engine.
‡ The Air Force P-80 jet fighter—later F-80—came into the Navy in the late 1940s. Initially it was designated TO-1, a trainer built by Lockheed. After the Navy changed the manufacturer Lockheed's symbol from O to T, the plane became the TV-1 Seastar.

through as fast as they could have, but I really pushed myself. I tried to get myself scheduled frequently. And I didn't take any extensive time off between phases. So I ended up, as I say, finishing first of that group of 25 that went in my class. I got my wings on the seventh of November 1952, about 13 months after I started my training.

Paul Stillwell: Who were some of the instructors you recall at the various phases?

Admiral Lawrence: Well, Gordon Smith was one whom I remember really well, and he went on to become a rear admiral in the Navy.[*] He was not Naval Academy. He was one of the flying midshipman. He became one of our top electronic experts in the Navy. So he was my instructor in F8Fs.

I had an instructor in all-weather flight school at Corpus Christi, who was Thomas Hudner, out of the class of '47, who was a Medal of Honor winner.[†] I got to know him right after he'd gotten his Medal of Honor.

Paul Stillwell: Any personal reflections on him?

Admiral Lawrence: Well, he's just a really wonderful guy, really one of the nicest guys you'll ever meet. And he was very, very modest; he would never even talk about getting the Medal of Honor. I learned from other people that he had gotten the Medal of Honor. But he was a very fine instructor. We became good friends and stayed friends since that time.

Paul Stillwell: How capable was he as an instructor?

Admiral Lawrence: Oh, he was good. This was all-weather flight training where we were really learning instrument training.

---

[*] Lieutenant (junior grade) Gordon H. Smith, USN.
[†] Jesse L. Brown was the Navy's first black aviator designated as a result of going through the Navy's basic flight training program. He had received his wings on 21 October 1948 while a midshipman. He was commissioned an ensign in the U.S. Navy on 17 March 1949 while a member of Fighter Squadron 32. He was killed in Korea in December 1950. Lieutenant (junior grade) Thomas J. Hudner Jr., USN, a member of Brown's squadron, crash-landed his plane near Brown's and made an unsuccessful attempt to save his life.

Paul Stillwell: Hudner tried to save the life of a black aviator named Jesse Brown, who frequently gets confused with Wesley Brown.

Admiral Lawrence: Yes, that's right. That's quite a story of how he crash-landed his airplane and tried to save Jesse Brown—and, of course, was not successful.

Paul Stillwell: What were the satisfactions from mastering these various stages?

Admiral Lawrence: Well, I think it's just the pride and satisfaction of developing a skill. That's the way it was to me. Here was a skill that had to be mastered and learned. I guess that's what is one of the rewarding aspects of flying, that there's a certain evolution you have to perform and do it in a skillful manner. Doing it successfully brings you immediate satisfaction, because you can see the results of what you did.

For example, going out and flying a good carrier approach and landing, having the LSO give you a good grade.* That was always very satisfying to me. And, yes, there's a very close correlation between flying airplanes and playing sports. Before a game, you get keyed up, and you might have a few butterflies in your stomach. Then you go out and do your best and you do well. Then there's a euphoric feeling that you have when it's over, like winning a game or having a successful mission. Always the nice appeal of flying was that it was a challenge, and then if you met that challenge, you had a euphoric-type feeling that put flying above just the routine activities of life. I always tried to do the ultimate challenge that was available. That's why, when I got out to the fleet, I wanted to get into the night-fighter thing. The squadron I was in did get the night-fighter mission. Alan Shepard and others really did some pioneering in night flying on the old straight-deck carriers.

Paul Stillwell: Could you describe your first carrier landing, please?

---

* LSO – landing signal officer, a naval aviator, who stands on a platform on the port side of the carrier at the aft end of the flight deck. He signals to incoming aircraft in order to coach them onto the deck for recovery.

Admiral Lawrence: Well, as I remember, landing an SNJ aboard a carrier was pretty simple.* It was just kind of like just shooting fish in a barrel. It really wasn't all that much of a challenge, but it was quite a thrill to complete it. I bet I completed it right around the Fourth of July in 1952, and then went on down to Corpus Christi to do the advanced training. Then my next carrier landings were in the F6F. It was much more demanding to do it in the F6F, as compared to the SNJ.

Paul Stillwell: In what ways?

Admiral Lawrence: Well, you had a heavier airplane; you had more difficult visibility around the engine. In the SNJ it was more like shooting fish in a barrel. In the F6F it required a lot more precision and finesse to get your pattern such that you would be able to see out of the airplane appropriately. But I never had any trouble with that; during my qualification, I didn't get a single wave-off in any of my carrier landings.

Paul Stillwell: What do you recall about the tactical work to transform you into a fighter pilot?

Admiral Lawrence: Well, I remember in the F6F we got exposed to the Thach Weave, which had been used in World War II.† I remember that it was kind of a thrill thinking I was doing the same thing in F6Fs that pilots had been during World War II. That's when I first became familiar with the name of Jimmy Thach.

Paul Stillwell: Great guy.

Admiral Lawrence: Yes, I guess he died, unfortunately.‡ But he was one of the old, original pilots who developed the early fighter tactics.

---

* Lawrence made his first carrier landing on board the USS *Cabot* (CVL-28) on 3 July 1952.
† The Thach Weave was developed shortly before World War II by Lieutenant Commander John S. Thach, USN, commanding officer of Fighting Squadron Three. It was a means of enabling the F4F Wildcat to counter the better-performing Japanese Zero fighter. Thach, who retired as a four-star admiral, described the origin of the maneuver in his Naval Institute oral history.
‡ Thach died 15 April 1981 at age 75.

Paul Stillwell: He left Pensacola not too long before you got there to take command of a CVE that went out to Korea.*

Admiral Lawrence: Yes, I remember he was out of the class of '27. He was in the same class with George Anderson and Tom Hamilton and Howard Caldwell—all those.†

Paul Stillwell: Did the aggressiveness that you'd had on the football field translate into that same quality in the air?

Admiral Lawrence: Yes, I think so. There's such a close correlation between flying and sports, and military sports in general. I had to tone down a little bit of that aggressiveness when I got out to the fleet.

For example, in my first squadron we used to do aerial gunnery against a rectangular banner.‡ In those days, the accuracy of the guns you were flying—I guess they were .50 caliber—wasn't all that good. It was really difficult to get hits on this banner, so I got frustrated. I thought I was doing everything right. I was maneuvering the airplane well and kept my pipper on the target, but then I'd come back, and there'd be no hits, or one and two hits. I said, "God, I thought I did everything right." So I was just determined, and something just said, "By Golly, I'm going to do better." One time I flew too close to the banner. The aerial banner was suspended on a metal rod. I was determined I was going to get in close and get hits, and I embedded that metal rod in my wingtip. [Chuckle] So I flew back and landed with this metal rod in my wingtip.

The commanding officer had a little chat with me. He said, "You don't have to be that aggressive and determined to get those hits." So I had to learn just to moderate some of this desire to achieve and always do everything right and well.

Paul Stillwell: I suspect, though, that the CO would prefer that task than trying to motivate a person who wasn't inclined to do it at all.

---

* Captain Thach commanded the escort carrier *Sicily* (CVE-118) in 1950-51.
† Admiral George W. Anderson Jr., USN, served as Chief of Naval Operations, 1961-63. His oral history is in the Naval Institute collection.
‡ In March 1953 Lawrence joined Fighter Squadron 193 (VF-193), the Ghostriders. Commander Donald E. Carr Jr., USN, was the commanding officer.

Admiral Lawrence: Yes, he didn't really chew me out all that much, but it was very embarrassing to come back with that metal rod embedded in my airplane.

Paul Stillwell: How much emphasis was there on aviation safety at that time?

Admiral Lawrence: Well, there was certainly strong emphasis but not anything like it is today. We now have much more definitive programs.

We have what we call the NATOPS now.* That really defines everything you do in an airplane. We didn't have that formal an approach to things. And we had a lot more accidents, because pilots weren't as proficient. It wasn't because of unreliability of the machinery. That was a factor, certainly, but I think the greatest factor was the pilot proficiency. But, also, it was more demanding in the sense that the carriers were smaller; we didn't have angled decks in those days. So the overall demands were greater, and we just didn't have pilots who were quite as skillful as they are today, because of the nature of our training.

Paul Stillwell: Wasn't there also a somewhat greater tolerance for flat-hatting then?†

Admiral Lawrence: Yes, there really was. There was a lot more of individualism, less regulatory aspect of what we were doing. I was Alan Shepard's wingman, and his great aspiration in those days was to be a Blue Angel.‡ In those days, academy graduates didn't go into the Blue Angels. This really bothered him, because he really wanted to be a Blue Angel. And this was before he even heard of space. So we formed our own acrobatic team, a four-plane division in our squadron. I flew in the slot; Alan Shepard was the leader; John Mitchell, out of the class of '52, was in the left wing.§ Preston Luke, who was an ex-flying midshipman, was on the right wing.** We got to be very proficient in flying formation acrobatics in that diamond. You would never even do that nowadays.

---

* The first NATOPS (Naval Air Training and Operating Procedures Standardization) manual was promulgated in July 1961 for the HSS-1. Manuals for other aircraft came out subsequently.
† "Flat-hatting" is a term for stunt flying closer to the ground than safety dictates.
‡ Blue Angels is the name of the Navy's flight demonstration team, which has done close formation flying for air shows and other events since 1946. Shepard was then a recently promoted lieutenant commander.
§ Lieutenant (junior grade) John R. C. Mitchell, USN.
** Lieutenant (junior grade) Preston Luke, USN.

Gosh, you'd be thrown out of aviation so fast, you couldn't believe it. But we used to spend most of our scheduled flights doing formation acrobatics in that diamond. We called ourselves the Mangy Angels.

One time we were deployed out in the Western Pacific on the carrier *Oriskany*.[*] When the *Oriskany* was in port, we off-loaded to Atsugi.[†] I forget which one of us conceived this idea of getting a picture of the Mangy Angels—we were flying F2H-3 Banshees—going up vertically with snow-capped Mount Fujiyama in the background.[‡] We could just envision this on the front of *Life* magazine—at least on the front of *Naval Aviation News*. So we pressured this photo pilot, Lieutenant John Romano, to fly an F2H-2P out and take pictures of us going up vertically in a diamond formation.[§] John was not all that keen on it, but he agreed, because he shared the ready room with us, and he knew he'd get a lot of flak if he didn't. So we went out and we decided we had to do a couple practice loops so that John could get his positioning. We did two practice loops, and then we heard this unintelligible transmission on the radio.

Finally, about ten seconds, later John said, "Hey, we're going to have to knock it off and go back to Atsugi."

So we went back and landed, and we ran over to John Romano, "What happened, John?"

He said, "I got sick and I threw up in my oxygen mask." See, he hadn't been doing all this acrobatics like the rest of us; he was a straight-and-level guy. So we were really upset, because we thought the world was denied the greatest aerial photograph in history. I thought that was a great idea, but we never really got that picture.

---

[*] USS *Oriskany* (CVA-34) was an improved *Essex*-class aircraft carrier, commissioned 25 September 1950. She had a standard displacement of 33,000 tons, was 888 feet long, 93 feet in the beam, and had an extreme width of 148 feet. Her top speed was 33 knots. She had eight 5-inch guns and could accommodate approximately 90 aircraft.
For more detail on this deployment, see Neal Thompson, *Light This Candle: The Life & Times of Alan Shepard, America's First Spaceman* (New York: Crown, 2004).
[†] Atsugi is the site of a U.S. naval air station near the port of Yokosuka on the island of Honshu, Japan.
[‡] McDonnell's F2H Banshee was a jet-powered fighter-bomber that first entered the fleet with squadron VF-171 in March 1949. The F2H-2 version was 40 feet long, wingspan of 45 feet, gross weight of 22,312 pounds, and top speed of 532 miles per hour. It had four fixed forward-firing 20-millimeter guns and provision to carry two 500-pound bombs.
Mount Fuji, also known as Fujiyama, is the highest mountain in Japan at 12,388 feet. It is considered sacred in Japanese culture. It is on the main island of Honshu, about 70 miles from Tokyo.
[§] Lieutenant John A. Romano, USNR.

My commanding officer of that first deployment on *Oriskany* was Captain C. D. Griffin.* I don't know whether you've ever interviewed him.

Paul Stillwell: No, but my predecessor did.

Admiral Lawrence: Well, he was a great skipper. He was old-school guy, had been a test pilot; he was a very famous naval aviator.

Paul Stillwell: He was a classmate of Thach's also.

Admiral Lawrence: Yes, he was '27. He used to wear an old railroad conductor's hat, and he'd have an ascot-type scarf.

See, jets were still fairly new on the carriers in those days, back in 1953. This was the first air group that had three jet fighter squadrons and one AD squadron.† We were having a problem with the wooden flight deck on the *Oriskany*. Mahogany, I guess, was the prime cover, and the bottom was Douglas fir. Anyway, we were gouging holes in that with the hard landings of the jets. The problem was that the LSOs were cutting us too close, and then we'd push over and land too hard, and it would start gouging out the flight deck. Captain Griffin was getting very concerned about the condition of his flight deck, so he assembled the whole air group back on the rear of the flight deck. And, boy, he really read the riot act to us about doing a proper type landing.

Our air group commander was Jig Ramage out of the class of '39.‡ He had won the Navy Cross during World War II, I think at the Battle of the Philippine Sea. He developed a phrase, "Don't dive for the goddamn deck." That became our motto for that cruise.

Paul Stillwell: He's a colorful individual.

---

* Captain Charles Donald Griffin, USN, commanded the aircraft carrier *Oriskany* (CVA-34) from June 1953 to July 1954. The oral history of Griffin, who retired as a four-star admiral, is in the Naval Institute collection. Dr. John T. Mason Jr. interviewed him.
† Douglas AD Skyraider propeller-driven attack planes first entered fleet squadrons in late 1946.
‡ Commander James D. Ramage, USN, Commander Carrier Air Group 19. The oral history of Ramage, who retired as a rear admiral, is in the Naval Institute collection.

Admiral Lawrence: Yes, he really is. He's one of the real naval aviators and a very good friend of mine.

Paul Stillwell: What else do you recall about him?

Admiral Lawrence: Well, he used to fly with my squadron in the F2H-3s. Our skipper was Commander Deke Carr out of the class of '41. One time Ramage was leading our flight, Al Shepard was flying as his section leader, and I was flying as Al Shepard's wingman. We were flying up through kind of a cloudy situation, and all of a sudden Commander Ramage started wandering off course. Al Shepard was perceptive enough to realize that he probably was having a hypoxia problem. So he called him and said, "Check your oxygen, check your oxygen." Ramage did and realized that his oxygen mask had come unplugged, that there was some problem. Al Shepard's very alert situation there probably saved Ramage's life.[*]

We had a lot of fun on that cruise.[†] We arrived out there shortly after the armistice had been signed in Korea.[‡] We flew in the Sea of Japan, and we did a lot of flying over land in Korea. But the armistice was in effect.

Paul Stillwell: Ramage strikes me as the kind of individual who would not be inclined to observe regulations that didn't make sense to him.

Admiral Lawrence: Not at all, not at all. He really espoused good flying and was a great proponent of naval aviation, but was a very charismatic leader. I always had great respect and admiration for him. He was a very intelligent guy; he was thoughtful about devising new tactics.

Paul Stillwell: Well, he did a lot to advance the heavy attack community.

---

[*] Ramage's account of this incident is in his oral history.
[†] The deployment began with the ship's departure from San Francisco on 14 September 1953. The *Oriskany* arrived in Yokosuka, Japan, on 15 October to begin Seventh Fleet operations.
[‡] On 27 July 1953 negotiators for the United Nations and the Communist North Koreans signed an armistice agreement at Panmunjom, Korea, to end the Korean War. It took effect at 10:00 that same date.

Admiral Lawrence: He really helped them. He was not a heavy attack pilot, but he perceived that they needed a lot of help. He really got them to become more professional. He's a really, really highly professional naval aviator.

Because the Korean War had just ended, one great experience I had when I was in the squadron was that we used to have a program where we'd have an exchange visit with the Army troops. We'd have some out to the carrier, and then we'd visit them. So I got to visit with the Second Infantry Division up on the front lines in Korea. We were there in November 1953, and it was really cold. That's where I got a appreciation of what the Army life was really like and how fortunate I was to be in the Navy then aboard ship. But that was an interesting cruise. I learned a lot about carrier flying and of course, I was, to a degree, involved in the Korean War, although the armistice had been signed.

Paul Stillwell: What more can you say about your squadron skipper?

Admiral Lawrence: Well, Deke Carr was a very stern guy. He was kind of taciturn, and he was a very technical type. He'd had a PG education in aeronautical engineering.[*] He was just exactly opposite from Jig Ramage; he was not as charismatic at all. But he was a good, solid, capable aviator, and he was really an operator. He loved to fly, and he was always in there leading the tactical situations. But he was just not an outgoing guy, so that it was hard to relate to Deke Carr. But he and I, of course, got along well.

My first job in the squadron was as the line division officer, being in charge of the plane captains. Then I was moved in to be the personnel officer. We had some reservists in our squadron who had been recalled to active duty because of the Korean War. They had come from Glenview and St. Louis, where they'd been flying in the reserves. When the war ended, those reserves who wanted to leave were allowed to go. About three of them left our squadron during that cruise, because the armistice was in effect. I had to move from being personnel officer up to being admin officer. So I got a chance to be a department head as a young officer, lieutenant (j.g.), so that was a good experience for me. I worked very hard at my ground duties, and I wanted to learn as much as I could

---

[*] PG – postgraduate.

about administration, being the personnel officer. So it was a good cruise as a learning experience. I really enjoyed that first cruise.

Paul Stillwell: Well, please tell me more about flying with Shepard.

Admiral Lawrence: Well, he was unquestionably the best naval aviator I ever saw during my career. Later we were test pilots together back in Patuxent, when they first announced the space program. I told everybody, "The first two guys I know they'll pick will be Al Shepard and John Glenn."[*] I was close to both of them. I knew that John Glenn was a superb aviator; he was a superb physical specimen and kind of the ideal man, Eagle Scout-type guy. But I always gave Shepard the nod on just raw flying ability. It was really a great privilege to be able to fly with him, and I'd learned so much about just the basic skills of flying, but also how you think to be a flight leader. He was very good in that respect.

One time we were out in the Sea of Japan there, and Shepard wanted to do something to boost the spirits of the people down there on the flight deck. It's a great rapport you have with the flight deck people, and most of them really respect and kind of idolize pilots. So you try to do good things for them, because they work so hard. He decided one day that he would bring our four-plane division back to the carrier in a diamond formation. We would break into the landing pattern out of a diamond instead of the echelon. Well, today that's an absolute no-no, but Shepard decided he would do this. As you come back, the left wing goes first, then the leader goes next, then the slot, then the right wing. You have to be very careful, because you're maneuvering close to each other. So we came back and did that.

The flight deck crew was thrilled, but Deke Carr wasn't. So he put Al Shepard in hack for a week, which used to be very common in those days.[†] I remember I used to go up and eat with Al in his room so he wouldn't be by himself.

---

[*] On 16 July 1957 Major John H. Glenn Jr., USMC, broke the transcontinental speed record when he flew an F8U-1P Crusader from Los Alamitos, California, to Floyd Bennett Field, Brooklyn, in 3 hours, 22 minutes, and 50 seconds. On 20 February 1962, as a lieutenant colonel and astronaut, Glenn flew the "Friendship 7" spacecraft on the first manned orbital mission by the United States.

[†] Being "in hack" means that an officer is suspended from duty and confined to his room for a period of time.

But the thing that was really the pioneering aspect of it was doing the night jet operations on those straight-deck carriers. That was by far the most demanding thing that I ever did in naval aviation. It was tougher than combat and the experimental test flying, because it demanded such a precision and more skill than anything else I've ever done. Because there was a straight-deck pattern, we were still using the landing signal officer, and you had to come in at night and maneuver to end up about 75 feet over the water and at a cut position. And at night, you were flying on instruments and visual and the confusion factor of radio. [End of tape, end of interview]

Interview Number 3 with Vice Admiral William P. Lawrence, U.S. Navy (Retired)
Place: U.S. Naval Institute, Annapolis, Maryland
Date: Monday, 24 September 1990

Paul Stillwell: Admiral, when we were finishing up last time you were talking about the night carrier work. Could you go into some more detail on that, please.

Admiral Lawrence: Well, the early '50s were really an interesting time to be in naval aviation, because at that time naval aviation was still only 40 years old. Of course, naval aviation had grown significantly during World War II. This was just shortly afterward, and here we were making the most significant step in naval aviation, I feel, with the introduction of jet airplanes. I was fortunate to be one of the pioneers in the commencement of night jet operations. We had started fairly extensive night flying in World War II with the prop airplanes. Then we had continued that, but flying the jets at night put a new dimension into naval aviation in terms of the challenge.[*] You were talking about airplanes coming aboard about 30 knots faster, in terms of approach speed, than the prop planes. That was about 30% greater speed in night carrier landings.

Paul Stillwell: Was that a psychological problem for some people?

Admiral Lawrence: Oh, yes, the psychological challenge was really great, because the hazards increased commensurate with the increase in the speed. Of course, the advantage in the jet was that you had basically a smoother-flying airplane because of not having that big propeller up there in front of you and all the torque effects of the reciprocating engine. But the increased speed really put a tremendous challenge into it.

When I came back from my first deployment out to the Western Pacific in 1953-54, in the F2H-3 Banshee, we were told that we would now become a dual-mission squadron. Our squadron would have both the night fighter and the special weapons delivery missions. That, of course, was a tremendous training challenge to get people

---

[*] For background on the progression, see Charles H. Brown, *Dark Sky, Black Sea: Aircraft Carrier Night and All-Weather Operations* (Annapolis: Naval Institute Press, 1999).

qualified to be proficient. In the special weapons area, you had significant training requirement to get people familiar with the nuclear weapons.

Paul Stillwell: Low-level navigation was part of it.

Admiral Lawrence: Well, we really didn't get as much involved in the low-level navigation at that phase. We were really concentrating more on the type of delivery. Initially we were looking at the high-level delivery of a nuclear weapon. Then people realized that to defeat the vulnerabilities of the air-defense systems, you would have to come in low level and do a loft maneuver.[*] We started doing that type of training, but it put a tremendous burden on our squadron.

Our commanding officer was Commander Mickey Weisner, out of the Naval Academy class of '41, who in his final assignment was CinCPac.[†] He realized that that was going to be a significant challenge. Only three of us returned from the squadron of '53-54: Alan Shepard, who had just made lieutenant commander; Lieutenant Don Long, out of the Naval Academy class of '50; and myself.[‡] As I mentioned, the squadron that went out to Korea in '53-54 had about 50% reserve officers who had been recalled back to active duty. So when we arrived out there, within a couple of months we saw that it looked like the armistice was going to endure, so they permitted the reserve officers to leave active duty. So we lost almost everybody from that first cruise, either from getting off active duty or going to shore duty.

Then Mickey Weisner really handpicked everybody that he brought into the squadron. We only took three officers out of the training command. Two of them were

---

[*] The loft bombing method was designed as a tactic to prevent airplanes from being damaged by their own nuclear bombs. The method called for the pilot to make a low-altitude approach to the target and pull up into the first part of a Cuban 8. The bomb would be released as the aircraft reached about 45-degree angle during the climb. The pilot then completed the half of the Cuban 8 and flew back in the direction from which he had made his approach. A nickname for the method was "idiot loop."
[†] Admiral Maurice F. Weisner, USN, served as Commander in Chief Pacific from 30 August 1976 to 31 October 1979. He had the rank of commander while commanding officer of VF-193.
[‡] Lieutenant Donald C. Long, USN.

out of the Naval Academy class of '52, John Mitchell and Dan Blide.* The third was Bill Brunhaver, an NROTC graduate out of the University of Washington.†

Paul Stillwell: How did Weisner have that opportunity? Did he have an in with BuPers?

Admiral Lawrence: Oh, yes. He had spent a lot of time himself back in BuPers as a detailer.‡ And he really impressed upon people the tremendous challenge that we faced, both the night fighters and special weapons. The special weapons then, as it is today, put a tremendous reliability imperative in there.§ He wanted to make sure every pilot he picked could measure up to the demands. It was tough; we really had to work hard to meet all of our qualifications.

Paul Stillwell: What was involved in those qualifications?

Admiral Lawrence: Well, first of all, doing the requisite amount of night flying, doing enough of the night field carrier landing practice. I was in the night fighter component with Alan Shepard. His primary role was in the night fighter element in the squadron. But as a result of his having been a test pilot at Patuxent River, Al also became dual qualified in special weapons because he had that capability. He was the only pilot in the squadron in both missions. You had to do a tremendous amount of night flying; yet, the night flying was not compatible with the special weapons training. It was hard to split the squadron in two—a day component and a night component—because that put a tremendous demand on your maintenance personnel. So we had to capitalize on every opportunity for good training.

---

* Lieutenant (junior grade) John R. C. Mitchell, USN. Lieutenant (junior grade) Dan C. Blide, USN. Mitchell eventually reached the rank of captain, commanded the carrier *John F. Kennedy* (CV-67) from 1975 to 1977, and retired in 1978. He recalls that one of the other new pilots when he joined VF-193 was Lieutenant (junior grade) George K. Farris, USN.
† Lieutenant (junior grade) William H. Brunhaver, USNR.
‡ BuPers – Bureau of Naval Personnel.
§ On 27 September 1991—a year after this interview—President George H. W. Bush announced a unilateral initiative to cease deployment of tactical nuclear weapons on board U.S. Navy surface ships, attack submarines, and land-based aircraft during "normal circumstances."

We made a deployment to Fallon, Nevada, where we did training.* Those of us who were in the night fighter component did air-to-air gunnery, and those who were in the weapons component did weapons training. Then we made another deployment down to Inyokern, California, the Naval Ordnance Test Station. That's when we did a lot of emphasis on the special weapon training, particularly doing loft work on their range.

Landing at night those old *Essex*-class straight-deck carriers was really tough, and, of course, night flying in any type of carrier is very demanding. We had to develop our own procedures. There was no real guidance for this. There had been a little bit of previous night jet work out of the Composite Squadron Three at Moffett Field.† We used to send out teams of four pilots and, I think, two airplanes to be night teams, but that just started concurrently with our taking this role in the squadron.

Paul Stillwell: What were some of the procedures you came up with?

Admiral Lawrence: Well, we flew in four-plane divisions, just like we did in the daytime. We would bring the four airplanes back in a right-echelon formation at 5,000 feet, and then, by our ADF radios—automatic direction-finding—we would locate the carrier. We didn't have TACAN in those days.‡ Then you would try to pick up the ship visually. You would fly over the carrier at 5,000 feet, and then about five miles aft of the carrier you would break out of your echelon formation. I think we gave ourselves a good one-minute interval between airplanes. Then as you turned back towards the carrier, you would descend and fly by the yardarm. You'd visually sight the yardarm, where the lights were not at bright setting. As you'd fly by that, you would try to set your altimeter very accurately. I think the height of the yardarm was about 200 feet, maybe a little bit more than that off the water. But, see, prior to takeoff, you would set your altimeter at 60 feet on deck. We didn't have any radar altimeters. We had radio altimeters that just didn't work. I mean, they were very new, and the technicians weren't able to maintain

---

* Naval Auxiliary Air Station, Fallon, Nevada, later upgraded to full naval air station status in 1972.
† Moffett Field Naval Air Station, Sunnyvale, California, was located ten miles north of San Jose, at the southern tip of San Francisco Bay. It was named in honor of Rear Admiral William A. Moffett, USN, first Chief of the Bureau of Aeronautics.
‡ Tacan – tactical aid to navigation, a homing signal broadcast by an aircraft carrier to aid returning aircraft in locating the ship.

them. So we totally relied on pressure altimeters. Today they have very sophisticated radar altimeters.

So you set the pressure altimeter before landing and then, as a check on your altimeters, you flew by the yardarm as you came back. Then you went ahead of the carrier, turned downwind, and we always had either a cruiser or destroyer over at the 180-degree position to mark where you should commence your turn. It was, I think, 2,000 feet abeam when you would start into your turn at, as I recall, a one-half standard rate. You'd set it on your gyro horizon and the needle of your needle ball indicator. Then you would come over that at the 180-degree point at 200 feet. And then from 180 in, you would start a descent, because you had to end up at the ramp at about 70 feet. So you'd set a half-standard rate turn.

By now you were flying half visual outside and half on instruments, which is the most dangerous situation you ever get into, because it's really a vertigo-inducing situation. But you would try to maintain that half standard rate turn and just hope like hell that there was just a even a faint outline of a horizon. Because if you had that horizon, that really facilitated the flying airplane well, because you wouldn't have to refer to your own gyro horizon, and it would be less conducive to having vertigo. But many nights you had no horizon, just like being in a damn punchbowl. But at the 90-degree position, where now you were getting to about 100 feet, you looked down to see if you could see the reflection of your belly light on the water. And you hoped that you'd have some whitecaps, because this would enhance the reflection. And somebody said, "Well, what if your belly light was out?"

Somebody else in the ready room responded, "Well, tough shit!" [Laughter]

Paul Stillwell: At what point in that sequence did you pick up the LSO?

Admiral Lawrence: Well, then at the 90-degree position, you were about 100 feet, and you confirmed that 100 feet on your pressure altimeter by seeing this reflection of your belly light on the water. Then from the 90-degree position on in, you started looking for the LSO, and by now you were principally concerned about your line-up. You wanted to complete that turn, so you rolled on up and you had a certain amount of straightaway, what they called the groove. But from about the 75-degree position, now you were really starting to look for that LSO, and you were flying more outside the cockpit than inside the cockpit. You were trying to maintain that turn so that you could roll out and be in a position lined up for the carrier. There was a great tendency to do what they call angling, where you would turn a little bit too much, and you would end up having to be angled over to the carrier, rather than being in a real straightaway. You really did not want to overshoot and come back, because then you'd have to have a steep turn, and then it would inhibit your ability to see the LSO.

Paul Stillwell: You're saying you didn't want to get too far to starboard on the approach to the carrier.

Admiral Lawrence: That's right—what they call overshooting. So the tendency was to end up angling, which was bad as well. But, anyway, from about the 75-degree position on in, you were really looking to the LSO, and now you were flying almost completely head out of the cockpit.

In that era, the LSOs just started using suits with little lights on them to facilitate seeing them. So now you were really looking for him in hopes that he would pick you up with a "Roger." The big concern on the part of LSOs, of course, was that, one, you would get too slow, and two, would be that he cut you so you were, in fact, over the deck.[*] So there was a tendency for them to cut you too close to the carrier and have you too fast. That's why you hated to be the first airplane to come back in a night recovery, because the LSO was just getting his eye. One night he put me into the damn barrier by cutting me too close, and he gave me a slow signal. He got me going too fast, and I ended up going into the barricade.[†] I wasn't hurt. The airplane went into the barricade, and it just bent the wings, but it really didn't significantly damage the airplane.

Paul Stillwell: But that diminishes the sense of trust you need in that LSO.

---

[*] The "cut" means cutting off the engine as part of the landing sequence.
[†] Straight-deck aircraft carriers had a barricade rigged across the flight deck, forward of the landing area, to prevent incoming planes from crashing into those parked at the forward end of the flight deck. This is not a problem in angled-deck carriers. If the plane has a problem landing, the pilot puts on power, takes off from the angled deck, climbs back into the air, and goes around again for another landing attempt.

Admiral Lawrence: Oh, yes. Well, of all the things I've done in naval aviation, that was by far the most demanding. I remember saying to myself, "You know, if I survive this, I'm afraid I'll be lucky, because I just can't believe that we can get through a full deployment doing this stuff."

Paul Stillwell: Were there, in fact, some casualties in the squadron?

Admiral Lawrence: Oh, yes, sure. John Mitchell went into the fantail one night, and he was in the second airplane to land after I landed. The Banshee had the J-34 engine, which was one of the last with a radial compressor, I think. Today's jet engines all have the axial-flow compressor, in which you compress the air through stages, stator rotor vanes. Whereas, the early jet engines had just a single centrifugal type of turbine arrangement that in one stage compressed your air. The basic problem with that was that it tended to cause residual fires in your tailpipe, because there was not enough airflow in there to blow out the fuel. At low RPMs, and you could tend to pool a little bit of fuel back there, and if you shut down from low RPM, you'd get a residual fire. So we always turned up to about 70% RPM before we shut down to prevent residual fire.

But for some reason on that night I got a residual fire in one of my engines when I shut down. Of course, it was a touchy situation, because they didn't want you to turn up too high RPM on deck, because you could blow people overboard. But I got a residual fire and John was right behind me. I think that residual fire just lit up like Fourth of July fireworks, and on a real black night. So I think that distracted him. Although he never said that it was a factor, I think it had to be a factor. Anyway, he got slow, and regardless of what the LSO was trying to do, he settled into the fantail of the *Oriskany*.

Well, the *Oriskany* had two 40-millimeter mounts back on the fantail. From just a foot or so beyond his cockpit, the rear of the airplane was broken off and fell into the water. From the cockpit forward, he reefed, as we found out. On the fantail of an *Essex*-class carrier were two ladders that went up into some spaces just underneath the flight deck. There was a vertical stanchion adjacent to that ladder. We found through his experience that that vertical stanchion is exactly one Banshee fuselage width from the ladder, because he wedged perfectly between that vertical stanchion and the ladder.

Paul Stillwell: He was a lucky man.

Admiral Lawrence: Anyway, this fuel sloshed up into the hangar deck, and, fortunately, it didn't ignite because it would have caused a catastrophic conflagration. But the firefighting team was deterred in going back there because of this sloshing up into the hangar bay. Finally, they went back there, and they looked in the cockpit, and there was no pilot. They saw the seat was still there, so he hadn't ejected. The shoulder harness and lap belt were just lying in the seat. John had realized that, having had a crash, the medics were going to check him. So he unstrapped himself, got out, went into the hangar bay and went down a ladder that led to sick bay. So, anyway, the people came back and said, "Where in the hell is the pilot?"

Of course, all of us up in the ready room just knew that he was dead. So we were all sitting around just very despondent, and nobody was talking to each other. The squadron duty officer was at the desk in the ready room when the phone rang. A very excitable guy named Wilmer Gilbert was the squadron duty officer.[*] He answered the phone and said, "Hey, Mitch, where are you calling from?" [Laughter] We all thought he was calling from heaven. [Laughter] We couldn't believe that John Mitchell had survived that crash. It was just extraordinarily good luck.

We had had a similar settling-on-the-fantail accident the previous cruise, which was during the daytime. That pilot, Frank Repp, hit the round-down on the flight deck and the aft part of his fuselage fell off, but he skidded up the deck, and it just so happened his cockpit came to rest in a clear area where there was no fire. He survived and got out.[†]

John Mitchell's crash was the major accident that we had at night. Luckily, we didn't lose a pilot.

Paul Stillwell: That was luck.

Admiral Lawrence: We really were lucky because, as I say, it was really hairy. Of course, within a year or two the angled deck came out and that just really made it much

---

[*] Lieutenant Wilmer R. Gilbert, USN.
[†] Lieutenant Frank J. Repp, USNR, crashed his F2H-3 Banshee on 31 March 1954.

safer. We simply could not have introduced the later breed of airplanes—the swept-wing airplanes like the F3H, the F11F, and all the supersonic breed—on straight-deck carriers.* So we were very thankful to the British for conceiving the idea of the angled deck.

Paul Stillwell: Where did the mirror landing system come in that sequence?

Admiral Lawrence: Well, it was after my time in that squadron tour over there. The mirror landing system and the angled deck were coincident developments. It would have been very difficult to use the mirror landing system on the old straight-deck carriers. You were pretty much committed to being under continuous LSO control in the old straight-deck carriers, because under the descending approach, there's much less control of your approach by the landing signal officer. So the angled deck and the mirror landing system were introduced at the same time, but that really put a significant increase in the safety of carrier operations. As I say, we were fortunate that we got through that whole deployment without any fatalities. But I think we really made a great contribution in that pioneering effort.

Paul Stillwell: Were you essentially writing doctrine in this field?

Admiral Lawrence: Oh, yes, we really were. We were pleased that we had Alan Shepard in the squadron, because he was a test pilot, and he had done a lot of the carrier landing tests back at Patuxent. So in addition to being just an absolutely superb aviator, he had the test pilot experience. So he was invaluable to us as we worked out this doctrine.

Paul Stillwell: Was that why he was doing both of the squadron's missions?

Admiral Lawrence: Yes, just because he was just that capable. The commanding officer, Mickey Weisner, just felt that it would be useful to use him in both missions. But he

---

* McDonnell's F3H Demon was a jet-powered fighter-bomber that first entered the fleet in 1956 but was relatively unsuccessful. The Grumman F11F Tiger was first delivered to Squadron VA-156 in March 1957.

didn't do a lot of flying in the weapons area, because we were so heavily committed to this night fighter work.

Paul Stillwell: Do you remember any specific incidents involving Shepard?

Admiral Lawrence: Well, I'm going to give you a copy of this article that I wrote that's going to be out any day now in our Naval Aviation Museum Foundation magazine called "My Reminiscences of Alan Shepard."[*]

I got a cold cat shot one time. When I joined the squadron, it was preparing for deployment, so we were heavily involved in weapons training: bomb delivery, rocket delivery, everything. When we got to Hawaii, we did our operational readiness inspection. One day I was fully loaded with bombs, and for some reason I didn't get enough pressure off the catapult. My airplane went off the bow and settled into the water. In those days we had just the reciprocating-engine helicopters. Today all of our helicopters are turbine-powered engines, but the reciprocating helicopters were not all that powerful. Fortunately, the airplane settled in, wings level, and it continued floating for a while, so I was able to get out of the airplane. But I forgot a lot of things I had been taught and should have remembered. I left my parachute on, so they had to pull me out of the water with my parachute, which put a lot more burden on the helicopter. I could just feel it really laboring to pull me out of the water. Of course, I was fortunate that this happened when the *Oriskany* was about 20 miles directly south of Barbers Point, so the water was a nice and comfortable temperature.[†] If you had to go in the water, it was a hell of a lot better than going in off the coast of Korea, I tell you.

They brought me back on deck, and the first thing they told me when I got out of the helicopter was that, "The captain wants to see you on the bridge." This was Captain Don Griffin, and I was sure that he was going to summarily take my wings away from me when I arrived on the bridge. But when I arrived on the bridge, he said, "Well done. You did a great job in handling that."

---

[*] "Reminiscences of Alan Shepard," *Foundation*, Fall 1990, pages 38-41. Much of the information in the article is also covered in this oral history.
[†] Barbers Point was the site of a naval air station at the southwest "corner" of the island of Oahu, Hawaii.

Subsequently I found out that the officer of the deck was Ensign Bob Denbigh, out of the class of '52 at the Naval Academy.* I was on the right catapult when this happened, and he had given an immediate rudder order for a left turn. Then the captain got into it, and he gave the turn back to the right, which was to swing the bow of the ship away from me and then turn immediately back to the right so the stern wouldn't hit me.

Paul Stillwell: So the screws wouldn't hit you.

Admiral Lawrence: Yes, that's right. So they did a superb job. I had known Bob Denbigh at the Naval Academy, and I might add that he later went into submarines. I'm sure that that experience convinced him that submarines would be better than aviation. Anyway, they did a superb job in avoiding me. But they refired that catapult many, many times, and they simply couldn't get it to repeat the malfunction. They would get a reporting of the pressure and the end speed for each catapult, which showed that I didn't have enough end speed, but they never could get the malfunction to repeat itself. So they put the catapult out of commission to thoroughly look at everything. Then we had our accident board, and Al Shepard was the senior member of it. They had to come up with a finding of undetermined as a result of that situation, because they simply could not get the catapult to repeat the malfunction. So it was just some quirk, an anomaly, that caused the catapult on that occasion not to give me enough end speed.

But the Banshee was a good airplane in the sense that it had a lot of stability, and as it slowed up, it didn't have a tendency to drop off one wing on the other, because it was a straight-wing airplane. It didn't have some of the adverse characteristics of the swept-wing airplanes, so I was a very lucky guy that the airplane settled in the water and stayed afloat in time for me to get out. In the swept-wing breed of airplanes that came in later, if a guy went into the water, he rarely ever survived, because the airplanes were heavier, and they usually fell off one wing. But that was another interesting experience from that deployment in those early years on the *Oriskany*.

Paul Stillwell: What can you say about Weisner as both an aviator and a leader?

---
* Ensign Robert S. Denbigh Jr., USN.

Admiral Lawrence: Well, you have to give Mickey Weisner a tremendous amount of credit, because he had been a multi-engine pilot back in World War II, and post-World War II, he flew seaplanes.

Paul Stillwell: Somebody told me he tried to hide that background when he went into carrier aviation.

Admiral Lawrence: Well, he wasn't going around advertising it, but he was, I think, proud of the fact that he got a command of a PBM squadron as a lieutenant commander, very early command.[*] Then he went back to BuPers and arranged to write himself orders to make a transition into carrier aviation. So you have to give him a lot of credit that he had the courage and the tenacity and all to do that, because to come into a, your first tour on a carrier squadron, particularly a fighter squadron, with a dual night and special weapons mission, as a commanding officer, takes a hell of a lot of guts, I'll tell you.

He was a good skipper, and he did all the flying that he should have done. He was in the weapons side; he didn't do any night work, but he got his night qual landings. Everybody in the squadron had to get the qualification landings. He was a very tough taskmaster. He worked us really hard, because we had a lot of work to do. We used to kid him about him being a "sundowner," as the old term used to be.[†] We used to say that in our squadron that we really should keep moving west so that the sun would never go down in our squadron.

See, we did a lot of night flying, so we'd have a schedule where we'd come to work at about 4:00 o'clock in the afternoon and then go home at midnight. That was the theoretical schedule, but there are just certain things that you have to do during the daytime, like interfacing with other units and everything. So, invariably, you'd find that although the working day commenced at 4:00, you'd be getting in there about noon, and sometimes you'd get there earlier than that. It ended up that we'd be working consistently 12-hour days.

---

[*] The Martin PBM Mariner was a two-engine flying boat that first entered fleet patrol squadrons in 1941.
[†] "Sundowner" is a Navy slang term for a very strict officer.

Paul Stillwell: Where was the squadron based?

Admiral Lawrence: Moffett Field. So it was a very tough, demanding schedule, and the pressures were really great, too, because of this night work.

My two deployments in that squadron aboard *Oriskany* were really very professionally rewarding, stimulating. You learned a tremendous amount about aviation. And, of course, the demands were very great on what we had to do. Even though we arrived out there after the Korean War, we were still very much in a wartime-type posture. I remember it was extremely cold in that first deployment out there. We got out in October, and then we were in the Sea of Japan and we went through a winter out there.* I had to wear exposure suits a lot, and the old exposure suits had this very tight rubber neck seal. It was very tough for a fighter pilot to have to wear those because of heavy maneuvering and turning and everything was really restrictive.

I remember when I first wore my exposure suit, I had to escort one of our photo airplanes on an overland photo mission just south of DMZ.† He was doing all sorts of maneuvering, and every time I would turn my head abruptly, it would cut off my blood and I would almost black out because of lack of blood. So wearing those exposure suits most of that deployment was really very uncomfortable.

The other wonderful, valuable experience I had was that we had a program of exchange visits with the Army units down on the front line. We'd bring some Army officers out on the carrier and some Navy pilots would go visit Army units on the front line. So I had the opportunity to go from the carrier to visit the Second Infantry Division, which was up there south of DMZ. It was north of Seoul and just south of the old town of Chorwon. And Chorwon had just been completely destroyed during the Korean War. So Second Division was in what they called the Chorwon Valley. We stayed for two or three nights with the Army unit on their front line. We went up to forward observation post and looked through the glasses and see the Chinese troops in their padded uniforms. I learned a lot from interfacing with the Army and realized how tough their life is, being

---

* The ship ended her deployment on 22 April 1954, when she arrived in San Diego.
† DMZ – the demilitarized zone that divided North Korea from South Korea.

in that Korean, cold situation. That was a very special experience in that first deployment.

Paul Stillwell: What highlights do you recall from the second deployment?

Admiral Lawrence: Well, of course, doing all the night work was very demanding. One problem is that you would go sometimes three weeks between night landings, and that just made it just that much more difficult because you weren't doing enough to really build up your proficiency.

Paul Stillwell: How were the carriers used in that peacetime period?

Admiral Lawrence: Well, by the second deployment, which started in the spring of '55, we were off the Korean focus.* They had pretty much of a stabilized armistice, and they had the Air Force units that were there in place of Army units. So we didn't really spend much time up off of Korea. We spent more time down in the Philippine-South China Sea area. I remember we did an interesting joint amphibious exercise, on the island of Iwo Jima. There were Marine units, and the carriers supporting the Marines. We did a lot of flying out of the Philippines. Cubi Point had not yet been developed.† They were working on it, so we had to go in the old Sangley Point Air Station. The carriers anchored off of Manila, and we went over to Sangley Point. So most of our work was south of Japan, just outside of Tokyo Bay in that area, and then on down in the Philippines area.

Paul Stillwell: Sounds as if it was largely training.

---

* The *Oriskany* departed Alameda Naval Air Station in March 1955 and arrived in Yokosuka, Japan, on 2 April. She completed the deployment by arriving back at Alameda on 21 September.
† Cubi Point Naval Air Station was at Subic Bay on the island of Luzon in the Philippines. The station went into commission on 25 July 1956.

Admiral Lawrence: It was largely training. One thing I should mention about that second deployment, too, is one time when they were having the Tachen Islands crisis.* These were in the islands between Taiwan and China's mainland.

Paul Stillwell: They were evacuated.

Admiral Lawrence: They were having a crisis, and we went into the Taiwan Straits in that '55 cruise. We were prepared to fly as the escort for the reconnaissance airplanes that were going to take some photographs over mainland China. At that time Marion Carl, who retired as a Marine major general, very famous aviator, had a Marine photo squadron that he deployed from Atsugi down to Taiwan. The Marines were flying those photo flights.† We got all geared up to do it, and for some reason at the last minute we were cancelled. But I was all prepared to escort these photo planes over mainland China.

Paul Stillwell: Carl has a very high reputation as a test pilot.

Admiral Lawrence: Yes, he was very actively involved in the test work period at Patuxent. He and I are in an organization called the Golden Eagles, who are the pioneers of the naval aviation organization. He lives out in Oregon and is still doing well.‡ But it was a pretty interesting time, because although we were off the Korean focus, there were still some tense times, particularly with Red China and Taiwan.

Paul Stillwell: What recollections do you have of being ashore in some of those WestPac ports?

---

* The small Tachen Islands, north of Taiwan were subject to attack from mainland China in the early 1950s. On 7 February 1955, on the advice of the U.S. Government and with the assistance of the U.S. Seventh Fleet, the Nationalist Chinese evacuated the Tachens.
† Lieutenant Colonel Marion E. Carl, USMC, commanded Marine Photo Squadron One (VMJ-1) from November 1954 to June 1955. For details on his service in the squadron, see Carl's memoir, written with Barrett Tillman: *Pushing the Envelope: the Career of Fighter Ace and Test Pilot Marion Carl* (Annapolis: Naval Institute Press, 1994), pages 80-85
‡ Carl, then 82, was shot and killed on 28 June 1998 while protecting his wife Edna from an armed intruder in their Oregon home.

Admiral Lawrence: Well, I remember we went to Hong Kong for the first time. And Hong Kong was nowhere what it is today. Of course, we got all caught up in the shopping and bought a lot of junk like everybody does. You always get misled by the merchants down there in Hong Kong.

One interesting experience I had was that I met a British officer who was in one of the British regiments that were quartered north of Kowloon, just south of the border with Red China. So I went up there and visited this regiment on the border. Then I had his family out aboard ship and gave them a tour. So that was an interesting experience in getting to know the British officers. I'd gotten to know them when I was the shore patrol officer on duty. They came up to me and started chatting with me, so I invited them to have a tour of the ship. Then they reciprocated by taking me up there on the border. Those were tense times with Red China in '55, so the British units up there were in a high state of readiness.

Paul Stillwell: Did you get to Japan?

Admiral Lawrence: Oh, yes, we, of course, spent quite a bit of time in Japan. Our squadron on two occasions during that period moved off to Naval Air Station Atsugi and did more training. That was when Al Shepard and John Mitchell and Preston Luke and I tried to get the picture of the Mangy Angels with Mount Fujiyama in the background.

There was another thing that was interesting. You may have remembered from reading *The Bridges of Toko-Ri* about how the carriers used what they called the pinwheel.[*] Well, that was primarily done by the reciprocating airplanes, because there's a very high degree of thrust from the reciprocating engines, even at medium power settings. But our commanding officer wanted to use the pinwheel with the jets. So we always had to come into ports such as Yokosuka, and Kobe, Japan, where there was kind of constrained maneuvering room around the piers. We'd always use our jets, as well as

---

[*] *The Bridges at Toko-Ri*, based on a novel by James Michener, was a 1954 movie starring William Holden, Grace Kelly, Frederic March, and Mickey Rooney. It was about carrier combat action in the Korean War. The movie included the "pinwheel" movement to maneuver a carrier in the tight spaces of the harbor at Yokosuka, Japan. Planes were set up in two groups on the flight deck, noses facing opposite directions, and tied down to prevent movement. Their propellers supposedly aided the twisting of the ship. Part of the movie was filmed on board the *Oriskany* during her 1953-54 Western Pacific deployment.

our AD props to do the pinwheel.* That was always a lot of fun, getting up on the flight deck and doing that.

Paul Stillwell: I got the impression that was mostly a stunt.

Admiral Lawrence: Well, I guess the commanding officer thought he got value out of it. I don't know, but I enjoyed doing it because it got you up on the flight deck, and you got to watch the evolution of coming into port.

The other thing is that the commanding officer, Captain Westhofen, who was out of the Naval Academy class of '30, was the CO for part of that second deployment, and he allowed the air group pilots to become qualified as officers of the deck.† So Alan Shepard and I stood those officer of the deck watches, and both of us got qualified. I remember many long night watches with Alan Shepard up on the bridge, where we said, "Fine. Why are we doing this? Why can't we be down there sleeping like everybody else?" But we did get our officer of the deck qualifications, and I'm sure that helped us in our future careers.

Paul Stillwell: Shepard has a reputation for a sense of humor. Did you see that?

Admiral Lawrence: Oh, yes, we always had a lot of fun with each other. And he got put in hack twice—one time because we came back and broke out of the diamond formation, as I mentioned before. He was a very exuberant guy, always cutting up, and he engaged in the repartee that you have in a ready room.

The thing that amazed me about Alan Shepard was his tremendous self-confidence. As dangerous and highly demanding as that night carrier work was, most of us who did it would have to go through a mental preparation period. It was kind of like before a football game, where you sit in the locker room and you really think very carefully about everything you have to do. I used to pre-fly those missions in my head.

---

* The Douglas AD Skyraider was a propeller-driven attack plane.
† Captain Charles L. Westhofen, USN, commanded the *Oriskany* from July 1955 to January 1957.

Shepard would sit there playing acey-deucy, cutting up, and laughing.* I said, "God, when does he think about what he's supposed to do on his flight?" But he was so good as an aviator, it came so naturally to him, that he didn't have to do all of this thinking like the rest of us did. He was a very remarkable man.

Paul Stillwell: It's really a gift to be able to do that.

Admiral Lawrence: Oh, yes, it really is a gift. He was just the best natural aviator. I guess NASA perceived this when it did all the screening tests, that he had all the prerequisites for being a good astronaut.†

Paul Stillwell: It's good when a person can find his niche that way.

Admiral Lawrence: Yes, and I think that it was fortunate for him because he would not have been a real good staff officer. That just wasn't his area of expertise. He could really fully realize his potential by being an astronaut, where he was really, permanently involved in the operational tests and all aspects of the space program, rather than being in a planning staff role.

It's very interesting that the Navy, in its infinite wisdom in career management, kept trying to shunt him off to some place out in left field. When he left our squadron, he wanted to come back to the Naval Air Test Center, and the Navy tried to send him to the special devices center up at Port Washington, New York, where he'd be working with simulators or something like that. Somehow he got somebody to intervene and canceled those orders, and they sent him back to the test center. But after he was at the test center for a couple years, they sent him down to CinCLantFlt staff, where he was doing something he just abhorred.‡ He was there when he got selected to be an astronaut, so he kept getting rescued from obscurity.

---

* Acey-deucy is a variation of the board game backgammon.
† NASA – National Aeronautics and Space Administration.
‡ CinCLantFlt – Commander in Chief Atlantic Fleet. Shepard served as the fleet's aviation readiness officer in 1958-59 before being selected for astronaut training.

Paul Stillwell: In addition to standing the officer of the deck watches, how else did you get involved in the life of the ship?

Admiral Lawrence: Well, I really tried to learn as much about the ship as I could. I always felt that it was important to be broadened as a naval officer. In those days we had required correspondence courses, because we were still taking promotion exams.

Paul Stillwell: I didn't realize that.

Admiral Lawrence: Oh, yes. Then you could qualify and get exempt from promotion exams if you took correspondence courses. So a young officer had to spend a tremendous amount of time doing correspondence courses. The Uniform Code of Military Justice was one; others covered subjects like operational tactics. But I just was so busy in my squadron work, becoming qualified as an officer of the deck, that I didn't have a chance to take all the correspondence courses I should. So I remember that to get promoted to full lieutenant, I had to take a promotion exam in 1956, and that was on naval tactics or something like that.

So you kept really busy as a young officer in those days. Of course, I had important division officer responsibilities in the squadron. When we were out at sea, we worked most of the time. The one thing that was inviolable was that any time you were not doing night flying, you always had a movie in the ready room. Of course, you always had a movie officer who was in there wheeling and dealing to get the best movies possible.

But it was a great learning experience. Mickey Weisner was a great commanding officer to learn from. I really got a good, solid foundation in my junior officer experience in the squadron.

Paul Stillwell: What do you recall about your dealings with enlisted men in that division officer role?

Admiral Lawrence: Well, I had three jobs in the squadron. My first job was as a line division officer. I was in charge of all the plane captains—the guys who did the daily preflight inspections on airplanes, strapped the pilots in, and did the post-flight inspections. I really enjoyed being a division officer of 20 or so young enlisted. We had one chief, one first class, maybe a couple of third class petty officers, and the rest were airmen.

Then after I had about six months in that job, they moved me to be the personnel officer of the squadron. I really enjoyed that, although I didn't have as much interface with enlisted as when I was a division officer. I still dealt with a lot of enlisted men because of maintaining personnel records and orders and all those sorts of things. But I very much enjoyed being the personnel officer, too, because that taught me a lot about personnel procedures and service records.

Paul Stillwell: And the foibles of the American sailor.

Admiral Lawrence: Yes. Then I moved from that job to being the admin officer of the squadron, which was good, because, as a jaygee, I got department head-type responsibility. Nowadays, it's always a lieutenant commander. But, because we had a small number of officers in our squadrons in those days, you could get to be a department head in your first tour. I got a pretty broad exposure to the Navy leadership and so forth in those three ground tours.

Paul Stillwell: We talked about how you operated around the ship at night. What did you do during the time you were in the air?

Admiral Lawrence: Well, we primarily ran what we call intercepts. You'd have two airplanes that the controllers on the carrier would separate by radar, and then we flew intercepts against each other. Sometimes you would do a nine-degree-type intercept or head on. We had the Westinghouse APQ-43 air-intercept radar. But the air-intercept radar was still in its infancy, and so we just didn't have the raw capability to really get much use out of the radars. You felt very fortunate if you could hit a contact within ten miles. But we primarily did air intercepts, where the radar controller on the ship would control us into a gun-firing situation. We didn't have air-to-air missiles, just guns. If you could pick him up on the radar and get a lock on him, then you'd fly it yourself. That was mostly what we did at night.

Sometimes, when there were targets available, we would do night weapons drops. Like out in Hawaii during our operational readiness inspection, we dropped bombs on the island of Kahoolawe. During our deployment, we very rarely ever had a chance to do any night weapons work from the ship, so it was all air-to-air intercepts.

Paul Stillwell: How much differently did the plane fly with bombs hanging on it?

Admiral Lawrence: Well, being a straight-wing airplane, it could handle them pretty well. But where you really noticed the difference was a lack of excess thrust going off the catapult. I think when I went in the water off of Hawaii, the fact that I had a heavy bomb load on it had to be a factor, because it was heavy taxiing onto the catapult, to give you the pressure with that bomb load. The Banshee was not blessed with a great amount of excess thrust.

Paul Stillwell: What sort of bombsight capability did the Banshee have?

Admiral Lawrence: It had just a regular fixed bombsight. In other words, it wasn't like the radar bombsights that came out. Those computed a solution, and you just flew the pipper, and that sight would calculate your speed and then just give you the amount of lead you needed. The one in the Banshee was a fixed optical sight, so you had to compute the lead in your head—the number of mils.[*] For example, if you're dropping bombs, you'd have to look in the tables in advance to see what they call the mil-lead was. You'd have to compute for your given speed and the altitude to drop your weapons. It was the same thing for air-to-air gunnery: you had to pretty much look in the tables in advance and see what type of a mil-lead that you'd have to put in.

---

[*] A mil is an angular measurement; as defined by the Navy, it is 3.44 minutes of arc, a minute is 1/60th of a degree.

Paul Stillwell: And this was level bombing, not any dive-bombing.

Admiral Lawrence: No, these were dive-bombing. The typical bombing run that we used in those days was a 45-degree angle dive-bomb. You'd roll in from about 10,000 feet, and release at maybe about 4,000 feet. Then you would try to be straight and level by about 1,000 or so.

Paul Stillwell: Did you have some flaps to kill your speed then?

Admiral Lawrence: We had a speed brake on the Banshee, which actually came out of the wing. The Banshee did not have a wet wing like the later breed of airplanes did. The wet wing has fuel inside of it. These speed brakes were just an iron frame that would come out of the top and bottom of the wing. Most later airplanes had speed brakes that came either out from underneath the fuselage or off to the side—two flaps that came out of the side. But the Banshee's were incorporated in the wings.

Paul Stillwell: Well, I've about run out of questions on that squadron tour. Anything else to add?

Admiral Lawrence: Well, when I was coming to the end of that squadron tour, I pretty much made up my mind that I really wanted to go back to the Test Pilot School. I had great admiration for Alan Shepard, and he and I were very, very close. From his influence, I determined that I really wanted to fly and go to Test Pilot School. But when I submitted my letter, and it was going up through the chain of command, I got orders to go to the training command as an instructor down in Pensacola. But then the results of the Test Pilot School selection board came in, and I received the information I was selected. That made me very happy, because I felt that I wanted to stay active in flying and become the very best naval aviator that I could. That's why I really was not all that interested in going to postgraduate school like several of the pilots from my previous deployment had gone to the postgraduate school down at Monterey.[*] I really wanted to

---

[*] Naval Postgraduate School, Monterey, California.

stay in naval aviation, and I felt that Test Pilot School, and being a test pilot, was the ultimate. So I was fortunate enough to get selected for that.

Paul Stillwell: That was the apex of the pyramid.

Admiral Lawrence: Yes, that's right. I never regretted going to Test Pilot School, because it really gave me knowledge of aviation and experience that I would never have gained otherwise. So it really helped me significantly in my aviation career.

Paul Stillwell: Please describe the curriculum.

Admiral Lawrence: Well, in those days the Test Pilot School was of six months' duration. I came in and started in the class in February '56. In this six-month curriculum, half a day was devoted to ground school, and half a day was devoted to flying. The ground school initially gave you a foundation and refresher in math and physics. After you got this refresher, then you started having courses in aerodynamics and performance, stability and control—those specific areas where you need knowledge to be a test pilot. Then you had a flight syllabus. Over the six-month period, it was probably about 25 to 30 flights, and they covered all phases of test piloting: stability and control, flying qualities, performance testing. For every flight you had to write a flight report.

It was a very, very demanding curriculum, because you had to make the flight reports very complete and really go into detailed analysis about what the airplane was doing. The academics were really tough. Some of the things that we were doing in those days were right out there on the leading edge—the state of the art in what was going on in naval aviation at that time.

Paul Stillwell: By its very nature, it would be.

Admiral Lawrence: Yes. And so it was very, very tough. I had to really study hard. The only time I really was able to give myself off while I was going to Test Pilot School was on Saturday, and then I had to spend most of Sunday studying.

I benefited greatly from going to the Naval Aviation Safety School for a month before coming back to Test Pilot School. At that time the Naval Aviation Safety School was at the University of Southern California.

Paul Stillwell: Admiral Dunn told me about going to that also.

Admiral Lawrence: So I learned a lot about aerodynamics and performance there that helped me very greatly.

Paul Stillwell: Well, you were in with the cream of the crop. How competitive an environment was that?

Admiral Lawrence: It was very, very competitive, because you were really with a handpicked group from the Navy and the Marine Corps. I was really fortunate. Physics, math, and those sorts of subjects were not too difficult for me, because I could remember them from my midshipman days. But a lot of guys were older. In those days some of the civilian test pilots would come from commercial companies. Several of those guys had been out of school for a long, long time, so they had troubles with some of the academic subjects.

Paul Stillwell: What do you recall about the flying part of it?

Admiral Lawrence: Well, it was really interesting. We did all of the typical things that you do in flying that are very comprehensive: the various types of stability, like the directional stability, pitch, longitudinal stability, lateral stability. You really got a good foundation in all of the parameters that contribute to a good, stable airplane and good flying qualities. So a great deal of that effort was devoted to stability and control, flying qualities testing. About an equal amount was devoted to performance testing, where you became very thoroughly familiar with what constitutes fuel consumption and designing wings and fuselage that are most economical from the fuel-consumption aspect. So you really got a thorough foundation in all aspects of aeronautical engineering. I really enjoyed it. I really learned a lot about it.

And you had to do an in-the-class project. It was what they call a Navy preliminary evaluation, just like you were a test pilot going out to fly an airplane for the first time. You had to write a comprehensive Navy preliminary evaluation on it. I chose the F9Fs. I was given the F9F-6 model, so that was a real challenge to do a Navy preliminary evaluation on it.[*]

So I learned a tremendous amount from the total demands of that course. We also took a field trip at the end of the course, where we visited various aircraft manufacturers, and went to places like General Electric Aircraft Engines at Evendale, Ohio. We went down to NASA at Langley. So we had a lot of interesting field trips as a part of that test pilot course.

Paul Stillwell: That F9F-6 was one of the early swept-wing planes, wasn't it?

Admiral Lawrence: That's right. That was really one of the first supersonic airplanes.

Paul Stillwell: What do you recall about flying that one?

Admiral Lawrence: Well, it was an interesting airplane to fly, but compared to the later breed of supersonic airplanes, it was very rudimentary. It basically had a fairly thick wing, and in order to go supersonic, you had to get into a steep dive and literally punch through Mach 1.[†] But it was just all a step towards the more improved quality performance airplane.

---

[*] The Grumman F9F-6/F9F-7/F9F-8 Cougar was first delivered to operational units in November 1952. The F9F-6 model was 42 feet long; wingspan of 36 feet; gross weight of 20,000 pounds; and top speed of 690 miles per hour. It was armed with four 20-millimeter guns. The Cougar had swept wings and was a substantial improvement over its straight-wing predecessor, the Panther.

[†] A Mach number, named for Austrian physicist Ernst Mach represents the speed of an object divided by the speed of sound, 768 miles per hour. Thus anything above Mach 1 is described as supersonic.

Paul Stillwell: We were talking earlier about psychological barriers. Ten years before that there had been a great psychological barrier about Mach 1.

Admiral Lawrence: Yes.

Paul Stillwell: The though was that people would be killed at that speed, it wasn't achievable.

Admiral Lawrence: Well, that's right. Everybody visualized a wall that you had to punch through. Of course, the early breed of airplanes, like the F9F-6 Cougar, had basically a thick wing. The thicker the wing, the more shock waves would be developed on there as the airflow became supersonic over the wing. So it was, literally, like hitting a brick wall, because as the shock waves developed on the wing of the airplane, the drag increased significantly. That's why you see pictures of a guy going supersonic, seeing his head turn around, and all sorts of violent reactions, skidding into the turbine airflow caused by these shock waves.

I remember going supersonic in the F9F-6, which was really quite something. You had to go up, turn over, and then point the airplane straight down. Then, of course, when I came over to the flight test division, I started flying airplanes like the F8U, which you could fly supersonic straight and level.* So I really saw quite an enhancement in the airplanes during that time at the test center.

Paul Stillwell: Who were some of your fellow students?

Admiral Lawrence: Well, I think that I was the only guy in the class to become a flag officer. Ted Doolin was out of the Naval Academy class of '45; he later on became skipper of a fighter squadron and retired as a captain.† Jack Herndon retired as a Navy

---

* The F8U Crusader was a jet fighter built by Chance Vought Aircraft Corporation, Dallas, Texas.. It first entered fleet squadrons in 1957. The F8U was 54 feet, 6 inches long; wingspan of 35 feet, 2 inches, gross weight of 34,000 pounds, a top speed of 1,120 miles per hour. It was armed with four 20-millimeter cannon and could also carry bombs, rockets, or Sidewinder missiles. In 1962 the plane was redesignated F-8.
† Lieutenant Commander Edward H. Doolin Jr., USN.

captain.* We had some civilian test pilots who went on to become fairly well known, including Hank Lank, who was from Chance Vought. I forget right now the names of the others, but those civilian test pilots were doing significant things. I remember the guy—I think he was from Lockheed—who flew the Sea Dart, which was a seaplane fighter on skis.† I think his name was D. J. Long, and he was an interesting guy. But none of our active duty naval officers really became famous.

Paul Stillwell: Was there class standing officially?

Admiral Lawrence: Yes.

Paul Stillwell: How did you do in that?

Admiral Lawrence: I stood number one in the class.

Paul Stillwell: Out of how many?

Admiral Lawrence: I think we had right around 25 students in that class.

Paul Stillwell: How did that kind of grind you describe affect your family life?

Admiral Lawrence: Well, it was tough. We had two young children, and then we were building a house in the middle of all of this.‡ So we had to accommodate all that. But my wife had grown up in the Navy; her father was a naval aviator, and she was really very positive about it all and a real good trooper. But we both had to work hard. That was just a way of life in those days. You just accepted the fact that you worked hard in those younger years. We were products of the Depression, and we didn't have the same

---

* Lieutenant John G. Herndon, USN.
† The Convair F2Y Sea Dart was developed as a seaplane fighter, the only seaplane to fly supersonic. Its landing gear was made up of hydro-skis. Four prototypes were tested in the 1950s, but the plane never went into production.
‡ William P. Lawrence Jr. was born 26 February 1953 and Laurie M. Lawrence on 20 April 1955. The couple's third child, Wendy B. Lawrence, was born 2 July 1959.

attitude that so many young people do today that you're entitled to so much leisure, the good life. The work ethic was really very strong. We grew up in a Robert E. Lee tradition: his famous statement was when a young wife with a child came up to him after the Civil War. The wife went over to the soldier, and she said, "Is there any message you'd like to pass on to our son?"

He said, "Teach him he must deny himself." That was a good discipline; as a young officer, you felt that you had to give up a lot of things in order to do the professional and family requirements. You didn't have a lot of time for leisure and fun. It was very much a nose to the grindstone.

Paul Stillwell: And the Navy reinforced that system with its low pay scales.

Admiral Lawrence: That's right, yes, but we were all happy. We didn't know any better. There was tremendous professional camaraderie. And, of course, I had these exciting aspects of the astronaut program starting while I was a test pilot. I went through all the astronaut selection tests with Alan Shepard, John Glenn, Wally Schirra, Scott Carpenter, and all those guys.

Paul Stillwell: Admiral Hayward told me he was in that, as well.[*]

Admiral Lawrence: Yes. Tom Hayward went through those tests. Tom Hayward and I and all the other guys were in the final 32 for the Mercury program. They detected a heart murmur in my case. One of the tests was to put you in a heat chamber, and they raised the heat to, I think, 120 degrees. You stayed in there for a half hour, and they wired you up to check your total body function. Apparently, one of the instrumentations they put on you was to record your heart sound. They heard what they called a murmur, which is indicative of leakage around your aortic valves. In those days it was before the electro-cardiograph, which can do an outline of your heart. They felt that probably the murmur and leakage were caused by a scar to the aortic valve, and so I was disqualified from the astronaut program because of that heart murmur. I was the youngest guy in that

---

[*] See the Naval Institute oral history of Admiral Thomas B. Hayward, USN (Ret.).

first group. At the time I was 29; John Glenn was 39, and the cut-off age was 39. They had not only that age limitation, but also a height limitation. I think it was 5-foot-11. Some of the taller guys resented the fact that they didn't go through it.

As a result of picking up this heart murmur, they sent me up to the top cardiologist in the Air Force at Andrews Air Force Base hospital.* He pored over me for several hours and confirmed that I did have a murmur, so I got disqualified, even though I was the youngest guy in the group. But I knew that John Glenn and Al Shepard would probably be picked, because they were the best pilots we had at Patuxent at that time, I felt.

Paul Stillwell: It was fascinating to read in Tom Wolfe's book, *The Right Stuff*, all the medical tests, men treated as guinea pigs.

Admiral Lawrence: Yes. Also, several of us were covered in Michener's book *Space*.†

Paul Stillwell: How did that come about? Did he talk with you?

Admiral Lawrence: Well, it surprised me. His book was not written until a good 20 years after I'd been at the test center.

Somebody mentioned to me one time, "Hey, your name is in the book *Space*." I was mentioned along with Shepard, Carpenter, Glenn, and Pete Conrad.‡

Paul Stillwell: It was a very favorable mention too.

Admiral Lawrence: Well, it surprised me, because I didn't know that he would even know about me. But I was fortunate when I was at Patuxent, because I did some of the really new things in the Navy. I was in the group of guys sent out to do the competitive evaluation of the F8U-3 and the F4H, which was the first Mach 2 breed of airplanes. I

---

* Andrews Air Force Base is located approximately ten miles southeast of Washington, D.C., in Prince George's County, Maryland.
† James A. Michener, *Space* (New York: Random House, 1982).
‡ Lieutenant Charles Conrad Jr., USN.

had been picked to be the project pilot on the F8U-3. The F8U-3 had the same basic plan form configuration as the F8U-1—the two-position wing, everything.* But it had a much thicker fuselage, because it had a J75 engine, which had the capability of about 28,000 pounds of thrust. The old F8U-1 had a J57, which was about 18,000 pounds of thrust. So you had a 10,000-pound thrust increase, and so that made it Mach 2 capable. I was selected to be the project pilot on that.

The F4H had the two J79 engines, and they gave it about 30,000 pounds of thrust.[†] Dick Gordon, who later on was an astronaut, was the project pilot for that.[‡] Other members of the team were Captain Bob Elder, who's one of the famous naval aviators; Commander Larry Flint, who went on to distinguish himself, some high-altitude records; and Commander Don Engen, who retired as a vice admiral.[§] We were the principal members of the team that did the joint evaluation.

So we went out to Edwards Air Force Base to fly these airplanes.** Captain Bob Elder, as our team leader, decided he would do the first flight in the F4H, and he would let Commander Larry Flint do the first flight in the F8U-3. The manufacturer was just McDonnell in those days; it wasn't yet McDonnell Douglas.[††] Mr. Mac, the old Mr. McDonnell who formed that company, controlled everything in that company.[‡‡] He was very, very conservative, so—even though his own pilots had flown the F4H on quite a few flights—he laid down the requirement that on that first flight by a Navy pilot, he

---

* The plan form is the view looking down from above the airplane.
† The McDonnell Douglas F4H Phantom II first entered fleet squadrons in 1961 as the F4H; it was redesignated F-4 in 1962. It was a two-seat airplane with the pilot in the front and the radar intercept officer (RIO) behind him. The F-4B version had the following characteristics: length, 58 feet; wingspan, 38 feet; gross weight, 54,600 pounds; top speed, 1,485 miles per hour. It was armed as a fighter with either Sparrow or Sidewinder missiles and also could carry bombs. It had a maximum external stores capacity of 16,000 pounds.
‡ Lieutenant (junior grade) Richard F. Gordon Jr., USN.
§ Captain Robert M. Elder, USN; for a detailed article on his career, see Barrett Tillman, "Where Are They Now? Bob Elder," *The Hook*, Fall 1989, pages 12-17. Commander Lawrence E. Flint Jr., USN; Commander Donald D. Engen, USN; his oral history is in the Naval Institute collection and includes discussion of the testing of the F8U-3.
** Edwards Air Force Base is on the border of Kern County and Los Angeles County, California, about seven miles east of Rosamond. It is located next to a dry lake that provides an extension of the base's runways. Edwards has long been used for experimental flight testing.
†† In 1967 the McDonnell Aircraft Corporation merged with the Douglas Aircraft Company to form the McDonnell Douglas Corporation. A merger with Boeing in August 1997 produced the Boeing Company.
‡‡ James S. "Mac" McDonnell (1899-1980) founded the McDonnell Aircraft Corporation in 1939.

should only go out to 1.5 Mach number. The pilot should just do some maneuvering and come back in and do some slow flight, practice landings, and so forth.

Well, it was my plan, as the project officer of the F8U-3, that on our first flight, if it felt comfortable, we were going to fly 2.1 Mach number. Larry Flint was going to take the first flight about the same time as Bob Elder taking the first flight in the F4H. We were briefing for the flight, and Larry Flint was very hoarse. Finally, he turned to me and said, "Hey, Bill, you're going to have to take this flight, because I don't feel too good. I'm coming down with some laryngitis and a fever."

I said, "Great, I'll take it." So I took the first flight in the F8U-3, and I got airborne just about the time as Bob Elder in F4H.[*] He went out to 1.5 Mach number, and I went out to 2.1, so I became the first naval aviator to go twice the speed as sound in a Navy airplane. Old Bob has always had his nose a little bit out of joint about that, although he did some very distinguished things as a naval aviator. I think he made the first jet carrier landing when he was executive officer in VF-5.[†] It always miffed him a little bit that we weren't restrained in the F8U-3 and chose to go Mach 2 on our first flight. It was very interesting, because we were the first guys, really, in the military aviation to explore a high Mach number flight in military type airplanes, as opposed to experimental airplanes, like the X-15 and those sorts of things. Because the F-102, which was the only Air Force airplane that was Mach 2-capable, could only go out to Mach 2, and you had to try to come back and land. It just didn't have much fuel capacity.

We'd had an airplane called the F11F-1F. We took an F11F, the Tiger Cat, manufactured by Grumman, in which the basic production airplane had a J65 engine. They took an F11F and put in a J79 engine. That airplane was Mach 2-capable, but we never really had the fuel to get out there. You'd run yourself out of fuel. The F4H and F8U-3 had enough fuel, but you could spend some time flying up there. So we learned some very significant things. The compressive effect on air due to high Mach number produced what they called ram effect, which gave you significant increase in thrust. So we had more excess thrust in the F8U-3 at 1.8 Mach number, than we did at .9 Mach, even though your drag was significantly higher. But you've got a greater increase in

---
[*] This test was in September 1958.
[†] On 21 July 1946, Lieutenant Commander James Davidson, USN, made the first jet carrier landings and takeoffs in a McDonnell FD-1 Phantom; the ship was the USS *Franklin D. Roosevelt* (CVB-42).

thrust than you did in drag. So you had your maximum rate of climb at 1.8 Mach number. So what you'd do, if you wanted to really climb to maximum service ceiling, the standard practice in a supersonic airplane was that you always climbed to .9, but just below the drag rise. We'd take it up to about 45,000 feet at .9 and then we'd push over in full afterburner, and then we would accelerate out to 1.8 and then we'd climb at 1.8 to go up to maximum service ceiling.

We found that out just by accident, and it was very, very high-risk flying, because the engines weren't really all that well developed. They had a lot of bugs in them. For example, you tended to get very bad compressor stalls when you shut down your afterburner at very high speed, because for the airflow through a jet engine to maintain itself smoothly, you have to have pretty stable conditions. So to be at very high Mach number and come out of your afterburner, you had to have a real what they call transient into the engine, where at full afterburner, you need this high airflow, and then suddenly you come out of afterburning, where you needed much less airflow, it tended to induce a compressor stall. That basically meant that the airflow in the vanes of that compressor was in stalled condition, so it would give very explosive bangs in the engine as that compressor was trying to get stabilized.

So we had the real problem in the F8U-3 is that if you came out of afterburner at point Mach 2, it would be in a very bad compressor stall, which could cause the engine to break up. So they put in a provision where you would open a bleed valve to start bleeding air out of the engine so that when you finally came out of burner, it wouldn't put as much of a transient in the engine. You had to make a conscious move back on the throttle, so your light would come out and kick the bleed valve, and then you'd come out of burner. Well, we had a couple of guys who got their procedures screwed up in their heads. They came out afterburner and got these horrendous pressure stalls at a very high Mach number, which is very scary.

Then we found out some other things that the contractors hadn't determined, like when you opened your speed brakes at a high Mach number, you induced a terrible turbulent airflow on the surfaces of the airplane that turned into a terrible vibration.

So it was really a very high risk, high-challenge flying. It took a tremendous amount of precision. I was the project pilot who basically worked with our project engineer and with the contractor reps to work out our evaluation program, and I had to write the report. So it was really a good learning experience as a lieutenant, because Dick Gordon on the F4H and I on the F8U-3 were the principal authorities on those airplanes. We'd go up to Washington as young lieutenants to the Bureau of Aeronautics, and we'd be briefing rooms full of admirals and captains about these airplanes, because they had to make decisions on which one to pick. Senator Johnson, who was the Senate majority leader, said we could only pick one airplane.[*] And even though he was from Texas, he really wasn't pressuring us to pick the F8U-3, which was a Chance Vought airplane.

It was really exciting to do all that very advanced test work as a young lieutenant. I did some other very exciting things there. We did a crosswind carrier trial, trying to determine if it was feasible to land airplanes and take off airplanes with a crosswind.

Paul Stillwell: Why would you want to do that?

Admiral Lawrence: So that the carrier wouldn't be committed to one course for a long, long period—in other words, what they call the SOA.[†] For example, it was a tactical requirement for you to go in that direction, although the wind was out of this direction, could you go and accept a crosswind. We found that a crosswind really put some limitations. I went out in an FJ-4 and flew into a crosswind condition, so I learned a lot from that.

I did a lot of exciting things, flew a rocket airplane. We had a rocket put in an FJ-4, the first real rocket flying that we did.[‡]

Paul Stillwell: Well, for those of us who haven't had the experience, what is the sensation of going that fast?

---

[*] Lyndon B. Johnson, a Democrat from Texas, served in the House of Representatives from 10 April 1937 to 3 January 1949 and in the Senate from 3 January 1949 to 3 January 1961. He was Senate majority leader from 1955 to 1961. He was later Vice President from 1961 to 1963 and President from 1963 to 1969.
[†] SOA – speed of advance. Normal procedure is for a carrier to steam directly into the wind.
[‡] The FJ-4 Fury, built by North American Aviation, was a swept-wing carrier-based jet fighter. It had increased fuel capacity and range over the FJ-3. Squadron delivery, mostly to the Marine Corps, began in 1955. Two of the planes were converted to the FJ-4F version to test auxiliary rocket engines.

Admiral Lawrence: Well, you notice things that you don't sense otherwise; one thing is aerodynamic heating. The friction of the air on the plane's skin has a heating effect that is proportional to the square of the Mach number. So if you're at Mach 2, you're getting four times the aerodynamic heating than you are at Mach 1. So as you get out there, you feel the heat starting to build up in your cockpit.

The other thing you see is that the airplane is much less tolerant of any vibration or anything like that. In aeronautical terms, the term for aerodynamic pressure is Q, and the high-Q flight, where there's tremendous pressure on that airplane, any vibration or out-of-balance flight produces very pronounced effects. So the margins for error in those high-speed airplanes are really decreased. As I say, we were getting into these airplanes fairly early. The contractors had flown just a certain amount of flights. In fact, I flew the 100th flight in the F8U-3, so that was how early we were getting in these airplanes.

One thing is that the F8U-3, with this tremendously high-thrust engine—28,000 pounds of thrust—when you went into afterburner at low altitude, high speed, it was a very explosive situation. Because you got all this burst of fuel into the tailpipe, and then the ignition—the burner light—was just almost like an explosion in the after part of the engine. So they had what they call ejectors behind the tailpipe of the J75 engine. That ejector was designed to facilitate the flow of engine exhaust out of your tailpipe. Because of the theory of a jet engine, when you're supersonic, you have supersonic flow only right at the minimum point of the jet exhaust. Then it has to slow down to supersonic flow and that sometimes can result in a shockwave, confused flow behind the engine. So they put in these ejectors to facilitate the transition from regular to supersonic flow at supersonic speed.

The ejector that they put in the F8U-3 actually floated until it determined optimum position. We found out at high-speed, low-altitude flight, if that ejector was just a little bit off center when you went into burner, it could put you in a tremendous yaw. One time I was out at about 600 knots, about 1,000 feet, and I lit my burner, and the airplane went into almost uncontrollable yaws. So these were the types of things that we were finding.

The other thing was that Alan Shepard and I did some of the pioneering in pressure suits. For some reason, the Navy was given responsibility for developing the full pressure suit, the type of suit that later on the astronauts wore. We did the first full pressure suit flying out in the F8U-3, and I got the responsibility for doing most of it, because I was the junior man. Nobody else wanted to put the damn thing on. But earlier than that, Al Shepard and I had gone out to fly the F5D. The F4D was the Skyray, and the F5D was the Sky Lancer, which never went to production.[*] He and I did some of the early partial pressure suit flying in that airplane. This was different from the full-pressure suit where your full body would be pressurized. In the partial pressure suit, the only place where you got direct air pressure was in pressure breathing. So if there was a decompression in the airplane, you would get pressure forcing the air into your lungs, but the pressure in your body was done by having these capstans down both arms and both legs. Then these capstans would fill with air, and it would pull these ribbon-like devices around your body. It would apply pressure to your body through these ribbons to prevent the air in your blood from coming out of your bloodstream. So Al Shepard and I did the early partial pressure suit work in the F5D, and did a lot of zoom climbs to high altitude.

One time I was given the task of doing a zoom climb in an F5D, where you go out to max speed of about 1.5 Mach number, and that airplane pulled up to try to go up to 60,000 feet, something like that. I got a very bad pressure stall, and I had to shut down my engine. Of course, the partial pressure suit started to go into operation. I tell you, that's pretty scary when you have to shut down your engine with a single-engine airplane.

But one of my favorite stories about Alan Shepard was when we were doing that partial pressure suit work. As a training measure, to prepare you for this, the survival technicians on the ground would subject you to the pressure just so you could feel the pressure on your body. But you also had to pressure-breathe, because when you were pressurized, as I say, the air was forced into your lungs under pressure. Then you had to eject it by applying pressure—just the opposite from normal breathing. So it's very exhausting to have to do pressure breathing. One day Alan Shepard and I were getting ready to go out and do some partial pressure suit flying, so he told the survival technician, "Give me the full pressure."

---

[*] The Douglas F5D Skylancer was a further development from the F4D Skyray and included the use of the Pratt & Whitney J56 engine for added thrust. The first flight, which was supersonic, was in April 1956. The plane was later used for testing by the National Aeronautics and Space Administration.

The technician said, "Well, you know, Commander Shepard, you don't want to do that. That's going to really be uncomfortable."

He said, "Give me the full pressure." So, sure enough, boy, the technician turned it up, and Alan just became rigid like a robot, because these capstans got really full, and these ribbons were pulled across his body, so he was just spread-eagled like this. They realized he wasn't having a very pleasant time, so after a while they cranked the pressure back. But then, when he finally took the suit off, he had all these stripes across his body, where these ribbons had marked him. So for about a month, he looked like a zebra. But that was typical of Alan Shepard; he always was looking for the ultimate challenge. I'll never forget that.

Paul Stillwell: One of the other themes that Tom Wolfe developed was the repression-of-danger aspect of test piloting, that you figure you're not going to be the one that crashes, because that only happens to people who screw up, and I won't screw up. Was that the kind of attitude that was prevalent?

Admiral Lawrence: Oh, yes. In order to be a good military pilot, jet pilot, I think you have to be very much of an optimist. I think we all basically had that attitude. But I wasn't naïve; I knew it could happen to me, so I always tried to have my personal affairs all organized. But it was a very high-risk time. And, of course, I was the first guy to come to the test center that had gone through safety school. So I became the safety officer for flight test, and we had a tremendous amount of our accidents while I was there.

We had an F8U-1 in which the pilot, Tim Kean, a Marine major, and I were working together on a control project, where he kept the airplane in afterburner at low altitude.* About five miles after takeoff, he got into what we call a pilot-induced oscillation. It just pulled the wing right off the airplane. He was killed, and then we found out that the ejection seat had an incompatible firing pin that was supposed to fire to release his seatbelt and shoulder harness to allow the ejection to take place.

---

* Major Timothy J. Kean, USMC.

See, in those days we were experimenting with the best type of ejection seat, and so a lot of changes were going into those seats. It just so happened that the survival technicians hadn't gotten the right type of firing device in that system, and so that's one thing that killed him. When the ejection seat went, he didn't get automatic separation of his harness, so that was one accident we had.

We had another bad accident when some helicopter pilots were practicing auto rotations in the old helicopter that had the radar on it for airborne early warning. So I was involved in many, many accident investigations, which really added significantly in my workload, because those accident investigations were very time consuming.

Paul Stillwell: A sobering job too.

Admiral Lawrence: Oh, yes. Gosh, it was tough. I didn't really enjoy that at all, but we did have a lot of accidents in those days. I know a lot of good friends of mine were lost.

I had a really close call myself. I was out on this carrier crosswind trial.* As I was coming in for a landing, fairly low state, the engineers blew the tubes and put all this smoke right into the landing area, so I had to wave off. They did what they call bingoed me ashore—sent me ashore. I had a fuel gauge malfunction, and I ran out of gas. I flamed out as I was coming in to land at Oceana.† I pulled my landing gear up and settled in short of the runway. Fortunately, I just slid up on my belly. I was really lucky on that one.

Paul Stillwell: That's stupid to blow tubes when somebody's making an approach.

Admiral Lawrence: Yes. It was on the carrier *Intrepid*, so I just couldn't believe that they would do that.‡

Then the old J65 engine, which was in the AD-4, A-4, and the FJ-4, was made by Curtiss Wright, but it was the duplicate of a British engine. And the British, essentially, hand-tool their engines. But when Curtiss Wright took it over, they put it through

---

* The ship was the aircraft carrier *Intrepid* (CV-11).
† Oceana Naval Air Station is in Virginia Beach, Virginia.
‡ For more detail on this incident, see Admiral Lawrence's memoir, *Tennessee Patriot*, page 50.

mass-production techniques. The airplane had a tremendous amount of vibration in that engine, because they couldn't get the tolerances that the British had through hand-tooling. I think it was called an Avon engine in it. But, anyway, so you'd get a lot of vibration in that engine. Many times I had to shut down that J65 engine and make a precautionary-type approach, where you'd do a flame-out landing and then light up the engine to make the final landing. It was really interesting because one of the things that I got heavily wrapped up in was to determine the minimum-distance takeoffs. That was one thing that we had to work out for the charts in the aircraft handbook. I don't know why I got selected to do that, but I became the specialist for doing minimum-distance takeoff. It took, of course, a very special technique, because you had to use the optimum technique to get the airplane airborne in the minimum distance. Then they would put various bomb loads on the airplane. To get several of these tests done, you would take off and then come back and land at heavy weight.

Then, also, in addition to doing this minimum distance takeoff work, often in some of the performance testing, I would come back with heavy bomb loads. You'd try to land on the 12,000-foot runway so you wouldn't have to use your brakes. But, still, some of those low-drag airplanes, like the FJ in particular, you'd have to use your brakes, so you'd build up heat in these brakes. And the FJ-4 didn't have a good wheel brake system. So I had two situations where the wheels exploded on me after landing.

One time I was taxiing at Patuxent down to flight test. One of the taxiways there goes across the road. As I was coming down, there was a car parked at the road just as my wheel exploded. So I immediately shut down the airplane because it swerved around. I walked over to the car to see if anything had happened. The driver wasn't in the car. When I looked out, I saw this small figure way out in the field shaking her fist. So I ran over, and it was a woman who had been in that car. She was almost incoherent, because I'd showered this car with all these metal fragments from that exploding wheel. She thought I'd done this on purpose, just to bring her grief. So I had to assure her that it was a complete accident. I remember her; she was the wife of a commander named Stoppelmann.[*] But that was a big problem in those early jet years. They just didn't design enough strength and heat resistance in those wheels.

---

[*] Her husband was Commander Renold W. Stoppelmann, USN, a naval aviator.

Another time I was out doing some work on the catapults out in the field installations there at Patuxent, and another wheel exploded on me. It was just an interesting time. Those were still early jet years, and then this testing was exploring a lot of unknowns. But it taught me a tremendous amount about flying.

In those days, in the '50s, we were introducing about six or eight new airplanes. Nowadays, the F-18 has been the only airplane we've been able to introduce into carrier aviation in the last 15 years.* So for the test pilots of that time, our opportunities exploring the unknowns were far greater than those today.

Paul Stillwell: Well, you got your wish. You said that the reason you sought aviation out of the Naval Academy was to get in on this cutting edge.

Admiral Lawrence: It was really an exciting time to be in the aviation game. We lived a lot with imminent danger. We lost a lot of people. Just like Tom Wolfe said, it seemed you were going to funerals all the time. It's a very heart-warming thing that naval aviation is so much safer today than it was in that time. We're about 25 times safer today, statistically, than we were in those days, if you look at the number of accidents per 10,000 hours.

Some humorous things happened. I spent the last six months of my tour at Patuxent on the Test Pilot School staff as the stability and control instructor and the assistant operations officer. My previous time had been in the carrier branch of the flight test division. When I got my orders to leave to come down and be the aide to Admiral Tom Moorer, on the Carrier Division Six staff, Pete Conrad was coming up from armament tests to relieve me.† I had been working with the Navy pilots who were going through postgraduate school at Princeton in aeronautical engineering. Three people were there at that time: one was Bob Mandeville, who was out of the class of '50; Bob

---

* The F/A-18 Hornet, originally built by McDonnell Douglas, is a jet aircraft capable of both fighter and attack roles. It first entered operational service with VFA-125, a fleet readiness squadron, in May 1980.
† Lieutenant Conrad was later in the second group of astronauts chosen by NASA, following the original Mercury Seven group. In 1965, on the Gemini 5 mission, Conrad became the tenth American to fly in space.

Cornwell, who was out of my class of '51; and Jim Foxgrover.[*] Jim Foxgrover and Bob Mandeville both became rear admirals. They used to send me a requirement for flying a particular profile or type of maneuvers in one of our instrument airplanes. In those days we had oscillographs and photo panels. I used to help them in their research, their thesis work. They would send me down a requirement. I would fly it, and usually I would send the report up to them by mail. But they asked me this one time to fly up there and to deliver this material. That way, I would be able to see what they were doing at the Forrestal Laboratories at Princeton. There was a grass field at Princeton, so I decided I would take a T-28, reciprocating prop airplane, and I'd land on that grass field. Well, Pete Conrad was in the process of coming up to relieve me. He had a BS in aeronautical engineering from Princeton. So I said, "Hey, Pete, do you want to fly up with me?"

He said, "Oh, yeah, sure." So we got into a T-28, and this was about April.[†] They told me the field would be a little bit soft, because it still hadn't dried out from the spring rains. They said I should be careful. So, with Pete in the back seat, I flew up there and landed on the grass field. We came in and spent the day at the Forrestal Laboratories. It was very interesting; that was one of the first places to do work on the ground-effect vehicle. They had a little circular vehicle that was a ground effect, and they could actually get it airborne; it would go up about a foot. I forget the name of the eminent aerodynamicist who was the head of the Forrestal Laboratories.

After we spent the day at the Forrestal Laboratories, being very magnanimous, I said, "Hey, Pete, do you want to fly home? You flew in the back seat; I'll fly in the back seat and you fly." The people there went through a very detailed briefing and were emphasizing that we should taxi only on the marked taxiways, because that was a compacted area. Everything else there was not compacted, and the ground was still moist. Well, I really liked Pete Conrad, but he was a cocky, brash guy; a lot of fighter pilots are. I could tell he wasn't paying attention to this briefing. Since he had gone to Princeton, he thought he knew everything about Princeton. I said to myself, "Well, I'm sure he knows what the hell he's doing." We got in the airplane and he started up. Pete immediately went off the compacted taxiways, and the airplane sank in. When you added

---

[*] Lieutenant Robert C. Mandeville Jr., USN; Lieutenant Robert R. Cornwell, USN; Lieutenant Commander James H. Foxgrover, USN;

[†] This event was in the spring of 1959.

power in the T-28, the nose went down, because it was a tail-wheel airplane. So he added power, the nose went down, and the prop hit the ground. I said, "Oh God, I can just envision us being up here for days on end while we're waiting for a replacement engine to be brought in."

So he shut down the engine. They pulled us out of the mud, and we came back to the line. I said, "Now what in the hell are we going to do?"

They said, "Well, the first thing you've got to do is to inspect the strainers in the oil system, because on a sudden stoppage, if there's engine damage, you see metal particles in the strainers. So I inspected the strainers; there were no metal particles.

This old mechanic, who had been there at Forrestal Laboratories for years and years, came out and looked at this three-blade prop. One blade was jagged where the metal had broken off, but the other two blades were okay. He said, "Look, I'm going to take a hacksaw, and I'm going to cut that jagged area off." So he drew a little line, and he cut it off. Then he made a template, and he cut each of the other two blades the same.

Then we got in the airplane and, as I recall, the maximum manifold pressure you could get in this airplane was 60 inches. I pushed it up about as high as I could and still hold it in place to about 45 inches. There didn't seem to be any vibration. I said, "Well, I probably ought to call up back down to Test Pilot School and tell them about this. But if I do that, they're going to say, 'No, don't try to fly the airplane. We'll have to truck an engine up here.'" I could just see us being there for days and days and all sorts of complications. I said, "Conrad, you get in the rear seat; you've had your chance. I'm going to fly this thing back." That's the only time I've ever seen Conrad quiet.

They towed us out to the end of this grass runway. I turned up the engine, and it still sounded pretty good. So I turned it up as far as I could to hold it in place, because I wanted to get the maximum initial impetus for the takeoff roll. Then I started rolling, pushed it up to full power, and got airborne. I got over the power lines, settled in, and started flying back. The whole time I was just imagining this engine was vibrating. We got all the way back to Pax River, and I parked it on the line. I could probably have avoided saying anything to anybody, and no one would ever notice. They'd probably continue flying the airplane. But, of course, I reported it. But here was this airplane that, instead of having the square-bladed props, they were all tapered.

Paul Stillwell: The old mechanic knew what he was doing.

Admiral Lawrence: That's right. So that's my favorite Pete Conrad story.

Paul Stillwell: There's one in Tom Wolfe's book—I forget if it was Conrad or Alan Bean—but undergoing psychological testing, and he's handed a blank sheet of paper, and the doctor said, "What do you see?"[*]

He said, "Well, I don't know; you've got it upside down." [Laughter]

Admiral Lawrence: Yes, that was what they called the Rorschach Test, I remember.

Conrad, Bean, Lovell, and Gordon were not in that first group of astronaut candidates with me.[†] As I say, I was the only real young guy in that group, because the first guys that went in there were Glenn, who was 39; Shepard, who was about 36; and Schirra, about 35. Because it was an older group of guys in that first selection, Tom Hayward and I were probably the two youngest guys in the group.

Paul Stillwell: And he was several classes ahead of you.

Admiral Lawrence: Yes, he was out of '48.

That was because I had come back to the test center as a jaygee, just right out of a squadron. I certainly regretted the fact that I was not selected to the astronaut program. It wasn't in the cards for me, I think. I took a different route in my career, but with hindsight, I don't regret it now

Paul Stillwell: Well, evidently, you were healthy enough to keep flying.

Admiral Lawrence: I came back after that, and I told my flight surgeon at Pax River, "Look, they picked up a heart murmur, and here are the results of all the tests. Do you want them?"

---

[*] Lieutenant Allan L. Bean, USN. The joker about the upside-down paper was Conrad.
[†] Lieutenant James A. Lovell Jr., USN.

He said, "Oh don't worry about them. Don't tell anybody in the Navy." Since that was what my flight surgeon said, I didn't. And so that was in '59.

Of course, the Navy listens to your heart and all that, out on ships and so forth, and the chipping hammers are going and everything. So they didn't seem to give the emphasis to the heart exam in the Navy. It wasn't till '66 that a Navy flight surgeon first took cognizance of that murmur. So I had to go through all sorts of tests.

In 1966, they sent me down to Pensacola, where the board of flight surgeons had to evaluate my case. They said, "Well, gosh, this guy's been commissioned for 15 years and he's going in to be an executive officer of a squadron. We've got a lot of investment in this, and there's no—" It's what they call hemodynamic insignificance. In other words, there was no detrimental impact on my cardiovascular capability. There was just the leakage. Of course, for the astronaut program, they wanted perfect specimens and they knew they could get them, so they wouldn't take somebody with a murmur. But the naval aviation flight surgeons decided to keep me in aviation. So I'm probably the only pilot in history flying with a heart murmur.

But it turned out in later years, when they got the echo-cardiograph capability and could do the outline of your heart, they found that I had what they call a bicuspid aortic valve. The normal aortic valve has three leaves; that's what they call the bicuspid. The three leaves enable it to open and close perfectly. But about 1% of the people in the world have bicuspid valves. It doesn't quite close with a complete seal, and there's a minor amount of leakage. That's what I have. Apparently, it's quite minimal in my case. It has never impacted on my cardiovascular health.

Paul Stillwell: Especially when you were an athlete too.

Admiral Lawrence: Yes. And, of course, having been an athlete helped me. The thing is you get older, up into your 70s and 80s, when your muscles start to lose their resilience, that condition can become more pronounced. There's a condition called stenosis that happens in older people. Your tissue becomes less viable, less pliant. So someday, a person who has my situation may have to go through a valve replacement. But they've been checking my heart very carefully now, since I came back from being a POW in

1973. They have seen no degradation in heart function. One of the principal things they look at is a change in your heart size. When there's a really great taxation placed on your heart, it will normally increase in size. They were able to superimpose heart X-rays in 1966 over ones that were taken in '59. There was no change in the size; I've had no change in the size. That's the key measure that your heart has been adversely affected.

Anyway, I think I'd better knock off here now.

Paul Stillwell: Can I ask one more question?

Admiral Lawrence: Yes, sure.

Paul Stillwell: We haven't talked about operating the F8U around the ship. Did you have that experience too?

Admiral Lawrence: No, I did not, because I was never in an operational squadron with the F8U-1. Of course, the F8U-3 never went into production. I did a lot of that around the field. I did field carrier landing practice. Probably one of the most significant things I did as a test pilot was to help in control system design. I became a stability and control specialist while I was at Patuxent, although I did a lot of performance testing—high-altitude engine evaluations and things of that nature. My principal expertise was in stability and control testing. When the F8U-3 was being developed, because I'd been the stability and control project officer in the F8U-1, they asked me to work very closely with Chance Vought in trying to develop the type of control system for the F8U-3. So I had a lot of recommendations based on my experience in the F8U-1. I actually went down to Chance Vought and sat in control system simulators as we worked out a new control system. That to me was one of the most significant things I did as a test pilot, to develop a control system for the F8U-3, which flew significantly better than the F8U-1. As a part of that evaluation, I flew the F8U-1 very extensively in a field carrier landing pattern, because the most critical demand on the flight control systems is in the landing pattern, doing carrier landings.

Paul Stillwell: Well, I've heard that the early version was not very stable on the glide path.

Admiral Lawrence: It was terrible. The two-position wing configuration just made the landing configuration terrible. It was a high drag; the stability requirements were really immense with that two-position plane. And I never felt there was a real imperative for having a two-position landing. I just think that Chance Vought got off on the wrong track. It was all put in to have a lower landing speed than they felt they could achieve with a fixed wing. But they bought themselves a tremendous amount of problems. They had to put in stability augmentation. In other words, they had to put in a roll-damping feature in the airplane, because the roll lateral stability was deficient. It was a very, very difficult airplane to fly in the landing configuration. It was just an absolute tremendous challenge to bring that on board at night; it was a tough, tough airplane to fly. That's why they didn't do a lot of night flying in the F8Us. It was really a day fighter. With that wing down and the plane configuration, boy, it was really a slick airplane. It did have the capability to go out to about 1.5 Mach.

Paul Stillwell: And it had the advantage that it fit in an *Essex*-class carrier.

Admiral Lawrence: Yes, that's right. And it shot down a lot of MiGs. I think it had more MiG kills than the F-4.[*] I think it was VF-211 that shot down quite a few MiGs in the Vietnam War. So it was a good day fighter, but it was not very valuable at night. It was just too unsafe to bring aboard at night.

Paul Stillwell: Well, thank you, Admiral, we covered a lot of ground today.

---

[*] F-4 was the redesignation assigned to the F4H Phantom II in 1962, prior to the start of the Vietnam War.

Interview Number 4 with Vice Admiral William P. Lawrence, U.S. Navy (Retired)
Place: U.S. Naval Institute, Annapolis, Maryland
Date: Tuesday, 2 October 1990

Paul Stillwell: Admiral, it's good to see you again today. We're ready to resume and finish up your time at Patuxent River, please.

Admiral Lawrence: Well, one project that I was involved was when they were looking at the feasibility of putting a rocket-type engine in airplanes, as a means of thrust augmentation. You can put a relatively small rocket engine in an airplane and get a fairly good amount of thrust—maybe, say, even up to 5,000 pounds of thrust for a relatively small engine, which wouldn't be as complicated as having an afterburning engine on a jet. So North American, which is now Rockwell, took an FJ-4, and put this small rocket engine right below the vertical stabilizer and right above the fuselage. I did some flying in that to evaluate it. Commander Don Engen and I were involved in that, and so was another test pilot, Lieutenant Burdick. It was really quite interesting to evaluate that.

Paul Stillwell: How well did it work?

Admiral Lawrence: Well, it worked fine. It really, significantly augmented your thrust. You could light that rocket, and you could go immediately out to supersonic speed. But I guess after the Navy looked at the safety requirements of having a second source of fuel on an aircraft carrier, it determined that it wasn't feasible to really explore that. It never really became a production installation; it was just an experimental concept that we evaluated.

Paul Stillwell: You probably couldn't use it for very long, either, could you?

Admiral Lawrence: No, it had a duration of only about three minutes, but in those three minutes, you could really do quite some interesting acceleration.

Paul Stillwell: What would be the tactical applications?

Admiral Lawrence: Well, the tactical application was in an air-to-air combat situation to give yourself a significant maneuvering advantage. In other words, you could put that rocket on and it would really give you added capability without losing speed. You could use that speed to give you an advantage in an air-to-air combat situation to climb; you could go faster. So it could have a valuable application, and it basically served the same function that an afterburner would in a jet airplane. Many of the airplanes we were getting in that era had engines didn't lend themselves to the installation of an afterburner. It made a lot of sense tactically, but I guess it was a logistics problem that shot it down.

Paul Stillwell: Well, did the afterburner essentially come along and serve that function?

Admiral Lawrence: Yes. Afterburners, of course, had already been in airplanes for two or three years, and we were getting a generation of airplanes that were virtually all afterburning airplanes, like the F8U, the F3D, F11F. But there was a period of time when no airplanes had afterburners. So they looked at those non-afterburner airplanes, like the FJ, to see if it was feasible to incorporate a rocket.

Paul Stillwell: In a way, it sounds like an attempt to extend the lifespan of a plane that had been a really good combat aircraft in Korea.

Admiral Lawrence: Yes. The FJ-3 and FJ-4 were first cousins of the Air Force's F-86. It's true that that airplane, in the F-86 Sabre jet version, had done well in Korea.

Paul Stillwell: Well, it has more of an Air Force reputation than Navy, I think.

Admiral Lawrence: Yes. We never really built a lot of FJ-3s and FJ-4s; and we also had a FJ-4B.* But we had ever more than a handful of squadrons of those airplanes.

---

* The North American FJ-4B Fury was a ground attack version of the FJ-4. The FJ-4B differed from the FJ-4 in that it had six under-wing stations capable of carrying a total of up to 6,000 pounds of fuel tanks, rockets, or bombs.

Paul Stillwell: How good a carrier plane was it?

Admiral Lawrence: Beautiful. The FJ-4, in particular, was a beautiful carrier plane. I took it out on that crosswind carrier trial, and it handled beautifully. It was one of the first airplanes that we put in an angle-of-attack indicator. When you fly aboard a carrier now, you use an angle-of-attack indicator and you fly angle of attack. Prior to that, back in the '50s, we always flew airspeed, so you had to look at the airspeed indicator. But an airplane stalls on angle of attack, not airspeed. For example, if you're heavier, or if you stall at the same angle of attack, your air speed will be higher. So the beauty about flying angle of attack is that that one angle of attack is your valid approach angle of attack. I did the first real angle-of-attack indicator flying when I went out on this carrier trial.

Paul Stillwell: What are your recollections of flying with Commander Engen?

Admiral Lawrence: Well, he was a very wonderful pilot, very enthusiastic pilot, loved to fly. Really a very fine person, really a nice guy. He had won the Navy Cross in World War II and was a really valuable member of our team. He had gone to the Empire Test Pilot School in England.[*] Most of us had to go to the U.S. test pilot school. The Brits don't believe in this working hard; they believe in these long lunch hours. Of course, the Test Pilot School was really a tough, tough grind. We always envied those guys who went there. A lot of our famous test pilots are graduates of the Empire Test Pilot School.

Paul Stillwell: Well, obviously he had talents beyond just in the cockpit, because he became a vice admiral and head of the FAA.[†]

Admiral Lawrence: Yes, very bright guy. He really has a deep professional knowledge of aviation. The whole orientation of his career has been in aviation. I think they picked him to be the head of FAA, because he does have this tremendous depth of knowledge in aviation. He was one of the really good early test pilots, and I enjoyed serving with him.

---

[*] See the Naval Institute oral history of Vice Admiral Donald D. Engen, USN (Ret.), for details.
[†] After his retirement from the Navy, Engen served as Administrator of the Federal Aviation Administration from 10 April 1984 to 2 July 1987.

He and I are very good friends. This weekend, he's going to be inducted in the Carrier Aviation Test Pilot Hall of Fame down in Charleston at the USS *Yorktown* Museum.*

Earlier I mentioned my being a safety officer at flight test since I was one of the early safety school graduates. We had a lot of accidents in those days. So I was very much involved in accident investigations. That really kept me quite busy, in addition to my regular project work. I was always the one who had to write the accident report. We're so much safer than we are now than we were back in those days. It's been a very heartwarming thing to see a significant improvement in aviation safety as compared to that era. We almost had, it seemed to me, one accident a month of some sort. So I was very heavily involved in the safety business.

This was a time when we were really getting survival systems better refined and improved. We always wanted to have a low-altitude ejection seat. While I was there, the British invented the Martin-Baker seat, which gave you ground-level ejection capability.† That was really quite a significant advancement in safety, just the realization that if you got into difficulty on the ground, you could eject with a strong likelihood of surviving.

I remember a young British Royal Air Force officer coming back and demonstrating the Martin-Baker seat to us.‡ He actually went out on a flight, and on the runway he activated it. We had a little plowed area beside the runway, and he landed in it. Honest to God, it takes a lot of courage to demonstrate that ground-level ejection capability.

Paul Stillwell: What became of the airplane?

Admiral Lawrence: Well, he was in the back seat, and the pilot kept flying the plane.

---

* The aircraft carrier *Yorktown*, which at various times carried the hull numbers CV-10, CVA-10, and CVS-10, was decommissioned on 27 June 1970 and placed in mothballs. In June 1975 she was towed to Charleston, South Carolina, to become the centerpiece of a naval memorial named Patriot's Point. She was formally dedicated in that role on 13 October 1975, the U.S. Navy's 200th birthday.
† Martin-Baker Aircraft Company, Ltd., is the British company that makes the seats.
‡ The individual who tested the seat was Flying Officer Sidney Hughes, who was in an F9F-8T trainer. For details, see "Science: Positively Wizard," *Time* magazine, 9 September 1957.

Paul Stillwell: Oh, I see.

Admiral Lawrence: So the Brits were traveling around the world demonstrating their Martin-Baker seat. So I remember that very, very much.

Paul Stillwell: Were there any other projects you were involved in before you joined the staff of the school?

Admiral Lawrence: I don't know if I talked about all the work I did in the minimum-distance takeoffs. That was quite exciting.

Paul Stillwell: I don't think so.

Admiral Lawrence: One of the areas I in which I became something of a specialist was when we were developing all the performance data on these new airplanes, the charts that they have in the handbook. One of the charts you have to develop is the minimum distance for takeoff. I had to do a lot of that work. What you would really try to do is get the absolute minimum distance that you could get an airplane in the air, so it meant that you had to fly in the air at the flying speed just above the stall speed.

I guess my real area, expertise, especially, was stability and control, analyzing the aircraft flying qualities and helping to put improvements in control systems. I was also helping to impact the new design of control systems to make an airplane fly better, in terms of flying quality, stability, and control. So I was brought up to the Test Pilot School staff to teach pilots how to do stability and control and flying qualities testing. I also served as the assistant operations officer for the Test Pilot School.

Paul Stillwell: What do you recall about that period as an instructor?

Admiral Lawrence: Well, it was really interesting, because as assistant operations officer, I had the responsibility for scheduling one of the two classes that we had in there at any one time. The operations officer was Commander Joe Moorer, who retired as a vice admiral. He was the younger brother of Admiral Tom Moorer.[*] He was the operations officer, and he had the scheduling responsibility for one of the classes. As the assistant, I had the scheduling responsibility for the other class. This involved scheduling the pilots for their flights and grading a lot of their flight reports and briefing them on the flights they were going to conduct. Then I would give regular lectures on the stability and control, flying qualities, testing the airplanes. It was really a very enjoyable period, because I got to apply a lot of the lessons I'd learned over the years down there in flight testing, and I gave these lessons to the new pilots coming along. It gave me a chance to do a little research and really solidify my knowledge of aeronautical engineering, test flying, and all that.

Paul Stillwell: Well, at least, to a degree, you do become an aeronautical engineer.

Admiral Lawrence: Well, you do. The good thing about the Test Pilot School is that it not only teaches you the practical applications of how to be a good, practical test pilot, but you learn a lot about the theory—aerodynamics, performance. I think it's one of the finest schools available to give you a good balance between the practical and the theoretical. It really enhanced my knowledge of airplanes. It helped me so much later on in my aviation career—being able to analyze why airplanes do certain things. It was of value in the tactical area as well.

Paul Stillwell: How much of a relationship did you have with the commander of the Naval Air Test Center?

Admiral Lawrence: Not really all that very, that much. We had two while I was there, and the second one was Admiral Thurston Clark.[†] And the first one was—gee, he's still living, too, but I can't think of his name right now. But he's retired, living down in Pensacola. So we had two while I was there. I had to go up and brief Admiral Clark one time because I was the project officer of the F8U-3. That was such a high-visibility

---
[*] Lieutenant Commander Joseph P. Moorer, USN.
[†] Rear Admiral Thurston B. Clark, USN.

program that all the admirals, and so forth, were quite interested in how the airplane was doing. But I didn't have all that much personal interface with him.

Paul Stillwell: Did you have much contact with John Glenn because of his work on the F8U?

Admiral Lawrence: Yes. John Glenn was over in armament test, but he and I were neighbors; he lived right down the street from us for over three years. We used to water-ski every weekend. Our families were really close. His children were a little bit older than ours, but we were quite close. John's a really very wonderful guy. I mean, he's the true Eagle Scout and had a wonderful family. I really admire him, although we don't have much contact with each other now. We move in different circles now that he's a senator.*

Paul Stillwell: Well, you two probably had a lot of similarities, because you're an Eagle Scout type too.

Admiral Lawrence: Yes. Well, we compared notes on the F8U. When he left Patuxent, he went up to the staff of the Chief of the Bureau of Aeronautics and became the F8U project officer. I was the project pilot on the flight test for F8U-3 and was really following it very closely, particularly during its fleet introduction. So I had occasion to get up and talk to him in Washington; he was what they called the class desk officer in the Bureau of Aeronautics.

Paul Stillwell: He's portrayed as a very competitive individual. Did you see that side of him?

Admiral Lawrence: Oh, yes. He's a real fighter pilot and a Marine.

---

* John H. Glenn, Jr., a Democrat from Ohio, served in the Senate from 24 December 1974 to 3 January 1999.

Paul Stillwell: What examples might you cite?

Admiral Lawrence: Well, he set the cross-country speed record in the F8U.[*]

Paul Stillwell: I think that's really when he came to prominence, and then he was on a TV program.

Admiral Lawrence: Yes, that's right. He and that little kid were on the television program. The kid came down to visit him at Pax River, and that was a big deal, because he came out water-skiing.

Paul Stillwell: "Name That Tune."

Admiral Lawrence: Yes. And that kid became famous.

Paul Stillwell: I think he was in a Broadway musical or something.[†]

Admiral Lawrence: Yes, he was. He was really a fine little kid, I remember.

But John's a fine man. I have great admiration for him. I hated to see him get into politics, because that's the fastest way in the world to get tainted a little bit, but it looks like he and McCain might slip out of this Keating scandal.[‡]

Paul Stillwell: Well, that remains to be seen; Keating's gone to jail.

Admiral Lawrence: Yes.

---

[*] On 16 July 1957, when he was a major, Glenn broke the transcontinental speed record when he flew an F8U-1P Crusader from Los Alamitos, California, to Floyd Bennett Field, Brooklyn, in 3 hours, 22 minutes, and 50 seconds.

[†] Child actor-singer Eddie Hodges made his Broadway debut in 1957 in *The Music Man* and was later in several movies.

[‡] The Keating Five comprised five U.S. Senators who were accused of corruption in 1989 in the savings and loan crisis of that period. They were charged with improper intervention on behalf of Charles H. Keating Jr., chairman of Lincoln Savings and Loan Association, when he was under investigation. Senators John Glenn and John McCain, both retired military officers, were eventually cleared of having acted improperly.

Paul Stillwell: What students do you remember from your time as an instructor?

Admiral Lawrence: Well, I had some students who did some good things in the Navy. I had a student named George Aitcheson, who became a rear admiral and retired.* He retired here back in about 1985. Most everybody whom I had in that class was a real solid citizen. They were the guys who really made the contributions out there in naval aviation. I remember another one was Earl Godfrey, who retired as a captain.† Let's see, John Tierney retired as a rear admiral.‡ They were all good guys, the real cream of naval aviation.

Paul Stillwell: Well, that must be a pleasure to work with people like that, because they wouldn't be there if they weren't good.

Admiral Lawrence: Yes, it really was quite a pleasure, a wonderful experience.

Paul Stillwell: You served closely with both of the Moorers. What comparisons might you draw?

Admiral Lawrence: Well, they're very similar persons. Admiral Tom Moorer is so brilliant that he's in a category by himself. He's one of the smartest guys I've seen. His brother was more a normal man like the rest of us. But both of them are just wonderful people, absolute salt-of-the-earth-type people. I really like them both. But Admiral Tom Moorer was more of a real intellectual, a broad, strategic thinker. Joe was more down-to-earth, hard working. I really like them both.

Paul Stillwell: Well, anything more to say about Patuxent before you moved to Admiral Moorer's staff?

---

* Lieutenant George A. Aitcheson Jr., USN.
† Lieutenant Commander Earl F. Godfrey, USN.
‡ Lieutenant Commander John M. Tierney, USN.

Admiral Lawrence: No, I really can't think of anything more about that; I think I covered all of the major projects that I was involved in. It was a wonderful tour. I really learned a lot from it and laid a foundation that really helped me tremendously in naval aviation.

Paul Stillwell: How did your next assignment as his aide come about?

Admiral Lawrence: Well, Tom Moorer was selected quite early for admiral. He's out of the Naval Academy class of '33. He was selected for admiral in 1957, just 24 years out of the academy. Of course, in those days it was absolutely unprecedented for anybody to be selected that early.

Paul Stillwell: He didn't even get a chance to command a carrier.

Admiral Lawrence: That's right. He had been earmarked for a particular carrier, and he got selected early. After he was ordered to command the carrier division, he asked his brother Joe if he had any recommendations as to a young officer to be his aide, and Joe recommended me. That was good for me, because I really needed a tour like that after being solidly in the cockpit for eight years. It really broadened me on his staff, the things that I learned and what we all did.

As I said, we went through the astronaut selections in the winter of 1959. When I was told I was not qualified because of the medical tests, shortly after that I detached to go on to Admiral Moorer's staff. He personally wanted to get me detached early and come in to staff before he arrived in August. The staff was due to deploy to the Mediterranean, so he wanted me to get there early to learn as much as I could before that.

I arrived on the staff in June, when Admiral George Anderson was still the carrier division commander.* Initially, I worked as an assistant under Admiral George Anderson's regular aide. Then, in view of the fact that I was there, he let his aide go ahead and detach. So I worked for Admiral Anderson for about two months. I learned a lot from him; he's quite a guy.

---

* Rear Admiral George W. Anderson Jr., served as Commander Carrier Division Six in 1958-59.

Shortly after I came aboard, we were faced with the military committee of the NATO Standing Group visiting our carrier. They were all four-star admirals from the NATO countries, and so I had to plan that visit. Of course, Admiral Anderson really wanted to make that go well, and he had a lot of ideas. One of the things he charged me doing was when we were out off the Virginia Capes operating area. He wanted to have a *Washington Post* newspaper outside the door every morning when the visiting admirals got up. [Chuckle] That meant I had to make arrangements to get *The Washington Post* flown down to North Carolina. Then we sent on a carrier-on-board delivery airplane—a COD—in to Cherry Point. It picked up the newspapers in the early, wee hours of the morning and flew them out to the carrier.*

Admiral Anderson was really quite a brilliant man. He had all these ideas. He was a different cut of a guy from Admiral Moorer. Both of them were pretty smart. Admiral Anderson really liked to do things like that to impress people, so that kept an aide really busy.

Paul Stillwell: What other things did he do?

Admiral Lawrence: Well, of course, he was heavily involved in tactics. While standing watches on the bridge, I learned a lot about naval surface tactics, as well as aviation tactics, and how to control a task force. I started standing watches initially as the assistant tactical watch officer. After about six months, I moved over and got my quals as a regular watch officer. I actually got the qualifications to be the number-one tactical watch officer. What I learned was immensely valuable to me.

Paul Stillwell: Well, the impression I have of Admiral Anderson is that he was very big on protocol and smartness.

Admiral Lawrence: Yes, he was. In fact, he wrote out something called "Are you outstanding?" He listed 20-some areas where you should ask yourself if you were

---

* Cherry Point Marine Corps Air Station, North Carolina—near Camp Lejeune.

outstanding. I've saved that in my files. It's a really good guide for how an officer should conduct himself, and I give a copy of that to my classes that I teach.* He's a real, real professional.

Paul Stillwell: Did you go along with him when he conducted inspections?

Admiral Lawrence: No, he didn't really conduct very many inspections. He just told you what he wanted you to do, but he was not a guy who went around to a lot of ships inspecting. He was so busy, he just couldn't carve out that much time.

Paul Stillwell: Anything specific you remember about the maneuvers when you had the NATO people on board?

Admiral Lawrence: We did, really, a very conventional type of air show for them, in addition to letting them watch what we call cyclic ops. They represented all the NATO countries. It was really quite an educational experience for a young officer to set all this up from a protocol aspect. Of course, one of the big challenges was always to keep the Turks away from the Greeks. I learned a lot with Admiral Anderson, later on with Admiral Moorer.

Paul Stillwell: My impression also is that Admiral Anderson would be a more impulsive type individual than Moorer. Would that be a fair statement?

Admiral Lawrence: Oh, yes, but I want to tell you when Admiral Moorer gets really keyed up, starts to really getting concerned about an area, he can be a really dynamic guy too. But he's a lot more of a southern gentleman than Admiral Anderson. It was good to have the opportunity and a very great privilege to work with those two men.

---

* At the time of the oral history interviews, Admiral Lawrence was teaching leadership classes to Naval Academy midshipmen.

Paul Stillwell: It's a rare thing for one future CNO to relieve another in a previous job.*

Admiral Lawrence: Yes. That's right, that's right.

I used to have a lot of very personal discussions with Admiral Moorer. He and I got to be very close because we often just traveled, the two of us together. So I learned a lot about him, just philosophy and approach to being a naval officer.

Paul Stillwell: Well, please, what do you remember?

Admiral Lawrence: I used to ask him, "How are you able to make decisions so rapidly?" For instance, in a tactical situation, he'd look at the situation and say, "Okay, let's do this."

He said, "Well, there are many ways to do everything. The important thing is to get a course of action identified and get everybody supporting that and involved in that. And you can make it succeed. The average mistake that many people in ship positions make is they delay making decisions. By the time action is taken, it's been overcome by events. So I don't waste time by trying to research every possible course of action and coming up with the best one. I'll see one that I think can accomplish the job and I'll very quickly get the decision made so that people can get on it and get it done." But that's so true. He said the average person is basically reluctant to make a decision, and so he will vacillate and delay. Then they delay themselves into a much more difficult situation, or they lose one of the great opportunities. So he could make decisions just like that.

Also, I learned a lot about just the manner of dealing with people. He never really lost his temper. He always maintained himself on a very even keel. I learned that when you come down to it, the best way to deal with people is to be approachable and not be afraid to let your hair down. One of the worst things you could be is too stuffy and formal. I learned a lot of that from him. He had probably the best breadth of knowledge of anybody I've ever seen in the Navy, in terms of knowing operational aspects of the

---

* As four-star admirals, Anderson was Chief of Naval Operations from 1961 to 1963 and Moorer from 1967 to 1970.

job—knowing the tactics, and by having this tremendous knowledge of strategic aspects of our job. He was very well read. So I was very lucky to have served with him.

Paul Stillwell: What do you remember about the deployment?

Admiral Lawrence: Well, I got there in June 1959, and we deployed in August. The good old *Saratoga*, which was our flagship, had an engineering casualty.* I think one of the enlisted men flooded part of a fireroom or something like that, so we had to move off of *Saratoga* and onto the USS *Essex*, which was the other carrier in our division.† We went over to the Mediterranean in the *Essex*, and the *Saratoga* later joined us and we switched back to *Saratoga*. So I had to spend about two weeks crammed up in the USS *Essex*. My roommate at that time on that cruise was the exec of a Marine squadron that was on board. So it was very austere living to have our staff suddenly thrust into the USS *Essex* that didn't have space to accommodate us.

But the *Essex* had a wonderful skipper, Captain Tom South, out of the Naval Academy class of '34.‡ Later, when he left the *Essex* at the end of his tour, he came over to be our chief of staff. So I really developed a very close relationship with him. He was one of the really wonderful men in the Navy, had a great sense of humor. Regrettably, he's dead now. The sad thing about it is that he lost his ability to speak after he had a stroke. It was a very sad thing. At a relatively young age, he had a bad stroke. We were just lucky on that particular staff to have some really, really quality guys. We had a great team, and everything we did we just did absolutely superbly.

We had that Mediterranean cruise, and we came back and went through a shipyard period up in New York, and then we came back from that and got the *Saratoga* and the air wing all pumped up and refreshed, and went out on a North Atlantic NATO

---

* USS *Saratoga* (CVA-60) was commissioned 14 April 1956. She had a standard displacement of 56,000 tons, was 1,063 feet long, 130 feet in the beam, and had an extreme width of 252 feet. Her top speed was 34 knots. She was originally armed with four 5-inch guns and could accommodate approximately 70-90 aircraft.
† USS *Essex* (CV-9), lead ship of her class, was commissioned 31 December 1942. She had a standard displacement of 27,100 tons, was 872 feet long, 93 feet in the beam, an extreme width of 148 feet on the flight deck, and had a draft of 29 feet. She had a top speed of 33 knots and could accommodate about 90 planes. By 1959 she had been reclassified CVA-9.
‡ Captain Thomas W. South II, USN, commanded the USS *Essex* (CVA-9) from 19 November 1958 to 29 October 1959.

cruise, which was really interesting. We had some great operations with the British and the other NATO countries. After that deployment we went into Southampton, England, and had a great in-port visit. So we were quite busy. We had that first deployment in the Mediterranean, which was eight months. Then we went up and spent two months in the New York Naval Shipyard. When we got out of that, we had to start working up for our NATO deployment, so just about the whole time I was on that staff, I was at sea.

Paul Stillwell: What were some of the things you did during the Med cruise?

Admiral Lawrence: Well, we just did the standard things in those days. We used to have a nuclear weapons exercise, which we called a strike-ex. We always would practice the nuclear target plan. We, really, very intensively, exercised ourselves—both the air wing and the carrier. So I really learned a lot being on that staff. It helped me so much in the rest of my time in the Navy, because it's hard to sit down and explain to young people what they have to do in their careers, unless they've smelled the jet fuel themselves.

Paul Stillwell: What sorts of things did you learn?

Admiral Lawrence: Well, I learned a lot about surface tactics. I became qualified as a surface tactical warfare officer. In other words, I ran the battle group, gave the orders, devised the tactics. I got qualified before I was on board even a year. And that's a good qualification to get, because it deals with all the broad aspects of fleet operations; you know how to use communications; you know all the circuits available to you; and you know about dispositions that you put the ships in. So being the staff tactical watch officer was a very valuable learning experience. And I learned a lot about protocol, which has really helped me so much, because every senior officer has to have a pretty good protocol sense. That made me study a lot about protocol and how you handle distinguished guests and entertain. So it really helped me, in particular, when I came back here to the Naval Academy, since I hadn't had much protocol responsibility.

Paul Stillwell: What specifics do you remember about, say, visiting guests or dinners or what have you? Did you have any royalty or heads of state?

Admiral Lawrence: Well, we had a constant flow of people through their congressmen—I'm just trying to think if any heads of state came out. I think we had at least two or three people up there in that category. I think one of the British princesses came out—I forget exactly who. The Mediterranean is a very popular spot for people to visit, so that kept us with a large influx of guests all the time. I ran the mess, and I had to really do all that planning, so that was a good education too. I guess that was just a wonderful learning experience because of the breadth of the things I did.

Paul Stillwell: What is the role between an aide and an admiral?

Admiral Lawrence: Well, there's no precisely defined thing. It's really what the admiral wants the relationship to be. Some flag officers use their aides in very much of a menial-type role, where you have to carry bags and things like that. Admiral Moorer was a very self-sufficient guy. He didn't need an aide doing a lot of things for him. He wanted you to be more a participatory member of the staff, somebody he could bounce off ideas on tactics and things like that. One reason he was happy he had me was that I really knew the airplanes. Since I'd been a test pilot, I knew all of the aspects of introducing these new airplanes, and he really appreciated the fact that he had someone with a good tactical feel could talk airplanes.

The way an admiral uses an aide is purely how he desires it to be, and how the relationships evolve. In other words, he and I both often traveled together, but there were times when he just determined it was better for him to fly alone. That way I could stay back and do some work and not get tied up being a bag carrier and door opener. He could do all those things for himself; he didn't have to have an aide to do menial stuff. That gave me an opportunity to learn a lot about other aspects of the operation of the staff, not just what was done at his level.

Paul Stillwell: Well, it was apparent he wanted more than a bag carrier when he asked for somebody from Test Pilot School.

Admiral Lawrence: Yes, that's right. He wanted somebody who knew the airplanes, because he wasn't current on the airplanes, and I knew them all.

Paul Stillwell: Was there any gap in his knowledge or experience level because he hadn't commanded a carrier? Did he depend on the chief of staff for that input?

Admiral Lawrence: Well, I think he's just so brilliant that he would make sure that things happen that way. He's just a remarkable man. It was really obvious to all of us at that time that he was really going to go to the high places. He was smart, but he also had so much common sense. He always knew the gut issue in every situation, as complex as it was. He could always shift the chaff away and really get to the heart of the issue. It was obvious to all of us there—when he was still a young man—that he would be a future CNO.[*]

But we really used to work hard too. I worked 18 hours a day every day when we were on that staff. But it was very rewarding work. I really enjoyed it.

Paul Stillwell: What do you remember about the exercises with the British?

Admiral Lawrence: Well, of course, the Brits had a pretty good carrier navy at that time. We operated with the Brits in the carriers down in the Med, as well as up in the northern Atlantic. They were very professional. They always had been professional in the Royal Navy. It's a shame that they've had to cut back so much. I'm just trying to think of some of the carrier operations.

They tend to have much smaller and simpler airplanes than we do, because their aircraft carriers were smaller. But it's very interesting because they always seemed to invent some things first, like the angled deck and the mirror landing systems. They're very sound technically.

---

[*] Moorer was born in 1912, so he was 47 when he took command of the carrier division.

I remember one thing that Admiral Anderson liked to do before Admiral Moorer came; I learned this from him. We had an F8U-1P photo airplane, and for night photos it could throw off explosive flares that would actually illuminate the sky at night. The F8U-1P had a bay of exploding flare-type systems that would be blown out of the airplane with a charge, and it would light up in the air. You could see this flash in the daytime. So one time he sent a message over to a foreign flag officer and said, "I plan to salute your flag at umpty-ump." And, of course, they were confused. They didn't see a ship around to do this, so he sent this F8U-1P over it, and fired out 15 of those flares. That was the way he rendered honors at sea. We had a lot of interesting experiences, both in the Mediterranean and also in the Northern Atlantic.

As I say, I felt very fortunate to have had that tour.

Paul Stillwell: Any specifics that come to mind would be welcome.

Admiral Lawrence: Well, we did a very interesting NATO operation in September 1960. The British Navy and the French Navy were still pretty strong, so we accumulated a lot of NATO ships up in the Northern Atlantic and did simulated nuclear weapons strikes against the Norwegians. Then we came back and went into Southampton, England, after it was all over. It was a very, very successful operation.

We had a radar picket submarine with us, the USS *Triton*.* It was commanded by Captain Ned Beach, who's a very famous guy. Admiral Moorer and I had gone up before that exercise, and we went on a little two-day deployment in that submarine. Admiral Moorer wanted to learn all he could about the radar picket capability of that submarine. Admiral Moorer had a mind like a sponge; he was always trying to learn things: new tactics, new concepts. So it was very stimulating and very inspiring for all of us to have an opportunity to serve him.

Paul Stillwell: You described the cramped situation you had in the *Essex*. How did things work out when you got on board the *Saratoga*?

---

* In the spring of 1960, the USS *Triton* (SSN-586), commanded by Captain Edward L. Beach, USN, made the first submerged circumnavigation of the world. Commissioned in November 1959, she was ostensibly a radar-picket submarine but actually a test ship for a two-reactor propulsion plant.

Admiral Lawrence: Well, it was okay. In *Saratoga* I shared the stateroom with a lieutenant (junior grade) who was the communications officer on the staff, Dave Marshall.* The staterooms there were much larger and more comfortable. But when we went on that NATO exercise in the fall of 1960, the *Saratoga* had another engineering casualty. We had to go up there on the USS *Shangri-La*, so we were crammed in on another *Essex*-class carrier.

Paul Stillwell: Who was the skipper in the *Saratoga*?

Admiral Lawrence: The first one was Johnny Hyland, who became, ultimately, CinCPacFlt, retired as a four-star.† The next was Al Fleming. He retired as a rear admiral, and he just died a few years back.‡

The first skipper of the *Essex* was Captain Tom South, and he came over to be our chief of staff. The skipper of *Shangri-La* was now Admiral Fill Gilkeson.§ Knowing these captains has really been a very heartwarming thing, because most of them made admiral, and I kept in touch with them as admirals. Having that initial time together as captains really was useful to me in my relationships with them as admirals. For example, Admiral Hyland came out and was Commander Seventh Fleet when I was flying as the skipper of a squadron.** I was shot down when he was Commander Seventh Fleet.

Paul Stillwell: Any specific recollections of him from this time in the *Saratoga*?

Admiral Lawrence: Yes, he was a very cool man. I remember one time we went into Istanbul. Of course, you have the Bosporus flowing through there, and it's about five knots, so it's kind of tricky coming in to anchor there. I remember being on his bridge,

---

* Lieutenant (junior grade) David M. Marshall, USNR.
† Captain John J. Hyland, USN, commanded the USS *Saratoga* (CVA-60) from 16 October 1958 to 9 November 1959. The oral history of Hyland, who retired as a four-star admiral, is in the Naval Institute collection.
‡ Captain Allan F. Fleming, USN, commanded the USS *Saratoga* (CVA-60) from 9 November 1959 to 9 November 1960.
§ Captain Fillmore B. Gilkeson, USN
** Vice Admiral John J. Hyland, USN, served as Commander Seventh Fleet from 13 December 1965 to 6 November 1967. The oral history of Hyland, who retired as a four-star admiral, is in the Naval Institute collection.

and as he was coming in they told him that, "Captain, there's a freighter in our anchorage." So he had to steer the ship very precisely and drop our anchor, not, of course, in our assigned spot, but he had to pick a place just as close as he could to where the tanker was that had stolen our anchorage. I remember his giving these orders up on the bridge, and he was just as cool as cucumber. A lot of skippers I've known would be jumping through their hats if somebody told them another ship was in their anchorage.

Paul Stillwell: He's a very enthusiastic individual.

Admiral Lawrence: Yes, he's really a wonderful man. I really like him. He and I used to play tennis together when he was the skipper of the *Saratoga*. He had privileges to play at these tennis clubs in the French Riviera. He'd take me with him. He and I became very close friends, and we've stayed that way over the years. I was the only guy he could find on the *Saratoga* to play tennis with him, because tennis was just not a popular game in those days.

But I was really fortunate, because many of the people I was associating with went on to very senior positions in the Navy, and it was good to know them and continue to interface with them as they became flag officers.

Paul Stillwell: Well, naval aviation was on the verge of coming to a period of real dominance in the Navy—CNOs throughout the '60s.

Admiral Lawrence: Yes, that's right. In some respects that was really the height of naval aviation, because it was right in the middle of the Cold War. We had the nuclear capabilities and exercised the nuclear strikes. Of course, the nuclear capability was really the number-one priority in those days. Naval aviation was really, clearly regarded at that time as the cutting edge. The nuclear submarines really hadn't gotten going in those days.* It was an interesting time to be at sea, developing tactics and so forth.

---

* The keel for the ballistic missile submarine *George Washington* (SSBN-598) was laid on 1 November 1957. She was launched on 9 June 1959 and commissioned on 30 December 1959. Her first deterrent patrol began in November 1960. She served until being decommissioned on 24 January 1985.

Paul Stillwell: It was about that same time when the nuclear targeting plans were being integrated, too, the joint setup out in Omaha.*

Admiral Lawrence: Yes, that's right.

Paul Stillwell: Did that have an impact at your level?

Admiral Lawrence: Well, not really. But Captain Hyland went out to Omaha to help set up that staff, directly from being CO of *Saratoga*. I remember when he left the ship he had orders to go out there, and he wasn't very happy about that. He didn't want to go there, but he did.

But that was a really good tour for me. It really helped me so much later on, when I became a fleet commander, to have all that knowledge about tactical operations.

Paul Stillwell: Well, I'd be grateful for any other insight you could provide on Admiral Moorer and the kind of leader he was.

Admiral Lawrence: He had one of the best overall dispositions I've ever seen. He would always operate on an even keel. He just was a true gentleman in every respect. He very rarely lost his temper with anybody or was curt with anybody. He was just very much a gentleman, but obviously a tremendous intellect. As I say, he was a very self-sufficient man, and I have offered over the years to do things for him in his retirement. I have access to officers or anybody, but he's just so brilliant that he can handle everything himself. I used to feel, as an aide, that I wasn't doing enough for him personally. But he didn't want anybody to do something personally; it made him feel better that I was becoming one of his top staff watch officers, learning tactics, and talking to people about airplanes, which I knew very well.

---

* In August 1960, at the instigation of Secretary of Defense Thomas Gates, the Joint Strategic Target Planning Staff was established at the headquarters of the Strategic Air Command, based at Offutt Air Force Base near Omaha, Nebraska. The JSTPS is discussed in the Naval Institute oral histories of several officers who were assigned there: Admiral John J. Hyland, USN (Ret.); Vice Admiral Gerald E. Miller, USN (Ret.); Vice Admiral Kent L. Lee, USN (Ret.); Vice Admiral Edward N. Parker, USN (Ret.).

But he knew everything. In fact, most naval aviators never learn communications, but he knew all about single sideband, the advantages of low frequency versus medium frequency, plus UHF.* He had a real sponge of a mind, because everything he read he remembered. So it surprised none of us that he moved very quickly up the ladder after that tour and then ultimately became the CNO.†

Paul Stillwell: Well, despite his southern gentleman manner, he left no doubt that he was in charge.

Admiral Lawrence: Oh, yes, there's no question about that. He really did. [Chuckle]

Paul Stillwell: Any examples along that line?

Admiral Lawrence: Well, I never saw him severely reprimand anybody, not to the degree that I've seen other admirals do it. But one thing that happened to us in the *Saratoga* was that after our first deployment, we went to the Mediterranean and came back in the spring of '60.‡ We were due for an overhaul, so we went into the Navy yard at Brooklyn, New York. There was really a morale problem, because normally most staffs had left the carrier and gone ashore at Mayport, but we had to stay aboard.§ And all this time, we were planning this big NATO exercise. That was really tough. I know Admiral Moorer had argued with Admiral Joe Rees, who was ComNavAirLant.** But Admiral Rees said, "You stay on the carrier."

So, anyway, we came out of New York. We had to pick up our ammunition load at Norfolk, over in the weapons station near Portsmouth. We got that done and were coming out at night on our way down to Mayport, Florida, and we had a collision with a

---

* UHF – ultra-high frequency.
† Admiral Moorer served as Chief of Naval Operations from 1 August 1967 to 1 July 1970. He was later Chairman of the Joint Chiefs of Staff from 3 July 1970 to 30 June 1974. His oral history is in the Naval Institute collection.
‡ The *Saratoga*'s Mediterranean deployment was from 15 August 1959 to 26 February 1960.
§ The ship was home-ported in Mayport, Florida.
** Vice Admiral William L. Rees, USN, served as Commander Naval Air Force Atlantic Fleet from 29 May 1956 to 30 September 1960. Prior to 30 July 1957 the title was Air Force, Atlantic Fleet.

German freighter.* This was really a tense time, a bad collision in the middle of the night, and some sailors were injured. Admiral Rees was really a tough guy, so I know Admiral Moorer dreaded having to tell him about this. He and I flew over in the chopper, and as we were driving up to Admiral Rees's headquarters as ComNavAirLant, he was driving down himself to get on a chopper and go out and see the damage on the *Saratoga*. So that was really embarrassing for Admiral Moorer, because Admiral Rees went out there, and Admiral Moorer wasn't on board. [Chuckle]

But he never let things like that faze him; he never got excited and blew a fuse or anything, always an even-keel guy. It was just so wonderful to work for him, because of his really gentlemanly treatment of you and not getting excitable. But you learned a lot from his example and his knowledge of various areas. That's where he was so good; he just had this breadth of knowledge on virtually anything that went on in the Navy.

Paul Stillwell: Did he strike you as politically astute?

Admiral Lawrence: Yes, he certainly was, but he was never a guy who really tried to capitalize on it. He certainly realized that whenever you have human beings interfacing each other, there's going to be an element involved. He never really, to the best of my knowledge that I could see there, never tried to play politics or go directly to a congressman or something like that. Although, I'm sure as he got to be more senior, he got a lot more astute as to things you have to do to accommodate Congress.

Paul Stillwell: What were the circumstances in the collision?

Admiral Lawrence: Well, we came out of Thimble Shoals and turned into the Virginia Capes area to head south. We were supposed to do a speed trial on that carrier, so the officer of the deck was really concerned about doing that. When you do a speed trial, where you're checking economy and all that, you're very reluctant to change course,

---

* On 25 May 1960 the carrier *Saratoga* (CVA-60) collided with the German freighter *Bernd Leonhardt* off the coast of North Carolina. The *Saratoga* then steamed to the Norfolk Naval Shipyard, where she was docked for collision repairs.

because that will induce more drag. So this officer of the deck was really concentrating on keeping his course and his speed. He looked down, and he saw a vessel coming at him out there about 20 miles or so. He turned to the right to open up a little distance so that this ship would be free to pass on his side. But for some reason, he got confused and he turned back. But because he'd shown this guy a red light that made that guy burdened, when he turned back like this, this other guy was still trying to be the burdened ship and go right under his stern, and so they ended up colliding.*

It was just a goof-up on the part of the OOD on *Saratoga* of changing his course, making the other guy the burdened ship, you the privileged ship, and then changing back. He should have held course. The people on the German freighter were trying their best to go behind the *Saratoga*, and *Saratoga*, which had opened the distance this way, initially, now wanted to try to go this way. So it was really a dilemma for the German freighter. The interesting thing about it is that the signalman on the German freighter at the time of the collision was transmitting bon voyage. He didn't realize that the collision was that imminent. The overhang of the carrier scraped the superstructure of the German merchant ship.

Paul Stillwell: What was the outcome? Did Admiral Moorer conduct an investigation?

Admiral Lawrence: Yes, he was appointed to be the head of the board of inquiry—whatever they called it in those days. He and another officer who was in Norfolk, Captain Eddie Outlaw, came over.† Moorer and Outlaw were the two principal members, and I think they may have had a captain. But I think it was only those two guys.

The commanding officer was, of course, faulted because, even though he was not on the bridge, he had to take the accountability. But he, later on, Captain Fleming made flag, so he outlived it.

Paul Stillwell: How much damage was there to the carrier?

---

* In the nautical rules of the road, the relative positions of the two ships determine which one is privileged—that is, obliged to maintain course and speed—and which one is burdened—that is, required to maneuver to avoid the other ship.
† Captain Edward C. Outlaw, USN.

Admiral Lawrence: Not all that great, but it really bent up the structure of the other ship quite a bit. So we had to go in and spend a week or so in the naval shipyard there at Portsmouth to get the repairs effected.* But it happened at midnight, and there was this really excruciating, uncomfortable sound. That was the most significant accident we had during that 18 or 19 months that I was on that carrier staff.

Paul Stillwell: How would you describe the relationship between the ship's company officers and the staff?

Admiral Lawrence: Our staff had been using the *Saratoga* as a flagship for quite a few years. We had pretty good rapport, and I really worked very hard to maintain that rapport. In my dealings with the ship, I really never tried to wear the rank of the admiral or use this horsepower of being on the staff.

I was mentioning some things about Admiral Anderson, some of the funny things that we had happen. The *Saratoga* had difficulty making a good ice cream to satisfy Admiral Anderson; he loved ice cream. It was always just a little bit soft, and he wanted it hard. One time we were operating in company with the *Essex*, our other carrier, and he flew by chopper from *Saratoga* over to *Essex* just to visit with them. While he was over there, he sent a flashing light message that came over and just said, "The *Essex* has good ice cream."

So Captain Hyland looked at this and called me up to read it. He said, "What does he mean by this?"

I said, "Captain, I think he's trying to tell you that you don't have good ice cream." [Laughter] So he summoned the supply officer up on the bridge, and they got their ice cream maker squared away, but that was the way Admiral Anderson told him that it needed to be improved.

Paul Stillwell: Was it better after that?

Admiral Lawrence: Oh, yes.

---
* Norfolk Naval Shipyard, Portsmouth, Virginia.

But Admiral Anderson, as I say, he had a different style of doing things and getting points across to people.

I remember one time after Admiral Anderson had moved up to be the commander of the Sixth Fleet.* His flagship was the USS *Des Moines*, and the *Des Moines* was tied up inside the sea wall in Barcelona.† It had gone in and they did what they called a Med moor, where it backed the fantail up to the pier. Everybody had to go on and off the ship on the fantail; there weren't separate officer and enlisted ladders.

Paul Stillwell: The ship was perpendicular to the dock instead of parallel.

Admiral Lawrence: That's right. That's what they call a Med moor. Admiral Anderson for some reason was ashore, and he decided that he was going to bring his guests back aboard the *Des Moines*. So he walked on the *Des Moines*, looked down, and here were all these drunken sailors laid out prone, just like cordwood. He really blew a fuse, because he was very much of a stickler for the conduct ashore and uniforms and all that. So he directed the shore patrol officer would be increased from the commander rank up to the captain's rank. So we had captains standing shore patrol officer watch. In those days we used to have destroyer division commanders in addition to destroyer squadron commanders. So the job fell to, usually, the DesDiv commanders who were young junior captains, and also to some staff captains got those jobs.

Paul Stillwell: As I recall, Admiral Anderson had a voice call sign something like "Fast Charger," and that described his manner of operation.

Admiral Lawrence: I think it was "Fast Charger." Yes, he had a very appropriate call sign that fit his personality. But he always wore summer whites, and they were always beautifully tailored. So that put a burden on the rest of the staff to have to wear whites all

---

* Vice Admiral George W. Anderson, Jr., USN, commanded the Sixth Fleet from September 14 1959 to 13 July 1961.
† USS *Des Moines* (CA-134) was the lead ship of a class of heavy cruisers. She was commissioned 16 November 1948.

the time. He was a real stickler for appearance and all those things. Distinctly different personality from Admiral Moorer, but both effective in their own way.

Paul Stillwell: How much did you learn about the logistics side of the job?

Admiral Lawrence: Well, I developed a pretty good feel for all of the fleet operations and what you have to do in terms of replenishment. I got to be pretty close to the staff surface operations officer, who was Jerry King.[*] Our staff ops officer was Roy Isaman, who retired as a rear admiral.[†] But I learned a lot from Jerry King, who was considered our senior watch officer and was trying to qualify us as tactical watch officers. He taught me a lot about the broader aspects of surface operations. I learned in depth about logistics, and I certainly developed an appreciation for what is required to maintain all your destroyers and other ships in an appropriate state of fuel and how you schedule your oilers and do your replenishments. I tried to learn as much as I could. I figured, "I'm out here on this cruise, I might as well work 18 hours a day and learn as much as I could."

After I got qualified as a tactical watch officer, where I ran the whole task force, because in those days we operated two carriers together from time to time. I remember one time we were coming into Mayport at the end of our Med deployment. We had the *Essex* and *Saratoga* in company, and I had just gotten qualified as the staff tactical watch officer. Because of the rotation, it so happened that I was the staff tactical watch officer when we were coming into Mayport. As the staff surface operations officer, Jerry King had to write the night orders, because he was also the staff navigator.

The requirement that was levied upon us was to fly the air wing off, and just as soon as we flew the air wing off, we had to hit the sea buoy, because carriers had to arrive in Mayport at high-water slack.[‡] Mayport only has just a minimum depth of water, so the carriers had to come in at high tide. I knew that I was going to have that watch, so we talked it over and determined how to best approach this. So we made a circle that, if

---

[*] Commander Jerome H. King Jr., USN. The oral history of King, who retired as a vice admiral, is in the Naval Institute collection.
[†] Captain Roy M. Isaman, USN.
[‡] High-water slack refers to the period when the tide is high and neither flowing in nor out.

the wind was a certain amount, then you would have to commence the launch of airplanes on this circle, and your course was just the reciprocal of the wind.*

So I had this all worked out the night before and knew exactly what I was going to do. I had the 4:00 to 8:00 watch, and I came up about an hour early just to make sure that everything was under control. But the officer who had the watch before me had not reset the dead reckoning tracer bug that they have on the plot. There's a little bug beneath the chart that has a light in it.

Paul Stillwell: Well, there are cams under there, aren't there?

Admiral Lawrence: Yes, you put a pitot tube down the water. That detects your velocity, and then there's an input from the gyro direction.

I thought that bug was indicating accurately. I came up, and I was using that bug, and everything worked out. Then, after I relieved the watch, I had the navigator go down to get the ship's latest position, and I found out that the bug was about ten miles off. They hadn't reset the bug to compensate for set and drift, the current and all that. By the time I got this all figured out, it was now about 5:00 o'clock, and we were supposed to start launching at about 6:30. So I just pushed the ship up to over 30 knots to get where we were supposed to be.

Jerry King heard the hull vibrating because he hadn't anticipated us going faster than, at the most, 20 knots. So he called in and said, "What the hell's going on up there?" I tried to explain to him. He was half asleep, so he just chewed me out. He said, "God dammit, I thought you had all this straight last night, and now you're off course. Boy, if you screw this thing up, it's really going to be bad. We have all those families waiting to see the carrier."

I said, "Oh, gosh, yeah, this is really something."

And, of course, Admiral Moorer called me up, and he said, "Why are we going so fast?"

So I explained to him, "Sir, I think we've got the corrective action taken."

---

* Aircraft carriers launch and recover planes while steaming into the wind in order to provide lift under the wings.

Of course, Admiral Moorer's such a gentleman, he said, "Very well. I'm sure you'll handle it." So, anyway, it turned out that we started launching those airplanes, after all this high speed that I had to use to make up. We reached the sea buoy just almost within a minute of when we were supposed to be there. Had the last airplanes launched, so I said, "Boy!" I looked at Jerry King and he looked at me, and he and I were the only two that realized that we'd really been out of position. We had to play catch-up ball.

But it was things like that really taught me a lot when I just as a lieutenant. Being a staff type of watch officer and running two carriers and all the destroyers—in a tactical sense, I really learned a lot. Later on, I was a surface ship navigator, and that knowledge I gained on that staff really helped me immeasurably.

Paul Stillwell: King was later Moorer's EA for a while, wasn't he?[*]

Admiral Lawrence: I think he was. Admiral Moorer had great respect for Jerry King as a professional.

Paul Stillwell: Sent him out to Vietnam to relieve Admiral Zumwalt.[†]

Admiral Lawrence: Yes, he had great respect for Jerry King. Jerry King was an NROTC graduate from Yale and a very smart guy. He was not as good a leader in all senses of the word as Admiral Moorer. He tended to be not as people-oriented and not as much of a gentleman. You had to handle him a little bit. I think that probably inhibited him in some ways, but he did have responsible jobs. He became the J-3 on the Joint Staff and retired from that billet.[‡] But he was wonderful in that job on the staff as surface operations officer. I learned a tremendous amount from him that really stood me in good stead for the rest of my career. Gave me a good, solid foundation in ship and task force-

---

[*] As a captain, King served from 1966 to 1968 as executive assistant to two Chiefs of Naval Operations, Admiral David L. McDonald and Admiral Thomas H. Moorer.
[†] Vice Admiral King served as Commander Naval Forces Vietnam/Chief of Naval Advisory Group Vietnam from 14 May 1970 to 5 April 1971.
[‡] J-3 – directorate for operations.

type operations that an aviator normally doesn't get. But I've been fortunate because I'd gotten qualified as an officer of the deck on a carrier. And I had a pretty good foundation and knowledge of ship operations.

Paul Stillwell: What do you mean by that phrase, you had to "handle him?"

Admiral Lawrence: Well, Jerry had a short fuze. He was a very intense, hard-driving guy, heavy smoker like a lot of hard-driving guys are. He'd come up on the bridge, and if things didn't look right, boy, he had a short fuze. So you had to kind of sit back and say, "Well, Commander, we've got everything under control here. This is going okay."

Paul Stillwell: Calm him down a little.

Admiral Lawrence: Yes, he was just a very intense guy, but he's smart; he really knew what he was doing. He could really help run the task force, because he was basically the guy who would set up all the replenishments, for example. Then he would go out with the messages to the replenishing ships, and he would go out to the destroyer squadron commanders and give them their assignments, and he'd do all the basic planning. He had one assistant, a lieutenant commander. The two of them ran all the surface ships in the task force.

Back in those days, we were still not operating as dispersed as we are in today's time. Often when we would replenish, we would have two carriers with a complete circular destroyer screen all around us. You'd have probably 16 destroyers— two destroyer squadrons and two carriers in what they call a formation 40. We'd have the standard replenishment formation—multiple lines with about six or eight replenishment ships. We would bring that circular formation in at 25 knots, and then use the term, "unzip the fly," where you'd have the destroyers on the right peel off and go around that way, and the destroyers on the left go off this way. Just as you were about ready to let advanced destroyer screen reach those replenishment ships, you'd execute the unzip-the-fly maneuver. I forget the term that we used—one of the signals was something like "Yankee Mike One," which meant, "Proceed independently on duties assigned," or something like that. In those days we used standard signals out of that signal book all the time. You very rarely ever used a plain-language message. You'd look up the signal, and you'd come out over the air with a signal. I really got to be very proficient in using the signal book. But we did some very demanding surface operations they never do today.

Paul Stillwell: Was this done by tactical voice radio?

Admiral Lawrence: Yes. We used to do it over what they call a primary tactical circuit, which is PriTac. You really prided yourself on the very formal usage of the PriTac like, "Signals follow, execute to follow," using that formal terminology. I got to be very proficient on using the radio. So it was 18 months of very intense education in all aspects of naval operations.

I really learned the tactical aspects of task force operations. At the same time, I was running all the protocol stuff when visitors came, so I developed a great knowledge of protocol. So it was an immensely valuable experience to me to get this broad experience, and to be associated with people of the caliber of Admiral Moorer and Admiral Anderson. It gave me a really good sense of how you had to conduct yourself as a senior officer, and it gave me some good guidance just as to how I should prepare myself for that rank. So it was a wonderful tour.

Unfortunately, though, in the about 18 months I was on the staff I was physically away from home for about 15 months. So it was tough on my family, and that really affected me later on in some of my attitudes, because I just didn't feel I could spend that much time away from my family in my career. I had to make some tough decisions about whether I wanted to continue doing that or not.

Maybe I'd better break here, and then the next time we can cover what I did after that staff tour.

Paul Stillwell: Well, if I can throw in two more questions about that.

Admiral Lawrence: Yes, sure.

Paul Stillwell: Did you have any encounters at all with the Soviets during that tour?

Admiral Lawrence: Well, the Soviets really were not actively operating their navy in those days. We had minimal contact at sea with the Soviets. In fact, I can't even remember seeing a Soviet ship back there in 1959-60. Of course, we were conducting these simulated nuclear strikes. About once a line period, or about once every month we would do a 36-hour strike-ex, where you would do the simulated nuclear strikes with our A3Ds and your A4Ds.* Basically, they would do a simulated profile for a mission. They would go into Italy, Turkey, and things like that, but it was a simulated strike against the Soviet Union. We were very much aware of the Soviet threat, but we never really saw any of the Soviet Navy.

Paul Stillwell: Well, you figure they must have had some means of knowing what you were doing.

Admiral Lawrence: Oh, yes. Yes, they certainly did. But we were very much aware that we were in a Cold War and that everything we were doing was basically oriented against the Soviet Union.

Paul Stillwell: In what ways had the air group and carrier operations evolved since you'd been in the *Oriskany* five years earlier?

Admiral Lawrence: Oh, really, really, significantly. We'd gotten the angled deck, of course, incorporated in the carrier. The *Saratoga* was the second *Forrestal*-class carrier, and it was significantly larger than the *Essex* class.†

Paul Stillwell: Higher performance aircraft.

---

* These were the designations of carrier-based nuclear-capable attack planes.
† USS *Forrestal* (CVA-59) was commissioned 1 October 1955 as the first of the U.S. Navy's big-deck carriers. She had a standard displacement of 56,000 tons, was 1,046 feet long, 129 feet in the beam, and had an extreme width of 252 feet. Her top speed was 33 knots.

Admiral Lawrence: Higher performance aircraft and much safer and much broader capability because of the larger deck. Now you had four catapults instead of just the two. What really impressed me was our ability to operate on a much broader scale.

Paul Stillwell: Were you getting more night work?

Admiral Lawrence: Oh, by that time, in 1959-60, every pilot in the air wing qualified at night. Admittedly, everybody didn't fly a lot, and there were some guys, the newer kids, who might have been a little bit lacking in those skills that they didn't fly at night. In the night fighter squadron everybody flew extensively at night. That was much more than we'd done back in my time. But everybody got qualified at night. We were really getting into night operations. Getting the *Forrestal*-class carriers out there just kind of gave the impetus to doing a lot more night work in the ships.

Paul Stillwell: Well, thank you, Admiral, I look forward to the next time.

Admiral Lawrence: Okay.

Interview Number 5 with Vice Admiral William P. Lawrence, U.S. Navy (Retired)
Place: U.S. Naval Institute, Annapolis, Maryland
Date: Tuesday, 9 October 1990

Paul Stillwell: Admiral, the last time we talked about your tour as aide to Admiral Moorer. Now you're going to get back into the cockpit again in VF-101.[*]

Admiral Lawrence: Well, this was a very difficult period in some ways, but it just shows you that some of the darkest times turn out to be the brightest times over the long haul.

When I was serving as the aide to Admiral Moorer, we were on the *Saratoga* out of Mayport. We'd owned a home in Patuxent River, Maryland, which we'd sold, fortunately, very readily, and then we bought a home down there in Florida. I had been told, while I was with Admiral Moorer, that they very much wanted me to come back up to Oceana to be involved in the introduction of the F4H to the fleet.[†] I wasn't happy with the prospect of having just been down in Jacksonville a little over a year and then having to sell a house, which appeared to me to be the prudent thing to do in order to move up to Norfolk.[‡] But I realized that I could make a good contribution to the program since I'd test-flown the F4H—not as much as I'd flown the F8U-3, but enough to really know the airplane pretty well.

The tour with Admiral Moorer had been a very professionally rewarding tour, but it had really been tough in the separation from my family. I reported to the carrier division staff in May of 1959, and I was gone just about all the time until I detached in October of 1960. I was away from them for virtually the entire 17 months, and I was really bothered now with my children coming along. Then I saw having to go up to Oceana and probably leave my family down at Mayport, because there was difficulty selling the house.

Another complicating thing was that my first wife, who was a very wonderful

---
[*] Lieutenant Commander Lawrence reported to Fighter Squadron 101 Detachment A in November 1960.
[†] Oceana Naval Air Station is in Virginia Beach, Virginia.
[‡] Mayport, Florida, which was the ship's homeport, is adjacent to the Jacksonville Naval Air Station.

person, really wasn't all that happy about my flying. I'd had some really close calls those first eight years in flying, because flying at that time was really a dangerous business. I'd had that cold catapult shot, and on a night landing I'd gone into the barricade. Then I had several cases back at Patuxent of having to make precautionary landings. I could tell that this was taking a toll on her. She just was not comfortable about all this. So I came to a point where I felt I really needed to do an assessment as to whether this was really the right thing for me to do.

But, anyway, I went on up to Oceana, and I was commuting down to Jacksonville as best I could. Fortunately, the CO of our detachment that was going to introduce the airplane was Commander Jerry O'Rourke, a very wonderful, wonderful guy.[*] He was very liberal about giving me an airplane to fly down there on the weekends. Then, after reporting there in November, in January we had to go out to Miramar for this fleet introduction.[†] And here I was faced with another long separation from my family.

Paul Stillwell: Why did you have to go to the West Coast?

Admiral Lawrence: VF-121, which was the replacement air group training squadron on the West Coast for the all-weather fighters, was designated to be the sponsoring squadron. We put together a team of people from VF-101 on the East Coast and VF-121 at Miramar. We would fly the airplanes back to Miramar, and we would set up our separate training in VF-101, and they would set up in VF-121. But we had the problem of having both F3H and F4H squadrons at that time. So that required us to have split units in those squadrons.

Paul Stillwell: So VF-101 was an existing squadron of F3Hs?

Admiral Lawrence: Yes, it was the F3H training squadron, which was down at Key West. But they put together our VF-101 Detachment Alfa for the F4H at Oceana, and we

---

[*] Commander Gerald G. O'Rourke, USN.
[†] Miramar Naval Air Station was near San Diego, California. It has since been turned over to the Marine Corps.

initially started training in the F3D at Oceana, the guys who were going to be our first radar intercept officers in the Navy.*

Paul Stillwell: Sounds awfully complicated.

Admiral Lawrence: Yes, it really was. I think that it was a problem of base loading at Key West, which is not a very large air station. That's why they decided to put the F4H training and the radar intercept officer training in the F3Ds at Oceana.

Anyway, my morale really went low at that point because of all the separations from my family. I came to the realization of the real demand of the naval career on the family situation. So I made a real soul-searching decision, thinking while I was out in California. I decided that I didn't want to stay with it. I was going to get out of the Navy, because I knew it was very tough on my wife and my kids.

Well, all sorts of people started going to work on me.

Paul Stillwell: Such as who?

Admiral Lawrence: Admiral Moorer, Admiral Anderson, and others. I told Jerry O'Rourke after I'd been out there a couple of months and we were in the program, that he really ought to send me back to Oceana and let me just go back to the parent squadron and think about this, which I did. I thought I'd already had all my decisions made, but then I realized that a lot of people had a lot of confidence in me and wanted me to make this contribution to the Navy. My sense of patriotism and all that made it very difficult for me to leave. But, also, I decided that out of deference to my wife, I would talk about going into the surface Navy.

I talked to a lot of people, and they said, "Well, if that's what you want to do, we want to accommodate you." So I did get permission to change my designator from 1310 to 1100.† BuPers would give me a job as the navigator on the USS *Newport News*, which was a heavy cruiser. So I took that, and it was very difficult, because I still wasn't sure I

---

* Radar intercept officer, a naval flight officer—not a pilot—who sat in the rear seat of the aircraft.
† The officer designator for a naval aviator is 1310; at the time 1100 was the designator for an unrestricted line officer.

was doing the right thing. I, of course, felt badly about leaving aviation, but I just felt that it was the best course of action for me to take, because I came to the realization that I couldn't make myself get out of the Navy entirely. But I owed it to my wife and my family to make this change, because aviation was really dangerous in those days.

Paul Stillwell: Well, before you get to the *Newport News*, could you discuss some of the substance, please, on your work on the F4H.

Admiral Lawrence: Well, one thing that they had me do when I came up there to the detachment at Oceana, when we were training the new radar intercept officers in the F3Ds, was to develop the syllabus that we would use in our fleet introduction program. This was a syllabus for the pilots from our squadron and from the squadron out there on the West Coast that were going to get oriented in the F4H, because they knew that I was the one who had the most experience. Of course, I worked with the other guys to develop the tactical part of the syllabus. Then we met with the guys from VF-121 out on the West Coast. It so happened that in 121, there at Miramar, was Dick Gordon, who'd been a test pilot with me at Patuxent and had actually flown the F4H more than I had—because I was flying the F8U-3.[*] He also played a big hand in it, and we had some very talented guys out there.

So I made my input, and we got together with them and formalized the syllabus. Then, of course, we all went out to Miramar and flew the airplane and did the missions that we'd formulated. When we saw that some of those missions might not be quite right, we readjusted them and changed them here and there. But after I'd been out there about two months—which was about two-thirds the way through the program—that's when I made my decision to come back to Maryland.

Paul Stillwell: Were you also writing doctrine in addition to the syllabus?

---

[*] Lieutenant Richard F. Gordon Jr., USN. In October 1963 he was accepted into the space program in the third group of astronauts selected. He subsequently went to the moon.

Admiral Lawrence: Yes, I was. My main input was primarily in stability and control, the flying qualities performance of the airplane, as I'd learned at Patuxent. As for the specific tactics, there were guys who were a little bit more knowledgeable than I in that area—missiles and missile capabilities. But I was the one who knew how the airplane flew, its performance: what you could do at 1.5 Mach number and 1.3, 1.7—how much fuel consumption was. That was where I had my greatest expertise, so I was able to work with the guys who really had more tactical expertise on missile capabilities and things like that as we developed the complete syllabus.

Paul Stillwell: Well, the man who knows the system needs to work hand in glove with the man who's going to say how it's going to be used.

Admiral Lawrence: That's right, that's right. Because, the Sparrow missile, for example, the APQ-72 radar, and then the fire control systems in the F4H were areas that I didn't have a lot of expertise in, because I didn't do any work at all on those at Patuxent.[*] So I had to really work very closely with those guys, but I knew performance and stability and control. I could tell them, for example, that contrary to what most people thought, even though you had a Mach 2 airplane, you were still going to be using the airplane more subsonically than you were supersonically, because when you went supersonic, you increased your fuel consumption by 50%. So we had to really think more of using the performance of the missile and the performance of the airplane.

The value of that high degree of thrust was first in your ability to climb to altitude rapidly. The other was to accelerate, but not for prolonged, high-speed operations. You would probably spend the vast majority of your flights at around .85 to .9 Mach number, and driven by fuel considerations, because at very high Mach number, you were going to be using about 100,000 pounds of fuel an hour. The fuel use goes up significantly with Mach number, and afterburner's at least a 50% increase in your fuel consumption.

Paul Stillwell: Was it viewed strictly as an interceptor at that point?

---

[*] Since the late 1950s the Sparrow has been the U.S. Navy's major long-range air defense missile. The Sparrow I version entered fleet service in 1956 on board F3H Demons and F7U Cutlasses.

Admiral Lawrence: Yes, it was viewed only as an air-to-air fighter. At that time, we didn't even seriously think about an air-to-ground mode for that airplane. In my first tour in the squadron, which I'll talk about later on, we considered ourselves only air to air. It was not until the Vietnam War that we really started using it as an air-to-ground aircraft.

Paul Stillwell: How was the F3D used to train the RIOs?

Admiral Lawrence: Well, it was a side-by-side, two-place airplane, and it had an air-intercept radar in the cockpit. The good thing about the F3D was that you were right next to the other guy; you could reach out and touch him. So you could do very good instruction in that airplane, because of your ability to talk and look in this guy's radar at the same time with him. Although it was a subsonic airplane, it still was very good for instructing basic air-to-air intercept and air-to-air tactics.

We didn't have any radar intercept officers in the Navy before that time. This was the first two-place fighter that we ever had. The F3Ds were really used principally by the Marines; there were a few Navy squadrons, but the F4H was really the first two-place fighter. So we had to develop immediately, high priority, these radar intercept officers.

Paul Stillwell: There wasn't an NFO community per se then.[*]

Admiral Lawrence: Not in jet aviation. We had them in some of the electronic warfare areas, such as the old AD Skyraider versions that did the electronic warfare.[†] And we had some in ASW, but not in so-called tactical aviation.[‡] So we developed the first group of them.

Paul Stillwell: Any specifics you remember on that training?

---

[*] The term naval flight officer had not yet been adopted; an individual with the 1350 officer designator was described as "A line officer, a member of the aeronautic organization who is not a pilot."
[†] The Douglas AD Skyraider was designed as a propeller-driven attack airplane.
[‡] ASW – antisubmarine warfare.

Admiral Lawrence: Well, they were really good guys. Actually, they were all volunteers who had come from various fields in the Navy. Some had come from multi-engines, some had come from ASW, and all of them had been through the radar intercept officers' course that the Air Force conducted, because the Air Force had the F-101 and F-102.[*]

So they were a very fine group of guys. They came to us well prepared through the Air Force training, and they were gung-ho. Many of them went on to become very successful in the Navy. Out of that group of early guys, we had produced at least one flag officer that I know of, a guy named Tom Johnson.[†] But all of them were just solid, salt-of-the-earth-type guys. So it was very professionally rewarding to work with them.

Paul Stillwell: Did the pilots have to adjust psychologically to the idea that they were no longer able to do it all themselves?

Admiral Lawrence: Yes, oh, yes. There was a little bit of a culture adjustment, but we very quickly perceived that it was really good to have a lot of that workload taken off of you. That was a situation where I felt I was often overtaxed—having flown the F2H-3 in a squadron and flown the F3H. Handling that radar and flying the airplane at night was very heavy burden on a pilot. To have a guy who was a real expert, true professional, in operating that radar and interpreting radar presentations I felt really enhanced your capability. That's why I felt that it was a very sound, very wise decision to build a two-place airplane, as opposed to the F8U-3 concept with a single place.

Paul Stillwell: Was the issue of whether or not to put a gun in the F4H taken up?

Admiral Lawrence: No, I think that we felt that the Sidewinder missile was really a fine missile.[‡] By that time, the Sidewinder had been out for about five years or more, and so we felt that the infrared heat-seeking missile really gave you much more capability in the rear hemisphere than guns. All of my experience with guns is that you had to be in there

---

[*] The F-101 and F-102 were Air Force jet fighters.
[†] Lieutenant Thomas J. Johnson, USN.
[‡] Sidewinder is an air-to-air infrared-homing missile with a speed of approximately Mach 2.5. It has been operational, in various forms, since 1956. It was used extensively in the Vietnam War.

around 1,000 feet to really get a good shot. Now, 1,000 feet in the air, particularly at night, is really close. But to be able to sit back at about a mile with an infrared heating-seeking missile, where you got a tone as soon as your seeker got that infrared signal, was far better. So I felt that the Sidewinder was a better rear-hemisphere weapon than the guns were.

Paul Stillwell: How did you go about developing the teamwork between the two men?

Admiral Lawrence: Well, there was a lot of just practical experience, and I have to admit we relied very heavily on what the Air Force had done in its two-place airplanes—the fighter interceptors. Of course, the Air Defense Command had a lot more experience already in this work with two crewmen.* That was their bread and butter. Although we had this capability in the Navy, we frankly just didn't have the airplanes that were as capable, or the pilots that had had that specific expertise in the air-intercept mission. The Navy still operated primarily day fighters, doing the best we could at night, as opposed to guys who could operate freely at night with great capability. The F2H and F3H were not all that capable, frankly. The F4H was a quantum improvement over the F2H and F3H.

Paul Stillwell: Well, not only in all-weather capability, but just pure performance.

Admiral Lawrence: Pure performance, yes.

Paul Stillwell: Did you get into air-combat maneuvering before you left the program?

Admiral Lawrence: Oh, yes. I developed a best approach to air-combat maneuvering. It showed how much excess thrust you would have, say, at .9 Mach number versus 1.2 versus 1.3, 1.4. What I really tried to convince everybody was that the perception you were going to be flying a lot at supersonic speeds was completely erroneous, because your fuel consumption would increase so greatly that you just couldn't afford to fly

---

* The North American Air Defense Command (NORAD), an Air Force command based in Colorado Springs, was responsible for detecting and attacking Soviet bombers headed toward the United States.

supersonic for a long time. So you would be doing most of your air-combat maneuvering down at .9 Mach number or below. Of course, that's the way it turned out. To provide enough fuel to do those things, as a standard practice with we ended up out in the fleet operating planes with external tanks off the carriers. But that fuel consumption prevents you really going at a very high Mach number.

Paul Stillwell: Did you get into any carrier work in that squadron?

Admiral Lawrence: No, in those early days we just weren't to that point of being rated to go to the carriers. Not only did we have to get ourselves checked out, we had to come back and get our syllabuses refined and start checking out the first fleet squadron. Then, after we had been in for several months, we had to bring in the second fleet squadron. The first fleet squadron was VF-74; the second one was VF-102.

Paul Stillwell: Jerry O'Rourke had been a fighter pilot for some time. How well suited was he for that role and in introducing the new plane?

Admiral Lawrence: Well, he had been ideally suited, because he had actually been in one of the very few Navy F3D squadrons in the Korean War. So he had the F3D background, and I think that was a factor as to why Jerry O'Rourke was chosen. Also, he was a Test Pilot School graduate. He'd been in electronic systems test, and so he had a very good understanding of radar and night, all-weather intercept tactics.

Paul Stillwell: How was he on the leadership side?

Admiral Lawrence: Oh, wonderful. He was a great officer. I have great, tremendous admiration for him. He and I were always very close, both at Patuxent River Test Center and when we were together in VF-101.

Paul Stillwell: He's really a gregarious, enthusiastic individual.

Admiral Lawrence: Very smart, very smart guy, good writer. He writes a lot for the Naval Institute, or he did in the past. Really a good man. He should have been a flag officer, but he had some bad luck. I think he just proves that getting to high rank is as much luck as anything else sometimes.

One of his other guys with us was Tim Wooldridge, who retired as a Navy captain—E. T. Wooldridge.[*] His dad was a vice admiral when he retired. Tim now works for the Smithsonian in the Air and Space Museum.

Paul Stillwell: He's a frequent visitor to the Naval Institute.

Admiral Lawrence: Yes, I would think he would be.

Another good man. There were some real good people, not only in VF-101, but also in VF-74, which was the first squadron. And, of course, when the squadron came back from the West Coast, we worked very closely with the guys who were going to be in the new VF-74, to help them get checked out and training them tactically.

Paul Stillwell: What specifically did you do as an instructor?

Admiral Lawrence: While we were out there at Miramar, we were just flying the types of flights we perceived would be in the syllabus flights that we would later on have the pilots train in. Then, of course, when we went to Miramar, then we actually had pilots whom we would train, brief, and help fly those missions. So our time out there at Miramar was just going through it ourselves to determine if they were, in fact, the correct type of flights, that would accomplish what we felt should be accomplished.

Paul Stillwell: Were people handpicked to form this first squadron?

---

[*] Lieutenant Edmund Tyler Wooldridge Jr., USN. After his retirement from active duty as a captain, Wooldridge concentrated on naval aviation history. He edited three books of first-person accounts on the subject: *The Golden Age Remembered: U.S. Naval Aviation, 1919-1941* (Annapolis: Naval Institute Press, 1998); *Carrier Warfare in the Pacific: an Oral History Collection* (Washington: Smithsonian Institution Press, 1993); *Into the Jet Age: Conflict and Change in Naval Aviation, 1945-1975: an Oral History* (Annapolis: Naval Institute Press, 1995).

Paul Stillwell: Were people handpicked to form this first squadron?

Admiral Lawrence: Yes, just like the group of us who went to Miramar. We were all handpicked, from Jerry O'Rourke right down to the new guys we got right out of the fleet squadrons. Most everybody who went into that first VF-74 was a handpicked guy. Even those kids out of the training command who came in there as ensigns and jaygees were the kids who stood high in the training command. The skipper of that first squadron was a fellow named Julian Lake, who later on became a rear admiral.[*]

Paul Stillwell: Electronic warfare expert.

Admiral Lawrence: Electronic warfare expert. His executive officer, as I recall, was Scott Lamoreaux, who retired as a captain.[†] The maintenance officer at that time was Lieutenant Commander Jim Foxgrover, who later on retired as a rear admiral.[‡] So that squadron had a lot a very fine people who made names for themselves later on in naval aviation.

Paul Stillwell: Did you work with BuPers to set up a training program for the rear-seat men?

Admiral Lawrence: Well, of course, what we did out at Miramar was to have both a pilot and a radar intercept officer syllabus. And, yes, we, of course, did set up a program for training those kids that came in the Navy. We set it up and had the Chief of the Naval Air Training down in Pensacola set it up as part of the Aviation Officer Candidate School. At AOCS down there, they have an NFO track, as well as a pilot track.

Paul Stillwell: Because fairly soon you would want to stop relying on the Air Force.

---

[*] Commander Julian S. Lake, USN.
[†] Lieutenant Commander Lewis Scott Lamoreaux, USN.
[‡] Lieutenant Commander James H. Foxgrover, USN.

Admiral Lawrence: Oh, yes, that's right. We didn't rely on the Air Force after we got that initial group of guys who came in as instructors in VF-101. Those guys had to come in as instructors, even though they didn't have the background. That's why we had to send them to the Air Force course. It was a, really a very outstanding group of people. Everybody was very competent professionally, and it was a real pleasure to serve with them. Except that, as I say, my morale was not very good at that point, because I was going through a really tough time trying to decide the best thing to do for my family and for me.

Paul Stillwell: Were you discussing this with your wife at the same time?

Admiral Lawrence: Oh, yes, yes. And she was a very, very fine person. Her father, as I say, was a career naval aviator, but he had been shot down in World War II and was missing in action for a while. He had to evade capture by the Japanese in the Philippines. Fortunately, he was kept by the guerrillas. So, because of her World War II experience, she just was not completely comfortable about what I was doing. I guess many wives are that way. I was very sensitive to her feelings, but the separation from family was the thing that really was a driving factor. I just didn't feel that I wanted to have a career where I'd have such minimal time with my children.

The other thing is that in my Patuxent years, I really developed this tremendous interest in the technical aspects of aircraft testing and development. I really loved that very much. I felt that I would like to get out of the Navy and get deeply involved and be very highly specialized in aircraft design and engineering development. But finally, after a lot of soul-searching, I realized that I couldn't leave the Navy. I couldn't step across that threshold. Call it patriotism or a sense of responsibility to people like Admiral Moorer and Admiral Anderson, so I said, "Well, I'll give it a try in the surface Navy"—even though that wasn't really what I wanted.

Paul Stillwell: It was sort of a compromise position.

Admiral Lawrence: Yes, it was a compromise. But I was accepted very warmly by the surface guys, because there was a real shortage of surface officers in that time frame. They were eager and happy for me to go in and be the navigator of this cruiser.[*] I really wanted to be the operations officer on a destroyer, but they said there was no way, because that was such a plum job for the surface guys.

Paul Stillwell: Did they harbor any of these latent animosities toward brown shoes?[†]

Admiral Lawrence: No, no, I was pretty warmly received.[‡] My first skipper was Captain Bennett, who later on retired as a vice admiral.[§] He was one of the real premier destroyer sailors in the Navy. The XO had just come from command of a destroyer—a guy named Galvani, who later made captain.[**] I had a very good rapport with them.

Then our second commanding officer was Captain Tom Kimmel, who was a submariner.[††] His father was Admiral Husband Kimmel of Pearl Harbor fame.[‡‡]

Paul Stillwell: The son lives here in the Providence area.

Admiral Lawrence: He and I are working together to get his father posthumously promoted to four stars, which I think we're going to be able to achieve.

I have to say that I really, thoroughly enjoyed my time as the navigator of a ship, because I love being up on the bridge and tactical operations and that sort of thing. That

---

[*] USS *Newport News* (CA-148), a *Des Moines*-class heavy cruiser, was commissioned 29 January 1949. She had a standard displacement of 17,255 tons, full-load displacement of 20,980 tons, was 717 feet long, 76 feet in the beam, and had a maximum draft of 27 feet. Her top speed was 33 knots. She was armed with nine 8-inch main battery guns and twelve 5-inch dual-purpose guns.

[†] In the early days of naval aviation, the aviators wore brown shoes with their khaki uniforms and green uniforms. They thus acquired the nickname "brown shoes" to distinguish them from the traditional surface ship officers, who are known as "black shoes."

[‡] Lawrence reported aboard in June 1961.

[§] Captain Fred G. Bennett, USN, served as commanding officer of the heavy cruiser *Newport News* (CA-148) from 15 July 1960 to 17 July 1961.

[**] Commander Amedeo H. Galvani, USN.

[††] Captain Thomas K. Kimmel, USN, commanded the *Newport News* from 17 July 1961 to 13 July 1962.

[‡‡] Admiral Husband E. Kimmel, USN, was Commander in Chief Pacific Fleet from 1 February 1941 until he was relieved of command on 17 December in the wake of the attack earlier in the month. He was essentially forced to retire in early 1942 as a two-star admiral, his permanent rank. Subsequent attempts to restore his four-star rank have been unsuccessful.

really appealed to me. I came in there in the late spring of 1961. We were immediately preparing to go on a Mediterranean cruise.* I went over on the deployment and got experience on all of the most demanding aspects of being a navigator.

Paul Stillwell: Still family separation, though.

Admiral Lawrence: Yes, I know, but I realized that you just had to accept that as part of the profession.

But that job was not completely satisfying to me. I had all of the aviator instincts, I guess, and it was just too slow a pace for me. Although I learned a lot and I enjoyed what I was doing, it was just not the same life. I guess I'd grown used to the risk and the challenge of aviation. I talked to my wife, and I said, "Look, this is not what I want to do." She, of course, had matured a lot by that time, and I could see that aviation was getting safer. We were going into the angled-deck carriers, and other features were being put into aviation to make it safer. So she gave me the indications that she could handle this well. It was just an unusual thing that here, her father had been a career naval aviator, her husband was, but both she and her mother were very squeamish about flying. You could never, to this day, get her mother into a commercial airplane. She had to live with that all those years.

Paul Stillwell: Had she known that you were going into aviation when you got married?

Admiral Lawrence: Oh, yes. Oh, sure.

Paul Stillwell: But the reality of it, I guess, was even stronger.

Admiral Lawrence: That's right. But, as I say, I'd had some real close calls in those early years. I don't know whether you ever read the book by Tom Wolfe, *The Right Stuff*.

---

* The ship departed Norfolk for the Mediterranean on 3 August 1961.

Paul Stillwell: Oh, yes.

Admiral Lawrence: See, that was about the years we were at Patuxent, and we went to a hell of a lot of funerals.

Paul Stillwell: Well, in a way it's harder for the person who stays behind.

Admiral Lawrence: Yes.

Paul Stillwell: Because the person who's taking the risk knows exactly what he's facing.

Admiral Lawrence: And you just lived with it in those days. About once every couple of months at Pax River in those days somebody got killed. I think, as a wife, as opposed to being a daughter, it's tougher for you, although I knew that World War II had been tough on her and her mother. But she and I talked it over, and so I sent a letter in to the Bureau of Personnel, just laid it all out, explained exactly what happened. They took me back, because I'd only been away a little over a year.

They sent me to VF-14 down at Cecil, which was the third squadron to get the F4H, but I got there before we were due to bring the F4H in.* They sent me to that squadron purposely to help them transition to the F4H. I had to go over and spend part of a Med cruise in VF-14, so I had the distinction of making one of the last Demon deployments of that squadron. That made me appreciate the F4H all that much more after flying the Demon, a single-place airplane with much lower performance.

Paul Stillwell: I'd be interested in your observations comparing surface officers and aviators, because you are better qualified than most to make a comparison.

Admiral Lawrence: Yes. Well, they have very fine, wonderful officers in the surface Navy. It's just a slower pace. I guess what I really missed in the surface Navy was that you just didn't seem to have the same excitement and challenge that you do in aviation.

---
* Cecil Field is part of Naval Air Station Jacksonville, Florida.

Out of those years in a fighter squadron at Moffett and being a test pilot, I'd gotten used to being out there on the edge, and I really got bored in the surface Navy. There are these long periods of boredom, of not very much excitement.

Paul Stillwell: The surface people didn't miss it because they'd never had it.

Admiral Lawrence: That's right, that's right. And I missed it, because I knew what it was like. I just told my wife, "Look, if I'm going to do this as a career, which I think is the right thing to do, I just have to go back in aviation." But that time in the surface Navy was immensely valuable to me.

Paul Stillwell: In what ways?

Admiral Lawrence: Well, it taught me a lot about surface ship operations that would have been hard for me to learn otherwise. I really learned navigation and ship handling.

Paul Stillwell: How much did the skippers let you handle it?

Admiral Lawrence: A tremendous amount. Within my first few days on board, Captain Bennett said, "You're going to make the next fueling approach."

I said, "Well, you know, sir, although I got qualified as officer of the deck on a carrier, I have not had a lot of ship handling."

He said, "Don't worry, you'll do it." So we came around in *Newport News*, which was really the Cadillac of ships in terms of its power plant. It was just a big destroyer; I think it displaced about 18,000 tons. He said, "We make all of our fueling approaches at 25 knots, which is full speed. There's a guy standing up there on the forecastle with a flag, and when he passes a point where you're supposed to go all back full, he'll drop that flag."

So I conned the ship around, and I got it lined up where I thought it was about the right distance abeam. He said, "Yeah, that looks okay."

I went in, the guy dropped the flag, and I just said, "All back full."

Then he said, "Okay, when you see yourself settling into position, where you're right opposite the proper point on the ship there, just say, 'Go all ahead standard.'" Just like an obedient officer, I did everything he told me and, gosh, the thing fell into place. It was just sheer luck.

Paul Stillwell: Well, there's more to it than luck, I think.

Admiral Lawrence: Well, of course, in aviation, you really develop an appreciation for relative motion. An aviator usually is a good ship handler, because you see relative motion so much in flying airplanes. So you can judge distances very well from aviation experience. So ship handling was a very natural thing to me.

Captain Bennett's predecessor had been Admiral John Victor Smith, whose father was General Howling Mad Smith of World War II fame.[*] They were still talking about John Victor Smith when I came on the ship.

Paul Stillwell: What were they saying about him?

Admiral Lawrence: Well, that he was really a tough, tough taskmaster. All the young officers were talking about him. Bennett was a tough taskmaster, too, but not like John Victor Smith. But he was a very fine, destroyer-trained officer, great tactical sense, and really knew how to run the ship from the bridge. Captain Kimmel had grown up in the submarine force, so he didn't have as good a background in the tactics, but he was a very fine skipper.

Paul Stillwell: What specifically do you recall about him?

Admiral Lawrence: Well, he knew his stuff; there wasn't any area where he lacked anything. He just didn't have the detailed knowledge of, for example, destroyer screens,

---

[*] Captain John Victor Smith, USN, commanded the *Newport News* from 18 July 1959 to 15 July 1960. The oral history of Smith, who retired as a vice admiral, is in the Naval Institute collection. His father, Lieutenant General Holland M. Smith, USMC, commanded the landing forces in several amphibious assaults in the Pacific during World War II.

and how you change station in a formation or disposition. Captain Bennett would hear a tactical order, even though it was given from the signal book, and he knew the signal right away. He'd do the maneuvering board solution in his head, and he would tell the conning officer the new course: "Okay, it's going to be 120."* So the conning officer turned to 120, and he would do the maneuvering board solution, and it might come out to 122 or something like that.

Captain Kimmel just didn't have that experience in close-steaming-type of fleet operations, but he knew seamanship. He'd been CO of a submarine, CO of a submarine division. So he knew practical seamanship and how to run the ship and be a commanding officer of a ship. But he just didn't have the broad surface tactical background that Captain Bennett had.

Paul Stillwell: How was the *Newport News* used tactically at that time?

Admiral Lawrence: Well, we were the last gun cruiser. We had automatic 8-inch guns, which were very rare in the naval forces of the world. They were automatic in the sense that the shell was brought up in the hoist and automatically loaded, as opposed to a battleship, which is a manual operation, and the powder is separate from the projectile.

Paul Stillwell: And the shell case was ejected underneath the barrel in the *Newport News*.

Admiral Lawrence: Yes. So, we were used primarily in a gunfire support role for amphibious landings. We would be involved very much in those. But we also had an air-defense capability as well. We had the 5-inch guns, and 40 millimeters, and the ship had a pretty effective CIC team.†

---

* A maneuvering board is a sheet of paper containing a compass rose, concentric circles, and logarithmic scales. It is used for working out relative motion problems for ships that are maneuvering.
† CIC – combat information center. By using ranges and bearings taken from a radar scope, the CIC team can develop fixes and plot the ship's course, either as a backup to the visual navigation or as a replacement for it.

Paul Stillwell: Did you practice in surface engagements against other ships?

Admiral Lawrence: Yes, we certainly were prepared for that role, and we did quite a bit of firing against sleds out on the gunnery range off Norfolk—what they call Virginia Capes operating area. We did some of that over in the Med, although the capability to do that in the Med is fairly limited. We did a fair amount of firing with our 5-inch guns against sleeves flown by airplanes.

Paul Stillwell: Had the *Newport News* yet gotten that flagship modification at that point?

Admiral Lawrence: No. We went over to the Med in August 1961, and then about November we were told that we would have to terminate our cruise, come back to arrive just before Christmas. Then we would be converted to become the flagship of the Second Fleet, because the *Northampton* was being converted to the alternate command element.[*]

So we had to come back across the Atlantic in December at fairly high speed. We had to make a 17-knot SOA.[†] We had to go rhumb line, which brought us up to fairly high north latitude, where the weather was pretty rough.[‡] We went through several days of that, where we simply couldn't sit down in the water, because we were being thrown around so much. I remember Captain Kimmel had to be up on the bridge virtually around the clock, because he would watch the waves and try to avoid taking a wave that could really do some damage to the superstructure. He had to really, very carefully conn that ship in that weather situation. But we had had an absolute imperative of a 17-knot SOA levied on us.

Paul Stillwell: That kind of speed doesn't help you in those seas either.

---

[*] USS *Northampton* (CLC-1), a one-of-kind command ship, was commissioned 7 March 1953. She had a standard displacement of 12,320 tons, was 677 feet long, and 70 feet in the beam, and had a mean draft of 19 feet. Her top speed was 33 knots. In the early 1960s she was reclassified CC-1 and given the role as a seagoing equivalent of Air Force One as an alternate command post for the President.

[†] SOA – speed of advance.

[‡] A rhumb line is a projection of a ship's course that intersects all lines of longitude at the same angle. At higher latitudes it provides the shortest distance between two points.

Admiral Lawrence: I know. We took a pretty good pounding, but we made it back okay and went through the modification to become the Second Fleet flagship.* They put in a lot of office space up in the superstructure and did a very fine job. It enhanced the ship significantly because of all the topside office space that they put in there.

Paul Stillwell: I spent a month on board the *Newport News* in 1974 on the Second Fleet staff, and I think that topside weight increased the rolling tendency.

Admiral Lawrence: I'm sure it did; I'm sure it really did. I know the metacentric height had to change.† That mod was done pretty rapidly. As the navigator, I really benefited from that, because I was able to get some enhancements, some of the spaces under my control, on the justification it was necessary to accommodate the larger flag staff. So we had all that done over at the shipyard in Portsmouth.‡

Paul Stillwell: You finally got some quality time with your family.

Admiral Lawrence: Yes, that was nice. And then we embarked the Second Fleet staff. We had previously had a cruiser division staff on board, and it was very small. The commander of Cruiser Division Two was a Rear Admiral Barney Sieglaff.§ Barney had been a big submarine hero from World War II. He was really a very fine person, and I enjoyed talking to him, because, as a navigator on a cruiser, you also did the navigation for the flag staff. They relied on you to go where they needed to go. So I got to know Admiral Sieglaff and his chief of staff and all his officers very well.

We did some interesting operations in the Med, varied operations, which I enjoyed. I remember one amphibious exercise that we did was over in the eastern

---

* The *Newport News* got back to her homeport of Norfolk on 18 December 1961 and on 20 December entered the Norfolk Naval Shipyard, Portsmouth, Virginia.
† Metacentric height is the distance between a ship's center of gravity and her metacenter; the greater the metacentric height, the greater the ship's stability.
‡ The cruiser completed the modernization and left the shipyard on 3 April 1962.
§ Rear Admiral William Bernard Sieglaff, USN, served as Commander Cruiser Division Two from 7 December 1960 to 7 December 1961.

Mediterranean at the same place as the landing at Gallipoli in World War I.* So that was interesting. And we went into some interesting ports. We went into Izmir, Turkey, which I'd never been into. I've been up to Istanbul, so I got to see a port that I'd never been to in the Med before.

When the Second Fleet staff came aboard, I learned even more, because, although we had a fleet commander on board, he didn't exercise tactical command. We were right in the center of fleet operations, and we did some very interesting things.

Paul Stillwell: What do you recall?

Admiral Lawrence: In the spring of 1962, we put on a big fleet demonstration for John F. Kennedy.† It was off of the North Carolina area. We did an amphibious landing at Onslow Beach, near Camp Lejeune, and we also had some demonstrations at sea, including an air demonstration off one of the carriers. That was interesting because we went through a full rehearsal and went back to Norfolk and then came out and did the real thing, because they really wanted to do the right thing by President Kennedy.

Paul Stillwell: Did he come aboard your ship?

Admiral Lawrence: No, he rode, I think, the carrier. That was going to be his primary vantage point. But, anyway, I had become pretty close to Captain Kimmel at that time. He admired the way I ran the ship tactically and really kept him abreast of what we were supposed to do, including the operations officer, operations orders, training, and so forth. He asked me to go with him to a critique of the rehearsal for this demonstration for President Kennedy. Admiral Dennison, who was Commander in Chief Atlantic Fleet, ran

---

* The Gallipoli Peninsula is a narrow tongue of land that extends southwest from the south coast of Turkey. It was the scene of an ill-fated amphibious landing by Allied troops, mainly Anzacs, on 25 April 1915. The campaign, which also included naval bombardment of Dardanelles forts, was ultimately unsuccessful. The last Allied troops withdrew in January 1916.
† John F. Kennedy served as President of the United States from 20 January 1961 until he was assassinated on 22 November 1963.

it.* So here I was, a lieutenant commander, and I was in there with all these flag officers. I was amazed at the things they were talking about it at this briefing, like what type of a sound system to have in President Kennedy's quarters?

I said, "Well, sir, there's no phonograph." They didn't have stereos in those days, I guess.

He said, "Get one!" [Laughter]

They were talking about things like some of the amenities in his stateroom, and I said, "My gosh, is this what flag officers worry about?"

But, also, there were some really tough things said about how the rehearsal went, because that had not all gone well. One of the things they had us do was to get into a column of ships at night, and I can't remember why in the world we did so.

Paul Stillwell: That was a pre-World War II formation.

Admiral Lawrence: Yes, but part of this was that they passed in review for President Kennedy. But I remember really being right there with Captain Kimmel as we were moving into a column formation at night and how really tricky that was. We had to watch our distance, and it took some pretty adroit ship handling. That demonstration for President Kennedy in the spring was one of the most significant things we did.

Paul Stillwell: Who was the flag officer embarked on the *Newport News*?

Admiral Lawrence: Vice Admiral John McNay Taylor was Commander U.S. Second Fleet.† The officer in tactical command was a carrier division commander, Rear Admiral Reynold D. Hogle, who was called Admiral Toby Hogle. I think he was out of the Naval Academy class of '29. So that was quite interesting.

After that we had just routine fleet operations, and later on in the fall they were

---

* Admiral Robert L. Dennison, USN, served as Supreme Allied Commander Atlantic, Commander in Chief Atlantic, and Commander in Chief Atlantic Fleet from 28 February 1960 to 30 April 1963. His oral history is in the Naval Institute collection.
† Vice Admiral John McNay Taylor, USN, commanded the Second Fleet from September 1961 to October 1962.

going to go up for a NATO exercise that Commander Second Fleet would really be running. I did all the preparation and planning, getting the charts ready to go up to those northern European ports, although I detached in July when we made a trip up to the port of Halifax. I remember worrying about going up to Halifax, because the incidence of fog is very high there. We didn't look forward to making a radar approach into Halifax.

Paul Stillwell: There was a famous collision there in World War I.[*]

Admiral Lawrence: Yes. I just didn't look forward to having to radar navigate, because any navigator likes to do it visually. The quartermasters who work for you are the ones who get out there on the alidades and take the sights.[†] It's a navigator-quartermaster evolution to do piloting. When you get into a radar nav situation, you have to rely on the CIC guys, but they don't work for you. So that's more of a coordination problem. Anyway, it turned out to be a beautiful, clear day when we went into Halifax.

In that job I learned a lot about ship handling and seamanship. I had to navigate into various ports and encountered some pretty demanding situations, because part of the previous cruise over there in the Med was in the winter. I remember that Rear Admiral Ellis was our cardiv commander—CTF-60, we called him.[‡] I could see what they called this mistral-wind situation. You have this situation in the Med, as the winter months approach, where you can get very high pressure over the continent. That differential in pressure between the air over the continent and what exists down in the Mediterranean causes a very strong northwesterly wind, which they call the mistral. Because the Med is just a big lake, it doesn't have the reach that you have out in the ocean; big waves can build up, and they can really be very damaging to ships.

---

[*] On 6 December 1917, during World War I, the French cargo ship *Mont Blanc*, loaded with munitions, collided with the Norwegian freighter *Imo* at Halifax, Nova Scotia, Canada. The collision resulted in a horrendous collision and fires that devastated the city and caused the deaths of some 2,000 people and injuries to an additional 9,000.

[†] An alidade is a circular device that fits over the top of a gyrocompass repeater and enables one to ascertain the bearing to a point on land. The bearings to a number of points ashore, and where the lines of position intersect is the ship's position at the time the bearings are taken.

[‡] Rear Admiral William E. Ellis, USN, served as Commander Carrier Division Two, 1961-62. While deployed to the Mediterranean, his operational title was Commander Task Force 60, the Sixth Fleet Carrier Striking Force.

We'd been caught in a mistral wind situation back when I was on the *Saratoga* with Admiral Moorer, so I knew somewhat about these mistral winds and the problem they caused for ships over in the western Med, between Sicily and Spain and that area. So when I saw this mistral wind situation developing, I tried, through Captain Kimmel, to get this warning over to the OTC, Rear Admiral Bill Ellis, who was in the carrier.* They didn't pick up on it, so we got caught in a hell of a rough sea, and one of the oilers lost a seaman. The seas were so high and so rough that the oiler couldn't turn around to try to find him. I really faulted the carrier division commander for not more timely action in responding to the mistral winds coming up. I felt we knew about it about six or eight hours ahead, and he could have had a lot of ships steam and get in the lee. But he and his staff didn't perceive this.

So all those experiences just go into your data bank and make you a lot more competent in the future. But, as I say, as a flag officer and fleet commander, having had that a little over a year of being a ship's navigator really was money in the bank. I learned a lot that the average aviator doesn't really pick up.

Paul Stillwell: Did you have any joint operations with NATO nations?

Admiral Lawrence: Yes, we had a fair amount of interface with, principally, the Royal Navy officers, and some with the French and the Italians, but primarily Brits. When I was with Admiral Moorer, I had some interface with the Germans.

Paul Stillwell: The British always have a very high reputation for their seamanship.

Admiral Lawrence: Oh, yes, they're the real pros, and unfortunately their navy has really been cut back. But even though it's small, they're still probably the most professional naval officers in the world. That tradition is very deeply ingrained in them.

Paul Stillwell: Were you able to use your aviator knowledge in that job?

---

* Ellis was on board the carrier *Independence* (CVA-62).

Admiral Lawrence: Oh, yes, I really did. I could tell them a lot, because they did a fair amount of air controlling from the cruiser. That cruiser division staff would serve as what they called the air defense commander. They used to come to me all the time and talk to me about fighter capabilities and that sort of thing.

So, yes, as an aviator, I was very valuable to them, teaching them a lot about aviation. I've often advocated taking aviators and giving them jobs on surface ships. It's good for the aviators; it's good for the ships. They never have made that a standard practice, although we will put aviators now on staffs that we previously did not. But, anyway, I had very good feelings about serving on that cruiser, really, professionally rewarding; I learned a lot. But after a year I was ready to go back to aviation.

Paul Stillwell: How sophisticated was electronic warfare in that era?

Admiral Lawrence: Very, very unsophisticated. We really had no jamming capability. No one had even thought about chaff, those sorts of capabilities.[*] We hadn't even really seriously thought about ASMs, the air-to-surface missiles from Soviet bombers. In those days the Soviet naval threat was very remote, because you just didn't see Soviet ships around you much in the early '60s. They just didn't operate much at sea.

Paul Stillwell: What do you remember about working with the enlisted men in the *Newport News*?

Admiral Lawrence: I had a wonderful senior chief quartermaster, Johnny Johnson, and he was really great.[†] He and I were very close. He was the old school Navy; boy, he ran those quartermasters with an iron hand. But most quartermasters are really fine kids. They're screened to go in that, and you put a lot of responsibility on them. They maintained the rough log, called the quartermaster's notebook. The officer of the deck would use that to write his own log, which, I guess, they don't do anymore. And the quartermasters had to know celestial navigation. I became very close to quartermasters.

---

[*] Chaff is composed of metal strips that are launched to deceive enemy radars.
[†] Quartermaster is a Navy enlisted rating that specializes in navigation.

And I developed a great respect—not only there but from previous times—for those ratings like the boatswain's mates and the gunner's mates. The men in those surface ratings are really solid guys. They're different from the airdales in a lot of ways. They usually don't have as high GCT scores and all that, but I love boatswain's mates.[*] They're just kind of a special breed.

Paul Stillwell: They're the bedrock of the Navy culture.

Admiral Lawrence: That's right. But I found, as a navigator, when I was running the bridge, that anything that I had as navigator to announce on the 1MC, that I just couldn't say, "Hey, boats, put this word out."[†] Because you never knew what was going to come out. [Chuckle] So I made a policy that said, "Look, anything that's said over the 1MC, write it out and make sure the boatswain's mate understands what you're giving him." Very few of the boatswain's mates had a high school education. But I've always really enjoyed interfacing with enlisted men. Leadership has always been my principal interest. On a surface ship, you have some advantages you don't have in aviation, because you are thrown in with enlisted men 24 hours a day. In aviation, you go off and away. Just by the nature of what you do in aviation, you can't get as close to enlisted men as you can on a surface ship. So that's what I really enjoyed about the surface Navy.

Paul Stillwell: How much did you learn about shore bombardment in that time?

Admiral Lawrence: Well, quite a bit. I really had to learn a lot about the procedural aspects of it, because, as the navigator, you had to position the ship properly. We maintained all the grid maps right there on the bridge. Of course, the captain would be right there on the bridge. The gunnery officer had a battle station in fire control, but he would often come down to the bridge and talk to the captain. So I had to really know exactly what we were doing to be able to support them navigationally.

---

[*] GCT – general classification test, a part of the battery of aptitude tests administered to Navy recruits.
[†] 1MC was the official designation for the ship's general announcing system.

I remember one time we were firing some type of competitive exercise. We were going to do a whole series of things, and we were firing on a sled as the target. Vice Admiral John McNay Taylor, who was a surface officer, came down on the bridge one time. I had been really busy with other aspects of navigation, so I hadn't been following this competitive exercise too closely. I didn't have it all in my head. He came up and asked me how things were going, and I didn't give him a quick answer. Boy, he got kind of hot under the collar, turned to the captain, and said, "It appears your navigator is not aware of what's going up here." But Captain Kimmel was a great guy, and he handled that in good style. Taylor was the old-school naval officer, boy, very stern. He never smiled very much. I was a little bit embarrassed. After that I really kept abreast of what the gunners were doing.

Paul Stillwell: Anything else you remember about Admiral Taylor?

Admiral Lawrence: Well, it just clearly came across to all of us on the ship that he was a stern taskmaster, and that you had best not get close to the flag bridge or the flag quarters. [Chuckle] So the junior officers and the sailors very carefully avoided going anywhere near the flag area.

Paul Stillwell: How much interaction was there between the fleet staff and the ship's officers?

Admiral Lawrence: Not as much as it had been when we had a cruiser division staff. For example, as a navigator, I never really interfaced very much, because they were never the OTC, so they really didn't have to keep a good navigational picture. So it was not as close a relationship as it had previously been. They were mostly planners and big-picture types. They weren't operational guys. We very rarely saw Admiral Taylor, so the fact that he came down to visit us on the bridge one time really was quite a surprise.

Paul Stillwell: The very possibility of his arrival would keep you on your toes.

Admiral Lawrence: Yes, that's right.

I can't think of anything else on that cruise of interest. And this might be a good break point, because I have to go to a Rotary dinner tonight, but I did bring my calendar if you want to talk about the next interview.

Interview Number 6 with Vice Admiral William P. Lawrence, U.S. Navy (Retired)
Place: U.S. Naval Institute, Annapolis, Maryland
Date: Wednesday, 31 October 1990

Paul Stillwell: Admiral, today we're ready to get you back into naval aviation and into squadron VF-14 after your time in the *Newport News*.

Admiral Lawrence: Well, after I completed that tour in *Newport News*, I expressed a desire to come back into naval aviation, which the Navy approved. They decided to send me to VF-14, which was scheduled to be the third squadron to get the F-4 Phantom airplane.[*] The first squadron had been VF-74, and the second was VF-102, which were both Oceana squadrons. Because I had flown the F-4 and had been involved with it at Patuxent in the testing world and then had been involved with it in the fleet introduction program, they felt this was where I could probably serve most effectively.

I joined the squadron in about November of 1962, while it was still flying the F3H Demon. We were scheduled to transition to the F-4 the following spring. An interesting thing happened to me when I was going through my replacement squadron training in VF-101 down in Key West. The Cuban Missile Crisis occurred, and so all of us there were very much aware, because Key West was such a key base.[†] We simply had to shut down our training in VF-101, because the base was so totally committed to supporting the Cuban contingency. A large number of Air Force and Navy airplanes were brought into the Naval Air Station Key West at Boca Chica. They basically put this air station into a gridlock situation. I remember some Air Force F-104 squadrons came in there. We brought VF-74, the first F-4 squadron down there, and we brought in several A-4s.[‡]

---

[*] On 18 September 1962, while Lawrence was in training before reporting to Fighter Squadron 14, The McDonnell Douglas Phantom II was redesignated from F4H to F-4. This was part of a U.S. tri-service designation system to standardize aircraft designators within the Defense Department. It was based on the Air Force system then current and did away with the previous Navy-Marine Corps-Coast Guard nomenclature system.

[†] The Cuban Missile Crisis was triggered in mid-October 1962, when a U.S. reconnaissance plane photographed a Soviet nuclear missile site in Cuba and the presence of Soviet bombers. On 22 October President John F. Kennedy went on national television to announce a naval quarantine of Cuba, to be implemented on 24 October. On 28 October Premier Nikita Khrushchev of the Soviet Union notified President Kennedy that he was ordering the withdrawal of Soviet bombers and missiles from Cuba.

[‡] The A-4 Skyhawk was a nuclear-capable attack plane.

Paul Stillwell: Probably some photo recon planes too.

Admiral Lawrence: As I recall, the photo recon planes were flying out of Homestead, up near Miami.* Most of our airplanes at Key West were the tactical-type airplanes—ground attack as well as the air-to-air fighters.

They set up a kind of a command center there at Key West, and I went up and volunteered my services, since our training had come to a halt. I helped them basically in keeping track of forces. But then they made a decision to send a detachment of the VF-101 airplanes up to Cecil Field and finish our training there.† The only real training that we had left was to go out and do carrier qualifications on board the *Antietam*.

But it was kind of interesting to be that close to the Cuban Missile Crisis and observe all the actions that were taken in the very massive, rapid deployment of U.S. forces into Florida: Air Force, Army, and Navy. We really thought there was a very strong likelihood we were going to go to war. Everybody had that kind of a perspective.

Paul Stillwell: What are you recollections of that time in the command center?

Admiral Lawrence: Well, the basic thing the command center was trying to do there at Key West was to maintaining the status of U.S. forces, and trying to develop the intelligence capability to determine what our enemy forces were doing. Really, the larger effort was being done up at CinCLant in Norfolk, and maybe up at MacDill Air Force Base.‡ That was a center of activity. But I don't think they ever developed a very advanced command center capability at Key West, other than just very local tracking of forces. But I did that for only a few days, and then we were sent up to Cecil Field to continue our training up there.

Paul Stillwell: What do you recall about the deployment that you made with the Demons

---

* Homestead Air Force Base, since renamed the Homestead Air Reserve Base, was six miles east northeast of Homestead, Florida.
† Fighter Squadron 101, then as previously, was the training squadron for the F-4. Cecil Field is part of Naval Air Station Jacksonville, Florida.
‡ MacDill Air Force Base is near Tampa, Florida.

before you made the transition?

Admiral Lawrence: Well, it was interesting. I had flown the Demon only a little bit at Patuxent River back in my test pilot years. But I really became aware, when we got out aboard the *Franklin D. Roosevelt*, what a limited capability that airplane had in terms of speed, range, endurance.* You look at the development of the Demon; it turned out to be much heavier airplane, and it was out of balance with the thrust of the J71 Allison engine. You may recall the debacle of the F3H-1 that had an engine that just couldn't get it into the air, and they had to basically terminate the F3H-1 program. It had a Westinghouse engine.† They tell the embarrassing story of having to barge the F3H-1s down the Mississippi River to send them to museums and air stations to become monuments. But the J71 engine had had so many problems that it had progressive thrust reductions as one means of solving some of the engine problems. So the airplane was very much under thrust. Every catapult shot had to be done at full afterburner. You just didn't have the endurance to really use the full performance potential of the airplane.

One thing, for example, when you went up at night, carrier operations were still very demanding and very tenuous. So you'd fly the whole flight at maximum endurance. You wouldn't even consider going into afterburner. So your capability to do a real air-defense mission was very much limited.

I was maintenance officer of VF-14. When I took over the job from my predecessor, our squadron was having terrible maintenance problems, because the Demon at that time was beginning to be an old airplane. It had been in the fleet for almost ten years. It had hydraulic leaks, and we were having a lot of communication systems failures. So I really had to take a round turn on our whole maintenance organization to get the availability of that airplane improved.‡ One thing I identified from the sources of

---

* USS *Franklin D. Roosevelt*, a *Midway*-class aircraft carrier, was commissioned as CVB-42 on 27 October 1945. She was reclassified CVA-42 on 1 October 1952 and extensively modernized from 1954 to 1956. Among other changes, she received an enclosed hurricane bow and angled flight deck. Following the modernization she was 974 feet long, 110 feet in the beam, extreme flight deck width of 210 feet, maximum draft of 36 feet, full-load displacement of 62,000 tons, and rated speed of 33 knots. She could accommodate 70-plus aircraft.
† The F3H-1 initially had the Westinghouse J40-WE-22 jet engine.
‡ In nautical phraseology, taking a round turn means putting two loops of mooring line over a bitt or bollard, thus restraining the ship. In a figurative sense it means restraining unwanted behavior.

our problems is that we would go into an in-port visit for about a week or so, and the airplane wouldn't be turned up. All the seals in the hydraulic systems would dry out, and we would have very massive hydraulic leaks. So the first day of flying at sea we'd lose all sorts of flights because of these hydraulic leaks. So I came to the conclusion that we had to turn up the airplane every day in port to keep the hydraulic seals from drying out. I presented this program to our commanding officer, Commander Cal Buck, and he said, "You're right. Do it."[*]

Of course, that was very unpopular with the pilots who had to get up in the morning all hung over and go up on the flight deck and turn up these airplanes. The air officer on the carrier wasn't all that pleased with this, because sitting in the harbor at Cannes on the French Riviera, with these jets going, didn't make you very popular with the tourists. But, anyway, I talked to the ship's air officer. He was Commander Forbes, out of the Naval Academy class of '45, now a retired vice admiral.[†] I said, "Look, if you want these Demons to fly, we're going to have to turn them up." I kept trying to convince him, and finally he bought it. Our air wing commander was Commander George Talley, out of the Naval Academy class of '44, also now a retired vice admiral, and he bought it.[‡] So that one act alone really helped our availability.

But over the period of that cruise, we went from being the squadron with the poorest availability to being the one with the best. We did so many other things, because we had some really fine maintenance personnel, and once we got them all pulling together we achieved results.

Paul Stillwell: Was there a way that the word of this could be spread farther so it wouldn't be just isolated to your squadron?

Admiral Lawrence: Well, this was commonly known in the Demon community. I think one reason our squadron was not turning up the airplanes in port was just because of complacency. We changed commanding officers at the time I came in. I think the

---

[*] Commander Clarence Carlton Buck Jr., USN, commanded the VF-14 Tophatters from December 1962 to January 1964.
[†] Commander Bernard B. Forbes Jr., USN. His oral history is in the Naval Institute collection.
[‡] Commander George C. Talley Jr., USN, Commander Carrier Air Group One.

preceding commanding officer just wasn't a dynamic person who insisted on maintaining a high state of readiness and availability. He was willing to accept not meeting all the scheduled sorties on our flight schedule. I'd gone through training down at Key West with the new commanding officer, we'd gotten to be very close. When I presented all these programs to him, he readily approved. We had some really fine maintenance personnel, and once we got them fired up and going in the right direction, we really improved the availability.

When I started flying in that squadron, a problem I saw immediately that we had to tackle was that we were having a lot of communication failures. We would lose our tacan, for example.* If you lose your tacan at night, that's an absolute emergency, because you can't locate the ship and you can't fly a night approach. The concept in those days was that you use your tacan to basically determine exactly where you should go to do what they call the marshal. That's where the airplanes were in a holding pattern. You'd use your tacan as a means of locating yourself, and then determining how you would fly your approach. You picked up radar only in the very final phases of your approach. We were having a large number of tacan failures, and we were having UHF radio failures. So I had to get the squadron avionics officer, Frank Taylor, who was an LDO, a very fine guy.† I said, "Look, we've got to square that problem away."

So we used our aviation electronic technicians who were responsible for the communication system. They took out every comm system in our airplanes and really basically overhauled them. Once we completed that over about a two-week period, we went the rest of our cruise without any significant communications problem. So I had to take a lot of measures like that, because the problems were indicative of just not strong leadership in the squadron, both at the top and in the maintenance department when I came in. But we ended up having a very successful cruise.

Paul Stillwell: This was before the Navy had really institutionalized some of these things with the planned maintenance system, wasn't it?

---

* Tacan – tactical aid to navigation, a homing signal broadcast by an aircraft carrier to aid returning aircraft in locating the ship.
† Lieutenant (junior grade) Frank Lee Taylor, USN. LDO – limited duty officer, a former enlisted man whose duties are limited to the area of his enlisted rating specialty.

Admiral Lawrence: Well, later on we developed what we called the Naval Aviation Maintenance System, where you had the three levels of maintenance: the organizational and the intermediate and then the depot level. We still didn't have an aircraft intermediate maintenance department on carriers. It was still called the V-6 division, I think. So squadrons did a lot of their own work that today is done in these intermediate maintenance departments, like avionics, testing radars, repair of the radars and communication systems. So we've really come a long way in our organizational concepts for maintenance. In those days it was still very much an individual squadron effort. If the squadron didn't have a good strong leader as the maintenance officer, or strong enlisted personnel, they really did not do well in terms of meeting the scheduled sorties.

But we really got that squadron turned around, and towards the last three months of that cruise, we were out-flying everybody in the air wing. We used to have these 36-hour strike-exes, they called them, where you would exercise the nuclear attack plan. Basically, you'd go against targets in Italy, sometimes over in Greece and Turkey if you were over in the eastern Med. You'd fly a simulated mission, like you would fly over the Soviet Union. Then, in addition to that, you'd have a very comprehensive air-defense exercise. You'd fly pretty steadily for 36 hours right around the clock. I remember in one of those, we set the sortie production rate for the entire task group in our squadron in flying around the clock.

Paul Stillwell: Earlier Commander Talley took the air group on board the *Enterprise* just for her shakedown.* What do you recall of him as air wing commander in your ship?

Admiral Lawrence: Well, I had known George Talley when he had been the skipper of VA-34 on *Saratoga*, an A4D squadron, back in 1959 and '60. Then he came back in '62 to be the commander of Air Group One on the *Roosevelt*. There was a different air group

---

* On 12 January 1962, the nuclear-powered aircraft carrier *Enterprise* (CVAN-65) got under way for her shakedown cruise following commissioning in November 1961. Talley took Carrier Air Group One aboard the ship to participate in the training. On 27 January, while flying an F8U-1 Crusader, Talley made the ship's first arrested landing and first catapult takeoff during fleet operations. There had previously been limited aircraft operations during sea trials.

on the *Enterprise* in the Mediterranean at that time. I know the F-4 squadron was VF-102.

Paul Stillwell: Well, Kent Lee had the air group when it made the first Med deployment.* Talley had it briefly before that just to get the ship shaken down.

Admiral Lawrence: They still had the first skipper of *Enterprise* in command in 1962.

Paul Stillwell: Yes, that was Captain DePoix.†

Admiral Lawrence: We were in the Med on that '62-63 cruise with the *Enterprise*.

Paul Stillwell: What do you recall of Talley?

Admiral Lawrence: Well, I have great admiration for him. He's a very competent aviator, real good leader, very people-oriented and outgoing guy. I really had very high regard for him from my observation of him earlier on the *Saratoga*.

Paul Stillwell: Well, he'd also been involved in that Joint Strategic Target Planning Staff at Omaha, so he had that additional background when he went into the Med.

Admiral Lawrence: Yes. See, when they established that Joint Strategic Target Planning Staff out there at Omaha, the Navy picked its very best people to send out there. Johnny Hyland, for example, went out there as a young flag officer. Then Jerry Miller was sent out there and George Talley.‡ Then Talley came back to command that air group after being out there at Omaha. He did a super job. I have always admired him. I was surprised that he seemed to retire prematurely, well before his peers. Often I've seen this

---

* Commander Kent L. Lee, USN, commanded Carrier Air Group Six, 1962-63. For details see the Naval Institute oral history of Lee, who retired as a vice admiral.

† Captain Vincent P. de Poix, USN, commanded the aircraft carrier *Enterprise* (CVAN-65) from the ship's commissioning on 25 November 1961 until 20 June 1963.

‡ Captain Gerald E. Miller, USN, was a Navy representative to Joint Strategic Target Planning Staff in 1960. The oral history of Miller, who retired as a vice admiral, is in the Naval Institute collection.

happen where a guy gets promoted early, as he was, that sometimes he gets his jobs and leaves before his peers come on. I guess he had two vice admiral jobs. He went out to be the Deputy CinCPacFlt. Then he came back to be OP-06. He retired in about '74 or so.[*]

Paul Stillwell: Beetle Forbes was a colorful character. What do you recall of him?

Admiral Lawrence: Well, he was a very good air officer on the *Roosevelt*, and really strong, tough, set high standards. As I say, when I went to him with this very unpopular plan to do these in-port turn-ups, he was smart enough to see that it made sense. He said, "Okay, we'll do it." And I know we were taking some criticism from the local communities, on the French Riviera there and down in Naples, and we also did it up in Livorno and places like that. But he was a very good air boss; he ran a very good flight deck. Yes, I've always admired Beetle Forbes quite a bit.

Paul Stillwell: Did it then fall to the captain or the admiral to go ashore and placate these communities?

Admiral Lawrence: That was above my pay grade. I didn't worry about that. All I wanted to do was get out the airplanes. But I suspect that the commanding officer probably had to do something along these lines. Since we didn't have an embarked flag officer, I think we were able to get away with some things that the flagship couldn't. The embarked flag was in the *Enterprise*, as I remember.

Paul Stillwell: John Hayward was in the *Enterprise*.

Admiral Lawrence: Chick Hayward, yes, was in the *Enterprise*.[†] He was Commander Carrier Division Two, as I recall.

---

[*] Vice Admiral George C. Talley Jr., USN, served as Deputy Chief of Naval Operations (Plans and Policy) from February 1973 to February 1975. He retired from active duty 1 March 1975.
[†] Rear Admiral John T. Hayward, USN, Commander Carrier Division Two.

Paul Stillwell: Well, that was pretty much a PR trip for the *Enterprise*, just to show off this new ship, and Hayward is very good at that.

Admiral Lawrence: Yes. I think they actually left the Med and went down around Africa. It was the all-nuclear task force, and they had the *Bainbridge*, and the *Long Beach*, and didn't they make an around-the-world trip?

Paul Stillwell: I don't know if it was that same time.

Admiral Lawrence: It seems to me that when we were with them in the Med that the Med period then was a part of their so-called around-the-world trip.*

I remember that one time I had to go over to the *Enterprise* to pick up an airplane they had brought over as a replacement airplane for us. So I got to see all my old friends, like Commander Jerry O'Rourke, who was the CO of VF-102, and Tim Wooldridge was in that squadron. They were all my friends from Patuxent River days. So I rode the *Enterprise* for a couple of days before I flew the airplane. In fact, I think that they came into the Med in the early part of 1963.† They were just coming in to have a brief period in the Med and then go out.

Paul Stillwell: How would you compare the *Franklin D. Roosevelt* as a ship with the *Essex* class you'd been in before, and the *Forrestal* class?

Admiral Lawrence: Well, it was certainly a more capable ship than the *Essex* class, because we had the third catapult, whereas the *Essex* had only two. Then it was more spacious than the *Essex* class. As I recall, it had a steel flight deck instead of the wood

---

* That cruise took place the following year. Operation Sea Orbit was an around-the-world cruise by the world's first nuclear-powered task force, which comprised the aircraft carrier *Enterprise* (CVAN-65), the cruiser *Long Beach* (CGN-9), and the frigate *Bainbridge* (DLGN-25). The cruise began 31 July 1964 when the ships transited through the Strait of Gibraltar from the Mediterranean into the Atlantic. The ships then proceeded around Africa and hits numerous ports. The cruise ended 3 October 1974, when the *Enterprise* and *Long Beach* arrived in Norfolk and the *Bainbridge* in Charleston. The commander of Nuclear Task Force One was Rear Admiral Bernard M. Strean, USN. See the Naval Institute oral history of Strean, who retired as a vice admiral.
† The *Enterprise* entered the Mediterranean on 16 February 1963.

flight deck. But it was not comparable in capability at all to the *Forrestal* class. And from a habitability perspective, it certainly didn't compare with the *Forrestal* class.

The other thing about the *Midway* class is that it was built with the kamikaze threat very much in mind, so it had a lot of damage control features, such as compartmentation that they didn't put into the *Forrestal* class. That excess compartmentation degraded habitability. You just killed yourself on that ship with the knee-knockers.* [Chuckle]

Paul Stillwell: Well, another thing I noticed was that it had low overheads too.

Admiral Lawrence: Low overheads. See, I made my first midshipman cruise on a sister ship, the *Coral Sea*, and I came back and made the Mediterranean deployment on the FDR. I came to the conclusion that I didn't want to be on those *Midway*-class carriers anymore, [chuckle] that the *Forrestal*-class ships were far more comfortable—and much larger flight deck. And four catapults really gave you much more capability to operate. The other big difference that I saw of the 85,000-ton carriers, opposed to the 60,000- to 65,000-ton that you have in the *Midway* was sea keeping. You could operate much more in heavy weather in the *Forrestal*, as compared to the *Midway* class. So I'm glad that we did go to the bigger class. And, of course, the *Nimitz* class is even an enhancement over the *Forrestal* class.†

Paul Stillwell: Anything you remember from the port visits other than antagonizing the locals?

Admiral Lawrence: Well, no, it was kind of uneventful; a winter Mediterranean cruise isn't the most desirable cruise. You spend a lot of time as the non-flagship carrier in Naples, for example. The flagship spends Christmas on the French Riviera; the

---

* "Knee knockers" is a slang term for hatch coamings that separate adjacent compartments. One has to lift the feet to step over the coaming into the next compartment.
† The aircraft carrier *Nimitz* (CVN-68), the first of her class, was commissioned 3 May 1975. She has a standard displacement of 81,600 tons, is 1,092 feet long, 134 feet in the beam, and an extreme width of 251 feet. Equipped with nuclear power, her top speed is 30-plus knots. She can accommodate approximately 90 aircraft.

non-flagship spends Christmas in Naples. Naples never greatly appealed to me as a port. So I didn't do a lot of things ashore. I did go back to Pompeii, which I have always enjoyed doing whenever I go into Naples.* But I've never been enthralled about the downtown part of Naples. But I did do some fun things up in Livorno. And I always enjoyed going to the museums and historic places in Florence. I don't even recall our going into the French Riviera. I'm sure we made one port visit there.

Paul Stillwell: Well, if you went to Cannes, you did.

Admiral Lawrence: For some reason, the flagship seemed to spend more time on the French Riviera than did other ships. I'm sure it had nothing to do with the admiral being embarked. [Laughter]

Paul Stillwell: What were the shortcomings of Naples?

Admiral Lawrence: Well, it's a dirty, congested city, and the telephone system doesn't work. And, of course, being the maintenance officer, I took advantage of a rework facility at the Naples municipal airport. They had a Navy rework facility, where we would do depot-level repairs on airplanes. So I had to fly some airplanes from our squadron that had been banged up on the carrier into that rework facility. It was always a hassle to get a taxicab and go there through the Naples traffic. So that was not a very pleasant experience. But I was so busy as maintenance officer on that cruise, trying to get the squadron really turned around, that I really didn't go much ashore.

I was very busy on that cruise, and we had some accidents too. We lost two pilots on that cruise, both off the catapult. So I got very deeply into trying to analyze what the problem was, because here was an airplane that had been in the fleet for over six years and was starting to develop a problem off the catapult. We found a problem with the holdback rings that the older airplanes used to use. Now we have the nose-wheel towing mechanism for catapulting most of our airplanes. The airplane taxis up, and the catapulting mechanism hooks into the nose wheel, and it pulls the nose wheel to catapult

---

* Pompeii is an ancient city about 15 miles southeast of Naples. It is near the volcano Mount Vesuvius.

the airplane. In the old days you had these fittings on the bottom of your airplane, and they put a heavy wire shuttle mechanism around those catapult fittings. Then you had a shuttle on the deck that this wire fit around. When the airplane was catapulted, you had a holdback ring that was a cylindrical shape with two flanges on each end. At a certain pressure, that holdback ring would sever it, and that was the way the catapulting worked.

Nobody was brilliant enough to think about just attaching to the nose wheel. This very heavy holdback cable would be attached to the deck. Then you'd have this holdback fitting that attached to the cable and to this holdback fitting in the airplane. For some reason, during that cruise, a disturbing phenomenon developed. When the airplane was brought under what they called tension, and that holdback cable straightened out, there was a twisting phenomenon that would roll these holdback tension bars out of the holdback fitting in the airplane. We had two airplanes on which that happened. One dribbled off the bow and the pilot was killed; the other guy went into the catwalk alongside the flight deck but survived.

We also lost an airplane on a night catapult shot. He flew into the water, ahead of the ship. In the wreckage debris after that crash, they found an airplane part still in the packing box that somehow was in that airplane, but we didn't determine how it could cause the crash.

Paul Stillwell: So this was the catapult mechanism, not that the plane was underpowered?

Admiral Lawrence: No, it was just the catapult mechanism. I was in charge of that investigation and did a comprehensive report and sent it back to the naval engineering facility at Philadelphia that had the cognizance over aircraft carrier-airplane compatibility. They sent a rep out there, and he couldn't determine why in the world, after six years, this unique problem was developing with these holdback tension bars being rotated out of the holdback fitting. So we had to take special measures to make sure that, when they took the tension on the airplane, that it was done more slowly so that wire would stretch without a twisting-type action that would roll the tension wire.

Paul Stillwell: It sure couldn't have done much for the peace of mind of those pilots until that was solved.

Admiral Lawrence: Yes, I remember how uncomfortable we all felt, particularly on a night catapult shot, because you knew that the flight deck people couldn't see as well. So it was not a happy cruise in all respects, because the weather was bad and the maintenance had been bad.

The other thing was that in 1962, night flying off an aircraft carrier was not a common, well-accepted practice. So every time we flew at night, there was a lot of excitement. The F8U airplane was still relatively new in the fleet, and that airplane was very poor at night. So every time the F8U pilots went out, it was just another aerial circus.

We had a really wonderful officer as the air operations officer, Commander Bud Nance, out of the Naval Academy class of '45.[*] He was one of my very favorite guys, really good friend. And his cool head, in being able to control those airplanes at night, probably averted quite a few accidents, because it was a very touch-and-go operation. We had the big A3D, the Skywarrior. I tell you, those were really a handful, operating those on the *Midway* decks. The dangers and the accident rate in naval aviation at that time were still pretty high—significantly higher than today.

But still, night flying was better than it had been on my first cruise out there on that old straight-deck carriers, just to be able to fly on the angled deck and make the descending approach, the glide slope was far better than doing the old level approaches.

Paul Stillwell: Anything you recall about the atmosphere in the ready room in that squadron?

Admiral Lawrence: Well, we were a good-spirited squadron. I had some wonderful young people. That was when I really first became aware of the healthy aspects of having a mix of young officers together from the Naval Academy, NROTC, and the Aviation Officer Candidate program. Because you got the interface and the cross-

---

[*] Commander James W. Nance, USN.

fertilization, and the different views of a kid who's gone to an Ivy League school or a big state school, as compared to the Naval Academy. It knocked some of the Naval Academy guys out of their arrogant posture, and it educated some of these kids from the Ivy League schools. We had some very fine NROTC kids along with the Naval Academy kids, and they were always arguing with each other about this and that.

The morale of the squadron was good, although, as I say, we had these accidents. In the early part of the cruise, we hadn't distinguished ourselves in terms of our flying, sortie rate and all that. As I said, our new skipper was Commander Buck, and he and the exec were really good people. The exec was Dick Savage.* Both of them are really fine, good guys. So I think, in retrospect, the full eight-month cruise turned out to be quite a productive phase.

Paul Stillwell: Do you remember any specifics on that cross-fertilization process?

Admiral Lawrence: Well, we had an NROTC officer out of one of the Ivy League schools—and I forget whether it was Harvard or Yale—Danny D. Burke, a very smart, smart guy. He was always kind of knocking some of the Naval Academy guys off their perch and trying to educate them on the real world. Because, in addition to D. Burke, who was an NROTC guy, we had two Naval Academy guys out of the class of '59, Dale Fendorf and Wally Logan.† This was in '62, so they had just completed flight training before coming to the squadron, and they had very much the Naval Academy perspective. D. Burke was an NROTC guy from Ivy League schools, who was always heckling them. It was good. I think they learned from each other.

Then we had a couple of guys who had come through the Aviation Officer Candidate program. They brought in a somewhat different perspective, so it was a very healthy process. As I got more senior and became the Chief of Naval Personnel, I said I think it's a healthy process that we have officers commissioned from these diverse sources, because they all bring in a healthy perspective. And that's why I've always been an advocate of not allowing the NROTC and the Aviation Officer Candidate officers to

---

* Commander Richard A. Savage, USN, who then succeeded to command of the squadron from January to November of 1964.
† Lieutenant (junior grade) Dale N. Fendorf, USN; Lieutenant (junior grade) Wallis M. Logan, USN.

feel like they were the second-class citizens in the Navy, and the academy kids are the favored few. That's why I've always said we must treat the officers commissioned from all the sources basically the same.

Here recently, things have happened that try to single out the academy's officers being different, like having a longer obligation for the service academy officers than the officers from NROTC. The rationale in the Senate was that because the cost of the academy education is greater, they should have a longer payback. But the downside of that is if you have a six-year obligation for a service academy graduate and four from ROTC, that conveys to the ROTC that you want to keep the academy guys more than you want to keep ROTC. And that's a bad signal to send to them. And I finally, I think, a lot of things I've written convinced the Congress that they shouldn't have these disparate obligations between service academy and ROTC. We need to keep those ROTC graduates, and some of them turn out to be very superb officers.

Paul Stillwell: Was there any correlation at all between commissioning source and airmanship?

Admiral Lawrence: Well, there really was. I found that most of the individuals from the Aviation Officer Candidate program were basically good pilots. These were guys who had grown up from the time they were young with great desire to fly. They just didn't have the opportunity to get into the Naval Academy or ROTC, but they were motivated more than the other guys by this intense desire to fly. Whereas, often a Naval Academy kid will just say, "Well, I think I'll go to flying, because that seems to be a career field that's more attractive to me." But he also debates about whether to go into the submarines or surface, but then he finally decides on aviation. The other thing about it is that the aviation officer candidates probably in some respects are held to a tougher standard in their flight training, because they weren't commissioned when they came in. They had to struggle through the regimen down there at Pensacola.

Paul Stillwell: Well, this cross-fertilization could be very useful for them, so they could get more polish in some of the leadership and management skills.

Admiral Lawrence: It very definitely is. I think the overall diversity of commissioning sources is a healthy process. I don't think we need to increase the number of Naval Academy graduates, or significantly increase the NROTC program. I think that you get very fine officers out of the Officer Candidate program.

Paul Stillwell: Were you doing things at this phase of your career to grow intellectually, so you wouldn't be completely bogged down in the technical aspects?

Admiral Lawrence: Yes. I've always had a very active reading program throughout my whole naval career when I can carve out the time. In those younger years I was really very busy, because I always gave my principal emphasis to doing my job, as opposed to these leisure pursuits. And when I went home I totally dedicated to my family. As I mentioned in an earlier interview, I've always had a very active reading program, principally of history and biographies. I've read every biography of every great military leader in the United States. I found that this has probably helped me more than anything else I've done in my career. Because I've learned, not only a lot about leadership qualities, but as you read those biographies, you learn a lot about the events that occurred in that era. That was really the only type of reading I had time to do in those younger years. I just couldn't really do a lot of professional reading. I've read very few novels in my life. [Chuckle] I just didn't have the time to do it.

Paul Stillwell: What do you recall about fleet operations there in the Mediterranean?

Admiral Lawrence: Well, in the early '60s, there was an absolute minimal Soviet naval presence. They were just starting to build up their navy at that time. I don't think they regarded their navy as a really serious component of their military, because we saw very few Soviet ships in those days. The Soviet Bear airplanes were starting to do overflights of our naval ships, but they never did it in the Mediterranean.[*] We were only concerned about the overflights out in the Atlantic. Apparently, what the Soviets would fly their

---

[*] "Bear" is the Allied designation for the Soviet Tu-95 strategic bomber and maritime reconnaissance aircraft.

airplanes over the Baltic and then out through the Skagerrak and into the North Sea. Then they'd fly all the way down to the Atlantic, and then fly back home the other way to overfly our naval forces, usually en route to and from Europe.

Of course, we were absolutely paranoid about these overflights, because the Navy was so concerned that they'd be charged by the Air Force as being vulnerable and not having an air-defense capability and so forth. We just didn't want to have any bad publicity about a Soviet overflight. So when we came back on that Mediterranean cruise, we came through the Straits of Gibraltar, ran south, and then came across, just to make sure we were beyond the Bear range. I guess we went almost 1,000 miles south to make our transit. We got down in the warmer regions of the South Atlantic.

Paul Stillwell: Wouldn't it have been easier to put up a combat air patrol?

Admiral Lawrence: Well, it really wasn't, because, it wasn't a question of shooting them down. We just didn't want them to be able to say that they overflew us. Even if we had a fighter airplane on their wing, the fact that they overflew us was bad publicity. I remember we had to stand condition watches all the way across the Atlantic. That was a big concern in those days, but I never figured out why they didn't fly their Bear airplanes and Badgers down into the Mediterranean to overfly us. But the Soviets had an absolutely minimal naval presence in the Mediterranean. I guess it must have been in the late '60s and early '70s, when they started operating their ships more in the Med. So we never really thought about the Russian naval threat very much in the early '60s. It was more an air threat. And, really, your thinking about the Soviet Union in those times was more in taking the nuclear strikes into the Soviet heartland.

Paul Stillwell: Well, things like NORAD and the DEW Line were also geared against a Soviet bomber strike.[*]

---

[*] The North American Air Defense Command (NORAD), an Air Force command based in Colorado Springs, was responsible for detecting and attacking Soviet bombers headed toward the United States. DEW Line – Distant Early Warning Line, a chain of radar sites built 1,200 miles from the North Pole in the early 1950s as a means of detecting Soviet bombers approaching the United States over the Arctic.

Admiral Lawrence: That's right. See, the Navy has always been paranoid about the allegation, principally by the Air Force, that the aircraft carrier is vulnerable. So they didn't want them to have any ammunition, such as a Bear overflying a carrier. I guess that period was still not too long after the revolt of the admirals back there in the late '40s, and we were still very much guided by that type of thinking.*

Paul Stillwell: And even though, logically, a Bear wouldn't be a very good anti-ship weapon.

Admiral Lawrence: Yes, that's right. That was still before the anti-ship missiles. I don't remember ever being too concerned about anti-ship missiles in that early '60s. They must have come on in the late '60s or in the '70s.

Paul Stillwell: Well, anything more on the Demons before you talk about the transition to the F-4?†

Admiral Lawrence: No, I think that pretty well covers that deployment. Our commanding officer was Captain Wally Clarke, who'd been a big ace during World War II.‡ Then he was succeeded right after that cruise by Jerry Miller, who came in to be the captain.§ Wally Clarke did not make flag, but he was a real nice guy. We all liked him very much as a skipper. So I guess that's about all on that deployment.

We came back in April of 1963, and after we were back about a month, our squadron went through the transitional training to the F-4.** They moved the F-4 training from Naval Air Station Oceana down to Key West, so we went through all of our training down there.

---

* The Navy and Air Force were involved in an acrimonious struggle in 1949 over the future of U.S. military aviation. See Paul Schratz, "The Admirals' Revolt," *U.S. Naval Institute Proceedings*, February 1986, pages 64-71.
† VF-14 made the transition from the F3D Demon to the F-4B Phantom II in May 1963.
‡ Captain Walter E. Clarke, USN, commanded the USS *Franklin D. Roosevelt* (CVA-42) from 1 June 1962 to 20 July 1963.
§ Captain Gerald E. Miller, USN, commanded the ship from 20 July 1963 to 25 July 1964.
** The *Franklin D. Roosevelt* returned to her homeport of Mayport, Florida, on 22 April 1963.

Paul Stillwell: Do you know the reason for that move?

Admiral Lawrence: Well, with the Demon being phased out, they wanted to have the F-4, which was now becoming the primary type of training conducted in VF-101, to be brought back into the parent squadron, which was down at Key West, rather than being done by a detachment up there at Oceana. With the Demon leaving, they could dedicate their total effort to the F-4.

Paul Stillwell: Well, because of your previous experience, you must have had a leading role in the squadron.

Admiral Lawrence: Yes, I did a lot to help educate the other officers on the systems of the airplane, and also some of the tactical concepts. That early familiarity I had with the airplane enabled me to help the squadron a lot. And I was still the maintenance officer.

It was really a significant challenge to get our maintenance personnel trained in this new airplane, because the F-4 was a quantum jump in terms of complexity. For example, the J79 engine in the F-4 was a lot more complicated in terms of variable geometry than the engine in the Demon. You had the variable stator vanes, and you had the ramps on the airplane for subsonic flight, and the afterburner nozzle was more complex. So it was really a challenge getting our maintenance personnel through all these schools. We transitioned some of our own maintenance personnel, but we got new people in, because the total number of enlisted personnel in an F-4 squadron was larger than that. So as maintenance officer I had a tremendous challenge to get this maintenance organization going.

I was really fortunate that I got a newly commissioned limited duty officer in the squadron named Harry Errington. He was absolutely the most competent, ex-enlisted maintenance officer I've ever seen in the Navy.[*] He came in to be my maintenance control officer as a young ensign. He just was worth his weight in gold, because he'd been a chief metalsmith before he got commissioned.

---

[*] Ensign Harry R. Errington, USN.

This was a time when we just started a new type of maintenance inspection system on airplanes. We went more into what we called phased maintenance. In the early days of maintenance, when you inspected an airplane, you just put the airplane completely down and you did every system. When they brought in the F-4, you did just a little bit at a time. You phased it, so that it meant that the airplane wasn't down for a long period of time. That used to be always a problem, because you'd put an airplane down for about three weeks for a full check, and being inactive just dried out the seals and gave you problems, so that the phased maintenance made a lot of sense. But we really had to train our people on this more sophisticated form of maintenance, where you used to check on cards that things had been done.

Paul Stillwell: Record-keeping is crucial.

Admiral Lawrence: Record-keeping got to be a lot more complex. So that was really a challenge as maintenance officer to get this squadron ready. And this was the first time I trained to be capable of maintaining this more complex airplane. And that was one good reason for me to be the maintenance officer, because I had had previous experience in the airplane. So I could be cut back a little bit in my flying study of the airplane to concentrate on this maintenance effort, because when we were going through the transition down there at Key West, we had our maintenance personnel right with us. I was very much involved in that training.

Paul Stillwell: How much support did you get from McDonnell on the technical side?

Admiral Lawrence: Well, we had at least one McDonnell rep assigned to the squadron. We also had a Westinghouse rep that handled the APQ-72 radar in the airplane. I don't think we had a GE rep for the engines. The Navy was then involved in what they called the NAMO training, the naval aviation maintenance organization training. They used the system mockups and everything to do both the pilot and enlisted training. They had a really good setup there at Key West, which was run by the Navy itself. It was not done by the contractor. We had transitioned that capability into the Navy. That was pretty much advanced at that point, because when we went through in the spring of '63, it had been almost two years since VF-74 had been the first squadron that transitioned.

Paul Stillwell: And, probably, the doctrine for two-seat operation in the plane was pretty well established.

Admiral Lawrence: That's right. I told earlier about how we had developed the training for the radar intercept officers. That had really come along well. And we, of course, got these new radar intercept officers into the squadron to go through training with us. Several of our pilots who'd made the Demon cruise were being transitioned into the F-4, in addition to getting in some new pilots. But all of our NFOs were new guys, so we had to integrate them into the squadron.

In a way it was an improvement, because you had more officers to do the work. You could have an officer as a division officer in all the maintenance areas. That was the advantage of the dual-crew concept, more people get the ground work done. And, of course, pilots are notoriously bad on doing paperwork and things like that. [Chuckle] So the pilots were elated to have somebody to take this load off of them. I've always found that naval flight officers take a much more rational approach to doing paperwork and ground duties than pilots. A lot of young pilots, all they want to do is fly. They don't want to be encumbered with anything else. In many respects, you get more production out of the NFOs in paperwork and ground duties than you do pilots.

Paul Stillwell: Was there any sense of rivalry between those two groups in the squadron?

Admiral Lawrence: No. I've been in two F-4 squadrons; one as a maintenance officer, and later on as an executive officer and a commanding officer. We always had excellent rapport between the pilots and NFOs—never any second-class citizen connotation.

Paul Stillwell: Well, that would depend on the leadership, certainly.

Admiral Lawrence: Yes. I think we got off to a good start back there in 1960, when we first started training those NFOs and imparting certain philosophies that have endured. Now you've got almost as many NFOs in command of squadrons as you do pilots. So I think the early work that we did on that paid off.

Paul Stillwell: Well, the pilot knows that the NFOs help him in two ways: the operation of the plane and in the paperwork. And he's grateful.

Admiral Lawrence: Well, I tell you, after two tours in the night fighter squadrons, where I did it all myself, it was really nice to come in where you had a guy to share the load, particularly to operate that radar, and do all the tweaking of knobs, and doing the analysis. Because, I tell you, as a pilot, that was really a burden to manage that radar and then fly the airplane at night in the weather. The NFOs used to kid us and call us the truck drivers. I said, "That's fine with me. I'm happy just to drive this airplane and let you handle the weapon system." It's always been a very healthy relationship between the pilots and NFOs in those dual-crew fighter squadrons.

Paul Stillwell: Did you deploy once you got into the F-4s?

Admiral Lawrence: We completed the transition into the F-4 in the summer of 1963 and were fully operationally ready. Then our squadron had to go down and be on the hot-pad duty at Key West. Even though the Cuban Missile Crisis was basically over, it was still less than a year afterward. So to protect the reconnaissance airplanes that were flying around at Cuba—both the photoreconnaissance and the electronic reconnaissance airplanes—they kept an F-4 fighter squadron down there at Key West. We were on a continuous alert, so that we could launch on a moment's notice.

Paul Stillwell: Did you ever see any Cuban or Russian planes while you were up?

Admiral Lawrence: I didn't personally, but the squadron had some near encounters with Cuban airplanes while we were there.

One time, when we were standing at hot-pad duty down at Key West—Cuban airplanes for some reason started attacking a freighter that was coming around the western coast of Cuba. I think it was a Liberian registry. So I was launched at night to go down and look at this situation. They informed me, when I got airborne, that this was being checked with the White House to see what I'd be allowed to do. I went down about a couple hundred miles, and they finally turned me around and brought me back when the White House said, "No, don't get involved." It was still touch and go in '63, because we really knew that we could get into a fracas by reconnaissance airplanes flying on the periphery of Cuba. The rules of engagement were very nebulous. It was kind of counseling the context that you don't attack a Cuban airplane until you get clearance to do so. We felt that we were in a no-win situation if a problem developed. If we shot a Cuban airplane down, we'd really get hell. On the other hand, if we sat back and allowed our reconnaissance airplane to be shot down, we'd get hell. [Chuckle]

But that was interesting, and that was very good for the squadron to go down there and stand at hot-pad duty, because we got a fairly intensive amount of flying. And the maintenance people got further opportunities to get checked out in the airplane.

Paul Stillwell: How much intelligence were you getting about the Cubans at that time?

Admiral Lawrence: Not very much. We were kind of at the end of the line. We just did what they told us.

Paul Stillwell: You were on the front line.

Admiral Lawrence: Yes, but they didn't tell us much about the broad intelligence picture. We just stood the alert duty and we didn't have to sit in the airplanes. We stayed in the alert trailer. We were always being exercised. Virtually, every four hours or so they would give us a no-notice launch just to check, test our capabilities. I will never forget one time getting launched and getting up in the air, and I looked down and the plane captain hadn't hooked up my parachute [chuckle], so I was sitting in the airplane without a parachute hooked up. I had a hell of a time getting the damn thing hooked up.

In the haste to get airborne, we'd overlooked that minor detail. But it was interesting. It was exciting, because you really felt like you were close to the action.

Paul Stillwell: Did the squadron have contingency plans in case it was called on to support a strike into Cuba?

Admiral Lawrence: No, we didn't have that. Our only role was to protect the reconnaissance airplanes. Never did they plan for us to support the attack airplanes going to Cuba.

I had one interesting flight. They got me airborne to check out a bogey—an unidentified contact—and they were bringing me in from astern. I noticed that my closing speed was just enormous. I kept throttling back, and I still had the high closing speed. Finally had to put my flaps down. As I came in, I saw that it was a C-46 two-engine, reciprocating transport from El Salvador. I figured it was probably going from Miami or someplace like that down to Central America. So I pulled up beside it and I was just calling down to the controller and telling him all about the markings. Then and I looked up, and about 15 miles ahead of me was Havana. The plane was going into Havana, not Central America. So they said, "Hey, break off; you're going straight into Havana." So I had to turn away. I looked up and saw the coastline of Cuba. That was exciting.

Paul Stillwell: So that must have been a rule about not invading Cuban airspace.

Admiral Lawrence: Oh, yes, we were still very conscious of that. We were respecting the territorial limits of Cuba. But I just completely lost sight of where I was; I was so transfixed with trying to look at this El Salvadoran airliner.

Well, Paul, I'm supposed to go over and have lunch with Colonel Harry Summers.* He's in talking to our political science people.

---

* Colonel Harry G. Summers, USA (Ret.), was an author and syndicated newspaper columnist. His best-known work is the book *On Strategy: a Critical Analysis of Vietnam* (Novato, California: Presidio Press, 1982).

Interview Number 7 with Vice Admiral William P. Lawrence, U.S. Navy (Retired)
Place: U.S. Naval Institute, Annapolis, Maryland
Date: Monday, 5 November 1990

Paul Stillwell: Admiral, last time we were partway through your discussion of VF-14, the F-4 squadron in which you were serving as maintenance officer. If we could resume that, please.

Admiral Lawrence: Okay. I think that I had pretty well covered the transition of the squadron from the F3H to the F4H, the great challenge that we had in training both the pilots and our maintenance personnel. The F-4 was certainly a step up in sophistication and much greater complexity, both from the aircrew aspect of using the weapon system and also from the maintenance aspect. So we really had to work hard in that transition to train the people properly.

We were the first squadron of F-4s at Cecil Field. Whenever you're the first squadron at a particular base, you have all the problems of supply, support, and getting the base acclimated to operating the airplane. Often people do things locally without really discussing it with other people. Naval Air Station Oceana was where the first two F-4 squadrons were and where the training squadron was located until it was moved down to the parent squadron at Key West.

At Oceana you could do what they called hot refueling, where they keep the engine running on the airplane and go through the fuel pits, which were adjacent to the taxiway. It was much more efficient than having to refuel the airplane with the engine shut down. At Oceana, they concluded that procedure was completely safe. You'd come in from a flight and go through the fuel pits to top off. Then you would go back to your line, and the airplane was ready to go for the next flight.

At Cecil Field they didn't want to do this. So you'd have to park your airplane after a flight. You'd have to put a tow tractor on it and tow it over to the fuel pits. You also had to have external power, because the airplane could be refueled only with power in it so all the pumps worked. That was much more inefficient. So one of my first projects as the maintenance officer was to get concurrence of the base to permit hot refueling. And, God, you would think that I was trying to change the naval regulations or something. It was really a tough battle convincing the fire marshal and the safety people down there, but we finally got that approved. So that really enhanced the efficiency of our operating the airplane.

Things really went well down there at Cecil. It's a good base in terms of operating area off the coast. You have a good operating area, and then you have Whitehouse Field, which is just about five miles north of Cecil, where you can do your night carrier landings. So even though it was a little difficult getting the squadron ready, about three or four months after we had returned to Cecil Field from Key West, where the transition occurred, the squadron was going pretty well. We were faced with going out on the *Franklin D. Roosevelt*, which was in Mayport. Our previous cruise in the Demons, of course, had been on the *Roosevelt* in Air Group One.

There's some history I recall very vividly from the fall of 1963. While we were there at Cecil Field, President Kennedy was assassinated.[*] This occurred a week before Thanksgiving. I remember coming back from a flight and walking into the ready room; and everybody was very dejected and downcast. They told me, "The President has been assassinated." This happened on a Friday afternoon. Then I remember going home and watching television all that weekend when Jack Ruby shot Lee Harvey Oswald.[†]

Another thing I might mention is they decided to have a 27-plane fly-over for the burial in Arlington.[‡] They decided to make it both Air Force and Navy fighter planes. They decided to have a column of nine three-plane V formations. You can imagine the tremendous coordination problem. The Air Force airplanes, as I recall, were coming out of Langley and Myrtle Beach Air Force Base, and then we had F-4s from Cecil Field and from Oceana.[§] So I and my two other guys were the ones who were designated to fly up from Cecil Field to do this. It was really quite an interesting experience to join up with the other airplanes in a column of V's. You tend to fall behind, then try to catch up, and

---

[*] President John F. Kennedy was assassinated in Dallas on 22 November 1963.
[†] Lee Harvey Oswald was the assassin who shot Kennedy. Jack Ruby was a local nightclub owner who shot and killed Oswald on 24 November while he was being transferred in the Dallas police station.
[‡] The funeral was on Monday, 25 November 1963 at St. Matthew's Cathedral in Washington. Burial was that afternoon in the Arlington National Cemetery in Northern Virginia.
[§] Langley Air Force Base, three miles north of the city of Hampton, Virginia.

you'd overrun. It was one of the toughest situations that I did, but I had a real sense of history in doing that fly-over.

The man who was controlling this was on the ground down there at Arlington. He would say, "Okay, you have five minutes for your fly-over." We were in a big circle over to the east of Washington, and then we flew in. When I got back down to Cecil Field, I had a chance to see the rerun on television showing the airplanes coming over as the caisson was arriving at the burial site. We looked pretty good.

Paul Stillwell: Getting back to your squadron, were changes made on board the *Franklin D. Roosevelt* to accommodate the transition to a new plane?

Admiral Lawrence: Oh, yes, we had to deal very closely with the carrier in building up the part support, working with the air department to make sure that they could handle the airplane. The Demon had been a big airplane, but the Phantom was an even larger, more difficult airplane to move around the carrier. We knew we were going to have some real challenges operating the airplane on the carrier, so we did a lot of interface with the carrier. In fact, I remember flying over to Mayport so they could load an airplane on board and work with it even before we even landed on board.

Paul Stillwell: So that probably involved you with Commander Forbes a good bit.

Admiral Lawrence: Yes, as I recall, he was still the air officer.

Then in the fall of 1963, we went up to Oceana and then flew out and got the squadron car-qualed aboard the USS *Forrestal*. That went very, very smoothly. We were really proud of our squadron in that everybody got both day and night qualified without any hitches at all. We really did well.

Then right after the first of the year, we were due to go out on *Roosevelt* and start the workup for the forthcoming deployment. The carrier was going to go down into the Caribbean for this training for us. I was due to move from being the maintenance officer, which I'd been for over a year, to become the operations officer of the squadron. I would replace Lieutenant Commander Dick Thompson, who was leaving the squadron.* But in early January, I got a call from my friendly detailer in Washington. He asked me, "How would you like to be the executive assistant to a four-star Army general?"

I said, "I wouldn't like to be the executive assistant to a four-star Army general. I've had an aide's tour already for Admiral Moorer, and I'm just taking over as operations officer of a squadron. They really need me to help them in initial shipboard work on the carrier *Roosevelt*." And I had been told that the plan for me was that the coming July, during the next Med deployment, I would be detached and come back and go to the Naval War College. So now he was talking about me departing six months earlier than originally planned. I really didn't want to do this at all, because I felt it was important for my own career to stay in that squadron for the full two years.

Paul Stillwell: Did you find out why you, of all people, were chosen?

Admiral Lawrence: Yes. I called my former commanding officer, who was now Captain Mickey Weisner and the senior naval aviation detailer in BuPers.† I said, "Look, skipper, I think this is unfair. I've had a previous aide's tour."

He said, "Well, let me look into it." He called me back a day later, and he said, "Well, you have been personally picked by Vice Admiral Smedberg, the Chief of Naval Personnel."‡ He said, "It's a very sensitive situation, that General Adams, who is commander in chief of Strike Command, has just been given full unified combatant command status, taking over the Middle East, Africa south of the Sahara, and South Asia."§ The Navy lost some of its responsibilities, like the CinCNELM responsibility.** It was quite concerned about naval ships in General Adams's area coming under his opcon.††

---

* Lieutenant Commander Richard G. Thompson, USN.
† As a commander, Weisner had been commanding officer of Fighter Squadron 193 on board the *Oriskany* (CVA-34) in the mid-1950s.
‡ Vice Admiral William R. Smedberg III, USN, served as Chief of the Bureau of Naval Personnel from 12 February 1960 to 11 February 1964. His oral history is in the Naval Institute collection.
§ General Paul D. Adams, USA, was Commander in Chief Strike Command, headquartered at MacDill Air Force Base, Tampa, Florida, from 1961 to 1966. The command was established in December 1961.
** CinCNELM – Commander in Chief U.S. Naval Forces Eastern Atlantic and Mediterranean.
†† Opcon – operational control.

General Adams did not agree with the Navy's concept of operating in support. When the Navy's supporting an amphibious operation, the ships remain under the opcon of the task force commander; they don't report to the theater commander. So it was a very strained time. The Navy had fought tenaciously to prevent this unified command status going to Commander in Chief Strike Command.

Paul Stillwell: Was this an initiative from Secretary McNamara?*

Admiral Lawrence: Yes.

Paul Stillwell: What was the rationale?

Admiral Lawrence: Well, the rationale initially was that we needed a rapid-reaction force. So the Strike Command was formed in 1961, right after the Kennedy administration came to office. It was a thrust to improve our conventional warfare capability, also unconventional warfare capability, but to take the emphasis off the strategic mission. In the decade of the '50s the country really built up the nuclear forces. When Kennedy came in, his perception was we didn't have a real rapid-reaction capability, because in the Continental U.S. the Air Force units were under Air Force command and the Army units were under Army command. You didn't have joint coordination in the event of a contingency. So they formed the U.S. Strike Command, General Adams had command of what they called the strategic reserve in the continental United States.

So then in 1963, McNamara decided to make him a full unified commander, because they had no one commander who had cognizance of the Middle East, Africa south of the Sahara, and South Asia. By South Asia, they meant Pakistan and India. CinCEur had North Africa down to the Sahara Desert.† Countries like Libya, Tunisia, Morocco came under the European command.

---

* Robert S. McNamara served as Secretary of Defense from 21 January 1961 to 29 February 1968.
† CinCEur – the joint-service U.S. European Command.

There was an organization called Joint Task Force Four, which was down at Fort Monroe, which is right there at Hampton, right across Hampton Roads from Norfolk. That was the location of the Continental Army Command. JTF-4 answered directly to the Joint Staff and did the contingency planning responsibility for the Africa area. Then you had Commander in Chief Eastern Atlantic and Mediterranean; it was a Navy command in London that had the Middle East. So everything—military assistance, contingency responsibility—was very much fragmented.

McNamara wanted to bring this under one commander, and he felt it was just logical to tie this to the Strike Command. The Navy realized that their relationships were very strained with this new commander. Admiral Page Smith, who was at Norfolk, and Admiral Don Felt out there in the Pacific—CinCLant and CinCPac, respectively—wouldn't even talk to General Adams.* They wouldn't have any interface. They refused to exchange liaison officers with him.

So General Adams, to show good faith, asked the Navy to give him a rear admiral as his chief of staff. Then both the Strike Command and the CinCMEAFSA functions were together.† He didn't separate the staff; everybody did both areas. So the Navy sent out Rear Admiral Forsythe Massey to be chief of staff. He was out of the class of '31, naval aviator. And Admiral Smedberg personally handpicked me to go down there as the peacemaker with General Adams. He knew me from my academy days, and I was a classmate of his son, Bill Smedberg.‡

Paul Stillwell: But, why you?

Admiral Lawrence: I don't know. I guess Admiral Smedberg just knew me personally and by reputation, and he felt that I was a guy that could go down there and help heal the division between the Navy and that command.

---

* Admiral Harold Page Smith, USN, served as Supreme Allied Commander Atlantic, Commander in Chief Atlantic, and Commander in Chief Atlantic Fleet from 30 April 1963 to 30 April 1965. Admiral Harry D. Felt, USN, served as Commander in Chief Pacific from 31 July 1958 to 30 June 1964. His oral history is in the Naval Institute collection.
† CinCMEAFSA – Commander in Chief Middle East, Africa South of the Sahara, and Southern Asia.
‡ Lieutenant Commander William R. Smedberg IV, USN.

Paul Stillwell: Was it his perception that Massey was not getting the job done?

Admiral Lawrence: Well no, Massey and I went down together.

Paul Stillwell: I see.

Admiral Lawrence: So Massey and I both were charged to go down there and improve the cooperation. It concerned me, because I felt it could jeopardize my career. Even though Smedberg thought this was a great idea, I might be adversely perceived by Felt and people like that, Page Smith. I said how much I hated to go down there, because I really hated to leave that fighter squadron and just felt it was unfair that I got tapped to be an aide the second time—although it was really more an executive assistant than an aide. But I said, "Okay, I'll go down there and make the best of it."

It was tough, really hard work, because General Adams was just getting into putting the Strike Command aspect of it under control, the rapid-reaction capability, and getting the Army and Air Force units really working together and accepting him as an operational commander. Because the Air Force guys felt they worked for the Commander in Chief of the Tactical Air Command; the Army guys felt they worked for the Commander of the Continental Army Command, which were both four-star commands. But, operationally, they worked for General Adams. So that was a sensitive relationship.

I decided, "Okay, I'm not even getting involved in any of this politics; I'm just going to go down there and do the best job I can." As I say, we were plowing new ground, both in the rapid-reaction capability, also in this unified command responsibility. Not only did we have to prepare the contingency plans for that area, we also had to administer the military assistance programs. And we were very much involved in all the politico-military affairs.

The first year that I was in that job we worked seven days a week without fail. The second year I was there, we worked only six days a week; we didn't work on Sunday.

Paul Stillwell: What kind of issues were you confronting during those seven days a week?

Admiral Lawrence: Well, gosh, there were a tremendous number. First of all, on the Strike Command side of the house, we were really working on this rapid-deployment capability. We had developed the joint task force concept, so that when you had a contingency, you would tailor a force of both Air Force and Army units, and you would call it a joint task force. You would have a joint task force commander and a joint staff that worked for him on both Army and Air Force. So we were developing those joint task force tactics, and doing things exactly like we did years later in Grenada or Panama.* So the rapid-reaction concept made, really, great sense. And we had, of course, units that were in a constant readiness status. For example, as it is today, the 82nd Airborne Division at Fort Bragg and the 101st Airborne Division there at Fort Campbell were our two rapid-deployment forces.

After I got there, we were involved in some major crises. The Dominican Republic crisis in '65 was one we had to deal with. I guess that was, really, the only one where we had to deploy forces during that time there out of the Strike Command.

Paul Stillwell: What do you remember specifically about that operation?

Admiral Lawrence: Well, I remember that right in the middle, once it got going, Admiral Moorer came in to be CinCLant/CinCLantFlt from being CinCPacFlt.† The first thing General Adams did after that change of command was to call Admiral Moorer on the phone. He would never have done that with Page Smith, because Page Smith wouldn't

---

* In October 1983 the United States mounted a joint-service operation to occupy Grenada in the Caribbean after a Marxist military coup overthrew the island's government. The overthrow and subsequent developments led to concern about the safety of approximately 1,000 U.S. citizens on the island.

Manuel Noriega was de facto ruler of Panama in the early 1980s and in August 1983 promoted himself to general. Relations between the United States and Panama deteriorated in the late 1989. Following harassment of U.S. service personnel in Panama in December 1983, the United States invaded Panama. Noriega was captured in December 1984. He was subsequently convicted in U.S. federal court and imprisoned.

† Admiral Thomas H. Moorer, USN, served as Supreme Allied Commander Atlantic, Commander in Chief Atlantic, and Commander in Chief Atlantic Fleet from 30 April 1965 to 17 June 1967. His oral history is in the Naval Institute collection.

even answer the phone. Admiral Moorer said, "I just want to assure you that I'm working with you; we've got everything under control." Because the Dominican operation not only involved Army and Air Force units, it also involved naval units. Admiral Moorer was very forthcoming, and then immediately, General Adams went up and made a call on Admiral Moorer. Then shortly after that Admiral Moorer came down to see us. It was just day and night when Moorer came in compared with Page Smith.

That's why I was really disappointed in Admiral Page Smith and Admiral Don Felt— that they weren't big enough to say, "Okay, the President's decided this is the way it's going to be, and we'll support it." Like Admiral Moorer.

Paul Stillwell: What do you think was the basis for their attitude?

Admiral Lawrence: Well, they looked upon the Strike Command and this U.S. CinCMEAFSA as really having degraded the Navy's responsibility. It was a roles-and-missions issue, and they thought the Navy had lost roles and missions. And it wasn't General Adams's idea; it was conceived by McNamara and the President. They ordered it to be implemented, but Page Smith and Felt directed their bitterness towards General Adams.

Admiral McDonald took over as the CNO in '63, and he was more forthcoming than Admiral Anderson had been, initially, when he was CNO.[*] Admiral McDonald came down one time with General Maxwell Taylor, the Chairman of the Joint Chiefs of Staff; and the Chief of Staff of the Air Force, General LeMay.[†] They all came down to learn about the Strike Command and the U.S. CinCMEAFSA. McDonald was starting to be more receptive to the idea, but, boy, old Page Smith and Don Felt didn't change.

That was one of the big reasons why I was sent down there: to make peace and to facilitate the communication between the Navy and the Strike Command.

---

[*] Admiral David L. McDonald, USN, served as Chief of Naval Operations from 1 August 1963 to 1 August 1967. His oral history is in the Naval Institute collection.
[†] General Maxwell D. Taylor, USA, served as Chairman of the Joint Chiefs of Staff from 1 October 1962 to 3 July 1964. General Curtis E. LeMay, USAF, served as Air Force Chief of Staff from 30 June 1961 to 31 January 1965.

Paul Stillwell: What could a lieutenant commander do with these four-stars grumbling at each other?

Admiral Lawrence: [Laughter] Beats me. Well, I was known by Admiral McDonald, who was the CNO, because when I had been the aide to Admiral Moorer, I had interface with Admiral McDonald. See, Admiral McDonald relieved Admiral Moorer as ComCarDiv 6. And so he visited us before he took over. I had been aide to Admiral Anderson before Admiral Moorer took over, so they all knew me. And I mentioned that Smedberg knew me from the academy days. So I guess they just figured that I was a guy who could help facilitate this improved communication.

Paul Stillwell: Do you think you did?

Admiral Lawrence: Oh, yes, I did, but I never, ever did any covert communication. I did it by working hard at my job every day. When I perceived some area where there could be improved communications with the Navy, I tried to make it happen. In other words, I would look for opportunities to have General Adams meet senior naval officers in putting together his speeches and things like that to ensure that he said the right words about joint cooperation.

Then, of course, we made some overseas trips. The first overseas trip I made with him was in the summer of 1964. After I'd been there about three or four months, we made General Adams's first trip over to the African-Middle East area. I guess initially we went to France to go to what they used to call the SHAPE in Paris, SACEur, and CinCEur.[*] I made sure that General Adams spent some time with Admiral McDonald, who was also there.

There was kind of an interesting sidelight when we left Paris, after spending a week there at the SHAPE and heading on down into the Middle East and Africa. We went down to southern France to a place called Montélimar. In World War II General Adams was the commander of a regiment in the 36th Infantry Division, which was

---

[*] General Lyman L. Lemnitzer, USA, served as NATO's Supreme Allied Commander Europe from 1963 to 1969. SHAPE stands for Supreme Headquarters Allied Powers Europe.

fighting its way up through southern France.* And the Germans provided some pretty tough resistance.

A lieutenant in this regiment of the 36th Division got a Congressional Medal of Honor in some pretty tough fighting.† So General Adams went back and visited this French family that made their chateau available to him as his regimental command post. He had kept in touch with that family ever since World War II, so we went over to their home and gave them a plaque he'd had made. So that was an interesting sidelight.

Then, I remember, I specifically encouraged him to go to Naples to meet with CinCSouth, who was a naval four-star commander, a NATO command. Admiral James Russell was CinCSouth.‡ He hosted General Adams very warmly, and I really worked hard to make sure that the two got together, and they hit it off beautifully, because Admiral Russell was a great guy.

Paul Stillwell: Well, he's a very gracious person.

Admiral Lawrence: Yes, really a wonderful man. He took General Adams out on his boat, and they went over to the famous isle of Capri. Admiral Russell's quite a physical fitness individual, and he did some scuba diving and things like that. General Adams was not inclined to do any of that. But that was a very useful visit, although there was no real professional tie between those commands, because CinCSouth was a NATO command. It was good to get the two of them together.

Paul Stillwell: What kind of a person was General Adams, just from having this close observation of him?

---

* In 1944-45, as a lieutenant colonel, Adams commanded the 143rd Infantry Regiment, 36th Infantry Division, in the Mediterranean and Europe.
† On 17 April Stephen R. Gregg, recently promoted to the rank of Army second lieutenant received the Medal of Honor. It was based on his actions while serving in battle as a technical sergeant in the 143rd Infantry Regiment on 27 August 1944, in fighting near Montélimar, France. In Operation Dragoon, the Allies had invaded Southern France from the Mediterranean on 15 August 1944.
‡ Admiral James S. Russell, USN, served as Commander in Chief Allied Forces Southern Europe from January 1962 to March 1965. His oral history is in the Naval Institute collection.

Admiral Lawrence: Well, he was the old-school Army officer. He was out of the West Point class of 1928, infantry officer; he always said that he had spent more time forward of artillery in World War II than any other officer. At the beginning of World War II, he was assigned to the First Special Service Force, which were to be our first commandos and special forces. It was a joint Canadian-U.S. group that formed up in Helena, Montana, and trained there. Their plan was to send them in as commandos into Norway. And the first commanding officer was a Colonel Frederick, and General Adams was his executive officer as a lieutenant colonel.[*] This was in early 1942.

Then the Aleutians campaign broke out, so they decided to send this First Special Service Force into the Aleutians, so they went and fought there. After the Aleutians, they put them on a ship, and they came down through the Panama Canal and went over and arrived in Italy about the time of Salerno.[†] So they went in at Salerno and fought up the Italian boot. Since they were so well trained in cold-weather operations, they were designated to do the mountain fighting in the central part of the Italian boot. Some of the fighting that was done up in the mountains in Italy was really tough fighting, and he was involved in that.

Then the 36th Infantry Division, which was a Texas National Guard division, was cut up so badly at Anzio.[‡] You remember that Mark Clark was very severely criticized for what happened at Anzio.[§] The division was very demoralized, because they'd taken a lot of casualties, so they changed all three regimental commanders, and General Adams was brought in to be a regimental commander in the 36th Division. They fought up and liberated Rome and then went over and then made the invasion of southern France. Then he fought all the way up through France, and then at the very end of the war, he was promoted to brigadier general and made an assistant division commander of the 45th Division, which was the Oklahoma National Guard division. So he had continuous combat from '42 to '45. As I say, he said he had more time forward of artillery than anyone. He was a very taciturn, very demanding, intense type of individual.

---

[*] The First Special Service Force was activated 9 July 1942 under the command of Lieutenant Colonel Robert T. Frederick, USA, a West Point classmate of Lieutenant Colonel Paul Adams, his XO.
[†] The Allies invaded Salerno, Italy, a seaport about 30 miles east southeast of Naples, in September 1943.
[‡] The Allies invaded Anzio, a city on the Italian coast about 35 miles south of Rome, on 22 January 1944.
[§] Lieutenant General Mark W. Clark, USA, commanding general of the U.S. Fifth Army.

General Adams didn't have a lot of close friends in the Army. He was handpicked by McNamara himself, because General Maxwell Taylor would never have picked him. General Adams was not an outgoing, hail fellow, well met. He was not part of the old boys' club. But very job he'd ever had, he proved himself, including being the Army commander in Lebanon in 1958.* He was sent down to run our intervention there.

Paul Stillwell: Well, it sounds as if he developed some outgoing traits just out of necessity.

Admiral Lawrence: Oh, yes, but I mean he was not . . .

Paul Stillwell: Not that way normally, naturally.

Admiral Lawrence: He was not part of the old boys' network that develops in the military, even though he was a West Pointer, and he was certainly respected as a fellow West Pointer. He didn't have close rapport with General Wheeler or General Maxwell Taylor.† He really made it on his own. He was a guy who grew up in a small town in Alabama and didn't have a lot of polish. He had some rough edges, but, boy, he was very smart, one of the hardest working guys I've ever seen.

So it was really a challenge for me to come in there as a naval officer in a primarily Air Force and Army command. I had to really work to learn all about the Army, Air Force way of doing business, the unit designations, and all of that.

General Adams had just the reverse philosophy of leadership from what you'd expect. The average senior officer boss assumes everybody's going to be okay, and you have to disprove yourself. General Adams had just the opposite. You had to prove yourself, so, as I told everybody, that was my second plebe year. I mean, he was really

---

* On 15 July 1958, at the request of Lebanese President Camille Chamoun, U.S. amphibious forces landed at Beirut to support Chamoun's government, which was threatened by both civil war and the prospect of foreign invasion. Two of the Sixth Fleet's three battalion landing teams went ashore within 24 hours. For details see the account of the U.S. ambassador to Lebanon, Robert McClintock, "The American Landing in Lebanon," *U.S. Naval Institute Proceedings*, October 1962, pages 64-79. Adams was then Commanding General, U.S. Army Forces in the Middle East.
† General Earle G. Wheeler, USA, served as Army Chief of Staff from 1 October 1962 to 2 July 1964.

tough on me the first three months.

Paul Stillwell: What kinds of things?

Admiral Lawrence: Well, he was demanding in the quality of papers that were brought in and the way I ran his schedule. See, I basically put his schedule together. And, boy, if anything was wrong, he'd be on me just like that, because he wanted to ensure that I quickly learned his requirements and his standards. He was very, very demanding on his schedule. The guy really tried to get the most efficient utilization of his time. He would normally have his meetings in the morning, and then he liked to have about two hours in the first part of the afternoon to write and think and dictate letters. That time was absolutely inviolable.

Well, in my early months on the staff, I was still learning the ropes. The Strike Force staff included a political adviser from the State Department, Mr. Hank Ramsey. He was a Foreign Service Officer One, which is one grade below ambassador. He was typical State Department-type guy, very verbose; he would write lengthy messages. He didn't use the terse military style. So I guess it was the practice in the State Department that they'd bounce in and out of each other's offices and talk at great length about things. So he would come down and demand to see General Adams. Well, I knew General Adams was very particular about how he used his time, so I tried to dissuade Mr. Ramsey from getting in there. But one time he said, "This is an absolute, dire emergency. I must see General Adams."

So I remember walking in General Adams's office and said, "Sir, Mr. Ramsey needs to see you."

We used to have to have a full glass of number-two pencils sharpened every morning for General Adams. He was writing something during this inviolable time, and he had this Plexiglas covering on his desk. He took his pencil and threw it down and he said, "Goddamn it, can't you keep that son-of-a-bitch out of here?" This pencil ricocheted by my head and fell down. Anyway, I got the message, and after that Ramsey would get in there only over my dead body. So Ramsey and I had a really unpleasant relationship, because he kept coming down and saying, "I must see him, dire emergency."

So, finally, after I worked with him, I said, "Sir, you know General Adams is very busy. The other thing is that the things that you have to tell General Adams would be of great benefit to the other senior officers on the staff, so what I suggest is that you just cover these items at the morning staff meeting." Finally, I got Ramsey trained, so as the general went around to key people at the morning staff meeting, Ramsey would do the briefing there. So I finally broke him of this habit of going in to see General Adams.

As I say, General Adams was kind of rough around the edges in some respects. He was not an articulate individual, and he kind of mumbled. They used to try their best to get the most sophisticated sound system for the morning conferences so they could record what he said. Then I was always asked to play these recordings back: "What did General Adams say? We can't quite understand him."

Even before the Dominican Republic crisis, in our unified command responsibility we had a lot of sensitive situations going on, particularly in Africa. For example, as you may recall, the Congo had just gotten its independence. They hadn't even renamed it Zaire yet; it was still called the Congo.* They had this guerrilla problem that developed back in the inner part of the Congo, and they actually captured the town of Stanleyville. Well, this had to be in 1964. We had to plan all of that rescue operation, to go in and liberate Stanleyville. We made the arrangements to use Belgian paratroopers, because we felt it would be better perceived internationally if the Belgians went in to rescue the hostages.† The Air Force provided the C-130s to pick them up, and they flew down to Ascension Island, and then staged from Ascension into the airdrop at Stanleyville. We were all involved in the planning of that.

During that 1964 trip, after Paris and Naples, we went down to Lebanon, because it was in our area of responsibility. This was the first time that General Adams had been back to Lebanon since the 1958 crisis, so he was very interested to see how the situation

---

* Belgium granted independence to its colony, the Belgian Congo, on 30 June 1960. The country was subsequently known as Zaire from 1971 to 1997.
† In the fall of 1964 Simba rebels seized the city of Stanleyville during the Congolese Civil War and captured more than 1,000 American and European hostages. On 24 November of that year five C-130 U.S. Air Force transports dropped in 350 Belgian paratroopers to recapture the city and evacuate the hostages who had not already been killed.

was working in there. At that time, Beirut was known as the Paris of the Middle East. It was just a beautiful city, and so we enjoyed our visit.

Then we went on down to Saudi Arabia, because we were just starting a very active military assistance program at that time. We went to visit with our chief of the military mission there and to meet the Saudi hierarchy, both military and the civil. It was really an interesting experience going into Saudi Arabia and observing their culture.

Paul Stillwell: Do you remember specific examples?

Admiral Lawrence: Well, you never saw a woman at any social event, for one thing. And all the women who were out publicly had the veils on. They had several receptions for us, and no women were present.

But the other thing that was very apparent to me when we went into Jidda over on the Red Sea was that the level of sanitation was really very poor, very low. The hotel rooms were very low quality. They did have inside plumbing, but the country was still very backward in '64. I guess today it's really advanced, very ultramodern. But the oil wealth, which was just becoming apparent at that time, hadn't really had the impact on the country that it did later.

One thing that really struck me was how austere the U.S. embassy and U.S. embassy compound were at Jidda, and the austere quality of the hotel we stayed in. It was obvious to me that the Saudis were not operating the equipment that we'd given them very well. At that time they had mostly British items, because the Brits had had a much closer relationship. I guess the Brits had controlled Saudi Arabia before they gave them their independence. The Saudis had their regular army, and then they had what they called a white army. The King and the princes of the Saud family very much wanted to ensure that they didn't have a challenge to their family. The white army I guess, really, was kind of the palace guard, and then they had their regular army. But the two of them kind of balanced each other out, because the royal family was very much concerned about keeping themselves in power. So that was really very interesting.

From Saudi Arabia, we went over to Ethiopia. At that time, the United States had very good rapport with Ethiopia, and Haile Selassie was still in office.* We had an Army brigadier general who was the chief of the mission, and we were really working hard to build up the Ethiopian Army and Air Force. The F-5 airplane was just starting to come out, I think, at that time.† So we had a very good working relationship with the Ethiopian military. General Adams had a chance to meet with Haile Selassie while he was there. He was just a little guy, but he had tight control of that country. But I was also very much impressed with how backward that country was, really backward. But we had a chance to go out of Addis Ababa and go down to one of their outlying military bases and observe some of their army and air force maneuvers.

We were flying in a C-118—four-engine prop transport, and it was really grim.‡ All of us were right on the edge of malaise all the time, because of incipient dysentery, and we never drank any water any place we went in the Middle East. Fortunately, in Ethiopia the Army had distilled this water, and they put that in our hotel room. But I remember going to receptions, both in Saudi Arabia and down in Ethiopia, where the food was just—you knew that you would probably get dysentery because of the flies and everything.

From Ethiopia we went over to Congo—this was before the Stanleyville problem. The United States had a very colorful ambassador to the Congo at that time named McMurtrie Godley.§ You may have read about him, because he became the ambassador to Laos. He was always a troubleshooter in the State Department, and since they were having this guerrilla problem in the Congo—but even before the guerrilla problem, you remember it was the province of Katanga had seceded from the rest of the Congo. They actually had to send in troops to subdue them and bring them back. I think the Belgian troops went in there and brought them back.

---

* Haile Selassie I was Ethiopia's regent from 1916 to 1930 and Emperor from 1930 to 1974. He was Commander in Chief of the Ethiopian Navy.
† In the 1950s the Northrop Corporation developed the F-5 as a lightweight single-seat tactical fighter for the U.S. Air Force. It was subsequently produced in a number of versions.
‡ C-118 was a four-engine propeller-driven Navy and Air Force transport built by Douglas as the military counterpart to the DC-6 civilian passenger plane.
§ G. McMurtrie Godley served as U.S. Ambassador to the Congo, 23 March 1964 to 15 October 1966, and as ambassador to Laos, 24 July 1969 to 23 April 1973.

Paul Stillwell: I remember Patrice Lumumba.

Admiral Lawrence: Yes, Patrice Lumumba. He was assassinated.* They felt that Patrice Lumumba was a Marxist, and he's kind of been held up as a martyr among the Communist world.

When we arrived there in July-August of '64, Mobutu had just become the President; he'd just led a coup as an army sergeant and taken over.† So it was really very interesting. The thing that was so exciting to me was that every day, you know, I'd read voluminous message traffic from all these places in Africa and the Middle East. And, of course, the Pakistan-India problem was still boiling.‡ And they later had a guerrilla war while I was a POW.

Paul Stillwell: I remember it being in 1971.

Admiral Lawrence: Yes, but in '64 they could see all the potential there for a real conflict developing.

Paul Stillwell: This was like a war college education for you.

Admiral Lawrence: Oh, yes, I tell you, I learned all about those countries in Africa and the Middle East, because every day I was reading, intensely, all the messages. And, of course, the Rhodesian problem occurred about that time, and Rhodesia declared its independence later on.§ Every day, you'd be briefed on these problems in Africa, the

---

* Patrice Lumumba was a Congolese independence leader and the first legally elected Prime Minister of the Republic of the Congo. In September 1960 he was deposed in a coup, imprisoned, and then killed by a firing squad on 17 January 1961. The U.S. Central Intelligence Agency was believed to be complicit.
† Moise Tshombe was president of the Katanga Province before going into exile and later returning as Prime Minister of the Congo in 1964-65. Mobutu Sese Seko was President of the Republic of the Congo/Zaire from 1965 to 1997.
‡ The Indo-Pakistan war over the disputed region of Kashmir was fought from April to September of 1965. The Bangladesh Liberation War followed in 1971.
§ Rhodesia, a British colony, issued a unilateral declaration of independence in 1965 and was formally granted independence by the United Kingdom in 1980. The countries in what was formerly Rhodesia are now Zimbabwe and Zambia.

Middle East, and so forth. And we were planning military assistance programs, plus contingency operations like the one in the Congo.

In addition to that, we were running this rapid-reaction mission. A key thing that we also been given responsibility for was the Joint Test and Evaluation Task Force. Under our cognizance, it was headed up by an Army major general named Rawson to develop the helicopter mobility tactics, which led to the First Air Cavalry Division being formed. So we had a tremendous amount on our plate. And here I was, a lieutenant commander thrust into being the executive assistant. It was quite a learning experience for me.

Paul Stillwell: How long did it take you to get over being sorry you were there?

Admiral Lawrence: Well, I didn't have time to even think about it, because I was so busy. I relieved an Army major, Richard Harris, who was out of West Point class of '51.[*] He was one of the superstars in the Army, had been handpicked to go down there and be the executive assistant to General Adams. But he and General Adams did not hit it off. The problem was that General Adams was so feared in the Army, because he was so tough, that Army officers couldn't relax around him. I used to see generals who dreaded to go into his office. They'd stand out and just quake. And this Army major had been a very competent guy; later on he became a major general in the Army. Because of the pressure, he couldn't bear up on the job with General Adams. When I got there, he was in the hospital, so the job was vacant. I was thrust in and didn't have a turnover or anything like that.

Paul Stillwell: Did Adams warm up to you after a while?

Admiral Lawrence: After about three months. But I used to say, "Well, gosh, I'm not going to worry myself about satisfying him. I'll work as hard as I can. The worst thing that can happen to me, he can send me back to a fighter squadron." [Laughter] I think he appreciated having somebody around him who wasn't uptight, because after a while I

---

[*] Major Richard Lee Harris, USA, had stood number four in the Military Academy class of 1951.

said, "The hell with it. If I get fired, I get fired." I was reasonably respectful, but I wasn't relaxed. But the Army officers absolutely feared him. I saw him chew out a three-star Army general one time, General Ralph Haines, who was the commanding general of the III Corps down at Fort Hood. Later on, Ralph Haines, as a four-star, was Vice Chief of Staff of the Army.* But General Adams got mad at him about something and just plastered him up against the wall. General Haines was braced up like a plebe, and General Adams was giving him hell. [Chuckle] So he was quite a tough taskmaster.

I had been in the job about four months when we made that trip through Africa, which lasted three weeks. Boy, that was a tough, demanding trip. I think when he saw that I was handling that trip okay, getting his schedule, and taking care of Mrs. Adams, that he started warming up to me.

When we were in the Congo, General Adams went over and had dinner with General Mobutu, the President. I went with a guy to a restaurant out in the hinterlands, and I had a piece of beef that really tasted bad. I'm sure that resulted in my getting a pretty bad case of the dysentery when I came back.

But after the Congo we went up to Nigeria, which had just become independent from Great Britain.† I was more impressed with Nigeria than any other nation, because they were far more advanced than Ethiopia or the Congo. The officials, the black people in Nigeria, both in the Army and the civil, were much better educated. The British did a much better job of training the locals.

Then we went from Nigeria over to Liberia, and that was, of course, interesting because Liberia had been settled by former slaves. It was really interesting to interface with these descendants of those ex-slaves, who really controlled the country. But that was not very advanced there at all. They had a U.S. rubber company in there; I think it was maybe Goodyear or Goodrich that had all these rubber plantations. That was their principle source of culture there.

From Liberia we went up to Senegal, which was a former French colony, and spent some time there. And then we flew from Senegal back to one of the Caribbean islands and then back to MacDill. When I arrived back at MacDill, I had a very bad case

---

* General Ralph E. Haines Jr., USA, was Vice Chief of Staff of the Army, 1967-68; Commander U.S. Army Pacific, 1968-70; and Commanding General, Continental Army Command, 1970-73.
† Nigeria received its independence in 1960.

of the dysentery. My temperature really soared, so they had to put me on a massive dose of penicillin. Fortunately, my fever broke in a couple of days, and I was able to go back to work.

I guess I really earned my spurs with General Adams on that trip to Paris and Naples and Middle East and Africa. We got to be pretty close after that. But he was not a person who really brought people in close to him. He was very formal, even with his own family. But the workload, as I say, was really demanding because those dual responsibilities were just immense. There was really probably more than just one individual should be doing in terms of span of control.

Paul Stillwell: Did he use you as a resource to learn about the Navy?

Admiral Lawrence: Oh, yes. Oh, yes. Sure, and one of the really sensitive issues that I had to work with was this aspect of the Navy operating in support of land operations. General Adams and his staff had conceived this joint task force approach to handling contingency operations, when, basically, they would put together an Army-Air Force team that they would rapidly deploy into a region of the world where there was a crisis. Of course, we had to develop not only an air-delivery response, but also to address this response of an amphibious force being part of this joint task force.

Well, this was really absolute anathema to the Navy to have naval forces come under the operational command of an officer of another service. Now the Navy's a lot more open about this, but back then there had just been a total standoff between the Navy and the Strike Command about amphibious forces coming under the opcon of a joint task force commander. I had to work that issue, and, finally, General Adams acceded to the fact that the naval forces supporting the amphibious forces and the carriers, but also the amphibious ships, would stay under the opcon of a naval commander. Only after the troops were ashore would they come under the opcon of this joint task force commander. So we worked out a doctrine for this, and I was very much involved in that, because for a while General Adams and his staff were hard over about this. They felt that since he was the unified commander that had that area, all naval forces involved in an operation in this area should come under his opcon, and also under the opcon of that joint task force commander. So we had to work out whether the naval forces stayed under the opcon of the Navy and operated what they called in support of. That had been the big point of contention between Page Smith and Felt and General Adams. With Admiral Moorer coming in, and Admiral Massey and I working on that, we got that pretty well solved.

Paul Stillwell: Another issue in that era was the forward-deployed logistic ships, which actually took another 15 years to come about. Was that one of the things you were addressing?

Admiral Lawrence: No, we didn't get involved very much with that.

The issue that the Navy fought and lost had to do with the Middle East Force—that old seaplane tender and two destroyers that were there in the early days.* The question was whether they should be under General Adams's opcon, because he controlled that unified command area. By the unified command plan, those ships should be under his opcon. So, finally, the Navy did agree on that, and General Adams had his own little three-ship Navy. But we were working those types of issues all the time. And it was really, as I say, quite fascinating.

We also had several Army exercises that we ran as part of the CinCStrike responsibility. One, we did the first large armor exercise since World War II. It was right around Needles, California, which is in the desert area in southeastern California, between California and Arizona. We did it on both sides of the Colorado River. Both the First and Second Armored divisions out of Fort Hood, Texas, came out with their tanks, and we had a big armor exercise.†

As part of the helicopter air-mobility tests, we had a big exercise out at Fort Leonard Wood in Missouri, and we also did tests down at Eglin operating the area in Florida, and in the operating area around Fort Jackson, South Carolina. We had some

---

* For many years the U.S. Navy maintained a small Middle East Force in the Persian Gulf as a show-the-flag presence. In the years since this interview, the size of the presence has varied, growing most notably during the tanker wars of the late 1980s and the Gulf War of 1991. The U.S. Fifth Fleet now has its headquarters at Bahrain in the Persian Gulf.
† This was Exercise Desert Strike in May 1964. It involved more than 100,000 men, 780 aircraft, 7,000 wheeled vehicles, and 1,000 tanks. For details, see "Armed Forces: Non-War Is Hell," *Time*, 5 June 1964. The article contains a quote from General Adams, whom the *Time* compared with German Field Marshal Erwin Rommel, known as "The Desert Fox" in World War II.

no-notice exercises, where we just on short notice got an Army battalion and an Air Force squadron deployed at some place to see how quickly they could react. We usually would get a unit from either Fort Campbell or Fort Bragg. We did a lot of traveling to various Army posts, like Fort Riley out in Kansas, Fort Campbell in Kentucky, Fort Bragg. So it was really quite exciting for me to get to learn all about the Army.

When we got into 1965, it was obvious that the Vietnam affair was developing. We were the ones who were charged with working with the Department of the Army and the Department of the Air Force to designate the Army and Air Force units that would be first deployed into Vietnam. I remember the first Army unit that we identified and earmarked was the First Infantry Division out of Fort Riley, Kansas.

Then the next was the First Air Calvary Division, which was the first to be called an air-mobile division. It had massive numbers of helicopters and all of their tactical concepts that they'd been developing under this Joint Test Evaluation Task Force. The First Air Cavalry Division was formed by merging the Second Infantry Division at Fort Benning with the 11th Air Assault Division. They had to take the colors from the First Calvary Division in Korea and bring them down to Fort Benning, and then take the Second Infantry Division and put them out in Korea. They just switched colors.

So that was really exciting, getting those units ready and sending them out to Vietnam. General Adams was the only senior military officer at that time who was predicting that that would be a long, tough war. Everybody else, from President Johnson on down—General Wheeler, Chairman of the JCS; Maxwell Taylor, who was the ambassador out in Vietnam—said, "Oh, we'll get a few Marine-Army divisions in here; we'll mop this thing up real fast."[*] Well, General Adams, who is quite a scholar, had very intensely studied the French-Indochina War from '46 to '54.

He wrote these very long letters to General Wheeler, giving his concern about our preparedness for that war, having the number of troops over there. Because he predicted it would be a tough, hard war, and nobody else would agree with him. I remember in November of 1965, when a brigade of the First Air Cavalry Division encountered some North Vietnamese regular units, in the Battle of Ia Drang Valley, which you may have

---

[*] General Earle G. Wheeler, USA, served as Chairman of the Joint Chiefs of Staff from 3 July 1964 to 2 July 1970.

read about recently in *U.S. News and World Report*. They had a historical coverage because it's the 25th anniversary of the Battle of Ia Drang Valley. These North Vietnamese regulars really bloodied this brigade of the First Air Cav, the Army's very finest. It opened a lot of eyes, and people said, "My God, those North Vietnamese can fight."*

But General Adams had read all about General Giap and Dienbienphu, and he knew that they could fight.† He was not very enthusiastic about going into Vietnam in the first place, but he supported it because he had to. I used to help him put these letters together. He dictated most of his letters, but, as I say, he tended to mumble. He was not articulate. We had a stenographer who was just unbelievable in her ability to get what he said. If she ever got sick, we were in big trouble, because no other stenographer could do it. Anyway, she'd come out and she'd type what she had, and there'd be all sorts of holes. We weren't about to go in there and tell him we hadn't got it. So I used to figure out what he was trying to say. So I would write the prose in these holes in her letters. And he never, ever sent one back. So these letters that were going to General Wheeler and Admiral Moorer and people like that, General Stone up at ConArc, and General Sweeney at Pac—a lot of those were written by me.‡ [Chuckle]

Paul Stillwell: Did they produce any results?

Admiral Lawrence: Well, we never got people to realize that that could be a tough war. By the time I left in January of '66, after being there two years, people were starting to really say, "Yeah, you know, this is going to be a little bit tougher than we thought."

But even though General Adams was happy that I was going to a squadron, I could see a little touch of sadness that I was going to have to go out and be in a war. He

---

* For an excellent first-person account, Harold G. Moore and Joseph L. Galloway, *We Were Soldiers Once – and Young: Ia Drang, the Battle that Change the War in Vietnam* (New York: Random House, 1992).
† General Vo Nguyen Giap, Vietnam People's Army, was the principal military commander during the First Indochina War (1946-54) and the Vietnam War (1960-75).
The Battle of Dienbienphu took place between 13 March and 7 May 1954 in what was then known as French Indochina. Communist Viet Minh troops defeated the French Army garrison at the time peace negotiations were getting under way in Geneva Switzerland. The French surrender on 7 May paved the way for French disengagement in the region and the later establishment of North and South Vietnam.
‡ ConArc – Continental Army Command; ArPac – U.S. Army Pacific.

knew all about the horrors of war, because he'd been in both World War II and the Korean War.

Paul Stillwell: Would you say that he perceived it as a futile effort in Vietnam?

Admiral Lawrence: No, I think he felt that we should be able to win it. He just felt that it was going to be a hard, tough war, based on his study of history.

Well, I'm going to go over to the Quarterback Club luncheon, so I guess I'd better stop here.

Paul Stillwell: Let me ask you one more question, if I may. How would you assess Admiral Massey's role in all this?

Admiral Lawrence: Well, he had a tough job because under the Army concept, the chief of staff runs the staff. Our staff was completely joint. We didn't have a group that dealt with the Strike Command people and a group that dealt with the CinCMEAFSA, although there were some people who really did only the one type of thing. It was a very completely unified staff. We had a J-1 through a J-7 in our staff, and the J-7 was a military assistance. The people in J-5, which is the planning, were mostly involved in the CinCMEAFSA. But they also had to develop the rapid-deployment contingency plans.

So Admiral Massey had a real burden, because he had to come in as a naval officer and learn about the Army and Air Force. But General Adams was really very good to Admiral Massey. He really bent over backwards to make his job as effective as possible. General Adams, as I say, was tough, really hard on the Army officers. But after making sure that I had the right stuff and I earned my spurs, he was basically very good to me. But he's a very intense guy. If you worked closely with him, he was going to spread some flak on you from time to time, because he was very caught up and intense. We had tough battles that we had to fight, trying to get things done where people just didn't agree with us. But I'll talk some more in a later session on some of the other trips I made. We made another trip through Europe and down to Naples. And we'll get into some of the other issues that we had to deal with while we were there, such as the Dominican Republic operation.

Paul Stillwell: Well, we'll get that next time. Thank you.

Interview Number 8 with Vice Admiral William P. Lawrence, U.S. Navy (Retired)
Place: U.S. Naval Institute, Annapolis, Maryland
Date: Wednesday, 7 November 1990

Paul Stillwell: Admiral, when we finished up a couple of days ago, you had gotten well into discussion of your time with General Adams at the Strike Command, and now I believe you want to phase into the Vietnam War aspect of it.

Admiral Lawrence: Yes, I want to explain what our role was in the Strike Command in the Vietnam War buildup. But I might mention that as part of General Adams's responsibilities as a unified commander, having cognizance over the Middle East, South Asia, and Africa south of the Sahara, he really played a very active role in an organization that used to be called CENTO.* It was kind of the Middle East-South Asia counterpart of NATO, but it never really gained the stature of NATO or had the cohesion and so forth. I don't think CENTO even exists nowadays. It dissolved back with all the Arab-Israeli problems and the Iran situation.

Paul Stillwell: Well, ironically, there was the Baghdad Pact, and now Baghdad's the thorn in our side.†

Admiral Lawrence: That's right. There was a Baghdad Pact too.
But, anyway, it was always interesting to participate in those CENTO activities, because, as I recall, CENTO was composed of the Turks and, basically, all of the Moslem nations in the Middle East and South Asia were members of CENTO. So it gave me a lot of good insight in dealing with the CENTO representatives and going to some of these CENTO meetings. We had one of them back in Tampa at our headquarters at MacDill

---
* CENTO – Central Treaty Organization. Originally known as the Middle East Treaty Organization (METO), it was established in 1955 by the Baghdad Pact as an alliance of Iran, Iraq, Pakistan, Turkey, and the United Kingdom. The United States joined CENTO's military committee in 1958. CENTO was dissolved in 1979, the year Iran seized U.S. embassy personnel as hostages.
† At the time of this interview, the United States was involved in Desert Shield, building up forces in the Middle East in response to Iraq's invasion of Kuwait in the summer of 1990.

Air Force Base. I learned a lot about the Moslem approach to military affairs, so that was a very interesting aspect of what we were doing.

Paul Stillwell: Did you get to fly in that job at all?

Admiral Lawrence: Oh, I flew a lot, of course, in airplanes going to and from. But I had to fly with the Air Force at MacDill. I flew the F-80, or what they called the T-33, which was the administrative jet airplane.[*] Of course, I was very experienced in the F-4, and when I arrived at MacDill, the Air Force was just getting the F-4, and the transition training unit was there. They had a very colorful colonel named Pete Everest, who'd been an ace in the Air Force.[†] So I approached him one time, and said, "Look, you know, I have a lot of experience in the F-4. I might be able to help you all down here." He wasn't interested at all in having a naval aviator get involved in the Air Force business. So I never got to fly the F-4s, although they were at MacDill. So all of my proficiency flying, as we call it, was in the T-33.

One time, General LeMay, who was the Chief of Staff of the Air Force then, came down to MacDill to visit with us. He used to fly an Air Force KC-130 that had no real refinements in it at all.[‡] It was just a straight, fleet-type airplane. He invited General Adams and me to accompany him back to Washington, because General Adams had to go there. He said, "Well, no sense in taking our separate airplane; we can go with General LeMay."

So I remember watching General LeMay when we got in the airplane, because I had always heard he flew his own airplane. But he sat in a single seat behind the pilot compartment, and he was reading a paperback and smoking a cigar. Then, when the airplane got out to the end of the runway, the pilot came back and said, "General, we're ready." So he stepped in, took the airplane off, climbed it up to a certain altitude, then came back out, sat down and resumed reading his book while chewing on a cigar. When

---

[*] The Lockheed T-33 Shooting Star Air Force trainer was designated T2V Seastar by the Navy. It was developed from the F-80 fighter.
[†] Colonel Frank K. Everest Jr., USAF, was a World War II ace and later a test pilot. From 1961 to 1964 he commanded the 4453d Combat Crew Training Wing at MacDill Air Force Base.
[‡] The KC-130 is the tanker version of the C-130 Hercules transport plane.

we got to the destination, they came and said, "General, we're ready." So he went back up and made the approach and landing. Then after the landing, he came back. So that's the way General LeMay flew the airplane. But he read a paperback the whole time he was in there. I expected him to be doing paperwork and things like that, but not at all.

I remember one time when we were out on this big armor exercise Desert Strike in 1964 that I told you about. General LeMay came out to visit us, and we had a little field mess. It wasn't very plush at all. As the senior aide to General Adams on that trip, I had to run that mess. So I came in there one time to see how things were going, and General LeMay showed up a little bit before everybody else. Just to be nice, I said, "Good evening, General, how are you?" He didn't even answer me. He's a very taciturn guy. I couldn't even hold a conversation with him, because he just was not inclined to speak to me, and he was the antithesis of small talk at all. But it was kind of interesting to see the famous Curtis LeMay.[*]

Paul Stillwell: Did you ever see any other side of him? Did you see the bombastic side?

Admiral Lawrence: No, I guess I never saw him in a role where he had to display that. But he was basically a very quiet and reserved guy in those type settings.

Paul Stillwell: The movie *Doctor Strangelove* came out about that time and had almost a caricature of LeMay in it.[†]

Admiral Lawrence: Yes. Well, that was an interesting aspect of that job that threw me in contact with some senior officers that I'd read about. Maxwell Taylor was the Chairman of the Joint Chiefs of Staff when I first came in with General Adams. Then he left to go out to be the ambassador to South Vietnam.[‡] I remember he made one trip as the

---

[*] During World War II, as a major general, LeMay was commanding general of the 21st Bomber Command, which was ran B-29 bombing strikes against the Japanese Empire.
[†] *Dr. Strangelove* was a 1964 movie that was a dark satire of the nuclear arms race between the United States and the Soviet Union.
[‡] Even though he had retired from active duty after serving as Army Chief of Staff from 1955 to 1959, General Maxwell D. Taylor, became Chairman of the Joint Chiefs of Staff on 1 October 1962 and served in that post until 3 July 1964. He was then U.S. Ambassador to South Vietnam in 1964-65.

Chairman before he left to go out there. Then, of course, I had a lot of interface with General Wheeler, who was the Chairman of the Joint Chiefs of Staff for six years.[*]

Also, there were some famous generals from World War II that I got a chance to see, like General Gavin.[†] And there was a General Jacob Smart, who had led the raid against the Ploesti airfields.[‡] That was kind of interesting, too, because in the mid-'60s the World War II-era leaders were still in power. I remember General Lyman Lemnitzer was SACEur. When we went over to these meetings in Paris, General Lemnitzer hosted a big reception. He, of course, was a very distinguished gentleman.

And I remember, in connection with one of our trips over to Paris to what they called the SHAPE, which was run by SACEur, we went over to England, and General Adams met with Admiral Mountbatten, who at that time was in a position that was comparable to our Chairman of the JCS—the Chief of Defence Staff.[§] So I had a chance to see Admiral Mountbatten, who was a very imposing figure.

Paul Stillwell: Any other impressions of him?

Admiral Lawrence: Well, he just exuded dignity and was just a very distinguished gentleman. And he wasn't arrogant. I mean, he had a warmth about him that I thought was very impressive. I always enjoyed going to London because the Navy headquarters over there is on Grosvenor Square, right across from the American Embassy. They're in the same building that was Eisenhower's headquarters during World War II.[**] So I always had a real sense of history when I went to London.

That was one of the really thrilling aspects about working with General Adams; it enabled me to meet people and be exposed to situations I just wouldn't have otherwise.

---

[*] General Earle G. Wheeler, USA, served as Chairman of the Joint Chiefs of Staff from 3 July 1964 to 2 July 1970.
[†] Major General James M. Gavin, USA, commanded the 82nd Airborne Division in World War II. He retired from the Army as a lieutenant general in 1958 and subsequently served as U.S. ambassador to France, 1961-62.
[‡] General Jacob E. Smart, USAF, served as Deputy Commander U.S. European Command, 1964-66. He was the architect of a raid that 178 B-24 Liberator bombers made against oil refineries in Ploesti, Romania, on 1 August 1943.
[§] Admiral of the Fleet The Earl Mountbatten of Burma served as Britain's Chief of Defence Staff from 1959 to 1965.
[**] In 1944-45 General of the Army Dwight D. Eisenhower, USA, served as Supreme Command Allied Expeditionary Force.

And it was very good education for me in so many ways, learning about the other services, learning about high-level planning.

But General Adams was the only senior officer in that time who perceived that the Vietnam War was going to be a tough war.

Paul Stillwell: We talked about that some the last time.

Admiral Lawrence: Okay. Well, I won't go over that again, but our role in that was to identify the units to deploy to Vietnam from what we call the strategic reserve in the Continental U.S. The thing that was interesting was that we had been so busy and focused on Africa and Middle East, and also that contingency down in the Caribbean— the Dominican Republic—that we really weren't aware of the problems developing over in Southeast Asia.

Paul Stillwell: Well, that was really CinCPac's area.

Admiral Lawrence: That's right. I remember the bombing strike there in August when Alvarez was shot down.[*] But I only took just casual note of it. But then, when it became apparent that the President wanted to increase our role over there, it was our responsibility to work with the Department of the Army and the Department of the Air Force and the Commander in Chief of the Tactical Air Command and Commander in Chief of the Continental Army Command to determine what units we would deploy. Then our director of logistics had to make arrangements for the transportation, both the surface transportation out to the port of embarkation, and then lay on the ships to send them over there.

I remember the first division we earmarked to go was the First Infantry Division out at Fort Riley. It was a kind of a fortuitous thing that we had earlier had done a study of an Army division that was what we called tailored for airlift. In other words, General Adams directed this study, and it showed how really brilliant he was. He could see these

---

[*] On 5 August 1964, while flying an A-4E Skyhawk from the carrier *Constellation* (CVA-64), Lieutenant (junior grade) Everett Alvarez Jr., USNR, was shot down and captured, the first POW of the Vietnam War. His oral history is in the Naval Institute collection.

situations—as we've seen here recently in the Middle East—where you would have to take an Army division that you needed to deploy somewhere. Then you would decide what people and components of that division would be sent by air and what others had to be sent by surface. We finished that study just before the Vietnam War buildup occurred.

As a part of that study, we went out to Fort Riley. They had the whole division, both personnel and equipment, laid out on a big parade field. The elements that would go by air were in one area, and they were laid out in an arrangement in the sequence by which they would be embarked and flown over. Then another component was laid out as a surface component. And that was laid out in a way that would be the logical sequence for embarking in ships. The title of that study was "An Army Division Tailored for Air and Surface Lift." It really helped us when the Vietnam War broke out. So that just showed you how perceptive General Adams was. He had a great logistical sense.

Paul Stillwell: Did you observe as time went on that the planners were spending more of their time on Vietnam?

Admiral Lawrence: Well, see, we weren't developing any real contingency operations for Vietnam, because that was not our area; that was CinCPac. The people who were doing most of our planning were the director of operations and the director of logistics, because the director of operations worked with the Tactical Air Command and the Continental Army Command, in determining which units should be sent, based on the force buildup plan. And, of course, they worked closely with the Joint Staff, and I'm sure CinCPac was actively playing. Once the unit was identified, like the First Division at Riley or the First Air Cav Division down at Fort Benning, our director of logistics had to determine the most feasible way of getting them over there. We did it mostly by surface, because we just didn't have the airlift at that time to take heavy equipment.

Paul Stillwell: Well, a lot of old ships came out of mothballs.

Admiral Lawrence: Yes, I'm sure they did. In fact, I know we did a lot of commercial charters to get those ships over there.

But, anyway, as we got that Dominican Republic crisis put to bed, and we saw the Vietnam buildup was coming on, General Adams wrote a series of letters to General Wheeler telling him that it was his perception that it was going to be a tough war, and we'd better get all the mechanisms in place to do it as successfully as possible. In other words, not only get the combat units over there but develop the logistics infrastructure as required to conduct that war as efficiently as possible. He was the only senior officer I saw at that time who had any air of concern or pessimism. Everybody else just kind of had the attitude, "Well, we'll get a few divisions over there, and we'll mop them up real quick." But General Adams had studied history; he'd studied about the Dienbienphu, the famous book about how the Vietnamese won over there—I think written by a Frenchman.*

Paul Stillwell: I don't know.

Admiral Lawrence: It was about how tough that war had been, and General Giap had been a brilliant, tactical general. General Adams knew all that; he studied that war very thoroughly. Here he was exhorting everybody to be prepared for a long haul, and General Wheeler and all these other people were—I could just tell they just had an air of cockiness about them that we'd mop them up in a hurry. General Adams's son was in the First Air Cav Division, which was the second Army division to go, and that was the first real air-mobile division, vast numbers of helicopters. So General Adams was very concerned about that division.

So, anyway, that's just an element of the Vietnam War preparation that I thought I would inject. But it was a great learning experience for me in every respect. And it really helped me tremendously, as I got to be more senior, in learning how to operate with the Army and the Air Force and make plans with the Army and Air Force.

Paul Stillwell: Well, they had different mind-sets; they approached problems differently. Could you expound on that, please.

---

* The book may have been Bernard Fall's *Street Without Joy: Indochina at War, 1946-54* (Harrisburg, Pennsylvania: Stackpole, 1961).

Admiral Lawrence: Well, the Air Force and Army—the Army, in particular—are better schooled than we are. In other words, they have a mandatory school requirement for every officer who's moving up. For example, as a young officer, you go to what they call the branch school, like artillery school down at Fort Sill, Oklahoma; armor school at Fort Knox, Kentucky; or infantry school down at Fort Benning. So as young lieutenants, they go to the branch schools and get all the basics—how to be effective junior officers in that branch.

As majors, they go through the Command and General Staff College out at Fort Leavenworth. Then as lieutenant colonels or colonels, they go to the Army War College or to the Naval War College or the Air War College. Those three schools are absolute prerequisites for promotion. It's very rare that any officer would be promoted to general, for example, who hasn't attended the Army War College at Carlisle, Pennsylvania. So the Army officers are much better schooled; they're better professional staff officers than the naval officers. The quality of their staff work is just absolutely superb.

Paul Stillwell: Would it be fair to say that they take a cookbook approach, because they've studied the cookbook?

Admiral Lawrence: Oh, yes, that's right. They do. They are much more prone to follow doctrine that's been formally established than naval officers are. Naval officers are more improvisers, and that's because of our tradition of operating often in single ships. A ship is always regarded as an autonomous unit, and the commanding officer of a ship is almost a god. Whereas, in the Army, everybody's within a larger organization. They're a lot more attuned and use doctrine than we do. We have tactical doctrine publications and all that, but naval officers don't study them and master them as Army officers do.

Paul Stillwell: Well, the naval officer doesn't have the luxury in peacetime of being able to just get away from things and study as much either.

Admiral Lawrence: That's right, that's right, because we're always operating.

Army officers also tend to be better professional staff officers in terms of writing staff papers, preparing briefings, and things like that. They're not smarter, but they're more competent, better-trained staff officers. But I found that naval officers, just in conceptual thinking, will often be vastly superior to Army officers, because they're not constrained to do things the standard way. We're used to operating more independently during our careers.

Paul Stillwell: Where would you put Air Force officers in that mix?

Admiral Lawrence: They're not quite as well schooled in staff procedures as the Army officers; they're more operationally oriented, I think. Often you'll find the Air Force pilots who stay pilots. But they are also very doctrinally oriented. In other words, the Air Force probably has the most detailed procedures on how you can operate an airplane and all that.

Paul Stillwell: Well, in that sense, the Navy does too. I mean there's a certain way to do an underway replenishment, a certain way to fly an F-4.

Admiral Lawrence: Yes. And the Air Force really led the way in its counterpart of what we now call NATOPS, Naval Aviation Training and Operation Procedures. We really kind of patterned that after the Air Force. But in terms of being professional staff officers, I'd rank it Army, Air Force, and Navy. But I learned a lot from them in that joint command. I'm a great advocate of giving people joint assignments. I think it really was a great preparation.

Paul Stillwell: Well, anything more on that before we get you back into the squadron?

Admiral Lawrence: Well, as I mentioned previously, I'd gotten knocked out of the astronaut program because I had this heart murmur that was detected in the selection tests conducted by NASA. They maintained the data that was obtained during our screening test and did not make it available to our services. I had learned, of course, from talking to the doctor, that I had a heart murmur. In fact, they sent me a copy of the report that this very prominent cardiologist did on me, and so I took that back to the Naval Air Test Center after the NASA tests were over. I showed that to my flight surgeon, and he said, "Ah, you're in good health, and just don't worry about it."

So I said, "Okay." So the Navy did not take official cognizance of the fact that I had this heart murmur in the NASA test in 1959. And no Navy doctor picked up my murmur for the next several years. But when I was getting my annual physical down at MacDill Air Force Base before I was leaving the Strike Command to go back to the squadron, this young Air Force doctor said, "Hey, I think I hear a heart murmur."

I said, "Well, you know, I'm going back to the Navy next month. Why don't you just fill out the form and then send it out to the flight surgeon down at Naval Air Station Miramar."

When I arrived out there at Miramar, my flight surgeon said, "Hey, you have a heart murmur and we have to pursue this, because it's a disqualifying condition."

So I said, "Okay. The guy down there at MacDill just called it as he saw it. I wasn't trying to influence him."

The flight surgeon said, "This is the type of ailment where you just simply have to go into the hospital at Balboa and get a thorough cardiological workup."[*]

Well, I went over to Balboa and checked in, and there were no flight surgeons there in the cardiological service. Their inclination was that, "This is disqualifying you. If a person had this applying to come in the Navy, he'd probably be disqualified. And that doesn't even mention going into aviation, which is even more demanding."

So I called up my friends who were flight surgeons and got in touch with Frank Austin.[†] Frank had been both a pilot and a flight surgeon, and he knew both the aviation and the medical side of it. So, rather than have Balboa declare me not qualified for flying, he convinced them that the board of flight surgeons down in Pensacola should evaluate my case.

So after arriving out in California in February of '66, ready to go to work, I was sent down to Pensacola and had to fight to stay in naval aviation. But the flight surgeons

---

[*] Balboa Naval Hospital, San Diego.
[†] Captain Frank H. Austin Jr., Medical Corps, USN.

analyzed the situation and said, "Hey, you've been in naval aviation for 15 years now, and you're healthy. Your heart murmur is what we call human dynamically insignificant, so we're going to give you a waiver to stay in naval aviation, service group one." They said I was the first guy that they'd ever known in history who had a heart murmur and was allowed to stay in a military field, aviation particularly.

But it appeared that my heart and respiratory system had fully compensated for this situation that I had.

Paul Stillwell: Your life certainly would have been different if you hadn't got that waiver, wouldn't it?

Admiral Lawrence: [Chuckle] Yes. I would have not, of course, been a POW. And it's always been kind of interesting to analyze that. But, anyway, I started to go through that and finally was declared okay for flying by the flight surgeons and came back to go into replacement squadron training.* Shortly after I got there, my squadron deployed out to the Pacific.† So, since I had a fair amount of F-4 experience, they rushed me through the replacement training, and it was just a refresher. Then I flew out to join the squadron.

Paul Stillwell: How had you gotten assigned to that particular squadron?

Admiral Lawrence: Well, I think it was just the luck of the draw. I told my detailer, "I definitely want to go to a PacFlt squadron, because I want to get out in the Vietnam War."

Paul Stillwell: Was there a command screening somewhere along with this process?

Admiral Lawrence: Yes, I'd passed the command screening at least a year earlier. And, of course, we have the executive officer-commanding officer fleet-up program in naval

---

* The replacement air group (RAG) squadron was Fighter Squadron 121 (VF-121), with which Lawrence had operated in the early 1960s during the F-4 transition training.
† Lawrence's permanent assignment, following refresher training, was to Fighter Squadron 143 (VF-143).

aviation. So I knew I'd go right in as executive officer, and then a year later I would move up to commanding officer.

Paul Stillwell: Well, that was still relatively new at that time. A few years earlier the exec didn't necessarily take command.

Admiral Lawrence: Yes, I think we probably put the RAG concept in around 1958-59, and I think that's the time we put the XO-CO fleet-up program.* It was all part of the effort to improve safety, because we were having a very high accident rate and got some of this new breed of airplanes out there, like the F8U and the F3D, where you really needed to have more experienced pilots and accrue the continuity in the squadron. The thing that I noticed in the early years when a guy would come in directly as CO, particularly out of a shore establishment, his credibility as a CO would be adversely impacted because of his lack of recent experience. And that would degrade his effectiveness as a leader. But in the XO-CO fleet-up, by the time the guy gets to be CO, he's really got his edge back.

Paul Stillwell: Well, another change was that you had previously been in the F-4 just when it was coming into use. Now it was a going concern.

Admiral Lawrence: Well, that's very true. And it was really playing a yeoman's role out there in Vietnam, both in doing bombing missions as well as the combat air patrol.†

But, anyway, I had to lag my squadron getting out there two to three months. I joined them in the middle of the summer and had the rest of the cruise out there on the *Ranger*.‡ When I got in there, we had stopped bombing in South Vietnam. We had built

---

* RAG – replacement air group was the designation of a squadron that trained pilots and other flight crew members in a specific type of aircraft before the personnel reported to a fleet squadron flying that particular plane. The current term is fleet replacement squadron.
† Combat air patrol is a group of fighter planes deployed in the air to intercept incoming air raids headed toward a naval force.
‡ USS *Ranger* (CVA-61) was commissioned 10 August 1957. She had a standard displacement of 56,300 tons, was 1,046 feet long, 236 feet in the beam, an extreme width of 249 feet on the flight deck, and had a draft of 37 feet. She had a top speed of 34 knots and could accommodate about 80-95 planes. The ship's deployment to the Western Pacific was from 10 December 1965 to 25 August 1966 with Carrier Air Wing 14 (CVW-14) embarked.

up the Air Force to the point that they could handle all of the South Vietnam bombing with their in-country assets. That's when the Navy moved entirely to bombing North Vietnam.

Paul Stillwell: Well, before that there had been this Dixie Station, and carriers sort of warmed up on that before they went to Yankee Station.*

Admiral Lawrence: We did away with Dixie Station; it became all Yankee Station, and that happened just before I got out there on my first deployment in 1966.

Paul Stillwell: Interesting, those terms were used from the Civil War 100 years earlier.

Admiral Lawrence: Yes, that's right.

But, boy, it was a tough battle getting those doctors to give me an up status, so I was really happy when I finished that RAG and I was heading out to the squadron and combat.

Paul Stillwell: Anything to say about that RAG time?

Admiral Lawrence: Well, it was good to give me a way to get caught back up and really become an expert on the weapon system and the F-4. And, of course, it was nice to have that time to spend with my family, because I'd been so busy in the Strike Command, and I was traveling so much that I had a lot of separation from my family. So going through the RAG, flying an airplane that I was really familiar with, I didn't have to work quite as hard as I would have otherwise. So it was a good family experience.

Paul Stillwell: Did you find any changes in F-4 doctrine as a result of the combat experience?

---

* During the initial stages of involvement in the Vietnam War, the U.S. Navy maintained aircraft carriers on two stations based on Civil War designations—Yankee Station off North Vietnam and Dixie Station off South Vietnam. The latter, which began on 16 May 1965, was dropped 15 months later once airfields were available ashore in South Vietnam.

Admiral Lawrence: Well, not really significantly. Of course, we got a lot more knowledgeable about delivering ordnance in the F-4. When I'd been in my first F-4 squadron back in '62-63, we didn't even consider carrying air-to-ground ordnance on airplanes. We knew that the capability existed there, but no fighter pilot [chuckle] really looks upon himself as a bomber. But we very rapidly geared up to use the F-4, in fact, as an attack airplane. It made eminently good sense.

Paul Stillwell: Because there wasn't that much of an enemy air threat.

Admiral Lawrence: Yes, that's right. That's right. So all my missions on that cruise were up in North Vietnam.

Paul Stillwell: Well, please describe what a mission was like.

Admiral Lawrence: Well, let me talk a little bit about the package setup they had up there in North Vietnam. For planning purposes, North Vietnam was divided into six zones—one being the zone at the very southern part of North Vietnam. What we called package six was the very northern part, and comprised of the area of Haiphong over on the coast and then Hanoi inland.[*] All of our targets were being assigned out to us from right in the White House. At an Air Force history symposium last week, I found that LBJ himself was making a lot of these target assignments.[†] Then the target assignments would come out to us the night before a mission.

On the '66 cruise, the majority of our targets were in the central part of North Vietnam, usually around package two or three. We really didn't get up there in the heartland of North Vietnam during that '66 cruise. We got back off the line just before

---

[*] Starting with the Rolling Thunder Campaign in late 1965, North Vietnam was divided into six Route Packages (RP). They were numbered one through six, running roughly south to north with the south edge of RP1 on the DMZ and the north edge of RP6 at the Chinese border. RP6 was divided into 6A and 6B, 6A from the Gulf of Tonkin to Hanoi, 6B between Hanoi and Laos. Generally, but not always, the Navy flew in Packages 2, 4, and 6A. The Air Force flew in 5 and 6B. The Marines flew mostly in country (that is, South Vietnam) and in Package One. Hanoi was the capital of North Vietnam. Haiphong, about 60 miles east of Hanoi, was a seaport in the Red River Delta.

[†] Lyndon B. Johnson served as President of the United States from 22 November 1963 to 20 January 1969.

the big escalation occurred out there, and they started hitting targets that had been off the list.

Paul Stillwell: How much of a SAM threat did you face?

Admiral Lawrence: Well, we really didn't see a great SAM threat in '66.[*] We knew they were there, but they had dispersed them pretty widely throughout the country. The other thing that became very painfully apparent to us was that if a missile was charging up the flight path towards you, we didn't have the electronic countermeasure equipment in the plane that could make it break lock.

Paul Stillwell: Did you at least have a warning?

Admiral Lawrence: No, in the F-4s we didn't. The A-4s had a lot more sophisticated electronic countermeasures capability than we had because of their nuclear weapons mission, where they would theoretically go overland in Russia. We had nothing because before the Vietnam War, the F-4 fighters were strictly for fleet air defense.

Paul Stillwell: So you had to see the missile coming.

Admiral Lawrence: Yes, that's right. We got no warning through the detection of its thrashing signal, that sort of thing. Fortunately, on that '66 cruise, we really didn't see many missiles, because they were so widely spread through the country that they couldn't really mobilize any real density in one place.

Paul Stillwell: What was the mix of day and night operations?

Admiral Lawrence: Oh, we had a schedule that when there were two carriers out there, one would fly from noon till midnight, and the other one would fly just the opposite. Sometimes we had three carriers out there, and then one would fly midnight to noon; the

---

[*] SAM – surface-to-air missile.

other would fly noon to midnight; and then the third carrier would fly 0800 to 1800. Really the worst time, of course, was to fly from midnight to noon, because, you'd wake up in the middle of the night and you'd not get acclimated to that sleeping schedule. So I hated the midnight to noon; I much preferred the other one.

That kind of program existed through most of the war. Then we were flying every 1.5 hours, so you'd get eight cycles a day. When you were out there on the line for about 30 days, you tried to settle into a number of sorties a day, a good, comfortable load to keep enough demand on the personnel and maintenance equipment to keep producing enough airplanes.

So the whole pace, when I went out in that '66 cruise was altogether different from the '67 cruise, because the intensity of our sorties, the risk associated with the nature of the targets that we were hitting there, they were just much more benign than they were when we came back in '67.

Paul Stillwell: On the other hand, it was a lot different from the peacetime cruises you'd been in.

Admiral Lawrence: Oh, yes, yes. I mean, you were always aware you were being shot at; I'll tell you that.

During the next cruise, when we went into the Hanoi-Haiphong area in '67, by that time, the North Vietnamese had brought all the missiles and concentrated a tremendous amount of fire in that Red River Valley Delta. And so, boy, in '67 it was really quite a tough air battle when you went in there.

I guess I probably shouldn't jump ahead here to '67 right now, but, as I say, the '66 cruise, in terms of risk and everything, to me was very manageable. In other words, I knew I was being shot at, but I didn't really feel there was a great element of danger. We knew, of course, that that lack of electronic countermeasures—the lack of ability to break lock, and all that—was a real detriment to us. Fortunately, we had a squadron skipper named Doc Townsend who was very technically oriented, so he did a lot of good work in defining what we really needed in those airplanes to help us detect the missiles.*

We needed, of course, a system that would detect the missile's basic search radar signal. Then, once it did lock on you, you also had to be able to detect the guidance signal. It was a very complicated system in the airplane to counter these missiles. So when we came back from that '66 cruise, we had to put all of our airplanes through the modification program to get this ECM equipment called the APR-25. It was a strobe indication that would tell you the direction of the threat, and it would have an audio signal to basically be able to tell you when the missile had gone to high PRF and it was getting ready to lock on you.†

We had to just really knock ourselves out when we came back in August of 1966, to get all these ECM systems in our airplanes. This was done over at the overhaul and repair depot there at North Island.‡ So it really reduced our capability to fly and train as much as we wanted to. But I think everybody who was going out on the next cruise in '67 was on board. This was in fall of '66, so although our flight training was reduced, we were able to get to nuggets, the new kids, a fair number of flights to get them up to speed.

Paul Stillwell: What do you remember about the relationship with the other squadrons in the air wing?

Admiral Lawrence: Well, that was a good relationship, and, of course, we had a sister F-4 squadron, and there was always a lot of kidding that went on, but there was still a lot of good camaraderie.

---

* Commander Marland W. Townsend Jr., USN, commanded the squadron from July 1966 to June 1967. Later, as a captain, he commanded the carrier *Kitty Hawk* (CVA-63) in 1972-73. For further biographical information on Townsend, see Gregory A. Freeman, *Troubled Water: Race, Mutiny, and Bravery on the USS Kitty Hawk* (New York: Palgrave Macmillan, 2009).
† PRF – pulse repetition frequency. The AN/APR-25 had a cathode ray tube in the cockpit that showed on the screen the threat's range and relative bearing.
‡ North Island Naval Air Station is on the end of the Coronado peninsula, across the harbor from San Diego.

I was in an interesting squadron that had always been known for its exuberance and sometimes rowdiness. It was VF-143.* The symbol of the squadron, the insignia that we always painted on the airplanes, was a creature from mythology called the "winged griffin."† It basically looks like a dog with a wing on its back, and the squadron insignia was this winged griffin bent over with its mouth open. So I guess it was just a natural that somebody called it the "pukin' dog." We had another nickname, which I can't even remember, because no one ever used it. I think the squadron kind of felt it had a reputation to live up to, because it was always a very flamboyant group and had wild parties—contrary to my image.

Doc Townsend, who was the skipper when I was the XO, was a very colorful character, very outgoing and flamboyant. But I wanted to clean up our image, because I could see a lot of ways where the young officers would come into the squadron, and they would feel compelled to maintain such a lifestyle of heavy drinking and all of that. So I was really trying to make us a little bit more sedate.

But one funny thing was that when I was told that this squadron was called the P-U-K-I-N dogs, I never connected it with puking. I thought, "Maybe this creature from mythology is from a province in China called the Pukin Province." I really thought that was it; I couldn't believe that it would be called the puking dogs. So, anyway, I came in the squadron; I sat down with the skipper, Doc Townsend, and I said, "Do we have any fact sheet or write-up about this? I want to know about the origin of the word 'Pukin.' Is it a Chinese term?"

He just rolled over in gales of laughter, and then he said, "Say, you know, that's a good idea. That's a good way we can clean up our image." So I sat down and I wrote out something that said, "Our squadron insignia is a winged griffin, but it's a creature from Chinese mythology from the Pukin Province of China." [Laughter]

We started distributing it around, and everybody said, "Ah, come on, you guys are full of baloney. You'll always be the pukin' dogs, so don't try to clean up your image or anything like that."

---

* For an article with a detailed history of the squadron, see Fred Tannenbaum, "Papa Wasn't a Rolling Stone. He was a Pukin' Dog," *The Hook: Journal of Carrier Aviation*, Fall 2001, pages 15-26.
† The mythological griffin (sometimes spelled griffon or gryphon) had the head, body, and talons of an eagle fused to the body, tail, and hind legs of a lion.

Paul Stillwell: So this was some modern mythology.

Admiral Lawrence: We actually had that thing written up and were sending it around all over the place, but nobody would buy it.

Anyway, this nickname was a detriment, because we'd fly all these missions, and at the end of the day the carrier would write up a news release to go back to the CONUS newspapers and wire services.[*] But we had to send it first down to the Seventh Fleet detachment in Saigon. Their public affairs people had to clear this news release before we could send it back to the States. So every day we'd send out a message and our public affairs officer, or whoever worked with him, always insisted the VF-143 Pukin' Dogs knocked out two bridges and did all of this. Then the message would always come back from the Seventh Fleet det saying, "To *Ranger*, your news release is approved except in line five, delete Pukin' Dogs, line ten delete Pukin' Dogs." No one would let us send Pukin' Dogs out in the news release.

So I saw Captain Buddy Yates, who later on became a rear admiral.[†] He was then the head of that Seventh Fleet detachment down there. I said, "Hey, you really ought to let us put Pukin' Dogs in there. That's how we're known all over the world, and that's an accepted nickname."

He said, "No, no, we can't do that. We don't want that to get back to the U.S. newspapers. It would be bad for the Navy's image."

The '66 deployment out there was tough in a lot of respects in the pace and intensity of the operations, but the element of danger wasn't there. I mean, you knew you were being shot at. You could see the flak and an occasional missile, because the missile installations were spread pretty widely. And, of course, the Russians were building up the numbers of missiles in there. So in the '66 deployment, I just never was really aware of the threat of their air defenses like I was when I came back in '67.

Paul Stillwell: What kind of tactics did you use to make this fighter plane into an attack plane?

---

[*] CONUS – Continental United States.
[†] Captain Earl P. Yates, USN.

Admiral Lawrence: Well, the original Phantom was going to be the AH1; it was going to be an attack airplane, and then the Navy had to use it as a fighter. So it had all the capabilities—wing strength and wing area—to be able to carry all this ordnance, in addition to the air-to-air missiles. The airplane, as I recall, would carry four missiles in the fuselage. These were basically submerged into the body of the airplane. Then you could carry two Sparrow missiles on your wings. But then you'd have these other wing stations, where you could carry all sorts of ordnance. So it was to be used very readily as a bomber.

Paul Stillwell: How large a section would you have going at a time?

Admiral Lawrence: Well, in the '66 cruise we did a lot of two-plane bombing missions. Sometimes we'd bring it up to four, but we weren't doing the large-scale attacks that we called Alfa strikes.

Paul Stillwell: What kind of altitude?

Admiral Lawrence: Well, our squadron doctrine came from our skipper, Doc Townsend. He was very astute, very fine technically; he had a master's in aeronautical engineering, and he knew the technical aspects of our profession very well. He developed a doctrine—and the other squadrons didn't all subscribe to this—that we would approach the coast at low altitude. The carrier, usually, was only about 100 miles out from the coast of Vietnam. In our doctrine, when we got within about 50 miles from the coast, we'd go up to about 15,000 or 20,000 feet and then come in. Then you'd lower down to about 50 feet off the water, and then when you hit the coastline, you would pop up. Most of our targets that we were getting at that time were within 15 to 20 miles to the coast. So we would pop up to 10,000 feet and then proceed in and make our bombing runs from 10,000 feet. When we hit the coastline, we would have our speed up to about 450 knots indicated air speed, which gave us about 500 knots true.

So we'd be going pretty fast when we hit over land to minimize the risk of the triple A and make it a more difficult solution then by going fast.* Then we would make our bomb run. Usually you used a 45-degree angle for a bomb or rocket run. It was a very interesting challenge, because you had no electronic navigational aids, so you had to do all your navigating to your target visually. You had to study that chart thoroughly beforehand, so that you could readily recognize the terrain features in helping you find that target. It was really imperative that you know exactly where you were and be able to hit the precise roll-in point that you'd selected. So, as a flight leader, I used to really study those charts very thoroughly before every flight. I just knew that chart so thoroughly that once I looked down at the ground, I could easily recognize where I was.

Paul Stillwell: That would really be a challenge at night.

Admiral Lawrence: Well, that's right. And this was one of my real sore points about that Vietnam War. We weren't allowed to mine Haiphong or to cut the northeast-northwest railroad link to China. So we would let the supplies get in country and then try to find the trucks, which they only rolled at night. That was absolutely the worst way in the world to prosecute a war. And those night missions were dangerous. The flares that were supposed to illuminate the targets often didn't work, and when they did they obliterated any horizon that you had and destroyed your night vision. It made your instrument flying much more difficult, and then, of course, you couldn't really see anything on the ground.

In two combat cruises in Vietnam, I'm yet to see my first truck on the ground [chuckle], but I sure hurled a lot of bombs at the ground. Some of the things we did were just unbelievable and just out of sheer dedication on the part of naval aviators to do the job you were assigned. We developed a tactic in our squadron that involved one of the EA-3 airplanes—an electronic version of the A-3 Skywarrior. When the EA-3 would pick up some emission that would indicate that there was a significant target on the ground, they would call an F-4 that was a mile in trail, flying behind them. The EA-3 would keep the target on the radar and say, "All right, I have this target." I guess he would drop the flare, and then you would go up into a big circle, come back, and try to hit

---

* AAA – antiaircraft artillery.

this target. But we were flying at about 800 to 1,000 in trail on the A-3, keeping position on the radar at night. I mean, the ultimate in risk and demand of our pilots. But we were so dedicated that we were trying to develop all these tactics to be able to find those trucks.

Paul Stillwell: You didn't have any kind of air-ground radar, did you?

Admiral Lawrence: Of course, our radar could be used against terrain, but it would not be able to discriminate between a truck on the ground. So you used your radar on the terrain purely as a navigational aid. It was really good to use that radar to be able to pick out the place on the coast—what we called the coast-in point—that you wanted to hit so you'd have a direct track over the ground. It was very effective out at 50 to 75 miles in being able to pick out the right point. But that's the only way we really used the radar in a non-air-to-air mode.

Paul Stillwell: How much did you get in the way of recon and intelligence support?

Admiral Lawrence: Well, it was actually very good. They always kept a very up-to-date chart on where the threats were: the antiaircraft installations and the surface-to-air missile installations, except that the enemy kept moving the SAMs around, so that was not real valid. I tried to teach myself to use the integrated operation intelligence center, because it really had some pretty significant capabilities.

For example, if you had a particular track that you were going to fly over the ground, you could tell an intelligence specialist, and he could get out the photographs that reconnaissance airplanes had taken. He could put them in this machine, and you could actually look and see what your approach to target would look like. It was a fantastic device. Only you usually were so hurried and time-constrained, that you never had a chance to do that. But if you did have time, that was a great way to really get firmly fixed in your mind what would appear to you as you were navigating to your target, because, as I say, that imperative for precision navigation was really great.

That was particularly true, as I will discuss later on in our '67 cruise, when you were taking in a large number of airplanes on an Alfa strike. You had to be right on your exact track and bring that large number of airplanes to a precise roll-in point, because everybody was basically flying on you and depending on you to get them to that roll-in point. It wasn't till you got them to that roll-in point that they started looking around where they were. So you had to be absolutely precise in that navigation. And of course, being a squadron executive officer and then commanding officer, I led every flight. So the pressure of preparing and planning for that flight was really great.

See, that got to be a real burden for us, because the targets were being assigned out of the White House. That's what we were always told. Frequently, we wouldn't get our target assignment till about midnight or 1:00 o'clock in the morning, then we'd have a 6:00 o'clock launch. That got to be a real burden, when, as a flight leader all the time, you had to wait till really late before you get the target and start planning. It really got to be a great fatigue problem on a 30-day line period, because in a fighter squadron, in addition to planning and flying that mission—or sometimes two in one day—you had to do what they called condition watches, where you went up and sat in the cockpit to be prepared to launch in case there were any incoming enemy air raids. So your day was really full of the operational activity and condition watches. But you had to keep your squadron business going.

Paul Stillwell: Well, we haven't talked about that at all. What do you remember about your role as exec?

Admiral Lawrence: Well, you're the guy who keeps the squadron going administratively. Of course, the good thing about it when you're out there at sea and on the line is that everybody's working and sailors aren't getting in trouble. But you still get letters in. So, as the exec, you really have to give attention every day to some paperwork. I remember some real burdens of trying to meet requirements for reports and things like that; it was usually operational stuff.

When we came back from that '66 cruise in August, the Navy had a system of trying to get everybody in the Navy some combat experience. So the kids who had had that one deployment were sent over to East Coast squadrons. Then we got people from the training command or East Coast squadrons coming into our squadron. This was part of the concept of spreading the wealth. So we had to really go through an intensive training effort. But we didn't have the airplanes available, so it was really quite a challenge to get the effective training done during that time between the end of that '66 cruise and the start of '67.

Paul Stillwell: That's tough that you don't get to use that experience that you bought so dearly.

Admiral Lawrence: Yes. And then we had an administrative material inspection, which everybody used to call the admat inspection. That was in December, so after doing minimal paperwork during the previous cruise, I, as exec, had to lead the effort to get ready for the admat inspection. I was really very pleased that right before the stand-down at Christmas, we completed the admat inspection and got an outstanding grade—the highest grade of any Miramar squadron. And, of course, fighter pilots aren't renowned for doing paperwork. So I had to really twist tails to get these guys to turn to and get ready for that admat inspection.

The other thing that I remember so vividly is that we really hoped so much that the war would end. In other words, we were very much aware of this strategy of gradualism. It was very apparent to us, when we were out there in '66, that we were part of what some people called "squeeze them and wait." Johnson would bomb and see the other side's willingness to negotiate. As you remember, they had these bombing pauses, and the one in '67 was at the time of their Tet, which was their Chinese New Year. But it's a very big, significant time during, in Vietnam. So in Tet of '67, Johnson ordered this bombing halt for a month. I remember that we were there at Miramar and we said, "God!" We really hoped that this would signal the end to the war, that this bombing moratorium would really be the thing that would bring about negotiations to end the war. I remember how disappointed I was when we started the darn bombing up again, because we didn't want to go back. We really had no eagerness to continue in the war.

As I say, between August of '66 and then when we went back in April, all our airplanes were getting modified. Then we had to go down to Yuma to go through our training, then out on the carrier for the work-ups prior to the deployment.* It was just a very, very difficult time.

You really became aware of how really different it is in wartime than peacetime. There's a much more seriousness on the part of your pilots and your enlisted personnel. That's where I came to realize that a lot of the old traditions of aviator happy hours and things like that go by the board when the war comes. I don't think we had a single happy hour in our squadron from the time we came back in August till we went, because everybody said, "Gosh, boy, if I get some free time, I'm going to spend it with my family. I'm not going out and sit around the bar at Miramar." That was a whole different attitude.

Anyway, that turn-around was really a tough time.

Paul Stillwell: Did you have much contact with Captain Max Harnish during his brief time as skipper of *Ranger*?†

Admiral Lawrence: Yes, I sure did. I'd known Max Harnish by reputation as being a real intellectual.

Paul Stillwell: Also a tough taskmaster.

Admiral Lawrence: A tough taskmaster, and, in fact, did Max go through nuclear power school? I think he did.

Paul Stillwell: Yes, he did. He'd been exec of the *Enterprise*.

Admiral Lawrence: Yes, and he just had a reputation for being a real bright guy. And, of course, he was our skipper for the last part of that '66 cruise.

---

* Marine Corps Air Station, Yuma, Arizona.
† Captain William Max Harnish, USN, commanded the aircraft carrier *Ranger* (CVA-61) from 7 June 1966 to 20 October 1966.

Paul Stillwell: Well, he really was just there long enough to get a ticket punched so he could go back to systems analysis.

Admiral Lawrence: That's right. That's right. I had occasions to talk to him, and I remember that he asked me what I felt was our biggest deficiency. I told him, "I think our biggest deficiency in the F-4 is we don't have a good bombsight. We have a very archaic gunsight; we don't have a radar bombsight like they do in the bombing airplanes. This is just an optical site. You have to put in your mil lead and all those things, just like we did 20 years before." I remember he went back to Washington with the aim of improving the bombsight on the F-4. And I remember having some big, long discussions with him about that.

But I felt he was a very impressive guy. He was a good skipper; he wasn't flamboyant at all. He was very serious, never really raised his voice; he was a real gentleman in that respect, although, as you say, he was a hard taskmaster.

Our air wing commander on that cruise was a man named Fred Palmer, who later on became an admiral.* He was a very colorful guy.

Paul Stillwell: Colorful in what way?

Admiral Lawrence: Well, he had a great sense of humor, very outgoing, somewhat flamboyant. He could get very serious, but he was a very outgoing, great sense of humor guy. Kind of a hail-fellow well met. But a real professional, really very competent air wing commander. He had been previously a skipper of our squadron, VF-143, so he liked to fly with us.

But we had some really fine young pilots. Something that really interested me was when we came back from that cruise—which was a long, long cruise—we had two pilots who volunteered to go right back out on another carrier, because in those days we had a shortage of pilots. I said, "I can't believe it; you guys been out there nine months and you're going to take a month's leave and go back out on another deployment."

---

* Commander Frederick F. Palmer, USN, Commander Carrier Air Wing 14 (CVW-14).

They said, "Yeah, we really want to do it." So I just realized that there are some guys who have this soldier-of-fortune mentality. I mean, there's something about the excitement of combat that appeals to certain guys. So these guys went back and did another long deployment; I forget what carrier it was.

Paul Stillwell: Were they married?

Admiral Lawrence: No.

Paul Stillwell: That would help.

Admiral Lawrence: No, they weren't married. And one of them had been my wingman, Terry Born.* I mean, he just loved every bit of it. After that they got out of the Navy, and Terry became an American Airlines pilot. Some years later, when I was a flag officer in Washington, he was flying in a reserve squadron out of Dallas. He went up in an F-4 and did some flat-hatting over an Indian reservation up in New Mexico. They were just about to hang him, and I had to intercede and save him on that one. I said, "God, you can't let your old Vietnam War wingman be court-martialed," so I bailed him out of that problem. He just had the warrior mentality and he loved it, every minute of it. I can handle combat okay, but I tell you, I had no desire to go back out again.

Paul Stillwell: You didn't thirst for it.

Admiral Lawrence: No, I didn't, but there were guys who thrived on it. And we had some really close calls, because we were doing so much flying at night. There was one study that wired up these pilots and took their pulse. They found that coming back and landing on the carrier at night, their pulse rate [chuckle] was higher than being over the beach getting shot at, because night carrier operations are always very, very demanding.

I remember where one time when I was up on the carrier deck getting ready to go in on a night mission. Someone raced out, just five minutes before launch, and said,

---

* Lieutenant Terry R. Born, USNR.

"There's a Russian ship up there in the northern Tonkin Gulf that we want you to go up and reconnoiter." We hadn't had a chance to plan for it, so my wingman and I went up there and flew around at low altitude at night, trying our best to see if we could find this Russian ship or trawler or whatever it was. Of course, we couldn't find anything, but the fact that we were at low altitude, we were really burning our fuel excessively. That bothered me, because in that time we just didn't have in-flight refueling capability to the degree that we developed a little bit later on. We came back to get ready to land, and we were really getting low on fuel. So, as it turned out, we had to go in and land at Danang, because we didn't have enough fuel left. And it was always touch and go going into Danang at night.*

Then later on one time, I had a hung bomb; I had to go in and land at Danang, being heavy with that bomb on the airplane, I had to really brake excessively, and I had blown a tire and I stayed a long time there at Danang. I never liked to go into Danang, because I was always afraid the Viet Cong was going to do a mortar attack on us or something.

But it was very tough and demanding out there in combat. And you always had this feeling of frustration that you weren't allowed to hit the targets that you really felt would do the good to end the war.

Paul Stillwell: What can you say about the maintenance and the flight deck people during that 1966 cruise?

Admiral Lawrence: Oh, they were really great. I've always been so impressed how the American sailors can rise to the occasion. The pilots were on a 12-hour flying period, but those maintenance guys would work as long as necessary. But, basically, you had your maintenance people on two 12-hour shifts. And they'd work those 12-hour shifts for 30 days at a time. The weather was hot out there in the Tonkin Gulf, and they weren't in the air-conditioned spaces. They never complained; they always turned to. And the flight deck crews, in particular, were doing heavy, physical-type labor. I used to always be amazed at how sailors would just lie down on a steel deck and go to sleep when they'd

---

* Danang is a seaport that was in the northern part of South Vietnam.

get a break. But they never complained. It's just a wonderful type of young person we produce in this country who will come out there and really come through for you when you really need them.

But we've always had these real demanding jobs that we've given sailors. One of the toughest jobs in the Navy, and it's one that usually goes to about a first or second class petty officer, is what they call the final checker. He's the guy who stands up in the catapult area, and when one of his squadron airplanes comes up there, he's the guy who looks all around the airplane for leaks or anything that would render the airplane unsafe to fly. And, gosh, the wind's blowing over the deck and jet blasts and noise. That guy looks around, and he comes out and gives you an up to convey to you that the airplane's ready to go on that catapult. I found over the years, you always pick your very best guy, and invariably it's a Midwest farm boy who gets that job. [Laughter] That's the type of guy we produce out in Middle America, and they're just unassuming guys who don't think anything at all about the danger. If an airplane turns abruptly and directs its jet blast wrong or if the blast defector doesn't go up at the proper time, I've seen guys like that just blown right over the side and lost. But these final checkers never manifest any fear and are just totally dedicated and loyal.

Paul Stillwell: And you were trusting your life to this checker.

Admiral Lawrence: Yes, and then, of course, we had the catapult crews. Every time you taxi up on that catapult, you know that your life is in the hands of those guys down there that are hooking you up and checking machinery. And you never have any doubt at all that they're going to be completely reliable. That's why there's such a great feeling of respect and affection the pilots have for the flight deck personnel. And, on the other hand, they have great respect for us, because we go out and do the dangerous stuff. So it's a real great respect, mutual respect and affection between the air crew people and those. They're primarily aviation boatswain's mates. They're really the salt of the earth, just like the surface boatswain's mates. I wouldn't take anything for my years on aircraft carriers and the great deal of respect that I have for American sailors from what I've seen the American sailor do when they're called on to do it.

Paul Stillwell: I wonder if this is a convenient breaking place so we can talk about the '67 cruise all together.

Admiral Lawrence: Yes, and then we'll get ready to go back to '67, because I have a lot of work to do today.

Interview Number 9 with Vice Admiral William P. Lawrence, U.S. Navy (Retired)
Place: U.S. Naval Institute, Annapolis, Maryland
Date: Tuesday, 20 November 1990

Paul Stillwell: Admiral, last time we just about wrapped up your 1966 cruise in the *Ranger*. At what point did you make the transition to command, and how did you spend the time between cruises?

Admiral Lawrence: We got back, as I recall, in late August of 1966, and we really had a tremendous amount to accomplish before we went back out the following April. In wartime circumstances, that might seem like it was a long turnaround, but we had to put all these electronic modifications into our airplane, because we just didn't have any real electronic countermeasures capability in that '66 cruise. When we saw that the North Vietnamese were putting in the surface-to-air missiles in greater numbers, the Navy really went on a very active effort to put in the electronic countermeasures.

We had to send our planes over to the overhaul and repair facility at North Island there in San Diego. The problem we had was that we didn't have very many airplanes to train in, and yet we got in these new pilots, because the Navy had a program under way at that time of trying to balance the combat exposure. So when we got back from the '66 cruise, all of our young pilots were sent to East Coast squadrons. Then we filled in with new inputs out of the training command. I think we also received some transferees from the East Coast. It was all part of a Navy effort to balance the combat experience and the combat exposure.

Paul Stillwell: Do you think that was a wise program?

Admiral Lawrence: Well, I think, fundamentally, it was probably a good idea to do that, because in those times we were going out there for eight- and nine-month deployments. It really was quite a strain on an individual. So part of it was just to balance that exposure and that strain.

Paul Stillwell: Well, and the other side of it is that the Navy was getting some of that experience into these other squadrons in case they would be called upon for combat.

Admiral Lawrence: That's right, that's right. It was a cross-fertilization move. But it really put a lot of pressure on us, because we had to do everything we could to maximize the training with our airplanes, which were tied up in the modification program.

Paul Stillwell: Did you get some inputs from the intelligence people on what kind of threat you'd face and various warning signals on the missiles?

Admiral Lawrence: Yes. We knew that even when we went out on the '66 cruise. They just didn't have an opportunity to put the mods in the airplane. And, of course, the A-4s and A-6 already had that capability. They both had the instrumentation that would indicate when you were receiving radiation and the radial from which that radiation was coming. Then they had this electronic equipment that would actually attempt to counter, or break the lock, of the guidance system that was trying to lock onto your airplane. Basically, they were just putting in our fighter airplanes what was already in the attack airplanes.

But it was a very extensive mod program. So we had a limited number of airplanes to fly. And, of course, in true Navy fashion, even though it was wartime, we still had to go through an admat inspection. So that occupied a great deal of our time, because during the previous deployment, we had done minimal paperwork. So from getting back at the end of August until the middle of December, we were frantically getting ready for this admat inspection. As the executive officer, of course, I was basically in charge of getting ready for that, so it was really a busy time.

That involved a lot of long hours of work and coming in on Saturday to see how the modification programs were going, and test-flying the airplanes that had received the mod work. Then we had to go down to the Marine Corps Air Station at Yuma, Arizona, to do some training. I think we went down as an entire air wing and worked up at Yuma. Before that our squadron had gone on a separate short-term basic weapons deployment, to fire some missiles and do some air-to-ground work.

Paul Stillwell: What was the attitude of the nuggets coming into the squadron? Were they eager to go into action, or did they have a little bit of trepidation?

Admiral Lawrence: Well, I think everybody was really impressed with the seriousness of what we were doing. We'd been in the war long enough, and we were incurring enough losses over there, so that the nuggets were certainly serious about their work. They didn't seem to have the great exuberance that often seems to go with peacetime operations.

I can remember during the Tet period—which was, I think, February of 1967—when President Johnson put a one-month moratorium on the bombing. This was an effort to get the North Vietnamese to come to a negotiating table, to take some action to reduce their involvement in the war. And, gosh, I remember how fervently we all hoped that we would not have to resume the bombing, and maybe we wouldn't have to go back out there. It was obvious to us that the war definitely escalated in 1966 under Johnson's policy of gradualism. In the reports that we were receiving when we went back out there in '67, it was going to be an entirely different war. It was solely oriented to strikes in the north and more strikes into the Hanoi-Haiphong area, which we used to call Package Six.

We had a young pilot in the squadron, Ensign Brown. He was kind of a quiet guy, not really very outgoing, but we could see that he was basically a pretty good pilot. He did some good things out on the ship and in his work at night. So we were quite impressed with him. One week before we were due to deploy, he went over to pick up an airplane at the overhaul and repair facility at North Island, which had just completed this mod, to bring it back to the squadron. He had a rear-seat naval flight officer with him who was a mustang. His father had been a Filipino messman in the Navy. On the way back from North Island, Ensign Brown went out and flew by the beach at La Jolla. At low altitude, high speed, he did a roll and went into the water. God, that just really devastated all of us, as hard as we'd been working, getting ready to go back to war, and then we were faced with this flat-hatting incident. We just couldn't believe that it happened. We thought that everybody was aware that you just didn't do things like that anymore—maybe back in the old days in the Navy but not now. So on top of the burdens of getting ready to go back to war, we had to deal with that accident. It just really demoralized our squadron.

Paul Stillwell: Were they both killed?

Admiral Lawrence: Oh, yes. He just did a roll and scooped out and POOH!—crashed before all these people on the beach at La Jolla. I mean, that really took its toll on me, to lose two fine young people. And the mustang lieutenant had a family; I think he had three children. So we had to go through the memorial service; we didn't recover either of their bodies. I remember bringing in Ensign Brown's father, who was an Air Force colonel dentist, and taking care of their families.

As we got under way from San Diego on the cruise, I remember the burden of having to prepare that JAG investigation, which I was responsible for doing, and the accident report.[*] It was really a very tough time emotionally.

Paul Stillwell: Well, certainly, a preventable accident.

Admiral Lawrence: Oh, gosh, it was just a tragedy. I tell you, it just really devastated me. It really took its toll on me to have to deal with that, and at the same time, saying goodbye to my family, going back out to war. I had to spend just about every waking moment on the way out to Hawaii writing that JAG report and supervising getting the accident report ready.

Our air wing commander was Commander Gene Tissot.[†] He told me that after our operational readiness inspection in Hawaii, he intended to fly out to WestPac with me, as the future fighter skipper, and with Commander Leo Profilet, who was the skipper of the A-6 squadron.[‡] He wanted us to have a little bit of advanced liaison with the people who were doing the fighting.

So just as soon as we finished our operational readiness inspection in Hawaii and came into port, the three of us got on an airplane and flew out to Clark Air Force Base.[§] We were taken down to Cubi and Subic Bay and flown out to Vietnam. We spent some

---

[*] JAG – Judge Advocate General.
[†] Commander Ernest Eugene Tissot Jr., USN, commanded Carrier Air Wing 14 (CVW-14) from January 1967 to February 1968.
[‡] Commander Leo T. Profilet, USN, commanded Attack Squadron 196 (VA-196) until he ejected from his A-6 Intruder when it was hit over North Vietnam on 21 August 1967. He was a POW until 1973.
[§] Clark Air Force Base was about 50 miles north of Manila, on the island of Luzon in the Philippines.

time on the *Kitty Hawk* and the *Enterprise*, which were deployed out there at that time. The skipper of the *Enterprise* at that time was Captain James Holloway.[*] The skipper of the *Kitty Hawk* was Captain Paul Pugh, a famous fighter pilot.[†]

So we flew some missions off those carriers just to get a feel for what the new procedure was going to be out there. The key thing that we noticed was that all our missions now were virtually large-scale strikes into the very north heart of North Vietnam, Package Six—Hanoi-Haiphong complex—what we called Alfa strikes.

Paul Stillwell: Did you have any impressions of Holloway or Pugh from those visits?

Admiral Lawrence: Well, I didn't get up on the *Kitty Hawk* bridge, but I got up on the *Enterprise* bridge, and I was really very impressed with Captain Holloway. He really had control, and he had tremendously good morale and a lot of very fine esprit. He was just a very dynamic leader. It was obvious he really loved ship handling and all of the challenges of running a ship in combat.

Paul Stillwell: Lots of self-confidence.

Admiral Lawrence: Yes, tremendously confident. And I had some real good friends on *Enterprise*. The skipper of one of the F-4 fighter squadrons was my classmate Jim Rough, and I actually flew with his squadron on a mission.[‡] But the trip out there was invaluable. We picked up a lot of good information. We waited out there then, of course, for our carrier to come out. We joined the carrier up in Japan.

Paul Stillwell: Was this the *Ranger* again?

---

[*] Captain James L. Holloway III, USN, commanded the aircraft carrier *Enterprise* (CVAN-65) from 17 July 1965 to 11 July 1967. He later served as Chief of Naval Operations, 1974-78.
[†] Captain Paul E. Pugh, USN, commanded the carrier *Kitty Hawk* (CVA-63) from 18 July 1966 to 28 August 1967.
[‡] Commander Jimmie L. Rough, USN.

Admiral Lawrence: No, it was the Connie—*Constellation*.*

We had a really good squadron. We brought back the same operations officer we had had on the previous cruise. And, of course, I'd been on the previous cruise, as had the commanding officer. So there were four of us who had combat experience. We had a new maintenance officer. Virtually everybody else in the squadron was new. Everybody was, from my perception, basically a very solid citizen. I didn't have any trepidation about anybody's ability to perform effectively in combat.

We had our first period on the line in late May and early June.† Then we came back into port, and the commanding officer, Doc Townsend, and I had our change of command there at Subic Bay. We went back out, and then I was shot down on the 28th of June 1967, midway through the second line period.

But things had gone well the first line period, and from everything I could see, our squadron was doing well. I had no reservations about any aspect of our operation. But it was a different level of intensity out there. Basically, in our 12-hour flying period, which would either be from midnight to noon or from noon to midnight, we would usually, during that period, fly two Alfa strikes. There would be about 30 to 35 airplanes each strike. We no longer had these two-plane missions or four-plane missions going after various targets in North Vietnam. We were doing all large-scale strikes.

Paul Stillwell: Was the idea to overwhelm the defenses?

Admiral Lawrence: No, it was just another notch up in the escalation, and I think it was just increasing the intensity and the destructiveness of our raids. But we still weren't striking the things that I really felt would hurt them. For example, we weren't allowed to go in and wipe out the piers in Haiphong. Instead, we'd strike a storage area back away from the pier. We still were not allowed to mine the harbor, and we weren't going up and

---

* USS *Constellation* (CVA-64), a *Kitty Hawk*-class aircraft carrier, was built by the New York Naval Shipyard. Her keel was laid 14 September 1957. She was launched 8 October 1960 and commissioned 27 October 1961. She had a standard displacement of 60,000 tons, was 1,048 feet long, 129 feet in the beam, an extreme width of 248 feet on the flight deck, and had a draft of 37 feet. She had a top speed of 34 knots and could accommodate about 80-95 planes. The *Constellation*'s 1967 deployment from her homeport of San Diego was from 29 April until 4 December.
† The *Constellation* was in combat operations off Vietnam from 28 May to 11 June. The next line period began on 19 June, after Lawrence had taken command of VF-143.

striking the railroad leading from Haiphong up to China. So we raised the intensity, but in other respects we didn't raise it to the point where we'd really inflict significant damage on them. It was very demanding for those of us who were squadron executive officers and commanding officers, because the executive officers and commanding officers were leading all these raids.

When you brought that many airplanes over the beach, you really had to plan very carefully what your route of flight would be and establish a roll-in point. And you'd have to assign, within the target area, specific targets for each group within the strike group. So the mission planning was very demanding, and it was made more difficult by the fact that the target assignments were coming out from Washington. Many times it would be midnight or 1:00 o'clock in the morning when we'd finally get the target assignments, because they'd come from Washington, and, apparently, out to CinCPac, CinCPacFlt, and then on down the line. Then you'd have to sit there with maybe your rear-seat guy and maybe one other, and plan this mission in the wee hours of the night. The time on target might be 7:30 in the morning.

So many times, when I was the strike lead, I'd finish the strike planning about 3:00 or 4:00 o'clock in the morning and get to bed for just a couple of hours. When you were the strike leader, once you planned the route and developed all the target assignments, then you had to sit down—probably by yourself—and really study that chart, because all the navigation to target was by reference to the ground—visual navigation. So you simply had to be able to look down at the ground and recognize exactly where you were and relate it to this symbology on the chart.

So I found I used to have to get at least a half hour to sit down and just really study that chart as carefully as I could so I could get a good mental picture of how the navigational track would appear to me.

Paul Stillwell: Did you ever get a chance to catch up on your sleep?

Admiral Lawrence: Well, one of the toughest demands of combat is programming adequate rest, because in addition to having to plan these strikes and then participate in them and go through the debrief, you had your duties during the day of running a squadron, being aware of the maintenance situation, taking your turn in standing the alert watches up on the flight deck. We always had two fighters in what we called condition one, to be prepared to launch in case of an enemy attack. So you just seemed to have trouble squeezing out any time in a day to get caught up on your rest. I used to try to slip down to my room and get a 20-minute to a half-hour battery recharge.

The real burden of combat is getting enough rest. It wasn't as bad on the junior officers as it was the commanders, because we were leading the strikes. And you simply had to do the flight planning yourself. It was something you couldn't delegate.

Paul Stillwell: How well did the airplane perform?

Admiral Lawrence: Well, we had really, no problems with our airplanes, maintenance-wise. Our maintenance personnel did a magnificent job. They demonstrated what the American sailor could do. You put him on a carrier, and he didn't have anyplace to go. He was working 12 hours on, 12 off. But the really key guys were working many hours longer than that. So we had very good availability of all of our full systems. I never, ever remember having radar fail on a flight or ever having a communications problem. The F-4 is really a very durable workhorse, so our airplanes held up pretty well.

Paul Stillwell: Was night carrier operation by then a routine thing?

Admiral Lawrence: Oh, yes. Everybody car-qualed at night. You had to be careful about your young pilots. You just didn't throw them out in an unrestricted manner. You had to make sure the conditions were right, that the weather wasn't marginal or anything like that. You flew your young guys with an experienced group of pilots until they started getting up to speed through experience. Night ops were very routine by that time.

The schedules officer tried to keep it pretty well even as to the number of night landings we were given, so that everybody would be able to maintain his proficiency. As I say, you had to watch the young officers and make sure that they were getting requisite experience and everything. But I was quite impressed with what our pilots and radar intercept officers were doing on that cruise up to the time when I got shot down.

I had an NFO named Jim Falvey, on whom the toll of the pressure of combat was starting to take its effect.* I had some long chats with him, where I was trying to stroke him to keep him going, but he made it through the cruise. But before I was shot down, I was really worried about him, because he'd come to see me and say he was seriously considering turning in his wings. It was an interesting thing that, after giving him as much encouragement and support as I could, then I got shot down. But when I came back, he was one of the first guys to look me up. He said, "God, I thank you so much for giving me the strength to keep going and hang in there during combat. Because if I'd have pulled myself out, if I'd quit, I'd never, ever have felt the same about myself as I do now." So he was very thankful that I helped him stay in there.

Paul Stillwell: Maybe the fact that you were lost got some of these guys to tighten up their belts and go a little harder.

Admiral Lawrence: Well, I'm sure it did. That's a very sobering experience for everybody, particularly for the young guys who were on their first time out there.

Paul Stillwell: Well, you were the father figure for them.

Admiral Lawrence: Yes, that's right. I was very pleased with the caliber of the pilots and radar intercept officer we had out there. I can't remember a single weak sister in the whole group.

Paul Stillwell: Well, a good deal of selectivity went on before they got to your squadron.

Admiral Lawrence: Oh, yes. That's right. Going through flight training and the RAG is a pretty effective weeding-out process. I think it's really to our credit in naval aviation that we train our young very well. We have a good tradition built up of picking the right people and training them well. They measure up to the very high standard in naval aviation. We had a few pilots who were a little bit shaky about some aspect of carrier

---

* Lieutenant (junior grade) Bernard James Falvey, USNR.

operations, like tending to over-rotate off the catapult or not being all that smooth at night. But they quickly rectified those little deficiencies, and everybody was really pulling his oar once we got pretty well settled into the cruise.

Paul Stillwell: What do you mean by over-rotate?

Admiral Lawrence: Well, when the F-4 has full external tanks, it tends to have a little bit of an aft center of gravity. So when the airplane comes off the catapult—when the bridle releases the airplane and it goes off the end of the deck—it tends to over-rotate due to this aft CG. Most of us at that time were making what we call hands-off catapult shots. Because of the type of control systems that we had, control surfaces were positioned by hydraulic pressure. Aerodynamic pressure had no effect on where they were pre-positioned. So you basically were better off to take a hands-off catapult shot and then, when the airplane rotated to where you had it in the proper position, based on how you trimmed the airplane, then you took the controls and held at that point.

The way I always took a catapult shot, I pre-positioned my hand behind the stick, because the tendency, because of the way you trimmed it, was to pitch up pretty rapidly. Then you would push forward on the stick, when you saw the nose coming to the right place above the horizon—or I usually made most of mine on instruments when I saw the gyro horizon indication coming to the right spot, and then I would just hold the stick at that point. A lot of young pilots couldn't acclimate to this hands-off catapult shot. It was foreign to everything they had ever learned. They had been taught that you always hold the stick when you're flying an airplane. So these guys would hold onto the stick, often just due to the inertia, and so the catapult shot would pull too far aft to the stick and combine with this aft CG so that they'd over-rotate.

Paul Stillwell: By over-rotate, you mean pulling the nose up?

Admiral Lawrence: You're too high in angle of attack. We had one pilot named Bob Hickey, who was later the skipper of the *Ranger*; he's now a rear admiral.* We used to call his catapult shots "Hickey loopers." He gave me a few very tense moments as I watched a plan form of his airplane.† When we took external tanks, we always took full afterburner shots. You didn't have a thrust problem; the airplane was accelerating okay. So even if you over-rotated and got a little bit close to a stall, you usually had sufficient flying speed to correct it okay. We never had anybody go into the water from the catapult. But a night catapult shot was particularly demanding. Fortunately, Bob Hickey overcame his over-rotation tendencies.

But the F-4 was basically a very good carrier plane. The only thing that made me feel a little bit uncomfortable about it was that the airplanes had become very heavy with all the racks and the bombs and so forth we were carrying. So your takeoff speed was very high, and, of course, your landing speed was very high. Just to give yourself as much safety margin as possible, you tended to come back and land at pretty close to 4,000 pounds of internal fuel, so your weight was quite heavy, and you were making your carrier approach up around 145 knots. That was a tremendous amount of energy, because energy is directly proportionate to the square of speed. So it bothered me that when hitting the deck and arresting, there was a tremendous amount of energy that had to be dissipated. It put much more of a burden on all the systems—the arresting gear, the landing gear, the airplane, and the airframe.

The F-14, for example, comes aboard at about 120 knots.‡ So there's a much lower energy dissipation requirement, but the old F-4, I tell you, it was strong and durable, because it took that pounding for a full cruise.

Paul Stillwell: Anything to say about Subic and Cubi Point?

Admiral Lawrence: Well . . .

---

* Captain Robert P. Hickey, USN commanded the aircraft carrier *Ranger* (CV-61) from 8 July 1988 to 13 February 1990. In 1967 he was a lieutenant (junior grade).
† The plan form is the view looking down from the top.
‡ The Grumman F-14 Tomcat fighter first entered training squadrons in late 1972. The Tomcat was operational until 2006.

Paul Stillwell: It was an enlisted man's paradise.

Admiral Lawrence: Well, that's right. The enlisted men all loved Olongapo with its dirt streets and the bars and the hospitality girls.* I spent minimal time in Olongapo. On my first cruise out there, I went out there just to see what it was like, and saw there was nothing out there for me. So I spent most of my time, when I went off the ship in Subic, maybe going around to some of the recreational activities there. And, of course, we had the officers' club at Subic, and another one over at the NAS Cubi. I liked the Subic club a lot more.

But I found, particularly as an executive officer, that when you came into port, you had to spend a lot of time aboard ship getting caught up with paperwork. Aviators are notoriously poor about doing their paperwork, particularly when they're at sea. So I had no desire to do anything on liberty, because I was out there to work and fight the war. So I really did very little at Subic or at Cubi. I would try to go in if there was another carrier and just see my friends from the other carrier and compare notes with them about what was going on in the war. Just a good kind of a cross-fertilization effort. As I say, I was geared up purely to fight the war and not to have fun. [Chuckle]

Paul Stillwell: Well, anything more to say about your shipboard time before you got shot down?

Admiral Lawrence: No, as I say, the big difference when we went out there the second time was the type of the large-scale Alfa strikes that were conducted, but also the intensity of the air defense. On the raids that we were making into the heartland of North Vietnam, the air opposition to us in all categories—air, missile, and gun—was very intense. So every mission that you took in there, in what we called "Indian Country," was really a tough challenge. The surface-to-air missiles put an entirely new aspect on the air war, because now we faced an antiaircraft system where you could see the missile from time of launch.

---

* Olongapo, the town right outside the U.S. naval base at Subic Bay in the Philippines, was noted for its raunchiness during the Vietnam War period and later.

In some ways it was good, but another way it was bad. It was almost better to be hit by what you didn't see, because you didn't worry about it till you get hit. When you were a flight leader, you had to keep your eye on the ground. If you saw a missile lift off, then you had to keep your eye on it, because if it was locked onto you and your flight, then you had to maneuver very abruptly to cause it to avoid you.

Paul Stillwell: Did you have sufficient equipment on that second cruise to tell you when a missile was locked on?

Admiral Lawrence: Well, we had the capability to know when the guidance system was locked on us and, also, the direction of the radiation. But when you came into the Hanoi-Haiphong area, there were so many systems radiating on you that your APR-25 system that it was not of value to you. [Chuckle]

Paul Stillwell: Saturated.

Admiral Lawrence: So you really had to keep your eye on the ground, because you just simply had to see that missile from time of launch to be able to see if it was tracking you, so you could outmaneuver it. But the big problem was maintaining that flight integrity at 30-35 airplanes and with several missiles coming up.

On several of our missions we just simply lost flight integrity. The airplanes were thoroughly dispersed before we got to target. People had to make individual efforts to drop their bombs. So it was tough; we were pioneering. This was the first time in the history of air warfare that we were facing surface-to-air missiles. So we were developing our own tactics as we went along.

We had what we called, Iron Hand airplanes that had the capability to attack missile sites by having weapons that homed in on their radiation.[*] I think Shrike was the

---

[*] Iron Hand was a type of mission designed to attack and destroy North Vietnamese surface-to-air missile sites. Often the aircraft used were specialized ones known as Wild Weasels.

type of missile used there.* But those missile-suppression aircraft were not sufficient in number to really help you very much. You just simply knew if you went into the Hanoi-Haiphong area, you were going to get a lot of missiles thrown up at you.

Paul Stillwell: How did you inspire your junior officers, when you yourself didn't believe you were getting the best targets to hit?

Admiral Lawrence: Well, it was tough. It really was, but it just shows you how very dedicated, faithful people are, that they really didn't complain much about this. But it bothered me from back in my '66 cruise that we weren't mining—particularly the main port of Haiphong—to interdict the flow of supplies. To have to go out and look for trucks at night was absolutely the worst way in the world to try to interdict the flow of supplies. But, as I say, I guess it's just for the type of guy who aspires to come into aviation, and all the things you give them while they're going through training, they're just dedicated, faithful, loyal, and obedient. There was minimal complaining. I never recall any pilot who really bellyached much about the situation over there.

Paul Stillwell: What do you recall about the last mission, the one on 28 June in which you were shot down?

Admiral Lawrence: Well, this was a 36-airplane mission. I was the flight lead and the navigational lead for the flight, and I was the leader of the eight F-4 flak suppressors. Our mission in the F-4s was to drop what they called the CBUs, the cluster bomb units. They dispersed fragments widely over the ground, kind of an anti-personnel type of bomb. That was the principal means that we used to suppress the flak, by impacting the people who were manning the guns and missile systems.

Paul Stillwell: Did you carry air-to-air missiles, even when you were in an air-to-ground role?

---

* Shrike, produced by a consortium of Texas Instruments and Sperry, was the Navy's first specialized tactical antiradar missile. It was essentially a Sparrow airframe with an enlarged blast-fragmentation warhead.

Admiral Lawrence: Yes, because after we completed the flak-suppression mission, we would go up in the direction from which we anticipated any air threat, any MiG-21s or MiG-19s.[*] Then we had usually four Sparrow missiles and two Sidewinders, as I recall. So we did both the flak suppression and what we called the MiG CAP mission.

In addition to those eight F-4s, I think we had probably 12 A-4s and maybe eight A-6s, and we had the photo airplanes. It came up to right around 35-36 airplanes. And on our missions, of course, that's when we did a very extensive briefing to all the aircrews down in the carrier's integrated operations intelligence center. Then we got airborne, and everything we did after launch till we were finally joined up in a big circle around the carrier, we did on radio silence. We really prided ourselves that we could launch all those airplanes and get them all joined up in individual four-plane sections without ever making transmission on the radio. Then once we headed in to the beach, there was maybe one transmission to indicate everybody was on board. But it was an awesome thing always for me to observe these airplanes going up in the air and all silent.

Our targets on that particular mission were going to be the transshipment points in Haiphong; it was where they would take the supplies off the ship, and they'd move them back to a storage area so they could be picked up by trucks. The rules of engagement would allow us to attack those storage areas, but they wouldn't let us attack the piers. And particularly if there was a foreign ship at the pier, you had to really be very, very careful about this. Apparently President Johnson was very worried about antagonizing the Russians and the Chinese and maybe precipitating their entry into the war.

We got the airplanes joined up, and we were heading in. Shortly before I got over land, I could see that there was very heavy cloud cover over Haiphong, and this was early in the morning. As I got closer, it was just apparent to me that we could not make satisfactory bomb runs. Our alternate target down to the southwest was Nam Dinh. We were principally hitting the thermal power plant in the city of Nam Dinh and the transshipment areas adjacent to the Red River. The Red River, which led down from Hanoi on out to the ocean, went by the little town of Nam Dinh. So I selected that as our

---

[*] The Mikoyan-Gurevich MiG-19 (NATO designation "Farmer") was a single-seat Soviet fighter, the first with supersonic capability. The MiG-21 (NATO designation "Fishbed") was a supersonic Soviet jet fighter that went into operation in 1959.

alternate target, because it was on the approved target list, and took the flight towards Nam Dinh.

Now at that time in the war, because of our repeated missions into Hanoi-Haiphong area, the North Vietnamese had brought all the missiles in from all over North Vietnam and ringed them right around Hanoi-Haiphong. So I remember when I turned down to go to Nam Dinh, I said, "Boy, I won't have to sweat the missiles today, because we'll be outside the missile zone." Instead, I was shot down by an 85-millimeter, which was a World War II gun. At the time, I was going 500 knots at 10,000 feet, a darn good shot for a guy to sight on you from ground level.

Paul Stillwell: Did they have radar fire control on those guns?

Admiral Lawrence: Some did and some didn't. I don't remember, quite frankly, getting an indication of being radiated before I was hit. But, of course, as a flight leader you're really busy, because you have to precisely navigate that flight into the target. And, of course, I'd done most of my planning and study for tracking to Haiphong. Now I was faced with going down to Nam Dinh. So I was really very much concentrating on keeping myself precisely located by reference to the landmarks on the ground. And then, of course, you have to be constantly turning the airplane, which they call jinking, to make it difficult for them to sight on you. So I was the one-armed paperhanger as a flight leader, because I had to make all this stuff come together. The pressure for precision navigation was really great, because you had to bring all 36 airplanes into this one roll-in point, so all 36 of them could make a satisfactory bomb run.

The other thing was that you had to have a really good sense of judgment, because you were coming in at high speed. So you didn't have the time to circle around the target to come to your roll-in point, because you would be exposed to much greater enemy fire. So you had to do a roll forward; you would come in and you'd pull the airplane over on its back, and then you would pull down and go on your run. So you had to really be very precise in your judgment as to when you pulled the airplane down and got onto your bomb run. That was why we only had commanders leading flights, because it was a tough thing to lead a flight.

When I was within about five seconds of my roll-in point, I saw my airplane just enveloped by flak, the small puffs of smoke, and I felt a jolt in my airframe. But the airplane seemed to want to keep flying. My wingman Tom Rodger called up and said, "Hey, skipper, I think you've been hit."*

I felt like saying, "Tell me something I don't know." [Laughter] Because in addition to seeing the flak puffs of smoke all around me, I felt this real jolt in my airframe. Well, the airplane seemed to be flying okay, and then, as I got closer to the roll-in point, I saw the hydraulic pressure warning lights come on, but the controls still felt pretty good. So I made a snap decision not to pull myself out of the flight and head back to the ocean, but to go ahead and complete my bomb run. I got pretty well to the roll-in point, and got rolled over on my back and got settled into my bomb run.

I could see out of the corner of my eye that those three hydraulic indicators for the two flight-control systems and the utility systems all showed red. So it looked like my two flight-control hydraulic systems had been severed. I could feel as I was pulling my nose down that the airplane's controls were starting to get kind of mushy. But I was able to get my pipper bombsight on the target and released. When you were dropping these CBUs, you didn't have to be all that precise, because it's an area weapon. It spreads these fragments all over the area, so it's not like dropping an individual iron bomb. But I still was able to get a pretty good bomb run by getting my pipper on the target.

But then I had a hell of a time getting the nose of the airplane to come back up. It was just unresponsive, so I was really afraid I was going to fly into the ground, because the airplane only slowly came out of the dive, and then the nose was coming back up. So I immediately headed back towards the water. I told my wingman that I was heading back to water, because I knew I'd been hit. Well, I got up to about 10,000 feet, and the airplane just went out of control. I guess, finally, the hydraulic pressure just went to zero. So that put me into a very flat spin. It was obvious to me that my controls were having no effect, so then I started using alternate afterburner. In other words, to stop this, there's a right rotation, so I went into full afterburner on my right engine and idle on my left, but that didn't have any effect. The airplane was really settled into a very heavy spin. At about 3,000 feet, it was obvious to me that the airplane probably was not going to come

---

* Lieutenant Thomas W. Rodger, USN.

out. So I told my rear-seat guy to go ahead and eject himself. When I got down to about 1,800 or so feet, I knew I was getting into a perilous situation, so I went ahead and ejected myself.

We always carried these hand-held radios, kind of a walkie-talkie. So as I was coming down in my parachute, I was able to get that walkie-talkie radio out of my integrated harness that we wore. I transmitted on that hand-held radio to my wingman and everybody in the air that I was out of the airplane and was okay. So that was very lucky, because that gave them a feel that I probably had survived and would be a POW, although my name was not released by the North Vietnamese for about three years.

Paul Stillwell: Who was your rear-seat man?

Admiral Lawrence: It was Lieutenant (junior grade) James W. Bailey.

Paul Stillwell: Did he get down okay?

Admiral Lawrence: Yes, he got down okay. He was 24 years old at that time, an unmarried jaygee. I saw his chute about a half a mile away from me as I was coming down, and so I felt good about that, and I made the point on my radio that I saw his chute. So they were very confident that we both had survived that situation.

Paul Stillwell: Would it have made any difference if you had elected not to drop the bombs and headed for the coast earlier?

Admiral Lawrence: Yes, I would probably have made it. When I was initially enveloped with that flak, if I'd just pulled up and gone back, we were about 20 miles inland, and I think there would have been a good chance that I could have made it back to the ocean. But I never really seriously considered it, because the airplane felt like it was flying. And all your training tells you that you should complete the mission.

Paul Stillwell: It's almost an instinct to fly at that point.

Admiral Lawrence: Yes, that's right. It's an instinct. I mean, I never even seriously considered it as long as that airplane was flying. And, of course, I was a flight leader, so I couldn't very readily pull myself out.

I never dwell on that very much. But I have to admit that my first several weeks as a POW, you go through this "Why me?" where you think you must have done something wrong to facilitate their being able to hit you. I used to think, "Gosh, was I jinking well enough?" I couldn't remember whether I was really jinking as much as I should.

So later on, when I got out, Tom Rodger and those guys said, "Yeah, you were jinking." But it was really a hell of a good shot, because if you calculate the mathematics, there's a very definite, finite amount of time it takes for that shell to depart the barrel of that gun and go up to 10,000 feet, considering you're going 500 knots.

Paul Stillwell: Well, on the other hand, it may be that you ran into the shell rather than the other way around.

Admiral Lawrence: Well, I think that's probably what happened, but, of course, being the lead airplane on a clear day, you're very vulnerable because you're the guy they sight on. That's why so many commanding officers and executive officers got shot down in this war, I think, because we were always the flight leaders.

Paul Stillwell: Well, if they put up a barrage, you might just catch one of the ones that's coming up.

Admiral Lawrence: Yes, and that was their common practice. I think they used barrage fire more than radar-guided fire. Every indication I got was that that was a manual shot; it was not a radar-controlled shot.

Paul Stillwell: Doesn't matter how it got there, though, it was just as effective.

Admiral Lawrence: That's right, that's right. [Chuckle]

Well, Paul, this might be a good place to break, because then I can start into the POW and the capture. Since I've been out, I was down at the University of Kentucky, because I do some work for the Patterson School of Diplomacy, International Congress down there. I was down there from Thursday till yesterday, so I'm getting caught up on things here in my office.

Paul Stillwell: All right.

Admiral Lawrence: But it's a good place to start into the, maybe in the next one, I can cover the whole POW experience, because I've got this book I kept to guide me.

Paul Stillwell: Good, I can look up the book in the meantime and do a little homework.

Interview Number 10 with Vice Admiral William P. Lawrence, U.S. Navy (Retired)
Place: U.S. Naval Institute, Annapolis, Maryland
Date: Monday, 26 November 1990

Paul Stillwell: Admiral, the last time you had just discussed ejecting from your Phantom on 28 June 1967 and riding the parachute down and notifying your shipmates that you were safe. At that point you were apprehended by a local militiaman. That's the point to resume, please.

Admiral Lawrence: That's right. I'd been shot down over the Red River Delta, which is a major rice-growing region in North Vietnam. I landed right in the middle of a rice paddy, and the water was up to my thighs as I was trying to get my bearings and prevent my parachute from entangling. I looked over, and there was this militiaman standing over at the edge of the rice paddy with an old rifle, so I had no chance to try to evade and escape. I was captured right at the instant I landed.

Paul Stillwell: Had you gone through any of that training back in the States?

Admiral Lawrence: Yes, I'd been through what they call SERE training—survival, evasion, resistance, escape—twice in my career. So I was well versed in what I should try to do.

Paul Stillwell: Do you think that training was useful for you as a prisoner, even if not for escaping?

Admiral Lawrence: Yes, it was useful, because it really introduced you to the problem and the fundamental difficulties that you would face, even though you just can't get thorough realism in that training to duplicate what you're going to encounter in a POW camp. I'd gone through the one up at Warner Springs in California in 1966, before my first deployment, and I thought it was good. They gave you a good appreciation for what's necessary to evade capture and how you do your own navigation over difficult terrain. In the prison compound situation, they gave you a sense for what interrogation was like, bad treatment, and all that. But, as I say, they just basically introduced you to the problem. They couldn't really make it emulate the actual conditions. But, anyway, I knew exactly what I should do in terms of trying to abide by the Code of Conduct.* I knew what the Geneva Convention on the treatment of prisoners of war stipulated. So I was all prepared, as soon as I hit that ground, to abide by those two documents.

I was taken immediately into custody. And it was obvious that this guy was very inexperienced at this. I was probably the first American he had ever seen face to face. The river delta there is filled with rice paddies, and they have these little huts, known as hooches, interspersed through the rice paddies. My captor took me into a collection of hooches that formed a little hamlet. Then he put me into the hooch that was the pigpen, and there was a big female sow pig in there. She must have weighed 400 or 500 pounds; it was one of the biggest pigs I've ever seen. He had me over in a corner, and I noticed the whole time I was in there, the sow was kind of was eyeing me like, "What in the hell are you doing in my bedroom?" [Chuckle]

Later on he came back with somebody who seemed to be more senior, had more authority, and this person took me in custody. One of the first things they did was to have me strip down. They took off my integrated harness, and they took my pistol and my hand-held radio and my flight suit, and they stripped me right down to my skivvies. I was barefooted, and they looked in my mouth to see if there was any gold in there. Of course, they took my watch. I always left my Naval Academy ring back in my stateroom on board ship; I never flew, ever flew with my ring. But they really stripped me down to just the bare essentials. Then they started running me across the countryside, which ultimately turned out the place where we were picked up by a truck. I could see that my rear-seat guy, Jim Bailey, had landed about half a mile away from me, but he was taken separately to a collection point.

---

* The Code of Conduct is a set of rules that American service personnel are expected to follow if captured. The code was established by the U.S. Department of Defense in the wake of the Korean War, in which many servicemen collaborated with the enemy and submitted to brainwashing. The code requires steadfast resistance and encourages escape if captured. In recent years the words of the code have been changed to gender-neutral language.

It was kind of interesting as we ran through these little hamlet areas that the young kids thought it was a big social event. They laughed and cut up. The kids thought it was a great experience. Most of the people there who were in their 30s or below were not aggressive. The only people who seemed to have any real hatred were the older people. They probably had gone through the first war against the French, or had experienced French colonialism. They were the only ones who stepped forward and tried to strike me.

The militia people basically had me trot until we finally reached this collection point. I'd been shot down right around 7:30 in the morning, because I remember our time on target was at 7:30. So this was still fairly early in the morning. They finally got my rear-seat guy and me to this old dilapidated truck. They blindfolded us and tied our arms behind us and put us in the back of the truck. They had a guard observe us, and they would not allow us to talk to each other. If we tried to whisper or anything like that, they'd hit us with the butt of a rifle. But it took us a fairly long time to get up to Hanoi. I guess Nam Dinh, the point where we were shot down, is around 45 miles southeast of Hanoi. But it seemed to take us an extraordinary long time, because the roads were full of potholes.

Paul Stillwell: Could you judge how much time elapsed for that? An hour, maybe?

Admiral Lawrence: No, it was well into the afternoon when we finally arrived at Hanoi, because we stopped at one intermediate point and went into a guard station. They put me before some official, probably a militiaman. He put before me a questionnaire, in English, he had typed up there. I was supposed to fill out this questionnaire giving a lot of information. I refused to do it. I said, "Under the Code of Conduct, I'm only required to give my name, rank, serial number, and date of birth." So the guy accepted it; he didn't really press me. So I thought, "Gee, maybe this is the way I'm going to be treated. Maybe they're going to abide by the Geneva Convention."

But then when we got up to Hanoi, I found it was a different ball game. But it seems to me that either they let me languish in this cell area up there in Hanoi, or it took a lot of time to get there. When I finally faced the North Vietnamese officials, it seemed to be in the early evening. It was getting dark. When we got to Hanoi, they brought us into this obvious large prison, which subsequently I learned was called Hoa Lo. That was the place that Americans came to call Hanoi Hilton.

The area where they took the new prisoners for the initial interrogation was what we later on have called Heartbreak Hotel. I guess the early prisoners named the places in that Hoa Lo complex. Since there were so many Air Force officers, a lot of the places in that prison were named after places in Las Vegas, because many of them had flown out of Nellis.* We had a name for each compound, the interrogation rooms, and everything. For example, Gold Nugget, Thunderbird, and Stardust were some of the names of the locations at camp.

Anyway, they finally brought me before three officers, one of whom spoke English. He started asking me questions, and, as before, I said, "I'm only required to give name, rank, serial number, date of birth." He kept telling me that I was an air pirate, that I was not a prisoner of war, so I would not be accorded the rights of the Geneva Convention.

Paul Stillwell: What kinds of questions was he asking?

Admiral Lawrence: Well, what was the ship that I was flying off of, what was my target, what type of airplane—those types of questions. He was trying to get more information about the mission. Another thing they were interested in was what would be the future targets that would be assigned. It was basically operational type of information and military tactical type of information, as opposed to other types of intelligence.

Well, I kept refusing, and then, after several confrontations, he left. And then the guy that we came to know over the years as the professional torturer came in. Our nickname for him was Strap and Bar; we nicknamed every guard we had in the camp. Surprisingly, we had essentially the same guards the whole time we were there. Apparently, that was their assigned duty in the Army, and they just stayed in it.

---

* Nellis Air Force Base is in North Las Vegas, Nevada, about seven miles north of the central business district of the city of Las Vegas.

Strap and Bar was kind of unreal. I mean, he was very laid back and phlegmatic, but very efficient at what he was supposed to do. We talked about why they picked a guy like this to be the torturer, as opposed to some vicious type of guy. I think the North Vietnamese realized that they had to have a very skillful guy who could induce this pain without maiming or killing people. An overzealous torturer could unquestionably seriously injure or kill somebody. But they knew we were hostages, and they didn't want to dispose of us, although I know that some prisoners were probably killed through torture by overzealous guards.

But this guy was very professional. He had the straps and a bar, and he would basically put your body into contorted positions. For instance, he would put your legs into shackles on this long, horizontal bar. Then he pushed your head over to go underneath the bar so your body was very much bent and compressed, and this induced a high level of pain. He pulled your arms behind you and tied you, and then just left you in this position so you had to endure this pain. I think all of us initially had the James Bond type of attitude: that we could resist to death if we had to, not give information. But we all learned that you can take pain for just so long, and then you had to think of another strategy.

I tried to endure as long as I could and probably passed out several times. I remember that I had some type of a strap around my neck. It was cutting off the blood flow to my brain, and that made me black out. But over about a three- or four-day period, I went through this torture, and then I finally got to where I felt I just had to talk. I'd get up and I'd try to still evade any answering, and then be subjected to more tortures. It's kind of dim in my memory, because I was in and out of it.

Paul Stillwell: Where were you in between these torture sessions? Did you have a cell that soon?

Admiral Lawrence: The interrogation room, which was fairly large, served as your cell. They had a simple table down at the end of it, and these interrogators came in. It was a fairly large room, as a matter of fact. It was actually larger than this room, and you just stayed in that room when the interrogators and torturer were not in there.

Paul Stillwell: So that was mainly for new people?

Admiral Lawrence: Yes. This was an area where they brought in the new people. It was totally isolated from the rest of the camp.

Paul Stillwell: How soon did you get any contact with other Americans?

Admiral Lawrence: Well, I think this initial torture interrogation went on for about three days. The type of information they were seeking from me was about the planned targets. Well, I didn't really know, because the targets would come out each day from Washington. So finally I realized I had no other alternative; I had to tell them something. So I just started picking out the targets that would do the most damage. For instance, I said we were going to knock the piers out in Haiphong; we were going to knock out Phuc Yen fighter base. We were going to bomb the government palace in Hanoi. [Chuckle] That seemed to satisfy them. I had no idea of the validity of the things I was saying, but it got them off my back.

But the thing that really worried me was that they were going to ask me some very sensitive intelligence things, because I had some very highly classified knowledge about some of the electronic systems that were planned and our electronic countermeasures and all that. Gee, the questions were not sophisticated at all; they were just very, very simple questions.

Paul Stillwell: That's surprising since the torturer was so sophisticated.

Admiral Lawrence: Yes, it is. I think they didn't want a guy to do us in, but just efficiently go do a job and get the answers out of us. I was subsequently worked over by Strap and Bar, and you'll hear Jim Stockdale talk about this guy, whom they also called

Pigeye.* In Jim's book he describes this professional respect between people doing their jobs professionally, because old Strap and Bar was a professional torturer.† But he was so unemotional about it. I remember saying to myself, "I can't believe that this guy is doing these things to me, and it's just like he's another workman, 'Ho-hum, this is my job.'" But I'm sure it was by design, because you really learn when you have one human being totally subjugated to the will of another, that, God, you can just do irreparable damage and harm to that person. So they needed a guy like that, I guess, to do the torture.

Paul Stillwell: Well, it sounds like the object was more to show that they could make you talk than rather than trying to get specific information.

Admiral Lawrence: Well, I think that might be part of it, but also I think that they were not very sophisticated. That was where I came to realize that the Chinese and the Soviets, or any foreign power, were not closely involved in the North Vietnamese, or they would have been urging them to get more sophisticated information from us.

Paul Stillwell: Well, another point you made before we started with the tape was that this seemed out of character for the Vietnamese people.

Admiral Lawrence: Yes. Well, they are basically young people. They're not a fierce culture, like the Koreans, for example. We only had, say, one or two guards who were just what you'd call brutal. I wouldn't say the others were kindly towards us, but they never really were vicious or brutal in their actions against us. But if they were instructed to punish you, or something like that, they would do it, because that was their job.

---

* Commander James B. Stockdale, USN, eventually a vice admiral, was a prisoner of war in Vietnam from September 1965 to February 1973. He was subsequently awarded the Medal of Honor for his heroism while in prison. His wife Sybil was active in publicizing the plight of prisoners in Vietnam and calling for more humane treatment than they had received from their captors. He was Ross Perot's running mate in the 1992 presidential election.
† Jim and Sybil Stockdale, *In Love & War: The Story of a Family's Ordeal and Sacrifice during the Vietnam Years* (New York: Harper & Row, 1984).

Paul Stillwell: Well, sometimes they might have been motivated by a fear that they would be punished if they didn't punish you.

Admiral Lawrence: Oh, yes. It was obvious that there was an attempt by the leadership of the North Vietnamese to keep their people incited all the time. They told them to rise up to fight the enemy, this foreign power that was trying to re-colonize them. I mean, they were constantly trying to get their people incited. But, even in spite of that, the guards basically never got really vicious with us. But if they determined that someone was part of the leadership of the camp, they wanted to do something with you, like get information or try to force a propaganda statement or things like that. And they would apply the measures to get it, principally through the torture, inducing pain and so forth.

But I was fortunate, and I think it was because I held out pretty hard initially and established my credibility. So they never came back and tried to get me to do something for propaganda, like go out and be part of a visiting delegation for Jane Fonda.* I got punished a lot, and I got put into leg irons and out and isolated, but it was usually because they knew I was running camp communications, and I was serving as a leader. But I never was forced to make a propaganda statement or anything like that, and I was very happy about that.

The other thing is that they never went after me for sensitive information. And that really perplexed me—that they wouldn't be interested in more military information. I wondered why they didn't ask what our bombing tactics were, what our tactics were to try to counter their airplanes. They never asked me anything like that. The only other time there was a big torture for information on my part was they wanted us to fill out a very comprehensive questionnaire on personal information about us, like members of our family and all that. There was nothing in there that I saw would be harmful to the United States. But, as a matter of principle, I resisted—to make them have to work to get anything out of me. You refused to answer so you could keep your credibility up, because you never knew when they were going to have some exploitation. As you may have seen, there were pictures in the international media of prisoners being forced out

---

* Jane Fonda, an American movie actress, publicly supported the North Vietnamese side in the war and in 1972 visited North Vietnam. In 1988 during a "20/20" with Barbara Walters, Fonda apologized for her judgment in going to North Vietnam and contributing to North Vietnamese propaganda.

and having to appear on stage and that sort of thing. I was fortunate; I never was put in that position.

Paul Stillwell: What was your view of people like Jane Fonda and others who visited?

Admiral Lawrence: Not very favorable. The two most prominent were Jane Fonda and Ramsey Clark.* They were the ones who got the most visibility. Jane Fonda made a tape that they played to us, and it basically said, "The U.S. government's wrong. You've been misled, being forced to be in this war." We got an awful lot of antiwar-type statements from Ramsey Clark.

I feel a large part of it is that they were just hopelessly naive, and that they just had no concept of the nature of the enemy and what Communism was all about. The thing that I resent mostly is that Jane Fonda, although she has later admitted that she, perhaps, made a mistake and was misdirected, she's never really taken positive action to overcome what she did. But Ramsey Clark was the one who came across to me as just being really naive. I was amazed that a man of his stature would have gotten so far off the track. We got statements read to us made by both Fonda and Ramsey Clark.

Anyway, after that initial torture session, I was really banged up. I really could not use my limbs very effectively, and it took me several months to heal up from that. I still had a bad shoulder where they'd fractured a bone in my shoulder, and I'd lost the feeling in the outside of my right leg. But they did take me over into the main camp, which we called Las Vegas, or Camp Vegas. I initially went into an area called the Thunderbird. I was put into a cell by myself, but very soon I could hear POWs talking. So I just had to kind of just pull myself over to the door, because I was really still kind of crippled from that torture.

I did get involved in some talking, and I found out that our senior officer in that compound was Jim Stockdale. He was down the hall, and he and I were old friends from our test pilot days. I was able to pass the word to him that I had seen his wife about four months before I was shot down; I saw her at the change of command of the USS

---

* William Ramsey Clark served as Attorney General of the United States from 1967 to 1969. Later he became an antiwar activist. In 1972 he visited North Vietnam to protest the U.S. bombing of Hanoi.

Constellation over at North Island. I was also able to tell him that his name had just appeared on the promotion list for captains. So that was kind of a boost for his morale, because he hadn't heard anything from his family. I noticed in Jim Stockdale's book that he comments on the fact that I told him about his being selected for captain.

Paul Stillwell: How soon did you learn the tap code?

Admiral Lawrence: Well, very soon, because, as I say, at that time they were talking in this compound. In the course of this talking, they did pass me the tap code.[*] Then I moved over to a room where I had a common wall with a POW named Ron Mastin, who was an Air Force lieutenant, so he and I started tapping to each other.[†] It was amazing to me how quickly you could become proficient in that tap code. Even in those early days I was able to transmit a fair amount of information to Mastin.

It was tough getting acclimated to the prison life—just the austere conditions, staying on a bare, wooden bunk, and the heat and the lack of sanitation. I started getting very bad sores in my scalp. And I remember at night, instead of rice at the time, they were feeding us this coarse, brown bread. I think they imported flour from other Communist countries. I remember one time I had my bread laid out on the bunk, and I looked up and there was a big rat one time just pulling [chuckle] this piece of bread. The rats that they had there were just unbelievably big.

Paul Stillwell: Ten inches long, a foot long?

Admiral Lawrence: Yes, I think some of them were as much as a foot long. They were really big. In later times, when I'd be down trying to communicate under my door or through some water drain in my cell, I'd look up and be face to face with a rat. I mean, the hygiene was just unbelievably bad. I think that was just the way people were

---

[*] For an explanation of the tap code, see an article by the first prisoner of the Vietnam War, Commander Everett Alvarez Jr., USN, "Sound: A POW's Weapon," *U.S. Naval Institute Proceedings*, August 1976, pages 91-93.
[†] First Lieutenant Ronald L. Mastin, USAF, was shot down over North Vietnam on 16 January 1967 while flying an RF-4C Phantom. He was released on 4 March 1973.

accustomed to living over there. It wasn't just within our cell. I think that was a fairly prevalent standard of hygiene throughout the country. But it was tough acclimating to that low level of hygiene.

Paul Stillwell: Did you get any medical care?

Admiral Lawrence: We had very rudimentary medical care. One thing the French did when they had these people colonized was introduce them to the rudiments of medicine. I was fortunate that I never got really, seriously sick. The worst thing that happened to me was I got a very bad eye infection; it was kind of a viral infection. They took me out to this guy who was our camp corpsman, in his little, filthy clinic. He got out a big needle and gave me an injection, which I think may have been penicillin. I broke out in really a bad rash, because I was allergic to that large a dose of penicillin.

But that was really the only time that I required medical care. I was so lucky, boy, because when I was shot down, I was in tip-top condition, because I'd kept myself physically fit. I think that really helped me get through the experience, because there are a lot of guys who were just sick the whole time they were POWs. They'd have dysentery or just malaise, and I didn't. I was charging every day.

The North Vietnamese kept me in solitary confinement from the time I was shot down, which was the 28th of June, through that summer. They moved me from cell to cell from time to time. But after I'd been there about a month, the communication just ended in Thunderbird. What had actually happened, I guess, was that the camp commander and his people had learned that Stockdale was putting orders out to the other POWs. Somehow they got this feedback through interrogation or something. So they took the 12 guys that they perceived were the kind of leaders of the resistance, and they took them all off and segregated them to a place called Alcatraz. You may have heard about Alcatraz, where they kept the 12 prisoners.

Well, when they pulled all those guys out, it just ended communication in Thunderbird. So I didn't communicate with anybody from about July to October. As I say, I was in solitary confinement, but I was trying to do everything I could to see as much as I could. One time I was looking out my window in this one cell, and lo and behold, I saw my Naval Academy classmate Byron Fuller.* He was being helped by another POW. That was the common practice. When we had one POW who was injured or sick or something like that, a POW would be assigned to be the kind of a nurse for him. So Byron was being helped out by his nurse. I was able to confirm that with Byron, and I said, "My God, that's the third guy out of my class who's been shot down." Al Brady had been shot down a few months before I was.† So I knew about that.

But one time, when I was looking out, trying to confirm about Byron, I got caught. That was the first time I got put into leg stocks, which were just basically iron shackles at the end of this wooden bunk. They put me into this real small cell, and I was in stocks. And it was, of course, terribly hot. That was the only time in the POW experience when my morale really got low, because I'd been there two months, and it was obvious they were not going to let me write or receive mail. From the discomfort of being in leg stocks and the heat, I really got well down, but somehow I was able to pull myself out of it. That was the only time in my whole six years I ever had anything like being depressed. Most of the time I was in there, I was trying to resist and keeping in contact with the other POWs, and those challenges gave me things to be upbeat about.

Paul Stillwell: How long did that period last in the stocks?

Admiral Lawrence: It was about a month. And then, in October of '67, there was a real significant escalation in the bombing; I guess President Johnson had just lost his patience. So he significantly escalated the bombing and we had massive raids that came into the heartland of North Vietnam, [unclear] and Hanoi, Phuc Yen, the jet base up there northwest of Hanoi.

I remember several times a day you could hear the air raids coming in and always

---

* Commander Robert Byron Fuller, USN, was shot down over North Vietnam on 14 July 1967 while flying an A-4C Skyhawk as part of Attack Squadron 76 (VA-76) from the carrier *Bon Homme Richard* (CVA-31). He was released on 4 March 1973.
† Commander Allen C. Brady, USN, was shot down over North Vietnam on 19 January 1967 while flying an A-6A Intruder as executive officer of Attack Squadron 85 (VA-85) from the carrier *Kitty Hawk* (CVA-63). He was released on 4 March 1973.

preceded by the air-raid siren. But as a result of these really intense raids there in October, quite a few pilots were shot down. So I guess they decided my punishment was up, with those leg stocks in that small cell, and I was put together with three other guys who had just been shot down. One was my classmate Chuck Gillespie, and the others were Tom Kirk and Dan Daniels.* They had all been shot down on raids into the heart of North Vietnam, so it was obvious that that was a real escalation of the war at that time. Chuck Gillespie was the commanding officer of Fighter Squadron 151. He was flying F-4s, same as I was, both out of Miramar. Tom Kirk was an Air Force lieutenant colonel, who was the commanding officer of an Air Force fighter squadron. He was flying F-105s. And Dan was a squadron executive officer.

Paul Stillwell: Well, that was an enormous difference then, having roommates after all this isolation.

Admiral Lawrence: Yes, it was. And then we basically stayed together on and off till the end of the war. But I went through long periods where I was just with Tom Kirk. Then I went through some more solitary confinement. My total number of months in solitary confinement over the six years was 14 months.

When I got together with those three guys, I was the senior in that group, and I said, "We've really got to start getting a communication system going." So we worked at that. I told them the tap code, and then we started doing a limited amount of talking, because we figured out a way to do the lookout for the guards. We knew that communication was just absolutely imperative to have a military organization and have effective resistance, but also to help guys keep their morale up.

After really analyzing the situation, we realized that the guards, during certain

---

* Commander Charles R. Gillespie Jr., USN, was shot down over North Vietnam on 24 October 1967 while flying an F-4B Phantom as commanding officer of Fighter Squadron 151 (VF-151) from the carrier *Coral Sea* (CVA-43). He was released on 14 March 1973.
Lieutenant Colonel Thomas H. Kirk Jr., USAF, was shot down over North Vietnam on 28 October 1967 while flying an F-105D Thunderchief as commanding officer of the 357th Tactical Fighter Squadron out of Takhli Royal Thai Air Force Base. He was released on 14 March 1973.
Commander Verlyne W. Daniels, USN, was shot down over North Vietnam on 26 October 1967 while flying an A-4E Skyhawk as executive officer of Attack Squadron 155 (VA-155) from the carrier *Coral Sea* (CVA-43). He was released on 14 March 1973.

times of the day, had stereotyped patrolling patterns where they'd go from one compound to another compound. We had three large compounds and two smaller compounds in this camp that we called Las Vegas. Some of the guards would use the same route, and it would take them the same amount of time. So by looking out of our door and out of our window, we could tell when that one guard that we knew left, that it would be about ten minutes before he came back.

So that's when we developed this capability to do some talking. That usually had to be during what they called the siesta period, which was a period from about 1:00 to 2:00. I guess the French had introduced them to the siesta, which is done in some of the European countries, and the North Vietnamese kept it as a part of their culture. So that's the time when the camp got pretty quiet, and they expected us to be quiet. So we would do most of our communications. So working on this, I got a pretty good communication system established within our compound, both by talking and by tapping.

That was when I really took command of the camp. I kept that command position for about the next three years, because Stockdale and those guys were all in Alcatraz and other camps. We really worked on maintaining good communication, both by talking when we could and by tapping. We also found we could take these stiff bamboo brooms that they gave us, and by using strokes of the broom, we could send that tap code. The tap code that we used was based on a matrix that we formed by taking the 26 letters in the alphabet, dropping off the letter K, and making C and K interchangeable, so that gave you 25 letters, so you could form them into five lines of five letters each. For example, the first line was A through E, the third was L through P, and the last was V through Z. When you wanted to tap a letter in that matrix, you would tap down the left side, then to the right. The letter M was the second letter in the third line, so you'd just go tap-tap-tap, tap-tap. By pressing your ear to the wall, you could hear this tapping as much as maybe 20 to 25 feet away, light tapping.

So we built up this fairly sophisticated communication system over time, and then we also had typical sounds you make when you have a respiratory ailment that we also used to transmit that code. The first line would be one cough; the second line would be two coughs; the third line would be a throat clear; the fourth line would be a very deep, what they called a hack; and the last would be the old spitting. So we would send messages with that version of the tap code. If we got a guy who was off by himself that we couldn't tap around to him on the wall. For example, a message we'd usually send something like GBU that stood for God Bless You, and that would be [demonstrating message with various sounds].

To keep the guards confused, we would be constantly sneezing, coughing, everything, just to mask the times when we want to send that voice tap code. Also, we were always bugging them to let us sweep out our cells, because that would be a chance to send messages by sweeping with a broom that could be heard all around the camp. The guard must have thought we were absolutely nuts on the subject of cleanliness.

We were in a constant confrontation with them. They were always trying to find some prisoners they could force to do something, like make a propaganda statement. There were a couple of prisoners—Marine Lieutenant Colonel Ed Miller and a guy named Gene Wilber—who eventually pretty actively collaborated with the North Vietnamese on making propaganda statements.* Miller was in my compound. I was talking out, and then suddenly he just went off the line, and I couldn't get him to come up and communicate. I really thought that was strange, but I guess he had made his decision that the pressures and so forth were so great that he was going to collaborate with the enemy to have a better life. But I remember trying my best to keep him on the communications, and he just stopped communicating.

It was a real challenge to keep everybody on the line. One of the first signs when a guy was having some problems with depression and so forth, would be that he would stop communicating. You just couldn't get him to come up, either a tap or talk. Another sign was when a guy stopped eating, and you had to use a lot of means to get these signals. We were in individual cells—about seven-foot-square cells—and then as you finished up your meal, they would have you bring your little bowls out to put one place. If I came out and I saw a bowl that was full of food near a door, I would say, "Better start

---

* Lieutenant Colonel Edison W. Miller, USMC, was shot down over North Vietnam on 13 October 1967 while flying an F-4B Phantom as executive officer of Marine Fighter Attack Squadron 323 (VMFA-323) from Danang, South Vietnam. He was released on 12 February 1973.
Commander Walter Eugene Wilber, USN, was shot down over North Vietnam on 16 June 1968 while flying an F-4J Phantom as commanding officer of Fighter Squadron 102 (VF-102) from the carrier *America* (CVA-66). He was released on 12 February 1973. His radar intercept officer, Lieutenant (junior grade) Bernard F. Rupinski, USNR, was killed when the plane was shot down.

watching that guy; he might be having problems." Because if a guy just lost his appetite, it was usually a psychological situation.

Paul Stillwell: Were there some that you were able to bring back through this communication?

Admiral Lawrence: Oh, yes, yes. The guys went through periods where they just would be very, very depressed and just didn't want to communicate. Also, there was this great fear of being caught communicating, because they'd really, really work you over in those early days up until about 1970. If you were caught communicating, boy, you really got punished. A lot of guys didn't relish the thought of communicating and getting caught, so I had to really be pretty firm as a senior officer in requiring people to communicate. Because I knew that if we didn't communicate, we couldn't have an effective resistance. Also, I knew guys would be psychologically healthier if we kept them communicating. My biggest challenge, as a camp senior officer, was keeping everybody on the line and just requiring people to develop innovative means of keeping the communication going. Because if you didn't work at it all the time, you just couldn't get the information passed around, because it was so hard, with the guards patrolling, to find those times to communicate. So you had to exploit every opportunity.

Paul Stillwell: Why did they try so hard to discourage communication?

Admiral Lawrence: Well, they knew that this would enhance our resistance. And they really wanted to exploit us to the absolute max for propaganda purposes. I think they had this feeling that if they could get prisoners to say that we were against the war, that this would be a valuable propaganda tool.

While I was a senior officer, no one under my command ever went out to see a delegation. I think we had a pretty tough resistance posture, and they just looked upon our camp there, Camp Vegas, as not being a good potential. Only one guy died in the camp while I was a senior officer, and that was a guy named Lance Sijan, who was shot down as an Air Force first lieutenant.* I guess after he'd been there a while, he was promoted to captain. But he had evaded for a long time after being shot down, so he was suffering very advanced exposure and everything. He had broken his leg, and so he had some gangrene. So he was brought into our camp, and then he eventually died there. It was obvious to us that, even though I could never get face to face with him, I could just tell, through the communication system, that he was on his final days. But then they took him out, and he did die, because he was not released. He was given a Congressional Medal of Honor, and they have a hall named for him out at the Air Force Academy.

But we had other prisoners who were taken out, apparently in good health, and just never returned. Somehow they died in the system.

Paul Stillwell: Well, they might have been victims of those overzealous torturers.

Admiral Lawrence: Yes. We never really knew all those situations.

Paul Stillwell: What other functions did you have as the commander besides maintaining the communications?

Admiral Lawrence: Well, I put out directives, things like, "You would not go out and see a delegation." We formulated the directive on how you resisted. In other words, by that time, we all knew that if they tortured us, that we didn't have the option of dying. You probably could endure the pain for only a certain amount of time, so we actually instructed people, "Don't hang in there till you lose your rationality, and do something where you really can be exploited." So the guidance was that, "When you're interrogated, have a cover story, but before you start using that cover story, go to significant pain." Because we wanted people to establish their credibility, and not look as a person as an easy mark. That was a standard policy—that when they were attempting to get you to do something, before you started maneuvering and using cover stories and

---

* First Lieutenant Lance P. Sijan, USAF, was flying in an F-4C Phantom when it was lost on a mission over Laos on 9 November 1967. Sources differ on the cause of the loss. Sijan was held prisoner and made several escape attempts. He died on 22 January 1968. His remains were returned to U.S. custody on 13 March 1974.

all that, you hung in there and took significant pain. But go to your fallback story while you still had your wits about you.

Paul Stillwell: Of course, that would vary for every individual.

Admiral Lawrence: Oh, yes, and, of course, I found that people's threshold of pain varied significantly with individuals.

One of my cellmates just absolutely just feared any pain; he just couldn't accept any. The rest of us were able to take far more than that. So you had to spend a lot of your time, as the senior officer, just really trying to boost people's spirits. When you were communicating with them, you had to project that you were with it and exhorting them to measure up. You were more of a cheerleader than giving specific orders.

I think our camp really had a pretty good, unified resistance posture. As I say, we had that one guy Ed Miller who was with us, and he went off the line. I think he was having psychological problems.

So I really ran that camp for between two or three years.

Paul Stillwell: Was that policy or practice of dealing with torture something you inherited from Stockdale or something you devised?

Admiral Lawrence: Well, it was kind of an extension of some of Stockdale's early policies. I just basically amplified and went into more detail about the torture thing. He had basically the same policy, but it was not as much detail. I was the one who formulated the instruction to take enough pain to establish credibility and go to the point before you lost your rationality, but don't give in easily. I mean, take enough pain that they knew that you were a tough nut, so they'd have to work to get something out of you. They were human, and they were trying to get something for the least cost.

Paul Stillwell: On the other hand, that gives you a good deal of internal pride that you can hold out for a certain time.

Admiral Lawrence: That's right. That's the other aspect of it. You have a better feeling about yourself, because when you finally had to give in after being tortured, you really felt low. That's where Stockdale talks a lot about the ability to be able to bounce back. I mean you're down, so you just have to build yourself up to bounce back. Actually, even though you're physically in great pain, you have a lot better feeling about yourself that you hung in there, rather than just capitulate right away.

Paul Stillwell: Are there any mental techniques that you can use to distract yourself while this is going on?

Admiral Lawrence: No. I used to compose poetry when I was a POW. And two things I said into the old poem, "Stone walls and bars do not a prison make; you mean to tell me this is all a fake?" And the other one was that, "Your mind can play tricks on you, but in the main, it's pretty goddamn honest when it comes to pain." [Laughter] No, I never found that you could get your mind on anything else once they had you to such a high level of pain.

But you just had to handle it the best way you could. But, fortunately, when the North Vietnamese released some POWs in the summer of '69 as a propaganda measure, these guys went back, and they revealed all this torture that was going on, mistreatment. And that release, which they thought would get them world sympathy, really backfired on them. They got so vilified in the international press, that in late '69 they started backing off on the physically harsh type torture. But they still punished you, particularly if you were caught communicating. And that's where I got most of my punishment, because I knew it was my job to keep communications going, and so I got caught a few times.

One type of punishment they would give you was just to have you sit in a chair. And then, well, you said, "God, that's not very difficult." But then after about 12 hours or so, when you're just sitting in a chair, the blood pools in your ankles, and they don't let you sleep, and you start almost hallucinating. That was a form of punishment, just sitting in a chair for days. That really got to be very painful.

Another thing was that I really felt that we got really smart and more sophisticated in that we'd just start passing some notes around the camp. Then we worked out a system of having a place to put the notes, a kind of a common place where POWs would go, like the outside bath stall. I got caught one time putting a note in a note drop, and they knew that I'd been one of the leaders of the resistance all those years. So I think they finally just decided they were going to break me. So they took me out into a six-foot-square cell that was unventilated, unlighted, and had this tin roof. We called it Calcutta, from the Black Hole of Calcutta. You had hardly any room besides your wooden bunk to even walk.

It was in August, and during the day the temperature would go up well above 100 degrees. So in the summer months, particularly those of us with fair complexions, we'd have this heat rash over our entire bodies. But on that occasion, that heat rash advanced into heat sores, and my body was covered with all these sores. I had to just lie immobile, completely flat on my back, to minimize the discomfort. I just realized that I had to get some good thought process going. And, of course, I'd known this from my early years as a POW when you're in solitary confinement, you couldn't daydream and fantasize; you had to have a good productive mental process.

In the earlier years, one thing I did at first was to relive my life in great detail. I did that about three times. It used to take me almost three weeks to go through my life in great detail in my head, trying to resurrect as much as I could remember, going back to my earliest recorded memory, which was as a kid in a crib. I remember seeing my parents; I had that as a mental picture. Then you'd do things like try to recall as many people as you could in your first grade class. And then you'd just brainstorm that for hours and hours, and it was amazing how these names would start coming out of your head—friends that you had. That was a great advantage to me in being able to resurrect a lot of my family history and things like that.

I remember when I went home for the first time after being released, people would come up to me and say, "Well, I'm So-and-so; I was in your elementary school class."

"Yeah, I remember you," because I'd resurrected their name. So that was a beneficial thing.

Paul Stillwell: How do you draw a distinction between that and the fantasizing and daydreaming?

Admiral Lawrence: Well, as I say, you just had to come to the realization after a while that you couldn't fantasize and daydream.

Paul Stillwell: Why was that destructive?

Admiral Lawrence: Well, you became almost like a vegetable. You just lay there and languished. It was just not good for me from a morale perspective. In other words, you had to have goals and projects that you were working on to keep yourself sharp. Most of the time when you were in the system, as we called it, you were communicating. And, boy, that was really keeping you on your toes and sharp. But the times you're off in solitary confinement, you were not having an opportunity to communicate, you just had to get your mind productively employed and not worry about your family.

What you basically did, as I describe it, was just shrink your world down to where at times it just encompassed that cell; that was your world. Your objective was to get through that particular day in the most effective way possible. I'd require myself to do calisthenics, even though it was hot and I was debilitated. Sometimes I would walk in my cell, and I got very much involved in these thought processes. I'd review history, do complex math in my head.

But in this one occasion in Calcutta, I knew that I had to really get deeply absorbed in something to get my mind off this pain. And, fortunately, the guards were leaving me completely alone. That was an era when they knocked off the harsh, brutal treatment. So they just basically left you alone in this terrible, uncomfortable, isolated situation. So you'd have all day. And that's when I conceived the idea of composing poetry in my head.

I had remembered from my tenth grade English, a great poet, Sir Walter Scott, who used an iambic pentameter. One of his poems is "The Lady of the Lake," which contains the line, "The stag at eve has drunk his fill." So I said, "I'm going to compose in my head a perfect iambic pentameter poem. Sir Walter Scott had genius, but I've got time, and I'm going to do whatever it takes." So I started really thinking deeply, and I came up with the line, "O Tennessee, My Tennessee," as a perfect iambic pentameter line. So that's when I composed this poem, "Tennessee, My Tennessee." In addition to making every line iambic pentameter, which is an eight-meter and rhyming with the sequential line, I also set as my goal to have every line in there describe something about my native state. It took me about three weeks to compose that poem in my head. Then I composed some other poems. Then I kept the poems in my head after that.

I finally got out of Calcutta after two months and was brought back into the camp and put back in with my old roommate, Tom Kirk. But I found out later on that the guy who had succeeded me was John McCain, because he'd gotten into some trouble.[*] So I've always been thankful to him for getting me out of Calcutta, but anyway I kept all these poems in my head over the years. When I finally was released, one of the first things I did when I went to the hospital at Clark Air Force Base in the Philippines, was to sit down and write out all these poems. As I'll describe later, "O Tennessee, My Tennessee" became the state poem. We don't produce many poets down in Tennessee; it's mostly country music people.

So that's just an example of how deep we were in thought, and the great capacity for doing things mentally that we developed. Our memories got to be so sharp, you couldn't believe it.

Paul Stillwell: Well, I've seen examples where returned POWs would recite long rosters of names, which was a great thing to do.

Admiral Lawrence: I was a memory bank for the names of POWs. There were about three of us who were designated to be the ones who tried to remember every name that we had in the system. About every third day I would go over these names, and I had

---

[*] Lieutenant Commander John S. McCain III, USN, was shot down over North Vietnam on 26 October 1967 while flying an A-4E Skyhawk as a member of Attack Squadron 163 (VA-163) from the carrier *Oriskany* (CVA-34). He was released on 4 March 1973. He retired as a captain in 1981. He became a member of the U.S. House of Representatives in 1983 and the U.S. Senate in 1987. He described his experiences in *Faith of My Fathers* (New York: Random House, 1999).

them in groups of five, alphabetically. We were so skillful at doing this, that if you got a new name, you knew how to insert it in the right place and then line up the fives again. I did that for years.

Also, memorization was a great way of keeping yourself mentally sharp. Any time a prisoner could pass you a poem or something like that, you'd just grab it eagerly and commit it to memory. I remember poems like "Gunga Din," and other Kipling poems. But memorization and those mental challenges or projects were absolutely essential. Gee, I designed houses and did all sorts of very mentally challenging things. Our memorization was unbelievable. We got so, when we were tapping on the wall, that we could tap for about 15 minutes and then turn and go over to the other wall and tap everything that you received, because you still had it committed to memory. The average person just doesn't ever use his mind quite like we did, because our whole society is attuned to exchanging information through very rapid means—television, radio, and telephone.

Paul Stillwell: Short attention span.

Admiral Lawrence: That's right. And the average person very rarely sits back for many hours and gets deeply involved in thought. I think that was one of the most useful things we did. We really learned what your mind is like, and how much information is in your mind if you really learn how to pull it out.

Paul Stillwell: Well, this activity also kept you from lapsing into self-pity, I would think.

Admiral Lawrence: Oh, yes, that's just right. You learned after about the first two or three months, you couldn't go through that "why me?" and feel sorry for yourself. You couldn't worry about your family. You just had to have faith that everybody was doing their best to take care of your family. I'm sure other POWs handled it differently. But that's the way I handled it. I had to get involved in all these productive projects.

Paul Stillwell: How did you mark the passage of time? Could you keep track of what day it was?

Admiral Lawrence: Yes. I never had any problem with that. Every morning when I woke up, I would say, "Today is Friday, March umpty-ump." I don't think a day went by that I didn't do that. As I say, I was really lucky, because I never had a serious health problem, whereas, many POWs did. They'd have very bad dysentery, constant malaise. I guess I was just lucky because I was shot down very physically fit, and I'm just basically a healthy person. So that, I never was really out of it for a long time. There were a lot of guys there that you just worried from one day to day whether they were going to survive. It wasn't as though we weren't being fed. It was just a bare subsistence diet, but their whole state of health seemed to just be at a minimal level. And you were always worried about their being able to make it.

Paul Stillwell: What was your diet, besides the coarse bread you've mentioned?

Admiral Lawrence: Well, it was essentially vegetables. And then supplemented usually by a small loaf of bread a day or rice. We were fed twice a day, and they did everything on that line for their convenience. So it was for the convenience of the cooks to wait from 10:00 o'clock in the morning till about 4:00 o'clock in the afternoon. And it was amazing how your system got acclimated to that. In other words, you would be just as hungry at 4:00 as you were at 10:00 in the morning, even though the time periods were not equal. I always made myself eat all my food, even though it wasn't very palatable. I really stressed and ordered some POWs to eat their food, force it down.

But even in spite of the limited diet, there were times of protest that we went on fasts. I fasted two to three days on two occasions as a protest. And still, in spite of fasting for two days, it didn't significantly impair my health. So I was really lucky because I think I was, just basically, had a good, strong constitution. By basically feeling good and not too debilitated, it really enhanced my capability to be a leader, a senior officer. I had periods when I had officers in the camp that were more senior than me, but they just weren't capable of assuming a leadership role, because they were physically debilitated or not willing to get active in the communications system.

Paul Stillwell: Well, this idea of honor that had been with you since childhood was probably a compass for you too.

Admiral Lawrence: Yes, and I think that I really saw the value of the Naval Academy experience, because the principal leaders in North Vietnam were Naval Academy graduates—guys like Stockdale, Denton, McCain, Shumaker.* I never saw a Naval Academy graduate not keep his head up and keep going. It really proved to me the value of what we do here, because I'd say that I think the Naval Academy graduates constituted about 5% of the total POW population, and yet got at least 50% of the very high medals, like Stockdale got the Congressional Medal of Honor; and several others got the Distinguished Service Medal, like Denton, Shumaker, myself. The key leaders up there were the Naval Academy graduates, because often I was aware of a Naval Academy graduate taking over and running the operation, even though there were people that were senior. I had three Air Force colonels in the camp, full colonels who just, for one reason or another did not want to act as the camp senior officer. But, anyway, I really think it validates what we do here at the academy.

Paul Stillwell: The point you made when you were talking to Al Santoli involved the usefulness of the age factor in your ability to resist and lead.†

Admiral Lawrence: Oh, yes, there's no question about that. I was shot down at just about the right age, in my middle 30s. I had enough experience to be senior and to have

---

* Commander Jeremiah A. Denton Jr., USN, was shot down over North Vietnam on 18 July 1965 while flying an A-6A Intruder as commanding officer of Attack Squadron 75 (VA-75) from the carrier *Independence* (CVA-62). He was released on 12 February 1973. His oral history is in the Naval Institute collection, and his memoir of the POW period is *When Hell Was in Session* (New York: Readers Digest Press, 1976). He subsequently served as a U.S. Senator from Alabama, 1981-87.
Lieutenant Commander Robert H. Shumaker, USN, was shot down over North Vietnam on 11 February 1965 while flying an F-8D Crusader as a member of Fighter Squadron 154 (VF-154) from the carrier *Coral Sea* (CVA-43). He was released 12 February 1973.
† Al Santoli, editor, *Everything We Had: an Oral History of the Vietnam War as Told By 33 American Men Who Fought It* (New York: Random House, 1981).

the authority of leadership. And yet I was young enough still to be healthy and vigorous and not be pulled down too much by the poor diet and just the poor sanitation.

Paul Stillwell: How much input did you get from new prisoners on how the war was going and how the national mood was changing against the war?

Admiral Lawrence: Well, in my early years, we really couldn't get all that much, because our communications involved just really sending the central type information. There wasn't a chance for a guy to give you comprehensive information.

Then there was a moratorium on the bombing in '68. The bombing was limited to the southern part of South Vietnam, so we had a very, just a trickle of prisoners coming in. And so our information on what was going on outside was limited. For example, when we put a man on the moon in 1969, the Vietnamese did not tell us about this, because they never gave us any good information.   [Interruption—end of interview]

Interview Number 11 with Vice Admiral William P. Lawrence, U.S. Navy (Retired)
Place: U.S. Naval Institute, Annapolis, Maryland
Date: Friday, 30 November 1990

Paul Stillwell: Admiral, when we stopped the other afternoon, you were on the point of telling how you got the news of the first moon landing in 1969.*

Admiral Lawrence: Okay, one thing they did with us over there in the POW camp was to try to convert us to their way of thinking. I guess you couldn't really call it brainwashing. I think it was actually motivated by a naive feeling that they could change our views on the war or turn us against the war. They felt this obligation to show us the light and the truth.

Members of the antiwar movement in the United States used to send the North Vietnamese movies of antiwar demonstrations in the United States. So one time in 1970, at nighttime, they took us out into the courtyard of our camp from the individual cells. They had us sit by cell, far enough away from the other cells so that we couldn't talk to people. It was dark, so you really couldn't see who they were. Then they showed us a movie of an antiwar demonstration, and it appeared to us it was in San Francisco, because you could see them going up the hills, and we could see the types of buildings alongside the street. One thing we always did make sure to do in watching antiwar demonstrations was to read the placards. We saw one that said, "Hey, Dick, you can put a man on the moon, but you can't stop the Vietnam War."

So we went back and said, "God, wonder what that means."

Someone said, "Well, Dick must be Richard Nixon."†

I said, "God, you think we really put a man on the moon?" I remember when I was shot down in '67, that was a goal that we had set for ourselves, to have a man on the moon by the end of the 1960s. But I never really believed that we could achieve it. I

---

* Astronauts Neil A. Armstrong and Michael Collins made the first human walk on the moon on 20 July 1969. During the time they were on the moon, Edwin E. "Buzz" Aldrin Jr., remained behind on board the Apollo 11 command module.
† Richard M. Nixon was President of the United States from 20 January 1969 until his resignation from office on 9 August 1974.

thought it was too much of a technological feat that might be beyond our capability to attain. But, anyway, we talked it over for several months, and, finally, when the bombing started up again in the very northern part of North Vietnam in the spring of '72, we got new POWs who confirmed for us that there had been a man on the moon. The Vietnamese had never told us.

Paul Stillwell: Almost three years then.

Admiral Lawrence: Yes, that's right.

This was all part of their education, brainwashing effort. In every cell in our camp we had small, rudimentary speakers that had bad fidelity. But for a half hour in the morning and a half hour in the afternoon, they would play us the daily Voice of Vietnam broadcast. I guess it was an international broadcast sent out over the radio waves. And Hanoi Hannah, we called her, was the one who presented the Voice of Vietnam. She spoke in basically very good English with a little bit of an oriental accent.

That was a broadcast that was very much oriented to pointing out all the bad things that were happening in the United States. So for six years I learned about every calamity and adverse thing that happened in the United States. Most POWs just tuned it out and didn't even pay any attention to it. But I always listened to it very carefully, because I wanted to get as much news from back in the United States as possible. But they also would talk about the war. I found that if you really analyzed what they were telling you, you could get a little bit of a flavor for how the war was progressing. When they reported U.S. casualties, if you would divide that by four, that was usually pretty correct.

The other thing that they gave us was a propaganda newspaper. That also told about engagements in the war. So I used to read that very carefully. So, surprisingly, from this an hour a day of intense anti-American broadcast, coupled with that newspaper, I really knew a lot about how the war had progressed on the ground in the South, which was primarily what this paper covered.

That was the type of information program they had for us. In the early years, we used to get periodic interrogations by some of the camp officers who could speak

English. After the first two years, they basically gave up on that; they realized that they couldn't be effective in changing our minds. But they did give us an hour a day of radio broadcast.

Paul Stillwell: Well, in fact, the U.S. public mood had turned dramatically against the war as time went on. Did you really believe that, or did you discount it because of their lack of credibility?

Admiral Lawrence: Well, I knew that some antiwar attitudes had developed in the country. But I think it was not anywhere near as bad as they expressed. Because we wondered how Nixon was able to keep fighting the war if people were so much against it. He came into office in 1969, and there was tremendous antiwar pressure at that time, but he was able to hold out for four years.

Paul Stillwell: Well, part of it was that all these negotiations were going on, and the feeling kept being that, "Well, just a little more, then we'll work it out."

Admiral Lawrence: They gave us some information on negotiations and how that was progressing, although we never really got much in detail about it.

Paul Stillwell: Did members of your family try to communicate with you?

Admiral Lawrence: Yes, yes, they did. I think I was there three years when they finally let me have a letter from home, and that was from my parents. I never was allowed to have any letters from my wife or children; it was always from my parents. I don't know why they chose to do it that way. As a result of not being sure where my children and my wife were, I sent all my letters to my folks, because that was the only communication I got.

Paul Stillwell: How regularly would you hear from them?

Admiral Lawrence: Oh, at the most, about once every three months. Some POWs got more mail than others. It didn't seem to be tied to prisoner attitudes. You couldn't say that the guy who was more cooperative got more mail. It was a very haphazard, hit-and-miss situation.

For a number of years after I was captured, I was listed as missing in action. Then Senator Kennedy did prevail on the North Vietnamese, around late 1969 or early 1970, to put out a list of POWs.[*] I think they felt he was an antiwar senator.

Paul Stillwell: Did your parents deliberately withhold the news about your wife's situation?[†]

Admiral Lawrence: Yes. They never mentioned anything at all about it.

Paul Stillwell: Probably wouldn't have helped you in the least.

Admiral Lawrence: No, it wouldn't. Everett Alvarez found out about his wife divorcing him. I'm sure if the North Vietnamese had known about it, they would have told me, because they took great delight in telling somebody that a parent had died or something like that. I really think it was in my best interest that I didn't find out there.

Paul Stillwell: Did Alvarez have some kind of status within the prisoners because of his longevity?

Admiral Lawrence: No, no, not that I could see. It certainly didn't cause him to get improved treatment from the North Vietnamese there.

Paul Stillwell: Well, I was thinking more in terms of how he was held in esteem by Americans.

---

[*] Edward M. Kennedy, brother of President John F. Kennedy, was a Democrat from Massachusetts. He served in the Senate from 3 January 1963 until his death on 25 August 2009.

[†] Lawrence's first wife, Anne, divorced him in absentia on 26 August 1971.

Admiral Lawrence: Oh, yes, sure. I never lived with him, but, sure, the people who lived with him held him in very high esteem and tried to be deferential with him, considering all he'd been through for so long.

Paul Stillwell: What did you do for physical exercise?

Admiral Lawrence: Well, it was just purely what you could do on your own. Every morning I would run in place to try to get my heart rate up. Then I would walk back and forth, and then I would do some calisthenics on my wooden bunk. When I'd wake up in the morning, I would do pushups, touching my toes, and just general calisthenics.

There was really no other opportunity for any organized activity with the other POWs. The conditions just weren't conducive; you didn't have enough open space or balls or anything like that. But I used to do a lot of walking in my cell too. That used to be a great pastime. Anything you did exercise-wise really had to be self-generated. The guards really didn't help you at all.

Paul Stillwell: Well, the combination of exercise and not many calories would certainly be conducive to weight loss.

Admiral Lawrence: Yes, that's right. We got acclimated to the diet, but we were never acclimated to the heat. It was the heat that was just really oppressive and the heat rash, even advancing to the point of heat sores, which were really very uncomfortable.

I guess the thing that interested me is how you can acclimate your system to a situation like that. I recall that I was able to exist day to day without feeling a great gnawing hunger. And, gee, we also fasted on two occasions. Designated senior officers just decided we were going to take off. One time, we did it for two days and another time maybe even closer to three. You just have this kind of a dull ache and uncomfortable feeling, but it's amazing what you can do.

Paul Stillwell: Did you get the feeling while you were there that the guards had a begrudging respect for the prisoners?

Admiral Lawrence: Yes, yes, you really saw this develop over the years, because they certainly admired the way we hung in there and took care of ourselves. We were very self-sufficient. I think the fact that they saw a lot of POWs take torture to avoid doing something gained their admiration.

Paul Stillwell: How did that respect manifest itself?

Admiral Lawrence: Well, it was just more considerate treatment. Among our group, we had one guard we called Big Ugh; I think they had another name for him in Vietnamese, but I can't remember it. He was with us the whole time we were there, and he had a vicious streak in him. He liked to take his keys and strike you on the head with them. But he wasn't always that way. He was more macho, more prone to use physical measures against us than other people. He was really the only one guard I recall who was a very brutal, tended to be somewhat vicious, because the Vietnamese, as I say, are inherently very gentle people.

Paul Stillwell: You had some people who, maybe, have had more threshold for pain. Did you see some people you perceived to be collaborators with the guards?

Admiral Lawrence: Well, we had, as I said, the two prisoners who did things for the Vietnamese and kept doing them: Colonel Ed Miller, Marine Corps, and Gene Wilber from the Navy. We really tried to bring them back in the fold, but they always refused. I think they got pretty good treatment from the Vietnamese as a result of it. Originally there were five who looked like they were growing apart from the fold, and we got three back. Three or four decided they wanted to be with the U.S. personnel in every way, I mean be part of us. There were those two we couldn't bring back.

Paul Stillwell: Is there any stigma attached to them to this day?

Admiral Lawrence: Oh, yes. Oh, sure. The Secretary of the Navy gave a letter of censure to each one of them, and didn't give them a chance to comment, which is not in keeping with due process. That's supposed to be a requirement: if you say something adverse about somebody that leads to adverse action, you need to give him a chance to give his side. It's the fundamental American way, but the Secretary didn't do that.

So Miller challenged that. Wilber, a retired Navy captain, never took any action. Miller got a lawyer and tried to publish a lot of information on his side of the story through his suit, but that suit was thrown out of court. It was a kind of a class action suit, or maybe that's not the right term, but there were multiple defendants and I was one of them, because I'd signed a petition that denied him the chance of being elected as a commissioner of Orange County in California.[*]

Paul Stillwell: Well, I don't see how that could be cause for legal action.

Admiral Lawrence: Yes, I know.

Paul Stillwell: I mean, signing a petition is also an American right.

Admiral Lawrence: Yes, that's right. Well, that was the basis of the suit, signing a petition.

Paul Stillwell: How useful was the Code of Conduct to you during your stay?

Admiral Lawrence: Well, we always held it up as a guide, and we exhorted people to live up to it. But we realized that it had its limitations in some respects. In other words, it kind of gave the connotation that you should hang in there until death and never start a cover story routine with your captors and that sort of thing. So Stockdale and I concluded while we were there that the Code of Conduct really needed to be addressed, principally, in the way of training for the cadets and midshipmen.

---

[*] In 1979 California Governor Jerry Brown appointed retired Marine Colonel Edison W. Miller to a vacancy on the Orange County Board of Supervisors. In 1980 Miller was defeated in his attempt to retain the seat in a regular election. He subsequently brought suit for libel against his opponent and lost it. In 1985 Federal Judge Gerhard Gesell ruled in Miller's favor in his attempt to clear his name after charges that he was a turncoat. Gesell ruled that the Navy Department had to remove a letter of censure that Secretary of the Navy John W. Warner directed to be placed in Miller's personnel record in 1973.

There were strong elements of us who said the wording of the Code of Conduct should stay exactly the same and the perceived deficiencies should be addressed through training. In other words, I felt that the basic wording was fine, because it gave you a goal to shoot for. But the counter side of that was that it seemed to be so inflexible—name, rank, serial number, date of birth—that under that Code of Conduct you couldn't say anything more.

I was on a commission that looked at the Code of Conduct—I think it was 1976—and we only made a very minor change. Part of it said, "When questioned, the answer I'm required to give only name, rank, serial number, and date of birth." They said take out the word "only." It was just a one-word change, but the change connoted that you should definitely think about going to fallback positions. It wasn't something that I would have fallen on my sword about it, but I expressed my opposition to the change. I thought the Code of Conduct as it existed was fine.

Paul Stillwell: Well, if you can treat it as providing guidelines, rather than as legal sanctions and regulations.

Admiral Lawrence: Yes, they tell me that it's been tried in federal court. In the general sense, the Code of Conduct is okay, but when they get down to some of the specifics, like prosecuting courts in the U.S. attorneys' offices, and things like that it's a little bit different ball game than it is just within the military.

Paul Stillwell: Well, one of the provisions is that you should attempt to escape. Was that any kind of an option at all for you?

Admiral Lawrence: Well, it sure would have been difficult, because it was a maximum-security prison, and each compound had quite a few guards.

Paul Stillwell: Plus what would you do once you got out?

Admiral Lawrence: Well, we had some guys who got out of the compound, but they were captured. One pair of guys got pretty far down the Red River, and they were captured.

Paul Stillwell: Was there retribution on the rest of you following escapes?

Admiral Lawrence: No. When John Dramesi and Ed Atterberry, two Air Force captains, escaped from a camp called the Zoo, they'd been preparing for this for years.[*] They were the ones who were captured alongside the Red River. Ed Atterberry apparently died during that punishment he received, and we were really sorry to hear that, because he was a great guy. John Dramesi slipped out of sight, and yet he bounced back strong a couple years later when he was our guy in charge of escape plans. John Dramesi was a really tough nut. He took a lot of abuse along with Ed Atterberry when they were caught after the escape, and Ed Atterberry didn't make it through.

Paul Stillwell: What difference did the Son Tay raid make?[†]

Admiral Lawrence: Well, it was obvious that they had been very concerned about this, because right after that happened, they pulled us all into the central Hanoi prison, Hoa Lo, to ensure maximum security and prevent any type of commando raid rescue operation. We surprisingly learned about the rescue attempt fairly early, because some South Vietnamese soldiers, army prisoners, learned about this and they passed this to some the other captives. We had a couple or three Thai prisoners in our prison who were airmen, and they could talk to the Vietnamese. So I think through those Thai prisoners,

---

[*] Captain John A. Dramesi, USAF, was shot down over North Vietnam on 2 April 1967 while flying and F-105D Thunderchief from Korat Royal Thai Air Force Base, Thailand. Captain Edwin L. Atterberry, USAF, was shot down over North Vietnam on 12 August 1967 while flying an RF-4C Phantom as a member of the 11th Tactical Reconnaissance Squadron out of Udorn Royal Thai Air Force Base, Thailand. The two escaped from prison in Hanoi on 10 May 1969 and traveled three miles before being recaptured. Both were heavily tortured. Atterberry died in captivity on 18 May 1969. Dramesi survived and was released on 4 March 1973.

[†] On 20 November 1970 a U.S. commando force landed at the Son Tay prison, 23 miles west of Hanoi, North Vietnam, in an attempt to free U.S. prisoners of war reported to be held there. The commandos did not recover any POWs, because they had been moved to another location shortly before the rescue attempt. For details, see Benjamin F. Schemmer, *The Raid* (New York: Harper & Row, 1976).

we got the word about the Son Tay raid. We didn't get all the details, but we really tied two and two together, that this was the reason why all the camps were consolidated in central Hanoi.

Paul Stillwell: How much of a factor was religion, religious thought or activity during your time in prison?

Admiral Lawrence: It was a sustaining element in our lives. For the first four years or so, we were not allowed to do any personal religious activity ourselves. I might just point out to you that we felt it was important to try to have these religious services to give everybody a chance to have maximum influence on each other. The guards, of course, patrolled us very carefully and thoroughly, and they really prevented us from having any group religious services.

But finally, we were all put together. We were in these separate rooms in Hanoi; in our room we had about 40, and I think there were about six or seven more rooms. Each one had about 40 to 45 POWs. So we were having our group religious service in our room, and Robbie Risner, the Air Force colonel, was conducting it.[*] George Coker was assisting him.[†] The guards saw us doing this religious service and they panicked. They came in and removed from our big room Colonel Risner, Commander Rutledge, U.S. Navy, and George Coker.[‡] They pulled them out and put them into confinement away from the rest of us. We were very indignant about this happening, and it was obviously an overreaction by the guard to seeing this religious service. So, to show our indignation, we decided that those of us who were the senior leadership would go on a two-day fast. We sent the word around the camp that, in the evening after the sun had gone down and everybody kind of settled down, that we would stand up and on a prearranged signal, we would, at the top of our lungs, sing "The Star Spangled Banner."

---

[*] Lieutenant Colonel James Robinson "Robbie" Risner, USAF, was shot down over North Vietnam on 16 September 1965 while flying an F-105D Thunderchief. He was released 12 February 1973.

[†] Lieutenant (junior grade) George T. Coker, USNR, was shot down over North Vietnam on 27 August 1966 while flying as bombardier/navigator in an A-6A Intruder from Attack Squadron 65 (VA-165) from the carrier *Constellation* (CVA-64). He was released 4 March 1973.

[‡] Commander Howard E. Rutledge, USN, was shot down over North Vietnam on 28 November 1965 while flying an F-8E Crusader as executive officer of Fighter Squadron 191 (VF-191) from the carrier *Bon Homme Richard* (CVA-31). He was released 12 February 1973.

We did that, and I'm sure that was heard throughout Hanoi, but, again, they were very embarrassed, and they overreacted by taking those who of us who were the senior group and putting us back to living in the small cells.

Later on, after they saved face by taking the leaders of us out, they did start allowing group religious service. So we thought that was one of our victories in the POW camp. That was the second time that I engaged in a fast, because in an earlier time, Jerry Denton had come back from Alcatraz, and I turned over the command of the camp to him. He ordered a two-day fast one time in a protest. But that last thing in the world we needed to do was to be fasting at that time, I tell you.

Paul Stillwell: But that was about the only weapon you had.

Admiral Lawrence: Well, we knew that we had hostage value. That's why we could do things like that and apply pressure to them. As I say, they did back down on the religious services issue.

Paul Stillwell: That's probably what kept John McCain alive, too—his hostage value.[*]

Admiral Lawrence: Oh, yes, yes.

Paul Stillwell: Because apparently he was in pretty bad shape.

Admiral Lawrence: Yes, he was really banged up when he was shot down.

I think in the early years, they weren't as sensitive to the hostage value as they were later on. But they got the max they could for us when they came around to negotiating.

Paul Stillwell: What do you recall about the impact of the B-52 raids?

---

[*] His father, Admiral John S. McCain Jr., USN, served as Commander in Chief Pacific from 1968 to 1972, so his death in captivity would have attracted much attention.

Admiral Lawrence: Well, they had great impact on the North Vietnamese. Prior to the B-52 raids and the years before that, the guards would just laugh and cut up out in the courtyard of the camp as the attack airplanes came over.* Now you could see real anxiety in their faces, a desire to really get that war over. I would try to engage some of the camp guards in conversation, because some of them could speak kind of broken English, but they really didn't want to talk in that period. They were really worried. You could just see it in their faces. I think they were really eager to get the war over at that point.

Paul Stillwell: It's interesting to contemplate, in retrospect, what might have happened if that kind of sanction had been applied earlier.

Admiral Lawrence: Well, I think it had a dramatic effect. If we had mined Haiphong and gone in and massively bombed and cut the two rail links to China, I think the war would have taken an entirely different course.

I want to cover that in more detail, because it was kind of interesting that we knew before December '72, when the B-52 thing occurred, that something was happening. In the early fall of '72, I was back living in the cells, because after that protest all the senior guys were moved out of the large rooms and put back in the small cells. But it was different from small-cell-living in the early part of the war. I think this protest incident had occurred around February 1971, two years before we were released. So, although we were living in small cells, they did progressively loosen things up. They even got to the point that they let us all come out of the cells together and do things out in a little courtyard together; whereas, in previous years only one cell would go out at a time, because they were really trying to prevent this communication between cells. So we knew that through this progressive improvement of our treatment that something had to be happening in the negotiations that they could perceive the war was going to end.

Paul Stillwell: Well, didn't the food improve too?

---

* Between 18 and 29 December 1972, the Navy's Task Force 77 and the Seventh Air Force conducted Operation Linebacker II, a heavy aerial bombing campaign directed against North Vietnam. More than previous bombing campaigns, this one emphasized the use of Air Force B-52 rather than tactical aircraft.

Admiral Lawrence: Well, the food improved about a year before we were released; they gave us more, and the quality was better. I think a lot of us picked up some weight. I figure I lost originally about 40 pounds; I probably gained about 20 of that back.

We were all together in December of 1972. By this time, they had finally taken us out of the individual cells, and they put those of us who were just the senior ones back into a smaller open room. We used to sleep on these concrete slabs with just a thin mat made out of bamboo, I guess it was.

All of a sudden, one night after dark, we heard this tremendous rumbling, and it went on and on. Everybody said, "God, what do you think that is?" Nobody in the room said, perceived, or guessed that it was a bombing attack. There were things like, "Well, it must be an earthquake," or other things. But no one, none of us really had any concept that it might be a B-52 raid.

Finally, they were playing the propaganda broadcast to us, and on subsequent nights they did reveal that North Vietnam was being attacked by the B-52s. As I mentioned before, you could just see the change in attitude of the camp personnel from that attitude of confidence, cockiness, to one where you could just see the fear in their faces. They started furiously digging holes. And as soon as dusk came, boy, every night, they went into those bomb shelters. I remember some of those camp personnel who spoke English, saying, "Why, why is your country doing to this to us?" You could really see the great impact on their morale with that B-52 bombing.

Paul Stillwell: Was there any concern at all on your part that these bombs would hit your prison?

Admiral Lawrence: Not really. I guess we were eternal optimists, that after going through the bombing for all those years and never having anything happen to our camp, we felt pretty confident they wouldn't hit us.

Paul Stillwell: Well, and you hoped that the U.S. intelligence was good enough that it would know where you were.

Admiral Lawrence: Yes, that's right, that's right.

But, anyway, that really, really gave us hope that things were really beginning to happen. After the bombing stopped, there were just so many signs that the end was in sight.

Paul Stillwell: Any other of the signs that you remember?

Admiral Lawrence: No, not until one night when they did have a broadcast saying that on January 27, 1973, that a peace treaty had been signed. One of the stipulations of the peace treaty was that they had to give us all the details. So they did it over the radio, and they also gave us a kind of a mimeographed sheet that gave all the details, the provisions of the treaty about how we would be released and all that.

Paul Stillwell: You mentioned Admiral Denton. He's known for transmitting that Morse code message about torture. Any other recollections of him from North Vietnam?

Admiral Lawrence: Well, yes, he was a tough resistor, and he was a very strong leader. Stockdale was senior to him, but there were certain times in the POW experience when they weren't together, and Denton had to be the senior officer.

Then one time when Stockdale and Denton and the guys who had been out there at Alcatraz came back into our camp. Stockdale got into a situation where he could not exercise leadership. He was put in as a cellmate to an Air Force POW who really had a great fear about getting caught communicating. He put great pressure on Stockdale not to communicate. So there was about a two- or three-month period there where Denton took over leadership of the camp, while Stockdale felt he was not in a position to exercise the leadership. Since I had been the previous senior officer of the camp before Denton and those guys came back, I was able to help Denton a lot and give him a lot of information about those of us who had been in the camp before and serve as his deputy commander for my area of the camp. So I really, although I'd only known him by reputation before being a POW and was not a good friend of his as I had been Stockdale's, I had great admiration for him in the camp. He was really a very, very strong, effective, tough resistor and a good leader.

Paul Stillwell: Are there any other individuals that you'd want to mention in that context?

Admiral Lawrence: Oh, yes. There were many who were really fine. John McCain was a very strong, active resistor. Jim Mulligan, who was Navy; and Harry Jenkins.[*] A guy named Howie Rutledge was just a real tower of strength. Most of the real strong senior POWs were Navy.

Now there was Robbie Risner, who was a shot-down Air Force lieutenant colonel; he was really a good strong, inspirational leader. But outside of Robbie Risner, your real strong leaders in the camp were mostly Navy, and they were mostly Naval Academy graduates. Often, when I'm lecturing to midshipmen, I tell them that the POW experience was one place that really proved to me the viability of the Naval Academy experience, because it was the Naval Academy guys who really carried the leadership load over there. Although the Naval Academy graduates probably comprise less than about 5% or so of the total POWs, the Naval Academy graduates got around 50% of the Congressional Medals of Honor, Distinguished Service Medals.

Of course, Stockdale got the Congressional Medal. And then Stockdale, Denton, Bob Shumaker, and myself got Distinguished Service Medals for our leadership in the camp. Bob Shumaker was shot down when he was a young officer; he's out of the class of '56 at the Naval Academy, and he was shot down in '65. I think Bob was a very junior lieutenant commander, but he was really a tower of strength as a POW, even though he was not a senior officer. But he was such a smart, innovative thinker. He was always devising effective tactics in the communications systems and things like that.

---

[*] Commander James A. Mulligan, USN, was shot down over North Vietnam on 20 March 1966 while flying an A-4C Skyhawk as executive officer of Attack Squadron 36 (VA-36) from the carrier *Enterprise* (CVAN-65). He was released on 12 February 1973.
Commander Harry T. Jenkins Jr., USN, was shot down over North Vietnam on 13 November 1965 while flying an A-4E Skyhawk as commanding officer of Attack Squadron 163 (VA-163) from the carrier *Oriskany* (CVA-34). He was released on 12 February 1973.

I don't want to sound disparaging about the Air Force guys, because they were tough in their own right, but their senior officers just didn't stand out. And four Air Force officers were shot down as full colonels. But until the very end, when we got everybody together, none of those Air Force colonels ever exercised a strong leadership role. They maintained kind of a low profile.

Paul Stillwell: Is there any explanation you can offer for that?

Admiral Lawrence: Well, it's just always perplexed me. It seems as though the senior naval officers were more caught up in the aspect of taking command. Because I think that's a very strong part of a naval tradition, being in command. The Air Force doesn't put the emphasis on command that we do. For example, commanding an aircraft squadron on a carrier is a big responsibility. The Air Force doesn't consider it any big deal to command a squadron. They don't have the screening boards squadron that we do; it's just kind of decided out in the field who's going to be the squadron commander. And he's just another pilot; he doesn't run the squadron like we do. The Air Force guys came across to me as considering themselves as pilots first and as leaders, second.

Paul Stillwell: In looking back afterwards, were there any recommendations you made as far as training or preparations that would affect you?

Admiral Lawrence: Yes, quite a few. We really felt there had to be much more realistic training about the best means of resisting. As I say, when we looked at the Code of Conduct, I was opposed to removing the word "only." After our deliberations, against my objection, they voted to change it. I felt that that kind of set a little bit of a bad tone, in that it only kind of connotes to you that that's all you give, you know, and you hold out—whereas, you say, "I'm required to give name, rank, serial number, date of birth," has a very distinctly different meaning to me. So I fought hard to not do that, but I was overruled. But the deficiency in training was in not clearly conveying to us that we could not resist torture forever. That they'd bring this level of pain until you eventually broke, and so you simply had to be prepared to give a cover story. That was one of the big things that we recommended in training, is to train people on how to go through the mechanics of resisting to the point where you have to break down and start talking, and then have preplanned cover stories.

Paul Stillwell: Any more on the Air Force officers?

Admiral Lawrence: The young Air Force guys there were tough, hard resistors, and there were several Air Force Academy graduates, because the Air Force Academy produced their first graduating class in '59. So there were several Air Force captains, academy graduates—like Lance Sijan, I was talking about, that got the Congressional Medal of Honor, was an Air Force Academy graduate. My key point is that the young Air Force officers outshone the senior officers in the camp.

Paul Stillwell: Well, there's certainly no correlation between rank and courage.

Admiral Lawrence: But I might mention, also, that the only time any foreign personnel came into our camp was after the peace treaty. They very strictly kept any foreign personnel out of our camp, and the Red Cross was never allowed in. But one stipulation of the peace treaty was that there would be a foreign team that would come in and look around the camp and ask the POWs about their health. But that was the only time in our whole captivity that anybody came in.

There was one time where there was a Cuban, and our nickname for him was Fidel. He didn't come into our camp; he came into the other camp. He was there to assist the North Vietnamese in propaganda. But we never saw any sign of any Chinese or any Russians. So, even though the Russians and the Chinese were actively supporting the North Vietnamese, we never saw any signs of their being in their prison camps.

But, anyway, I think that covers the POW time.

Paul Stillwell: Next time we can talk about the homecoming, which was certainly more pleasant than being in captivity.

Admiral Lawrence: Yes, that'll be interesting.

Interview Number 12 with Vice Admiral William P. Lawrence, U.S. Navy (Retired)
Place: U.S. Naval Institute, Annapolis, Maryland
Date: Monday, 3 December 1990

Paul Stillwell: Admiral, the last two sessions we've been talking about some less-than-pleasant times when you were a prisoner of war. It's now time to discuss the very happy occasion of getting out of prison.

Admiral Lawrence: Well, I just might mention that the cease-fire was signed on the 27th of January 1973.* One of the stipulations of the agreement was that the North Vietnamese had to give us a copy of the treaty and explain it clearly to us. So they did that. They were so eager to get us out of the country—the withdrawal of all U.S. armed forces was a provision of the peace treaty—that they, from our perception, fully abided by every aspect of that peace treaty. In fact, they released some people held in North Vietnam whom they probably could have gotten away with not releasing. For example, at the last stages of the war, a non-military civilian had strayed into North Vietnam and been apprehended. He was held with us, and they released him, although, for one reason or another, they could have held onto him.

So they seemed to be quite eager to do everything right. They allowed, as I mentioned the other day, some foreign military—I think Swedes and Swiss—to come in and inspect the camp. In the final month or so that we were there, they grouped us by the order in which we had been shot down, because that was one of the stipulations of the treaty. We lived together with our contemporaries, in terms of the time that we'd been shot down. Previously, we'd been basically lined up by rank, but then they put us into this chronological order of shoot-down for about the last two months of our captivity.

---

* The Paris Peace Accords (or Paris Agreement on Ending the War and Restoring Peace in Vietnam) were signed on 27 January 1973 by the governments of North Vietnam, South Vietnam, the United States, and the Provisional Revolutionary Government, which represented indigenous South Vietnamese revolutionaries. The results were an immediate cease-fire (to take effect at 8:00 A.M. Vietnam time on 28 January), U.S. military withdrawal from Vietnam, and the later repatriation of prisoners of war.

Then the release, as I recall, was conducted in four segments. The first was in the early part of February 1973, and I was released as part of the third group on the fourth of March of 1973. And I think there was a final fourth group that was released.*

Paul Stillwell: Why was it done in that sequence, rather than all at once?

Admiral Lawrence: I just don't know why they chose to do it on a progressive basis, whether it was administrative requirement, or whether they wanted to be assured of good-faith compliance. The release of prisoners may have been tied to the phased withdrawal of the U.S. troops. The troops couldn't be withdrawn as rapidly, of course, as we could. I never really dug into the fact that they did this release over about a three-month period, but that's the manner in which it had been conducted.

Of course, by that time, we were emotionally hardened individuals. We had experienced so many ups and downs during the time we were there. In the early years, any sign of change would get your hopes up that maybe release was imminent. Particularly when the negotiations started in 1968, we would often get our hopes up just by some sign, as sometimes they'd just change the diet in the camp. But by 1973, we refused to allow ourselves to get too euphoric, even though the peace treaty had come out. You just didn't want to have your hopes dashed.

So we were still a very reserved, restrained group of individuals. You'd so conditioned yourself over those years, as I mentioned before, just living in your own little world in that camp, where you stopped really thinking about your family. So I just refused to allow myself to think a lot about the reunion with my family, because, for one thing, I hadn't been allowed to receive any mail from my wife or my children the whole six years I was there. I got a handful of letters from my parents that were very short—six lines were all they were permitted—and they were just noncommittal-type letters, no real substantive information in them.

I think over the last three years I was there, I was allowed to send out maybe about ten letters. Again, they were very short letters. I had no idea of what the status was

---

* Altogether, 591 American POWs were released from captivity between 12 February and 1 April 1973. Included were 457 from North Vietnam, 122 from South Vietnam, nine from Laos, and 3 from China.

of my wife and my children. I just had the basic optimistic hope that they were all okay, that the government and my other family members had taken good care of them.

When the release occurred, all of us in my group were taken over in buses to the commercial airport in Hanoi, Gia Lam. It's just across the Red River from the main part of Hanoi. When we got there, they had us all lined up in the order of release, which was the same order as we had been shot down. They'd given us a new attire to put on in place of the striped prison dress that we wore. We got cotton trousers and a simple jacket, but they did give us leather shoes, as I recall.

Then there was a very formal procedure, where they had a desk with a register. Your name was announced, and you had to come and check out at the desk, and then an Air Force officer escorted you out to the C-141 that was waiting.* We all got aboard the C-141, and it was not until the airplane got airborne on the way from Hanoi, headed down to Clark Air Force Base in the Philippines, that we really allowed our exuberance to come out. I think we were all very guarded that until we saw that coastline pass under us, we wouldn't allow our emotions to come unrestrained.

Paul Stillwell: Well, please describe that celebration.

Admiral Lawrence: We just yelled and shouted. In fact, there's a famous picture that appeared in the paper of a POW sitting in the airplane, shouting and yelling as—in a term we use in aviation—"we went feet wet" past the coastline. So that was a very joyous event.

While I was flying on the airplane, there was an Air Force colonel or lieutenant colonel who was a public affairs officer or something like that. He started talking to me and said, "My wife is from your home town of Nashville, Tennessee," and he named her.

I said, "Yes, I remember that family."

He said, "Well, I understand that you're going back to the naval hospital at Memphis, Tennessee."

Although I really didn't think seriously about it, I said to myself, "Gee, why am I going down to Memphis, Tennessee, when my family's in the San Diego area?" Because

---

* C-141 Starlifter is a jet-powered Air Force transport plane.

my squadron had been at Miramar, I expected to go back to a hospital in San Diego. Anyway, it just didn't even register with me.

We went on in and landed at Clark, and got a very, very warm reception. As we came off the airplane, Admiral Noel Gayler, who was Commander in Chief Pacific Command, was there, and Lieutenant General Bill Moore, U.S. Air Force, who was his deputy.[*] Both of them greeted us as we came off the airplane. I forget who the senior officer was in our group, but I don't think they required the senior officer to make a statement. Jeremiah Denton had been the senior officer of the previous group that was released. He had made a statement that became very famous when he said, "God bless America." Anyway, Admiral Gayler and General Moore greeted us, and a large crowd of people there was observing this and cheering. Of course, it was all televised.

By this time it was getting late in the afternoon, and they took us by bus immediately over to the hospital at Clark Air Force Base. This was a fairly new hospital. The young school children from around the country—and I guess there at Clark Air Force Base—had all these little welcoming posters that they had stuck around the hospital. So that was a very, very pleasant touch.

Then they took us up to the ward, but since it was now late in the afternoon, they didn't have any formal things planned for us. I remember that we had our places designated where we would stay. They essentially put four POWs to a room; it was sort of a large hospital room. As we were standing around out in the hall just chatting, I sensed that some people were observing me, but I really didn't think very much about it.

But then, Ross Trower, a Navy captain who was the chaplain for Service Force Pacific Fleet, came up to me. He later on became the Chief of Chaplains in the Navy.[†] He said, "I'd like for you to go with me into this room." So he took me in the room and sat me down. Then he said, "I'm going to tell you that your wife divorced you while you were a POW, and she's now Mrs. Ralph Haines. Her husband is an Episcopal minister, and she lives in Encintas, California."

---

[*] Admiral Noel A. M. Gayler, USN, served as Commander in Chief Pacific from 1 September 1972 to 30 August 1976. Lieutenant General William G. Moore Jr., USAF, was Commander 13th Air Force from 1 September 1972 to 1 October 1973. He then became Gayler's CinCPac chief of staff.

[†] Captain Ross H. Trower, CHC, USN. Later, as a rear admiral, he served as the Navy's Chief of Chaplains from June 1979 to August 1983

Of course, this was an absolute shock to me, because I never even considered that my wife might divorce me. In prison I lived with Tom Kirk, this Air Force lieutenant colonel, for almost four or five years. For three of those years we were actually close together, and he worried the whole time that his wife was going to divorce him. I used to keep assuring him, "Don't worry, Tom, she's going to hang in there with you." I never even considered it in my case, because my wife had been the last person in the world I ever expected to do this. Because she'd grown up in the Navy and she was really "duty, honor, country." If there was anybody who was, it was my first wife.

Paul Stillwell: You had taken it for granted that she would stay the course.

Admiral Lawrence: That's right. It just never even entered my mind, because she had grown up in all of the fine traditions of the Navy. Her father was a Naval Academy graduate, a naval aviator. He'd been shot down in World War II in the Philippines and had to evade with the guerrillas for six months before he got out of the Philippines. She was a trouper if there ever was one, so I absolutely couldn't believe what I was hearing.

Paul Stillwell: Did you feel bitterness when you got the news?

Admiral Lawrence: Well, no. Initially it was just great perplexity. And then, of course, they observed me very carefully as to how I would react to this. After that meeting was over, I don't remember exactly what I did, but I remember when I finally went to bed, the impact of this really hit me and it was a very tough, very emotional night for me. I didn't sleep very much, but then as the morning came, I said to myself, "Gosh, you've been through a hell of a lot for six years, and you simply have to get this behind you. You just can't let this really pull you down at this time. You've just simply got to do what's necessary to get through this." It was like what I'd done so many times in six years as a POW. So I really got the emotional aspect of it behind me that first night.

Then I remember calling and talking to my three children first. Of course, they were all living out in the same area where my wife was—in Encinitas, California. When

I heard them, I didn't like the sound of their voices; I mean, they just seemed to have no enthusiasm. And these had been fine, young, exuberant children when I left.

Paul Stillwell: Did they seem guarded or what?

Admiral Lawrence: Well, no, but they just seemed to be completely lacking in any zest or enthusiasm about what they were doing in life.

Paul Stillwell: What a letdown for you.

Admiral Lawrence: So I said, "Well, boy, I'd better take that one on." Of course, I talked to my parents, and they were happy, and I was happy to find that they were both in good health. Not too many of my relatives had passed on in those six years. I think I'd lost one great aunt out of all of my relatives during the time I was gone.

Anyway, I sat down and started really thinking seriously about what lay ahead of me. Of course, I had to inform the POWs whom I'd been very close to, like Tom Kirk; he and I became just like brothers those years that we lived so close together. But it was a very rapid situation there at Clark, because we had to get as much done on the physical exam as we could during about a three-day period.

Paul Stillwell: What did that physical turn up in your case?

Admiral Lawrence: Well, it turned up, first of all, that I needed glasses. My vision had declined. I think it was just a natural thing for the age I was; at 43 everybody's eyes start to degrade.

Paul Stillwell: Lack of nutrition, probably.

Admiral Lawrence: Lack of nutrition and being in a small cell, where you couldn't get the eye exercise you should have. So I had to get glasses; I had to have dental work done. They did some very rapid dental work, because I have to wear some partials; I lost some teeth playing football. There was just a very cursory total look, but they confirmed that all of us had these intestinal parasites. That was the principal finding. Then they gave us one trip over to the Air Force exchange, where we bought a lot of things. I bought a watch because I didn't have one. We were able to make only that one trip.

Then it was pleasant, because one of my old friends from my test pilot years, Rear Admiral Don Shelton, was the Commander Naval Forces Philippines and Commander Naval Base Subic.* He came up and visited with me in the hospital. And, as I recall, there were some other friends who came up from down at Subic to say hello.

Paul Stillwell: Did you have to start off with a bland diet?

Admiral Lawrence: Well [chuckle], a lot of people have asked, "How long did it take you to get acclimated to getting typical American food and sleeping on a soft bed?"

I said, "About five seconds." No, that was a very easy transition.

Paul Stillwell: I understand Admiral Stockdale had a hard time adjusting to regular beds.

Admiral Lawrence: Well, I remembered it was very pleasant to get into a soft bed.

But on the diet thing, I perceived that in some respects it was better to be on the type of low-fat diet that we had been on. So I was determined that I was not going to rapidly get back into eating a lot of beef. I remember right from day one, I was eating principally fruit and vegetables and salads. Those were the things that I enjoyed the most, that I had actually missed the most. So from that day on, I basically stayed on a very low-fat diet, and I've kept a very low cholesterol, always under 200. I think my cholesterol when I came back was about 140, and now it's around 180. So that was one good thing of the POW experience, that it basically gave me some good dietary habits that I think have been useful to me health-wise.

So it was a very quick period there at Clark, and they told me that the plan was that I would go back to the naval hospital at Memphis, even though my family was out in

---

*Rear Admiral Doniphan B. Shelton, USN, served 1973-75 as Commander U.S. Naval Forces Philippines. His oral history is in the Naval Institute collection. Like Lawrence, he was an early night fighter pilot.

the San Diego area. They just felt it would be better for me to be close to my parents down in Tennessee than to be out there in California.

We were put on Air Force airplanes to fly back to Stateside, and these were medevac-configured airplanes. They had a bunk for each one of us, and they had really planned this well. They had done everything for our health and comfort. We could easily have come back on passenger-configured airplanes, but they had bunk-configured airplanes, because they wanted to be prepared for any contingency. We flew from Clark Air Force Base and landed at Hickam in Honolulu.*

It was about 2:00 o'clock in the morning when we arrived at Hickam, but still a large number of people turned out. The Deputy CinCPacFlt at that time was Vice Admiral George Talley. He and a rear admiral by the name of Larry Heyworth were out there to meet me.† All my classmates who were stationed in that area came out, and so we had a nice pleasant session in the middle of the night, talking to them. After the refueling, we got back on the airplane and flew to Scott Air Force Base in Illinois. Apparently, the group that I was in was coming back to the central United States, as opposed to California.

I remember that as we flew across the California coastline, it was daylight, and I looked down, and it was great to see San Francisco. That was a real thrill. After we landed at Scott, we transferred out of the C-141 airplane, and they put us into C-9s.‡ About six of us were going on down to Memphis, where we would have our convalescence. I was the senior one in the group, so when I landed at Naval Air Station Memphis, I had been told it was expected that the senior POW of the group would make a speech to the assembled people, because we knew there'd be a large mass of people.

Paul Stillwell: By this time, you were a captain, weren't you?

Admiral Lawrence: Yes, I was a captain, and we had been outfitted with uniforms at Clark; they'd given us one set of khaki and one set of blue. That was another magnificent effort on their part that they brought these tailors in with a stock of uniforms.

---

* Hickam Air Force Base is adjacent to the Pearl Harbor Naval Base on the island of Oahu.
† Rear Admiral Lawrence J. Heyworth, Jr., USN.
‡ The C-9 Skytrain II, built by McDonnell Douglas, is a military version of the DC-9 civilian aircraft.

When I arrived at Memphis, there was a rear admiral who was the Chief of Naval Technical Training and really a wonderful guy. He was the one to greet me as I came off the airplane. I guess the other POWs came off and just stood behind me, but the rear admiral and the commanding officer of the naval air station, who was a captain, escorted me over to a microphone, and all these assembled people there. I got to the microphone and looked across, and there were my parents and my two brothers and my three children and my son's wife, all standing in front of me. So I had to make this speech while I was looking at my parents—before I'd even greeted them—and that was really a very emotional experience. But I'd rehearsed my speech pretty thoroughly in my head coming down from Scott Air Force Base, and I guess, maybe, flying from Hawaii back to Scott, so I was able to give this speech. And, of course, I was reunited with my family. Then they took us up to the hospital to get us checked in there. At that time we met an intelligence team; these were principally reserve officers who'd been called back to active duty to do the debriefing.

Then my family and I were given rooms over in the Navy lodge there. I told them, "Look, I'd like to spend the night in the Navy lodge with my family as opposed to the hospital." So I was allowed to do that. That began the process of really getting caught up on all the voids I had about how my family was doing.

Paul Stillwell: Were you children more enthusiastic then than they'd been on the phone?

Admiral Lawrence: Yes, they were much more enthusiastic. But I just knew that they had some problems. My two daughters, for example, were overweight, and I just sensed that things weren't really right. And we talked some about the situation with my wife. It was a progressive thing of getting caught up.

Paul Stillwell: One interesting phenomenon—you making this speech and receiving so much attention—I think this was one of the few wars where returning POWs were treated as celebrities.

Admiral Lawrence: Yes, that's right. And the unfortunate thing about it is that the POWs were the only real heroes of that war. Everybody else was treated very cruelly, so it always bothered us very much that we were treated differently from the other veterans. I guess that was because so much concern had been directed to the POWs while we were still in prison. I think that the country wanted to have some heroes from that war, so it just turned out that we were the ones thrust into that position.

Paul Stillwell: I think it was mainly a matter of circumstance. The others didn't come back in groups to be greeted that way.

Admiral Lawrence: That's right. My younger brother Tommy had received a commission in the Army and was in the 82nd Airborne Division in Vietnam. He said that after he finished up his year in Vietnam, he came back to the Oakland Army Depot. He switched immediately into civilian clothes, made his transportation arrangements to fly back, flew back to Nashville in civilian clothes, and got off the airplane. My parents met him, and they were the only people who said anything. Then he just went back in civilian life as though nothing had happened.

Most veterans wanted to come back to America quietly with no fanfare, because there was such an antiwar mood. But I said, "Isn't that terrible, a guy just comes back after a hard year in Vietnam, switches to civilian clothes, and probably if somebody saw him on the street, wouldn't even remember the fact that he'd been in Vietnam." Terrible, terrible way the veterans of that war were treated.

Paul Stillwell: What kind of a program was set up for you in Memphis?

Admiral Lawrence: Well, it was very comprehensive—physical exams and intelligence debriefs.

Paul Stillwell: What did the intelligence debriefs include?

Admiral Lawrence: Well, they covered everything they felt would be useful to the intelligence community on the type of interrogations, covert communications procedures, and our overall resistance posture. I gave them all the names that I had in my memory bank, so they could match that with those who had actually been released. It was just basically milking our brains for every bit of information we could provide.

Paul Stillwell: Do you have any views on this current concern that there are still Americans in Southeast Asia?

Admiral Lawrence: Well, it's very perplexing to me, because all the signs that we got over there indicated that the Vietnamese were more than eager to release everybody, that they did, in fact, release everyone we knew of who was in captivity in North Vietnam.

Paul Stillwell: You had fulfilled your hostage value by then.

Admiral Lawrence: Yes, because they got what they wanted, which was the withdrawal of the U.S. military from Vietnam. So I'm perplexed as to the allegations that the U.S. Government has been indifferent about the fact that POWs are still there.

When I was the Chief of Naval Personnel, I got very comprehensive intelligence briefings by intelligence officers who had no reason to conceal anything.[*] All the indications I got from my intelligence community were that, although there were some reported sightings, we never had any confirmed information that indicated POWs were still there. And I think the intelligence community was being completely open and honest. They had nothing to gain by trying to conceal this information by cover-up. Yet a recent book has come out that accuses the U.S. Government of a cover-up. I mean, there would be nothing to be gained by covering up.

The other thing is that you would think that if there were POWs being held, that some government over there or some group would be seeking to get some leverage from them. And I've never seen that. So it's very perplexing to me, because there are a lot of people whom I respect, like Ross Perot and Red McDaniel, former POW—he's a retired

---

[*] Admiral Lawrence served as Chief of Naval Personnel from 28 September 1983 to 31 December 1985.

captain—who very sincerely feel that there are still POWs there, because Ross Perot told me this one day.* In fact, he headed up a little group the President appointed to look into this. So that's really confusing to me because the intelligence reports—and I think I got all the intelligence that they had—certainly did not indicate this.

Paul Stillwell: What kind of culture shock did you have? This was certainly a different America from the one you'd left.

Admiral Lawrence: Well, we were disappointed in some respects, because by the time we got back, the skirt lengths were on the way down. [Laughter] We'd missed the real ultimate mini skirts, but they were still pretty short, and that was an eye-opener, seeing women walking around in these short dresses. That was the most dramatic sign. Of course, seeing my son with his long hair was a shocker. I guess I was surprised by the fact it was apparent that young people were doing things out of a sense of rebelliousness as much as anything. I think a lot of wearing long hair was rebellion against the establishment. But I realized immediately that, boy, I had to be on the fast track; there was no sitting back, relaxing, or anything like that, because I had all these family requirements—my children—before me. Then it was obvious that, boy, the public relations activity was going to be very demanding.

Paul Stillwell: In what sense?

Admiral Lawrence: Well, right away, at the hospital, a group sat down with me and said, "We're going to have this welcome home day for you up there in Nashville." Then the requests for speeches started flowing in. I think we all felt obligated to get out and make speeches. I felt that responsibility to thank the American people for their support, and try

---

* Lieutenant Commander Eugene B. "Red" McDaniel, USN, was shot down over North Vietnam on 19 May 1967 while flying an A-6A Intruder as part of Attack Squadron 35 (VA-35) from the carrier *Enterprise* (CVAN-65). He was released on 4 March 1973. His memoir, written with James L. Johnson, is *Scars and Stripes: the True Story of One Man's Courage in Facing Death as a Vietnam POW* (Irvine, California: Harvest House Pub., 1975). McDaniel retired from active duty in 1982 as a captain and became president of the American Defense Institute, a non-profit organization in Washington, D.C.

to have some impact on the younger people. So I just could see that the public relations commitments were going to be heavy.

Paul Stillwell: Did the Navy have a program to bring you up to date on those missing six years?

Admiral Lawrence: Well, they provided us with some reading material that gave us the news highlights of the years we were in captivity. It was fairly skillfully done; they cut out clippings from the key newspapers in the country and put them in subject groupings and printed them up for us to read. But I just didn't have time, initially, to get into that, because I had these other commitments. This welcome-home day, for example, was going to be about five or six days after our return. I think during that day I was going to make something like four speeches—one to a combined session of the state legislature, then one up on the city square, one at a luncheon. So I really had to start thinking about this, because I just couldn't give an off-the-cuff speech to the state legislature.

Anyway, the initial physical examination was completed, where they felt that I could be cleared to go up to my hometown. I was so much wrapped up in that physical that I really didn't have time to think about a speech. Then I was also very concerned about things to do with my children, just finding out what their needs were, what the future living arrangements were going to be.

This welcome-home day was interesting. For one thing, Admiral Thomas Moorer, who at that time was the Chairman of the Joint Chiefs of Staff, and for whom I had served as his first aide, flew down from Washington with his wife to attend that day.[*] Then the governor was involved, the local congressman, and other state dignitaries.

I remember arriving in Nashville the day before, and the commander of the recruiting district there really helped me very much in giving me support, transportation, and some clerical help. One of the first things I had to do was go over to his office and compose the speeches I was going to give the next day. I knew I had to do a fairly decent job. In looking at the speech to the combined state legislature, I had to make it of

---

[*] Admiral Thomas H. Moorer, USN, served as Chairman of the Joint Chiefs of Staff from 3 July 1970 to 30 June 1974. His oral history is in the Naval Institute collection.

respectable duration, so the idea of presenting the poem I composed on the state of Tennessee came to me as a way of making the speech a little bit longer. At the end of it, I quoted this poem. Then, lo and behold, about a week or ten days later, they adopted it as the state poem of Tennessee.

After I gave that speech, they printed it in the Nashville newspaper. And in my head, when I composed that poem, I had thought that the word "renowned" was spelled R-E-K-N-O-W-N-E-D. It's actually R-E-N-O-W-N-E-D. But it got printed in the paper with the wrong spelling. They used to call me Billy down there, and I got a letter from my fourth grade teacher, who wrote, "Billy, that was a lovely poem, but you misspelled the word 'renowned.'" [Laughter] Once a fourth-grade teacher, always a fourth-grade teacher.

Paul Stillwell: Did the Navy give you any freedom, or were you pretty well programmed during that period?

Admiral Lawrence: Well, that welcome-home day I was completely programmed because all these events that were going on. But then I was basically staying at my parents' house.

One of the first priorities, when I got to Nashville, above all else, was that I talked to my daughter, Laurie, who was just completing her senior year of high school. I said, "What are your plans for next year? What are you college plans?" She said she wanted to go to nursing school, and she had applied to UCLA, but she hadn't gotten a lot of help from her mother.[*] A neighbor had helped her plan for this, but her plans had not finalized for her going to college, and she was getting a little bit tentative about the whole thing. So I just took the bull by the horns and said, "Look, I'm going to enroll you in Vanderbilt University here in Nashville in their nursing school." So one thing we did was to go over and sit down with the director of admissions at Vanderbilt University. She just verbally gave him her SAT score numbers and everything.[†] So I think out of

---

[*] UCLA – University of California at Los Angeles.
[†] SAT – Scholastic Aptitude Test, widely used in measuring the ability of high school students to do college work.

deference to me as much as anything, he said, "Yes, we will accept her." So we got her enrolled in college, and that was one of the first priorities.

Then, of course I did a lot of talking to my other two children. My son Bill, who had been out of high school for two years, had married his high school sweetheart the year before, when he was 19 and she was 18. It didn't make me very happy that he was married. But I accepted it, and I realized that he wasn't really on a serious course. He was taking a few courses at a local junior college, and he was working as a gardener at the church of the minister my wife had married. So I really started talking to him about what he was going to do.

Then I started talking to my other daughter, Wendy, who was at that time in the eighth grade. I could just see that my kids weren't happy. They didn't have a real sense of purpose and all that. So I knew that that was one of my top priorities. I really had to get them going in the right direction. Of course, getting Laurie into Vanderbilt University was the first step.

But one thing that kept coming through in those initial discussions is that my children actually had thought that I was dead. And this perplexed me, because, although I was listed as missing in action for three years, Senator Ted Kennedy got the North Vietnamese to release our names, so my name was actually released in 1970. I had sent ten letters back. I asked my children, "Didn't you all see my letters, even if you hadn't heard that my name was listed as being a POW in 1970?"

"No," they said, "we'd only seen one letter from you, and our mother said that that appeared to be contrived. She said it just didn't appear to be in my handwriting or sound like me."

Well, anyway, as I dug into this, I realized that nine out of ten letters my wife apparently had not been shown to my kids. I said, "My God, this is just unbelievable. I thought that she was such a fine, honorable person; I can't believe that she would have done this." So I talked to her parents, who were now living out in Sun City. Her father was a retired tombstone rear admiral, they also had thought that I was dead.* I said, "Gosh, there was a POW office in Washington that knew I was alive, and my parents

---

* Rear Admiral Macpherson B. Williams, USN (Ret.). His highest active duty rank was captain; he was given a one-grade promotion at the time of retirement on the basis of combat decorations.

knew I was alive. I'm perplexed that this feeling of my children and my in-laws was that I was dead." And so, anyway, that was very upsetting to me that my wife, obviously, had acted dishonorably.

So after I'd completed my initial medical examinations down in Memphis, they got me on a treatment regimen. Basically, the only real problem I had was intestinal parasites, and I had to go through some medication.

Paul Stillwell: Did your heart situation require any attention?

Admiral Lawrence: No, my aortic insufficiency, heart murmur, had not worsened at all; it stayed about the same. I had this numbness in my outer calf here due to nerve damage, probably when I was in leg irons at one time. And I had a shoulder broken that had not healed correctly, but it wasn't limiting to me. And I had some teeth problems. I had a condition they called resorption, which is an unexplained phenomenon, where your teeth just seem to dissolve away slowly, and I had some problems with that. It lasted for about ten years after I came back, and finally it apparently stopped. And it's a phenomenon that they really don't completely understand what causes it, but usually it's a trauma.

After about a week or two, they allowed me to spend most of my convalescent leave up in my parents' home in Nashville, Tennessee. But we had to spend sessions with psychiatrists, as well as the intelligence debriefers. The intelligence debriefers completed their work in about three days.

Paul Stillwell: Was any of the information that came out of the intelligence debriefs considered classified?

Admiral Lawrence: Oh, yes, yes, because I was involved in some covert activity while I was there. It was very sensitive, highly classified. So much of this debrief was kept classified.

Paul Stillwell: In a sense, I'm surprised that so much has come out on the tap code, because that might be useful for some future captive nation.

Admiral Lawrence: That's right, there's no question about it. We, perhaps, revealed a lot that we shouldn't have. Of course, Stockdale's book, *In Love and War*, was very, very controversial, because he got into some of the sensitive communications. In fact, when that book came out in 1984, it was really a very tense time back there in Washington, as to how that was going to be handled.[*] I was very concerned that some official action would be taken against Stockdale, but apparently sane heads prevailed and nothing happened. But in that book he and his wife covered some very sensitive areas, means of communicating between the States and the POWs.

But all the time I was trying to get my medical exams completed and get my course of action with regard to my children, the PR demands were really, very heavy. I just felt I had an obligation to respond to these, to show appreciation of people and try to favorably influence the young people. So I was ripe to be in there. I was having to go out and make speeches and appear at various places.

But then I just felt I simply had to go out to California and meet with my wife and try to resolve a lot of those issues, because, for one thing, all of my clothes that I had at home and had been sent back from the carrier were still packed up in a cruise box. They were in a neighbor's garage out in California. My wife had not taken any initiative to have them shipped to me, so I had to go out there for one thing to make arrangements to have my clothes sent back, and I was, of course, buying some new items for a wardrobe. My dad's tailor there did me a very nice gesture in giving me a complete outfit.

So I went out to California within three weeks after I first got back. Then I made arrangements to meet privately with my wife. I determined from analyzing all this that she had acted just completely contrary to her makeup. It was obvious to me that she was a casualty of the war as much as anybody else, and that I had an obligation to try to help her in this situation. So I went out there with the plan to offer her the opportunity to come back to me, and just say, "Look, what's happened has happened, and we'll get it behind us, and out of consideration for the children we should seek to go back together and resume a normal life."

---

[*] Jim and Sybil Stockdale, *In Love & War: The Story of a Family's Ordeal and Sacrifice during the Vietnam Years* (New York: Harper & Row, 1984).

My father just violently objected to this plan, because he's a very principled individual, very strong will. He really felt that my wife had acted dishonorably, and she had, there's no question. She withheld letters from me, she never told my parents that the divorce was under way, and they were talking to her every week. They went out to see her one time.

Paul Stillwell: Was she remarried by this point?

Admiral Lawrence: Oh, yes, she was. But during that whole time that the divorce action was in progress, my parents were talking to my wife every week, and she never revealed to them that she was doing this. There were some major gaffes here. The POW office that had been established in Washington knew that the divorce proceedings were under way, but they never informed my parents. That was a grave omission, because if they'd informed my parents, my parents probably could have prevented the divorce. I'm sure the POW office in Washington was swamped, but they really dropped the ball.

Paul Stillwell: Well, they might have had a reasonable expectation that your wife would have communicated with your parents too.

Admiral Lawrence: Yes, I guess so. And then the court-appointed attorney, out in Oceanside, California, should have thought about talking to my parents or talking to her parents, but he didn't. Overall it was poorly handled from the aspect of what was for my benefit. But having accepted all that, I just felt the right thing to do, the best thing was to try to do, was this reconciliation with my wife. So when I first met with her, I presented it to her. I said, "Look, you were a victim of the war, and my perception is you acted completely contrary to what I know you really are. I think we should try to go back together for the benefit of the kids. I'm sure we can get an annulment on your marriage, or if we have to go through a divorce, that's what we'll have to do."

She didn't just categorically say no. It was very difficult to communicate about this; it was very difficult for her.

Paul Stillwell: Did she try to provide some justification for what she had done?

Admiral Lawrence: Well, no, she was finding it really difficult even to talk it over with me. Finally, as we were terminating the thing, she just finally broke down. She said, "Look, I really tried hard; I really tried to be strong. I'm sorry I couldn't, but I couldn't." Anyway, then she left and she did muster up. She said, "I just want you to know that I think you're the finest man I've ever known," and then walked out. I had no positive feeling that she would agree to come back, but I thought there was still a possibility.

Anyway, it was apparent to me that she simply had been seduced by this Episcopal minister. We were going to St. Peter's Episcopal Church in Del Mar, California, before I was shot down. The reason we settled at Del Mar, when I came back for sea duty, was because the chaplain who had married us, Matt Curry, had retired from the Navy and had settled in Del Mar.* And we'd kept in touch with him over the years.

So when we got out to California, we looked him up, and he said, "I'll help you find a place in my parish here." He helped us find a place to live in Solana Beach, not too far away. And so we, of course, attended that St. Peter's Church. I remember one time, the Episcopal bishop of southern California, came down to that church, and Chaplain Curry made a point of introducing our family to that bishop, because he looked upon us as the model young family in his church.

Also, let me say that while I was a POW, there were some very terrible, internal problems developing in that church. There was a group that was in opposition to Chaplain Curry, and it got to be so unpleasant that my wife just decided to remove herself from that congregation and go to a church up in Encinitas, California. The minister of that church, the Reverend Ralph Haines, was a newly widowed individual. His wife had died of cancer, and he had two young sons. As part of his ministerial duties, he came over to give solace to this POW wife, and over a period of time they apparently fell in love. At the time, my daughter Laurie was old enough to be pretty perceptive of what was going on; my other daughter was just too young to really understand. As Laurie told me after I got back from Vietnam, this man really violated his position of trust and responsibility as a minister. I felt that he actually seduced my wife and got her into a

---

* Commander Matthew A. Curry, Chaplain Corps, USN (Ret.).

situation. She was very vulnerable; she was a very honorable person, and once she'd compromised herself, I think it was just all downhill from there.

Anyway, when the divorce action was taken, her position was that our marriage was irrevocably broken before I left. Of course, that was just utter nonsense, as my children would attest; Father Curry knew us very well, and he would attest to that.

Paul Stillwell: Well, the fact that you wanted to be back with her suggests otherwise also.

Admiral Lawrence: Yes. But the thing that bothered me so much was the Episcopal Church seemed to be complicit in that the bishop accepted this. So did the California judge. But to show you the extremes they had to go through, under California law, if a woman initiates divorce proceedings against her husband, she has to show desertion. So one thing her attorney had to help her do was put an ad in the paper requesting that I appear in court, and run that ad for X number of weeks. She had to show evidence that she had sent a letter to my last known address, and the letter was returned. So she sent a letter to the USS *Constellation*, and it had been returned, of course. I couldn't believe that she had gone all through this.

So one thing I did, while I was out in California, I just went over to visit her attorney. I said, "You knew that I was a POW. It was commonly known in Washington that I was a prison of war. How could you, as an attorney, with any sense of ethics, do something like that? You know, I could probably get you disbarred."

Paul Stillwell: It was obviously a charade.

Admiral Lawrence: Yes, and he gave me some mealy-mouth thing. I said, "You're dishonorable and you should know it, and I hope you'll carry that to your grave, the knowledge that you've been very dishonorable." And I just walked out.

I wrote a letter to the bishop we had been introduced to as the model family in that church. I told him, "It's just salacious to make the point that our marriage was irrevocably broken. There's every indication that one of your ministers in your diocese acted dishonorably. I feel the Episcopal Church should officially address this. Letters were withheld from my children," and so forth. I gave him all this information.

Paul Stillwell: Did you communicate with the chaplain who'd married you also?

Admiral Lawrence: Oh, yes, Father Curry fully supported everything I was doing. He had retired from that St. Peter's, and the new minister who came in there was very sympathetic with me. He said what went on was commonly known among the Episcopal ministers down there. I wanted to get the bishop to officially address this issue, and this was while my wife was still considering whether to come back to me or not.

Anyway, my father was very, very upset about this whole thing. He hadn't done anything till I got back. He had some very prominent Episcopal friends back in Tennessee, and they got in touch with the Episcopal bishop in Tennessee. He was under the impression that there was a larger bishop who had cognizance over all the Episcopalians in the United States. Well, that's wrong. There might be somebody who's nominally, at any time, the number-one Episcopal bishop. But actually every bishop is totally autonomous in his own diocese.

So the bishop of Tennessee simply told my father, "I have no authority over that bishop in Southern California, nor does anybody else. He acts as he feels he should. I cannot bring any pressure to bear." But he did write this bishop in Southern California a letter and said that if any minister in his diocese in Tennessee had done something like that, he would have been defrocked.

But, anyway, this bishop of southern California sent me back one of the most mealy-mouthed letters you've ever seen. It started out, "I welcome you as you return to observe the culture that has developed in your absence."

I said, "God, what does that mean?"

He went on to say, "My heart goes out to those who have experienced pain and suffering." It was just a mealy-mouthed letter, and it got me irritated.

So I wrote him a letter back and said, "I'm going to expose all of this to the press unless the Episcopal Church shows me that they're going to take corrective action."

Boy, he came back immediately and said, "Don't do anything like this; it could really have adverse impact on your family." He was pleading with me not to take any more action.

Meanwhile, by this time my wife and her husband had gone up and talked to the bishop. And somehow, I guess through my son, she transmitted to me that she did not want to come back to me.

I thought it over and I said, "Look, I could just absolutely destroy that minister. I could go to the press and just really make this into a big thing and put all sorts of pressure on the Episcopal Church." But I thought it over a long time, and I concluded, "I really don't want to destroy my former wife. Gosh, if I do something like this to her husband, it's going to have a very severe impact on her. She was a good wife, hung in there with me all those years, and, unfortunately, due to the conditions in the war and the situation she got herself into, this has happened. She acted dishonorably; this is very unfortunate. But in the interest of her health and welfare and my own morale and my children, I'm just going to back off and not take any action."

So I wrote to the bishop and said, "I'm not taking any further action. I'm resigning from the Episcopal Church." I had joined for my wife's benefit, because I'd grown up as a Methodist.

I also wrote my wife's husband, this Reverend Haines, and said, "Look, I accept what's happened, and I'm not taking any further action. But I don't think my wife is in good sound condition, and I think you should very seriously seek to get some medical assistance in her case."

Her parents by this time had disowned her, and they really just severed all relationships with her. So I wrote them and said, "Look, she's your only child, and I think you should not sever your relationship with her. You should really accept what's happened, that it's an unfortunate occurrence during the war, and reestablish relationships with her and get it all behind you." Then I told my wife that I was going to take custody of my youngest child, Wendy, because my two older children were above the custody age, which is 18 in California. So I took custody of my youngest child, because it was an unsavory situation.

Paul Stillwell: Where did the law stand on that? Did you have to go to court to get that?

Admiral Lawrence: Yes, I had to go to court. We just got a simple court order, where if she didn't contest it, it would happen. The court-appointed attorney I had out there had been a Marine officer. He understood this situation, and he regretted the fact that he hadn't been more skillful at getting information. Because, see, he never communicated with my parents or her parents. He just talked to the Navy, and he realized that he dropped the ball, because when the case first came up, if he'd gone to my parents and talked to her parents, a lot of this might have been averted. So he was very upset that the situation happened, but he helped me in terms of getting custody of my youngest daughter.

In this overall process, I talked things over with my son and said, "Look, you simply have to get into college. You just can't pursue the type of life you are right now—just going to school part time and working as a gardener, and you've got a wife. You've simply got to get in school and get your degree. You tell me what you want to do."

He had a great love of music, and he said, "Well, I'd like to really major in music."

I said, "Okay, they have a very fine school of music down at Peabody College in Nashville. Come back to Nashville, and I'll support you going to school, and you'll be with your sister, who's going to be at Vanderbilt." Then I decided, since I'd been told I was going to the National War College in Washington, that I would send my daughter Wendy back to live with my parents and go to a private school in Nashville. So, anyway, the plans were under way to get all my kids to go back to Nashville.

Paul Stillwell: It sounds like they needed more direction than they had been getting.

Admiral Lawrence: Oh, gosh, yes. Of course, this had been a really traumatic thing. Here was my wife, going through a divorce from a POW, and trying to keep concealed from her children that their father was still alive. I can't believe that she actually did all those things to make this happen.

So it was a very tense time, and my older daughter, who was old enough to be aware of all that was going on, was very upset, and she was very vocal in her opposition to what her mother was doing. She didn't like her mother's new husband, and as unbelievable as it sounds, my wife and this Episcopal minister had a formal church wedding. Can you imagine in World War II an Episcopal minister marrying the wife of a POW in a formal church service?

Paul Stillwell: No.

Admiral Lawrence: But, actually, as you look through this, pull out the string on this, the Episcopal Church actually was supportive of this.

Paul Stillwell: In effect, they sanctioned it.

Admiral Lawrence: They sanctioned it. They wanted my older daughter to be in the wedding, but she said, "I absolutely am not going to be in that wedding. I refuse." My younger daughter actually was in the wedding. It was just unreal. So I knew that I simply had to get those children out of that home situation. I knew that their only hope of having a viable future was if I took total control, because if I left them in the custody of my wife, I knew that they just wouldn't get the supervision and the care and attention they needed. Because she'd just taken over as the wife of a man who had two children, and they needed a lot of help too. So I just said, "Hey, I'm taking them out of that situation."

So I made arrangements to send them back to Tennessee. They stayed out in California during the summer. I got out there as often as I could, and I did a lot of things for them. During their spring break in school, I took them all down to Disney World, because there were all sorts of these gratuitous things that were given for the POWs, like Holiday Inns and Disney World, so I was able to take them down to Disney World, essentially free.

When my older daughter graduated from high school, as a kind of graduation gift, I took them all back to New York City and used some of these gratuitous things for several days in New York City, because none of them had ever been there. So I did a lot of things with them during that summer. Also I was making a lot of speeches, and I was studying, trying to fill in the voids, getting my personal finances and personal affairs in order, and making plans for the future.

Most of the POWs pretty well felt that there'd be no hope of our being able to reestablish our careers. But, anyway, the leadership—Admiral Zumwalt was Chief of Naval Operations; Admiral Moorer was the Chairman of the Joint Chiefs of Staff—gave us every indication that they wanted to give us the opportunity to get back and have viable careers, so I said, "I'll give it a good shot."[*]

Paul Stillwell: Before we get into that, I'd like to just get your observation from the perspective of these years since. Are you comfortable with the way you handled things in relation to your family members?

Admiral Lawrence: Oh, yes, I think that was the only way I could do it. Of course, my kids have turned out to be remarkably successful in their personal and professional lives. I knew all the ingredients were there, but I think if I hadn't taken complete control of them, they would never have experienced their potential, because they just were not getting the support and the leadership out there. I couldn't have given that to them if they'd stayed under the custody of their mother.

My son Bill's a very prominent computer engineer, one of the most knowledgeable persons in the country on netware. He's written two books on netware. The last one has sold about 35,000 copies. My older daughter Laurie's a medical doctor at Vanderbilt Hospital in Nashville. My younger daughter, Wendy, graduated from the Naval Academy, and is a lieutenant commander in the Navy.[†] So they've all done really well, because I gave them every opportunity to really succeed and realize their potential.

I think I did the right thing in not really forcing some retribution type of action against my wife and her husband. I could easily have destroyed his career, but it would not have served a useful purpose. The last thing in the world I'd want to do is destroy my

---

[*] Admiral Elmo R. Zumwalt, Jr., USN, served as Chief of Naval Operations from 1 July 1970 to 29 June 1974. His oral history is in the Naval Institute collection.
[†] Wendy subsequently became an astronaut and retired as a Navy captain.

wife. His career as an Episcopal minister has not been very successful, and I think that was because there were those who perceived that he had done a dishonorable thing. Although the bishop of southern California didn't have enough courage to take it on, Reverend Haines's career has not been quite successful; he had only small churches. So I feel sorry for my former wife, because her life has not been as good as it could have been in terms of the economic situation. And she really has not had much interface with her children because of the difficulty of being close to them. My older daughter has no communication at all with her mother. My former wife felt so uneasy about any relation with her, because Laurie was the one who was most aware of what was going on. So it's unfortunate for her; I really feel sorry for her.

Paul Stillwell: So she's living with the choices she made.

Admiral Lawrence: Well, that's right. I hope that her life is as happy as it can be under the circumstances. I've really encouraged the children to maintain close relationships with her. My older daughter, the one who's a doctor now, was married while I was superintendent at the Naval Academy. My former wife came back for that with her husband, and that was the only time I had any personal face to face with her husband, but we had no discussion. When my daughter graduated from the Naval Academy, my former wife came back by herself for that. So she has been able to participate in some of the key events in their lives. I think she's doing reasonably well, but I can just tell that she's a distinctly different person from what she was before I was shot down. She's a casualty of the war, and it's unfortunate. But among the tragic aspects of war is the fact that a lot of people suffer besides those on the battlefield.

Paul Stillwell: Did the Navy offer you some kind of counseling to deal with all this turbulence?

Admiral Lawrence: Well, not really. I could have had it; there was psychiatric care constantly available. But I remember when I met with the first psychiatrist down in

Memphis, after about 15 minutes, I felt like he needed the help more than I did. [Laughter]

Paul Stillwell: You felt sane.

Admiral Lawrence: Well, he seemed to be kind of a flaky, different guy, so I said, "Hey, this isn't helping me at all." So I very quickly conveyed to the Navy that I didn't need that type of psychiatric help. But I got an awful lot of wonderful support from my parents. My parents were just stalwart; you can't imagine during this whole thing the way they conducted themselves. So I had wonderful support from my parents and my brothers and cousins and aunts and so forth. So I really didn't need any medical support. It was just obvious what had to be done.

As I say, my family rallied around to help with the transition of my kids back into Tennessee. My daughter Wendy was in the ninth grade when she came back to live with them; that was really a pleasant experience for my parents to have a granddaughter living with them and no children at home. I told her, "God, if there was ever a young woman who was treated like a queen, it was you." My father would drive her to school every day and drop her off, and he'd come back in the afternoon. And she had her own bedroom. My mother would help her go out and buy clothes, and that was really a good deal.

By this time, after the four or five months of recuperation, I came back to Washington to go to the National War College. I talked this over with the Navy, and I just felt that this was the best transition back to the real world. Because I always felt the National War College was the most prestigious of the colleges, even above the Naval War College. So I pretty much made my choice that that was the place where I could make the transition. I'd always wanted to get my master's degree and never had the chance, and I could get my master's at George Washington while doing that program.

Paul Stillwell: Were you offered a range of choices?

Admiral Lawrence: Yes, I could have done anything. Many of the POWs just took the easy way, like those in San Diego who got the Navy to send them to school or just to have some plush job.

Paul Stillwell: They wouldn't send you to sea right away, would they?

Admiral Lawrence: Well, I don't think anybody went to sea right away. Well, actually, my classmate Byron Fuller, after about four or five months, I think he got screened for a deep-draft command. He went right back on the sea track. I had been screened for a carrier command when I got back, and the plan was that I would go to a carrier after I left the National War College. Byron Fuller got screened for a deep draft, and he went right away. He didn't go to school. I have to give old Byron a lot of credit, because he really wanted to get back on the operational track, but I just felt I had to go to the National War College. It gave me a chance to give some supervision to my children, because I could commute from Washington down to Nashville, which was not a long commute. And I knew I had them under real good supervision of my parents.

It was really a busy time, because I did a lot of things for my kids, including making arrangements for my younger daughter to go to summer camp. I was trying to do things to get them out of that home environment, because it was very difficult for my wife to have to face my children, when it was revealed that she concealed the fact that I was alive. On top of that, I was making all these speeches; just one request after the other was coming in. I felt somewhat of an obligation to meet as many of these as I could. I told people, "I'm not going to go out and just speak to adult groups. If I'm going to speak, I want to speak to the young people to try to help them learn from this experience."

Paul Stillwell: What were the substance and tone of the speeches?

Admiral Lawrence: Well, the substance of most of my speeches was, "These are the qualities that enabled us to handle that experience. As a young person, you should be seeking to acquire these type of qualities." It was oriented to help them then shape their lives. That was the principal speech I gave. But I got caught into a lot of the towns around there. For instance, my mother had grown up near Parksville, Tennessee. Well, Parksville had to have a special ceremony for me, and so did Springfield, Tennessee. So I kept getting caught up in these special dinners and so forth, recognizing me. I was really one of two POWs who came back to middle Tennessee. One was an Army enlisted man who'd been captured at Hue, and I was, of course, a Navy pilot and more senior. So more of the attention was focused on me than, unfortunately, this poor Army enlisted man, although, I tried to make sure he got included in the recognition. But it just seemed more natural for me to get more recognition.

Paul Stillwell: Sounds like that was a healthy thing for you at that point.

Admiral Lawrence: Well, I think it was; I think it was a good thing for me to do. It really kept me extremely busy, because in addition to doing these things with my kids and these public-relations things, I was trying to get my personal affairs squared away, simple things I had to do like buying a new wardrobe. And I had to go through all the finances, which my wife had not handled very well.

Paul Stillwell: Deal with the IRS.

Admiral Lawrence: Yes, but the government bent over backwards. They really helped us; they gave us dedicated IRS support. The Veterans Administration, Social Security, all these things just really bent over backwards. So we got a tremendous amount of help. Ford Motor Company gave us the use of a car for a year; my hometown gave me a new car as my homecoming gift. So all sorts of things were done to make it easy for us to make the transition.

But I was just really pressed the whole time. And, of course, there are always people who are extremely sympathetic that you don't have a wife, and they feel they have this tremendous obligation to get you remarried. So I was always getting these calls, "Hey, I want to introduce you to somebody." So I got to where I had to go out on a lot of dinners, obviously for the purpose of introducing me to somebody.

Anyway, I went on back to Washington to enter the National War College, and I rented myself a little apartment over in Arlington. Actually, it was with an Army couple. He was an active duty major; she was an active duty major in the Nurse Corps at Fort Belvoir. They rented out their house, and I got to know them through a classmate of mine who'd been staying there. Initially I was renting just a bedroom with kitchen privileges and house privileges. Then I was commuting back to Tennessee virtually every weekend and embarked on this massive program. So that was really a very intensive, really busy time.

Then a fellow POW named Jim Bell, out of the Naval Academy class of '54, who was a commander at that time, whose wife had also divorced him, was going to the Industrial College of the Armed Forces, which was also at Fort McNair in Washington.* He had bought a condo over in Alexandria, so after I was there for about three months, he invited me to come over and live with him, because he was kind of lonely, and he wanted somebody to share the house with. So then I moved in with Jim Bell, which was just a natural, because we both could drive to Fort McNair every day together.

Paul Stillwell: How well could you focus on the program there with all these distractions?

Admiral Lawrence: Well, I don't know; I was able to do it. One thing that really helped very well in that situation was this sense of mental discipline I learned in the POW camp. I was able to really get involved in very deep mental activity, highly disciplined. We'd learned over six years that you just acclimated yourself to not very much sleep. And I just seemed to have a very high level of productivity during that time. So even though I'd been through a lot of traumatic things, I had a really positive outlook, because I'd gotten a very tough thing behind me, and I'd come through it well. It just seemed to give me a lot of enthusiasm. It made me very productive, and I had a lot of energy. I was just so lucky that my health had not really been seriously affected.

Paul Stillwell: What do you remember about the substance of the course you took?

---

* Commander James F. Bell, USN.

Admiral Lawrence: Well, I really enjoyed all of it. It was very much national security oriented. At that time we were still very heavily keyed on the Communist threat, principally the Soviets and the Chinese.

In my master's program at George Washington, I determined to do my thesis on that aspect of the law of the sea that dealt with deliberations and negotiations that addressed deep-sea mining. At that time it was a very interesting thing that all the manganese nodules and all these other metals that were down there on the ocean floor constituted the future in mineral exploration development. So I got all focused on that and did my master's thesis on the deep-seabed negotiations for the aspect of law at sea. I got all wrapped up in that, and that was really, I really enjoyed that.

My fellow POW National War College classmate John McCain kept coming to me every day. He was getting physical therapy for all these injuries that he had taken. His wife had been injured badly in a car accident, and she had gone to a physical therapy company called Rehab, Incorporated, down in Alexandria. When he came back, this same company offered to treat him so he wouldn't have to go up to the naval hospital in Bethesda. His physical therapist, who had offered to do this treatment free of charge, was Diane Wilcox. She had been previously married to a nuclear submariner named Chick Rauch, but they had divorced.[*]

John would come to school and say, "Hey, Bill, I've got to introduce you to Diane Rauch; she's just really great."

I said, "Hey, John . . ."

Paul Stillwell: That was one of many you'd heard.

Admiral Lawrence: I said, "Look, John, I just don't have any time right now to be involved with a woman. I'm up to here with this course here; I've got my three kids I'm trying to get on a track. I just simply don't have time."

But John—like all the McCains—is very persistent. So he kept working on me, and he was spending two hours a week of getting really intense physical therapy from her. He couldn't bend his knee, and she wanted to make sure he'd get the full 90-degree

---

[*] Rear Admiral Charles F. Rauch Jr., USN.

rotation in his knee, and his shoulder was bad. And he'd keep saying, "Diane, I've got to introduce you to Bill Lawrence; I've got to . . ."

She'd say, "Hey, John, I will never, ever again get involved with another naval officer." And so, finally, after four months of very indifferent reception on my part, he arranged a dinner party, and we were dinner guests. When we met, I was impressed with her as being a very classy gal, and very refined, intelligent. We hit it off well, but it was no big deal. I just chalked this up as another date in Washington.

But then, about two months later, she had a dinner party to reciprocate the McCains, and so she invited me to come over. And I really admired her, because she was obviously a very quality person. But still, no bells were ringing. And then, I guess maybe a month or so later, I had her out for a date. By this time I'd turned my master's thesis in, and my kids were really doing well, and the load was starting to reduce. I guess I was starting to get more interested in ladies. So we started dating more, and you could just see we had very unusual common interests, and a great deal of mutual respect. So that just kept growing and growing, until, finally, I guess it was in July, after meeting in December, after I'd finished the National War College course, but I was still finishing up my master's program, that we really started getting serious about each other and made the decision in July that we were going to get married.

Another big factor was that my two daughters had come up to visit me in Washington during their spring break, and they had really gotten along extremely well with her.

But it had been a tough year in some respects with my kids. The daughter who had gone to Vanderbilt had a terrible adjustment problem. She'd grown up in California, and, as I say, when I came back from being a POW, I made my first visit out there. I went to her high school, and here these kids were walking to high school barefooted, wearing these flowing robes, their hair down to their shoulders. I said, "My God, I'm getting you kids out of this environment, getting you back and subjecting you to a little bit of that southern Bible-belt culture."

But, anyway, it was a tough readjustment period growing up in California and being thrown into a southern private university with all these southern gals who had grown up as these southern belles. She had a tough adjustment, so I had to do a tremendous amount of stroking with her. For the first two years there she really wanted to leave; she just didn't like it. Finally, it all worked out.

So those are the principal aspects of the readjustment and return to American society.

Paul Stillwell: What was your thesis on?

Admiral Lawrence: Well, the deep-seabed.

Paul Stillwell: So it tied in with those negotiations that were going on.

Admiral Lawrence: Yes. It was "The Deep Sea Bed, the Current Status, and Future Prospects." That was where I did an analysis of negotiation and the potential wealth and so forth.

Paul Stillwell: Well, do you want to break it here?

Admiral Lawrence: Yes, we can break it here and then I can tell you about getting selected for flag that first year. I really couldn't believe that happened.

Interview Number 13 with Vice Admiral William P. Lawrence, U.S. Navy (Retired)
Place: U.S. Naval Institute, Annapolis, Maryland
Date: Wednesday, 19 December 1990
Interviewer: Paul Stillwell

Paul Stillwell: Admiral, the last time you finished up your discussion of the study at the National War College, and you said you had some discussions with Admiral Zumwalt about getting your career back on track following your time in prison.

Admiral Lawrence: Well, I really didn't have extensive discussions with him, except that he clearly conveyed to me and other POWs that he intended to give us every opportunity to reestablish our careers. We, of course, were very thankful, because most of us felt there was just no way we could ever catch up from what we lost during the many years that we were there. But, more than any other service, the Navy's position was that you gained a lot of value there that you could use effectively for the naval career.

So the Navy really bent over backwards to help us resume our careers. I think Admiral Zumwalt certainly has to receive a lot of personal credit, because the Navy did this to a far greater degree than the Air Force. In fact, unfortunate, negative attitudes towards POWs developed in the Air Force. I've been told of reluctance to take the risk of giving them operational commands, such as commands of wings and things like that.

Paul Stillwell: Well, in a sense there was some risk, because you didn't have the experience base your contemporaries did.

Admiral Lawrence: But Admiral Zumwalt set the Navy's policy on that, and they really were very forthcoming. I had been selected for flag while I was in the National War College, and right away they gave me a fleet command out at Light Attack Wing Pacific Fleet. I really felt good about going to that command; I didn't have any reservations at all. It had really been a busy year for me: going through the National War College, getting my master's at George Washington, commuting home to take care of my kids.

Paul Stillwell: And meeting your future wife.

Admiral Lawrence: Yes, meeting my future wife. But it really felt good that my efficiency and productivity were probably better than they had ever been during my whole career, my whole life. I think maybe all that pent-up productivity and energy from the POW years were starting to come out.

Paul Stillwell: Did you have any sense of disappointment over not getting the carrier?

Admiral Lawrence: Well, I guess you never can be disappointed about getting promoted to flag rank. [Chuckle] I would have liked to command a carrier, but when I got selected for flag, that foreclosed that opportunity. It's, of course, a regret, because I think commanding a carrier is the ultimate peak for a naval aviator.

Paul Stillwell: I've talked to any number of flag officers who cited that big ship command as really the most satisfying period in a career.

Admiral Lawrence: Oh, yes, it is, and it's probably one of the greatest leadership challenges, because you have 5,000 people on that ship. Not only do you have to know all the operational aspects of your assignment, but you really have to exercise very fine leadership, because of such a very large contingent of people whom you have to get inspired and motivated to perform. To me, it's probably the most challenging operational command in the military.

Paul Stillwell: It says something for the flag board's opinion of you that they would promote you, even before you really had an operational test after being out of prison.

Admiral Lawrence: Yes, I think it was. I think the evaluations I got from Colonel Flynn, who was a senior Air Force POW, and from Stockdale and Denton and guys like that were very helpful for me in that regard.* As I say, I think Admiral Zumwalt really wanted to demonstrate that he was willing to bet on the POWs. His rationale was that, even though we missed some experience, that was outweighed by the value of leadership challenge and so forth we had as POWs.

Paul Stillwell: Well, another aspect to Zumwalt, of course, was the Z-grams and all that kind of initiative.† Did you have a culture shock coming back to that kind of a Navy?

Admiral Lawrence: Well, I admit, when I went out to Lemoore in the summer of 1974, I found a different world out there.‡ Of course, I did not perceive this while I was in the National War College, because that was a cloistered environment. But when I went out into the operating Navy, I really saw quite a few differences from what I'd seen before I was shot down. By this time Admiral Zumwalt had retired. He retired in July of 1974. But I had to spend a lot of time going back and reading those Z-grams and getting myself caught up on the policies.

I didn't find any real difficulty in assuming that command. It's amazing just how much the basic expertise I had gained all those years stood me in good stead for the operational aspect of it. Even though I'd been a fighter pilot, I didn't find it all that much difficult to make myself proficient in the attack tactics, because I . . .

Paul Stillwell: You were an attack pilot also when you were in the F-4.

Admiral Lawrence: Well, that's right. Fighter pilots had to be attack pilots in the Vietnam War. And, of course, in my Patuxent River experience, I flew all sorts of different airplanes, so it was really no difficulty to take cognizance of the attack mission.

---

* Colonel John P. Flynn, USAF, was shot down over North Vietnam on 27 October 1967 while flying an F-105 Thunderchief in the 388th Tactical Fighter Wing. He was released on 14 March 1973. He subsequently reached the rank of lieutenant general. Flynn died 5 March 1997.

† Z-grams were consecutively numbered policy directives from Chief of Naval Operations Zumwalt that attempted to deal with such issues as enlisted rights and privileges, equal opportunity, and Navy families. Junior personnel viewed them much more favorably than did their seniors. See U.S. Naval Institute Proceedings, May 1971, pages 293-298.

‡ The headquarters for Commander Light Attack Wing Pacific Fleet was at Lemoore Naval Air Station. Site of a master jet base, it is in the San Joaquin Valley, ten miles west of Lemoore, California, and about 45 miles southwest of Fresno.

It was a very, very satisfying command, because I had a total of 23 squadrons under me. We had the two replacement air group squadrons, one for the A-7C and the other for the A-7D.* And then they had an instrument training squadron.

Paul Stillwell: Was the A-4 not a factor anymore?

Admiral Lawrence: The A-4 was phasing out when I got there. They were not sending anybody through the RAGs anymore for A-4s. At that time, we had two remaining A-4 squadrons, and they made their last deployment while I was there at Lemoore.

Paul Stillwell: I think the *Hancock* was just winding up then, wasn't she?

Admiral Lawrence: Yes, the *Hancock* and the *Oriskany* were the *Essex*-class attack carriers that were still operational when I went out there. I can't remember which one of them had the A-4s on it, but, anyway, that was the end of the A-4.

But, as I say, I had a total of 20 fleet squadrons or so under me, so it was a chance to really interface with the young pilots. That was a very satisfying aspect of it, because it was really good leadership experience in trying to motivate and inspire young people.

Paul Stillwell: Do you recall specifics from that kind of interchange?

Admiral Lawrence: Well, I really tried to get around and visit with every squadron there, go down into their spaces and have them brief me on what they were doing, their training program, and try to walk around and talk to the enlisted personnel. And I tried to participate in every official function that I could, such as changes of command. There were frequent changes of command with that large number of squadrons. I really tried to be a hands-on, highly visible leader in that environment, and that's what made it so pleasant, because I could do that.

---

* The Vought A-7 Corsair II was a jet bomber that went into service in light attack training squadrons in 1966 and fleet squadrons in 1967.

I had to get caught up to speed on a lot of things. Drugs were starting to be a new concern that we'd never had before I was shot down. So I had to start learning about the drug issue.

Paul Stillwell: I think '74 was about the nadir, and after that the policy started getting tougher as a tool to help commanders.

Admiral Lawrence: That's right. There was no real means of enforcement or deterrence at that time. The urinalysis and all that started later. We were just starting to get into the counseling and assistance function, where we had these counseling centers. That's when we really began to really wake up to the fact that we had to be cognizant of drugs out there. It really was a personnel concern. I was very much involved in helping our counseling center out there get off the ground and get going.

The thing that was so enjoyable about that job was that it included all the broad aspects of command: the administrative, personnel, and the operational aspects of it. In addition to the 23 squadrons, three air stations were under my command: the naval air station at Lemoore, the naval air station at Alameda, and the naval air station at Fallon, Nevada. So I was continuously going around and visiting those air stations.

Paul Stillwell: That's quite a geographic spread.

Admiral Lawrence: Yes, and I flew everywhere in a TA-4, a two-place A-4.* My aide had been in an A-4 squadron, so he was very current, and we always flew together. So one interesting aspect of it was that I got to fly quite a bit in that job.

I got out there and took over in August. My future wife and I had decided we were going to get married, and we were trying to set a date. But we were having a lot of difficulty, because my parents had commitments and her parents had commitments. We found that the first mutually agreeable date was out in September or something like that. And we couldn't really determine a feasible place to have it. Finally, one day I said, "We're doing all this for everybody else's convenience. We should do what's best for

---

* The TA-4 was a trainer version of the A-4 Skyhawk attack plane.

us." So I just picked out a date, the 29th of August. I called her up and I said, "Hey, your know, this is absurd trying to find dates that our parents can be there. They'd probably just as soon not have to travel anyway. [Chuckle] We've both been through the formal service in the previous marriage; we don't have to do that again. So you come out here, and we'll just have a private service out here."

Diane said, "Hey, that sounds great to me." So I didn't ask my parents. I just told them, and that was fine with them, because, as I say, they had other travel commitments. By the time we made that decision, it was about two weeks away, and so I contacted the senior Protestant chaplain there at Lemoore and asked him if he would conduct the wedding service. He was a Lutheran, and I'm sure most faiths have this requirement that before they marry someone, they want to be assured that it's, in fact, going to be a Christian wedding. So he had to tactfully tell me that he didn't marry people unless they went through some counseling with him. And, of course, this was going to be difficult to do, because Diane was back on the East Coast, where she was working. She really couldn't get out there till the day before the wedding. So we had to go into some kind of deliberations on this. Fortunately, she was Lutheran also, so she wrote out her concept for a service, and he reviewed that. I think he became convinced that he wouldn't be put in a "Marryin' Sam" role.[*] [Laughter] So he waived this premarital counseling requirement.

It turned out that my wife really couldn't fly out until the day of the wedding, which was going to be in the evening. She had quite an experience flying out, because in those days you couldn't fly directly into Fresno, which is the closest commercial airport. She had to fly through Los Angeles and then change and fly up to Fresno. And she was bringing a dog out with her. [Chuckle] They have a stipulation in the Los Angeles airport that they do not automatically change a dog from one airline to the other. She had to supervise getting the dog switched in the cage and almost missed her connection. So she had a real hassle.

---

[*] "Marryin' Sam" was the local Dogpatch minister in the satirical comic strip "L'il Abner," which was produced for many years by cartoonist Al Capp. Sam specialized in $2.00 weddings, though fees were negotiable.

Then I had to go up to Whidbey to an Air Force Pacific Fleet commanders' conference.* I flew back from Whidbey in an A-4 that day, and she flew out. Our plan was to get married that evening, but when I took off from Whidbey to come down, I got a barber pole indication on my landing gear, which indicated it wasn't up. I thought, "God, if I have to go back in to get that fixed, I'm going to miss the wedding." But we recycled the landing gear and it came up. She arrived in the early afternoon, and I arrived in the early afternoon, and we had to rush out and get the marriage license at the county courthouse in Hanford, California.

We ended up having this small wedding, and two people stood up with us. The husband was Jerry Solomon, a fellow out of the Naval Academy class of '50 who played on the baseball team.† He was a commander stationed at Lemoore. Jerry was Jewish, and his wife was Nativa Solomon, who was Portuguese. The Catholic chaplain came just to be present, and he was Polish. Of course, the Lutheran chaplain was German, and I'm Scotch-Irish and English. So I said, "Boy, this is really an ethnic wedding." But those were all the people who were there—the Protestant chaplain, the Catholic chaplain just observing, and the two people who stood up with us.

It was really a hectic day, but we finally got married. It was a very pleasant way for us to start our married life, because we had a nice set of quarters, and it was really great to be with the young people. My daughter Wendy, who's now a lieutenant commander in the Navy, was living with us there. We had a very fine experience during the time we were there.

But to get back to the Z-grams, the thing that I really noticed right away was the reluctance of commanding officers to take forceful action with regard to people. There seemed to be this fear that if they were too tough or too harsh on their enlisted personnel, that they'd get put on report. It was apparent to me that the concept of the hotline back to Washington, which existed in those days, had commanding officers reluctant to really take forceful actions.

---

* Whidbey Island, the site of a naval air station, is north of Seattle, Washington, in the Strait of Juan de Fuca.
† Commander Jerome E. Solomon Jr., USN.

Paul Stillwell: Well, that's an understandable concern.

Admiral Lawrence: One of my first priorities was to get commanding officers to take more initiative. I went around and looked at some barracks, and I was really upset with the basic cleanliness and overall condition of barracks. I really had to get tough on the commanding officers to get them in there to set standards. It appeared to me that the chain of command had been weakened in those years.

Paul Stillwell: That was a common perception.

Admiral Lawrence: Yes. But commanding officers were really afraid their troops could get them in trouble if they were too hard.

Paul Stillwell: Well, they may have felt caught in between, in that they had these people below them who could put them on report, and you were breathing down their necks to raise their standards.

Admiral Lawrence: But we got that pretty well squared away, and the commanding officers started being more assertive. We really didn't have any bad disciplinary problems there. I had read all about the racial problems that they'd had on the *Constellation* and the *Kitty Hawk*.[*] So I was very attuned about the racial situation at that time, as a result of those problems that they'd had on those two carriers. I kept my eye on it. The one place everybody perceived might get a little explosive was in the enlisted men's club. So we maintained a very strict security and decorum in that club. The commanding officer of the air station was Jack O'Hara.[†] He required the shore patrol to really maintain a very strong presence in there, because there was still very much a

---

[*] Racial disturbances broke out in the carrier *Kitty Hawk* (CVA-63) on 12 October 1972; in the oiler *Hassayampa* (AO-145) on 16 October 1972; and in the carrier *Constellation* (CVA-64) on 3 November 1972. See Captain Paul B. Ryan, USN (Ret.), "USS Constellation Flare-up: Was it Mutiny?" *U.S. Naval Institute Proceedings*, January 1976, pages 46-53. See also Gregory A. Freeman, *Troubled Water: Race, Mutiny, and Bravery on the USS Kitty Hawk* (New York: Palgrave Macmillan, 2009).
[†] Captain Jack F. O'Hara, USN.

concern about racial problems. Fortunately, we didn't have any while I was out there. I think the racial problems started getting squared away about that time.

It was a great command experience for me. It was a great way to get back into the operating Navy. I went out on a carrier while I was there, just to really have some opportunity to observe my squadrons operating in that environment. Then I made a trip out to WestPac with Admiral Baldwin, who was ComNavAirPac, and had a chance to visit with the two attack squadrons that were on the carrier *Midway*, out of Yokosuka.* That trip out to WestPac was a very good experience, and I enjoyed that.

Paul Stillwell: Was there any innovation in the light attack community then, or was it mostly just managing a going concern?

Admiral Lawrence: We were doing a lot of new initiatives in the maintenance area, which I got very actively involved in. The TF-41 engine, which is in the A-7C, is an Allison engine. It was trouble-prone, and it had problems with cracked vanes. So we developed a procedure out there that put this fiber-optic scope into the combustion area and the turbine blades. It's kind of like the arthroscopic surgery on the knee. This inspection capability in engines really revolutionized your ability to detect an engine problem or determine whether or not it was necessary to take an engine out and repair it.

I got very much involved in the maintenance and logistics aspect of what I was doing. But in terms of tactics and so forth, we were kind of phasing out of the Vietnam War, which had just been over for a year or so, and getting back more to the Cold War concerns. We were getting more emphasis on nuclear strike planning and that sort of thing. Because for years the principal focus was on fighting that war over in Vietnam.

Paul Stillwell: I've talked to Vice Admiral Steele, who was Commander Seventh Fleet at

---

* Vice Admiral Robert B. Baldwin, USN, served as Commander Naval Air Force Pacific Fleet from 31 May 1973 to 12 July 1976.
The aircraft carrier *Midway* (CV-41) and her escorts arrived in Yokosuka, Japan, on 5 October 1973 to begin the first overseas home-porting of a complete carrier task group. The forward deployment was the result of an accord arrived at on 31 August 1972 between the United States and Japan. In August 1991, after nearly 18 years of service out of the Japanese port, the *Midway* left Yokosuka for the last time and was replaced by the *Independence* (CV-62) as the forward-deployed carrier.

that time, and he said he had to make a deliberate reorientation back to the ability of attack pilots to hit ship targets; whereas, they'd been oriented to attacking land targets.* Was that one of your concerns also?

Admiral Lawrence: Well, yes, that's right. The big term that we were using at those times was "war at sea." Right after the Vietnam War, we suddenly woke up to the fact that there were other areas we had to be concerned about. In addition to attacking ships, we also had to start emphasizing the nuclear strike planning at the light attack weapons school we had.

Unfortunately, the Navy let me stay there only about ten months, because I think there was a perception that since I had never had any Washington duty I had to get back there to get that credential---a check in that box.

Paul Stillwell: Do you have any impressions of Admiral Baldwin from working for him?

Admiral Lawrence: Yes, I really had the highest regard for him. He was a superb ComNavAirPac—very smart, and he had fine leadership style. He was very much aware of what was going on. Of course, I had known him from previous years. Although we hadn't served together, we had known each other professionally. He was a test pilot graduate, so we had common backgrounds. I was very, very impressed with him. These were some tough times out there because the war ended and there were a lot of cutbacks in funds.

We had a flap over the aircraft carrier *Coral Sea*. The carrier was due to deploy in January of 1974, and, of course, the *Coral Sea* had gone really hard during the Vietnam War. It was tired from the trip, and the material condition was not very good. Two or three of the young wives of the crew members of *Coral Sea* were engaged in a very strong protest that the ship wasn't safe to go back up there on that deployment.

That got to be a problem for the senior commanders out there, because the press in San Francisco picked this up. And, of course, the press out there tends to be a little bit liberal, and they just blew it all out of perspective. So Admiral Baldwin had to get in

---

* Vice Admiral George P. Steele, USN, served as Commander Seventh Fleet, 28 July 1973 to 14 June 1975.

there and try to deal with that issue, and keep the press from getting just totally out of hand. It was unfortunate, because Captain Tom Rogers, who was CO of the *Coral Sea*, was a fine guy.* I think his career was adversely impacted by this bad press the ship was getting out there. It was a bad scene for a while. I was not involved in that, because I was not in that chain of command. But Alameda was under my command, and, of course, Alameda was the base for the *Coral Sea*. So I was very much aware of what was going on. I tried to help where I could by making the commanding officer of NAS Alameda, Ed McKellar, use his public affairs resources to try to deal with the problem.†

Paul Stillwell: Were you or he able to turn it around to any extent?

Admiral Lawrence: Well, it finally died out in the press, and the *Coral Sea* went ahead and deployed on schedule. But the press was just trying to have some sensationalistic coverage, more than anything else. But it just showed you, shortly after the Vietnam War, how the press was still very rabid and very liberal-leaning. I remember Admiral Baldwin or somebody called up the publisher of the *San Francisco Chronicle*, who was a very respected individual, to talk about these sensationalistic articles. This man's answer was, "I can't control those liberal reporters." That was probably the most unpleasant thing that happened. Everything else was very, very positive.

That tour of duty was a great way for me to phase back into the real Navy, and get my feet wet operationally again. I found that even though I was away six years, I still had not lost that much touch with the operations, tactics, and that sort of thing.

Paul Stillwell: Well, the *Coral Sea* had a successful cruise. She went out and supported the evacuation from Saigon.‡

---

* Captain Thomas S. Rogers, Jr., USN, commanded the aircraft carrier *Coral Sea* (CVA-43) in 1973-75.
† Captain Edwin D. McKellar Jr., USN.
‡ On 29-30 April 1975, as Saigon, the capital of South Vietnam, was being overrun by the North Vietnamese, U.S. Navy and Marine Corps helicopters evacuated almost 9,000 people. Included were 1,373 Americans, 6,422 of other nationalities, plus 989 Marines inserted to cover the operation. Graham Martin, U.S. ambassador to South Vietnam, was among the last to leave from the rooftop of the American embassy.

Admiral Lawrence: Yes, she had a very fine cruise. It was just two or three disgruntled wives who didn't want their husbands deployed. They started making noises, and they got all this audience in the news media. It was just amazing how things were at that time. They tell me that San Francisco had been the site of a lot of the antiwar protests, and so those attitudes were still very prevalent there.

Paul Stillwell: Up to this time you had focused more on operational-type billets. Now you had quite an administrative load. What did you learn from that?

Admiral Lawrence: Well, the administrative load in that job was not all that great. I was the court-martial authority and certainly had some disciplinary responsibility. But the average squadron is very much self-sufficient administratively, so I did not have to do a lot administratively.

Paul Stillwell: What about financial management?

Admiral Lawrence: The way the financial management occurs out in the fleet is that flight hour funds and things like that are dispensed at the NavAirPac level, so I was not a fund manager. The operations and maintenance account I had was not all that great, because the principal individuals who managed the O&M funds were the COs of the air stations. So the financial management was not really any challenge at all.

The big challenges were in maintenance, logistics, and operations. You had to take a very heavy role in trying to make the supply system work better. If there were maintenance problems, we interfaced with the type commander's staff and Naval Air Systems Command. As I say, we were having a lot of engine problems, and that's when we learned about the fiber-optic inspection capability. In the area of operations, I used to go up to Fallon frequently to observe the performance of the squadrons to find out if they were doing their weapons training, working on the targets and ranges there.

Another significant operational responsibility we had was that Washington directed the Pacific Fleet to do a joint electronic warfare test, and we were designated to run that test. Basically, it entailed determining the best type of electronic countermeasure support for a strike force, whether to have area jamming or to have the jammers escort strike group. Of course, the Navy's approach with the EA-6B is to have the jammers accompany the strike force.* The Air Force, with its large jammers, tends to do the standoff jamming. This test was to evaluate the relative merit of the escort versus the area type of ECM. We had to prepare extensively for that. One officer in my staff was the test director, and I think we got some very useful lessons learned about electronic warfare, but we had to work with the Air Force.

Paul Stillwell: Do you recall any of your conclusions?

Admiral Lawrence: We came to the conclusion that for the Navy's purposes, standard Vietnam War overland-type mission, having the jammers escort the strike force was by far the most effective. We just basically validated our approach. The Air Force did feel with some of the jamming capability they have in some of their large airplanes, like the EC-135, that they were willing to do it through this standoff area jamming. That was about the principal finding that I recall.

Paul Stillwell: Probably if they'd done the test, they would have come to the opposite conclusion. [Chuckle]

Admiral Lawrence: I guess they would have, yes.

Paul Stillwell: Any issues you remember on safety or training?

Admiral Lawrence: Well, one thing, of course, in that particular job, you very carefully monitor your safety program, and every accident that you have, of course, is very thoroughly investigated, because you're concerned about your accident rate. We had several accidents during that year, but there were no significant trends that were apparent. Of course, we gave a tremendous amount of emphasis to enhancing our safety. So I spent

---

* The Grumman EA-6B Prowler was the electronic countermeasures version of the A-6 carrier-based bomber.

a lot of time in monitoring that, and we always had at least a weekly all-commanding-officers' meeting in which safety was a big aspect.

While I was there, we looked at all of the factors that I felt constituted excellence—administratively, maintenance, logistics, and operations. I developed a system somewhat similar to what we have here in the Color Company at the Naval Academy. You're graded in all these various areas, and then at the end of the year you give the colors to the company that stands the highest. Well, I developed a similar concept for the squadrons out there. I felt that this would be a good thing to do to enhance the spirit of competition among that large number of squadrons.

I had a guy who was waiting to go be a CAG, and he was going to be on my staff about two or three months. So I laid out this concept for him. I said, "Look, why don't you work on this and try to take a cut at developing waiting factors and all that." That's what we did, and it turned out to be very good, because we looked at things like reenlistment rate and AOL rate in the personnel-admin area.[*] Then we looked at their operational readiness rate and all these broad factors that demonstrate the proficiency and excellence of that squadron in the broad sense.

Paul Stillwell: Didn't the battle efficiency competition cover that?

Admiral Lawrence: Well, the battle efficiency is very heavily oriented to operations and safety; in fact, it doesn't take your reenlistment rate into consideration. So I just basically broadened the criteria. It was interesting to work out all the concepts to do this. I forget what type of award we had, but we kept this going throughout the year, and then we had a ranking that was posted up in my headquarters all the time. That generated a lot of interest, although some commanding officers were not happy with it. I guess every commanding officer wants to have as good a record as possible during his time in command and is not always pleased to have things like this that might give him some bad publicity. But it was fun to develop the ranking criteria for our squadrons.

I thoroughly enjoyed those ten months; they just went by too fast. Lemoore was a great place to start out our married life, although Diane had to commute back and forth to

---

[*] AOL—absent over leave.

Washington. She'd spend about two to three weeks out there and then go back for about a week or so. She got a little bit tired of the commuting.

Paul Stillwell: Was she still running her business?

Admiral Lawrence: Yes, yes. She has a partner, so her partner took up some of the slack, but still she kept aware of what was going on. Her partner, of course, has really helped her a lot in those times when I was away and she had to commute. Later, when I went out to Hawaii, it was even a greater challenge. She's been able to keep those balls in the air somehow.

So, even though I hated to have that tour end, it was good for us, from a personal family aspect, to get back to Washington. My daughter Wendy was in the ninth grade then, and that was the first time that she had lived with me for seven years. She loved the high school at Lemoore. The San Joaquin Valley is very different from the coastal belt of California. It had some basically rural areas. You find a lot of the old grassroots values of patriotism and work ethic out there. For instance, the 4-H clubs are the big things. So my daughter really loved that type of attitude and approach, because she's very much into sports and has a strong work ethic, so it was a good high school for her to attend. That's about all on that experience.

Paul Stillwell: I have one more question, and it has to do with base-loading. The idea of basing similar type squadrons together came along, as opposed to basing air wings together. Do you have any thoughts on that?

Admiral Lawrence: Well, of course, the Pacific Fleet took the initiative first to go to the single type at a given base, and I felt that it made a lot of sense from several aspects. In the areas of maintenance, logistics, and training, it makes a tremendous amount of sense. I thought it worked very fine at Lemoore. The East Coast finally emulated that procedure. It really simplifies your supply problem, I'll tell you, that you don't have to have so many spare parts and inventory and storage areas out there. So I thought that was a good concept. I supported it.

Paul Stillwell: Well, the down side is that the air wing doesn't develop a sense of teamwork till it gets aboard the carrier.

Admiral Lawrence: Yes, that's right. But usually in the normal peacetime mode, you get a pretty good workup before you go out on deployment, so you have plenty of time on ships. That was the pattern we settled into. I'm sure that now has been gone by the wayside with this Middle East crisis.[*]

Paul Stillwell: Did you have any input into the tests that were going on then for what eventually became the F/A-18 strike fighter idea?[†]

Admiral Lawrence: No, that was just a little bit before that time. When I got back to Washington in the summer of '75, they were starting to get serious about the F/A-18. Northrop and General Dynamics had their prototypes, but we hadn't taken much cognizance of that in the fleet. We were still actively working to try to prove A-7 tactics there.

Paul Stillwell: The F-18 was seen initially as a lightweight fighter, and only gradually it evolved into a strike fighter.

Admiral Lawrence: Well, that's right. The initial language in the bill that set it up called it a lightweight fighter. The term that was used in those days was this was a low-cost complement to the F-14.[‡] Admiral Zumwalt used the term "high-low mix," but a lot of

---

[*] In January 1991 U.S. and Allied Coalition forces attacked Iraq to get it to retreat following its August 1990 invasion of neighboring Kuwait. The holding action in the meantime was Operation Desert Shield. The conflict itself became known variously as Operation Desert Storm and the Gulf War. Coalition forces won the war in February 1991.

[†] The F/A-18 Hornet, originally built by McDonnell Douglas, is a jet aircraft capable of both fighter and attack roles. It first entered operational service with VFA-125, a fleet readiness squadron, in May 1980. The F/A-18C model has a wingspan of 37 feet, 6 inches; length, 56 feet; gross weight of 36,710 pounds in the fighter version and 49,224 pounds in the attack version; top speed of 1,190 miles per hour. It replaced the F-4 Phantom and A-7 Corsair in fleet units.

[‡] Grumman F-14 Tomcat fighters first entered training squadrons in late 1972. The F-14A version was 64 feet long, wingspan of 38 feet, normal takeoff weight of 55,000 pounds, and top speed of Mach 2.34. It was equipped with a 20-millimeter cannon and was designed to carry a variety of types of missiles—Sparrow, Sidewinder, and Phoenix—and later equipped to deliver bombs as well.

people didn't like to use that term. I know my boss in OP-5, Vice Admiral Houser, used the term "low-cost complement," not the high-low mix.[*]

But it was clearly Congress that did this, and the principal reason was economics. They perceived that we just couldn't afford to develop a very sophisticated-type airplane. I think they did us a service, because my big problem right now is that we're going to break the bank with the A-12.[†] The cost of weapon systems today is just mind-boggling. I think the carrier *Enterprise* cost something like $500 million when it was built back in late '50s, and now it's going to cost $2 billion just to refuel it. The astronomical increase in the prices of these weapon systems has put us in a position where we can't afford to bring new systems into being.

Paul Stillwell: What job did you head toward then in Washington?

Admiral Lawrence: Well, I came back to be the director of the aviation programs division in the Office of the Deputy Chief of Naval Operations for Air Warfare. I had cognizance over broad areas: the maintenance and logistics program in naval aviation; all air stations, targets, ranges; the Navy aerospace program, and then I had to manage the aircraft inventory. I made the assignments of airplanes to various squadrons and maintained the historical records of naval aviation. I was counted on as the utility man of OP-05. [Chuckle] But I enjoyed it, because I enjoyed this breadth of responsibilities.

Most of these areas I was managing were not the high-visibility, glamour areas, so I was unencumbered. I did what I thought was right, and my boss didn't demand a lot of reports. So I had a lot of autonomy. I enjoyed that job, and I had some real challenges.

Paul Stillwell: Can you get into some of the specifics from things that you drew satisfaction from?

---

[*] Vice Admiral William D. Houser, USN, served as Deputy Chief of Naval Operations (Air Warfare) from 5 August 1972 to 30 April 1976.
[†] On 7 January 1991, a few weeks after this interview, Secretary of Defense Richard Cheney canceled the Navy's A-12 Avenger stealth aircraft, which was behind schedule and over budget. At a projected cost of $52 billion, it was the largest defense contract ever canceled. The A-12 was to have been the replacement for the A-6 Intruder attack aircraft that finally left the fleet in 1997.

Admiral Lawrence: Well, we did a lot of good work in the area of maintenance and logistics. First of all, improving the efficiency of supply support aboard our carriers. A great challenge we had was that we had a new test system, which was called the VAST, which stands for the versatile avionics systems test. The VAST was used on the F-14, the S-3, and the E-2C—those new airplanes that were entering the fleet about that time.* That had tremendous amount of problems, so I just spent a lot of time making the VAST concept work. So we had a lot of maintenance and logistics concerns. I put together the maintenance-logistics budgets. That included, for example, the amount of money we put out there in the depot maintenance areas and the amount of money we would spend on spare parts. I had a tremendous budgetary responsibility in putting together the so-called POM, and then defending the POM through the DoD wickets—all these other budgets that you have to do right in the building there and the various reviews with the Navy and so forth.† I learned a lot about how the PPBS works, because I had that total responsibility in the area of maintenance-logistics funding.‡

I ran the Navy flight hour budget, which at that time was around $800 million, and now I think it's well over $2 billion. We put together that budget to determine how much fuel money was given to AirPac, AirLant, and so forth. It was a very detailed effort to allocate money by type of airplane and so forth. I also had, as I say, cognizance of the Navy aircraft inventory, and the people who worked for me would make the specific aircraft assignments—ComNavAirLant, ComNavAirPac, and so forth. Also, I had cognizance over the aircraft stored out in the desert. At that time, it sorted out that they were at Litchfield Park, and then we moved them over to Davis Monthan, which is a short distance away in Tucson.

I had to deal with some really major things. The F-14 was in deep trouble at that time—accident-rate-wise, and it was having in-flight fires. Everybody was really

---

* The S-3 Viking was a jet-powered, carrier-based antisubmarine aircraft with a four-person crew. Built by Lockheed, its first delivery to a fleet training squadron was in February 1974. The S-3A had a wingspan of 68 feet, 8 inches; length of 53 feet, 4 inches; maximum gross weight of 52,539 pounds, and a top speed of 514 miles per hour. The E-2C Hawkeye is a propeller-driven carrier plane that has a look-down radar in order to track and manage the air picture from aloft.
† POM – program objectives memorandum, an element of the budgeting process.
‡ PPBS – Planning, Programming and Budgeting System, which was started in January 1961 by Secretary of Defense Robert S. McNamara. For details, see Gordon G. Riggle, "Looking to the Long Run," *U.S. Naval Institute Proceedings*, September 1980, pages 60-65.

concerned that the whole program might be canceled, because it was still a fairly new airplane. So I had to develop a get-well program for the F-14. It was a very comprehensive program that involved the Naval Air Systems Command, the Supply Systems Command, and a lot of laboratories. They just carved the money to do this out of the Navy overall accounts, which we couldn't afford to do, but we simply had to get that plane going, because it was running the risk of being completely canceled. So that turned out to be a $300 million program.

Paul Stillwell: Do you remember any of the fixes that you put in?

Admiral Lawrence: Oh, yes. One thing was that the TF-30 engine in the F-14A was throwing compressor blades right through the side of the engine casing. This was causing damage that might cause a blade to hit a fuel tank and ignite. So we had to develop a fix that put a heavy band of metal around the compressor section, where this disintegration of blades was commonly occurring. We had to put fire-retardant material in the plenum chamber around the engines. It was just a very detailed, comprehensive effort to improve the F-14 across the board.

Paul Stillwell: There was also some consideration of a more powerful engine, wasn't there?

Admiral Lawrence: Well, the original F-14 was supposed to have an upgrade from the TF-30 engine, but they just ran out of money, and they had to keep the TF-30 engine. We talked about a replacement engine for it, and the money just simply wasn't available. We were told we would have to keep what we had going. So that was when I started making more trips to get out there and find out what the problems were and who the key players were. But getting that F-14 going again was one of my top priorities.

Associated with this material maintenance improvement was that we were tasked to conduct a test called AIMVAL/ACEVAL. AIMVAL stands for air intercept missile evaluation, and ACEVALs are air combat evaluation. A lot of people in the Navy were reluctant for us to get into these tests, which were conducted out at Nellis Air Force Base, because they felt the Air Force's F-15 would look so much better than the Navy's F-14.[*] So I talked to a lot of people, and I came to the realization that we simply had to do that test, that the Congress wanted us to do those to get a better definition of the airplane and the capabilities desired in the future. My boss, Admiral Houser, didn't want to do it, because he thought the F-14 was just in too bad a material condition and would look so bad that the program could risk being canceled. But I said, "I think we can do it well."

So I set up a new supply system dealing out the contractor's plant up in Long Island.[†] I got a really good guy on site out there to supervise the operation. It turned out that over about a four-month period, we had about a 90% operational ready rate with all those measures we took. That operation was the first time the F-14 had ever shown any real potential. Somehow we got everything together in terms of part support, the type of enlisted personnel we had out there, and that just infused new life in the F-14 program. Our operational readiness capability was far better than the F-15 flying against it.

So that was a big achievement. I also ran a readiness improvement of the S-3, the ASW airplane. But a lot of my cognizance was over maintenance and logistics.

Paul Stillwell: Were these essentially teething problems, because you did have these three new planes?

Admiral Lawrence: A lot of it was teething problems, particularly one on the test equipment, the avionics. It was just basically not having systems that were completely compatible.

Paul Stillwell: Were you involved in the implementation of the CV concept?[‡]

Admiral Lawrence: No, it had already been done before I got there, but, as I say, we were introducing the S-3 into the carrier world for the first time. The S-3 was new, so it

---

[*] The F-15 Fighting Falcon was the Air Force's top-of-the-line fighter.
[†] The Grumman Aerospace Corporation plant was at Bethpage, Long Island, New York.
[‡] Up to that time the Navy had been operating two types of aircraft carriers; The CVAs were the tactical attack carriers; the CVSs were dedicated antisubmarine carriers. The CV concept, instituted in the early and mid-1970s, combined both roles in the big carriers, and the CVSs left the fleet.

was a real challenge to get the S-3 going well.

But the maintenance logistics, doing these readiness improvement programs and then monitoring the ship's performance out at sea and what kind of part support they have, that was one of my biggest responsibilities on that job. The maintenance and logistics were more taxing and more demanding.

I had some problems with the air stations' target ranges responsibility. Kahoolawe out in Hawaii is an uninhabited island we used for target practice, and the environmentalists and the native Hawaiians started complaining about our doing that, because they felt we were inconsiderate of them. So I had to fight that Kahoolawe problem while I was back there.

But it was a great job. I had that for two years, and then I moved over to be the Assistant Deputy Chief of Operations (Air Warfare), which they called OP-5B. You're the number-two guy in OP-05. I didn't like that job as much, because even though I had a breadth of concerns, I didn't get into any one program really well. As the number two to OP-05, I ran the place when he was out on the road but didn't have the amount of direct responsibility that I would have wanted.

Paul Stillwell: How would you characterize the relationship between OP-05 and Naval Air Systems Command, especially when Houser and Kent Lee were the commanders?[*]

Admiral Lawrence: Well, any time you have ComNavAirSysCom senior to OP-05, it's a bad thing. I think Kent Lee was about one number senior to Admiral Houser.[†] It was not anything unpleasant, because both of them are intelligent guys, and they would make accommodations as necessary. But I always felt that Admiral Houser bridled a little bit at being junior to ComNavAirSysCom, who theoretically, works for the CNO. I agree with Admiral Houser. I think that if OP-05 can't be the senior guy in naval aviation, that he's inhibited, and the whole program suffers.

Paul Stillwell: Did you see some suffering in the program?

---

[*] Vice Admiral Kent L. Lee, USN, served as Commander Naval Air Systems Command from 31 August 1973 to 29 August 1976. His oral history is in the Naval Institute collection.
[†] Lee's date of rank as a vice admiral was 29 January 1972; Houser's was 5 August 1972.

Admiral Lawrence: Oh, I can't say I saw any real faults, but I know that with ComAirNavSysCom being just a little bit senior to OP-05, OP-05 just didn't have the freedom to make things happen like he does when he is the big daddy of naval aviation, someone who can get on the phone and say, "Do this, do that." It just diminished the stature of OP-05.

Paul Stillwell: Well, Lee's argument is that if OP-05 had had its way, the money would have been put into more F-14s, and the F/A-18 wouldn't have come along.

Admiral Lawrence: Well, OP-05 is ruled by the tac air guys, that's for sure. But I think the aviators put aside their past backgrounds and they get in there and try to be totally objective. Our problem in naval aviation is that we can't get anybody to come back to Washington in the younger years, as a lieutenant and lieutenant commander, because there are so many billets out there that have to be filled. So that's one thing that always worked a little bit against OP-05, we don't build up this expertise like some of the other communities do, where they have guys who have had previous Washington duty and are more skillful at what they call playing the game of Washington.

Paul Stillwell: The submariners really don't have that opportunity either.

Admiral Lawrence: Well, they don't except that many of them will finish up their operational seagoing time as commanders and get an SSN, SSBN.[*] A fraction of them get a submarine squadron as captains. But they don't have anywhere near the number of commands an aviator does; first of all, an aviator has the XO-CO fleet up, and then he is a CAG, and if he has a deep draft, then a carrier. So there are essentially five commands. That precludes the aviators from getting back to Washington at the younger years, like the submarines. This has really worked against naval aviation, because we just haven't been too skillful the way we conduct our business, where the submariners always have it all together. But it's different when they just bring one new submarine into being, the SSN-21, and you're doing all these other things in OP-05.

---

[*] SSN – nuclear-powered attack submarine; SSBN – nuclear-powered ballistic missile submarine.

When I got to be Chief of Naval Personnel, I really worked on trying to give aviators more of the opportunity to get into that Washington arena at the younger ranks.

Paul Stillwell: What are your recollections of working with Admiral Houser?

Admiral Lawrence: Well, he's a wonderful man. He's a true gentleman, very smart. He knows all aspects of the job, and I have the greatest admiration for him. I like him a lot; he's great.

Paul Stillwell: Any specifics on your dealings with him?

Admiral Lawrence: Well, he pretty much concentrated on the high-visibility problems, like the new airplanes and keeping airplane programs going. He didn't get into my areas, dealing with the maintenance, logistics, targets, air space, and that sort of thing. He pretty much let me run my own show, which I appreciated. But when I needed his support, he really helped me.

For example, being the manager of the Navy airspace, we started having some real problems. As the airline traffic increased, we had problems with some Navy airplanes getting into the airways and having some near-miss incidents with the airliners. The FAA told us that we simply had to get better, more efficient management of our airspace.* So one of my big responsibilities when I first came in was to develop a concept for more positive control in the Navy-controlled air space. The FAA was very forthcoming, and they tried to help us on this, but we had to fight a battle to prevent losses of some much-needed equipment and things like that too. But we had some very dedicated, professional civil servants who helped us locate some excess Air Force equipment and get it transferred to bases like NAS Jacksonville and Oceana. We developed a concept for the positive control of our offshore areas in the East Coast similar to what we'd started out in San Diego.

Admiral Houser backed me 100% on that. I'd go in and lay out a concept and brief him and say, "I think we need this to put this amount of money to it." He was right

---

* FAA -- Federal Aviation Administration.

with me all the way. So I have great respect for him. He's smart, he's a good delegator, and he doesn't mind standing up and supporting you when the occasion arises. I was always very disappointed he didn't make four stars.

Paul Stillwell: Then his successor didn't last very long; Admiral Petersen then went over to NavAir.[*]

Admiral Lawrence: Well, what happened is that I think they brought in Petersen to be OP-05 as a holding operation until Kent Lee retired and he could go over there. I didn't know all the ins and outs of it, but Admiral Fox Turner, who finally came in to be OP-05, maybe wasn't available or something like that.[†]

Paul Stillwell: Well, my understanding was that they were going to have Lee and Petersen work together, because they were old friends, but then Lee retired sooner than expected, so Petersen went over to take his place.

Admiral Lawrence: Yes, it had to be something like that.

Paul Stillwell: Do you have any impressions of Petersen? He's also a respected test pilot.

Admiral Lawrence: Yes, he and I had been together at the test center, so I knew him really well from then. He was a very fine, technical-type individual. He had advanced degrees. He had done the flying of the X-15 out there at Edwards.[‡] He was really good. Yes, I had great respect for him. But also, I think that going over to ComNavAirSysCom was probably the best place for him to go and to have Fred Turner come over to OP-05,

---

[*] Vice Admiral Forrest S. Petersen, USN, served as Deputy Chief of Naval Operations (Air Warfare) from 1 May 1976 to 5 October 1976. Vice Admiral Petersen, USN, served as Commander Naval Air Systems Command from 29 August 1976 to 30 April 1980.
[†] Vice Admiral Frederick C. Turner, USN, served as Deputy Chief of Naval Operations (Air Warfare) from 6 October 1976 to 30 June 1979.
[‡] The X-15 was a North American-built experimental rocket plane that set speed and altitude records before the space program came along. Edwards Air Force Base is in California.

because Fred Turner was really operationally oriented. He'd come from being Sixth Fleet, and he'd been a test pilot himself. But they were a good combination. And, of course, Turner was senior to Petersen, which is good to have OP-05 senior.

But these were tough times because we were really cutting back in the '70s, the Carter years.* I remember one time they were talking about cutting back the aircraft carriers.

Paul Stillwell: Well, I remember when President Carter vetoed a nuclear carrier. Was OP-05 involved in that?

Admiral Lawrence: Oh, yes. I don't remember all the details about it. But those were really lean funding years, because I remember participating in a study about cutting back to eight aircraft carriers. Then I guess the Carter experience with the Iran hostage situation and some other things that happened in the world immediately brought him to the realization that he had to have strong defense.† So the last couple years of his administration, he actually put money into defense. But the years I was there up until '78, when I came to the Naval Academy, boy, defense budgets were really getting to be lean, and we were procuring the lowest number of airplanes we had in many years in OP-05.

Paul Stillwell: Well, there was also a study or consideration then of what they called a mid-size carrier to try to save some money.

Admiral Lawrence: Well, of course, earlier than that Admiral Zumwalt had tried to get the sea control ship, and that got canceled. But there was a lot of consideration given to smaller carriers. Admiral Holloway, who was the CNO, had an initiative to really make a massive effort to go to V/STOL, and with the V/STOL-type aircraft, we would go back to

---

* James E. Carter, Jr., who had graduated from the Naval Academy in the class of 1947, served as President of the United States from 20 January 1977 to 20 January 1981.
† When the Shah left Iran in January 1979, the Ayatollah Ruhollah Khomeini seized power and declared the nation to be an Islamic republic. On 4 November 1979 Iranian militants seized the U.S. embassy in Teheran and took the staff members there as hostages. The hostages were ultimately released on 20 January 1981, the day President Carter left office.

smaller carriers.* But we actually had a plan laid out in an office called OP-05B that was set up to really have cognizance over this transition to the V/STOL. But I just felt down deep inside it couldn't happen, because I knew that major funds would have to be put into this research, because major breakthroughs had to occur. For one thing, they had to find the metals to have significantly higher engine outlet temperatures to get that significant increase in thrust. They give a better thrust-to-weight ratio, and they had to make some strides towards miniaturized components and composites to get weight down. I knew that was just going to be a very, very expensive R&D program.[†] It pretty much died a natural death when Admiral Hayward became CNO in 1978, because he just saw we just couldn't afford it.[‡] But we did a lot of looking at that. Admiral Holloway was a great proponent of moving the Navy entirely to V/STOL, or at least STOL capability.

But those three years in OP-05 were very good years for me, because I learned thoroughly how the Pentagon worked. I learned all about how you deal with the Congress, because I had to go over and appear before the Congress a lot, primarily in the maintenance-logistics airspace target area. I learned how congressional staffs are organized, and I got a little sense of how the political game is played over there. And I pretty much mastered the so-called PPBS system, which stood me in good stead later on.

Of course, I had this concern of moving into my first Pentagon job as a flag officer. But I never had any real difficulty, frankly. A lot of it was just good common sense. I do remember another interesting aspect when I first came into OP-05. When I had been there just a week or two, Admiral Seiberlich, who at that time was OP-05B, called me in.[§] He said, "Look, we just had this GAO report that Senator Proxmire ordered us to look into the Navy back in September '74 [the year before I got there] flying all these C-9 airplanes to take people out to the Tailhook convention in Las Vegas.

---

* Admiral James L. Holloway III, USN, served as Chief of Naval Operations, 29 June 1974 to 1 July 1978. V/STOL – vertical or short takeoff and landing aircraft.
† R&D – research and development.
‡ Admiral Thomas B. Hayward, USN, served as Chief of Naval Operations from 1 July 1978 to 30 June 1982. His oral history is in the Naval Institute collection.
§ Rear Admiral Carl J. Seiberlich, USN.

You're responsible for responding to that GAO report."* [Chuckle]

Well, of course, that was not a very fun thing, and it hit me the first thing when I came into the Pentagon. I looked into it, and it was a clear-cut case that we just designated C-9 airplanes to fly as many people as we could to the Tailhook convention. It was simple.

Paul Stillwell: Was your answer acceptable?

Admiral Lawrence: Admiral Holloway said, "Well, why don't we just say that this was a part of our training, that in conjunction with training flights for these reserve squadrons and the active duty C-9 squadrons, they just brought these people to Las Vegas?"

I said, "Sir, you don't have 32 designated C-9 trips going to Las Vegas for training purposes. I think we should just stand up and tell Senator Proxmire that we thought it was important enough to bring our pilots to Las Vegas for this. We designated airplanes to do it. Sure, we got some training for the pilots, but the principal reason was to get these guys to the Tailhook convention."

He said, "Yeah, you're right." So that's what we did; we just told it like it was, and I went over with the report to brief Proxmire's staff. By this time he was on another witch-hunt, so they weren't even really interested. They'd received their publicity.

Paul Stillwell: Well, he had that Golden Fleece Award he used to give out.

Admiral Lawrence: Well, and see, I was upset because we had received the Golden Fleece of the Month Award, but we didn't win it for the year. The Air Force won it, and so I was really disappointed because I thought we were in competition to get it for the year. But, anyway, it took about two weeks out of my life responding to that GAO report.

---

* William Proxmire, a Democrat from Wisconsin, served in the U.S. Senate from 28 August 1957 to 3 January 1989. GAO—General Accounting Office, since changed on 7 July 2004 to Government Accountability Office.
The Tailhook Association is an organization of naval aviators and naval flight officers with aircraft carrier experience. The name comes from the tailhook at the rear of a carrier plane that arrests its landing on the flight deck.

One of the requirements in that GAO report was that we had to give the name of every Navy flag officer who had been flown out there by government transportation. I had paid my way to and from Tailhook, because just prior to that convention, my wife and I were married, and I was trying to minimize the time away from her. So I flew over on my own expense on a Saturday morning, because I only wanted to come over and attend the banquet on Saturday night; then I flew back on Sunday morning. So I didn't use government transportation. So they'd picked the right guy to run the report. But I recommended to Admiral Holloway that we not list the names of the flag officers. We just stonewalled it, because I didn't feel that was germane for the investigators. So we did, and Proxmire didn't push the issue.

Paul Stillwell: What is the value to the Navy of the Tailhook convention?

Admiral Lawrence: Well, it was really a kind of a morale spirit in those days. Now we've moved it more towards a professional symposium-type thing. During the Vietnam War years, I guess they did it for the morale of people who'd been involved in the war.

Paul Stillwell: An R&R type thing?

Admiral Lawrence: Yes, kind of an R&R thing.[*] It really started out nothing more than morale and spirit thing, but over the years, it's been moved into more of a professional endeavor. I'm going to get more active in the Association of Naval Aviation here in the near future. I'm going to look very carefully at trying to bring the Association of Naval Aviation and the Tailhook Association together, so we will have only one kind of professional organization in naval aviation. I think we're diluting our resources by having a separate magazine. They have *The Hook* magazine; we have the *Wings of Gold*, and each sponsors an annual meeting. I think we can better use our talent and resources if we look at something like merging those two organizations and then establishing a

---

[*] R&R – rest and recreation.

closer linkage to the Naval Aviation Museum Foundation organization down in Pensacola.*

Paul Stillwell: Of course, some of the people in Tailhook look down their noses at anybody who doesn't fly a carrier plane.

Admiral Lawrence: I don't think we can justify or condone that type of thinking anymore, because everybody in naval aviation has to be on the team. But the point is that Tailhook Association spends a lot of money for its magazine. They're talking about now building a separate headquarters. I think we could serve naval aviation better if we merged the organizations.

Paul Stillwell: Well, you could probably help overcome some of that idea that VP people, for example, are second-class citizens.

Admiral Lawrence: Yes, that's right.

But, anyway, I worked hard those three years in OP-05. Every day was basically a standard 12-hour day type of operation. I traveled but not a great deal. Because of the imperatives of meeting all the budget requirements in Washington under the PPBS system, you just couldn't afford to get out of town very much. The first two years I was OP-15, the director of OP-51, the director of the Aircraft Program Division, and my last year I was the OP-05B, which is the number-two guy. Those tours really gave me a good foundation in the ways of the Pentagon and Washington. But when I went over to the Naval Academy, I was happy to leave.

Paul Stillwell: Well, it sounds like troubleshooter is a good characterization of those first

---

* Admiral Lawrence's plan did not come to fruition. Following the Tailhook Association's September 1991 convention in Las Vegas—some months after this interview—a number of women complained of being mistreated by naval officers in attendance. There were other allegations of inappropriate behavior. A long, largely inconclusive investigation followed. The upshot was damage to the Navy's overall reputation and to that of naval aviation in particular. On 29 October 1991, the month following the convention in Las Vegas, the Department of the Navy ended all official ties with the Tailhook Association. The ties were restored on 19 January 1999.

two years.

Admiral Lawrence: Yes. Well, in most of your jobs in the Pentagon, you're a problem-solver. There's just a limited amount of effort that a flag officer can apply. I mean, in having these broad responsibilities, you really devote yourself principally to problem-solving.

Paul Stillwell: Management by exception.

Admiral Lawrence: Yes, that's right. Then you're in there trying to make the management matrix work, because you see the importance of what I call lateral communication in Washington. One of your responsibilities as a flag officer is to make sure the people under you are having lateral communication with the other organizations, like the Naval Air Systems Command, the Supply Systems Command, the Aviation Supply Office. Because you simply can't get involved in everything, you have to make your people do all the necessary coordination. All I did with the three years in Washington was basically trying to get things back on the track that were off the track.

Paul Stillwell: How well did your daughter Wendy adjust to that environment in the Washington area?

Admiral Lawrence: Oh, she really was happy, because she got to spend two years—her junior and senior years—in the same high school, and that was good for her. Then my last year at the Pentagon, she came over to have her plebe year at the Naval Academy. So she enjoyed living in Alexandria and going to Fort Hunt High School.

Paul Stillwell: Please describe the process of getting a daughter into the Naval Academy. That was certainly a novelty at that point.[*]

---

[*] Women were first admitted to the Naval Academy as midshipmen in the summer of 1976, the year the other federal service academies admitted women cadets. Wendy Lawrence entered in the summer of 1977.

Admiral Lawrence: Well, I had no idea about her going to the Naval Academy. All the plans had been made for her to go to William and Mary, and she'd applied and had been accepted at William and Mary.

Then, I guess around January or February, she brought up the Naval Academy—that the previous year they had introduced women, and this was the second year. She asked me what I thought about the Naval Academy. And, of course, Diane was really supportive of this. Being a professional woman, she was always looking at expanding the role of women. I always had a lot of reservations, because I had seen how opposed the senior leadership of the military was to women going to the service academies.

Admiral McKee, who was the superintendent, was my classmate.[*] He really spoke out against it. Of course, once it was directed, he turned to in order to make it viable. But I just felt that it would not be a wholesome experience for my daughter. I said, "Gee, you're coming into an environment where the senior leadership of the Navy's opposed to it, and you're just such a small number of women. I'm just afraid it won't be a viable experience for you."

But I came over and I talked to some of the women who were here; I talked to Admiral McKee and other people, and they convinced me they were really trying to make it work. And these young women I talked to seemed to be challenged. Diane was very, very supportive. So finally, I said, "Okay, if you want to go, I'll give my support." So she applied for a Presidential appointment—since her father was a career officer—and was accepted. She just basically sent in her application. She had been a straight-A student. She was the valedictorian of her class, she was an athlete, and her SAT scores were really high. So I felt she would probably be pretty competitive. But it was not very difficult. All we did was really, basically, make out the application, but, as I say, I had a lot of reservations about it.

Paul Stillwell: Did your first wife make any input to the process?

---

[*] Rear Admiral Kinnaird R. McKee, USN, served as Superintendent of the Naval Academy from August 1975 to August 1978.

Admiral Lawrence: No, and, of course, her grandfather was a Naval Academy graduate. We basically handled it ourselves.

Once she was a midshipman, she really ate it up from the day one. In fact, I remember when she was a plebe, she wrote a letter home one time telling what fun they had, the fun and games they were doing in Bancroft Hall, and described all the uniform races and the various things they were doing. The next time I saw her, I said, "Boy, something must be wrong with you if you're enjoying plebe summer." [Laughter] But she really enjoyed almost every minute of her time here at the Naval Academy. So that made me feel good that we'd really done the right thing. It was a lot of fun watching her go through her plebe year.

Paul Stillwell: Well, you certainly didn't push her into it.

Admiral Lawrence: No, not at all. And her grandfather didn't at all either. Boy, he was adamantly opposed to women at the Naval Academy, like most of the old-timers were.

Paul Stillwell: Not just her, but all of them.

Admiral Lawrence: All of them. And then, boy, he thought it was really a bummer that she wanted to go. But once she got here, he became her most ardent supporter. But that's so typical—the people who become the most ardent supporters are the fathers and grandfathers whose daughters are admitted to the academy. They do a complete flip-flop.

Well, I think that might be a good place to knock off and then the next time I can go into my years as superintendent here.

Paul Stillwell: All right. Well, I know that will be interesting. I look forward to it.

Interview Number 14 with Vice Admiral William P. Lawrence, U.S. Navy (Retired)
Place: U.S. Naval Institute, Annapolis, Maryland
Date: Wednesday, 26 December 1990

Paul Stillwell: Happy day after Christmas, Admiral. We're ready to resume the narrative at 1978, when you came to the Naval Academy as superintendent. I'd be interested in some of the factors that led to your selection, as far as you were informed of them.

Admiral Lawrence: Well, I came over in August of 1978, and the CNOs changed around 1 July of 1978.[*] At that time, I was just completing three years in OP-05 at the Pentagon, and I guess it was pretty clear that I wouldn't go out and get a carrier group. Admiral Holloway, who was the CNO, and Admiral Hayward both pretty much held the line that a person who did not have a previous carrier command wouldn't get a carrier group. So I pretty much had given up the thought that I would go back to sea. But I had no idea what my next assignment would be. My classmate, Admiral McKee, was the superintendent of the Naval Academy, and he was coming up on the end of his third year here in 1978.[†]

Then, suddenly, in the spring of 1978, it was announced that Admiral McKee was being promoted to three stars and was going to stay here for another year. I took note of that, but I wasn't even thinking that I would be considered for the Naval Academy. It had not even entered my mind to be superintendent of the Naval Academy.

But, anyway, Admiral Hayward took over, and then shortly after that, he had a party on his barge. He lived in the Washington Navy Yard, and he used to take his barge out on the Anacostia River and down the Potomac. So he invited me to go on one of those. He got me off to the side, and he said, "Look, I very much want to promote you to three stars. But I just don't have the available numbers and positions right now to do that. I plan to send you over to be superintendent of the Naval Academy."

I said, "Well, that's wonderful. I'd really enjoy doing that." It turned out

---
[*] Admiral Thomas B. Hayward, USN, served as Chief of Naval Operations from 1 July 1978 to 30 June 1982. His oral history is in the Naval Institute collection.
[†] Rear Admiral Kinnaird R. McKee, USN, served as superintendent of the Naval Academy from August 1975 to August 1978.

that when Admiral McKee was finishing up his third year anticipating orders, the Chief of Naval Personnel, Admiral Watkins, was trying to get a nuclear-qualified aviation admiral to come over as superintendent of the Naval Academy.* But the Secretary of the Navy, Graham Claytor, did not want this to happen, because he felt that it would give Admiral Rickover inordinate influence at the academy.† So Secretary Graham Claytor would not approve this nuclear-qualified aviation admiral coming over here.

Paul Stillwell: Why was aviation supposed to be part of it, rather than a submariner.

Admiral Lawrence: Well, they felt that they had to have another warfare community come over here. So they picked a former commanding officer of a nuclear carrier—who was a rear admiral at this time—as the guy who was going to succeed McKee. Admiral Watkins wanted to have a nuclear-qualified officer over here, because he felt that he would encourage more midshipmen to go into the nuclear program. At that time, they just hadn't made any progress increasing the accessions in the nuclear program while Admiral McKee was here.

Anyway, Secretary Claytor just said, "I refuse to do it." So, as solution to the problem, they decided to keep McKee another year. McKee resisted this; to mollify him, they promoted him to his third star.

Then Hayward came in and said, "I don't want to keep a guy over there for another year, and I don't want to waste a three-star on the academy, because I need a three-star out in other places in the Navy." So he talked it over with Claytor. Hayward, of course, knew me from the previous years, and so he picked me to be the superintendent.

---

* Vice Admiral James D. Watkins, USN, served as Chief of Naval Personnel from 10 April 1975 to 21 July 1978.
† W. Graham Claytor Jr., served as Secretary of the Navy from 14 February 1977 to 24 August 1979.
Hyman G. Rickover was considered the father of the nuclear Navy. He ran the U.S. Navy's nuclear-power program for many years, from 1948 until he eventually left active duty in 1982 with the rank of four-star admiral on the retired list. Rickover Hall at the Naval Academy is named in his honor, as is the nuclear-powered attack submarine *Hyman G. Rickover* (SSN-709), which was commissioned 21 July 1984.

Paul Stillwell: What had been your tie with him previously?

Admiral Lawrence: We had been test pilots together down at the Naval Air Test Center at Patuxent River back in '56. That's where we initially met. Then we were both in the flight test division together. We lived near each other in Navy housing over in Solomons, a little housing complex across the Patuxent River at the Naval Air Test Center.

Paul Stillwell: Well, he was also part of that astronaut screening.

Admiral Lawrence: Yes, that's right. He and I were part of the group that went through the screening of the astronauts.

I think he felt I was well qualified to go over and be superintendent. So he just, I guess, told Admiral Watkins, "This is the way it's going to be. We don't have to send a nuclear-qualified guy." This also made Admiral McKee happy, because McKee told me he had proposed my name as his relief.

So on relatively short notice, I did come over here to be the superintendent. Admiral McKee was then assigned to go out and be Commander Third Fleet in the Pacific.* Of course, I was happy about coming over here to be superintendent, because I felt I could make a good contribution and knew I would very much enjoy that job.

Paul Stillwell: Had you ever written down an agenda of things you might do if you got the job?

Admiral Lawrence: No. For some reason, I just never seriously thought I would be sent over here. I just don't know why I had discounted the possibility. The other reason it made me happy was because my daughter Wendy was just completing her plebe year. I remember telling her about this. She had gone on her summer cruise and then had gone over for a tour of the British Isles. I met her at the airport when she flew back from England and said, "I just wanted to tell you that I'm going over to be superintendent of the Naval Academy."

---

* Vice Admiral McKee commanded the Third Fleet from September 1978 to October 1979.

She said, "Oh, no." [Laughter] Because she knew that it was going to make her life a lot more difficult.

Paul Stillwell: Did it, in fact, make it more difficult?

Admiral Lawrence: No, it turned out to be a wonderful family experience, because she handled it well. Of course, I never, ever tried to call attention to the fact that my daughter was here. She was pretty well respected as a mid, and I think that reduced the amount of kidding she received. She never tried to ever take advantage of it. Several professors told me that they had her in their classes and didn't even realize she was the superintendent's daughter, because she tried to keep a very low profile.

Diane and I really had to scramble around to get ready to come over here. We had the change of command in the latter part of August, but the McKees needed a few more days after the change of command to finally move out of their quarters. So we stayed in our house over in Alexandria, which we had arranged to rent while we were in Annapolis. The first Sunday after I had taken over as superintendent, we were still moving over from Alexandria.

On that Sunday morning, my wife and I drove over with a van with all sorts of boxes and moved them into the superintendent's house. And we decided that we were going over to chapel service. This was the first time I attended chapel in my official capacity as superintendent. I knew Wendy was serving as a chapel usher, and I looked forward to seeing her. So Diane and I decided we'd go over about 20 minutes till 11:00, because we were kind of tired. We wanted to sit there and just enjoy the music and the beauty of the chapel. Of course, I was in uniform. We went up the chapel steps, and I saw my daughter right at the door with her white gloves on like the ushers wear. She said, "Stop, you can't come in."

I said, "What do you mean?"

She said, "You're too early. You're supposed to get here about two minutes till 11:00 and lead the procession at the beginning of chapel. Nobody's ready, the choir's not ready, the chapel's not ready. So just go walk around the yard and come back." The midshipmen who were with her didn't realize she was talking to her father, and they just about had apoplexy. [Laughter]

I said, "Well, okay." So Diane and I went out and walked around the yard a while, and then we came back at about two minutes till 11:00. Sure enough, we led the procession down there and sat in the superintendent's pew. Then a few minutes later, I noticed a figure in a blue uniform sliding down the pew. There's a little rail that partitions off the superintendent's pew, and so Wendy had to slip under that. She was whispering all these things into my wife's ear. I saw her leave, and then she came back again. I turned to Diane and said, "What's going on?"

She said, "Wendy's giving us instructions on what you're supposed to do when you leave." [Laughter] The reason she had to go out and come back was that she'd been telling my wife that at a certain time in the service the ushers would come and take us out.

Diane asked, "Well, is it before the postlude or after the postlude?"

Wendy said, "Oh, I'll have to check it." So she came back.

We went over to the quarters after it the service was over. She came walking in, and here was this new youngster at the Naval Academy.* She said, "I can't believe it." "You've been here for a week and nobody's briefed you on how to act in the chapel." [Laughter]

I said, "Young lady, get this straight. You can tell this to the chaplains and everybody. This is one superintendent who's going to get to that chapel when he darn well pleases, and I'm not going to lead a procession down the aisle. I'm going to come over there when I feel like it. You tell them that, okay?" So that was the last time I led the procession down. I left that up to the chaplains, not the superintendent. That's one of our favorite family stories.

Paul Stillwell: What overall observations do you have of the role of the chapel and the chaplains in the life of the Naval Academy?

---

* In this context, "youngster" refers to a midshipman's second year at the Naval Academy.

Admiral Lawrence: Oh, they're certainly really important. Actually, since we've done away with mandatory chapel, there really isn't a large number of midshipmen who attend chapel, and I can understand it. The midshipmen are so busy and really pressed for time that they look forward to Sunday morning as a free time. And, of course, many of the upper classmen are off on weekends. The ones who have a strong church identification often go to a church of their own denomination out in town. So you really don't get a large number of midshipmen at church.

The real impact of the chaplains is in their counseling. I've found that if midshipmen have a problem, they often go to the chaplain and sit down for advice and counsel more than to anybody else. So the chaplains' influence is probably greater outside of the formal church services on Sunday morning. Also, they support Sunday school programs and other religious groups that are here, like the Fellowship of Christian Athletes, the Navigators, and things like that. They have a very important influence here.

Paul Stillwell: Well, they can provide a sympathetic ear when that's very much needed.

Admiral Lawrence: That's a very important role for them and fills a need for midshipmen. I found if I really wanted to get the pulse of the academy, I would ask the senior Protestant and the senior Catholic chaplain, because they picked up a tremendous amount in their counseling. I often got just the two senior chaplains in to have them give me their impressions of a lot of things. It was valuable for me.

The other thing is that I always felt it was important to have a black chaplain at the Naval Academy. The black midshipmen, of course, are completely integrated in the academy, but they need some special help here, because many of them don't have strong academic preparation, and they're kind of sensitive as to how they'll be accepted in the military. They need a role model or figure here whom they can look up to. The chaplain is often the one who can fill that role. So the whole time I was here, I insisted that we have a black chaplain. So we established that as a tradition. So that's one facet of the role of the chaplain. And, of course, now we even have a Jewish chaplain.

Paul Stillwell: Do you remember examples of the kinds of feedback you received from the chaplains?

Admiral Lawrence: Well, when I initially arrived here, one of the first things I asked in my turnover was, "What's the drug situation here?" Because drugs were starting to build up as a problem out in the fleet.

I was told, "Ah, there's no drug problem here at all." Well, after I'd been here about two or three months, I just started getting fragmentary reports from the NIS and other sources that some were midshipmen involved with the drugs.[*]

This was one area I got the chaplains in. I said, "What's your view on this? Do you think that we have a drug problem here?" And I called them in and asked them, "How do you feel racial integration is working here? What's your view on that?" These are typical types of issues that I would get their opinion on. I made it very clear to the both of the senior chaplains—Catholic and Protestant—that when they were with me, they could let their hair down. They didn't want to have to worry about giving me bad news, or some unfavorable observation or opinion on their part, because I really wanted their frank views.

Paul Stillwell: What were the things you found out on those two topics—race and drugs?

Admiral Lawrence: Well, on the drug issue, it became increasingly apparent to me that midshipmen had some involvement. So after I'd been here about five or six months, I got together all the senior leadership and said, "Look, contrary to what I've been told when I got here, I think we have to have a more aggressive anti-drug program." There was no drug-abuse education when I got here; no training was given the midshipmen. The attitude was that midshipmen were above this. Their caliber was such that they would not be involved in drugs. So I said, "Using NIS and our own capability, we're going to dig into this."

Well, unfortunately, by the time all these investigative efforts came to fruition, graduation week in 1979 was just starting. This report came to me that there were

---

[*] NIS – Naval Investigative Service.

indications 18 first classmen were involved in drugs. The first decision I had to make was whether to withhold them from graduation while we completed this investigation. I made the decision, "Yes, we're going to withhold them from graduation."

So I called up the Vice Chief of Naval Operations, who at that time was Admiral Bob Long.* I said, "This is what I found, and this is what I'm going to do. I recommend that this information be provided to the Secretary of the Navy very quickly because we're going to get some repercussions on this."

Sure enough, the parents contacted their congressmen, and congressmen started pinging on the Secretary of the Navy. Boy, I really was so fortunate, Secretary Claytor said, "I support Admiral Lawrence. If that's what he feels is the right thing, I support him." Because he was getting all sorts of flak.

Paul Stillwell: What was the upshot of that?

Admiral Lawrence: Well, then we realized we had to go into a thorough conduct investigation. Basically, the midshipmen were charged with this, and we had to do what we call an Article 32 investigation.† So I called the Judge Advocate General of the Navy and I said, "Look, my JAG resources over here are overtaxed." So he sent me over a commander, JAG officer, to assist my own JAG officer and his assistant in prosecuting this whole thing.

After about a month, we got enough information that we could bring the case to completion. We just simply did not have enough evidence to obtain a conviction on more than two. So we separated those two and then had a late graduation for the 18. We did it in a really formal manner, and I got up and treated them just like nothing had happened, because they'd been essentially acquitted.

But it was a worthwhile thing to go through this, because it sent some signals to the rest of the brigade. After that we never had a serious drug problem. That was really an agonizing thing to go through, but I felt we simply had to do it. I had no other alternative, because I was getting enough information that convinced me there was some

---

* Admiral Robert L. J. Long, USN, served as Vice Chief of Naval Operations from July 1977 to September 1979. His oral history is in the Naval Institute collection.
† This refers to Article 32 of the Uniform Code of Military Justice.

drug involvement, so we had to dig into it and get it all out in the open. Then we went to the media right away and gave them a statement. And, really, it got minimal play in the media. That's why I keep telling people here that the best thing you can do when you have something you know is going to be of media interest is *you* make the contact with the media. You write the statement and give it to them, and half the time they'll print it."

The reason the Naval Academy had so darn much problem with this woman chained to the toilet was that they wouldn't put anything out.[*] It leaked to the press and then it was "Katie, bar the door."

Paul Stillwell: What was the source of your information on this drug use?

Admiral Lawrence: NIS. There would just be some fragmentary information about indications of midshipmen purchasing drugs from some source in town. Most of it was just marijuana; it was not hard drugs. But midshipmen were buying marijuana and then bringing it into Bancroft Hall. It really was concentrated principally in one company. There were some first classmen in that one company who really were in town and had learned about the contacts and sources. I tell you, it really took a tremendous amount of time and effort on my part and the JAGs' parts, but I felt we simply had to go through it. I told Admiral Hayward at that time, "You know, if midshipmen are involved in drugs, I'm sure that the people out in the fleet are very much involved in drugs." But I couldn't get him focused on the fact that drugs could be a real problem in the fleet. Just four months after that, the DoD survey came out that said 48% of the Navy enlisted personal, E-4 and below, admitted drugs on their confidential DoD survey.[†]

Paul Stillwell: "Pride and professionalism."[‡]

---

[*] Midshipman Gwen Marie Dreyer, USN, was handcuffed to a urinal in the Naval Academy dormitory, Bancroft Hall, on 8 December 1989. She resigned from the academy in May 1990. In July 1990, as the new Chief of Naval Operations, Admiral Frank Kelso, USN, ordered an investigation of discipline at the academy. The incident was fresh in mind, because it happened just a year before this interview.
[†] E-4 is an enlisted pay grade, petty officer third class.
[‡] Admiral Hayward subsequently initiated a strong anti-drug program and coupled it with the term "Pride and professionalism."

Admiral Lawrence: That's right. I told Admiral Hayward this when we were together at a football game in the fall of 1979, when we finally got all this cleaned up over here. I said, "If we have a problem with midshipmen, who are the very best in American society, I know we've got a problem out in the fleet." But he was focused on so many other things, and it wasn't until that confidential survey came out that the leadership of the Navy got going. But as a result of that, we put in very extensive drug abuse education program here at the academy. When I got here, nothing was done at all in the area of drugs, which surprised me. So these were the types of things I would talk to the chaplains about.

Another thing taught me a good lesson, and it happened very early in my tenure, after I'd been here only about a month. On a Sunday morning, the day after a football game, the commandant, Captain Jack Darby, called me up and said, "I'd like to come over and talk to you."[*]

I said to myself, "The commandant doesn't normally come over on Sunday morning for some polite chitchat." Anyway, he came over and he told me about a case of rape alleged by a plebe woman. She had gone to a company tailgate party, and apparently they served some beer or something; this was before the 21-year-old alcohol law. She got a little bit inebriated. I guess maybe she just never had much to drink before. So this chivalrous first classman said, "Well, I'll take her back to the Bancroft Hall." When they got in Bancroft Hall, they ended up in bed together; it was apparently in his room. Then she got up, went to her room, and told her roommates that she had been raped. So this was reported up to the officer of the day. Then the commandant came over the very next morning to tell me about it.

So then I went to general quarters. I said, "Look, rape is bad stuff. We simply have to proceed on the basis that this is a court-martial offense."

The first thing I did was to designate Captain Frank Donovan—who's now a three-star admiral and was then the deputy commandant—to be the individual to talk to her parents.[†] The reason I picked him was because he was Catholic, and this young

---

[*] Captain Jack N. Darby, USN, was the Naval Academy's commandant of midshipmen in 1978-1979.
[†] Captain Francis R. Donovan, USN.

woman was Catholic. She'd gone to a Catholic girls' school and had a very sheltered life. So it was obvious she just had gotten into a situation she didn't know how to handle.

Paul Stillwell: She didn't have practice at saying no.

Admiral Lawrence: No. So I got Frank Donovan, and I said, "You contact those parents and you maintain a very close dialogue with them about what's going on and what happened, because we have to be in close communication with them."

Then the other thing I did was say, "Okay, we prepare a statement for the press."

Everybody said, "Oh, you shouldn't do that."

I said, "Look, you just have to learn that you bite the bullet in cases like this, and you go to press." So we went out to the Annapolis *Capital* about this, and they didn't even print it. But, see, that set a pattern with them of knowing that we were completely open, and that we weren't ever going to try to hide things. It did finally come out in the media several months later, but it never got any sensational news coverage. You're far better off to put the information out than you are if you just sit back and hope it doesn't come out, because it probably will. That's probably how they got killed in the media on this chaining incident.

Paul Stillwell: What was the outcome of that case?

Admiral Lawrence: Well, I convened an Article 32, to go to court-martial. Because we had had this real close discussion, and Frank Donovan established such rapport with the parents and they had such respect for him, after about two weeks they came to us and said, "We do not want our daughter to testify; she does not want to testify." So we had no case, and so we terminated the Article 32, terminated the possible court-martial, and then punished this first class midshipman. We really slapped him hard under the conduct system. We gave this young woman some demerits too, because her conduct was not above reproach itself since she got inebriated. But the case died.

But an interesting sidelight to that is that when I was Commander Third Fleet, about three years later, I went out to visit the cruiser USS *Fox*. Captain Les Palmer, who later on came back here to be commandant, was then the skipper.* I came in by helicopter and landed on the fantail. He met me and said, "I'd like to take you up on the bridge." So I walked up there, and he said, "I'd like to introduce you to my officer of the deck." Well, he looked at me and I looked at him, and the wheels started spinning. The OOD turned out to be this former first classman who was involved in the rape charge. I didn't say anything to indicate I remembered this incident, but later on I was talking to Les Palmer, and I said, "Tell me, what kind of an officer is that officer of the deck?"

He said, "The best officer I've got aboard, the best officer of the deck that I have on this ship."

So I said to myself, "That guy had the entire first class year to study the rules of the road, because he didn't get any weekend liberty after that fall of his first class year. [Laughter]

Throughout the history of the Naval Academy, some of the kids who get into some of the worst conduct offenses turn out to be pretty decent officers.

Paul Stillwell: Did Palmer know the background, or did he just introduce the officer because he was so good?

Admiral Lawrence: No, he just wanted to introduce me to the officer of the deck of the ship at that time. I never told Palmer. It was just between that midshipman and me, because we had some good sessions in my office about his conduct.

Paul Stillwell: The sessions that you had with him would also send a message about how women should be treated.

Admiral Lawrence: Oh, yes. But that was a very sensitive issue that took very special handling. And that established the practice and the precedent that with every serious midshipman conduct case, we always went to the parents right away. Either the commandant did it or the deputy commandant.

---

* Captain Leslie N. Palmer, USN, commanded the guided missile cruiser *Fox* (CG-33) from March 1980 to April 1982.

Any time anything sensitive with a midshipman happened at the academy, I knew about it immediately. I told the commandant, "Look, that has to be the case, because the potential for news, unfavorable to the academy, the national coverage, that we're so highly visible here, that anything newsworthy is going to get into the national media." So I had as a standard practice that I find out right away. The commandant, the JAG, the public affairs officer, and I all put our heads together. We mapped out a strategy on the best way to handle it.

Paul Stillwell: Was Wendy able to keep you informed on possible things also?

Admiral Lawrence: No. I never, ever used her for that purpose at all. Sometimes we'd have some philosophical discussions. But I would never discuss anything sensitive like that.

Paul Stillwell: That would put her in an awkward position if she were perceived as a stool pigeon.

Admiral Lawrence: That's right. But she was valuable to me, in the sense that midshipmen would often come over to my house. Because she was a female, we'd get a lot of women midshipmen in the house at any one time. Often, when they weren't aware of it, I would listen to them talk. I could just tell by the nature of their conversation, and the fact that they would laugh about this and cut up, that women weren't really oppressed over there, because they were having fun about a lot of things. So that was comforting to me to have midshipmen in my house and hearing them just talk among themselves. That's the best way to find out from midshipmen how things are. Never ask them a direct question, because many won't give you the right answer. Some of them will.

When my wife and I moved in, she noticed that most of the upper level of the superintendent's house was just used for storage. So she cleaned out all the bedrooms up there and got just simple beds from other places here at the academy and set up several bedrooms in the upper level. Then she made them available to midshipmen's dates to stay on weekends. She had a little ledger book that midshipmen could call over, and she'd just say, "Okay, I've got a three-bedroom on this night." And she'd write the name in the little ledger book. The midshipmen initially couldn't believe this would be the case, so it took a while for them to understand they could keep their drags at the superintendent's house. But, finally, they did, and so every weekend, we had the house filled with midshipmen and their drags.* Since I was so busy going around to the various events, I didn't have all that much interface with them. But that was a good thing to do, because it helped us really keep our finger on the pulse of midshipman thinking.

Some of those kids who kept drags at our house stayed very close with us and now have married and have families. So that was a very pleasant aspect of it. It got to be interesting because sometimes you'd get to know these midshipmen just from seeing them every weekend. Diane and I would find that we'd start saying to each other, "Well, gee, we don't think she's right for him." [Laughter] And I'd say, "Can you imagine if a midshipman ever knew that the superintendent and his wife were critiquing his date?"

I remember the first time a female midshipman called over and had a male date. Diane said, "Gosh, what are we going to do if we put that male up there with all those women?"

I said, "Hey, let them work it out. They'll figure out how to make it happen, who gets into the bathroom at certain times. Don't get involved in things like that." So they did; they worked it out.

The other thing that she did was to minimize the labor involved. She put in replacement bed linens, so on the weekends they had to remake the beds and she had a closet where they would put soiled towels and all that. So it worked out beautifully. It turned out to be a really wonderful thing. It was good to have midshipmen in your house on the weekends. It was valuable to me, because the best way you can learn about midshipman attitudes and morale and all that is to hear them just talking among themselves.

But, anyway, although it was traumatic to have to go through that alleged rape case and that drug situation, it really taught me some good lessons that became standard practices here.

---

* "Drag" is a slang term from many years ago for a midshipman's date. It is also used in the verb form, meaning "to date."

In my tenure as superintendent, one of the biggest challenges was media relations. You simply had to have a very skillful capability for handling some of the public affairs aspects of what went on. Even though I took a lot of heat from the Annapolis *Capital*, that's just their propensity, because they figure that's going to help them sell newspapers. But I still had very good rapport with Phil Merrill, the publisher. When something very serious happened here, I'd go to him right away and say, "Look, Phil, we've had this situation here. It's not indicative of a serious problem at the academy. But on the surface, it appears to—" That really helped set the tone of whatever article appeared. And, of course, many times we might just write the statement. Things like that that kept it from being blown into the national media, because anything that gets into the Annapolis *Capital*, any sensationalistic tone, will probably get in *The Washington Post* and the *Baltimore Sun*. Then the next thing, AP and UPI would pick it up, and it would be going to be all over the damn country.[*]

I remember one time we had a case of group sex. It involved a young woman—I think a youngster, second year—who had not done well at the academy. We probably made a mistake in admitting her, and she had submitted her resignation. But she had a knee injury, so rather than just letting her go right away, they kept her here while resolving the physical problem. She was basically not going to class, and she got bored. So one night on a weekend, she decided to have a little farewell party for her male buddies in the company. It turned out it was group-sex incident. Two of the first classmen had come in pretty inebriated. They got involved in group sex with her, and they brought in some other guys. One guy went out and took the photos of this.

That could have really been a national sensation, but I learned about it right away and went right to the Annapolis *Capital* with a statement and to *The Washington Post*. The thing got in the papers and died within a couple days. So that's just the way you have to handle them here. If the people at the Annapolis *Capital* get their noses out of joint, because they feel you didn't tell them, they'll just beat you to death. That's, unfortunately, what happened here this last year.[†]

---

[*] AP, Associated Press, and UPI, United Press International, were the major wire services for the media.
[†] This is a reference to the urinal incident mentioned earlier.

I used to tell everybody that my definition of euphoria, as superintendent of the Naval Academy, was when your executive assistant walked in and said, "Sir, the staff judge advocate and the public affairs officer need to talk to you."

So I said, "Oh, God, what's this one?" [Laughter]

Anyway, that gives you some examples of the approach I took to being superintendent, because it was very apparent to me right away that one of my biggest responsibilities here was media relations, to project the right image of the academy. I knew there were going to be times when we'd take the hits. So I was always working to get money in the bank for the media. Anything good about midshipmen, boy, I pushed it into the press to counteract those few times that you got some bad press. And, inevitably, you're going to get bad press, because we're so highly visible, and people expect such a high standard here.

But, anyway, just to go on with that first year, I was really fortunate that when I arrived, 1978 was the year George Welsh hit the peak in his football reign here.* That fall, we were 7 and 0 after the first seven games. I said, "My God, I can't believe we're really doing that well in football." At homecoming, we upset Pitt, which was nationally ranked; we beat them 21 to 11. So I knew we really had something good going for us that season.

Then, unfortunately, we got beat by Notre Dame out in Cleveland, but I kind of expected that because they had a really good team, and Joe Montana was the quarterback.† The next game we played was against Syracuse, which I really thought we should have beaten, but we lost, 20-17. Then we played Florida State, and I expected them to beat us, because Florida State's always strong. We beat Army in the last game of the regular season. If we could have beaten Syracuse and ended up 9 and 2, we would have gone to a good bowl, the Gator Bowl or something like that. But we ended up 8-3, and we went out to play in the inaugural Holiday Bowl. We beat BYU in that game, a

---

* George T. Welsh was the Naval Academy's head football coach for the 1973 through 1981 seasons. The team's overall record in those years was 55-46-1, a percentage of .544.
† Montana went on to a highly successful career with the San Francisco 49ers in the National Football League and was elected to the Pro Football Hall of Fame.

really stunning upset, 23 to 16.*

Paul Stillwell: Did athletics, and particularly football, play as important a role when you were superintendent, as when you were a midshipman?

Admiral Lawrence: Yes, they did.

Football is a big source of spirit here at the academy. It always has been, and if you're winning, of course, it really has a very favorable influence on the midshipmen. I feel very strongly that if the Naval Academy is going to compete in intercollegiate athletics, we should strive to do as well as we possibly can, because of our national image. I think people look to the performance of the service academies on the athletic field, particularly football field, to get impressions about the school. If you play credible football, this is a comforting thing to the national public that the academies are producing individuals who have the right stuff.

I don't think we should go overboard to have strong football teams here. We should completely play by the rules and observe recruiting standards and all that, and bring in athletes who can succeed in the total program. But I think it's important we have credible programs and that we not be looked upon as unfavorably in the way we play intercollegiate sports. So that's why I was happy that we really had a very strong football program when I came here in 1978. I also was convinced that we were, in fact, following a tradition here producing student athletes, because all of our football players were, I felt, good, solid citizens. I got to know them pretty well, and I didn't see anybody on the team whom I felt was below our standards here at the academy. Sure, a lot of them weren't scholars, but they all handled themselves okay in the total program.

Paul Stillwell: Well, it became more and more difficult to compete, because the nature of collegiate football had changed so much, to almost quasi-professional status. Other schools let in people who clearly were not qualified as students.

Admiral Lawrence: That's true, and that's why we simply had to lighten our schedule here, because we just couldn't consistently compete against the really top Division I

---
* BYU – Brigham Young University.

teams. So that's why I support the fact that we took teams like Pittsburgh and Syracuse off our schedule, because we just can't consistently maintain competitiveness with that type of team.

Anyway, I had the benefit of three fine football seasons when I was here: 8 and 3 the first year, 7 and 4 the second year, and 8 and 3 the third year. Then we went to bowl games at the end of my first and my third years here. We won the bowl game in '78, but we lost the one in 1980, against Houston.

Paul Stillwell: How much dealing did you have of Bo Coppedge over that time?[*]

Admiral Lawrence: He and I worked very, very closely together in the athletic program. The Naval Academy organization is somewhat unique in comparison to those at other institutions. The superintendent did not have a chief of staff or a deputy to whom the subordinates answer and deal. Several key executives report directly to the superintendent: the academic dean, the director of athletics, the dean of admissions, the deputy for operations, the deputy for management, and the CO of the naval station. All of them deal essentially directly with the superintendent.

A lot of people said, "Well, this is organizationally unsound to have all these top-level executives reporting directly to the boss. But I found that the system worked well. Admiral Calvert had established this back in the 1970-71 time frame.[†] I thought it was good, and I supported it. Of course, it keeps the top guy pretty busy, but if you have a very competent executive assistant, he and you working together can really administer that type of a command arrangement pretty effectively. I made it very clear to those top executives, like Bo Coppedge, director of athletics, and the academic dean, and the dean of admissions—boy, if they wanted to see me, I was immediately accessible.

I contrasted that to West Point, which had so much more layering. They had a chief of staff and a deputy superintendent. The director of athletics at West Point told Bo Coppedge one time that it took him about two weeks to get on the superintendent's

---

[*] Captain John O. Coppedge, USN, became the Naval Academy's director of athletics in 1968. He retired from active duty in June 1970, then remained in the job in civilian status until his retirement in 1988.
[†] Rear Admiral/Vice Admiral James F. Calvert, USN, served as Superintendent of the Naval Academy from 20 July 1968 to 16 June 1972.

schedule, because he had to go through all these intermediate layers. Bo Coppedge could be in my office in 10-15 minutes if he wanted to, if I was in town.

Paul Stillwell: The director operations during part of that time that was one of your fellow POWs, Captain Dick Stratton.* What do you recall about his service here?

Admiral Lawrence: Well, he did a wonderful job. He was ideally suited for that job. We did some important things while I was here. His wife had a degree in social work. With the help of Dick Stratton and his wife, and working with the CO of the naval station, we did the prototype family service center here at the naval station. That concept is now used throughout the Navy. He helped me a lot, because he's a very effective manager. He also did a lot of lecturing to midshipmen, which was very effective.

I'll give you an example of how I used him very effectively. One time we had a yacht that made a transatlantic cruise and was in the Fastnet Race over in the Irish Sea.† An unusual storm came up very suddenly and damaged a lot of sailboats that were in that race. Well, the first we learned about that freak storm was on television. I said, "My God, I've got a crew over there that's got seven midshipmen on a yacht in that race, and we don't know what the status of it is."

So I called Dick Stratton and I said, "Look, we're going to set up a crisis-management watch system here, where we, first of all, make contact with the parents of every one of those midshipmen to tell them that we've learned about this, and we're doing everything we can to find out the information concerning their son. Dick Stratton was the crisis-management team leader and really started getting people to serve on that with him. Then they started communicating with the parents and making contact as necessary to find the status of that boat.

---

* Lieutenant Commander Richard A. Stratton, USN, was shot down on 5 January 1967 while flying an A-4E Skyhawk in Attack Squadron 192 (VA-192) from the carrier *Ticonderoga* (CVA-14). He was released 4 March 1973. He retired as a captain in 1986. His oral history is in the Naval Institute collection. See also Scott Blakey, *Prisoner at War: the Survival of Commander Richard A. Stratton* (Garden City, New York: Anchor Press/Doubleday, 1978).

† In August 1979 the Naval Academy's 56-foot sloop *Alliance* was one of 303 yachts that began a 600-mile sailing race from the Isle of Wight off the coast of England to Fastnet Rock off the Irish coast. A force 10 storm hit the racers, with the result that 15 people died and five yachts sank. Only 85 boats finished the race. For details see John Rousmaniere, *Force 10: The Deadliest Storm in the History of Modern Sailing* (New York: W. W. Norton, 1980).

It so happened that my plebe at the academy, from the class of '54, was Charlie Hunter. At that time of this yacht race, he was a captain serving as the deputy for operations or something on the CinCUSNavEur staff.* So I got on the phone, and I said, "Hey, Charlie, we've got this problem. Do whatever you can to find out the status of that yacht we have there." So he called the British Coast Guard and had them do everything they could.

Charlie called me back and said, "Hey, the boat's okay; nobody's hurt. They got through it okay." So I used Dick Stratton in situations like that. That was in addition to his regular job of running the operational aspects at the academy, because the supply officer and the public works officer worked for him as the deputy for operations. So the buildings and grounds and logistics and all that came under him. It's a broad job, but because I knew he was such a talented guy, I used him in special ways. He's a good man.

Paul Stillwell: Do you want to proceed sequentially on the rest of that year, or do you want to get into some individual topics?

Admiral Lawrence: Well, I think that just about covers the key things that happened that first year.

Paul Stillwell: I'd be interested in more on the idea of women in general at the academy. They were still a novelty at that time.

Admiral Lawrence: Well, okay. That's something, of course, I really monitored very carefully, because when I got here in '78, the third class of women was coming in. That really kept my eye on all this. Of course, we were doing all sorts of special programs of indoctrination, and we had a very interesting section on sexual harassment training for midshipmen.

The other thing we did was add a role for the director of professional development, a Navy captain. We had three departments under him: the leadership and

---

* Captain Charles B. Hunter, USN, was on the staff of Commander in Chief U.S. Naval Forces Europe (CinCUSNavEur).

law department, seamanship and navigation, and the training department. Then I gave him the additional duty and called him "The Dean of Women."[*] He was recognized as the principal authority at the academy on women and kept track of everything that involved them. I did this for several reasons: one is I wanted to send a signal that I felt strongly enough about women here at the academy, that I made a Navy captain a principal point of contact and a principal cognizant official on the integration of women.

I think it was unfortunate that we let that practice die out sometime after I left, because this guy kept track of everything going on. He always had his ear to the ground. If he heard about some disciplinary offense involving women, he got into it and learned all the aspects of it. I think it served many useful purposes.

Also at the time, we had a consultant named Edie Seashore, who came here at least once a year to advise us and look into all aspects of integration of women.[†] It was going pretty well during my time here. I never had any real major problems, although there were things that, of course, I had to deal with. It was apparent to me pretty soon there was subtle harassment of women. It manifested itself in a lot of ways. One would be cruel pranks and derisive comments about women. A lot of times you'd be in a mixed male-female situation. For example, at a Forrestal lecture or other type of lectures, if a woman got up and asked a question, you'd hear kind of a hum or something like that, also I'd get feedback about pranks being played on the women.

So I said, "Look, this is something I'm just going to have to take head on." So I started to practice after I was here about six months or so, that when I got up and addressed each class, I said, "I will not tolerate at this school any group or person being treated in an undignified manner. If it happens, I'm going to be tough." I made it clear to them, boy, that that was my stand. It helped a lot to hear it from the supe, because I just knew soon after I was here that it was a natural tendency of the guys to want to subtly harass the women. It's a complex phenomenon, one that's just basic prejudice. A lot of

---

[*] The individual who served as "dean of women" was Captain Richard C. Ustick, USN.
[†] Edith Whitfield Seashore is a specialist in the discipline of organization development. She is a consultant in the field and an adjunct professor at American University. She was involved in the Naval Academy's planning in 1975 for the impending accession of female midshipmen. In 1976 briefed the first women when they arrived as plebes.
H. Michael Gelfand, *Sea Change at Annapolis: the United States Naval Academy, 1949-2000* covers the racial and gender integration of the Naval Academy.

the young kids here tend to be very macho. They resent the women being here, because it degrades the macho image of the place.

I felt it was very important that the top individual here at the school—myself—address this with the midshipmen in a very forceful manner. So I really didn't have any bad sexual harassment problems after I was here, after the initial period and I got a feel for things. One, because I had a Navy captain who was the women's advocate, and what he did and what all the other principal leaders did here, I think, helped prevent some of the unfortunate harassment. But I still had things that came up, including, of course, the alleged rape situation.

I had another situation one time where a plebe woman alleged she was raped. We dug very deeply into this thing and found that it was just a fictitious thing; she concocted this for some reason. We never could figure what her motivation was, whether she was trying to get attention or just what it was. But she actually staged a situation to make it appear like she was assaulted.

Paul Stillwell: Was a specific male identified as the culprit?

Admiral Lawrence: No, she didn't identify the male. But some male names came out through some of the investigation we went through. We ended up separating that young woman, primarily for psychological problems. The superintendent simply has to get into those types of incidents, and you orchestrate the whole thing, because it's so media-sensitive. As I used to tell everybody, "There should be no doubt in anybody's mind the public affairs officer at the U.S. Naval Academy is the superintendent. The guy who's listed as a public affairs officer is my assistant."

Of course, the summer of 1979 was interesting, because that's when women first came into leadership roles. Actually, as future first classmen, they were involved in the plebe summer. So that got all sorts of national media attention; we had to very carefully manage that.

There happened to be three women in the class of 1980 who could have been fashion models. One was Sandy Irwin, who was a very, very attractive gal.[*] Another

---

[*] Midshipman Sandra Colette Irwin, USN.

was Tina D'Ercole, and the third was Laurie Rampp.* All three had been cheerleaders. They were really good super mids, very competent people. *The Washington Post* came over and said they wanted to cover women in leadership roles in plebe summer. So I said, "Okay, here are the three women I want to have them talk to." I did this a little bit tongue-in-cheek. First of all, because I knew they were very competent midshipmen; they were good, strong leaders, but I also knew that the fact that they were so very attractive would have additional appeal. What I was trying to do was to dispel the impression that only very masculine women were attracted to the service academies, that we really did have attractive, feminine midshipmen who were very competent leaders.

Paul Stillwell: The Naval Institute did some oral history interviews with members of that class of 1980, and they almost unanimously said that they were made to feel unwelcome. So you couldn't be apparently 100% successful in your efforts. You cannot legislate attitudes.

Admiral Lawrence: No. But I wanted them to know that the top man would not tolerate any monkey business. Still, I had a constant problem. Liz Belzer was the first woman graduate; she stood about 35 in the class, and she was a so-called first classman.† She was a five-striper, and she commanded one plebe summer training division. She had a constant problem in her company with guys playing pranks on her. Finally, this came to my attention, because she and my wife were pretty close. One time when she was over at our house, she was reluctant to go back to Bancroft Hall. Diane said, "What's wrong, Liz?"

She said, "Well, I know if I go over there, these guys are going to play some prank on me."

So I called Frank Donovan, who at this time was the director of professional development. I said, "Frank, you take Liz Belzer back to Bancroft Hall, and you tell those guys that if they don't knock that stuff off, we're going to throw all of them out of here." [Chuckle] So you had to do that sort of thing.

---

* Midshipman Tina Marie D-Ercole, USN; Midshipman Lynn Mary Rampp, USN.
† Midshipman Elizabeth Ann Belzer, USN, stood number 29 of the 947 graduates in the class of 1980.

Paul Stillwell: What kinds of pranks were they playing?

Admiral Lawrence: Oh, they used to like to get pies and smash them into her face. You can't imagine how the bullying instinct in young males is a very pronounced thing, the macho-type of guys. They'd rationalize it, "Oh, we're just having fun." But they wouldn't have gone to a varsity football player and smashed a pie in his face. I mean, you just have to deal with that. You can't be subtle about it. I found that, boy, whenever I found out about things like that, I just came down with both feet. The chaining incident we had here was a manifestation of the bullying instinct. As I say, the guys have to know that senior leadership is really going to be tough on them when things like that happen. Bullying is a big factor in sexual harassment.

Paul Stillwell: Well, the definition of bullying is that you intimidate somebody who can't fight back.

Admiral Lawrence: That's right. And so, I had to fight that problem the whole time I was here. But it really wasn't a serious problem, and it tended to get better as time went on, because once we got women in the four classes, that really alleviated the situation.

Before the class of '79 graduated, I had some interesting situations. See, that was the last all-male class. In fact, on their ring they have "all male." So the word got back to me on what the class of '79 was contemplating. When they threw their hats up at graduation, they planned to have ping-pong balls in their hats—the last class with balls. So I mulled that over and I said, "What's the best way to handle that one? Should I just come head on and deal with it directly or be subtle?" So that's when I developed an approach for graduation rehearsal, which we had a day or so before graduation. It was principally for the benefit of the first classmen—how to line up and the procession up to get your diploma. So I went up at practice and gave them a little philosophical discussion. This was completely separate from what I would do at graduation, when I introduced the guest speaker. But the tenor of what I said at the rehearsal was that, "Your class has a good reputation; you've done a good job here, but I can tell you that if you do something dumb at graduation, you will put a stigma on your class that might take you many years to overcome, so don't do something at graduation your class is going to be ashamed of that you're going to have to live with for many years after that. Graduation is a happy but dignified occasion." So I figured that was the best way to get this across. But I tell you, when those hats went up at graduation . . .

Paul Stillwell: You held your breath.

Admiral Lawrence: . . . I was holding my breath, but there were no ping-pong balls there.

Paul Stillwell: Did you have any question of different standards for men and women while you were superintendent?

Admiral Lawrence: No, I never really considered this a problem. I certainly didn't do anything to try to be more lenient with women. But it was apparent to me, carefully looking at the data while I was here, that women basically tended to be more obedient than the men. They were more disciplined, and they didn't do some of the real irrational-type things that young guys would do. They tended to have fewer honor cases. I don't think it was because the system was trying to protect them. I think it was just the nature of the women. But the integration of women here was not a great problem with me.

There was one problem for me that was created by James Webb.[*] The director of the department of English and History was Colonel Frank Zimolzak, Marine Corps. In December of 1978, after I'd just been here a few months, Frank came to me and said that a graduate of the academy who was a novelist, a Marine officer named James Webb, had expressed some interest in coming here for an 18-month contract in the English classes. They were going to give him a title, writer in residence, and he would be teaching some courses. I said, "Well, gee, that's wonderful, a former graduate and everything." As a matter of fact, I met him and expressed my appreciation that he was coming.

---

[*] James H. Webb Jr., Naval Academy class of 1968, was decorated for heroism as a Marine Corps officer in combat in Vietnam in the late 1960s. He later became an author and served as Secretary of the Navy from 1 May 1987 to 23 February 1988. For details see Robert Timberg, *The Nightingale's Song* (New York: Simon & Schuster, 1995). In 2006 he was elected to the U.S. Senate from Virginia.

But then, in February, after signing a contract in December—I mean, two months later—he announced he was going to leave in June at the end of one semester, instead of staying three semesters. So I said, "Well, okay. Everybody's plans change." But the English faculty members noticed that he had a tremendous number of midshipmen coming in his office, male and female, all the time. The departmental chairman asked him, "Why are you interviewing midshipmen so much?"

He said in February that the reason that he wanted to leave because he got so much involved with midshipmen that he wasn't getting his writing done. Anyway, he left at the end of semester in June, and then a few months later, this explosive article hit the street in *Washingtonian* magazine, "Women Can't Fight."[*] He had sent me a letter saying that he had an article coming out in *Washingtonian*, and that it might appear a little bit controversial, but he wanted to let me know.

I wrote him back and said, "Don't worry about it; we can handle it." I never expected the thing would be like it was—just really sensationalistic. It contained a lot of what I considered to be incorrect information, misrepresentation of facts. It had a statement that Bancroft Hall was "a horny woman's dream" and that midshipman sex was rampant in Bancroft Hall. I knew all that was wrong, because even if midshipmen wanted to, they couldn't have sex openly in Bancroft Hall. We really had our finger on the pulse of things. We knew that there was not flagrant sexual activity in Bancroft Hall. So the article was really, really a very poor representation of the situation.

Paul Stillwell: Well, more than that, it challenged the whole premise for having women at the Naval Academy.

Admiral Lawrence: And it really was very demoralizing to women here. This book I reviewed here recently, *In the Men's House*, I found out it was also demoralizing the women at West Point; it was just not the Naval Academy.[†]

So it really upset me. I felt that Jim Webb really, in my opinion, acted very dishonorably, to come to the academy on the premise of staying here 18 months, and then

---

[*] James Webb, "Women Can't Fight," *Washingtonian*, November 1979, pages 144-148, 273-282. For Lawrence's follow-up letter to the editor and Webb's response, see January the 1980 issue, pages 19-29.
[†] Carol Barkalow, with Andrea Raab, *In the Men's House: an Inside Account of Life in the Army by One of West Point's First Female Graduates* (New York: Poseidon Press, 1990).

making a decision to leave after two months. That really indicated to me he had no desire ever to stay here the full 18 months. And then using that time here, he had the confidence of midshipmen to get information for his book and then dropping it on us like a bombshell. It really upset me.

Then after that, he was telling everybody that he was banned from the Naval Academy. Well, the first time he put out the word that he had been banned from the Naval Academy, I told my staff, "You send him an invitation to every event we have here at the academy—every Forrestal lecture, every parade, you make sure you send him an invitation." He never, ever accepted a single one of them, yet he kept saying he was banned from the Naval Academy. So I really felt that that guy has a problem. I hate to say he's dishonest, but, boy, he sure acted to us in a dishonorable fashion.

I was picking up the pieces from that article for the whole time I was here, and it still has an adverse impact on the academy. The librarians told me one time, after I gave a little presentation to them, that it's one of the most popular pieces of material they have at the academy. They have to keep a stack of them, because male midshipmen are coming over and looking at them. So his influence here has been very adverse in the anti-woman attitude engendered here.

Paul Stillwell: How ironic then that his book should be called *Sense of Honor*.[*]

Admiral Lawrence: Right.

Paul Stillwell: What was your reaction to that?

Admiral Lawrence: Well, I'll tell you about that. One day I was in my office and Admiral Minter called me up—former superintendent Admiral Minter.[†] He said that General Greene, a former Commandant of the Marine Corps, had just called him and he

---

[*] Webb, *A Sense of Honor* (Englewood Cliffs, New Jersey: Prentice-Hall, 1981).
[†] Rear Admiral Charles S. Minter, USN, was superintendent of the Naval Academy from January 1964 to June 1965. The oral history of Minter, who retired as a vice admiral, is in the Naval Institute collection.

had read the galleys of Webb's book, *A Sense of Honor*.[*] General Greene was very upset; he said, "God, this depicts the Naval Academy in a manner that I'm just not familiar. It's not the Naval Academy I know."

Admiral Minter just wanted to make me apprised of this book. At that time, the executive director, Commander Bowler, called me and said that the Naval Institute had been approached to see if they would co-publish the book.[†] Bowler and his people had read the book and just decided that that was not a book that they wanted to publish, because it was not representative of the Naval Academy.

I said, "Well, I certainly agree with you, Bud, because I think it's very bad. One thing it depicts the faculty in a very negative way; it degrades nuclear officers; it has some sexual activity in there of an officer having an affair with his former roommate's wife. God, I mean, that's really a bad image of the academy. I sure agree with you. You shouldn't publish it."

But I kind of forgot about it. Well, the next thing I knew when the academy's supply officer contacted me. He said, "The publishing company up there in New York is accusing us of banning the book at the Naval Academy. The background is that we learned about Webb's writing his book after his previous book, *Fields of Fire*.[‡] We were contacted, we said, 'Yeah, we'll sell it at the midshipman store,' so we got the initial order in and we read the book. We just came to the conclusion that, although we'd sell the book, we didn't figure it would be all that attractive. So we called them back and said, 'Reduce the follow-on orders.' So the publishing company came out to the press right away and said the Naval Academy had banned the book."

Then Webb picked up on this and said, "Yeah, I've been banned from the Naval Academy in previous years." That was totally false; we didn't ban the book. So I had the midshipman store officer write out a statement that reported exactly everything he did. I had to go out to the press and say, "These are the facts." And I wrote to the publishing company. But, here again, I felt Webb tried to exploit us very badly over this book.

---

[*] General Wallace M. Greene, Jr., USMC, served as Commandant of the Marine Corps from 1 January 1964 to 31 December 1967.
[†] Commander Roland T. E. "Bud" Bowler Jr., USN, became secretary-treasurer of the Naval Institute and publisher of the *Proceedings* in 1962. He retired from active duty in 1964, then remained with the Naval Institute until 1984.
[‡] Webb, *Fields of Fire* (Englewood Cliffs, New Jersey: Prentice-Hall, 1978).

Anyway, Webb and I had quite a large amount of correspondence with each other while I was here. He was critical of the way we were doing things here at the Naval Academy. I really felt that he acted in a less honorable fashion with us here at the academy. I just simply have to come to the conclusion he was doing much of this to enhance the sale of his books. He was motivated by financial gain. So I do not have a great deal of respect for James Webb, because of the way he treated us. Nobody can tell me a person signs an 18-month contract in December, then two months later determines he has to leave. I think he knew all along he wasn't going to stay here. He kept going out saying he was banned from the Naval Academy, but I never had done anything at all to indicate to him that he was not welcome. In fact, I wrote him a letter and said, "I want to assure you that you're welcome here at the academy just like any other graduate."

Yet when he became the Secretary of the Navy, he made the statement, "Now is the first time that I'm warmly received at the Naval Academy." So you never know what people's motivations are, but I was really very upset about my relationship with Jim Webb, and he knows how I feel towards him to this day.

Well, I guess I'd better knock off there, Paul.

Paul Stillwell: Thank you very much.

Interview Number 15 with Vice Admiral William P. Lawrence, U.S. Navy (Retired)
Place: U.S. Naval Institute, Annapolis, Maryland
Date: Monday, 14 January 1991

Paul Stillwell: Admiral, from being an observer here on the yard, back during your tenure as the academy superintendent, I remember how very popular your wife was and much thought of by the midshipmen. What do you recall about that aspect?

Admiral Lawrence: Well, I think she really was a wonderful influence here. One thing she did was try to make the midshipmen, and everybody on duty here, aware that the superintendent's house was open to them. In other words, the superintendent's house belonged to the academy. It was the focal point of the academy's representational influence, not just the private residence of the superintendent and his family. As I talked before, when we came here, the top level of the superintendent's house was just a storage area. There are 32 rooms in that house, so she converted the entire top floor into a dormitory area. So that was a good thing that was done; it brought a lot of midshipmen and families into our house on weekends.

We did a lot of things, in addition to the standard receptions that you have through the year for the first and second class, and a lot of other initiatives to bring midshipmen to the house. For example, we used to have the chapel choir and the midshipman glee club come over and perform when we had guests in the house. We used to have cookouts for the drum and bugle corps, and have events for athletic teams. We wanted to make the midshipmen aware that the superintendent and his wife were very much concerned about them and were human and not aloof figures whom they rarely saw.

I remembered that when I was a midshipman, about the only time we saw the superintendent was when we marched into the chapel. On Sunday morning, he was standing out there on the steps. I never saw the superintendent's wife, never had any thought that I'd ever be inside the superintendent's house. I guess that was kind of the modus operandi in that period: naval officers were aloof, familiarity breeds contempt—

that kind of philosophy. It kind of turned me off when I was a midshipman, that there was not a closer relationship between the midshipmen and the officers.

There was a very negative image on the part of the midshipmen towards the company officers, because they were mostly cast in the role of duty officers, who were roaming the academy trying to put you on report. I felt that was a negative form of leadership, so I worked hard to turn that around. I made it clear to company officers, "You're not here principally as disciplinarians; you're here as role models. You demonstrate to midshipmen the proper type of leadership, and the essential attribute of leaders is to be concerned about their subordinates. That's the style I want you to have. Don't feel that you will be judged by the number of midshipmen you put on report, like they were in my time." I tried to establish that as a philosophy, and I felt that Diane and I had to, above everybody else, set the example.

So my wife was very active in things within the academy, and she also worked very hard to improve the relationship with the local community. She analyzed the situation and realized that there were certain key groups in town, like Historic Annapolis, that did most of the renovation of the historic homes here. Then there were the Annapolis Symphony and the other arts-type groups. She made an effort to have them in our house during her time here. I think that helped build rapport with the local community. Our basic approach was that we'd probably be here three years, and we'd really give it the max effort to do everything we could—not only to inspire the midshipmen, but also to improve the image of the academy. To do that we had to work hard; we gave up a lot of personal things.

Paul Stillwell: Such as?

Admiral Lawrence: Well, we just didn't have leisure time, because most every evening we were probably involved in some type event, and many of our weekends were given up. We didn't have the time to take leave and go on trips. But we justified that on the basis that it was for the good of the academy. So probably, in a lot of ways, the job as superintendent—for both my wife and me—was one of the busiest times we had. It was virtually a seven-day-a-week total effort. It was mostly rewarding and fulfilling, so we didn't resent it, but it would have been hard to maintain that pace.

Paul Stillwell: Well, you viewed it as an investment in the future of the officer corps.

Admiral Lawrence: Yes. Well, I perceived two challenges when I came here that I started working on right away. One was that we had a very high attrition among midshipmen, which also existed at the other service academies. Part of it was fallout from the Vietnam War period. We had about 30% attrition, and I said, "I think we can do better than that here. When we lose these kids, we're wasting a lot of the government's money." The end of the second year is when they start to incur active duty obligation if they stay. We had quite an exodus of midshipmen, and that was driving our attrition up. So that was a major objective that I articulated to everybody here at the academy. We simply had to lower the attrition, and it was across-the-board-type of effort. A big part of it was conveying to the midshipmen that the officers, starting with the superintendent here, were human and concerned about them. We had to demonstrate to them a good image of leadership.

Another thing I perceived as driving midshipmen out was that they knew they would incur an active duty obligation if they voluntarily resigned during the third or fourth year. So I really concentrated my effort on the second-year midshipmen, the third class. I would have the entire class together, and I would give them a rationale that went like this, "I'm not sitting here and telling you that you should make the Navy your career. I'm basically saying to you that, in my opinion, if you decide to stay after your third year and complete the academy, and then assume that five-year obligation, you're going to be better off seven years from now regardless of what you do after that. You're going to be better off than if you leave now and try to do something else. Unless you have a specific desire to be a lawyer or a doctor or something like that, but if you have no specific desire what you want to do, I can tell you that at age 27, having completed the academy and having five years of active duty, you're going to be far more desired, not only within the Navy and Marine Corps, but in any field in the country. So if you leave here after the second year because you were concerned about the seven-year obligation, you're throwing away a lot."

I didn't get up there and talk about patriotism and all that, I just gave the pragmatic facts: "This is what I'm telling you, based on my experience." I'd tell them what service academy graduates did, not only in the military, but I would say, "Look at Ross Perot and other captains of industry."[*] That was just one effort. But I told everybody here that when kids are coming to the end of the second year, they basically have shown they have the right stuff to stay here. That's where we should concentrate our efforts in trying to influence them to stay. Over a four-year period, the class of '82 graduated with only 22% attrition.

Paul Stillwell: So it was a measurable improvement.

Admiral Lawrence: Yes. We lowered it 8% in four years. And there probably were other factors other than what we did here at the academy. It may have been a national change in attitude, but I think we saved the country millions of dollars by lowering that attrition rate.

Another area of concern when I came here was that we had a very high attrition among junior officers on the staff. When I got here, every nuclear submariner had resigned while he was here. So I felt I had to go on a major effort with the young officers here at the academy. We sat around and brainstormed this, and I came up with a concept of having a junior officer study group. Now, I didn't want the junior officers to get the perception that they were running the place. On the other hand, I wanted to convey to them that I was concerned about all aspects of their careers and their duties here at the academy. So we got a very fine group of young officers together.

I forget the name of my personnel officer at that time. He was a young surface commander, very fine officer. And then Captain John Butterfield, who was the director of U.S. and international Studies, was very active in this effort.[†] I met with that junior officer study group periodically to get their perceptions on what we could do to improve

---

[*] Midshipman H. Ross Perot, USN, was president of the Naval Academy class of 1953. He resigned from the active Navy in 1957 and became a successful businessman.
[†] Captain John A. Butterfield, USN.

their duty and their lifestyle here at the academy. Nothing all that startling came out of that effort, but it's just the fact that it thoroughly conveyed to junior officers here that the superintendent and the top leadership were very concerned about them. I think it had a salutary effect, because we also got a very pronounced reduction in the resignation rate of junior officers. So those were two areas where I felt good about our achievements.

Paul Stillwell: Well, related to that is the business of service selection, going into the nuclear power program or aviation or surface. What input did you have in that?

Admiral Lawrence: Well, I always tried to play the role of the purple-suiter.* I never, ever espoused any particular career field. In other words, I never got up and tried to be the naval aviation advocate. I just felt my record itself would be enough for that. I didn't have to ever actually talk about it. In fact, if I did anything, I encouraged kids to go in the nuclear power training more than anything else.

Paul Stillwell: What kind of pressures were you getting from BuPers on that?†

Admiral Lawrence: Well, there was constant pressure, not in the adverse sense, but there was emphasis, I should say, on getting an increased input into the nuclear power field. There was a shortage of nuclear-trained officers, particularly nuclear submariners, in the commander-captain level. The fundamental problem was poor retention between the five- and ten-year times in a career. I felt there should be a more active effort to try to solve that rather than trying to increase the input from the Naval Academy. But there was a continuous pressure to get increased numbers. So I was supportive of that, but, unfortunately, the nuclear submariners went on a very strong effort—and I'm sure Admiral Rickover must have been a player in this—to draft people into nuclear submarines. We had a big debate on it, and I felt I should not take an active role in this debate. It was really a decision for the Chief of Naval Personnel and CNO.

---

* "Purple" is a slang term to describe joint-service staffs, purple supposedly being the color that would emerge from blending the uniforms of the various services. In this context, Admiral Lawrence was saying that he wasn't pushing any specialty—surface, aviation, submarines, or Marine Corps.
† BuPers – Bureau of Naval Personnel.

The nuclear submariners had convinced the Chief of Naval Personnel, who was Vice Admiral Baldwin, that manning the nuclear submarines was getting so critical we simply had to do this.* Admiral Baldwin asked me, and I said, "I am philosophically against requiring midshipmen to go into a particular curriculum. It violates everything we've done here in modern history. But if you feel it's in the best interest of the Navy, I'll do everything I can to make it work."

Well, Admiral Baldwin was sold and Admiral Hayward, who was Chief of Naval Operations, had great respect for Admiral Baldwin. So they directed that in the class of 1980 we would have mandatory assignment of midshipmen to nuclear submarines. I made every effort to make that as palatable as possible. I got the class of '80 together and gave them the rationale. I tried to tell them that nuclear submarine operations were some of the most exciting operations we did in the Navy, and there was a very high degree of professionalism and pride in that service. I tried to tell them it was in the best interests of the country that we have this draft, but the midshipmen were very upset about this. They were very bitter, because you'll find there are midshipmen here who, from the time that they've been little kids, wanted to fly. The attractiveness of flying is such that you're always going to get that element of midshipmen for whom that's been their aspiration. That's one of the big reasons they came in the service academy. So it really hit those midshipmen hard who wanted to fly and had worked hard to get into aeronautical engineering and all that.

But the thing that was devastating was that Admiral Rickover did not change his traditional approach. I can tell you from working very closely with Admiral Rickover and his office over many years that his sole criterion for picking midshipmen to go in his program was academic standing. He couldn't care less whether the midshipman was a leader, an athlete, or anything else when he was here. That was a minor consideration. He went for people who stood high academically. When the midshipmen got into the interview process with Admiral Rickover prior to service selection, I learned he was taking non-volunteers and turning down volunteers.

---

* Vice Admiral Robert B. Baldwin, USN, was Chief of Naval Personnel from 21 July 1978 to August 1980.

So I talked to him and said, "Admiral, in my opinion, I feel that whether a midshipman is a volunteer or not should be a major consideration in the selection. I think you could trade off academic standing in a case of a kid who's a strong volunteer."

He said, "No, that's immature. A midshipman should take whatever assignment we give him and do it well."

Well, that was a recipe for disaster, because the midshipmen saw kids who greatly aspired to come into nuclear submarines, who had a lower quality point rating than midshipmen who wanted to be aviators, and he'd take the non-volunteers. One midshipman was the son of a classmate of mine, who was a nuclear submarine admiral. His only desire since he was a little kid was to follow in his father's footsteps and be a nuclear submariner. But because he had a little bit lower QPR, even though he was a marine engineer, Admiral Rickover turned him down. He took a non-volunteer who was in aeronautical engineering.

So we had some very unpleasant situations then, because we had a couple of midshipmen who went in to interview with Admiral Rickover and made it very clear they had no desire to go into nuclear submarines. They just told him outright.

I remember one midshipman who was an all-American lacrosse player who did this. Admiral Rickover wanted him court-martialed because of insubordination. I told the Vice Chief of Naval Operations, Admiral Watkins, "Look, if that happens, you're just going to destroy the relationship between the academy and the nuclear power program and greatly exacerbate the ability to have midshipmen come in nuclear power in the future."[*] So we had a real shootout with Admiral Rickover. He finally backed off and agreed just to have that midshipman write him a letter of apology. So that was the solution to that problem.

Paul Stillwell: Did he take him anyway?

---

[*] Admiral James D. Watkins, USN, served as Vice Chief of Naval Operations from 1979 to 1981. He had been a nuclear submarine skipper earlier in his career.

Admiral Lawrence: No, he turned him down, because he didn't want an insubordinate. So I told this kid, "It's tough, but you've probably—you won." He's a very fine naval aviator today.

Paul Stillwell: Did you have other cases of damage control to do as a result of this?

Admiral Lawrence: Oh, yes, I had to do all sorts of damage control. He got a kid over there who was the honor chairman at the academy. He tried to force that midshipman to resign his honor chairman position, so he could improve his academic standing. This was earlier, when Admiral Long was the Vice Chief of Naval Operations.[*] I went to Admiral Long and said, "You know, Admiral, Rickover's on record for being against sports, sex, and now if you put honor in there, I don't see any way you're going to attract midshipmen to come."

So Admiral Long, who probably had more influence with Admiral Rickover than anybody I knew, got him to back off on that. Another time, he tried to get a kid to leave the track team. He was a black, and we really needed to get blacks in nuclear power. I had to work with Admiral Long on that one. Yes, I had very many damage control situations with Admiral Rickover. But I can tell you, I don't care what anybody says, his sole criterion for picking people on that program was academic performance. As a result, he lost some very outstanding midshipmen leaders here whom he could have taken into that program.

Paul Stillwell: Well, and he ignored the aspect of motivation.

Admiral Lawrence: Well, particularly in that volunteer situation in 1980. The fallout from that was very, very adverse. We even had midshipmen who got into nuclear power training and perceived that the thing that would get them out of there quicker than anything else was to say they used drugs. We had a kid who actually said he used drugs, so he'd get kicked out of there. I found out about it, and I knew he was a good kid, so I

---

[*] Admiral Robert L. J. Long, USN, served as Vice Chief of Naval Operations from 1977 to 1979. His oral history is in the Naval Institute collection. He had been a nuclear submarine skipper.

went to the aviation people and said, "Look, you really ought to take this kid." We saved that one, but I'm sure there were others who bilged out of nuclear power and eventually got out of the Navy because they were so disillusioned.

Paul Stillwell: What can you say about your relationship with the Marines here and getting people into the Marine Corps?

Admiral Lawrence: Well, that was another objective I set for myself, to really help the Marines get their 16⅔% of each graduating class. When I came, they were getting around 14% or so. So I talked to Colonel Zimolzak, who was the senior Marine and director of English and History. One of the first things I did when I came here was to ask to have a Marine officer as my flag lieutenant and aide. I wanted to convey to everybody that the academy existed to produce Navy and Marine officers. I got a very fine young Marine captain named Gordon Jackson, who was out of the Naval Academy class of '70; he was my aide for two years.[*] That was one thing, to project the right image. I did everything I could to show support for the Marine Corps.

The other thing I did, when they were building the new natatorium, was conceive the idea of naming that Lejeune Hall.[†] I really had to push it through because there were a lot of old-timers, senior admirals, who didn't want to name a building here after the Marines. I said, "Well, the Naval Academy has produced Marine Corps officers throughout our history, and we still produce a percentage of our graduates here who are Marines. I think we should have at least one building here named after a Marine." The CNO and the Secretary of the Navy supported me on that, and we got that building named Lejeune Hall.

But I have to be honest in telling you that I was very disappointed at the attitude of the senior Marines towards the Naval Academy. First of all, I found it very difficult to get any senior Marines to come over here.

---

[*] Captain Gordon R. Jackson, USMC.
[†] Major General John A. Lejeune, USMC, served as Commandant of the Marine Corps from 1 July 1920 to 4 March 1929. He was in the Naval Academy class of 1888.

Paul Stillwell: You mean more senior than your colonel in charge of English and History.

Admiral Lawrence: Yes, I'm talking about people up at the Commandant, Assistant Commandant level. It became very apparent to me while I was here that the senior leadership of the Marine Corps didn't have all those warm feelings towards the Naval Academy. For example, I tried to get General Barrow to come over and review a parade.* One time I gave him four months' advance notice, but he didn't accept. For other events here at the academy, people at the general officer level just wouldn't come over. They wouldn't accept invitations to come to football games and to attend football banquets and all that. So I wondered a little bit about that.

When we had the groundbreaking for Lejeune Hall, I sent out all these invitations. Only one Marine general came to that, and that was General Bronars, who was out of the Naval Academy class of 1950.† General Lejeune's grandson, a retired Marine colonel, came. There were only three of us there, including General Bronars and myself.

I can tell you that I've subsequently come to the very painful conclusion that there is an anti-Naval Academy bias in the Marine Corps. It's a very subtle thing, but I can give you all sorts of facts. If you look at the success rate of academy graduates in the Navy and Marine Corps, the disparity is very dramatic in terms of the percentage of O-6 or above in the Navy, as opposed to the Marine Corps.‡ That fine young captain out of the class of '70, one of the finest young men that I've ever known, got passed over for lieutenant colonel. Colonel John Ripley, great hero in the Vietnam War, *The Bridge at Dong Ha*, didn't get selected for general.§ From the era of the classes in the '60s, only three Naval Academy graduates have been promoted to general officer, and there are 77 in the Navy. So it's a subtle thing, but . . .

---

* General Robert H. Barrow, USMC, served as Commandant of the Marine Corps from 1 July 1979 to 30 June 1983.
† Major General Edward J. Bronars, USMC.
‡ O-6 is the pay grade for Navy captains and Marine Corps colonels.
§ Captain John C. Ripley, USMC, was awarded the Navy Cross for his heroism in blowing up a key bridge at Dong Ha during the North Vietnamese Easter offensive in 1972. He eventually retired as a colonel and served as Director, Marine Corps History and Museums. See John Grider Miller, *The Bridge at Dong Ha* (Annapolis: Naval Institute Press, 1989).

Paul Stillwell: That doesn't sound too subtle.

Admiral Lawrence: Well, it's subtle in the sense that a lot of people are not aware of it. I am because I've lived with this situation for 15 years now, observing from a superintendent's perspective, and then as a Chief of Naval Personnel and back here. The thing that's made this very apparent to me is that my wife and I keep in touch with many of the young people who were midshipmen when we were here. Invariably, those who went into the Marine Corps tell me that immediately after their commissioning, they perceived resentment towards Naval Academy graduates.

A kid named Steve Bessler was an ex-Marine, and he was one of the six-stripers in the class of '79.[*] He refused to have his picture in the Naval Academy *Lucky Bag*, and did not buy a ring, because he knew from being enlisted that Naval Academy graduates were not well received in the Marine Corps. This past year I tried to point this out to the senior Marines and say, "You've got a problem that you should address, because you're losing a lot of very fine talent in the Marine Corps, because these kids resign; they don't stay in." General Gray came across to Admiral Hill and others as not being a great advocate.[†] He told Admiral Hill that he couldn't care less whether or not he got any Naval Academy graduates in the Marine Corps.[‡] I think the Marine Corps is losing a lot of fine talent because they don't warmly receive Naval Academy graduates.

One of the things is that there is not a great deal of regard in the Marine Corps for academic achievement. There's a resentment towards the academy graduates who come in the Marine Corps with these fine academic educations by the officers who have the degrees in physical education and very soft academic programs.

Paul Stillwell: It's interesting that you had the nuclear submariners and the Marines at opposite poles on the value of academics.

---

[*] This name does not show up in the Naval Academy alumni register.
[†] General Alfred M. Gray, Jr., USMC, served as Commandant of the Marine Corps from 1 July 1987 to 30 June 1991.
[‡] Rear Admiral Virgil L. Hill, Jr., USN, served as Superintendent of the Naval Academy from 18 August 1988 to 15 June 1991.

Admiral Lawrence: Oh, yes, that's what makes your life interesting as superintendent, and all these little nuances of your role here. So that covers some areas of interest.

Paul Stillwell: Just to get back to your wife for a minute, did she have to put her business on the shelf to have this active role you've described?

Admiral Lawrence: Yes, she really turned more over to her partner in that business. She got out of much of the personal patient care herself and was more in an administrative role. Her partner came over to Annapolis often, and they had meetings here, but she still had to go over to her office a lot. I tell you, she's a remarkable woman, her ability to manage. She has tremendous energy, and she drove herself really hard, because, as I say, both of us felt that it was important to give our max effort to that job. She kept her business going all those years.

Paul Stillwell: My vivid memory from that period is seeing those banners that she put up on the side of your house. It was a nice personal touch that let people know that this was not a stuffy place.

Admiral Lawrence: Well, and that's one of the big reasons she did that. She and I both were conscious of trying to convey to the midshipmen and their families that the superintendent and his wife were very human people. I remembered from my midshipman days that I looked upon the superintendent as almost being a deity. And then, of course, the average civilian out there thinks a Navy flag officer is just in another world almost. I didn't want that to happen, and so doing things like that was a way of bringing a superintendent and his wife closer to the midshipmen. And, of course, the wife could do something like that, where the superintendent couldn't. She just wanted the midshipmen to know that she personally was concerned about them.

On the other hand, I did not want the midshipmen to perceive me as being less than a strict disciplinarian. In other words, I didn't want them to feel I would be a soft mark. Because while my wife and I were doing those sorts of things, I didn't mince any words when I got midshipmen together. If I saw they were doing some things here that I didn't like, I got up and talked to them about it. For example, I was really very direct and very firm with them about discrimination. I normally didn't talk in terms of race or sex. I just said, "If I see any examples here in this school of anybody being treated with disrespect for their personal dignity and so forth, I'm not going to tolerate it. If it happens, I'm going to beat up on the offender."

Because I really knew about the pressures here, particularly to discriminate against the women midshipmen. You had these macho young guys who tended to resent the women being here. I felt they had to hear it from the boss. Even though I did that, I still had to keep constantly fighting the cruel pranks and the derisive comments. Whenever I saw anything like that, I'd send the word back to the commandant, "You put out to those battalion officers and company officers that I don't want that stuff happening here. Anybody who does something in a group that he wouldn't do individually is the ultimate coward as far as I'm concerned." This was the type of message I kept constantly sending the midshipmen.

Paul Stillwell: What can you say about the acceptance of black midshipmen and their role at the academy?

Admiral Lawrence: Well, I never saw any overt racial discrimination here, but I used to very carefully observe things. I used to try to do those things that prevented midshipmen from grouping themselves racially. For example, the first time we had a football banquet here, I noticed that the football players and other midshipmen were sitting at tables by themselves. All the blacks would sit together, and all whites. This was the type thing that I really wanted to prevent happening, because I think there was a natural inclination of the blacks to tend to do things together, so I had to, in a very artful way, try to do things to facilitate integration.

Paul Stillwell: So it was kind of a voluntary segregation.

Admiral Lawrence: Oh, yes, and it's very much a thing that will occur. You hear the term on college campuses right now, what they call de facto segregation. So at the next year's football banquet, I solved that problem. I said, "Look, I want the football team, regardless of color or anything else, to be spread out among the guests. Don't have the football team just sit together, which leads to racial grouping. Let's just spread the midshipmen out and have a black at this table and a few whites." So I was constantly doing things to try to promote better integration, although you still had to respect the fact that there's going to be a black studies group, and you're going to have to observe Martin Luther King's birthday. Plus you're going to probably have a gospel choir. I mean, you had to allow the blacks, of course, to do things together. And, as I say, I really insisted on having a black chaplain, but I tried to always work to do things to facilitate integration without playing too heavy a role in the thing. It was a tough challenge, because many of the blacks who come here don't understand the middle class white culture. The most comfortable thing for them is to seek out a black who comes from a similar background, but you just can't let the natural process occur. You have to do some things that facilitate integration.

But we never had any racial problems that I recall. We had some disciplinary cases that involved blacks and whites getting into somewhat of a fracas, but I never saw it as a racially inspired thing. The far greater human relation challenge involved the women.

The other thing I don't know whether I addressed, but tell me if you recall my talking of this, is that I became aware very early that, because of our location close to Washington, that our ability to be in the national limelight was far greater than the other two service academies.

Paul Stillwell: You did talk about the media relations.

Admiral Lawrence: And that's why I just came to the conclusion early on that anything that happened here at the academy that was newsworthy, I had to have a system so I knew about it right away, because it required the most skillful management of those situations to ensure we didn't get a negative image in the press. As I say, the press can distort the image of these schools more than anything else by blowing a particular disciplinary problem out of perspective. So I managed every one of those. And there may have been those who said, "Well, gosh, you violated due process."

I'd say, "Look, my uppermost interest is to protect the rights of those midshipmen, and the quickest way their interest can be negatively served is to get something blown up in the media. So I don't care what the incident was, whether it was just something some people would say was a minor fracas within the company, but it was a black-white situation, as we had one time, where a black pulled a knife on a white kid, and there was no racial aspect to it at all. But, boy, I knew about it right away, and we started a plan as to how we would manage it. The commandant, public affairs officer, the staff judge advocate, my executive assistant —we'd sit around and say, "Okay now, what is the proper thing to do to it? Should we go to the media right now?"

Paul Stillwell: You talked about when you were a midshipman instituting the honor concept 30 years earlier. How had it matured or evolved by the time you were superintendent?

Admiral Lawrence: Well, the basic principles and the basic philosophy had really endured, essentially unchanged. The area that had matured after I left was that a much more formalized structure of boards existed. See, when I left, we had just reached the point where we had the brigade honor board. In that first year, we hadn't really conceived the idea of having class boards like they do now. The brigade board just did it all in those days. I guess after I left they came to the realization that they had to have a little bit different board structure. But it was basically still the same.

The counseling option we have here was something that I insisted on when I was a midshipman, because I saw so many cases up there at West Point of young plebes doing very minor things and getting thrown out. West Point had this almost zealous, religious fervor about its honor code, that anybody who had a violation should be thrown out. I said, "That's unfair. I mean, a lot of immature plebes are going to make mistakes here, and to have them thrown out just doesn't make sense. We should have the capability for an older, mature midshipman to sit down and explain the situation to them and not get it thrown into the formal arena."

The administration here bought that counseling concept. The non-toleration clause at West Point and the Air Force Academy, I think, is an impediment to their programs. They do a lot of things to work around it. I used to get asked by some of the people at West Point and Air Force Academy on the honor counseling option, "Doesn't it bother you that you have midshipmen at the academy who are making honor violations and you don't know about it?"

I said, "No, it doesn't bother me at all. If midshipmen are handling it and they know what the standard is, we don't let somebody graduate from here who has character deficiencies. That to me is a great strength of our concept. The best way you learn in this world, I found, is by making mistakes. God, we shouldn't throw a young 17- or 18-year-old kid out for just a minor mistake. It just doesn't make sense." In those two schools they tried to change this, but they always allowed the cadets to vote on it. And for some reason, the cadets won't vote to do away with the non-toleration clause. I used to ask the other superintendents about this: "Why do you have the cadets vote on this?"

They said, "Well, because it's their honor code."

I said, "Well, you know, I feel here at the Naval Academy, if there's something that I, as a superintendent, think is the right thing to do, I say we're going to do it. I'm not going to put it in the hands of young, inexperienced kids to vote on it." I mean, that's a philosophical difference.

Paul Stillwell: How much interchange did you have with your counterparts on other issues?

Admiral Lawrence: Well, quite a bit, because we had an annual superintendents' conference at one of the academies. General Goodpaster was the superintendent at West Point while I was here, and General Tallman was the superintendent at the Air Force Academy.* Of course, I saw them at the superintendents' conference, but, invariably, through the visits for athletic events and things like that, you'd see them through the year. And we'd talk to each other on the phone.

---

* Lieutenant General Andrew J. Goodpaster, USA (Ret.), was superintendent of the Military Academy from 1977 to 1981. Lieutenant General Kenneth L. Tallman, USAF, a 1946 West Point graduate, was superintendent of the Air Force Academy from 1977 to 1981.

Paul Stillwell: Goodpaster had been brought in after they had a big scandal up there.

Admiral Lawrence: Yes, he was brought in in 1977, put back on active duty as a three-star and was told he would be there four years. He was there from '77 to '81, and I was here from '78 to '81. And the whole time I was here, General Tallman was the superintendent out at the Air Force Academy. But we had very close rapport. And then, of course, the deans and the commandants and directors of athletics were always interfacing and had separate meetings.

Paul Stillwell: Do you remember any specifics from dealing with either of those two?

Admiral Lawrence: Well, one thing we did, just as an example, was deal with what we called an "out-of-district nomination" for a cadet or midshipman.

For example, if you had a congressman down there in Mississippi or Louisiana who couldn't get ten nominations for a vacancy here, the number allowed under the law, and you had a kid up here in Pennsylvania or New Jersey where the congressmen used all his nominations, if the nomination of the congressman in Pennsylvania was filled, then they would go down to this congressman from Mississippi and say, "Nominate this midshipman." That was one way they brought in athletes. The law didn't specifically state that that couldn't occur, but the spirit of the law was that a congressman and a senator would only nominate somebody within their district or their state. So we got together and mutually agreed, to the great unhappiness of the athletic people, that we would not have any out of district nominations, because I used to feel that that practice was really stretching the ethics.

The other thing was that General Goodpaster and I really had to band together very strongly to prevent moving the Army-Navy game from the Thanksgiving weekend until later. Of course, after I left, that was lost. Now we play up to the seventh or eighth of December, somewhere in there. Our feeling was that it was wrong to have the Army-Navy right before examinations. So he and I stood down ABC for all the three years I was here. They wanted to move us out of the Thanksgiving weekend, because they wanted to put some big game like Alabama-Auburn or one of the big, traditional rivalries. Now we play usually on the Saturday before examinations start, and it's really not fair to the midshipmen.

Paul Stillwell: Anything more to say on the business of admissions? How did you work with that organization?

Admiral Lawrence: Well, Admiral McNitt was our dean of admissions, and I certainly was very much aware of all that was going on and the whole process.[*] He was so effective that I personally had to get involved to only to a limited degree, because he had everything under control. I tried to do everything I could to support him. We built up the Blue and Gold officer structure. Those are the reserve officers who help us all so much in counseling the candidates. We had about 1,700 of these officers around the country. They were the principal interface with the young people, and not only counseled those who had applied, but also helped put the word out about the academy.

Paul Stillwell: Well, this could have an effect on your campaign to reduce attrition, by vetting the people who come in.

Admiral Lawrence: Yes, and the fact that Admiral McNitt had developed a very viable admissions process. So he has to get a lot of the credit for that lowering of attrition as well, because he had, in my opinion, the most effective process in the three academies in his development of the proper criteria for selecting people and the weighting system that he developed of the criteria for admission.

Paul Stillwell: What do you recall about the role of Admiral Loughlin and the Naval Academy Foundation?[†]

---

[*] Rear Admiral Robert W. McNitt, USN (Ret.), served from 1972 to 1985 in the civilian post of dean of admissions at the Naval Academy. His Naval Institute oral history discusses the admissions process in great detail.
[†] Rear Admiral Charles Elliott Loughlin, USN (Ret.). The role of the foundation in that era was to raise funds to support the cost of sending prospective midshipmen to private preparatory schools. Loughlin's oral history is in the Naval Institute collection.

Admiral Lawrence: Well, about 100 midshipmen a year came through the foundation process, and I thought that was a good thing. Initially, it was oriented toward athletes, but we found we needed to broaden that focus to really good, young kids who just needed some academic reinforcement. The kids who came through the foundation, about 8% of a class, turned out to be really good midshipmen, because they were the kids who had a strong desire to come, although they didn't quite have the academic qualifications.

So that program, I think, is a very viable part of the overall admissions, to a lesser degree than the Naval Academy Preparatory School at Newport. We get a larger input out of there. The good thing about the Naval Academy Preparatory School is that's the type of program that really helps you increase your minorities. Because it's basically a senior year of high school type of program up there.

Paul Stillwell: But geared very specifically to Naval Academy requirements.

Admiral Lawrence: That's right. And it really helps that young minority get the academic reinforcement and be ready to come in. So the Naval Academy Preparatory School is the most important prep school type of program that we have, because of the great help that it gives us on minorities.

Well, Paul, I think I'm going to have to knock off.

Paul Stillwell: All right. Thank you.

Interview Number 16 with Vice Admiral William P. Lawrence, U.S. Navy (Retired)
Place: U.S. Naval Institute, Annapolis, Maryland
Date: Friday, 25 January 1991

Paul Stillwell: Admiral, we've been talking about various facets of your time as superintendent of the Naval Academy and haven't gotten into the academic side at all. Could you talk, please, about your relationship with the academic dean, the various department heads, and so forth.

Admiral Lawrence: Well, when I was here, of course, I tried to maintain very close contact with the academic side of my responsibility. Prior to my coming in as superintendent, my predecessor, Admiral McKee, who had been here from 1975 to '78, had done a very comprehensive review of the academic curriculum. A fairly major restructuring occurred as a result of the Admiral McKee initiative. It cut down the number of majors and did several things with regard to the electives that were offered. It basically pared down the total course offerings that were available prior to that time. I think Admiral McKee's feeling was that we shouldn't dilute the academic program by offering so many majors, that we didn't achieve the degree of excellence we could in a smaller number of majors. That was when he arrived at the conclusion we'd have four humanities and social science electives, six in the math and sciences, and eight in the engineering disciplines.

Admiral McKee's emphasis was in the area of engineering. He felt the Naval Academy developed this reputation as being an outstanding engineering school, and we should seek to maintain this excellence and give our concentration to the engineering disciplines. That was why we ended up with the eight engineering majors. I came in right after that, and my perception was that we didn't need another superintendent looking closely at the curriculum with the thought of changing things. I felt we really needed some stability to allow those major changes that had been put in effect to mature and be fully realized. So I didn't really do much in the changing of the curriculum.

But one thing I felt really strongly about when I came in here was that we needed to have more history in the core curriculum. When I arrived, we had only two required history courses. They were done in the plebe year, and they were basically a modern history that started back in the 1600s and came forward. In addition to that broad history, there was naval history, and I felt that midshipmen should be exposed more to earlier history. We had an Under Secretary of the Navy at that time named James Woolsey.* He was a very fine scholar, he was a lawyer, and he had been a Rhodes Scholar. He also felt we should have more emphasis on history over here.

So when I came in, the only change in the curriculum I directed was when I said, "Look, we need to put in another required course in history." There was some resistance. The dean was concerned that we were just adding another requirement to the core, and his concern was that midshipmen were already overtaxed. But we made some compensation within the required electives area and the humanities.

Then, over the first year I was here, I worked with the history department as we developed that required course. It basically went back to antiquity, back to the Greek, Roman, Athens, and Sparta period. The focus was on how cultural values developed in society. It was basically a course that could be almost considered an ethics course, because it looked at the values of ancient societies and how those values were developed, what caused them to erode for a time, and those sorts of things. We point to that today as a part of the formal ethics program we have here at the academy. But that was really the only change I made in the curriculum in the three years I was here.

I tried to work closely with the academic faculty.

Paul Stillwell: What sorts of contacts would you have?

Admiral Lawrence: Well, I had always perceived, even back from my time as a midshipman, that one of the great strengths of the academy was the fact that we had a mixed civilian and military faculty, while West Point and the Air Force Academy had all-military faculties. I felt it gave us our higher degree of academic excellence, which, I think, is the common perception in the country. For one thing, if you have only military

---

* R. James Woolsey served as Under Secretary of the Navy from 9 March 1977 to 7 December 1979.

officers, you can't get the number of PhDs and the amount of academic experience you need to develop a quality curriculum.

Paul Stillwell: Well, I think it's easier in the other services, because they don't have to operate ships in peacetime.

Admiral Lawrence: Well, that's right. But they still do not compare with us in the percentage of the faculty with PhD degrees. Our faculty is 50% military and 50% civilian—we've been there about ten years—and every one of our civilian faculty members will have a PhD degree. I think that gives us a better program. There are very fine advantages to this military-civilian faculty mix in terms of having a civilian component of the faculty provide the continuity. Then by rotating the military to and from sea duty, they bring in a fresh approach, what I call a fleet perspective.

Paul Stillwell: Well, they also serve as effective role models.

Admiral Lawrence: Role models, of course.

The problem they have at West Point and the Air Force Academy is those tenured military faculty members lose credibility. They get into what I call neither a fish nor fowl mode. They're not accepted as academicians; they're not looked on with respect by people in the other academic circles in the country. And they're not accepted by the combat arms officers. They have a problem at West Point, in particular, and a resentment developing between the combat arms officers—who come back in a two- or three-year tour—and the tenured military. They don't mesh well, because the combat arms resent a guy who spends most of his career at West Point, and under law he gets a one-hike promotion on retirement. That's a law that goes back in the 1800s. It was put in there as an inducement to get officers to accept that role. But the combat arms officers resent that. It's a tombstone promotion, but still, for a colonel to retire and call himself brigadier general is a prestigious thing. So I've sensed a lack of good rapport at West Point, and I know that institution pretty well.

We had very fine cooperation between the civilian and military members of our faculty. It was a very harmonious relationship. But the fundamental problem is that our civilians, particularly those who had never been in the military, don't understand the system a lot. They're out in left field a lot here at the academy. So I really made an effort when I was superintendent to make the civilian members of the faculty feel they were an integral part of the team; they're not the stepchildren here at the academy.

Within the first three months I was here, I went around and met with every faculty department, and I think we have 16 faculty departments here. I went into each departmental conference room, sat down, and basically gave some introductory remarks. I told the faculty how proud I was to be here and how much I looked to working in the academic program. Then I just let them ask me questions. That helped me more than anything I ever did here at the academy, even though I didn't learn anything of great significance. Just the fact that I showed the interest to go out there and visit with them and let them unburden their souls really enhanced my linkage with the faculty and got their support. You sometimes have to do things here that do not make the faculty happy, because they perceive that you're giving too much emphasis to the military side or to athletics or something like that. So, anyway, within the first three months here, I met with all 16 faculty departments. That really got to be a drag because it was in the fall, which is a very busy time. But it paid off tremendously.

The other thing is that any academic endeavor, such as the naval history symposium, the foreign affairs conference or anything of that nature, I always made myself present to help in any way I could. I just wanted to show the faculty that I was visible and interested, and I really was.

Paul Stillwell: Did you sit in on any classes?

Admiral Lawrence: Oh, yes, quite a few, and I participated sometimes by giving the lecture in the class. Many professors asked me to come over and lecture on a particular topic. So I made it known I was readily available to come into classrooms and do those sorts of things. I also made it well known to the academic dean that any member of the faculty who wanted to come up and talk to me was free to do so. But not too many did that. Most of them really respected the so-called chain of command, but several came in with grievances. Several wrote me letters, and I was always very careful to answer them. I didn't want the faculty to think in any way that they were not an integral part of the team. So I think the main thing I can point to is that we did maintain stability those three years, and let all the changes that had been made get fully institutionalized.

The other thing that was an achievement while I was here was that we got the first Rhodes Scholars from the Naval Academy in many, many years.[*] I think the Rickover influence was a factor in the academy not putting any emphasis on producing Rhodes Scholars. Admiral Rickover had contempt for Rhodes Scholars and things like that. When I came in, I said, "Look, I think it's a matter of prestige to produce Rhodes Scholars from this school. I know we have midshipmen who can do it." So we started a Rhodes Scholar prep program here for the midshipmen. In their second or third class year, they would indicate their interest. Then we would have a member of the faculty---Professor Marshall, I think, from the English department---work with them. He would have a reading program to get them prepared so they would compete effectively in the screening process, including the interviews. So we produced our first Rhodes Scholar in over 15 years when I was here, and that was really good.[†]

We also started putting more kids in the medical programs. For some reason, even though the nuclear people certainly feel academics are important, they normally won't support anything that's non-engineering or non-science. That's why they didn't support the Rhodes Scholar thing. And they were very much against Naval Academy graduates going into the medical program. I said, "I firmly agree that the Naval Academy exists to produce line officers, but I think we can gain by sending students in a small number into things like the medical program, because individuals who go through there are probably going to turn out to be good career naval officers. But, also, I think it's good for the prestige of the school. The biggest problem you have with the Naval Academy around the country is the trade-school perception. If we can point to the fact

---

[*] Cecil J. Rhodes (1853-1902) was a British administrator and financier who made his fortune in the South African diamond trade. In his will he left 6 million pounds for public service and endowed 170 scholarships at Oxford, to be used by young people from the British Empire, the United States, and Germany.

[†] Midshipman Stuart W. Swetland, USN, class of 1981, received a Rhodes Scholarship. The last Naval Academy graduate prior to him was Midshipman Dennis C. Blair, USN, class of 1968.

that we're producing Rhodes Scholars, we're sending kids to medical school, and things like that, that helps our image in the country and it will help our recruiting. So what we gain by getting better kids in here more than compensates for the loss of people in the nuclear power program." But Admiral Rickover and the nuclear guys normally didn't see it that way. They have a very narrow focus on engineering.

Paul Stillwell: What do you remember about the issue of what portion of the student body should major in hard sciences versus humanities?

Admiral Lawrence: Well, really, during my time it was not an issue. It had been very thoroughly established that 80% would go into engineering, math, and science. Never in my time here did we have to require a midshipman to go into a technical major. And Dean McNitt had assured me that through the admissions process, he could make that happen just by the weighting of the admissions criteria. So it was not a contentious issue while I was here. It was not until Secretary Lehman had been in office for a while that he took that on.[*]

Paul Stillwell: What can you say about your relationship with Dean Davidson?[†]

Admiral Lawrence: Well, it was very good. We had very good rapport, and I extended his contract while he was here.

I instituted something while I was here, which was kind of a management-by-objectives approach. At the beginning of each year, I had the elements of our organization here—like the dean of admissions, the commandant, the athletic people—come up with objectives that would guide them during that year. I didn't want it to be in minute detail; I wanted major areas where they felt progress needed to be made. I had trouble getting the academicians to do this, because they, by nature, don't like to operate this way. That was the only area where I had to push the dean a little bit, because he would want to come in with just some three or four general things like improve academic

---

[*] John F. Lehman Jr., served as Secretary of the Navy from 5 February 1981 to 10 April 1987.
[†] Dr. Bruce M. Davidson was the Naval Academy's academic dean.

excellence. I had found in reading about large organizations that it helps to come out with objectives that require people to use their thoughtful analysis in key areas where progress needs to be made, where corrections need to be made. But I had trouble getting the academic dean ever to come up with anything very detailed.

Paul Stillwell: Did you succeed at all?

Admiral Lawrence: Oh, yes, he's a good and loyal, obedient guy. He would finally go back to drawing boards and produce something. But it wasn't anywhere near as good as you'd get out of the deputy for operations or the deputy for management. The dean of admissions always kept, as a matter of course, the objectives that he was working for.

Paul Stillwell: Over on the other side of the house, what do you remember about the work with the commandants and the Bancroft Hall organization?

Admiral Lawrence: Well, I had very good rapport with the two commandants who were under me.* As I think I've alluded to before, I had a very firm understanding with the commandant that, although he was the so-called commanding officer of the midshipmen, that I was the commander of this whole command, and there were times when things would go on here and I would make the decisions. That was why I didn't allow the process, which I've seen with subsequent superintendents do, that things that happen in Bancroft Hall were purely within the province of the commandant. After the commandant reviewed the situation, a recommendation would come to the superintendent. I found that if you did that, you would often be presented with a fait accompli.

I knew the importance of our image here, so if something happened in Bancroft Hall that had the potential for affecting the image of the school through the media coverage and so forth, I knew about it right away. They knew that I wanted to know immediately when something like that happened in Bancroft Hall, and then under my

---

* Captain Jack N. Darby, USN, served as the Naval Academy's commandant of midshipmen in 1978-1979. Captain/Rear Admiral William F. McCauley, USN, was the commandant, 1979-1981

guidance, we would develop a plan to handle it. I would not let something like that go into the system to grind away and work at it. You couldn't let one lieutenant, and inexperienced officers come up with an approach to dealing with things like that. Your potential for bad publicity here exists all the time, and you just can't allow something to get in the media that has the potential for really giving us a black eye.

Paul Stillwell: Well, you have to strike a balance too. You don't want the lieutenant to feel that he's powerless, that it doesn't matter what he does, because somebody's always looking over his shoulder.

Admiral Lawrence: That's certainly right. I would say the vast majority of midshipman conduct cases were handled in there. But the commandant well knew that anything with the potential for adverse media coverage, I got into it right away.

I could give you countless examples. While I was here two women alleged they were raped. Well, I knew about that right away, and we had a plan being mapped out. As I say, we never really got a bad media coverage from either of those cases. When I came over here, I told people, "There are probably about four or five things that can happen while I'm superintendent of the Naval Academy that will ruin my career. One is a rape situation. Others are a cheating scandal, a drug scandal, or a homosexual scandal."

Well, within the first six months, I had all of those. [Laughter] But, because I was thinking about this when I came over here, and how I would handle them, as soon as one of those situations occurred, I immediately started to have a plan.

Paul Stillwell: What was the approach on the homosexual situation?

Admiral Lawrence: Well, this was an allegation that there was some homosexuality on the women's basketball team. I forget how it was reported, but I found out about it very quickly, and so I said, "Well, the traditional way you handle things like this is put the NIS into a situation." That's the Navy's investigatory body. Then I let the NIS work the problem, and if you have any experience with NIS, you know they are not the smoothest individuals in the world. They're . . .

Paul Stillwell: Intimidating.

Admiral Lawrence: They're like a burro and burrowing a hole or something; they grind away. They're very results-oriented. They were getting these women in and really treating them pretty roughly. The feedback I was getting from that was not very good. Also, they wanted to do a stakeout of the coach of the women's basketball team when they didn't get the confirming information that they were looking for.

I looked at this, and I said, "You know, there's a lot of elements of just rumor and smear tactics, because a lot of guys in those times resented women here; they were prone to do things like that, say "Ah, those women athletes are just a bunch of homosexuals." So finally, I just said, "Hey the NIS is out of this. Thank you for what you've done; your role is over. I'm not going to have a stakeout of the women's basketball coach. She's a very fine officer." Well, I took flak in some circles from people who said I tried to cover up a homosexual situation here. I just accepted the flak, but I felt it was the right thing to do. I wasn't going to have these heavy-handed investigators intimidate these women. That could have destroyed their reputations to find out that the women's basketball team's coach would have her house staked out.

See, that's the NIS mentality. If they don't get results, then they want to escalate the action. And so that was really the only case of that.

Paul Stillwell: Was there any evidence to support the allegations?

Admiral Lawrence: We never really had confirming evidence. It started out with some allegations that members of the women's basketball team were all going over to the coach's house on the weekends, and there was some hanky-panky going on there. And the Naval Academy is a ripe place for rumors, I'll tell you. But none of the women on the basketball team confirmed this was going on. The most allegations were from people who were not on the team. I just felt we didn't have enough evidence to confirm it. I felt we had done enough so-called digging, and I didn't feel it was warranted to go any further. I said, "If something else comes up, we'll certainly pursue it, but I'm not going to destroy the reputations of these women or subject them to this inconsiderate type of treatment." That happened my first year here, and nothing ever came up again. But things like this are coming up all the time here. You've got 4,400 highly charged teenagers, and there is potential for unusual events to occur.

Two really, very traumatic things happened. When I arrived here, the academy was allowing midshipmen to drink beer over in Dahlgren Hall, and I didn't like it.* It was against all of my instincts and principles as the right thing to do. This had been going on for several years, and I didn't want to come in and just change things. But it became apparent to me that midshipmen were drinking too much, and the minimum legal drinking age at that time was 18. We hadn't yet gone to 21.

In spring of 1979 two midshipmen drove off the seawall down here by the library; one was drowned and the other got out. The driver of that car was inebriated, so I separated him through the administrative conduct system. I should have gone to court-martial, but it was within my authority to handle it through the administrative conduct system. I did it under the provision of law that allows the superintendent to dismiss midshipmen from naval service. Well, it turned out that was a law that had been passed back in 1800. So this kid filed suit in the federal courts, and that was a sticky court battle.

Two years later, another midshipman was inebriated. He came into the yard at high speed, ran into a tree right by the parade ground, and another midshipman was killed. I put that to court-martial, because I felt it was of the gravity to justify judicial-type proceeding, as opposed to administrative conduct-type proceeding. I also recalled my having to fight that suit. But it was amazing, when I put that to court-martial and it got coverage in the media, the number of letters I got in with great sympathy towards the midshipman who was inebriated driving the car, and from a lot of old grads from the Naval Academy—even a former CNO, who had the attitude that, "There but for the grace of God go I."

I said, "Hey, that's not the right attitude. I mean, hell, you don't go around killing people through getting drunk and have it just passed off." But some alumni were putting a lot of pressure on me just to dismiss the case.

---

* Dahlgren Hall is a former armory that has been converted for use as an ice rink and snack bar.

Paul Stillwell: What was the outcome?

Admiral Lawrence: Well, I sent it to court-martial, and the court-martial found him guilty; the sentence was dismissal from the naval service. I concurred but gave a suspended-type sentence. In other words, I put him on a year's probation, and if his conduct was satisfactory that year, I would suspend the sentence. I put him over in Luce Hall, and he worked in alcohol-abuse programs.

But at that time we had a constant battle with the midshipmen drinking. Drinking was sweeping the country in the college set at that time. Subsequently, we terminated the midshipmen drinking beer in Dahlgren Hall. I just felt it was too much.

The other problem we had was that first class midshipmen were going over into the officers' and faculty club here getting too much to drink. So we put some controls on that. And we went into a major alcohol abuse education program. I don't know whether I talked about the actions I had to take with regard to drugs while I was here too.

Paul Stillwell: No, I don't think so.

Admiral Lawrence: Well, maybe I'll do that the next time I'm here, because that's a little extensive.

Paul Stillwell: Well, let me ask you one more on this. Did you suspend the sentence because of this feedback you were getting from the alumni?

Admiral Lawrence: No, no. He was a good young man, and he had just got caught up in this national attitude among college kids about drinking heavily. I felt that he was worth redeeming, but I was going to make him go through a year's probation, where he could absolutely prove to me that he was worthy of this consideration.

Paul Stillwell: Well, did you see this taking him to court-martial as a useful example for the rest of the people?

Admiral Lawrence: Oh, sure. And I passed on to my successor, "Look, I was the first superintendent that used a court-martial in 100 years. Don't hesitate to use court-martial, because first of all, you'll prevent getting a suit filed against you, because when you take an action administratively, you can point to a provision of law. You just don't have the strength of your position that you would from something that's determined by a court."

Paul Stillwell: Which is due process.

Admiral Lawrence: That's right. And so on the administrative option, this doesn't have the due process, just looks like one individual making that decision. I said, "A court-martial is a jury." Since that time, all the academies were receptive to using a court-martial.

Paul Stillwell: Who was the former CNO who wrote to you?

Admiral Lawrence: Admiral Anderson.[*] This kind of surprised me, because Admiral Anderson was a . . .

Paul Stillwell: He had a very strait-laced reputation.

Admiral Lawrence: But the old-school attitude about drinking in the military was that everybody drank. I had other old grads respond when I suspended the sentence, "Boy, you did the right thing." I kept hearing "There but for the grace of God go I."

You really learn a lot about human nature when you're superintendent.

As superintendent of the Naval Academy, of course, it's a real challenge to run everything effectively. The other challenge is to really be very skillful in preventing the image of the academy from being tarnished, by some midshipmen conduct cases getting blown out of perspective. And here, you are in a much more difficult position than the guys out there at Colorado Springs and up at West Point in these remote locations.

---

[*] Admiral George W. Anderson, Jr., USN, served as Chief of Naval Operations from 1 August 1961 to 1 August 1963. His oral history is in the Naval Institute collection.

Because we have all these newspapers and news services looking over our shoulder. So that's a big challenge is to handle things like that in as skillfully as you possibly can.

Paul Stillwell: Well, I'll look forward to hearing more about it the next time.

Interview Number 17 with Vice Admiral William P. Lawrence, U.S. Navy (Retired)

Place: U.S. Naval Institute, Annapolis, Maryland

Date: Wednesday, 30 January 1991

Paul Stillwell: Admiral, I think an appropriate place to start today would be to talk about the physical plant and long-range planning you did during your time as superintendent.

Admiral Lawrence: Long-range planning with regard to the physical plant was a key part of what you were doing. First of all, you really had to work hard to ensure that you got an adequate amount of money in the budget every year for maintenance and upkeep of facilities. This was in that part of the '70s when there were all sorts of fiscal constraints. The physical plant was an area that often suffered, so I had to use a lot of personal influence, requesting that we be not cut excessively.

This was not just for the long-range durability of our buildings, but also because we are essentially a national historic site here, almost like a national park. I think it's important we project a good appearance to the national public. We get about two million visitors a year at the Naval Academy, so I had to work hard to get enough in our maintenance and upkeep budget to keep the Naval Academy looking well. We were usually pretty successful in that area.

There were two big challenges while I was here in terms of new buildings. One was getting the final approval for a physical education center. It's principally the natatorium we now call Lejeune Hall. And, of course, that had to go through all of the approval chain over there within the Navy and the Defense Department, and then get in the military construction budget. As I recall, we paid right around $12 million for that building. It was certainly difficult to justify to some people because of fiscal constraints. But we were able to keep it in the budget and finally get it approved.

When I was here, we had the groundbreaking and started the construction of Lejeune Hall. It was actually completed after I left.* As I mentioned earlier, I was the

---

* Lejeune Hall is the first Naval Academy building named for a Marine Corps officer. It was built at a cost of $13.5 million and opened in 1982. It provides seating for 1,000 spectators and has facilities for swimming, diving, water polo, and wrestling.

one who initiated the idea to name it Lejeune Hall, because we didn't have any buildings here named for former Marines. John Lejeune was a Naval Academy graduate and probably in many respects the most famous Marine officer in history. He commanded the Second Division in World War I, which combined a Marine regiment and an Army regiment. Then he was the Commandant of the Marine Corps during the '20s. Since he was so famous, I felt we should name a building after Lejeune. I had a little difficulty with some of the senior retired admirals and so forth: "Why are you naming a building at the Naval Academy after a Marine?" But the opposition wasn't too great. It was approved pretty readily. The big challenge was defending it in the budget arena.

Then the other challenge I had was that we knew we wanted a building such as this new brigade activity center. We had great difficulty with convincing the historic preservation people that we had to tear down the old Isherwood Hall to make room for it. Isherwood Hall was one of the original buildings from the 1900 to 1910 period when the academy was rebuilt.[*] It was a part of the Beaux Arts architectural style used in that time frame, although under the Beaux Arts style, you have this perfect symmetry, including two perpendicular axes. Isherwood Hall was not what you would call a principal edifice. It was actually behind Mahan Hall, so if there was any building here from the original Beaux Arts plan that you could tear down, it was Isherwood Hall.[†] It wasn't all that ascetically appealing anyway.

But the historic preservation people just really dug their heels in and said that they objected to tearing down Isherwood Hall. We had studied it very carefully. At the time they built Rickover Hall, the conclusion was that you simply couldn't modernize Isherwood Hall, put in all the laboratory facilities needed to make it an engineering building.[‡] So we felt we had sound justification for tearing it down, and it wouldn't seriously degrade the historic preservation aspects of the Naval Academy. But there is a National Council for Historic Preservation. The members are political appointees, and they work directly under the President. They approve all controversial destruction of

---

[*] Isherwood Hall was built in 1905 and used for teaching the discipline of steam engineering. It was joined by two other engineering buildings: Griffin Hall in 1918 and Melville Hall in 1937. All three were razed in 1982.
[†] Mahan Hall, which for many years housed the Naval Academy library, is still in existence. Among its features are a large auditorium and a clock tower.
[‡] Rickover Hall opened in 1975.

historically significant buildings. So Isherwood Hall was placed in that category, and it was determined that this decision had to go up to the National Council for Historic Preservation.

Initially they were not very receptive to this, and we were not getting any help from the National Trust for Historic Preservation, which is a private organization over in Washington. The National Council for Historic Preservation had a maritime section that was headed up by a retired Navy captain, Naval Academy graduate. He was adamantly opposed to tearing down Isherwood Hall. There is also a Maryland historical preservation authority, and it got into the act. I said, "How do they have any cognizance over us as a state activity?" But I learned that all these preservationists are networked.

Then we had Historic Annapolis out here. It was headed up at that time by Mrs. St. Clair Wright, whose father was a Naval Academy graduate.* She and I were on good terms, and so I talked to her and explained all this. So she basically stayed neutral, although I don't think she was really in favor of tearing down Isherwood Hall. At least, she didn't weigh in heavily when I had all these historic preservation groups against me. The National Council for Historic Preservation was really giving us the bureaucratic stall. They actually forced us to have a historic preservation architect come in and review the situation. So we found an architectural firm in Boston that specialized in historical preservation and historical buildings. They came in, and we paid them $100,000 to do a study to tell us everything we already knew. We had to present that study to the National Council for Historic Preservation.

Paul Stillwell: What was the finding of the study?

Admiral Lawrence: The finding of the study was that that building did not lend itself to being modernized, and the loss of that building would not serious degrade the historic preservation aspects of the Naval Academy. See, the architect was Ernest Flagg, who

---

* Anne St. Clair Smith Wright (1910-1993) was one of the founders in 1952 of an organization called Historic Annapolis, Inc., now the Historic Annapolis Foundation. She served the non-profit in a variety of volunteer leadership roles over the years. Her father was Rear Admiral Arthur St. Clair Smith Jr., USN, Naval Academy class of 1897. Her husband was Captain Joseph Martin Pickett Wright, USN, Naval Academy class of 1924.

was trained in the Beaux Arts School. The study said the loss of the building didn't degrade the overall Flagg plan for the reconstruction of the Naval Academy between 1900 and 1910.

But then, while we were fighting this big battle, President Reagan won the election.[*] He was very much against government regulations, you recall. So all these regulatory bodies went into a low profile mode when Reagan came into office, because they were all afraid he was going to cut them or something. So the opposition just died away, and finally, in early 1981, we got permission to tear it down. We got $1 million or so in the budget to tear it down, so it was torn down after I left in August of 1981.

But I had some tough battles with the preservationists. I found that, like a lot of special interest groups, they play hardball. I mean they actually got dirty in some of the things and made some false statements. That was very frustrating, but we did win that battle. But to show you how cost escalation is, at that time we were talking of a cost of the brigade activity center of about $12 million dollars. Now the final cost is $27 million.[†]

Paul Stillwell: How far along was the conceptualization for the new building?

Admiral Lawrence: Oh, we had a complete plan for the brigade activities center at that time.

Paul Stillwell: Was that cost growth all attributable to the delay, or were there other factors?

Admiral Lawrence: Well, it's just normal cost escalation, the delay, and I'm sure that when they finally got the architect's detailed plans, there were features in there that they probably determined were more costly than they had originally anticipated. But the cost

---

[*] Ronald W. Reagan served as President of the United States from 20 January 1981 to 20 January 1989.
[†] The brigade activities center is named Alumni Hall, a multipurpose building at the Naval Academy. It was financed partly by government funds and partly by private donations. It was completed in October 1991, several months after this interview. The seating capacity is 5,710 for basketball and 6,500 as a multipurpose auditorium.

growth in defense type of systems, both weapon systems and construction, is way above national inflation. For example, for the past two decades, the cost of a ship and aircraft has been rising an average of 12% to 13% a year. There's the cost escalation in military defense systems that no one can really define, and I think one reason is that there seems to be a tacit agreement among people there that you overcharge the government. Anyway, we really expected to get that building for $12 million dollars, about the same as we did Lejeune Hall, because Lejeune Hall is not all that much different.

Those were the principal challenges, getting the maintenance and upkeep money and taking charge of those new two facility developments. While I was here, we always had a master plan for long-range facility construction. Many of the items on the list were wishful thinking, but I think now that we have the brigade activity center, that satisfies all the major facility needs of the academy. I don't think we really need or have room for any more. You could put some things across the river, but I don't think we need anything to support the program at the academy.[*]

Paul Stillwell: Could you just talk briefly, please, about that area across the river, the naval station, and what it accomplishes?

Admiral Lawrence: Well, of course, it's a very valuable real estate to us, because, in addition to the naval station that supports the Naval Academy, we have the David Taylor Research and Development Center over there, which does important work for the Navy in the research and development area.[†] Then there's an Air Force electronic facility over there called ECAC.[‡] And we have a naval communication station over there. The naval station, of course, is essential to us here at the academy, because they maintain all the waterborne craft that support the academy professional training. They maintain the yard patrol craft and provide the personnel who man those yard patrol craft. They maintain

---

[*] In 2008, long after this interview, the Naval Academy dedicated the Wesley Brown Field House, a large new sports and physical education facility. Its name honors the Naval Academy's first black graduate.
[†] The David Taylor center was closed by the Navy in 1998 as the result of the work of BRAC – base realignment and closure, a process for reducing the number of U.S. military bases. The property has since been transferred to Anne Arundel County, Maryland.
[‡] ECAC – Electronic Analysis and Compatibility Center.

our sailing craft, and so they have a very extensive, complex, maintenance responsibility. And, of course, they support us in a sense of having a rifle range and pistol range for midshipmen. It's a very active, going concern.

When I was here, the commanding officer of the naval station also had cognizance over the Naval Academy sailing program. So we picked a guy who had sailing expertise. He spent probably as much time focusing on the overall sailing program that supported the midshipmen as he did on the naval station itself. This was during the academic year training—both formal training, also recreational sailing—and in the summer training, which was a very extensive offshore element. We have Naval Academy yachts that make transatlantic cruises. So it's a very important operation and takes a very good commanding officer to run that sailing program.

Paul Stillwell: What attributes does the sail training contribute to the overall development of the midshipmen?

Admiral Lawrence: I think it makes a very important contribution, because you learn a lot during sailing, just about basic seamanship, respect for the sea, develop a seaman's eye. You learn a lot about the important qualities you need, like self-reliance. It's very good leadership development, because midshipmen have to show initiative and dependability and those types of qualities when they're out there sailing.

One example of something that happened while I was here was the Fastnet race I told you about earlier. We were just getting into the offshore sailing program very heavily when I was superintendent. We sent a yacht on a transatlantic cruise over to the British Isles, and the plan was to go from the British Isles down to the Azores and then to Bermuda, then back to the United States. But they got caught in a freak storm in the Irish Sea. Captain Ned Shuman was the CO of the naval station and commander of the Naval Academy sailing squadron.* He was the senior officer there with another young officer with him, and he had seven midshipmen. I told you how I contacted Charlie Hunter in London to get information on our midshipmen. That was a very harrowing experience

---

* Captain Edwin A. Shuman III, USN, was commanding officer of the Annapolis Naval Station from March 1978 to July 1982. He was a prisoner of war in North Vietnam from 17 March 1968 to 17 March 1973.

for them. They really handled themselves well, and I was so fortunate to have Ned Shuman.

What that experience brought out to me was that we really needed to have the ability to communicate with our offshore yachts anywhere in the world. I knew we had single sideband communications capability that could do that. But the sailors' attitude was, "Well, you shouldn't send us out if you don't have faith that we can handle it."

I said, "Okay, I understand all that, but I want you to report in every day. Every ship in the Navy is in continuous communication, every airplane, and you're no different from the rest of the Navy. Before any ship can go offshore here, they have to have the ability to communicate with us here at the Naval Academy on an instant basis, if necessary." They really grumbled about this. They told me about how much money it was going to do this. I said, "I don't care about the money; you do it."

Well, it turned out that we have a system now where retired naval officers on a volunteer basis man a communications center on a continuous basis when we have offshore yachts. Every yacht has a capability for single sideband radio to communicate with that control communications center. And, of course, the retired guys love it; they're ham radio-type people anyway. They eat this stuff up.

So it has really improved a lot, in the sense of putting everybody's mind at ease. But it put a discipline in the system. Before we did that, a sailboat would sight a merchantman, and it would send a radio signal and say, "Hey, would you call the Naval Academy and tell them we're okay?" It was a very ill defined situation, so that's one of the imperatives I imposed on that, and I think it's really paid off. The sailing program is a very fine professional development mechanism. It has become even better organized since I left here, which is a good thing.

Paul Stillwell: What do you recall specifically about Captain Shuman and Captain Grosvenor?

Admiral Lawrence: Well, Shuman was here when I arrived, but Grosvenor's the guy who came in and laid the groundwork for developing a fine, well-organized sailing program, and getting the Naval Academy back to being competitive in national intercollegiate sailing.* During my time here, the Naval Academy dominated intercollegiate sailing. We won the national sailing championship every year I was superintendent. I think we won it five straight years, so Grosvenor was the one who really got that off the ground.

Paul Stillwell: Dean McNitt had a big hand in it too.

Admiral Lawrence: Well, sure. Of course, Dean McNitt, even though he was the dean of admissions, played a very active role. But we have the Fales Committee that has the oversight of the Naval Academy sailing programs; it's an advisory committee, and Dean McNitt has always been active in that. He certainly brought his wisdom to bear in helping the commanding officer of the naval station and everybody who had cognizance over the sailing program.

And, of course, Ned Shuman has done a great job. He's one of the best sailors in the country and a good strong leader. So he did a fine job in running the naval station and expanding the sailing program, getting more professional contribution out of the sailing program.

Paul Stillwell: What else do you recall about the athletic program and working with Bo Coppedge?

Admiral Lawrence: That was a very smooth-running operation. Having been a former athlete here at the academy myself, I, of course, was quite interested in it and tried to stay very close to it while I was here.

I was the beneficiary of George Welsh's very fine capability. He was the football coach during the three years I was here. I left in August of '81, and then George terminated his employment here after the '81 season. So the whole time I was here, George Welsh was here, and our won-loss record during that time was 25-11. We went to two bowls, so George kind of hit his peak while I was here. It was really a very heartwarming to be involved in a football program and see what we had done here. But I

---

* Captain Alexander Graham Bell Grosvenor, USN, was Shuman's predecessor.

use that as an example of what I feel we can achieve at the Naval Academy. If we have the right management and leadership, I think we can achieve it. Because in 1978 season, we ranked 17th in the country. I think that's achievable, while still maintaining the high admissions, academic standards that the school requires. It's just a question of good leadership, in my opinion.

We didn't really have a lot of athletic problems while I was here. Bo Coppedge, as director of athletics, ran a very good show, and there were several areas, of course, that I had to get into. I discussed previously how General Goodpaster and I were able to fend off the ABC network when it was applying pressure on us to move the Army-Navy game away from that Thanksgiving weekend. Bo Coppedge would come and wring his hands and say, "They're going to take us off national television if we don't comply with this."

I said, "Bo, Army-Navy game will never be taken off national television. Just mark my words. I mean, it's a national tradition, it has great national appeal, and it always ranks up with very top in television ratings."

He said, "Oh, yes, it's going to happen. They're going to take us off."

I said, "No, Bo, they're not going to take us off national television. If ABC came to me and said that they're going to take the Army-Navy game off television, then I'd get the Secretary of Defense to call the President of the United States, and he'd do it, and tell them they can't do that." So, anyway, we fought them, and finally, after I left the academies had to back off. Now we play them up around the seventh or eighth of December. The bad thing is that it's right before the midshipmen take exams. But we played Army this year on Saturday, and the midshipmen started exams on Monday. That's a terrible burden on a football player: get all primed for the Army-Navy game, his whole thinking is on that, and then have to take exams two days after the game.

Paul Stillwell: Well, the rest of the midshipmen also because they're there at the game.

Admiral Lawrence: Sure, I'm talking about all the midshipmen, but it really has impact on the football players themselves.

Paul Stillwell: One of the remarkable things about the athletic program is that it embraces so many different sports. That's quite a challenge to administer that many.

Admiral Lawrence: Well, it really is, and it's quite a business challenge, because the Naval Academy Athletic Association is a private organization, so it has to make a profit to succeed. It takes a very good business management. I didn't get intimately involved in a lot of that, but I knew well what the challenges were and how important it was for us to have good attendance at games and to try our best to get on national television. So I did all I could to support those activities that generate revenues.

Of course, my big challenge while I was here was progressive expansion of women's sports. When I arrived, women were in two classes, plebes and third classmen. Just as I arrived, we started the women into a third class. So that brought us up to around 200 women. So we had to sit down to see what varsity sports we could support. Initially, we started those traditional sports like basketball and volleyball. Then we started women's crew and women's softball. Very early, of course, we had started indoor-outdoor track and across country. But we had to think this through carefully.

I was a great advocate for establishing as many women's varsity sports as possible, because it wasn't so important to me that we have a great won-loss record as it was to have those sports. It was my perception that women here at the academy, in an integrated living situation and professional situation, being a very small minority, needed to have those opportunities in which they interfaced just with women. It's just the nature of the sexes, I think, that although you can have really good integration, they need those times when they are just women themselves, because the uniqueness of the sex requires that they interface with themselves. So women needed those opportunities just to be together as a group. Sports were the best medium for making that happen here at the academy. There were guys who said, "Oh, we can't establish women's softball team, because we don't have enough women to do it."

I said, "I don't really care. If we have just enough to fill the team, that's fine with me." But it turned out that probably between 50% and 75% of your women are varsity athletes, because the women who qualify to come here normally have an interest in sports. I mean, there seems to be a connection that women who are attracted to the military profession are also interested in sports.

Paul Stillwell: Well, another explanation could be that there are so few that you can be highly selective.

Admiral Lawrence: Well, that's true. And, of course, the coaches look for the good athletes to try to get them to come here. Anyway, this is a little bit of a problem with the guys. Whereas, about one-tenth of the males here will get a varsity letter, about 50% of the women do. It burns the guys up, "Oh, those girls got their varsity letters," because every time they see a gal walking around with a letter sweater on, it raises the hackles. So I did a lot of stroking of the guys and said, "You have to understand that only 8% of the brigade are women, and so they have greater opportunities to participate."

But the sports program here is a valuable aspect of life. I mean, you have to keep it in perspective and not give too much emphasis to it. But sports—in a proper balance with academics—are very important in developing those qualities you need in a military profession. Not only do you get all the things you learn on the athletic field—the will to win, teamwork and all those things—but the great value of the emphasis on sports and physical education here is that most graduates develop this lifelong dedication with fitness. So the carryover aspect of what we do here is important. I mean whether he's in sports, like tennis, golf, and things that like, which they play during their adult years, it is really important in a person's career. They asked me when they were interviewing me about the POW situation, what advice would I give to anybody in the military to prepare him to be a POW.

I said, "The first thing I'd advise someone is to keep yourself in the best physical fitness you can, because you get in a POW environment, health and fitness are big things that keep you going. Those guys who were shot down and were heavy smokers, alcohol abusers—they had a tougher time enduring that experience.

But, anyway, I was very, very pleased with almost every aspect of the sports program while I was superintendent.

Paul Stillwell: What can you say about Coppedge as an individual? He and Rip Miller were institutions here for years and years.

Admiral Lawrence: Well, they were both wonderful men. Rip Miller was largely responsible for helping me get my appointment as a midshipman, because he was trying to recruit me as a football player.[*] The big thing he did when he was assistant director of athletics was try to help athletes get appointments and help the coaches in their recruiting. So I've known Rip Miller all the way back to 1947. And, of course, when I was playing football, he was still coaching. I think he ended his coaching career in 1947, which was my first year here. So I got to see him as a coach and was very close to him all those years. And particularly when I was superintendent, I tried to stay close to him. He was a great institution, made a great contribution.

And, of course, so did Bo Coppedge, who really brought some wonderful qualities in there. He had some good, astute business sense. But I think his great strength was in human relations. He really knew how to get along with people, work with people, and he just was a very astute individual in the broad relationships you have to maintain in a job like that. He was very highly respected in intercollegiate circles, very highly respected in television industry. He was the chairman of the NCAA television committee for several years.[†] He made a great contribution here in his 20 years as the director of athletics.

Paul Stillwell: What do you recall about your relationships with Naval Academy alumni while you were superintendent?

Admiral Lawrence: Well, it was a very good relationship. I tried very hard, while I was superintendent, to help the alumni in some of the projects they were working on, particularly in the fundraising. This was just as we were conceiving the idea of getting

---

[*] Edgar E. "Rip" Miller was a Naval Academy institution. He had played college football at Notre Dame, where in 1924 he was one of the "Seven Mules," the linemen who played in front of the "Four Horsemen" of the backfield. In 1931 to 1933 he was the Naval Academy's head football coach. For many years thereafter he worked as a coach and assistant athletic director.

[†] NCAA – National Collegiate Athletic Association.

more active in fundraising for facility development and so forth. Before I came here, they had implemented some facility renovation through private donations, like the Crown Sailing Center was donated to the academy by the Crown family. I think Ross Perot paid for the renovation of Dahlgren Hall over the years. So the precedent had already been established for these privately donated funds.

When I was here, we were talking about doing it on a much larger scale, which ultimately led to the funding of the brigade activity center, in which Congress authorized us to do that on half appropriated funds and half on donated funds. That was the first time in anybody's knowledge where you had a government facility half funded by the government, half through private donations. The brigade activity center established that precedent.

So I worked really closely with them in that area, tried to get around and speak to alumni chapters as superintendent, to the absolute maximum extent that I could. This was the aspect of trying to keep the alumni informed and interested in what we were doing. And, of course, we derived a tremendous amount of support from the alumni association. They use a lot of funds they gain through donations to enable midshipmen to do a lot of things. Bill Busik, who's been the executive director of the alumni association for about 20 years now, is always looking for ways to help in certain aspects of midshipmen program here at the academy.*

Paul Stillwell: Do you have any specific examples?

Admiral Lawrence: Well, for example, he used to help fund sending the glee club around on tours. During the spring break and Christmas break, we'd go out and sing around the country. This is great public relations for the Naval Academy to do this. There are all sorts of areas that the alumni funds will help midshipmen, like maybe summer travel to foreign countries to support language training. But there seemed to be, throughout the year, situations that come up—very highly desirable things for midshipmen to do, a good opportunity, but you just don't have the government appropriated funds to pay for it. So

---

* Captain William S. Busik, USN (Ret.), was the executive director (redesignated president and CEO during his tenure) of the Naval Academy Alumni Association from 1971 to 1994.

the alumni will step in and say, "Yeah, we'll handle that." So there's a very, very close linkage between the superintendent and his staff and the alumni and their staff in terms of looking at cooperative endeavors. For example, if an alumni class or an individual alumnus wants to use their money in a certain way, Bill Busik will interface very closely with the academy to ensure that the most productive endeavors are taken on.

I think the biggest improvement we've seen is that most any memorial-type things constructed now at the Naval Academy serve a useful purpose. We just don't have granite monuments put in the yard that don't really contribute much to the midshipmen. A good example is the columbarium at the cemetery, where cremated remains can be stored; that was an alumni endeavor. And, of course, for the brigade activity center, they're paying I think about $14 million through donated funds. So we really get very fine support out of the alumni, and under Bill Busik's leadership, they progressively expanded the role of the alumni association. So it's a very fine relationship; it's a very wonderful operation that occurs here.

I think there is more that they aspire to do, like funding endowed chairs. For example, for five years I filled an endowed chair in leadership here at the academy, which is endowed by Ross Perot, and which I just terminated on 1 January. But other endowed chairs are future possibilities, because several quite wealthy alumni have expressed an interest in endowing chairs. Bill Busik and his people are orchestrating all that to make it all come together effectively. So it's a very fine operation for the Naval Academy. There are many things we couldn't do here without donated funds. They really enhance the whole program at the academy.

Paul Stillwell: Where did you take your direction from during your tenure? Was it CNO, BuPers, SecNav?

Admiral Lawrence: Principally, the CNO and the VCNO. My principal interface on a continued basis was the VCNO, if I had anything of interest occurring. On occasion, I had direct interface with the CNO, but mostly with the VCNO. And then up in the Secretariat, I had very rare, direct access with people there, because I felt my chain was through the VCNO and CNO up to the Secretary. But on midshipmen disciplinary cases—the way the law reads is the superintendent recommends disciplinary action, and the Secretary approves it. That law was written before there was even a Chief of Naval Operations. The position of Chief of Naval Operations came into being around 1915, but the law that governs the discipline of the midshipmen and cadets goes back to the 1800s. So it says the superintendent will recommend dismissal, and the Secretary of the Navy will approve it.

Well, this got to be a little bit of a sensitive issue one time when Admiral Watkins was the Vice Chief of Naval Operations. The CNO wasn't in the chain, but I said, "Well, the CNO can give any orders he wants to give. If he says, 'Send those through,' that's the way it'll be done. I don't care what the law reads; I'm going to do what the CNO wants me to do." But that kind of miffed Admiral Watkins one time. He found out that for years the superintendent had been sending these things directly into the Secretary of the Navy's office, and it didn't come through the CNO. So one time after he had calmed down a little bit, I said, "Why in the world do you want another problem to worry about? Don't you have enough already?"

He said, "Yeah, you're probably right." We kept sending them directly to the Secretary of the Navy.

So that was one time we directly interfaced with a lawyer or somebody like that up in the Assistant Secretary of the Navy for Manpower was the one who handled these things. Most of them were just basically formalized approval. But some of them are sensitive, particularly if a midshipman was filing suit, which happened several times while I was there.

I think I mentioned one time, when it was reported to me just a few days before graduation of a possible involvement of a midshipman with drugs.

Paul Stillwell: You did mention that one.

Admiral Lawrence: And that one, boy, Secretary Claytor and I were directly involved in a three-way combination: CNO, Superintendent, Secretary of the Navy. When James Woolsey was the Under Secretary of the Navy, he had a lot of interest in the academic program here, and I directly interfaced with him on occasion.* But anything I did, I always tried to keep the VCNO and CNO informed.

I developed a practice while I was here that in July of every year, I would go over and give the CNO and the VCNO and the Chief of Naval Personnel—all three of them together, and anybody else they wanted to hear it—a very comprehensive briefing on what was going on at the Naval Academy. I'd go into every aspect of the program. It would be about an hour briefing, and I'd cover everything from academics, athletics, admissions, disciplinary, financial. I'd tell the EA what I wanted, and he'd say, "We can't tie up the CNO for an hour."

I said, "Look, I only do this once a year, and I think the academy is important enough to the CNO that he should be willing to sit there and get a 45 minute to an hour briefing on the Naval Academy."

"Yeah, you're right." The CNO and the VCNO were always happy to go through it, because at those times, there were a lot of challenges in the Navy, the CNO would always say afterward, "My God, at least there's one place in the Navy that seems to be running without a lot of problems." Because we were basically trouble-free over here. When we'd get a few midshipmen disciplinary problems that would get in the press for a few days, that really didn't present the CNO any great worries. But occasionally, when Admiral Rickover would complain about something, then the VCNO would get involved, because Admiral Rickover was so powerful by that time that when he said something, we usually got the response, at least from the VCNO.

Paul Stillwell: Where did you get your policy guidance from in running the academy?

Admiral Lawrence: The CNO. In 1975, the CNO wrote a policy statement on the Naval Academy. That was the time when the superintendent of the Naval Academy was taken out from under the Chief of Naval Education and Training and brought directly under the CNO. When the Chief of Naval Education and Training was established in the early '70s, he was going to be the big czar for all training in the Navy, so not only was all the

---

* R. James Woolsey served as Under Secretary of the Navy from 9 March 1977 to 7 December 1979.

pilot training, enlisted training and all those things be under him, he also got the Naval Postgraduate School, Naval War College, and they gave him the Naval Academy.

When Admiral Holloway came in as CNO in 1974, he just didn't feel that was a viable thing to do. He felt that the Naval Academy was being neglected in terms of budgeting and that sort of thing. So he brought it under him, and he also put out a policy statement. In that policy statement was the famous requirement that you heard about, 80-20.[*] The reason that got in there was because Admiral Watkins was the Chief of Naval Personnel; he was in nuclear submarines.[†] Admiral Holloway was nuclear trained and then the CO of *Enterprise*. They felt that would enhance getting people in the nuclear program in the Navy, so that was how that got through.

Paul Stillwell: One of the features in the spring and fall are the dress parades. What do you remember about the value of those?

Admiral Lawrence: Well, I think if you ask any midshipman, he would certainly question whether it was of any value to him, or just harassment. But it was valuable to the Naval Academy in a lot of respects. First of all, it was a very impressive spectacle that tourists and others could watch, and so it was a patriotically inspiring event. So from that aspect it was good.

But also you could help the Naval Academy by the people you brought back to review parades and that sort of thing. I mean the most ego-massaging event is to have somebody review a Naval Academy parade. You stand out there and you see 4,400 midshipmen before you. So I used to give a tremendous amount of thought to those individuals I brought back here to be the reviewing officials for those parades. I'm not saying it was all PR-motivated, but you had to consider a tremendous number of factors. One, you wanted to honor a distinguished individual; you also were thinking about establishing some rapport when an individual was in a place to help the Naval Academy. The other thing, of course, was the importance of in getting individuals whose example would inspire the midshipmen. So all these factors were woven into it.

---

[*] That is, 80% of the majors were to be in hard sciences and 20% in humanities.
[†] Vice Admiral James D. Watkins, USN, was Chief of Naval Personnel, 10 April 1975 to 21 July 1978.

I used to start thinking about reviewing officials, both for the fall and the spring parades, six to eight months before to be sure to send a timely invitation. As examples of people that I brought back to review parades is—of course, I had the CNO, himself; the Secretary of the Navy, himself; the Assistant Secretary of the Navy for Manpower. I invited the Commandant of the Marine Corps, General Barrow, but he never accepted. He sent the Assistant Commandant in his place. The Governor of Maryland, who was Harry Hughes, came over.* Then I brought back all the Naval Academy graduates who were astronauts—as many as I could get. Then I had all the Naval Academy graduate Medal of Honor winners. And I had all the former superintendents. Then I had all the former CNOs. Also I had Mr. Ed Meese, who came for plebe summer parade.† I'd gotten to know Ed Meese from previous years when he was on Reagan's staff out in California. His son was at West Point at that time, and he sent a signal to me that he'd love to come over and review a Naval Academy parade. So I had him review a plebe summer parade.

That's the category of people I had. As I say, I tried to get the invitations out several months in advance, because I was going after the type of people who would be hard to get, because they were much in demand, heavy schedule, so I gave a lot of thought to that. Also, I gave a lot of thought to the people I brought back to give Forrestal lectures to the entire brigade and try to get the very maximum impact on the midshipmen.

I also gave a tremendous amount of thought to the people I invited to pre-game luncheons at my house and attending the football game. I tried to get as many members of the Congress to come over as I could. It's hard to get them, because most congressmen go back to the districts on weekends. I made that comment to you the other day that the superintendent was a public affairs officer, in my opinion, and that's an example. I didn't let that adversely impact my other duties here, but I sure gave a lot of thought to those types of activities, because you're always thinking, first, of inspiring the midshipmen, and, secondly, projecting a good image of the academy. That was just one of many ways you could do it.

---

* Harry R. Hughes, a Democrat, served as Governor of Maryland from 1979 to 1987.
† Edwin Meese III served from 1981 to 1985 as counselor to the President and a member of the National Security Council. From 1985 to 1988 he was U.S. Attorney General.

But I tell you, the biggest ego trip in the world is to review a service academy parade. I used to watch those guys standing out there and see the great feeling of pride. And, of course, all of them merited that type of honor. It's quite a stroking event.

Paul Stillwell: One of the other topics or themes, that I remember from your time as superintendent is the great emphasis on energy conservation in the Carter administration.[*] [Laughter] How was that manifested here?

Admiral Lawrence: Well, the Carter administration imposed some requirements on us. We had to realize something like a 20% energy saving over X number of years. We looked at it and said, "My God, how are we going to do it?" Then, as we were brainstorming it, that's when we came up with the determination that if we actually shut down our plant over Christmas, we could achieve quite a quantum savings. I realized that was going to be an inconvenience to a lot of people, but I'd seen so many times over Christmas where a lot of organizations just went down to a very skeletal staff, but the academy kept all the utilities going.

I'd gone through one Christmas at the academy as superintendent, and I said, "Hey, I think we can make it work. For those people who have to come in, we can provide a way to maybe heat a single space in a department to permit people to continue working." There was quite a bit of grumbling and complaining, but I kept putting it in a patriotic context. I said, "Gosh, we've got to save energy, and we just had the Iran crisis—the Shah was overthrown—a quantum increase in oil prices, and the President is pleading for national conservation. I guess from a patriotic perspective we need to do this."[†] But, also, we had a 20% requirement imposed on us, so for two Christmases while I was here, we really sent the civilian staff on leave, and the military were allowed to take all the leave they could. Those who felt they had to work, we'd provide them a way to

---
[*] James E. "Jimmy" Carter, Jr., a Naval Academy graduate in the class of 1947, served as President of the United States from 20 January 1977 to 20 January 1981.
[†] When the Shah left Iran in January 1979, the Ayatollah Ruhollah Khomeini seized power and declared the nation to be an Islamic republic. On 4 November 1979 Iranian militants seized the U.S. embassy in Teheran and took the staff members there as hostages. The hostages were ultimately released on 20 January 1981.

work. But I understand after I left my successor just didn't continue doing that. I guess there were enough grumbles.

By that time Reagan had come into office, and Reagan was not advocating conservation. Our memories are very short in this country, so the Iranian thing—the hostages had been released, the oil prices were going down, so there was no emphasis on conservation anymore.

But I felt that a Christmas shutdown was the right thing to do. Like this Christmas, for example, I worked every day during the holidays and was going in to the office. Often I was the only guy in Luce Hall over several days' period, and yet we had all the utilities going. It just doesn't make sense.

Paul Stillwell: I remember the paid parking program was a big pain during that time.

Admiral Lawrence: I couldn't believe that some civilian in OMB who put together the President's budget came up with this idea of paid parking.* He sold it up the line, and I think President Carter approved it. The initial program was going to be put in in Washington, D.C., and then the Naval Academy was considered part of Washington, D.C. So we had to put it in here. I fought it as hard as I could, and my rationale was that we are a national park, a national historic site. I said, "We can't impose a paid parking program on a place where we have a lot of tourists and visitors and things like that." It didn't fly.

Finally, we got the guy in OMB who had conceived this idea to come over and we showed him the Naval Academy. We sat down and said, "Here are the reasons why it won't work. The ill will that you will generate to U.S. public will be far worse than any income you're going to derive from this." Finally, they backed off, but we were already into the thing. People were paying and—boy, no wonder Jimmy Carter didn't get reelected after he let things like that happen. I guess in theory things like that sound good, but in practice things like this just fall flat on their rear end, because you have to think about good will and things of that nature. I mean, I think anybody who works for

---

* OMB – Office of Management and Budget.

the United States Government, or something related to the United States Government—the military—is entitled to park free of charge.

Paul Stillwell: One event that we haven't discussed, and I know it's a highlight for you, is your daughter Wendy's graduation in 1981. What do you recall of that?

Admiral Lawrence: Well, that was certainly a very wonderful experience, as well as having her during the three years we were together here. But, as I said, we didn't see her all that much, because she was quite busy while she was a midshipman.

Did I tell the story earlier about my first chapel attendance while I was . . .

Paul Stillwell: Yes, you did.

Admiral Lawrence: Well, that was just one example of some of the fun aspects of having a daughter here. She did quite well as a midshipman. She became the deputy brigade commander, which was a five-striper, and she stood 12th in her class. I think she stood number one militarily, but 12th overall. She was the number-one graduate in the ocean engineering major, so she got the class of 1924 prize for top graduate in ocean engineering. And she had three years on the varsity crew team.

Vice President Bush was the speaker at that graduation.[*] The way we work it at graduation is the speaker gives out the diplomas for the distinguished graduates, who are the upper 10% of the class. My daughter was among the distinguished graduates, so I was not giving out those diplomas. After the distinguished graduates, the superintendent shares giving out the diplomas, either with the principal speaker or somebody like the CNO designated to do that. I wasn't designated to give out the diplomas, but when my daughter got her diploma from Vice President Bush, and she started walking across the stage, I came up and gave her a hug. I just felt it was an appropriate thing to do.

Well, anyway, a picture taken of that by AP, UPI, spread all over the country, and I got many great letters back. But it also turned out that somebody got a snapshot that showed Vice President Bush smiling on the right part of the picture, and on the left side

---

[*] George H. W. Bush was Vice President of the United States from 20 January 1981 to 20 January 1989.

of the picture I was hugging my daughter. I kept that among our pictures for several years. Then last year I had it blown up, and I sent it over to my friend, Chase Untermeyer, in the White House.* I said, "Chase, would you see if the President would sign this to my daughter Wendy. I think it'd be a nice thing." He ended up signing a picture to Wendy's grandparents, one to Wendy, and also one to me. So that was a nice touch. But it was a really pleasant experience for the family, not only having Wendy here, but also during the graduation week, because her grandparents and her mother all came back and had a great time.

Paul Stillwell: I remember seeing a picture in the paper with her mother and stepmother each pinning on one shoulder board.

Admiral Lawrence: Yes, that's right. So that was really pleasant.

One other thing I did while I was here was a very pleasant experience. I was disappointed that this past year, in 1990, nothing was done. But 1980 was the 135th anniversary of the Naval Academy. We had a 135th anniversary celebration. It wasn't all that big a deal, except that we had each department at the academy make a historic exhibit for display. I found that a lot of these departments, like math and physics and chemistry, have equipment that goes way back in the 1800s. And then there were old books in the library.

The other thing we did was have a parade to commemorate the 135th anniversary of the Naval Academy. I generated this idea of having the brigade staff wear the midshipman uniforms from around the era of the founding. Of course, a lot of people probably thought I was a kook with some of these ideas I would generate around here. Professor Jeffries was kind of honchoing all this, and we found somebody who could produce replicas of the old uniforms.† And part of them had to be the fore-and-aft hats.

---

* Chares Graves "Chase" Untermeyer served from November 1988 to August 1991 as director of presidential personnel for George H. W. Bush, who took office on 20 January 1989. In the 1960s, as a Naval Reserve officer, Untermeyer was aide to Rear Admiral Draper L. Kauffman, USN, whose sister was married to George H. W. Bush's older brother. Untermeyer's recollections of that duty are in the Naval Institute's oral history collection.

† Professor William W. Jeffries was on the staff of the Naval Academy from 1942 to 1989. In 1971 he became the institution's archivist and later was director of the Naval Academy Museum. The academy's archives are named in his honor.

So here in this parade, the brigade staff was wearing these 1850s-type midshipman uniforms, and there was a very heavy wind that day in the fall. Those cocked hats were just like sails, and these midshipmen would be marching with a crosswind and they'd be leaning over. [Chuckle] So the brigade staff, I'm sure, thought that the superintendent was off his rocker. But I thought it was a nice touch. We got some publicity, but it wasn't bad.

You know, I'm a great one for history and tradition, and I was disappointed in 1985 that we didn't celebrate the 140th birthday of the Naval Academy. It just went by. Throughout the world the West Point graduates have a Founders Day dinner on the anniversary of the founding of the Military Academy. Some day I'm going to push to have more of that type thing among Naval Academy graduates.

Paul Stillwell: Admiral I'm about out of questions.

Admiral Lawrence: Well, I think we've got about all I could possibly say on the Naval Academy. Next time we can start on the Third Fleet. I think I can finish up the Third Fleet in probably a couple hours, because it was not as complex totally as the Naval Academy experience. So I think I can see the light at the end of the tunnel.

Interview Number 18 with Vice Admiral William P. Lawrence, U.S. Navy (Retired)
Place: U.S. Naval Institute, Annapolis, Maryland
Date: Monday, 4 February 1991

Paul Stillwell: Admiral, to begin, I'd be interested to hear how you went about getting a three-star fleet command after not having had a two-star sea job at all.

Admiral Lawrence: Well, I don't know; I never really expected that would happen. After having spent those years as a POW, I had no great illusions that I would have a chance to restore my career or do those things that someone who had not been gone for six years would have been able to do. But, anyway, I guess they decided to give me that opportunity, which I was, of course, very thankful for, felt very humbled to do it.

Paul Stillwell: Do you think that this was in part because Admiral Hayward knew you?[*]

Admiral Lawrence: Well, I'm sure that was a big factor. He and I had served together as young officers at the Naval Air Test Center, and we had kept in touch with each other in our careers over the years. At times, when I would say that the POW period had probably caused me to miss a lot of experience, he would say, "Well, you gained some things there that nobody else did in terms of seasoning for command and that sort of thing." He felt pretty confident that, through application, I could learn the tactical side of the house, and I had a good, thorough foundation in that.

Paul Stillwell: Do you know how much, if any, input Secretary Lehman had in the process?[†]

Admiral Lawrence: I don't think he had very much at all, because he was still quite new in the job. I think it was more Admiral Hayward than anybody else, quite frankly,

---

[*] Admiral Thomas B. Hayward, USN, served as Chief of Naval Operations from 1 July 1978 to 30 June 1982. His oral history is in the Naval Institute collection.
[†] John F. Lehman Jr., served as Secretary of the Navy from 5 February 1981 to 10 April 1987.

because I think Lehman was still kind of getting his feet on the ground. I really didn't know Secretary Lehman prior to his becoming Secretary of the Navy. He came over to the Naval Academy on only two occasions in my last six months or so as the superintendent, and we really didn't have a chance to sit down and talk privately. But since he was associated with naval aviation, he probably would have been supportive of my doing something like that.*

Paul Stillwell: Well, he evidently liked what he'd seen of the job you did at the Naval Academy.

Admiral Lawrence: Maybe so, maybe so. Anyway, I felt very thankful, because, first of all, I was surprised when I got promoted to flag. Then I was surprised when the Navy gave me an operational command out in California when I made flag, and I was surprised when I was sent to the Naval Academy. I was also surprised when I went out there to Third Fleet, so I think I was just very, very fortunate. I think the big factor, of course, was that Admiral Hayward had served with me, and he knew me for many, many years. That probably allayed any concern about the risk he was taking in doing that.

Paul Stillwell: What sort of briefings or learning experiences did you have en route?

Admiral Lawrence: Well, I did a lot of things to prepare myself. One thing I did was to take off several days right after graduation, which usually is one of the quieter periods at the academy. This was about two months before I was due to detach. I went out to California and spent several days talking to the type commanders out there, ComNavAirPac, ComNavSurfPac.† Also I went up and spent a couple of days at the Tactical Warfare Training Center on Point Loma and talked to them a lot about tactics.‡ I went over to the Navy Operational Intelligence Center in Suitland and got a lot of

---

* As a Naval Reserve officer, Lehman was trained as a bombardier/navigator in the A-6 Intruder.
† ComNavAirPac – Commander Naval Air Force Pacific Fleet; ComNavSurfPac – Commander Naval Surface Force Pacific Fleet.
‡ Point Loma is a strip of land that juts southward at the western edge of the entrance to San Diego Harbor.

briefings on Soviet capabilities and some of our own highly classified capabilities.[*] And I started doing as much study as I could about our forces' capabilities and that sort of thing. So I tried to prepare myself as well as possible.

Of course, in my three years in the Pentagon, and then prior to that in the aviation command, I was thoroughly up to speed on capabilities of airplanes and tactics. What I basically had to fill in was more on the area of ASW, submarine capabilities, and surface ship capabilities.

Paul Stillwell: Well, some years back the First Fleet and ASWForPac were combined.[†] So ASW was really a substantial part of the job, wasn't it?

Admiral Lawrence: Well, by that time, the old vestiges of the ASWForPac were starting to end, because our perspective was much broader in terms of fleet capabilities and tactics. One of the really important responsibilities as Commander U.S. Third Fleet is that you're the Pacific Fleet Commander in Chief's agent for the tactical doctrine development. You have a resident staff of people who develop inputs that go into the various tactical doctrines. Second Fleet is the one that does it for the Atlantic Fleet, so you work very closely to the Second Fleet.

For example, we got heavily involved in developing new doctrine for the Tomahawk cruise missile.[‡] We had to lay the early groundwork for command and control, the tactics both for the antiship missile and the land-attack missile.

Paul Stillwell: Can you provide some specifics on that, please, in the case of the Tomahawk?

---
[*] Suitland, Maryland, is a suburb of Washington, D.C.
[†] On 1 February 1973, the Navy's First Fleet, headquarters in San Diego, was combined with the Anti-Submarine Warfare Force Pacific Fleet, based at Pearl Harbor, to form the U.S. Third Fleet. Third Fleet headquarters essentially remained in Hawaii from 1973 to 1991, when it shifted to San Diego.
[‡] Tomahawk is a long-range cruise missile that entered the fleet in the early 1980s, capable of delivering either conventional or nuclear warheads. Originally conceived to have both antiship and land-attack versions, the antiship type is no longer in service. The original guidance system relied on the missile matching its course with the terrain below its path. Navigation now is guided by satellite.

Admiral Lawrence: Well, our initial emphasis with the Tomahawk was the antiship missile, because that capability was theoretically coming on the line first. What we had to do was to interface very closely with the people back in Washington—not only in the cruise missile project office, but also over in OpNav in the Pentagon—as to what the basic command-and-control concept was going to be. At that time we were developing what they called the combined warfare commander concept. You had, of course, the OTC—the battle group commander—and then under him you had an ASW commander; you had an AAW commander; you had an antisurface ship warfare commander. So we had to determine just how to integrate the command and control for the cruise missile into that whole structure. And, of course, we were getting the missiles on both surface ships and in submarines. So from the first time I arrived out there, we started giving very serious emphasis to the Tomahawk.

I was disappointed when I arrived out there that Third Fleet wasn't really pushing this concept very actively. The Third Fleet staff was not coming back to Washington for the Tomahawk cruise missile team meetings. They kind of rationalized, "Well, it's too far to go back to Washington. We'd pay a lot of money in travel payments."

"Look, we have to go and participate in everything, because that's the weapon of the future, and we have to do all we can to facilitate its introduction to the fleet."

Paul Stillwell: Well, this was still in the groundwork stage, really, wasn't it, before the introduction of the missile?

Admiral Lawrence: Oh, yes, this was well before the fleet introduction of the missile, and I don't think that we really had had very many firings of the missile at that time. I think they probably had had some firings, so it was all basically conceptual, except that I felt we had to very well define what the command-and-control procedures were, and make sure about the very complex mechanisms that allowed you to put the targeting information into the missiles. We pushed to get that developed so we could have all that in place by the time the missile became operational.

I felt good that my staff took the lead in the Navy in the development of the concept for the use of the Tomahawk. In fact, I insisted in our fleet exercises that we have a provision for the exercising of the Tomahawk command-and-control operational capability, even though they were basically simulations. I just wanted people to start thinking cruise missiles, because I could see a great application for this. The problem is that people in the fleet are so busy with day-to-day things that it's hard to get them to look out to the future, and they don't like to do simulations. They like to deal with real-time things.

Paul Stillwell: The real things are a lot more satisfying.

Admiral Lawrence: So I had to push hard to tell them we were going to do this, because we simply had to be prepared to rapidly introduce this weapon system to the fleet and use it right away. I think a lot of the work we did there is paying off now in terms of the contribution that the Tomahawk is making over there in the Middle East.[*] Of course, our principal effort at that time was on the antiship missile, because in at-sea exercises it was more appropriate to do that type of capabilities evaluation than the power projection, because we were doing a lot of our operations in the middle of the ocean.

Paul Stillwell: How did you address the problem of over-the-horizon targeting? That had shown some flaws for the Argentinians, for example, in the Falklands.[†]

Admiral Lawrence: Well, of course, in all of our tactical doctrine development, in discussions back in Washington and so forth, we really worked hard to develop that capability. By that time, we pretty well had in place very good overhead satellite capability for tracking any surface target throughout the world. So we used, primarily, overhead systems to do the long-range targeting for the Tomahawk. The antiship version had a very fine inertial navigation capability, as well as a terminal-guidance capability.

---

[*] The first combat use of Tomahawk cruise missiles was early on the morning of 17 January 1991 when the battleships *Missouri* (BB-63) and *Wisconsin* (BB-64) fired from the Persian Gulf at Iraqi command centers and radar installations. All told, U.S. warships fired 297 Tomahawks during Operation Desert Storm.

[†] The event that triggered the 1982 Falklands War was the Argentine occupation of South Georgia Island on 19 March 1982, followed on 2 April by the occupation of the Falklands. The British then mounted a long-range expedition that made an amphibious assault on the islands and recaptured them. Argentina surrendered on 14 June. Some Argentine missiles hit targets other than those intended.

Then, of course, for the land-attack missile, you had terrain contour matching as one of its principal targeting systems. That so-called TerCon concept had not really been fully developed at that time, so most of our effort was in the antiship missile, using overhead satellites.

Paul Stillwell: What do you do on a cloudy day when you can't keep constant surveillance?

Admiral Lawrence: Well, of course, this is a problem, and you just have to depend on all the systems, including aircraft reconnaissance and surface ship reconnaissance. Feeding it into your overall command and control system provides as precise a location as you can. That enables the Tomahawk's terminal guidance, which is, I guess, primarily a radar type, to be used. I found out in the fleet, frankly, that if you relied on all the targeting capability you had—overhead, aircraft, surface ship, submarines—there were very few times where the weather prevented you from getting reasonably accurate data to do that over-the-horizon targeting.

Paul Stillwell: I guess the problem would come when there were targets fairly close to each other and they were hard to discriminate.

Admiral Lawrence: Yes, that's right. I don't remember all the technical aspects of the Tomahawk, whether it had some IFF capability in there or not, but it's a pretty remarkable weapon, and, of course, we're seeing what the land-attack version is doing.* That terrain contour-matching feature requires the Defense Mapping Agency to develop this precise contour type of targeting capability that could guide the missile. To me it's one of the most remarkable things in the world. The only way they can defeat that terrain contour matching, which is the final guidance in the targeting, is to have about a million bulldozers change the contour of the land. [Chuckle]

---

* IFF – identification, friend or foe.

Paul Stillwell: The downside on the contour matching is that it somewhat robs your flexibility. Conventional bombs or projectiles can be used anywhere; whereas, those have to be programmed specifically.

Admiral Lawrence: That's right. Once you fire, you're committed to that particular target. In other words, you're always programmed into the targeting console, and once that goes, it's going to that particular target. But I think the beauty about the cruise missile is that it's a very fine complement to the other systems. As we've seen over in Iraq, you can bring the cruise missile in with a 1,000-pound warhead. It has built-in stealth because it's so small and it goes in so well it can take out the key elements in the command-and-control system. That reduces the enemy's targeting capability, so you don't have to have stealth in all of your airplanes. Maybe there are a few airplanes you want to have stealth in. They put in the Tomahawks and bring in stealth aircraft to knock the systems out. Then you bring in airplanes that can deliver masses of bombs in a degraded air defense environment. That's what's happened over there.

We sent the Tomahawks and the F-117s in first and so thoroughly degraded the air-defense systems that we could bring in the airplanes heavily loaded with ordnance, like the A-6s and the B-52s.[*] So I think an advantage of cruise missiles is that you can build simpler, cheaper airplanes, and you don't have to put this stealth and advanced ECM and that sort of thing into all the systems.

Paul Stillwell: Did you get someone assigned to your staff who had particular expertise on the Tomahawk?

Admiral Lawrence: No, we developed our own. I had two officers who became the fleet experts on the Tomahawk missile.

Paul Stillwell: In your command-and-control planning, how far down did you delegate the authority to fire a Tomahawk? Could it go to the skipper of a ship?

---

[*] The Lockheed F-117 Nighthawk was a U.S. Air Force stealth ground attack aircraft. The A-6 Intruder was a carrier-based bomber and the B-52 a long-range land-based Air Force bomber.

Admiral Lawrence: For example, the surface warfare commander would have the authority to use Tomahawks. See, under your overall officer in tactical command, in what they call the combined warfare commander concept, the commander who was in charge of antisurface warfare would be the guy who would have that authority to fire.

Paul Stillwell: What about against the land target?

Admiral Lawrence: The land target would be a decision of the OTC, because at that time we didn't have a power-projection warfare commander. Now they do have a power projection warfare commander, along with the ASW, AAW, and anti-surface. So I guess now it would be the power-projection warfare commander, but at that time it was basically a decision for the officer in tactical command and his staff. As I say, it was just a little bit premature for us to get very much involved in the land attack. It was mostly an antiship missile.

Paul Stillwell: What has been your evaluation of the effectiveness, based on that experience, of the composite warfare commander concept?

Admiral Lawrence: Oh, I think it's a very viable concept. It's particularly important if you assemble a large number of forces, because, for example, if you have two or three carriers operating in close proximity with one OTC, you simply have to have a commander who takes cognizance of a particular area. It's really the most efficient way to handle it. You couldn't have that centralized control in just that one staff. It's the delegation of responsibility to the most qualified people who do it. So we used it very, very effectively.

I had an opportunity to test it, because in the fall of 1982, I did a two-carrier group battle group operation up in the northwestern Pacific.* The reason we did that is that when I came out in '81, I was bothered by the fact we had not had much of a naval presence up in the Northern Pacific since World War II. We had entered into a mode of

---

* This exercise, in late September-early October 1982, involved the *Enterprise* (CVN-65) and *Midway* (CV-41) battle groups. The *Midway* was then home-ported in Yokosuka, Japan.

having these very stereotyped deployment patterns, like two carriers in the Mediterranean and one carrier out in the Far East in the Japan, and Philippines, area.

Then we started putting a carrier out in the Indian Ocean when the Iran crisis developed. I felt we had gotten too stereotyped, too predictable, in our deployment pattern. So I talked this over with CinCPacFlt when I got out there.* I said I thought we should vary our deployment patterns—somebody else coined the term "flex-ops" for flexible operations. And he agreed with me. We proposed this to Washington, and that's when we started having carrier battle groups go up in the Northern Pacific, and we did the two-carrier battle group operation in the fall of '82. We came back and did a three-carrier-battle-group operation in the spring of '83.

I proposed this, first, to give our personnel more experience operating in places where they hadn't been before. But also, I felt that we could learn a lot by doing these operations up off the periphery of the Soviet Union, up near Petropavlovsk, and really try to see what the Soviet reaction would be. Because, actually, the Soviets didn't do much in the way of blue-water ops with their navy. They stayed in port; they had these new ships and new submarines and new ships, but they really didn't go to sea anywhere near as much as we did. And they very rarely did task-force-type operations in deep water. The only regularly deploying units they had were their ballistic missile submarines. The Yankees came over close to the United States, and then the Deltas, which had the long range, would go up into the more remote spots.†

Paul Stillwell: As I recall, they had the big Okean exercises in the '70s, but the Soviets didn't hold the one in 1980 that we expected.

Admiral Lawrence: No, the Russians just didn't operate their navy extensively at the time. So in addition to varying our operational pattern and letting our people learn about

---

* Admiral Sylvester R. Foley, USN, was Commander in Chief Pacific Fleet, May 1982 to September 1985.
† Soviet Yankee I and Yankee II-class nuclear-powered submarines entered active service from 1967 to 1974. They displaced 7,900 tons on the surface and 9,600 tons submerged; length, 426 feet; beam, 39 feet; draft, 28 feet; speed 27 knots. They were armed with torpedoes and ballistic missiles. Soviet Delta I-class nuclear-powered submarines entered active service from 1972 to 1977. They displaced 9,000 tons on the surface and 11,750 tons submerged; length, 459 feet; beam, 39 feet; draft, 28 feet; speed 25 knots. They were armed with torpedoes and ballistic missiles.

areas that they had little familiarity with, I wanted to see what the Soviet reaction would be. I was trying to get as much intelligence about them as I could.

Paul Stillwell: Did you go to sea in any of these exercises?

Admiral Lawrence: No, I did not have a dedicated flagship, but I knew we had the command and control to do it right from Pearl Harbor, because we had the most advanced capabilities you could possibly have right there in our Third Fleet headquarters.

Paul Stillwell: What are your recollections of those exercises from the standpoint of what you learned about the Soviets?

Admiral Lawrence: Well, we got minimal reaction from the Soviet Union. They did no overflights of either of those exercises. Here we came within several hundred miles of Petropavlovsk, and we didn't go over into the Sea of Okhotsk, but we were right just outside of the Kurile chain. The intelligence people thought a Backfire bomber came out, but then he turned around and went back.* He never really penetrated the Kurile chain.

Then we went back with the three-carrier battle group operation in the spring of '83.† I surely thought the Soviets were going to do something, because we purposely planned the track of those three carriers to go right up into the approaches to Petropavlovsk. In fact, the officer of tactical command was Rear Admiral Tom Brown.‡ Tom got a little bit too zealous. I had to get on the radio and say, "Tom, come on, back off," [chuckle] because he was going right up into the approaches of Petropavlovsk. But the best we could determine, they sent only one Victor submarine, which actually

---

* The Tupolev Tu-22M Backfire was a long-range, high-performance bomber that was flown by Soviet Strategic Aviation and Soviet Naval Aviation. The Backfire-B, which entered service in 1975, had a cruise speed of 560 miles per hour, and a range of about 3,000 miles. It was armed with either bombs or missiles.
† FleetEx 83-1 took place near the Aleutian Islands, 22 March-16 April 1983. The aircraft carriers involved were the *Enterprise* (CVN-65), *Midway* (CV-41), and *Coral Sea* (CV-43).
‡ Rear Admiral Thomas F. Brown III, USN, Commander Carrier Striking Force Seventh Fleet; Commander Carrier Group Five.

broached adjacent to one of the carriers in that operation.* We did pick him up. That was the only Soviet unit that reacted. We got no airplanes, no surface ships, and to the best of our knowledge, that one Victor submarine.

So after watching the Soviets two years and conducting those two operations, in addition to an amphibious operation in the Aleutians, which was the first amphibious operation in the area since World War II, I came away with the conclusion that the Soviets were really very benign. They had no really aggressive posture, because you would think they would react when we brought that number of forces that close. So it was obvious to me by '83 that the Soviets had no real desire to get involved in anything with us.

I think the shoot-down of that Korean airliner that occurred in the late summer of '83 was just an anomaly.† I think it was just a big mistake.

Paul Stillwell: How would you explain this benign behavior of the Soviets?

Admiral Lawrence: Well, by that time they were up to their ears in the Afghanistan problem.‡ I just think their national leaders saw that we didn't really represent a military threat to them—certainly not in terms of attacking their homeland or threatening their interests in any other place. I talked to attachés who came back from Russia, people whom I knew, and they told me that the Russians had very serious internal economic and social problems. I just think that the Soviets clearly saw, even in '83, that it was not in their interest at all to have any military incident with the United States. We'd already, in

---

* Soviet Victor I-class nuclear-powered attack submarines entered active service at a rate of two a year from 1968 to 1975. They displaced 4,300 tons on the surface and 5,100 tons submerged; length, 312 feet; beam, 33 feet; draft, 23 feet; speed 30 knots. They were armed with torpedoes and SS-N-15 surface-to-surface missiles.
† On 1 September 1983 a Soviet SU-15 fighter aircraft shot down a Boeing 747 passenger plane over the Sea of Japan. The 269 people in the plane were all killed. The Korean Airlines plane was on flight 007, which was en route from Anchorage, Alaska, to Seoul, South Korea, but strayed off course and violated Soviet airspace over Sakhalin Island.
‡ The Soviets intervened militarily in Afghanistan in December 1979 and were ousted by U.S.-supported guerrilla actions some years later. See George Crile, *Charlie Wilson's War: The Extraordinary Story of the Largest Covert Operation in History* (New York: Atlantic Monthly Press, 2003).

the years before, executed an Incidents at Sea agreement.* But, anyway, I thought our doing this flex-ops concept served a useful purpose, because it broke us in the Navy out of some of our stereotyped thinking.

The other thing we did that was quite interesting was every two years the Third Fleet conducts a RimPac exercise, where you bring in all of the Allied navies, like Australia, New Zealand, Japan, the Royal Navy, the Canadians. You all do a major exercise in the Central Pacific area. Over the years we kept expanding it till the ships got under way out in California, and then it culminated in a major exercise in the general area if Hawaii. So I did a RimPac exercise in the spring of 1982, and that was a very, very satisfying exercise.

It was the second RimPac the Japanese participated in. And, of course, you know the sensitivities back in Japan about any offensive use of their forces. Their constitution says that their forces are all for defense. It isn't called a navy; it's called the Maritime Self-Defense Force. So we had to be very careful about how we utilized the Japanese forces in that RimPac, because we knew their press would leap right on the fact if they were used in offensive way. So our staff developed a concept, and I approved, of using the Japanese as the escort for the amphibious force that was going to do a landing on the island of Kahoolawee in the Hawaiian chain. I said, "This is a good utilization. It gives them an independent job to do, where I don't have to integrate them with the U.S. surface ships or protecting the battle group."

But the Japanese press said, "Yes, they're in a defensive role, but for an offensive mission."

Paul Stillwell: Which was true.

Admiral Lawrence: Their press over there, as you know, is very rabid. Democracy and free media are new concepts in that country. [Chuckle] They're still trying to work it all out. I found that their military just had absolute intense distaste for the media. The

---

* U.S. and Soviet officials signed the Incidents at Sea agreement in Moscow in May 1972. See John Erickson, "The Soviet Naval High Command," *U.S. Naval Institute Proceedings*, May 1973, pages 66-87, and David F. Winkler, *Cold War at Sea: High-Seas Confrontation Between the United States and the Soviet Union* (Annapolis: Naval Institute Press, 2000).

Maritime Self-Defense Force's approach was to lie whenever they could to deceive the press. So this got to be a sensitive issue with the Japanese media personnel who were out there with this amphibious force. So they started firing some articles back to the Japanese papers, and the senior leadership of the Maritime Self-Defense Force got to be kind of hyper about this. I was designated as the guy to have a press conference with these Japanese media people to put this all in perspective. So I kept getting calls from the Japanese CNO and his staff, telling me what I should tell them, and what they were suggesting was flagrantly false.

Paul Stillwell: What were you supposed to say?

Admiral Lawrence: It was supposed to be something very deceptive, and I forget exactly what it was, but I had to tell them, "Look, we don't lie to the media in our country. I have to tell them the facts; that is, that you're escorting an amphibious group, and although the amphibious group is a power projection, the Japanese are exercising a defensive role. The type of mission that they're prepared to do is to defend a group of ships, a battle force." But, boy, the Japanese admiral kept wanting me to tell them some completely false story, and I had to tell the Chief of Naval Operations over in the Japanese Navy that I just simply could not do this. Well, anyway, it finally blew over.

Paul Stillwell: How did the press conference come out?

Admiral Lawrence: It was fine. The Japanese media are typical Japanese. They're really polite; it's just that what they write is bad. [Chuckle] So they weren't tough on me in the questions. Really, it was a mountain out of a molehill. But the big problem is that the professional military and the media in Japan just don't get along at all, because the media represent a very anti-military feeling in Japan, like you see the problem that they're having right now doing anything in the Middle East. Like this $9 billion they're going to give for the war, they put on the stipulation it could be used only for logistics purposes; it couldn't be used for the offensive prosecution of the war. The media very much project the tip of the Japanese anti-military attitude, and it's really been a constant adversarial relationship with their professional military. So I got caught in the middle of that.

Paul Stillwell: That's really a legacy from the constitution that the United States imposed on Japan.

Admiral Lawrence: It's very true; it's very true.

Paul Stillwell: Could you please describe what it was like to monitor one of those exercises from your command-and-control spaces.

Admiral Lawrence: Well, actually, in the RimPac exercises, I spent quite a bit of time at sea, because it was in the Hawaiian area, and it was easy for me to get around from ship to ship. I spent a lot of time out on the carrier and on the amphibious command ship; I would alternate back and forth. But I had a very fine command-and-control capability in my headquarters, not only just be able to communicate, but also we had the latest state-of-the-art overhead systems that could project an instantaneous display of where every unit in our operating area was.

Paul Stillwell: Did you do management by exception—just let things run except when you had a case like this incident with Admiral Brown getting too close to the Soviet Union?

Admiral Lawrence: That's right. As a fleet commander, I was more or less a force commander. When I did this big exercise in the Northern Pacific, I called myself a theater commander. I had the two-star admiral out there who was the officer in tactical command, giving the minute-to-minute tactical orders. Even he, essentially, delegated to these various warfare commanders, but I kept very closely abreast of what was going on and knew exactly where the forces were at any one time. If I felt I had to inject myself into it, I did, such as when I gave him orders to change course, not to go too close to Petropavlovsk. I could talk to him on the phone instantaneously as I did from time to time. But mostly I delegated the responsibility to the tactical commander. It was very much like it was in World War II in the numbered fleet, kind of like the relationship between Admiral Spruance and Admiral Mitscher. Admiral Mitscher really ran the operation while Spruance did the overall planning and put out the basic op order.*

I thoroughly enjoyed the numbered fleet responsibility. You were into the tactical doctrine development area, but then you were running the day-to-day fleet exercises. One of your principal responsibilities as Com3rdFlt is to get the battle groups prepared, what we call worked up, to be able to go out and spend six months or so deployed out in the Western Pacific. So it was a good breadth of responsibility.

The only drawback about it was that I had to go to California all the time, since so many of our units were stationed in California, and there was so much a concentration of naval power, so to speak, of responsibility in California. So there was somewhat of a limitation on being out in Hawaii when most of the people with whom you had to deal were on the West Coast. See, all of our commanders' conferences, our scheduling conferences, were done in San Diego. So I did a tremendous amount of traveling in that job. I can't remember the number of times I had to come back to San Diego.

I also went out four times to Japan to meet with Commander Seventh Fleet. I felt it was really important that Com3rdFlt and Com7thFlt—the two numbered fleet commanders in the Pacific—have very close interface, particularly when we were doing these new concepts of varying deployment patterns. I had to propose to Admiral Holcomb about bringing the *Midway* out of the Seventh Fleet area to do that exercise where we had three carriers up in the Northern Pacific.† So I went out to see him, because it was difficult for him to come back to Hawaii, because it was traditional that the Seventh Fleet Commander stay in his area. Previous commanders of the Third Fleet just stood on protocol, and they wouldn't go out to visit. But I said, "Well, gee, that's important that he and I talk to each other." So I went out there.

Paul Stillwell: What are your impressions of Admiral Holcomb?

---

* In 1944-45 Admiral Raymond A. Spruance, USN, was Commander Fifth Fleet, and Vice Admiral Marc A. Mitscher, USN, was in tactical command as Commander Task Force 58, the fast carrier force.
† Vice Admiral M. Staser Holcomb, USN, served as Commander Seventh Fleet from 15 September 1981 to 9 May 1983.

Admiral Lawrence: Oh, I think he was one of the best; he was superb—very bright, well founded tactically, and a really strong leader. I had the greatest respect for him. Actually, I had a small overlap with Admiral Hogg, when he came up to the Seventh Fleet.* So one of my visits was out to see Admiral Hogg and three with Admiral Holcomb.

I also made a visit up to the Aleutians, to Adak, which is one of our principal ASW patrol plane bases up there. That was really an interesting experience. I enjoyed that, because it gave me a full appreciation for the tactical significance of Adak.

Paul Stillwell: What is the tactical significance of Adak?

Admiral Lawrence: Well, that's the only base that gives you the capability to go up in the Bering to look for the Delta-class submarines. Because we don't have much surface ship presence up there, and our other surveillance capabilities don't extend up in the Bering Sea. So you really, vitally need that base.

Paul Stillwell: I've heard that Admiral Holcomb was supposedly on a fast track for four stars but got bushwhacked by the submarine mafia.

Admiral Lawrence: No, it wasn't the submarine mafia. No, no. It was Secretary Lehman. See, Secretary Lehman and Admiral Hayward just clashed. So anybody whom Secretary Lehman perceived had been close to Admiral Hayward, his future was not very bright in the Navy. When we talk about my time as Chief of Naval Personnel, I'll go over some of that.

Paul Stillwell: All right.

Admiral Lawrence: Yes, I thought Admiral Holcomb was a clear four-star contender. Then when he left and became the Deputy Commander in Chief U.S. Naval Forces

---

* Vice Adm. James R. Hogg, USN, was Commander Seventh Fleet from 9 May 1983 to 4 March 1985.

Europe, I knew something was really wrong, because that was no longer a job for somebody on the track.

Paul Stillwell: What kind of feedback did he give you on the preparation that his ships were getting from your training for deployment?

Admiral Lawrence: Oh, he was very pleased, because he knew we were working hard to develop this combined warfare commander concept. We actually structured exercise concepts for him to use out there—to make sure we gave as good as we could on exercising the combined warfare commander concept. I was pushing for doing more multi-carrier operations than we had been, because I felt it was conceivable in certain types of warfare situations, where we would want to bring them into the same area though not close together; we'd bring them in the general area to get more synergism out of having operating carriers together. So that put more complexity on the command and control. But, yes, he was very much supportive of and felt good about what we were doing to prepare units to go out there.

Paul Stillwell: Did you see benefits from the Reagan defense buildup as far as readiness levels and ammunition or personnel?

Admiral Lawrence: Well, that was just a little bit premature to start to see much benefit from it. A big infusion of money started that first budget year, which was a fiscal '81 budget, but the real big leap up was in '82. And, of course, I left there in '83. So it was just a little bit too premature for me to be able to see all those effects. Of course, it really pleased me, and, of course, the thing that particularly pleased me when they had that very significant increase in the pay of people; that was really well received.

Paul Stillwell: You said some of the vestiges of the old antisubmarine type command were fading out. Did that mean there was a de-emphasis of that mission?

Admiral Lawrence: Well, no. From the way the command and control was set up and the intelligence capability that existed prior to my coming there, it was obvious a great deal of emphasis was given to try to detect the Soviet SSBNs patrolling in the Eastern Pacific.* There was an extraordinary amount of the staff effort over the years. You could just see from the way the spaces were arranged and the orientation of the intelligence function, command and control, that that had been a really strong emphasis. But my predecessors were starting to increase the emphasis to the broad fleet responsibilities.

Paul Stillwell: So it wasn't being neglected.

Admiral Lawrence: Oh, no, we spent a tremendous amount of effort trying to detect the Soviet SSBNs in the Eastern Pacific.

I was one of the first Third Fleet Commanders to do really extensive traveling, and I felt it was important for me to get out at sea in those battle group exercises off San Diego. So I spent a tremendous amount of time back on the West Coast, whereas, my predecessors, under that old ASW mission, had been sitting there very intensely focused on picking up those SSBNs. I just felt that I had to have a much broader focus than that.

Paul Stillwell: Your immediate predecessor, Vice Admiral Waller, was an ASW specialist.†

Admiral Lawrence: That's true.

Paul Stillwell: Did you feel confident that ASW was being given the attention it needed?

Admiral Lawrence: Oh, yes, it certainly was. We actually did some very good work in ASW. We developed the capability to do very intensive battle group ASW type of exercises out in the underwater range we had in Barking Sands. We developed the

---

* SSBN - nuclear-powered ballistic missile submarine.
† Vice Admiral Edward C. Waller, USN, commanded the Third Fleet from October 1979 to August 1981. He and Admiral Lawrence essentially swapped jobs. Waller went from command of the Third Fleet to become superintendent of the Naval Academy.

capability to put battle group units in there and with a programmable target really do integrated battle group ASW. The staff previously had been focused to a large degree on VP antisubmarine warfare.* We didn't neglect VP ASW, but we pushed to get more into battle group ASW. That's where we developed a type of exercise to do in the undersea range they have out west of the island of Kauai.

Paul Stillwell: How much can you say unclassified about ASW successes against the Soviets?

Admiral Lawrence: Well, I think reasonably well, but I was disappointed in the success with the SSNs. I got a very intensive evaluation of SSNs when I did that three-carrier battle group operation and had six SSNs. Admiral Foley was CinCPacFlt. I asked him if he could give me a large number of SSNs. He gave me six, but they didn't perform in their direct support role of the battle group as effectively as I felt they should. Primarily because of lack of Soviet submarine activity, I didn't get a chance to work with Soviet subs very much. I felt that the best ASW platform I had out there was the surface ship with the towed array, and the LAMPS helicopter.† That was your best ASW team.

Paul Stillwell: How well was the S-3 working?‡

Admiral Lawrence: Well, it just didn't have enough actual Soviet target opportunities for us to get a chance to evaluate its effectiveness. But it was still improving as we put in some systems improvement, but it really wasn't a principal player, frankly. They tell me they've got some updates in there now that make them much more effective than they were back ten years ago.

---

* VP – land-based patrol planes.
† LAMPS, which stands for light airborne multi-purpose system, is an antisubmarine helicopter carried on board destroyers and frigates.
‡ The S-3 Viking was a jet-powered, carrier-based antisubmarine aircraft with a four-person crew. Built by Lockheed, its first delivery to a fleet training squadron was in February 1974. The S-3A has a wingspan of 68 feet, 8 inches; length of 53 feet, 4 inches; maximum gross weight of 52,539 pounds, and a top speed of 514 miles per hour.

Paul Stillwell: What do you remember about living and working in Hawaii during those few times you were there?

Admiral Lawrence: Well, certainly I was there a lot. Oh, it was great to have your headquarters on Ford Island and live in a pre-World War II house.* You could look out and see the *Arizona* memorial. So it was really inspiring to live there and work there. In Hawaii, of course, the climate's beautiful, and the lifestyle there is just really great—the old aloha spirit. You get caught up in the sense of history there. It just seemed like a natural thing for me to learn all about the history of Pearl Harbor. Because you were there where it all happened. In fact, we had houses over in Luke Field, the west side of Ford Island, that still had the places you could see where the bullets hit in the buildings.† So it was a very inspiring experience.

Paul Stillwell: Was your wife able to join you then?

Admiral Lawrence: Oh, yes, oh yes. She had to commute back and forth, but she spent a lot of time out there. It was pleasant, because when she came out there, she was going to thoroughly enjoy the whole bit. Of course, one thing, when you get in Hawaii, family, friends you haven't seen for years [chuckle] suddenly reestablish contact. The thing that was interesting about that house was when World War II broke out and all the families went back to the mainland, they converted those homes into bachelor quarters. They put a bathroom in every bedroom. So I had five bedrooms and five baths, and it was a great place to have guests stay. Many people came out to see us, and they'd be gone for long periods of time, doing their own thing around the island. We'd just say, "Okay, you come and go as you please."

Paul Stillwell: How much of a social or diplomatic side to the job was there?

---

* Ford Island is in the middle of Pearl Harbor, Hawaii.
† When Japanese naval forces attacked Pearl Harbor on 7 December 1941, the aircraft strafed ground targets with machine guns in addition to attacking ships with bombs and torpedoes.

Admiral Lawrence: Well, you had a very heavy social life, because so many people come through Hawaii all the time. Admiral Long, who was CinCPac, and I were very good friends and had been for years.* So he often would have Diane and me come over when somebody like Secretary Weinberger would come through or some senator or some congressman.† So you very much got involved in the entertainment of these dignitaries if you were in town.

The local people in Hawaii maintain a close interface with the Navy, so you get very much involved with them. So you had a very, very active social pace. But the nice thing about Hawaii is it's become a tradition there that most every evening social event ends at 9:30. Maybe it's the climate or that people end their social activity early and they get up early. I used to be at work at 6:00 o'clock every morning. Then I usually would try to get out on the tennis court between 4:30 and 5:00 whenever I could. I thoroughly enjoyed that environment; I loved every minute in Hawaii. It was extremely busy in the breadth of things that I was doing and the fact that I had to travel so much. But I really, really enjoyed that. It's a very healthful lifestyle, because the climate's so good, you can go outside a lot.

Well, I guess we'd probably better knock off there.

Paul Stillwell: All right. See you next week.

---

* Admiral Robert L. J. Long, USN, served as Commander in Chief Pacific from 31 October 1979 to 1 July 1983. His oral history is in the Naval Institute collection.
† Caspar W. Weinberger served as Secretary of Defense from 21 January 1981 to 23 November 1987.

Interview Number 19 with Vice Admiral William P. Lawrence, U.S. Navy (Retired)
Place: U.S. Naval Institute, Annapolis, Maryland
Date: Wednesday, 13 February 1991

Paul Stillwell: Admiral, today we resume our discussion of your time in command of the Third Fleet, and one of the items you mentioned beforehand that you wanted to talk about was the arrival of the first Trident submarine.

Admiral Lawrence: Yes, the first Trident submarine was the USS *Ohio*, and it was due to be home-ported at the submarine base at Bangor, Washington, which is out west of Seattle near Bremerton.[*] This was a very fine new submarine base that had been built principally to accommodate the Trident submarines.

This posed some interesting challenges for me, because the *Ohio* was under my operational command as Commander Third Fleet. Greenpeace, principally, and other activist groups out there were scheduling protests concerning the arrival of the Trident submarine. This was the first submarine to be out there with a nuclear strategic missile capability, and Greenpeace was very upset about this. The Catholic bishop of Seattle had a very strong anti-military bias, and he was very vocal. So we had the problem of how to handle this protest. I just happened to be out in the area for the Seattle Seafair, which the Navy tried to participate in by sending a cruiser and a couple destroyers.[†]

I was interviewed by the local Seattle paper, and the reporter asked, "Well, how are you going to handle all these protests that you're going to have here? Are you going to bring the submarine in in the middle of the night? Are you going to have it come through Puget Sound submerged?"

I said, "Of course not. We're going to come in in broad daylight, and we're going to announce it in advance." For one reason, there are people there—families and other supporters—who want to greet the ship as it comes in. Out of deference to them, I want

---

[*] USS *Ohio* (SSBN-726), the first of a class of nuclear powered submarines armed with the Trident ballistic missile, was approved in the early 1970s. She was laid down 10 April 1976, launched 7 April 1979, and commissioned 11 November 1981. The ship is 560 feet long and displaces 18,750 tons submerged.
[†] Seattle Seafair is an annual summer festival that comprises a variety of activities. The Navy's flight demonstration team, the Blue Angels, sometimes performs as part of the fair.

to bring it in right in the middle of the day at the appropriate time. We'd never even consider bringing it in submerged up at Puget Sound."

He said, "Well, what about these dissenters?"

I said, "Well, we'll do our best to respect the safety of the dissenters, and we'll have the Coast Guard out there to remove the protesters who are in boats in the path so their safety's not jeopardized. I respect the right of the people to protest. I mean, that's a fundamental right in our country. Gosh, I served in two wars and spent six years as a POW preserving the freedom of speech in this country. I'm not going to be one who advocates restricting protester dissent."

They put a big, beautiful editorial in the paper praising me: "Finally, we have a military officer who's open. He's not trying to conceal things, and he respects the protests." That article had a great effect in disarming the dissent. When the *Ohio* finally arrived in Bangor, there was a very mild protest effort by Greenpeace. There were just a couple of people, and a couple of rowboats out there and the Coast Guard took care of things.* So it went through very smoothly, and the Trident was very well received.

But as soon as the *Ohio* arrived out there and was getting prepared to go out on its first patrol, a Soviet trawler positioned itself there. So we had to take some actions to ensure we weren't having our interests jeopardized by the presence of that trawler.

Paul Stillwell: What sort of actions?

Admiral Lawrence: Well, first of all, we took some classified intelligence actions to try to neutralize what they were doing. Also, we picked up signs there might be some special type of sonobuoys that they were placing in the water.† So I sent out the mine craft that we had up there. I think we had a squadron of about six mine craft that were stationed in Seattle. As reserve ships, their crews were half active duty and half reservists. So I got them under way to go out and use their minesweeping capability, to try to see if they were putting in special type of sonobuoys. We never found any, but a

---

* The *Ohio* arrived at Seattle on 12 August 1982. The protest was more vigorous than Admiral Lawrence remembered but was stifled by Coast Guard intervention so the submarine could make the trip unimpeded.
† A sonobuoy is an electronic device that picks up sounds in the water for the purpose of detecting submarines. It is normally dropped from a patrol aircraft and then transmits sounds back to the plane.

fisherman or somebody found one sonobuoy that washed up on the beach. We did some very highly classified ops involving our SSNs that came up there, because in addition to that trawler, we think we also detected a Soviet Victor submarine.

The height of all this activity occurred when my staff and I were under way in a cruiser to be involved in a fleet exercise. As I say, occasionally I took elements of my staff and embarked in a ship. Sometimes it was just a small number of us. But on this occasion I put several of the staff in there, because we really wanted to test our command-and-control capability as an embarked staff. So we had to handle all this surveillance of that Soviet trawler and that Soviet submarine while we were embarked, and it worked out quite well. So that was the whole Trident submarine introduction to the Pacific Northwest area, but after a while the operations just became routine.

Another thing we did was organize the first amphibious operation in the Aleutians since World War II. We had an amphibious squadron go up there with an embarked Marine battalion landing team. And we got some Air Force airplanes to fly out of their bases in Alaska to provide close air support and combat air patrol. The Coast Guard came out and participated. So, in addition to the other operations we did with the carrier battle groups up there, that was just another effort for this greater presence up in the Northern Pacific region.

Another interesting challenge I had involved an uninhabited island in the Hawaiian chain named Kahoolawe, which is used for target practice. The Navy took it over right around the World War I time frame, and they used it for target practice and very extensively used it in World War II. Well, some native Hawaiians, called the Ohana, strenuously objected to our use of Kahoolawe as a target island. They contended that there were some historical artifacts on there, which were of religious significance. So they had a very strong continuous protest.[*]

Even before I got out there, the Navy had made special accommodation to the Ohana. We gave them escorted, supervised visits to the island so they could search for

---

[*] The protestors formed an organization called Protect Kahoolawe Ohana (PKO). In 1990 President George H. W. Bush directed that the Navy stop using the island as a target for live-fire exercises. In 1994, the Navy transferred the title of Kahoolawe to the state of Hawaii. Vice Admiral Samuel L. Gravely Jr., USN, who was Commander Third Fleet from 1976 to 1978, also faced problems with protestors on the island. For details see Admiral Gravely's Naval Institute oral history.

religious artifacts and protect these artifacts. A large portion of the island was not an impact area, either for air or surface use. The main organization was Ohana, which is a small group—not all native Hawaiian—and there were some other ethnic groups that got involved as well.

Anyway, this protest got to be kind of a nagging problem for us. One time, when we did this RimPac exercise, we had some ships going over and doing target practice there, and the Ohana had a big demonstration out in front of the gates of Pearl Harbor. I looked very carefully at this, and I said, "From my perspective, I don't think this is a big issue in Hawaii." Only a small fraction of the people were really aware of it, but because the Ohana were getting attention in the media, their protests had caused the Navy to do some things that I didn't think were in the Navy's best interest, because we really needed Kahoolawe. It was a vital training area.

So I got my public affairs people together, and I said, "Look, we simply have got to go more proactive on this. We're continuously on the defense. We're responding to articles in the paper. We need to generate some favorable publicity." So we went to the editor of the *Honolulu Star-Bulletin*, and he turned out to be very sympathetic. He had been a World War II naval officer, and we convinced him that he should do a very extensive interview with me. He asked me questions that we suggested he ask, and he gave us a full page in the *Honolulu Star-Bulletin*. After the article came out, it just completely defused the Ohana. I think the large mass of people out there were basically indifferent on the subject, read the article, and said, "Hey, why are we letting this small group of people out here tie the Navy in knots?"

Paul Stillwell: Did you find out what the motivation was?

Admiral Lawrence: It was because of this intense desire to resurrect the native Hawaiian era and respect the native Hawaiian traditions. It involved a lot of strong religious fervor, a lot of zealous-type approaches to things. But over the years, it had really tied us in knots. Our proactive public affairs policy really did a lot to defuse the Ohana. But still, about twice a month, on Saturdays and Sundays, we provided support for people going out to Kahoolawe. They had to provide their own boats, and they'd leave from Maui, which was only about five miles or so from Kahoolawe. We sent people out there to ensure their safety was respected, because we didn't want them steering off into the impact zone for unexploded ordnance.

Ohana and environmental groups applied pressure on another issue—the goats on Kahoolawe. When Captain Cook, the British explorer, traveled around the Pacific with his crew, they put goats on these islands, so they'd have a source of meat when they came back.[*] Goats are the number-one enemy of Hawaiians, because they eat plants and shrubbery, and they cause a bad erosion problem. The goats have almost decimated all the foliage on Kahoolawe, so we had tremendous pressure on us to reduce the goat population.

We set traps, and we also had goat hunts, which, of course, the Marines loved. Periodically, we'd send Marines over there with rifles, and they'd walk through and shoot goats. We always had more Marine volunteers to do that than we needed. I used to sit back and say, "It's really interesting how things are in this world. Here in Hawaii we're getting criticized because we're not killing the goats fast enough. On San Clemente, we were criticized because we weren't taking care of the goats.[†] We had to collect them all at a cost of a couple million dollars and remove them from the island. [Chuckle] It's a crazy world, depending on where you live." But we often let these special-interest groups just tie us in knots. And that's a good example—saving the goats on San Clemente, but killing them on Kahoolawe. So that was an interesting challenge.

The other thing I wanted to talk about was a time when my knowledge of history, I think, really stood me in good stead. In November of 1982, a typhoon was detected several hundred miles southwest of Hawaii. Naturally, we started watching it carefully. Lieutenant Commander Moe Gibbs, my staff meteorologist, came in, and he was kind of relaxed about it. He said, "Don't worry, Admiral, there hasn't been a typhoon in history in this part of the Pacific that, on a northeast track, didn't turn to the northwest after it passed 19 degrees north latitude. So there's very little chance that this will come to Oahu."

---

[*] Captain James Cook (1728-1779) was an English mariner and explorer.
[†] San Clemente is an island off the coast of Southern California, southeast of Los Angeles. The Navy uses it for target practice.

So I said, "Okay. Well, let's just really watch this now." But then the wheels started turning in my head and I remembered my predecessor, Admiral Halsey, [chuckle] when he got caught in that typhoon in 1944, over 700 people lost and three ships capsized.* Another typhoon hit his fleet in 1945.

So I started thinking about this, and in every meeting with my meteorologist he said, "Don't worry, Admiral, don't sweat."

Finally, I started doing the mental calculations. I said, "If I order all the ships in Pearl Harbor to sortie and go to sea, it's probably going to take 24 hours, because of the queuing to get out of the mouth of Pearl Harbor. And there are ships in maintenance and so forth. Of course, we can get the airplanes flown out of Barbers Point and out of Kaneohe pretty quickly. But it's the ships and the submarines that concern me."†

Anyway, we had a meeting and we came in, and the staff meteorologist just gave me the same thing. I said, "Sortie the ships."

He said, "Oh, admiral, you don't have to do that. Think of the impact on morale, and you're going to have to call all the people off of liberty, and that's just going to have an impact on the men."

I said, "Sortie the ships. That's my decision."

He said, "Aye, aye, sir."

Of course, I'm the type of commander, kind of like Nimitz, where I want people to tell me if they don't agree with something.‡ I don't make decisions by consensus, but I tell everybody, "If you don't agree with me, you speak now or forever hold your peace." So my staff would openly challenge me. But, finally, after about the third time, I said, "Sortie the ships! That's the decision."

"Aye, aye, sir." So we sent the order out.

---

* While operating off the Philippines, ships of the Third Fleet, commanded by Admiral William F. Halsey, ran into a ferocious typhoon on 18 December 1944. In all, three destroyers—*Hull* (DD-350), *Spence* (DD-512), and *Monaghan* (DD-354)—sank, and a number of other ships were damaged. The Third Fleet suffered further typhoon damage in June 1945. See C. Raymond Calhoun, *Typhoon: The Other Enemy: The Third Fleet and the Pacific Storm of December 1944* (Annapolis: Naval Institute Press, 1981). Hans Christian Anderson and George F. Kosco, *Halsey's Typhoons* (New York: Crown Publishers, Inc., 1967).
† Barbers Point was the site of a naval air station at the southwest "corner" of the island of Oahu, Hawaii. Kaneohe Naval Marine Corps Air Station is on the eastern side of the island.
‡ Fleet Admiral Chester W. Nimitz, USN, served as Commander in Chief Pacific Fleet and Pacific Ocean Areas, 1941-45.

Finally, as the last ship went out through the mouth of Pearl Harbor, a large wave that had been generated by the winds down to the southwest hit the ship broadside, and one person was killed.* But, anyway, everybody else got off. There wasn't a single ship or airplane damaged. That typhoon came cracking right across Pearl Harbor, took a lot of roofs off of Schofield Barracks, a lot of damage to downtown Honolulu.† And I tell you, my staff members really had sheepish looks on their faces, like, "Did you have some special powers, Admiral?"

But I had read what happened to Admiral Halsey, and I said, "The consequences of our being wrong far outweighed the impacts of making a conservative decision." And, of course, that really paid off. But I don't think I would have done that if I hadn't been a very keen student of history. I had read about the impacts of making bum decisions with regard to weather.

Paul Stillwell: Nimitz put out a very good letter after that 1944 typhoon, saying it's better to take a precaution that's not needed than the other way around.‡

Admiral Lawrence: Yes, and I talked to them about the Nimitz letter. But that could have been a really bad thing, because we had winds of over 100 knots. Big trees—I mean, two or three feet in diameter—were blown over in our area. Houses were damaged on Ford Island.

Paul Stillwell: What are your own recollections of living through the typhoon?

Admiral Lawrence: Well, interestingly, I had a real malaise. I just really felt bad on the day of the hurricane. I remember in the afternoon, before the typhoon came across, a big limb had blown onto a house on Ford Island, and a family had to evacuate. I had this big

---

* On 23 November 1982, a large wave hit the guided missile destroyer *Goldsborough* (DDG-20) and killed Seaman Jose Cantu. The same wave broke one of Lieutenant Ray Beard's arms and washed him overboard. He managed to swim safely ashore near the Honolulu airport.
† Typhoon Iwa hit the islands of Oahu and Kauai on 24 November 1982 and caused some $250 million in property damage. Schofield Barracks is an Army post in the center region of Oahu.
‡ For the text of "Admiral Nimitz's Pacific Fleet Confidential Letter on Lessons of Damage in Typhoon," dated 13 February 1945, see the website of the Naval History and Heritage Command.

home, and my wife was back on the mainland, so I was just there by myself. This was the Schindler family, and the grandmother was visiting. I said, "Look, just have as many as you want of your family come over here and stay with me." But, as I say, I was really feeling bad. So I turned in and I was kind of out of it when all the wind and everything blew across.

But I felt real badly about that one person being killed. A freak wave hit just as the USS *Goldsborough* was going out through the narrow mouth of Pearl Harbor. The wind was blowing, and the sea was starting to build up from the west-southwest. *Goldsborough* was the last ship going out. A seaman who was up on deck was crushed against the superstructure, and the internal injuries killed him. But the SAR helo from Barbers Point came over with a flight surgeon, and those pilots landed on that fantail in that heavy sea.[*] The flight surgeon was the son-in-law of Vice Admiral Ed Waller, who was then the superintendent of the Naval Academy.[†]

I recommended to Admiral Foley that we give them a medal. I initially recommended that we give them the Navy-Marine Corps medal, which is for lifesaving. Admiral Foley didn't have the authority to grant that, but he had the authority to give Air Medals, so he gave Air Medals to the helo crew and the flight surgeon for doing that, because he wanted very properly have it done quickly and in a timely manner.

So, as I say, if I hadn't known a little bit of history, I think I would have just probably bought what my staff was telling me.

Paul Stillwell: What do you think the consequences would have been if the ships had still been in the harbor?

Admiral Lawrence: Well, I think there's no question that we would have taken some damage to our ships. Of course, the crews would have tied everything down, but I think that the wind's velocity was such that there would have been some form of damage to the superstructure and things of that nature. I think just the fact that we got all the ships and their crews out of there enabled the naval station to batten down the hatches, because they

---

[*] SAR – search and rescue.
[†] Vice Admiral Edward C. Waller, USN, was superintendent of the Naval Academy from 22 August 1981 to 31 August 1983.

didn't have to have people supporting the ships. So the whole naval station really had time to get into their anti-typhoon posture.

That episode demonstrated the loneliness of command, because sometimes you're the only one who has that wealth of experience to make the proper decision in a situation. Very few times have I ever had to go against my staff, but it has happened, because that's why you're the commander and have the experience. Of course, that's one thing that concerns me today is that we have a lot of flag officers who are promoted when they're so young. They haven't been through these experiences and sometimes don't have enough seasoning or the preparation to make those lonely decisions.

Paul Stillwell: Did the death of that sailor weigh on you for a while?

Admiral Lawrence: Oh, yes, it bothered me, because I kept saying, "Well, maybe if I'd made that decision 12 hours earlier than I did, it would have been before the buildup of the sea. At the time the typhoon was still quite a distance away, but the winds had caused the sea to build up. And, of course, the *Goldsborough* was in a hurry to get out. If they had been a little bit more prudent, talking on the radio to the port control office or something like that, maybe they could have anticipated a buildup. But we didn't take any official action against the skipper of the *Goldsborough*.

I did say that if we'd really been thoughtful, we could have been talking to somebody about what the sea conditions were, because Pearl Harbor, as you know, is unique. It has that very narrow entrance, and only one ship can come through at a time. So it stays very calm inside, but as you transit there's sometimes a very abrupt transition from very calm waters to heavy seas.

Paul Stillwell: You were talking earlier about the Trident submarine. What was the operational control arrangement when the SSBNs went on deterrent patrols?

Admiral Lawrence: They were basically under my opcon, because they were Pacific Fleet assets, and I was the fleet commander who had that area of responsibility. But any strategic asset is tied into the national command center back in Washington, and they have strategic communication links. So, although you know those assets are on patrol, you're never told the number and where they are. So you don't have any hour-to-hour, day-to-day responsibility. But they are in your area of responsibility, because, the Third Fleet has everything from about Guam back to the West Coast of California.

Paul Stillwell: But I guess it wasn't really considered a need for you to know.

Admiral Lawrence: No. You didn't have any real tactical responsibility; it was just an area responsibility. For example, if that Trident submarine got into difficulty and needed support, I would be the commander who would order that support to be given. Or if they were under attack, I would be the one who would be immediately informed so I could take action.

Paul Stillwell: One of the incidents I recall from that period was a very public grounding of the *Enterprise* at San Francisco. How did you get involved in that?

Admiral Lawrence: Well, the *Enterprise* was coming back from a deployment.[*] The skipper was Captain Robert Kelly, whose nickname is Barney.[†] He had been selected for flag rank in a board that had convened in February, and I was on that board. Admiral Schoultz was also a member of that board, so both of us had talked about Captain Kelly and what a good job he did.[‡] Of course, the grounding occurred in April, and at the time the *Enterprise* was under my operational command. Administratively, she was under Admiral Pete Easterling, Commander Naval Air Force Pacific Fleet, as the type commander.[§] Both Admiral Easterling and I were quite concerned about that incident, and both of us were quite impressed with the way Captain Kelly handled the situation.

---

[*] On 28 April 1983, when the aircraft carrier *Enterprise* (CVN-65) was about a half mile from the Alameda Naval Air Station, she ran aground in San Francisco. She remained there for about five hours before she was freed by tugboats and a rising tide.
[†] Captain Robert J. Kelly, USN, commanded the *Enterprise* from 23 February 1980 to 17 June 1983.
[‡] Vice Admiral Robert F. Schoultz, USN, who had served as Commander Naval Air Force Pacific Fleet from 31 January 1980 to 4 August 1982.
[§] Vice Admiral Crawford A. Easterling, USN, served as Commander Naval Air Force Pacific Fleet from 4 August 1982 to 16 August 1985.

As you know, after coming under the Golden Gate and then the Oakland Bay Bridge, as you head south into San Francisco Bay and the Oakland area, you have to make a 90-degree turn to come into the piers at Alameda. The current was often very tricky, and you had to dredge Alameda a lot to get the required depth there. It has an inherent silting problem. But, anyway, the ship was a little bit late in turning, and they had some engineering casualty. I don't remember exactly what it was, but this casualty was occupying the attention of the captain and the people on the bridge. I think it contributed to a late turn that put them over into shallow water, and they slid aground in a mud bank.

The thing we all admired about Captain Kelly was that just as soon as it happened, he sent communications out that said, "I accept full responsibility. It was my error." He didn't sit back and wait for people to ask him questions or wait for a board or anything like that. He just immediately said that, and he gained a tremendous amount of respect by virtue of taking that position. I sent him a letter telling him, "It was regrettable that this happened. I admire the way you conducted yourself, and I have every hope for you in the future."

Paul Stillwell: He's done very well since then.

Admiral Lawrence: When I was Chief of Naval Personnel, after that, he came up for his first assignment as a flag officer. In addition to being nuclear trained, he had a master's in aeronautical engineering and had a very strong technical background. So I put him into the office of the director of R&D in the Navy in the staff of Chief of Naval Operations, what we used to call 098. That made him in charge of the R&D for tactical aircraft. He so distinguished himself in his Washington assignments that he just kept getting increased responsibility. He was sent out to command a carrier group, and, of course, he's now a four-star admiral.[*] But it made me feel good that the system didn't destroy his career for making a mistake. Admiral Nimitz is a good example of somebody who went aground.

---

[*] Admiral Kelly served as Commander in Chief Pacific Fleet from 15 February 1991 to 6 August 1994.

Paul Stillwell: But that's really an exception. Usually, the consequences are severe for an incident like that.

Admiral Lawrence: Yes, they usually are. I think he got a letter of reprimand. He was not relieved for cause in that situation, but I had to convene the JAG investigation on the thing. I can't remember whom I put in charge of that. I think it was one of the carrier group commanders—rear admirals—who did that. That was, of course, an unpleasant incident.

The other unpleasant incident I had was when a P-3 airplane from VP-1 flew into the side of a mountain on Kauai.* Everybody was lost. I, of course, ordered an immediate JAG investigation, and I put Rear Admiral Wolkensdorfer in charge of that.† That unearthed some very disturbing information about improper leadership within that squadron. Admiral Wolkensdorfer recommended that the CO of VP-1 be relieved for cause and the executive officer as well. Because the investigators perceived that there had been some internal problems, because just a week or so before that accident, there'd been a wheels-up landing, which is virtually unheard of in the P-3 community because the plane has two pilots. That was very unpleasant, because I knew the CO of that squadron and his father—and I had for years and years. But that was a very proper action.

Paul Stillwell: Who was that?

Admiral Lawrence: Gosh, the name escapes me right now.‡ He was a Naval Academy graduate, and he was the son of a naval officer.

But the thing that was interesting in this was the officer who was sent in to take command of the squadron is the current commandant of midshipmen here at the Naval

---

* On 16 June 1983, a P-3B Orion land-based aircraft from Patrol Squadron One (VP-1) crashed into a mountain on the island of Kauai, Hawaii. All 14 crew members on board were killed.
† Rear Admiral Daniel J. Wolkensdorfer, USN, Commander Patrol Wings Pacific Fleet.
‡ Commander Jon D. Holzapfel, USN, commanded VP-1 from October 1982 to June 1983. He was in the Naval Academy class of 1967.

Academy, Captain Haskins.* He went in as a direct-input CO and really turned that squadron around. They won the E. But that was really a very tragic incident, because the entire crew was lost.

Paul Stillwell: By improper leadership, do you mean laxity?

Admiral Lawrence: Well, it was really hard to define all the elements of the squadron, but you didn't have a good, effective team effort on the part of the CO and the XO. The CO tended to be a one who delegated excessively, and the XO was someone who tended to really irritate and aggravate subordinates. They had a morale problem in that squadron. There was not enough attention to detail on the part of the CO, poor leadership style of the XO, and that produced all the elements for poor performance.

Wolkensdorfer pointed out the wheels-up landing and other poor performance in the mission. As you listened to the flight-recorder tapes of the period prior to that collision with the mountain, it was obvious that that crew was just not well organized. The other thing was that they violated crew integrity when they didn't have a copilot ready and available. They quickly summoned a guy from another crew and plugged him in, which you can do, but it's not good to violate crew integrity without getting a guy well prepared to move in. Within the squadron, they had violated all sorts of NATOPS procedures like that, so all the elements were there for a problem.† That was a very sad, tragic thing to have.

Paul Stillwell: It's unfortunate that the system could not have discovered that before it took that kind of an accident.

Admiral Lawrence: Yes, you have these NATOPS inspections that are conducted by the wing staff. And they had a patrol Wing Two staff located there at Barbers Point and does those sorts of inspections.

---

* Captain Michael D. Haskins, USN, served as the Naval Academy's commandant of midshipmen from 1990 to 1992.
† NATOPS – Naval Air Training and Operating Procedures Standardization.

Another interesting thing during that period involved the arrival of USS *New Jersey*. The *New Jersey* had been recommissioned, and because the crew had done so much work to get that ship ready, we wanted to do something to reward them for all their hard work.* So I talked it over with my staff and CinCPacFlt and Commander Surface Force Pacific Fleet. We arranged a four-month shakedown cruise for them, which, initially, they'd come to Hawaii and spend five to seven days in Hawaii, then they'd go out to the Philippines, Singapore, Thailand, operate over with the Seventh Fleet, and then come on back.

When the ship came out to Hawaii, we really rolled out the carpet for the crew.† They had public visiting, and the lines for the visitors queued all the way outside the naval station. Everybody wanted to come and see the *New Jersey*. That visit to Pearl Harbor was very, very successful, and they did some training in the Hawaiian area.

But one thing that was reported to me by an officer who was riding the ship as an observer was that the navigational procedures on the *New Jersey* didn't appear sound. This officer reproduced some tracks that showed that when they were using the Pacific Missile Range on Kauai, they came close to shallow water. So I had to write Captain Fogarty a letter and just say, "Look, you need to really review and get your navigational watch team better trained and under control."‡ I guess it paid off, because they didn't have any more problems. But it was alarming to me to view this great capital ship, which everybody was watching so carefully, but seemed to not have good sound navigational techniques.

After the observer made his report on the navigational tracks, it came to the attention of my staff, and they came in and felt they had to tell me. My chief of staff was a surface officer, Captain Taylor Keith—R. T. S. Keith Jr.—and, of course, he knew all the surface people. So he got the information, and he gave it to me. I chose to handle it personally with Captain Fogarty, instead of making a big official thing about it.

---

* As part of the defense buildup by the Reagan administration, the battleship *New Jersey* (BB-62), which had originally gone into service in 1943, was pulled out of the mothball fleet in 1981 and reactivated and modernized by the Long Beach Naval Shipyard. She was recommissioned 28 December 1982.
† The *New Jersey* arrived at Pearl Harbor on 17 June 1983.
‡ Captain William M. Fogarty, USN, commanded the battleship *New Jersey* (BB-62) from 28 December 1982 to 15 September 1983.

But it shows you that often some areas are frequently just not well covered in training ships that you think would do well. But there is a tendency, I found over the years, for people to rely excessively on radar navigation when operating in close to land, because you just take a radar distance, and maybe they don't rely on visual fixes and other navigational aids such as the Fathometer.* The ship came much closer to shoal water than it should have, because they just didn't have an effective organization that was assessing information so the navigator and assistant navigator could make the right decisions and give them to the officer of the deck, the conning officer, and the captain.

Paul Stillwell: What kind of response did you get from the skipper?

Admiral Lawrence: Oh, Fogarty is a very sharp guy. He took it aboard, and, of course, they went on out to WestPac. I'm sure they took efforts to correct the situation. But the thing is that I'm leading up to is that when they got out there, there was a problem with rebels in El Salvador in Central America.

Paul Stillwell: There was also concern about Soviet supplies to Nicaragua.

Admiral Lawrence: Yes. So the decision was made to bring *New Jersey* back at high speed to go to Central America. It bothered me that we had to terminate their shakedown cruise early. That was one aspect of that. But they also had designated a CruDesGru commander, Rear Admiral Hekman, to go down and be the on-scene commander.† They wouldn't take my recommendation to have him embark in *New Jersey*, which I thought should be his flagship. That was because there was all this sensitivity to allegations that we were bringing the *New Jersey* battleship back into service to be a plush flagship for flag officers. I guess I'm just not enough of a political animal, because my reaction was just tell the congressmen it's the best flagship, and that's where he ought to be. But the people in Washington don't act that way, I guess.

---

* A Fathometer is a device that measures the depth of water under a ship's keel.
† Rear Admiral Peter M. Hekman, USN, Commander Cruiser-Destroyer Group One.

Paul Stillwell: Who was it, OpNav, that was saying not to do that?

Admiral Lawrence: Well, it was CNO, but I'm sure Secretary Lehman was very much in it. But it upset me they terminated that fine cruise that we'd planned after the in-port visit in Thailand. I know it was a political thing that the Navy wanted to get some high visibility for the battleships, because I know that *New Jersey* had no impact on the situation in El Salvador. I can't believe it did have. But it went down at high speed from WestPac, stopped briefly in Hawaii, then went on out to Central America. After it was there for a while, the Lebanese crisis started heating up, and then it was directed to go at high speed through the Panama Canal and out to Lebanon. But the upshot of this thing was that it left in June of 1983, and it didn't get back until the following year.*

Anyway, I had come back to Washington in August to become the Chief of Naval Personnel.† When I got back, she was on station over there off of Beirut. And here we could see that she was going to go on beyond Thanksgiving and beyond Christmas. And this was for, as I say, what originally was planned as a four-month cruise. The families were all upset. So we developed plans to have volunteer recalled reservists go over on *New Jersey*, so we could get some people home. But, anyway, that was something that really upset me as Com3rdFlt, because I felt that what we did was politically motivated to get high visibility for battleships. We put that above what was the best for the crew. And that's the way thinking is in Washington.

But the other thing is that they were considering sending a carrier down there to Central America. And so I had a carrier that was deploying.

Paul Stillwell: I think the *Ranger* did go down there, didn't she?

---

* The *New Jersey* left her homeport of Long Beach, California, on 9 June 1983 and arrived back there on 5 May 1984. For details, see Paul Stillwell, *Battleship New Jersey: An Illustrated History* (Annapolis: Naval Institute Press, 1986).
† Vice Admiral Lawrence was relieved as Commander Third Fleet in August 1983 and then served as Chief of Naval Personnel from 28 September 1983 to 31 December 1985.

Admiral Lawrence: Yes, that's right.* And I remember the CarGru commander was named George Aitchison.† I had to change orders to him about three times as to whether he was to terminate his training off of San Diego and go down there at high speed or continue training. What was happening was that people were trying to help you by calling you directly. They'd say, "Hey, Bill, I'm going to give you a heads up; this is going to happen." But they were hurting me by giving me erroneous information.

Admiral Hardisty was the N3, and he thought he was helping me, and he'd give me a call and say, "Bill, get the *Ranger* ready because I think we're going to order them down there."‡

So I'd call Aitchison and say, "Hey, George, knock off flight operations; get ready to go."

He'd knock off flight operations and then he'd call back and somebody else would say, [chuckle] "Well, I'm sorry; that was wrong. He can continue—"

So finally, I said, "No more. We do everything by message. I don't give any orders to ships unless I get an order from CinCPacFlt, my boss." That was a good example of how people can be too helpful sometimes.

Paul Stillwell: I'd be interested in your personal impressions of the *New Jersey* and Captain Fogarty. I remember being on board when you came to visit the ship in May '83.

Admiral Lawrence: Well, that ship had the best spirit of any ship I think I've ever been on. I mean, the pride of the sailors at being on the *New Jersey* was just great—from the youngest seaman up to the E-9s.§

Paul Stillwell: How would you explain that?

---

* The carrier *Ranger* (CV-61) deployed to Central American waters in late July 1983, when Lawrence was still Commander Third Fleet.
† Rear Admiral George A. Aitcheson Jr., USN, Commander Carrier Group Seven.
‡ Rear Admiral Huntington Hardisty, USN, Deputy Chief of Staff, Plans and Operations, staff of Commander in Chief Pacific Fleet.
§ E-9 is the Navy's highest enlisted pay grade, master chief petty officer.

Admiral Lawrence: Well, I think it was the pride of being in the top surface capital ship in the Navy. I think it was all of that. Also, I think Fogarty had done a good job of building up morale and spirit on that ship. They all wore the same type of work uniform; they had their own special coveralls instead of the dungarees. I think that was an element in it. And there were recalled people we brought out of retirement who had the experience on the 16-inch guns. As I recall, we had at least one fellow who had been in the Korean War.

I think it was good leadership from Fogarty and good petty officer leadership, because the seamen we sent on that ship were not pre-selected. They were just what we call the general-detail sailors whom the system sent out there. But I think it was good, strong leadership by the commanding officer, the executive officer, and the senior petty officers. So that's why it really, really made me feel bad when they terminated that shakedown cruise. I just didn't see the justification was there to do it. Perhaps, it made some of the case for Lebanon, but I just didn't see making a case for Central America.

But you know how things are in Washington. Everybody's in there fighting to protect his image, and Lehman is a very much image-conscious guy. I'm sure he was in there pushing hard to get high visibility for the *New Jersey* to justify reactivation of battleships.

Paul Stillwell: Exactly, because he was trying to sell the other three.*

What do you recall about your relationship with the various type commanders in the Pacific Fleet, as far as using their assets to best advantage?

Admiral Lawrence: Well, I had very good rapport with the type commanders. Admiral Schoultz was initially Commander Naval Air Force Pacific Fleet, and he was relieved by Admiral Pete Easterling, who came from being the ops guy on CinCPacFlt staff.

Admiral Baggett was the first ComNavSurfPac, and he was relieved while I was out there by Harry Schrader, but we didn't overlap a great amount, as I recall.† But I had good relationships with those type commanders. I had very good relationships with all of

---

* Following congressional approval, the Navy recommissioned the *Iowa* (BB-61) in 1984, the *Missouri* (BB-63) in 1986, and the *Wisconsin* (BB-64) in 1988. All were again decommissioned in the early 1990s.
† Vice Admiral Lee Baggett Jr., USN; Vice Admiral Harry C. Schrader Jr., USN.

the cruiser-destroyer group commanders, and the carrier group commanders, and very fine relationship with the CinCPacFlt staff. It couldn't have been better. Of course, Admiral Watkins was CinCPacFlt during my first year, and then Admiral Foley was the next year. Admiral Foley and I had been friends back from midshipman days, and we were very, very close.

Paul Stillwell: What can you say specifically about working with those two?

Admiral Lawrence: Well, it was just that I had very fine support. When I had an idea for something, they were very receptive, particularly Admiral Foley, because when he came in, I'd had a year on the job, and we were really getting up to speed on some of these new initiatives. So I had the ability to go in and talk to him and say, "Look, this is the concept I have." And he was very open, very receptive.

Paul Stillwell: Do you remember examples of some of those ideas?

Admiral Lawrence: Well, when we did the three-carrier battle group operation up in the Northwestern Pacific in April of 1983, I particularly wanted to test the *Los Angeles*-class submarine in the direct-support role.* That was the mission of providing ASW protection for battle groups. I felt that this was an area we had not fully assessed, because the submariners were philosophically opposed to having submarines being the screen, so to speak, for the battle group. They liked to go out and operate independently. But I felt that we needed to know this. I didn't feel, as a fleet commander, that I really had a good knowledge of the capabilities of the SSNs to protect the battle group. So Admiral Foley directed SubPac, Commander Submarine Force Pacific, to make six *Los Angeles*-class submarines available to me. That was unprecedented. I'm sure that caused all kinds of anguish.

We put two submarines off the approaches to Petropavlovsk to try to pick up the Soviets' sortieing submarines, and we had four that were in direct support. As I say,

---

* USS *Los Angeles* (SSN-688) was commissioned on 13 November 1976 as the lead ship of a class of 39 nuclear-powered fast-attack submarines.

Admiral Foley fully supported me on that initiative when I laid out the concept. He had a very good deputy, Vice Admiral Dick Kinnebrew.[*] He was a very solid citizen, and he and I had known each other. His predecessor was Vice Admiral Briggs, and he and I knew each other from midshipman days.[†] I just had wonderful cooperation from all elements of that staff, and, of course, I had great advantage of being co-located with them on Hawaii. We had a lot of interfaces, professionally and socially. So I had a lot of advantages over Com7th Fleet in my ability to get things done. Of course, on the other side of the coin, he had an advantage in that he was out there and they couldn't see what he was doing. [Laughter]

Paul Stillwell: Whichever you prefer.

Admiral Lawrence: That's right.

Paul Stillwell: Well, you mentioned before that you were disappointed by the performance of these direct-support submarines.

Admiral Lawrence: Yes. They had such a great problem with water-space management and the difficulties of instantaneous communication between surface ships and submarines. I found they were nowhere nearly as effective as I had hoped they would be in that close-in protection of the battle group.

Paul Stillwell: That's the kind of thing that you want to find out from an exercise.

Admiral Lawrence: That's right. But I tell you, it was hard to force the submarines into a position where we could find it out, because I think they themselves knew of their limitations. That was why they preferred to be basically out in single-submarine operations: careful, patient, searching, detection, tracking. But we found that, as I say, with water-space management it was a problem just making sure you kept submarines

---

[*] Vice Admiral Thomas R. Kinnebrew, USN.
[†] Vice Admiral Edward S. Briggs, USN, who had also served temporarily as Commander Third Fleet in August-September 1981 during the transition between Admiral Waller and Admiral Lawrence.

from colliding by giving them certain depths to operate in. The ambient noise problem impacted their acoustic detection capability. And there were limitations on communication. We often had to communicate with them by naval message, as opposed to an instantaneous tactical communication. But I found in that exercise and other experiences, that my best ASW asset was a *Spruance*-class destroyer with a towed array and a LAMPS helicopter.*

Paul Stillwell: LAMPS has a dipping sonar.

Admiral Lawrence: That was the best ASW asset I had.

Paul Stillwell: Did you have much direct interface with ComSubPac?

Admiral Lawrence: Oh, sure. We had very close relationship. And, of course, theoretically, I had opcon of their submarines in our area of operations. They did a lot of highly classified special operations.† They always kept me informed on them, and some of the things that they were doing were really exciting. I have the greatest respect for submariners, and don't think I'm being critical of them, because you don't have a group in the Navy that's more professional than the submarine force. But their whole orientation is towards operating singly. They just don't like to get in a battle group support situation. They love to go out under ice, special ops, sniff out Soviet submarines. I guess it's all part of their tradition of independent operation, silent service, and so forth. But, still, it didn't lower my respect for them in any way, or my feeling about them didn't change in my close relationship with ComSubPac.

Paul Stillwell: Did this lead to any idea of corrective measures as far as their work with battle groups?

---

* A towed array consists of passive sonar sensors, as opposed to those mounted directly on the ship's hull. By being on a towline, the passive array has the advantage that it can be lowered through thermal layers that would otherwise inhibit sound propagation and reception.
† For examples of these special operations, see Sherry Sontag and Christopher Drew, with Annette Lawrence Drew, *Blind Man's Bluff: the Untold Story of American Submarine Espionage* (New York: Public Affairs, 1998).

Admiral Lawrence: Well, of course, we made the appropriate analyses and reports. But it really didn't change things, because at that time the Navy was being run by a submariner, and I think he basically supported their approach.* I mean, the submariners are philosophically opposed, as I say, to having submarines controlled by anybody other than a submariner, and being put in a group operational situation. They prefer and they feel their capabilities are maximized when they operate singly.

But, as I point out, because of concentration of ships in a battle group and what the battle group represents to the Navy, we have the responsibility to protect those as well as we can. And, indeed, there are assets in the proximity of the carrier and escort ships in the battle group to give them this ASW protection. A single submarine that's out 100 miles away can help, but that's not the most effective way to do the ASW protection. But the submarines prefer to be in a single-ship operation situation, under the control of a submarine commander ashore, and not the control of anybody else. I was out at sea several months ago, talking to people about operations, and that's still the way submariners like to do it.

Paul Stillwell: You mentioned your chief of staff, Taylor Keith. He was the son of a sort of a predecessor of yours in that he had been Com1stFlt.†

Admiral Lawrence: Yes.

Paul Stillwell: How was his son to work with?

Admiral Lawrence: Oh, he was really superb—very smart tactically, technically, and administratively. He was a very superb chief of staff. I really gave him a most glowing fitness report that I could ever write. I really tried my best to get him promoted to admiral. After he was with me, he came back and had some really plum jobs, including being a surface captain detailer. For reasons I just cannot understand, he was not selected for flag rank, and he retired as a captain. Somehow he was not high on their list of some

---

* Admiral James D. Watkins, USN, served as Chief of Naval Operations, 1 July 1982 to 30 June 1986.
† Vice Admiral Robert Taylor Scott Keith, USN, served as Commander First Fleet from 5 May 1962 to 11 December 1963.

elements in the senior surface warfare officers. And I never could figure out why, because he'd done all the right things tactically, he had gone to postgraduate school, and he had a strong technical foundation. Somehow, he did not make it into the inner circle. You never know why those things occur.

Paul Stillwell: What other staff members do you recall?

Admiral Lawrence: Well, I had some very, very fine officers. One officer on that staff later on became Rear Admiral Bill Mathis.[*] He was on there as a commander, and he was one of the guys I tasked to gear up our cognizance involved with this Tomahawk. He really picked up the ball and ran with it. He was in the ops section of our staff, and he was responsible for putting Tomahawks into exercises and using Tomahawk tactics. But I think he was the only officer on my staff at that time during my tenure who went on to become a flag officer.

I had some really solid, really fine people on that staff, and I think we did some very good, innovative thinking while we were there. The most significant thing we did, I think, was to get people really focused on the flexible operations. Because that exercise that we did—the three-carrier battle group exercise—that we did up northwestern Pacific, Admiral Foley, right after it was over, had Jerry Johnson—who at that time was a captain and is now an admiral—go back and brief that all over Washington: to the Secretary of the Navy and the Center for Naval Analyses.[†]

I mean, that exercise really got a lot of play, because not only was the flexible ops concept new, being up to the Northwestern Pacific and very close proximity to the Soviets, it was one of the best examples of joint operations up to that time. I had this very good rapport with the commanding general of the 15th Air Force, and he took the concept on up to the Chief of Staff of the Air Force. They gave us tremendous number of assets. We had KC-10 tankers that provided our tanking support; we had AWACS that were out there providing our airborne early warning; and they were actually controlling

---

[*] Rear Admiral William W. Mathis, USN.
[†] Admiral Jerome L. Johnson, USN, served as Vice Chief of Naval Operations from May 1990 to July 1992. He was VCNO at the time of this interview.

Navy airplanes.* And we actually had F-15s flying out of that airfield that's out on the very tip of the Aleutians, providing combat air support for the battle groups. The Canadians were involved, and the Coast Guard was involved. It was a wonderful example of joint operations, so that was another thing that they briefed all over town.

As I said, the Chief of Staff of the Air Force had to dedicate a lot of Air Force assets to doing that. And that was because we had laid all the groundwork, like establishing this rapport with the 15th Air Force there at March Air Force Base. Then he went on up to the air staff and sold them. We laid the foundation back there in 1983 for much of what you see happening in the Middle East right now in terms of joint cooperation, like the use of tankers, AWACS, and having one air plan. So it was really a very personally rewarding tour. Very busy in terms of the tremendous amount of traveling you had to do to cover your area of responsibility. But I really thoroughly enjoyed that whole experience.

Paul Stillwell: Well, anything else to mention on the Third Fleet?

Admiral Lawrence: No, I think this is probably a good place to stop.

Paul Stillwell: All right.

---

* AWACS – airborne warning and control system. This is an aerial look-down radar and tracking system carried on board the Air Force's E-3 Sentry, a modified Boeing 707 airliner with a rotating radome on top.

Interview Number 20 with Vice Admiral William P. Lawrence, U.S. Navy (Retired)
Place: U.S. Naval Institute, Annapolis, Maryland
Date: Wednesday, 20 February 1991

Paul Stillwell: Admiral, we talked the last two sessions about your time in command of the Third Fleet, and now you just want to wrap up that experience.

Admiral Lawrence: Yes, just one final thing that was one of the very significant achievements we made there. We certainly gave a strong emphasis to antisubmarine warfare there. It was more than just the fact we were descendent of the old ASW Force Pacific. We really were trying to improve the battle group ASW—in other words, how a constituted carrier battle group pursued the ASW mission in an integrated manner.

The problem in the past had always been grading performance. So we developed a concept for using the underwater range we have out there in the Pacific Missile Range facility to the west of Kauai—a place called Barking Sands—to do graded, assessed battle group ASW. Of course, we couldn't put the entire battle group in the range there, even though it was a fairly large range. But, for example, we could put the carrier there. We used to put the supporting surface ships in the battle group and submarines in there with opposition friendly forces and do a graded battle group ASW problem, a coordinated, integrated approach. So we had a practice that every battle group that was deploying to the Western Pacific would do a graded battle group ASW exercise on that range when it came through Hawaii. I felt this really made a great contribution to improving battle group ASW. That was one of the things we instituted in my time as Commander Third Fleet.

Paul Stillwell: Was the range instrumented so you could see the moves the various units made?

Admiral Lawrence: Yes, it was. It was one of two or three undersea ranges that we have in the Navy. I think one is down in the Bahamas at a place called Eleuthera.

Paul Stillwell: Yes, right.

Admiral Lawrence: This is the one out in the Pacific area. And there is some limited capability, I think, off the West Coast to do some of this around San Clemente. But Barking Sands is a fully instrumented range, where you can duplicate the tracks and do a complete assessment of the performance of every ship. From a shore-based control room you could do a graded exercise and track every ship that was in there.

Paul Stillwell: Do you have any assessment from that period on the value of the P-3s, the land-based patrol planes?

Admiral Lawrence: Well, quite frankly, in the area of assessing their performance against the Soviets, we just didn't have the Soviet threat. The Soviet Yankee SSBNs used to patrol off the West Coast of California in what we called the Yankee patrol area. But the Soviets were reducing the number of Yankee patrols. Then they had built the Delta SSBN, which had a longer-range missile, so we didn't really get much opportunity to work against Soviet submarines.

In the battle group exercises where the P-3s were involved, the number of detections they got was just not very great. I think it just shows you the great difficulty detecting submarines from an airplane, where you're relying on sonobuoys and MAD, magnetic anomaly detection equipment. In two years I could remember only a handful of submarine detections for the P-3.

Paul Stillwell: You said before that the ships and planes that could put sonar into the water were more effective.

Admiral Lawrence: Well, what I'm saying, really, is that I think the airplane ASW problem is much more challenging, much more difficult than the surface ship and submarine ASW, because the airplane is largely relying on sonobuoys in the water, plus using his MAD gear. MAD is based on magnetic signatures, and you have to fly close to a submarine. The problem with sonobuoys, of course, is a technical problem, of the sound being picked up and then transmitted by radio and converted into gram type of readings. You also have the problem of sonobuoy placement, achieving the right pattern. So the airplane ASW problem is great.

Paul Stillwell: Well, any last benediction on Third Fleet before we move to Washington?

Admiral Lawrence: No. The change of command we had was a very pleasant one, because Admiral Crowe had just come over from Naples to be CinCPac.[*] He was an old friend. Then my successor, Admiral Jones, had been the former EA to Deputy SecDef Thayer, so Thayer came out and gave the principal speech.[†] And, of course, I had known Thayer back in my test pilot days when he was the vice president of Chance Vought Aviation. So our final days, the change of command, and all the farewells in Hawaii were really very pleasant.

Paul Stillwell: That was before Thayer got his very unpleasant comeuppance.

Admiral Lawrence: Yes, that was all before that.

Paul Stillwell: How did you wind up with the job as Chief of Naval Personnel?

Admiral Lawrence: Well, frankly, I was surprised when they gave me that assignment, because I had never served in the Bureau of Naval Personnel and never had any job there in Washington that prepared me for it. Although when I was in D.C. in air warfare, I got very much involved in aviation personnel matters. But I really thought if they were going to reassign me after the Third Fleet, I would go to some other job, maybe go up into one of the JCS spots or something like that. But I guess, because of the fact that I'd had the

---

[*] Admiral William J. Crowe, Jr., USN, served as Commander in Chief Pacific from 1 July 1983 to 11 October 1983, when he left to become Chairman of the Joint Chiefs of Staff.
[†] Vice Admiral Donald S. Jones, USN, was Commander Third Fleet from August 1983 to August 1985. W. Paul Thayer was chairman and chief executive officer of the now-defunct LTV Corporation from 1970 to 1982. After he left LTV, he was U.S. Deputy Secretary of Defense in 1983-84. He was also the subject of a 1980s government insider-trading investigation in which he pleaded guilty. He entered prison under a plea agreement in 1985 and served 19 months of a four-year sentence.

tour as superintendent of the Naval Academy, the CNO, Admiral Watkins, perceived that that was pretty good preparation for being the Chief of Naval Personnel.

But, also, I think I had a reputation for being people-oriented, and had been throughout my career. But it really surprised me when I got the job. [Chuckle]

Paul Stillwell: Well, that's not the kind of job one asks for, is it?

Admiral Lawrence: No, you never ask for a job as—I guess some vice admirals may ask for their jobs. But normally the decisions on three-star assignments are made by the CNO and the Secretary of the Navy after talking things over. A lot of it is just based on timing—what's available. Really, it was a surprise to me, but I was very enthusiastic, because, as I say, I've always had a great interest in people. I looked forward to trying to get some good things accomplished for sailors in the job of Chief of Naval Personnel, because I had a lot of ideas of things I had seen over the years that I felt that would enhance the morale and effectiveness of the Navy.

Paul Stillwell: Well, maybe that's a good place to start. What were some of the things on your agenda?

Admiral Lawrence: Well, I always felt that we could make the detailing process, the career management, and the issuing of orders much more effective. I wanted to have our people much more responsive to individuals and trying to fill their needs, encouraging people to talk freely with their detailers.

Throughout my whole career, I talked to my detailer only one time. That was when I was at the lieutenant commander level. I had just felt that this was something a junior officer shouldn't do. I felt that whatever they decided back there, I would accept and would do that.

I really wanted to work to achieve the situation where every young officer in the Navy had no inhibition about getting on the phone and calling the detailer. That was one thing. We were on a concerted effort to get the information out to junior officers, "This is your detailer; this is his phone number, and you call." That policy put a real burden on our detailers, because they were on the phone a lot. But, anyway, I just felt that more personalized career management was something that needed to be done.

Paul Stillwell: Did you have to get more detailers just to handle that extra phoning?

Admiral Lawrence: I'm sure over time this happened, because we were building up our numbers of personnel during the time I was there. But I just made it clear to everybody that an integral part of their duties was talking personally to young officers. In those days we were calling it the Naval Military Personnel Command, and I wanted to ensure that organization became more responsive to individuals.

My executive assistant was Captain Mike Boorda, who's now the Chief of Naval Personnel.[*] We were brainstorming this, and that's when we came up with the "never say no" policy. We promulgated it with the people who worked there, based on the principle that if somebody contacted you, your first inclination was to say yes, and then you had to prove it to yourself why you had to say no and really made it clear that was the attitude we wanted everybody to have. If we learned of anybody who was not taking that approach, we would take appropriate action, because I'd always been very much turned off by the poor response when sailors asked for something. We'd try to get some help from the bureaucrats back there, the people who responded often took the attitude, "Why are you bothering me?" so people got short shrift, so to speak. So I really worked hard on that when I came here and was engendering that attitude to be helpful and responsive to sailors.

Paul Stillwell: Admiral Boorda came over here a couple months ago, and he was talking about the idea that he uses, that you try to let common sense prevail over regulations where possible. I wonder if that was part of your philosophy.

Admiral Lawrence: Oh, yes, that was all part of our approach that we really tried to personalize the whole thing.

---

[*] Vice Admiral Jeremy M. Boorda, USN, served as Chief of Naval Personnel from 9 August 1988 to 6 November 1991. He was later Chief of Naval Operations, 1994-96.

Paul Stillwell: I'd be interested in some specific recollections about Captain Boorda and his role with you.

Admiral Lawrence: Well, he, of course, had probably the best foundation of personnel experience of anybody in the Navy, because, even at that time as a captain, he had had, I think, at least three prior assignments as a detailer, working on a high-level staff and personnel. So he was really good, because he knew personnel in and out—in addition of being just a very intelligent guy with a lot of common sense and a very human individual. He had a great deal of compassion and concern. He had been a prior enlisted man, so he knew the enlisted situation very thoroughly. So he was a great asset to me.

We worked very closely together, because, as the Chief of Naval Personnel, you have cognizance over manpower, personnel, and training. See, we had changed the organization to put the Chief of Naval Education and Training underneath the Chief of Naval Personnel. My additional title was a DCNO for Manpower, Personnel, and Training.* In past times the Chief of Naval Personnel did not have cognizance over training. Then we separated the DCNO for Manpower, Personnel, and Training, OP-01, from the Naval Military Personnel Command and made two distinct organizations. Then we brought training under the DCNO for Manpower, Personnel, and Training hat. So that made a great breadth and depth of responsibility in that job. I relied very heavily on people such as my EA and, of course, the flag officers who worked for me. It was a very, very demanding job.

One thing that increases the degree of difficulty of that job is that you personally do the detailing of flag officers in the Navy—everybody below the three-star rank. And, of course, you get involved in the three-stars in discussions with the CNO, but that means you have to know everything there is about the legislation governing the flag officers. We have 258 flag officers, but at that time, we were frocking.† So your number of flag officers at any one time was probably about 350, because you had around 100 or so who had been selected and frocked. We don't frock anymore.

---

* DCNO – Deputy Chief of Naval Operations.
† "Frocking" a naval officer refers to the practice of allowing him to wear the insignia and assume the title for which he was recently selected. The officer does not receive the pay for the higher rank until a vacancy appears on the lineal list so he can be officially promoted.

But, anyway, it meant that in your head you had to know all about every one of those 350 flag officers. And, of course, in the restricted line and the staff corps—like the Medical Corps, Supply Corps, and so forth—although you detailed those flag officers, you relied very heavily on the Chief of the Medical Corps, the Chief of the Dental Corps, and so forth, to help you in that process. But that was the only time you relied on somebody else. You managed the careers of the unrestricted line, which is the vast bulk of flag officers. It was a very interesting, fascinating responsibility. But it consumed a tremendous amount of your time.

Paul Stillwell: Can you give some examples of how that process worked?

Admiral Lawrence: Well, on an everyday basis, you maintained what we called a slate. You knew the jobs that were becoming available because of people who needed to be reassigned, those who were retiring, and, of course, the new promotions. So on a continuous basis you had to be selecting people to go into the different positions. You literally had to devote some time to that function virtually every day. Because it was so demanding and so complex, you had to carve out periods where you could devote a long period of time—several hours—just sitting down and really brainstorming it, talking it over with the captain who was your special assistant for flag matters—the two of you. And, of course, you'd have meetings with the community leaders, the DCNOs for air warfare, submarine warfare, surface warfare, to get their inputs on how they felt about their flag officers who worked with them and were in their communities.

Of course, you talked probably about two or three days a week with the Vice Chief of Naval Operations and the CNO, where you gave them your proposals for flag officer assignment. In that process were a lot of discussions, because the CNO wouldn't buy a lot of the proposals I made. That would result in a pretty in-depth discussion about the billet and so forth. He and I had many sessions every week, either face to face or on the telephone, where we talked about what we were going to do with flag officers. That whole process was significantly complicated when I was the Chief of Naval Personnel, because the Secretary of the Navy, John Lehman, and the CNO, Admiral Watkins, didn't communicate well. It was obvious to me when I came in. I'd heard also that Admiral Hayward and Lehman didn't get along, and they had minimal communication.

My job was greatly made more difficult by the fact that the CNO and the Secretary did not have good face-to-face discussion on the matter of flag officers. Basically the CNO would send a nomination down to the Secretary and just wait for his action. Of course, the Secretary had all sorts of opinions about this, and the more time he spent in office, the more personally involved he got in the whole process. When I arrived there in '83, he had been in office for a little over two years, and so he was really beginning to feel his power. One of the first things Admiral Zech, whom I succeeded, informed me about in the area of flag detail was that a certain number of flag officers were on the Secretary of the Navy's disfavor list.[*] That meant you could not give them meaningful assignments.

I'd ask questions like, "Gosh, I know that individual. Why is he on the disfavor list?"

The reasons would vary considerably. Sometimes it would be something simple: "Well, he voiced up his disagreement with the Secretary at a meeting, and so he's on the Secretary's list." Or "The Secretary doesn't like him because he perceives that he's close to Admiral Hayward." So my job was greatly aggravated, made more difficult, by the Secretary of the Navy's involvement in the process and his favoritism to certain individuals and other people whom he didn't like.

Paul Stillwell: Do you remember any specific cases?

Admiral Lawrence: Oh, yes, many. For example, Admiral Weaver, who was an AEDO, had been the F/A-18 project officer.[†] And, of course, in later years, he became the commander of the Space and Naval Warfare Systems Command, which is a very significant job. But he had disagreed with the Secretary at a meeting on the F/A-18, and

---

[*] Vice Admiral Lando W. Zech, Jr., USN, served as Chief of Naval Personnel from August 1980 to September 1983.
[†] AEDO – aeronautical engineering duty officer. Captain John C. Weaver, USN, was program manager for the F/A-18 from 1980 to 1984.

so he was on the disfavor list the whole time I was Chief of Naval Personnel. Of course, when Lehman retired he went on and got a very significant responsibility.

A former executive assistant for Admiral Hayward, Admiral Cockell, one of the smartest guys in the Navy, was one of our really fine Sovietologists in the Navy.[*] Now he works in the White House. But because he had been the executive assistant to Admiral Hayward, and Lehman and Hayward didn't get along, Cockell was on the list. We had to send him to be Commander Training Command Pacific Fleet—far beneath his intellectual capabilities. And there were others.

Paul Stillwell: I heard Admiral Rowden was supposed to get a fourth star and never did, because he was on the bad list.

Admiral Lawrence: Well, I'm sure that that was the case. When I came back in '83, Rowden came in from being Com6thFlt and he came in to get the Military Sealift Command. And, of course, later on he got the Naval Sea Systems Command.[†] I think he was certainly a clear contender for four stars.

Paul Stillwell: Well, it was even in *Navy Times* that he was going to get NavMat, and then he wound up with Sealift Command instead.[‡]

Admiral Lawrence: Yes. That happened before I got back there, because Admiral White had already taken over NavMat. But I'd heard that George Sawyer, who was Assistant Secretary of the Navy for Shipbuilding, was close to White.[§] They'd both been in the nuclear program. He was instrumental in getting White in there, but it was a very unhealthy process that was going on.

The other thing that really concerned me about Secretary Lehman is his involvement in manipulation on promotion boards. I ran the flag boards, basically—got

---

[*] Rear Admiral William A. Cockell Jr., USN.
[†] Vice Admiral William H. Rowden, USN, served as Commander Naval Sea Systems Command from 1985 to 1988.
[‡] NavMat – Naval Material Command, a four-star billet.
[§] Admiral Steven A. White, USN.

the precepts prepared and appointed the officers. The first flag board I had when I was the Chief of Naval Personnel, it was clear to me that the president of the board had direction from the Secretary of the Navy to pick his EA, Paul Miller, who at that time, had been in the Navy only 20 years.[*] He'd been a captain for a relatively short time. He'd been, of course, a very bright officer, but it really upset me that the president of that board went in virtually on order from the Secretary of the Navy to pick that individual.

Of course, I saw the Secretary of the Navy's influence reflected on other boards, where he had conveyed in one way or the other how he wanted board results to come out. For example, it was a kind of a standing thing that if you didn't pick enough NFOs, naval flight officers, the Secretary would probably send you back.[†] So I felt that presidents of boards felt they were unduly influenced in the actions they took, because of their perception of what the Secretary wanted. They all had this fear that they would be called before the Secretary of the Navy and dressed down or maybe even sent back in session. As I say, the first flag board knew the president had directions.

On the second flag board, the Secretary wasn't happy with the results, so he sent the board back into session. They had a big argument between the president of the board, who was Admiral White, and the Secretary. The Secretary ended up giving an additional number for flag selectees. So if you get one more aviation flag, apparently there was a guy whom the Secretary wanted to select.

I felt we were violating the spirit of the law by the Secretary of the Navy's actions, and it concerned me very much. I talked to the CNO; I talked to the Vice Chief all about this, and it was one of these things, "Well, you know, we have to try to do our best to get along with the Secretary."

The other thing that concerned me was that the Secretary would delay approval of flag nominations. As I say, he and the CNO did not have good communication with each other. They basically communicated through the executive assistants. The CNO's executive assistant would go down and talk to the Secretary of the Navy's executive assistant, and that's the way the information was conveyed. So, because of that poor communication, we simply never, during my time, could develop a long-range flag slate.

---

[*] Captain Paul David Miller, USN. He entered Officer Candidate School in 1964 and became a commodore, then the title for one-star flag rank, in 1984.
[†] Secretary Lehman, a Naval Reservist, was a naval flight officer.

Normally you like to be able to look at least a year ahead and determine where the flag officers were going, but that wasn't possible.

Paul Stillwell: And you like to look even farther than that and groom some people.

Admiral Lawrence: Oh, sure, much longer than that. The arrangement they have now is that every flag officer will get his orders about six months in advance, so everybody can make the plans and have an orderly turnover. Back then, the relationship between the CNO and the Secretary got to be so poor with regard to flag assignments that I always felt lucky if I could get a month's advance notice for orders. The Secretary would string us along with a guy, knowing he was going to get orders, his relief being on board, and the Secretary wouldn't approve the new orders.

It was a terrible, terrible situation. Secretary of the Navy Lehman appeared to have absolutely no concern about the impact and inconvenience he was subjecting people to. I can give you an example after example what I'm talking about.

Paul Stillwell: Well, please do.

Admiral Lawrence: Okay, I'll give you a good example.

In 1985, the Secretary of the Navy wanted Vice Admiral Ace Lyons to be made a four-star admiral and put down to be the first CinCLant, when we separated CinCLant and CinCLantFlt.[*] Well, Admiral Watkins was very much against this. He didn't feel that Ace was the right person for the job. Admiral Crowe was against it; Secretary Weinberger was against it.[†] Well, apparently, Secretary Lehman was so upset that Watkins, as the CNO, did not support him in this, he started a practice that prevailed

---

[*] For a number of years prior, one four-star U.S. admiral simultaneously held the posts of Supreme Allied Commander Atlantic (SACLant), a NATO billet; Commander in Chief Atlantic Command (CinCLant), a joint-service U.S. billet; and Commander in Chief Atlantic Fleet (CinCLantFlt), a Navy-only U.S. billet. In 1985, the commands were divided, with one four-star admiral serving as SACLant and CinCLant and another four-star admiral as CinCLantFlt and Deputy CinCLant. The nominee for the SACLant/CinCLant job required international and U.S. Joint Chiefs of Staff approval because it was not Navy-only. Vice Admiral James A. Lyons, Jr., USN, served as Deputy Chief of Naval Operations (Plans, Policy and Operations) from July 1983 to August 1985.

[†] Admiral William J. Crowe, Jr., USN, was Chairman of the JCS from 1 October 1985 to 30 September 1989. Caspar W. Weinberger was Secretary of Defense from 21 January 1981 to 23 November 1987.

much of the time, where he held Watkins hostage by not approving flag nominations. One time we had about 25 flag nominations on his desk that he wouldn't approve. People were subjected to all sorts of inconvenience.

A good example is Admiral Mauz, who recently came back from being Com7thFlt.* He was the naval commander of the Middle East during Desert Shield. Back in the mid-1980s, I guess he was a one-star. He was in a job on the CinCEur staff, and because he was a really sharp guy, I had ordered him and gotten the CNO's approval to send him down to command Cruiser-Destroyer Group 12 in Mayport, Florida.† Admiral Donnell, who was in the job, was coming up to be the deputy J-5.‡ Well, Mauz's orders were in the group that Secretary Lehman was not approving, and he wouldn't say why he wouldn't approve them. It was a way of putting pressure on the CNO to make the CNO do things—or a way of punishing the CNO, because the CNO had not sided with him on the Ace Lyons situation.

Mauz's relief was actually on board, and Mauz had to move out of his quarters and into the VIP suite there. But I couldn't tell him where he was going, because we had a policy that you couldn't tell anybody until the Secretary of the Navy approved orders. I just would have my assistant for flag matters call him and say, "Look, we're doing our best to get the orders approved."

Finally, through the efforts of the Secretary of the Navy's executive assistant, Captain Paul Miller, who was begging him, he finally approved Mauz's orders. Mauz flew down to Florida and had a brief office turnover with Donnell, who had to fly up to Washington, because he had to relieve a guy up there, who was from a different service, as Deputy J-5 on the Joint Staff. No leave was allowed; families were put to all sorts of inconvenience, and this was a very typical thing. So we were really grossly mistreating flag officers during the time of Secretary Lehman, because we couldn't get enough advance notice on issuing orders. He had those who were on his disfavored list, and he had his favorites he tried to always take care of. So it was a very poor time. It took

---

* Vice Admiral Henry H. Mauz Jr., USN, served as Commander Seventh Fleet from 21 October 1988 to 1 December 1990.
† CinCEur – Commander in Chief U.S. Forces Europe. Rear Admiral (Lower Half) Mauz became Commander Cruiser-Destroyer Group 12 in May 1985.
‡ Rear Admiral Joseph S. Donnell, USN, became Vice Director J-5 (Plans) on the Joint Staff in May 1985.

several years after Lehman left office for us to get things back on the right track.

Also, we really made some gross mistakes on flag assignments. As I say, after Lehman had been in office two years, he made a lot of assignments himself. He just directed that they be done. Some of them turned out to be real bummers. Admiral Lyons is a good example. He went out to be CinCPacFlt as a four-star because Lehman couldn't get approval from the Joint Chiefs on Lyons going to CinCLant.[*] Then Lyons got fired from the job, because of, basically, insubordination.

On the Persian Gulf problem, Admiral Hays, who was CinCPac, directed that certain action be taken, and Lyons refused to take it.[†] He was actually giving orders to ship commanding officers in the Persian Gulf, but they were under the Central Command's authority. But since they originally belonged to the Pacific Fleet, Lyons felt he could give them orders in the Persian Gulf. It was a very untenable situation, so Admiral Hays fired him from his job. We had another gent whom Lehman put in to be Com6thFlt, and he was the one who got summarily relieved for flying his girlfriend around with him in an airplane.[‡] It was a very unsavory situation.

So it was a very bad time during Lehman's tenure with regard to management of career flag officers.

Paul Stillwell: Well, despite his pulling strings for Miller, Miller's done very well since then, so he must have been a capable officer.[§]

Admiral Lawrence: Yes, and of course, the reason they put Miller in there is because we knew it would be very tough for his executive assistant to work with John Lehman.

---

[*] Admiral James A. Lyons, Jr., USN served as Commander in Chief Pacific Fleet from 16 September 1985 to 30 September 1987.
[†] Admiral Ronald J. Hays, USN, served as Commander in Chief Pacific from 18 September 1985 to 30 September 1988.
[‡] Vice Admiral Kendall B. Moranville, USN, became Commander Sixth Fleet in June 1986. On 20 August 1988 Vice Admiral Kendall E. Moranville, USN, was relieved as Commander Sixth Fleet. He had been under consideration for another three-star job until 19 August, when he received a letter of reprimand as the result of an admiral's mast. He was charged with improprieties involving travel claims and for being accompanied by an unauthorized female Italian civilian while flying U.S. military aircraft when he was Commander Sixth Fleet. The Chief of Naval Operations, Admiral Carlisle A. H. Trost, USN, forced Moranville to retire as a rear admiral, one level below his highest active duty rank.
[§] Admiral Paul D. Miller, USN, served as Supreme Allied Commander Atlantic and Commander in Chief Atlantic Command from 13 July 1992 to 31 October 1994.

Miller had the reputation for being a very brilliant officer, and, of course, he had worked as executive assistant to Admiral Bob Long out at CinCPac, and so he'd proven himself as an EA. The unfortunate thing about it was that he spent a long period as an executive assistant.* He didn't have a command in the rank of captain, and I have found that a lack of experience, regardless of how smart a guy is, is a detriment to him.

Intelligence cannot replace experience, but Miller's highly respected, and I don't think anyone should criticize Miller because he happened to be Secretary Lehman's EA. He was basically doing his duty. I think, because he's a very smart, capable guy, he made a bad situation somewhat better, because he was the principal conduit for communication between the Secretary of the Navy and the CNO.

I'm sure it would be absolutely unbelievable for many people to know that during my three years as Chief of Naval Personnel, I observed that the CNO was not even involved in major deliberations on weapon systems acquisition. The CNO actually had no involvement at all in aviation decision-making. It was done entirely by the Secretary of the Navy. And, of course, we see today the disastrous results—the A-12 cancellation and the P-7 cancellation—because of Lehman's policies on fixed price development of contracts.† If there had been a greater review and broader scrutiny and questioning of decisions, I don't think some of the adverse things that are happening now, perhaps, would have occurred.

Secretary Lehman disestablished OP-96, the systems analysis group that we had there in OpNav. One of the big reasons was that he couldn't tolerate any disagreement. The people in OP-96 were our honest brokers, and they would say, "We don't feel this is a proper course of action. This is what we recommend." He took enough of that and he disestablished them. So there were no checks and balances in the high-level decision-making of the Navy, particularly in the area of aviation. Lehman and Paisley took it upon themselves to make all the decisions with regard to naval aviation.‡

---

* Miller was executive assistant to Admiral Robert L. J. Long, CinCPac, from October 1979 to August 1981 and for Secretary Lehman from September 1981 to February 1986—an extraordinarily long period as EA.
† The A-12 attack plane was intended to be the replacement for the A-6 Intruder and the P-7 for the P-3 Orion. Neither program came to fruition.
‡ Melvyn R. Paisley served as Assistant Secretary of the Navy (Research, Engineering and Systems) from December 1981 to March 1987.

Paul Stillwell: You alluded before to Admiral Demars and his being willing to stand up to Lehman.[*] Could you talk about that, please?

Admiral Lawrence: Well, Demars was the first president of a selection board who refused to abide by an order for Lehman to go back in and change the board results. It had been going on for years, and, as I say, it bothered me significantly. Demars basically said, "No, I'm not going to do it." I have to give a lot of credit to Demars, because he was jeopardizing his own career. I guess the Secretary of the Navy could have taken punitive action against him if he chose to do so. But Demars knew he was right. It was a violation of the spirit of the law to direct him to go back and change the results once the board process occurred and the results were reported out. So it took a lot of courage, but Demars did the right thing.

Then the Senate Armed Services Committee threatened to get in and investigate the situation. I think that threat caused Lehman to back down, because he realized that basically the majority was against him on that particular issue. Subsequently the Congress passed a law that restricted the Secretary of the Navy from changing the selection results, and that was specifically aimed at John Lehman for what he did.

I think Demars's action on that board really was a factor that led to Lehman's retirement, because there were indications that there may be an investigation by Congress and of what he did in manipulation of boards.

Paul Stillwell: Well, another factor was that the budget forecast was starting to look gloomy.

Admiral Lawrence: That was, of course, a big factor, because the Reagan buildup peaked in '85, and then Lehman left office in '87. One thing that was quite clear to him was that the aviation plan he had developed just could not be achieved.

Paul Stillwell: Well, and the 600-ship Navy was not looking very good either.

---

[*] Vice Admiral Bruce Demars, USN, was OP-02, Deputy Chief of Naval Operations (Submarine Warfare).

Admiral Lawrence: Yes, yes. If you look back on the Lehman years, a lot of those decisions are really coming back to bite us, because in that great buildup, in the kind of a kid-in-a-candy-store type of attitude that people had those five years of Reagan buildup, Lehman committed us to some high-cost systems that we simply couldn't afford in the budget realities after 1985.

Two good examples are the A-12 airplane and the SSN-21 submarine.* The A-12 was going to cost us about $100 million per airplane. The SSN-21 now is going for $2 billion dollars. So if we continue with those expensive programs, our force level is going to be reduced to the point that the Navy will be significantly weakened. The CNO just came out with a directive here recently saying that we have to procure lower-cost airplanes and ships, and he's specifically referring to SSN-21 submarines.

So some of those decisions that were made by Lehman—principally by him and the small group he had around him, like Paisley and George Sawyer and those people—have turned out to be really bad decisions. They didn't have the fiscal sense that they should have had in jobs like that. If they had subjected their decisions to broader scrutiny and used the systems analysis people, had the CNO more involved, I think we could have prevented some of those proceedings from the beginning.

We've always had a high-low mix in the Navy, where we'd have a few highly capable, sophisticated platforms, and then with them, we have less capable, lower-cost systems. For example, the A-4 airplane is the low end of the aviation mix. We couldn't have fought the Vietnam War without the A-4 airplane. And we had hundreds and hundreds of DEs in World War II, along with the battleships and the heavy cruisers.† Lehman had absolute contempt for this concept. He didn't believe that there should be a low component, even with everything we've gotten now. Nothing we're buying now is less than $1 billion dollars—the *Burke* is a billion dollars; SSN-21 is $2 billion.‡ Of

---

* USS *Seawolf* (SSN-21), the first of a three-ship class of nuclear-powered attack submarines, was commissioned 19 July 1997 after construction at the General Dynamics shipyard in Groton, Connecticut. She displaces 7,460 tons surfaced and 9,137 tons submerged. The ship is 353 feet long, 40 feet in the beam, and has a maximum draft of 36 feet. Her top speed on the surface is 15 knots; top speed submerged is 35 knots. The submarine is armed with Tomahawk missiles and has eight 26½-inch torpedo tubes.
† DE – destroyer escort.
‡ USS *Arleigh Burke* (DDG-51) was commissioned 4 July 1991. She has a standard displacement of 6,624 tons, is 504 feet long, and 67 feet in the beam, and maximum draft of 31 feet. Her design speed is 31 knots. She is equipped with the Aegis system; a 90-cell vertical launching system for missiles; two quadruple Harpoon canisters; one 5-inch gun, ASROC, and two triple torpedo launchers.

course, the carriers have always been expensive. The A-12 airplanes would have absolutely bankrupted us.

Someday the scholars will get in there and look very carefully at what happened back in the '80s, but at the present time, I think the average layman—L-A-Y-M-A-N—thinks that John Lehman was a great Secretary of the Navy. We're in a lot worse shape today than we would have been because of John Lehman—some of the actions that he took, both with regard to the personnel, flag officer selections, and the weapon systems decisions.

Paul Stillwell: On the selection boards, I remember there was unpleasantness, also, on a Naval Reserve board where there was a perception of undue influence. I don't think it was from Lehman.

Admiral Lawrence: No, I don't think Lehman had involvement in that. It happened before I came into office, but apparently somebody not on the board tried to make contact with or influence somebody on the board.

Actually, during my time in there, the boards went pretty smoothly, except, as I say, Lehman's personal manipulation and involvement, principally, in the O-6 captains' board and the flag boards. Those were two areas where he got personally involved. But he also reviewed carefully the results of other boards. He would always ask the question, "Well, how many NFOs are on it? How many A-6 pilots and NFOs?" So the Vice Chief of Naval Operations started having us give a very detailed breakdown of the board results, and that had the subtle effect of putting pressure on presidents to try to make the numbers come out even in these communities. So we were violating the principle of law that you pick the best fit, regardless of their designator or the type of airplane they flew or anything like that. You pick the best fit.

Paul Stillwell: Well, you have to have a reasonable distribution.

Admiral Lawrence: Well, but the law really says that you pick the best fit, and because of the nature of our Navy—the relative balance among submariners, aviators, and surface guys—it usually comes out okay. But when you get to the point that within aviation, for example, you want to try to balance between the types of airplanes that people flew—pilots and NFOs—this really, grossly deviates from the best-fit criterion. As I say, if you let the process occur naturally, things will usually come out. There may be occasions when more submariners are promoted than aviators, but it balances out over time.

But, anyway, his personal involvement in most everything that was going on in the Navy was often in a very adverse way. As Admiral Trost one time told some people who discussed it with me, "It will take us ten years to recover in the Navy, get the decision-making process relationships between the active duty Navy officers and the military and the civilians really back in the proper order that they should be."[*] In his forecast, it would take ten years to recover from the effects of the Lehman years.

Paul Stillwell: In the late '70s when NMPC was created, there was an idea of separating the policymaking from the policy execution.[†] How did that work out in practice?

Admiral Lawrence: Well, we really worked hard at having it occur that way. But because of the nature of the personnel business, you just cannot make that precise a delineation between execution and policymaking. For example, in the area of career management of people, the detailers who make the day-to-day assignments of people——what we call the distribution function—have to be very much policymakers themselves. They are the experts in that particular field, and they see the day-to-day aspects of certain policies, so they're the best judges of how viable a policy is, whether or not it should be changed. We had people in OP-01 organization, so-called policymakers, who would make these broad policies. But the people in NMPC, the detailers, had to be very much involved in the policy process, so that meant that the executors and the policymaking people, even though they were in separate organizations, were very close together. The NMPC people were doing both policy and execution type of actions.

---

[*] Admiral Carlisle A. H. Trost, USN, was Chief of Naval Operations from 1 July 1986 to 29 June 1990.
[†] NMPC – Naval Military Personnel Command.

Paul Stillwell: And now they've been brought back together, so it was a divorce that didn't last.

Admiral Lawrence: Well, and the key point is that it was really a little bit of idealistic.

Paul Stillwell: In what way?

Admiral Lawrence: In the sense that people read books on management and said, "Oh, you should always have policy and execution separated." But I think there are some organizations where you just can't make that clear delineation. I think Admiral Boorda, who had so much experience in personnel and came back in as Chief of Naval Personnel, just realized we hadn't really succeeded in making a distinct separation between the policy and execution. We were having a lot of overlap of functions of where people were doing a little bit of both. So you probably have more efficiency and could reduce personnel by merging policy and execution and going back to the old Bureau of Naval Personnel concept. So I guess you could prove that the guys back there in the olden times who established the Bureau of Naval Personnel knew what they were doing.

Paul Stillwell: Were there any benefits from the separation?

Admiral Lawrence: Well, of course, one thing you pretty much have to have as a separate, distinct entity, is the budgetary development process, what we call the POM process.* You have to have those people who are pure programmatic people who determine what resources are needed and put budgets together.

Paul Stillwell: Planners.

Admiral Lawrence: Planners and programmers. And so that's the function you basically have to have as a separate function. And that's what we used, as I say, on the OP-01 side of the house.

---

* POM – program objectives memorandum, an element of the budgeting process.

Then you have to have the people in NMPC who expend funds in their execution role. That was another thing that made the Chief of Naval Personnel job distinct, because you really did have two hats. One was the Deputy Chief of Naval Operations for Manpower, Personnel, and Training, and the other was the Chief of Naval Personnel. A lot of people just thought that you had two titles, but they were one job. But as the Chief of Naval Personnel, you were a second-echelon commander under the Chief of Naval Operations, just like CinCLantFlt is a second-echelon commander. So I had a budget that I managed, and my subordinate under me as Chief of Naval Personnel was the Commander Naval Military Personnel Command. So that made me unique among all the three-stars on the CNO staff in that I was both a member of his staff, but also I was a second-echelon commander. As a second-echelon commander, I was what they call a major claimant, which meant I had claimancy on dollars and I had to expend them.

So that's where the budgetary financial aspect has to be separated. You can't integrate the guys who do the programmatic work—putting resources together and funding the budget—be the same ones who go and expend the money. These are relationships that, for all those years, were in the Bureau of Naval Personnel. Well, it worked out pretty well, and they were being done within the same organization. And, as I say, we went on the kick of clearly separating policy and execution.

One thing that led up to this was a plan that was developed back in the '70s to put the Bureau of Naval Personnel down in New Orleans. You may have heard about it.

Paul Stillwell: Right. That's when Hebert was the chairman.[*]

Admiral Lawrence: That's right, and, of course, there seemed to be some relationship to Hebert's being from New Orleans. [Laughter]

But, anyway, that's what drove them to this policy execution. They would put the executors down in New Orleans, but the policymakers would stay in Washington. So it was that desire to go down to New Orleans that drove us in this direction. But I think

---

[*] F. Edward Hebert (1901-1979), a Democrat from Louisiana, was elected to the U.S. House of Representatives in 1932 and came to Washington as part of the Democratic sweep that led to the New Deal legislation of 1933-1935. He retired from office in 1976 after being stripped of his chairmanship of the House Armed Services Committee.

after a decade or so of experimenting with that, Admiral Boorda's decision was really proper at the time. We needed to come back together; we could probably reduce the number of people and probably be more efficient.

Paul Stillwell: How would you describe your relationship to Commander NMPC during that period?

Admiral Lawrence: Oh, it was very good. He and I used to meet just about every day, and we had very close rapport.

Paul Stillwell: Who was the commander?

Admiral Lawrence: Admiral Dave Harlow had that job while I was there, and he was really superb.* And we had some really tough challenges. When I came into that job in August of 1983, in the previous year we had had an overrun on our military pay budget—what we call a MPN budget, where you pay salaries and you pay travel costs and permanent change of duty cost. We had over $200 million overrun on that. Of course, that's a multi-billion dollar account. I think it's $5 or $6 billion in that pay account.

Paul Stillwell: How does something like that come about?

Admiral Lawrence: Well, if you haven't predicted the number of reenlistments accurately, that's one of the big factors. If more people stay in through reenlistment than you have projected, that's going to cause you to spend more money. The changes in cost of certain items have to be paid. But I think the big factor is not projecting accurately what the numbers of people in the Navy are during the course of the year. If you under-predict that, you're going to spend too much MPN money.

Paul Stillwell: What percentage of an overrun did that represent compared with the total?

---

* Rear Admiral David L. Harlow, USN.

Admiral Lawrence: Oh, it was probably only about 1%. I mean, in most national corporations, if they hit a budget within 5%, they feel that's very, very good. But under our budget, and Naval Military Personnel Command, particularly the pay and so forth, we had to hit in less than 1%. That was really a tough challenge. So that was one of the big things I had to do when I came in.

Paul Stillwell: What did you do to solve that?

Admiral Lawrence: We just developed a much better day-to-day monitoring capability of how we were expending funds. When a person would execute a permanent change of station orders and then put in a travel claim and all that sort of thing, I guess it could take months sometimes for the old system for the information to get back up to use how much was actually expended. So we really developed a much more responsive system so that we could get very quick reporting to us for costs. We had to develop ADP capabilities to give us better day-to-day monitoring of how we were expending that budget.[*]

Admiral Harlow, who had a pretty good solid foundation of financial management, took a very key role in doing this, but he also had some very fine professionals who managed that account. A Navy supply captain headed that section, and he had some very fine civilians. So that next budget year we managed that account right down to within, probably $15 or $20 million, which is just a fraction of 1%.

The total resources under me were about $12 billion. That's pretty scary when you're spending that much of the taxpayers' money, so you have to do it right. And, of course, the thing that makes it so complex is that you have to very carefully study the defense appropriation bill for your particular year just to make sure you know exactly where the funds have been allocated and how Congress directed they have to be spent.

The variable reenlistment bonus is a big thing, because it is the valve you use to control the number of people at a given rate. For example, if you see your reenlistments are going right down in the machinist's mate rating, you're going to have some shortages and crank up the variable reenlistment bonus to get more machinist's mates to stay in.

---

[*] ADP – automatic data processing.

And, of course, when you crank that up, you're going to spend more money out of that account. You have to know exactly what money's in that account.

It's a very, very complex function, and it takes real experts to work in that field. You need civilians who have been doing it a long time, and you need to bring in naval officers who have the expertise. That's why in these financial management jobs you often will bring in Supply Corps officers, because they have that capability. I spent a great deal of my time with the Commander Naval Military Personnel Command reviewing the whole financial plan and how we were executing it. At the same time, I worked with the people in my OP-01 side who were putting the budget together to make sure that we were getting the resources in the various areas where they were needed. So the financial management aspect of that job was a very great challenge.

Paul Stillwell: What do you remember about selling that budget to Congress?

Admiral Lawrence: Well, it was a great challenge, because you not only had to justify it up through the Navy, but then you had to justify to the Office of the Secretary of Defense, and then, of course, over to the Congress. It was a big challenge dealing with the Congress at a time when we were building up the Navy, putting more ships in, just getting the personnel we needed. They had a great reluctance to give us additional personnel in the Navy. I think in my three years back there I was able to increase our personnel only about 10,000, where we were trying to put about 40,000 more people in as we were increasing the ships.

Paul Stillwell: Well, the *Iowa*-class battleships certainly drew on that, because they're very manpower intensive.

Admiral Lawrence: Yes, and, of course, we were building new aircraft carriers, where they're very manpower intensive, including new air wings.

Well, Paul, I guess I'd better stop here, because I have to go over to Washington this afternoon.

Interview Number 21 with Vice Admiral William P. Lawrence, U.S. Navy (Retired)
Place: U.S. Naval Institute, Annapolis, Maryland
Date: Monday, 4 March 1991

Paul Stillwell: Admiral, the last time we talked about some of the flag detailing situations you had as Chief of Naval Personnel. One of the names we mentioned in a previous interview was Admiral Holcomb. What do you recall about him?

Admiral Lawrence: Well, I've talked previously about these flag officers who were on the Secretary of the Navy's blacklist, so to speak. Vice Admiral Holcomb had been the Director of Navy Program Planning when Admiral Hayward was CNO, and then he went out to be the Commander of Seventh Fleet, and from there he went to be the Deputy Commander in Chief U.S. Naval Forces Europe.*

Admiral Small was Commander in Chief of the southern NATO command over in Naples, Italy. He had been Vice Chief of Naval Operations under Admiral Hayward and moved over to be CinCSouth.† Well, I never realized they were on Secretary Lehman's blacklist. But I guess it made sense, because Admiral Hayward had so many disagreements with him. But, anyway, in late November '84, the Secretary of the Navy put out an order through his executive assistant. It passed through the CNO's executive assistant, to the CNO, and then it was passed on to me. The order said he wanted Admiral Holcomb and Admiral Small to be out of their current billets by the 31st of January—two months' advance notice. It really upset me that two men who had been in the Navy almost 35 years or more, were being given two months' advance notice to get out of their jobs and prepare to retire.

---

* Vice Admiral M Staser Holcomb, USN, served as Deputy Commander in Chief U.S. Naval Forces Europe from June 1983 to February 1985, when he was relieved by Vice Admiral Robert F. Schoultz, USN. Holcomb then reported to the Pentagon as a special assistant to the Chief of Naval Operations in February 1985, pending retirement from active duty on 1 May 1985.
† Admiral William N. Small, USN, served as Vice Chief of Naval Operations from 1981 to 1983. He was Commander in Chief Allied Forces Southern Europe/U.S. Naval Forces Europe from May 1983 to May 1985. He retired from active duty 1 August 1985.

This would have brought Admiral Holcomb up to a few months short of two years in his assignment. It was obvious that the Secretary of the Navy, John Lehman, was just waiting for those guys to get close to the two-year time so he could have them retire. I very strenuously objected to this as just really very callous, cool treatment of two superior flag officers. Admiral Holcomb and Admiral Small were just superb individuals. At one time everybody thought Admiral Holcomb was a future Chief of Naval Operations. I think he would have been a contender if it hadn't been for John Lehman.

The CNO, Admiral Watkins, protested about these moves. But we couldn't get Secretary Lehman to back off, so we really had to scurry around, because Admiral Schoultz, who was DCNO (Air Warfare), was going to go over to relieve Admiral Holcomb. This was kind of unprecedented, because Admiral Schoultz was in his second three-star job. He was a senior naval aviator, and this was, you might say, a demotion for him to go to that job. But it was the Secretary of the Navy taking care of one of his boys, so to speak. I objected to that, because we should have sent a young flag officer to that job and given him an opportunity, rather than Admiral Schoultz have serve a third three-star job.

We argued very much about this, basically through the EAs, but we couldn't get the Secretary of the Navy to turn around. So we had to get Admiral Holcomb out of London shortly. We were able to get a little bit of delay for Admiral Small—maybe another month or so—because of the difficulty in getting Admiral Baggett over to relieve him.* We really had quite a timing problem, because with Admiral Schoultz, who was DCNO (Air Warfare) going over to be Deputy CinCUSNavEur, we were bringing Admiral Martin in from being Commander Sixth Fleet to come be DCNO (Air Warfare).†

John Lehman also said he wanted Admiral Kelso to go to be Com6thFlt. Of course, Admiral Kelso was working directly for the Secretary of the Navy in the Office of Program Appraisal. That really surprised me, because Admiral Kelso had never had any sea experience as a flag officer. He had very minimal battle group operations, so it

---

* Admiral Lee Baggett, Jr., USN, served as Commander in Chief Allied Forces Southern Europe/U.S. Naval Forces Europe from May 1985 to November 1985.
† Vice Admiral Edward H. Martin, USN, commanded the Sixth Fleet from July 1983 to February 1985. He was Deputy Chief of Naval Operations (Air Warfare) from 25 February 1985 to 14 January 1987.

concerned me to have him sent into the Sixth Fleet, which is a very highly volatile area.[*] We had problems in Lebanon at that time. The Secretary of the Navy wanted him to go. Kelso was a wonderful man—very hard working, smart, honest guy, but it just concerned me that he didn't have the requisite experience to go over there. So we really had to make sure we backed him up with the best operators that we possibly could on that staff. So we picked a post-carrier commanding officer to be his chief of staff, someone who was a real operator in a lot of combat.

Paul Stillwell: Who was that?

Admiral Lawrence: Bobby Lee, who became an admiral.[†] I think he's still an admiral today. So that was a really traumatic time.

Paul Stillwell: That was quite a bit of disruption in that one geographic area, when you changed CinCSouth, Deputy CinCUSNavEur, and the Sixth Fleet commander.

Admiral Lawrence: That's right. We changed them all in the period of two months. And it was just abruptly announced by Lehman, because this was not something we had planned. I basically thought both Holcomb and Small would stay three years in their jobs, not less than two. And we knew that Martin would probably change in the summer. I was planning to get on that, and the man I had in mind to relieve him was Admiral Edney, who was coming back from commanding a battle group.[‡] He had a tremendous amount of sea time, battle group time, operational time. He would have been an ideal Sixth Fleet commander, but Lehman had other ideas. So, anyway, it was really a very traumatic time. It upset me that we treated two very superb flag officers so shabbily. But that was Secretary Lehman's style. He was very ruthless in his treatment of people like

---

[*] Vice Admiral Frank B. Kelso II, USN, served as Commander Sixth Fleet from February 1985 to June 1986. His oral history is in the Naval Institute collection.
[†] Captain Bobby C. Lee, USN
[‡] Rear Admiral Leon A. Edney, USN, Commander Carrier Group One. Instead of Commander Sixth Fleet, in 1985 he became OP-05B, the job Lawrence had earlier held as Assistant Deputy Chief of Naval Operations (Air Warfare). In 1988 he became a four-star admiral as Vice Chief of Naval Operations, though he had no sea duty as a three-star.

when he removed the three people out at Miramar.

Paul Stillwell: Well, we haven't talked about that. Do you want to discuss that?

Admiral Lawrence: That happened a few months before I retired. This was at a time when the press was criticizing the military about the high cost of things like hammers and toilet seats. As I recall this incident, it was an ashtray that was going to go to an airplane at Miramar, and the price turned out to be over $100.00 for this ashtray.* One of the personnel who worked in supply reported this on the fraud, waste, and abuse hotline. It got up to the Washington level, and I guess it came to the Secretary of the Navy's attention. So he called a press conference and apparently talked Secretary of Defense Weinberger into being with him there. At this press conference, he announced he was relieving the flag officer, Admiral Cassidy, the commanding officer at Miramar, and the supply officer at Miramar; he was relieving them from their jobs.

It turned out subsequently that these three people were not responsible at all. It was the Navy supply system that had done this, because the basic price had been contracted with the contractor for each part. So it was really a very unjust course of action. It probably was the worst thing I've ever seen in terms of lack of respect for rights, due process, and all that. But it was never reversed. Those guys never had a chance to give their side of it or appeal the situation.†

Paul Stillwell: How much personal dealing did you have with Secretary Lehman?

Admiral Lawrence: Not very much. He was not all that interested in personnel matters in general. He just basically liked to dabble in the assignments of flag officers and those

---

* Miramar Naval Air Station, near San Diego. Sources vary, but reports indicate the ashtrays cost more than $600.00 apiece. In June 1985 Lehman relieved three individuals from their billets: Rear Admiral Thomas J. Cassidy Jr., USN, Commander Fighter, Airborne Early Wing, Pacific Fleet; Captain Gary E. Hakanson, USN, commanding officer of Miramar Naval Air Station; and Commander Jerry L. Fronabarger, USN, air station supply officer.
† Contrary to Admiral Lawrence's memory, the Navy did investigate the firings, and the three officers appealed. Secretary Lehman subsequently reinstated Admiral Cassidy, but by then Cassidy had retired.

at the commander-captain level. But he gave his directives out through his executive assistant, who went to the CNO's executive assistant. That's the way his principal communication was with the CNO on personnel matters. He would call in certain people like the DCNO (Air Warfare) and Commander Naval Sea Systems Command to talk about procurement matters. But there was minimal face-to-face communication with the CNO or people at my level.

I went to several meetings in his office, but mostly the things I got were directives that were relayed from him. I'm sure he took that action out at Miramar purely for political mileage, to impress the public that he was taking forceful action on this. You talk about scapegoats in history, like Admiral Kimmel and others, those three guys really were in the one of the worst scapegoating incidents I've ever seen. There was no investigation. They didn't have any opportunity to give their side of it, but the removals stood. They took it and never complained. I think it'll come out some day when the scholars write the history of that era. Of course, Secretary Woolsey covered that in his book review of Lehman's book, but Lehman didn't cover it in his book.[*] So that was one example of other things like that that I saw Lehman do.

One time I was at what they call an air board, which is conducted by the DCNO (Air Warfare) for all the senior aviation commanders. If the Chief of Naval Personnel is an aviator, he is invited to attend. I happened to go to this particular meeting, which was down at the Naval Air Test Center at Patuxent. Secretary Lehman came to that meeting, because he wanted to brief on his perception of some of the errors we'd made in some of our air attacks into Lebanon, where we got a couple of airplanes shot down.[†] He was also giving his concept of a naval Strike Warfare Center that was going into Fallon.

While we were there, there was something in the paper quoting the first commanding officer of a Naval Reserve F/A-18 squadron. He was a reserve commander.

---

[*] John F. Lehman, Jr., *Command of the Seas* (New York: Scribner's Sons, 1988). R. James Woolsey served as Under Secretary of the Navy from 9 March 1977 to 7 December 1979.

[†] On 4 December 1983, the aircraft carriers *Independence* (CV-62) and *John F. Kennedy* (CV-67) launched a 28-plane strike against Syrian antiaircraft positions in Lebanon. A-7 and A-6 attack planes were shot down. The pilot of the A-7 was rescued. The A-6 pilot, Lieutenant Mark A. Lange, USN, was killed; his bombardier/-navigator, Lieutenant Mark O. Goodman, Jr., USN, was captured. Goodman was released early in 1984.

Secretary Lehman didn't like the tenor of his remarks, and I heard him turn to Admiral Dutch Schoultz and say, "You call that son-of-a-bitch and tell him he's fired." And it happened. The guy never had a chance to express his side. There was no investigation, no due process or anything like that. I'm absolutely amazed that the Secretary of the Navy got away with things like that, which in the private sector would probably have resulted in some type of suit, because of the violation of due process—human rights, civil liberties, and all those sorts of things.

Paul Stillwell: What had the CO of the squadron said?

Admiral Lawrence: Well, I didn't think it was all that bad, but it was a statement where he disagreed with some Navy policy like the rate of introduction of F/A-18s to the reserve, or something or that nature, nothing that was a big national issue. He just said some things John Lehman did not agree with, and John Lehman reacted to it by just summarily firing him. He didn't even have anybody investigate, just based on a quote in the paper similar to what happened there at Miramar.

Paul Stillwell: Do you have other examples of the Secretary's intervention?

Admiral Lawrence: Well, those were probably the most dramatic. Of course, as I mentioned in my last discussion, he made his influence felt in flag boards and in captains' boards. Those were the two boards he was most interested in, because he knew people at those ranks, where he didn't know people at lower ranks. But his desires were well known by those board presidents. What worried me was that by Lehman's personal manipulation or intimidation of board presidents and things like that, we were violating the spirit of law. It was not until Admiral Demars headed up that captains' board and refused to change the results that somebody stood up to Lehman. But that was going on very commonly prior to '87 when DeMars did it. The previous five years Lehman was taking actions like that very commonly. Of the two flag boards that were under me while I was Chief of Naval Personnel—the first one, as I mentioned, the board president had absolute orders from the Secretary of the Navy to pick Captain Paul Miller, who was his executive assistant. And the second flag board a guy whom Secretary Lehman wanted selected wasn't selected, so Secretary Lehman gave him another number and sent them back in session. They damn well knew whom they should select, and that was just completely contrary to the spirit of the law.

Paul Stillwell: Well, I would think to the letter of the law, too, isn't it?

Admiral Lawrence: Well, the letter of the law was not as precise on promotions and things like that. Now it is, as a result of the Lehman experience, Congress passed a law specifically restricting the Secretary of the Navy from intervening in board actions. I mean, it made it very specific by spelling out what service Secretaries can do. Senator Sam Nunn took that action based on the experience with Lehman over the years, and then brought to a dramatic head by his confrontation with Admiral Demars on the captains' board.[*]

Paul Stillwell: Were you involved during your watch in the business of setting up the material professional community?

Admiral Lawrence: Oh, very much. Yes, I really conceived the basic details of that program. We got the general overall conceptual guidance from the Secretariat. I think it was partly Secretary of the Navy and partly Mr. Melvin Paisley, who was Assistant Secretary of the Navy. Lehman basically wanted to have people become material professionals at a junior rank, like lieutenant commander. I very strongly held out for having people to go into it after they had a squadron or ship command. Because I knew that if they went in before that time, they just wouldn't have the credibility and the experience and be as competitive for promotion as they would if we waited till they were senior commanders then. Many of them would have had a commander command.

We debated this quite extensively, and I got Admiral White, who was the Chief of Naval Material, to agree with me. We sold the Secretary and his Assistant Secretaries on

---

[*] Samuel A. Nunn, a Democrat from Georgia, served in the Senate from 8 November 1972 to 3 January 1997. He was chairman of the Senate Armed Services Committee from 1987 to 1994.

this concept of bringing people in primarily to senior commander rank. I was the one who had to go around and brief all the flag officers as to what we were doing. But the thing that worried me about the material professional is that we established another small community of officers, similar to the aeronautical engineering duty officers or the engineering duty officers. Being so small in number, they would have difficulty competing for flag promotions and that sort of thing.

Paul Stillwell: What is the incentive for an individual to go into that?

Admiral Lawrence: The only incentive is if he just wants to spend all of his duty in technical areas and not go back to sea again. So if he's a line officer, he's done all the right things up until being a senior commander, but then decides, "Hey, I want to specialize in technical acquisition areas," then he can move into that and spend the rest of his naval career in that field. I guess it has worked out fairly well, from all I can see. But it was just another small community, in addition to engineering duty officers and aeronautical engineering duty officers.

Now, of course, the law has come out and established an acquisition corps, where you will have people at the lieutenant commander rank and major rank, go in and become in the acquisition corps and spend the rest of their years in acquisitions. So it's not clear whether the Navy's just going to do away with the material professional program and just use this acquisition corps. I just assumed that they would, because you can't have MPs separate from the acquisition corps people. But they're trying, in the Navy's implementation of the acquisition corps, to use the same concept, even though you have a person go in as a lieutenant commander, still keep him operationally oriented till he gets a squadron or ship command. Then after that they can do all acquisition billets.

Paul Stillwell: Were you involved at all in the abolition of the Material Command and the establishment of Space and Naval Warfare Command?

Admiral Lawrence: Well, yes, quite a bit, because I had to keep closely abreast of what was going on so I could give it the personnel support that was required. It was something that was done very hastily. Admiral White and Secretary Lehman had a disagreement on some issue, and in response to some order Lehman had given to White, White said, "I'm not going to do it; I'll retire first."

Lehman said, "Okay, go ahead and retire."* So when he put in his retirement, Lehman decided to use that as a time to dissolve the Naval Material Command.† He had Admiral Hays, who was the Vice Chief of Naval Operations, head up a whole small team that also included Admiral Baggett.‡ But over a weekend they basically made this decision. It was done very hastily, and it took us a very long time to get the personnel fallout from that stabilized. The Space and Naval Warfare Systems Command, which came into being to replace the Electronics Systems Command, really was a nonentity for a long, long time. I'd say it took as much as a year it to get going.

A lot of the people who have been around a long time say that the impact that caused on the Navy's acquisition program is really severe, because you essentially had people not sure exactly to whom they were accountable and what the organization structure was. The coordination all broke down. I know I kept talking to the new commander of this Space and Warfare Systems, who was Admiral Glenwood Clark.§ I said, "You've got to tell me what your billet structure's going to be, so I can be ordering the flag officers there." It took many months before he could even tell me what he wanted to do. So the disruption and turmoil caused by that very abrupt termination of the Material Command and standing up that new command were severe.

Paul Stillwell: So the move was made first and the planning afterward.

Admiral Lawrence: That's right, that's right. The real impetus, the key event that precipitated all that was the retirement of Admiral White. It probably would not have

---

* Admiral White retired 1 May 1985.
† In 1985, Secretary of the Navy John Lehman disestablished the Naval Material Command and redistributed functions among the various systems commands. For a summary of the reorganization, see Norman Polmar, "The U.S. Navy: Command Changes," *U.S. Naval Institute Proceedings*, December 1985, pages 156-157.
‡ Admiral Ronald J. Hays, USN, served as Vice Chief of Naval Operations from 1983 to 1985.
§ Vice Admiral Glenwood Clark, USN, became Commander Space and Naval Warfare Systems Command in June 1985.

been done if he hadn't retired.

Paul Stillwell: Or at least not have done it then.

Admiral Lawrence: That's right. But I think Secretary Lehman perceived this would be politically attractive. He could point out, "I have done away with this layering we have." He was very astute politically and knew the things that would appeal to the newspapers.

Paul Stillwell: Well, leaving aside his personality, wasn't it a good thing to get rid of some layering?

Admiral Lawrence: I really can't say that it was a good thing, because of the fact that you lost a lot of oversight of the systems command that would have been beneficial. Some Air Force and Army officers have told me they felt they lost a lot when they didn't have a Navy four-star at the same level as the Air Force and Army four-stars who had their material commands and systems commands, too, for the advocacy of dealing with the Congress and so forth.

Several people have told me that the Space and Naval Warfare Systems Command has never really ever become a viable organization. I think where the error was made was in not in putting together a blue-ribbon panel to look at what the best structure should be in our systems commands. Maybe they could have made a case that we should do away with the Chief of Navy Material, but they should have tried to well define the decision-making relationships that existed in the lines of authority in communication. That's what really became very confused after the Material Command was done away with.

Then, on top of that, they went to this Defense Management Review, just right on the heels of that action, where all the program managers were put underneath the Assistant Secretary of the Navy for Acquisition. They didn't even work under their systems command commanders. They didn't even have to answer through the CNO. So all the changes that were made in such a short amount of time—everybody tells me they've had a very detrimental effect on the Navy.

Paul Stillwell: Well, speaking of another strong personality, Admiral Rickover had been forced into retirement shortly before you got into that job.*

Admiral Lawrence: That's right. He retired when I was Com3rd Flt.

Paul Stillwell: What did you observe in the running of the nuclear-power program, once you were Chief of Naval Personnel?

Admiral Lawrence: Well, I had a lot of contact with Admiral McKee's organization in terms of personnel matters but not much direct interface.

One thing that I noticed while I was Chief of Naval Personnel was that we had very stable personnel posture, good reenlistment rates, and manning in our submarine force, but our enlisted retention and officer retention rates in the nuclear surface Navy were bad. So I said, "If we've done this in the submarine force, we should be able to do it in the nuclear surface role." I realized the DCNO (Surface Warfare), OP-03, didn't give the same support to the nuclear component of the surface Navy that OP-02 did to his submariners. Many of the people in DCNO (Surface Warfare) came up through a conventional background, so there was not an exact analogy, but I knew that many of the practices we used in the submarines should be able to translate on the surface ships.

I put my deputy, Rear Admiral Larry Burkhardt, who was a nuclear submariner, in charge of a blue-ribbon panel, so to speak, to look at what we had to do to get the nuclear surface Navy well, personnel-wise.† We used a lot of Admiral McKee's expertise. He would come during our meetings, and we would discuss with him what we were doing. And, of course, I would call on him from time to time to get his input on a lot of issues that were working. That action that we took by having Admiral Burkhardt look at the nuclear surface Navy, it turned out they weren't doing a lot of things that they were in the submarines. So we directed that those practices be implemented in the surface Navy, and we very dramatically improved our retention.

---

* In March 1982, Admiral Kinnaird R. McKee, USN, succeeded Admiral Rickover as Director of the Naval Nuclear Propulsion Program. For details, see Lehman's *Command of the Seas*.
† Rear Admiral Lawrence Burkhardt III, USN, Assistant Deputy Chief of Naval Operations (Manpower, Personnel and Training), OP-01B.

Paul Stillwell: Do you have examples of what those practices were?

Admiral Lawrence: Well, one thing was that the submariners used to over-man in the enlisted force. Their rationale was that people have to work so hard on submarines when they come back into port because of maintenance, that if you sent these guys to sea and then worked them as hard as you do at sea, when they came back in, had to continue that, it just would not be fair. So they actually got approval and committed the resources to over-man the submarines. And sometimes when a submarine was deployed, they'd keep part of the people back. Then when the submarine came back from deployment, those were the guys who had to turn to and work the whole time the ship was in port.

Paul Stillwell: Sort of like the refit crews in World War II.

Admiral Lawrence: Yes. And so that was an eye-opener for me. I didn't realize the submarines were over-manned. So we translated that into the surface Navy.

We also looked at the reenlistment bonuses. We found the surface guys didn't have bonuses as high as the submarine guys, and so we improved those. We did a very, very comprehensive look and really, completely translated the practices of submarines over into surface nuclear world. Also we strongly stressed to the DCNO for Surface Warfare that he simply had to give more advocacy to his surface nuclear people, and he started doing that.*

Paul Stillwell: There were all those reports of the trauma to prospective nuclear power program people under Rickover. Did you have the perception that that went away when McKee replaced him?

Admiral Lawrence: Oh, yes. A lot of the practices that Rickover employed of going directly to commanding officers, kind of berating commanding officers, keeping commanding officers off balance and everything—I think a lot of that went away.

---

* Vice Admiral Robert L. Walters, USN, was Deputy Chief of Naval Operations (Surface Warfare) from June 1981 to September 1984. Vice Admiral Joseph Metcalf III, USN, had the billet from September 1984 to December 1987.

Admiral McKee tried to work through the chain of command. In other words, if he had a problem with a nuclear submarine over in the Atlantic Fleet, he would work through ComSubLant, follow a chain of command, rather than Rickover getting on the phone and talking directly to commanding officers. I think Admiral McKee brought a lot more of a levelheaded approach to things. I mean, he was a stern taskmaster, but he was not harsh like Rickover was. I think he brought in a better style of leadership. He was still very strict in maintaining standards, but I think the personnel were a lot more relaxed with Admiral McKee.

Paul Stillwell: What do you remember about the war on drugs during your time?

Admiral Lawrence: Well, by the time I'd gotten there, we had fully implemented the urinalysis. Of course, for several years we'd had the drug counseling centers, and we have the drug rehabilitation center out at Miramar. We had had some problems with the urinalysis as we initially started, in that laboratories we had established to do the analysis of the urine specimens made some mistakes. Some false positives were reported, so we had to spend a couple of years getting that cleaned up. By the time I got into my job as CNP, we were just getting those labs up to a proper professional standard, and we were no longer having the false positives. We were finally getting the whole urinalysis program working well. Of course, I always felt that urinalysis was a big, big factor in reducing drugs out there.

Paul Stillwell: But you've got a real problem if you've got false positives showing up.

Admiral Lawrence: Yes, I know. So we really had to work that problem pretty hard. Rear Admiral Mulloy headed up that area of the Navy as OP-15, and by the time I got in, they really turned the corner on getting all these drug labs up to a proper standard, and we were not having the false positives problems anymore.[*] But because there had been these false positives, we had to go back through all sorts of records and send out letters to people and reverse some disciplinary actions.

---

[*] Rear Admiral Paul J. Mulloy, USN.

Paul Stillwell: How did you reverse a disciplinary action?

Admiral Lawrence: Well, if you separated somebody without a valid basis, then you would offer him an opportunity to come back in or change the nature of the discharge to an honorable discharge if it had been an admin discharge. A lot of personnel corrective action had to be taken because of some of these false positives.

But the other thing we did while I was there, we tightened up the policy in the sense that those who would be separated automatically if they had drug offense—I forget exactly what the percentages were—but I think we extended it down, say, to a second class petty officer. The first offense would be a separation. We had that with officers and chiefs, and I think we pushed it on down to some lower rated. The drug abuse program took a lot of my attention, because I really kept very close to that. We basically tightened it up, as we did with the alcohol problem.

But we couldn't get a strong policy statement out of the Secretary of the Navy on alcohol abuse. We felt it was the right thing to do, but it was also the trend within the Defense Department. The Army had taken a very forceful approach to alcohol abuse. They had removed all package stores from Army bases and wouldn't allow alcohol to be served at noon in officers' and enlisted clubs. So we wrote up a good, strong policy statement ourselves. It took us a year to get that approved by Secretary Lehman. The perception was that he was concerned about his image with the junior pilots out in the fleet if he came across as being too tough on alcohol, because I think one of the things we wanted was to do away with happy hours in the clubs. I guess he just couldn't bring himself to approving that, because he used to go down and fly at Oceana during his active duty time. I know that the JOs down there would tell him all these things. He loved to go to happy hours and drink with them. So, as I say, it took us a year with constant pleading and begging for the Secretary to address it before we got the policy approved by him.

Paul Stillwell: Well, in fact, he actually relaxed the prohibition against serving alcohol on board ships.*

Admiral Lawrence: Oh, yes, yes. He was a happy hour advocate who loved to go out with the young troops, which was just counter to everything that was going on with the other services.

Paul Stillwell: Well, you had the potential for some real injustice on those drug analysis reports that indicated a person had used when he really hadn't.

Admiral Lawrence: Oh, yes, it was a messy thing. Fortunately, I came in at the time when they were pretty much getting the problem under control, but for about a year there from late '81 to late '82, it was really messy as they had to get this whole system of drug analysis, laboratory analysis, and so forth squared away.

Paul Stillwell: What do you remember about the business of dealing with the growing number of married Navy couples in which both were service members?

Admiral Lawrence: Well, that really didn't pose a problem during my time. We knew that we were getting an increased number of single parents, and that sailors were marrying each other. We knew that was occurring, but at that time we really couldn't see any problem that was impacting our readiness.

The one problem that I had to address with regard to women was that the Bureau of Medicine and the Surgeon General had come out with a policy that just as soon as a woman found out that she was pregnant, that she'd be removed from shipboard duty. The rationale was that because of the radiation concerns on ships—from radars and so forth—this would be detrimental to the fetus. That was really causing a lot of problems, because sometimes a woman who was in a responsible position would learn that she's

---

* On 1 July 1914 a general order from Secretary of the Navy Josephus Daniels went into effect. It abolished the traditional wine messes on board U.S. Navy ships, resulting in a prohibition against drinking alcoholic beverages on board. The ban was relaxed in the 1980s to permit the serving of beer and wine—but not hard liquor—at official receptions on board.

pregnant, and she would tell her commanding officer and he'd have to order her off without relief. So we debated that one, and certainly with the Surgeon General. We finally got them to back off on this concern about the radiation hazard, because we really couldn't see that that existed. That was the biggest complaint that my ship commanding officers had when we had women on there. They were moving people without relief.

Paul Stillwell: Wasn't there a challenge in detailing to try to keep couples together?

Admiral Lawrence: Oh, yes, that, of course, was getting to be more and more of a challenge—particularly in the officer arena. But we were handling that okay. Our major problem was when they were cross-service marriages, like Navy-Marine Corps.

Paul Stillwell: Worse would be a Navy-Army or Navy-Air Force.

Admiral Lawrence: Yes. We, of course, had very active sexual harassment training. One interesting thing is that we decided in the Navy Department we needed to have a more explicit policy on fraternization. Gosh, we tried our best to write up a directive on fraternization, but it never sounded right. Every version we'd send over to the CNO, he'd say, "No, I can't sign that." It just basically came down to the fact that we really didn't need a specific directive on fraternization, because it was something that was very difficult to define in words. But it was something that was easy to recognize when it existed, because it was just nothing more than improper leadership. If a person exercises the proper leadership with his or her subordinates, peers and superiors, they're not going to do something that would be regarded as fraternization. So we never did get out a firm policy on fraternization, because it was just so hard to put the appropriate words together.

Paul Stillwell: Was the Navy's policy against homosexuals reviewed during your time as chief?

Admiral Lawrence: No, we pretty much maintained the policy that had been changed in the late '70s. The policy that went out when Secretary Claytor was the Secretary of the

Navy relaxed the harsh tone of the homosexual policy. It put it more as a medical-type problem as opposed to a disciplinary problem. The only time you could make it a disciplinary offense was if a person physically abused somebody; it was aggression, or something like physically assaulted somebody. If it was just a homosexual approach, that would be an administrative separation. But we didn't have a real problem with homosexuality while I was there.

Paul Stillwell: There were a lot of problems in the area of Navy medicine.[*] Do you want to address those, please?

Admiral Lawrence: Yes. I was aware that the Secretary—primarily the Under Secretary of the Navy—was heading up a group looking at the reorganization of Navy medicine. Actually, it was a long-term action, because even when I was out in the fleet, they came up with this regional concept, where you had a commander of a region and all of the medical arts were integrated, like the dentists and nurses and the doctors were integrated. Any of those three groups could command anything in the Medical Corps. That had basically happened before I got back to be the Chief of Naval Personnel, and that was working pretty well.

The big flap that I had when I was there was over the Billig case.[†] After they sensed there might have been some malpractice on the part of Billig, then the issue came up of how he was recruited. So I had to have the commander of the Naval Recruiting Command do a very thorough investigation into how Billig was recruited. As a result of that— and this happened after I retired—I think one recruiter was court-martialed for improperly recruiting Billig.

Paul Stillwell: And the head of Bethesda lost his job.

---

[*] During the mid-1980s the Navy's Medical Corps was beset by charges of negligence, incompetence, and malpractice. See Arthur M. Smith, "Are We Losing Confidence in Navy Medicine?" *U.S. Naval Institute Proceedings*, May 1986, pages 120-131.

[†] Commander Donal M. Billig, MC, USN, was found guilty by a military court-martial in February 1986 of involuntary manslaughter in the deaths of two patients and negligent homicide in the case of another in 1984. He had been a heart surgeon at the National Naval Medical Center in Bethesda, Maryland.

Admiral Lawrence: Yes. And, of course, Billig lost his job and then went to court-martial, but the court-martial occurred after I retired. The thing I had to go through was that when it appeared to me that there had been some malpractice in the recruiting, I had to have the Commander Naval Recruiting Command, who was Admiral J. D. Williams, do a JAG-type investigation.* The first time it came to me, I didn't feel it was thorough enough so I sent it back to him. It turned out as a result of that investigation that there were two recruiters who either falsified or misrepresented information for Billig to get into the Navy, and they were disciplined.

Another area that I really spent a lot of time in was trying to improve the training in the Navy to have their top-level management—both from the aspect of resource allocation and policy direction—but also improving the various command relationships that exist in the Navy. Because some of the training is conducted by the fleet and the other part is done by the Chief of Naval Education and Training. And then, of course, we have our Postgraduate School and the Naval Academy. So the interface between these training organizations and the overlap of functions and all that, we really tried to look very carefully at avoiding this duplication and having better communication between all the people who conduct training. Also, better resource allocation up at the Washington level decided which budgets would get certain amount of the money for training.

But training in the Navy is immensely complex. You have the problem with the people who conduct training out in the fleet under the commander TraLant or TraPac often don't communicate well enough with the people under the Chief of Naval Education and Training. Because one does kind of the schoolhouse-type training, and the people out in the fleet do more of the operational and hands-on-type training. But I used to try to devote a lot of time to improving the overall training organization, preventing redundancy, improving the flow of information, and the whole resource allocation.

Paul Stillwell: What do you recall about working with the Naval Reserve—the one Navy idea of integrating both active and reserve forces?

---

* Rear Admiral James D. Williams, USN.

Admiral Lawrence: Well, I spent a lot of time working in that area, trying to get the best integration that we could between the reserve and the regular—what we called the total-force concept. We did some new things while I was there. We developed what we called the Seaman-Airman Program—the SAM Program—where we would bring in these young recruits, send them through recruit training and maybe some post-recruit-type training, like the training is conducted in Great Lakes and the places like that after recruit training—the A schools and all that. Then we put them directly into the drilling reserve, and we called them SAMs. Secretary Lehman was a great advocate of that. So we had to spend a lot of time on how to best implement that. Just exactly what do you give a kid after recruit training just so he can go back as a drilling reservist, being reasonably effective and having enough of a base to build on? So that was a very challenging thing.

I very carefully monitored reserve recruiting, because we were building up the reserve in those days, and Admiral Kempf was the Commander of the Naval Reserve for most of the time I was there.[*] I started applying a lot more of the management practices to the reserves that we had with the regulars. For example, I had him attend our monthly briefing on how recruiting was going. And I made him put his briefing on his reserve recruiting in the same format as I did the active duty recruiting reports just to help some discipline in his personnel administration reserve, particularly with regards to recruiting. But it was a challenging time, because the reserves were building, and we were trying to give them more modern equipment, like frigates and airplanes. I always got very good response from reserves.

I guess one of the real big challenges in the Chief of Naval Personnel job is the putting together of your budget, the amount of money that you have to allocate to certain things. I spent a lot of time in that, particularly the areas like compensation—both in terms of salary compensation, but also the special benefits and so forth, to make sure we had a valid amount of money to put into that area so I'd be prepared to defend it as my budget was reviewed, both within the Navy Department and up in DoD, and finally over in the Congress. That resource allocation in putting together what you call the POM and all that was one of the real big challenges of that job. At that time I think my resource base was about $12 billion.

---

[*] Rear Admiral Cecil J. Kempf, USN.

Paul Stillwell: What do you remember about the reaction to the Walker spy case?*

Admiral Lawrence: Well, that happened in the latter part of my tenure, and I got a lot of informational-type support. But that was almost purely handled by the Director of Naval Intelligence, and he worked directly with the CNO and the Secretary on that issue. I really didn't get pulled into it, although I certainly provided as much information as I could of their service records and that sort of thing.

Paul Stillwell: What about the implementation of tightened security standards and clearances?

Admiral Lawrence: No, I really didn't get involved in that. The only thing that I really got involved in was security. We made a decision to establish what we called the Security Command in the Navy, where we put the Naval Investigative Service under that and have a Navy flag officer head that up. We got a SEAL, special operations officer, and gave him that first flag job. But I really didn't get involved very much in that Walker thing. That was held very much close to the desk by the Secretary of the Navy and the Chief of Naval Operations and the Director of Naval Intelligence.

Paul Stillwell: Obviously a great embarrassment to the Navy.

Admiral Lawrence: Yes, it really was.

One area that was really a very traumatic thing for me was that we had two sailors who died out in the Indian Ocean due to very strange type of maladies. This happened on small ships where they had just one or two hospital corpsmen. But the first class corpsmen in both cases just didn't diagnose these ailments properly, and they delayed in transferring their sick sailors over to a carrier. Two sailors died at sea within several

---

* On 20 May 1985 Chief Warrant Officer John A. Walker, Jr., USN (Ret.), was arrested and charged with selling classified information to the Soviets. He ran a spying organization that included his brother Lieutenant Commander Arthur J. Walker, USN (Ret.); son, Seaman Michael L. Walker, USN; and a friend, Senior Chief Radioman Jerry A. Whitworth, USN (Ret.). For details, see James Bamford, "The Walker Espionage Case," *U.S. Naval Institute Proceedings*, May 1986, pages 110-119.

months of each other. I got the Surgeon General of the Navy in to just make darn sure that our independent-duty corpsmen—the single corpsmen who go out on those destroyers and frigates, were being selected and trained properly. Because it reflected adversely on us in the Navy when you lose two people like that.

Paul Stillwell: Another area involved people who had died in abusive situations in brig management. How was that handled during your tenure?

Admiral Lawrence: The situation that happened on the *Ranger*, for example, was the case of a sailor who died of heat prostration. He was in the brig and he was being exercised up on the deck. That happened before I became the Chief of Naval Personnel, but my problem with regard to brigs was that I realized as I was traveling around in the Navy that we had some brigs that were just antiquated and converted wooden barracks, and I felt they were distinct fire hazards. So we needed a brig construction program, but nobody wanted to do it. It wasn't a glamorous thing. So I really had to fight hard to keep that in the budget so we could build some new brigs and make brigs that were more efficient, because they were to be designed as brigs as opposed to being barracks. My major effort with regard to brigs was getting new ones constructed. I had, of course, this anti-drug program that I was involved in and all my time there, I was looking at what we would do for brigs for the incarceration of people who may have a drug problem.

Paul Stillwell: Well, and the prison at Portsmouth had been closed. What do you do about the hard-core cases?

Admiral Lawrence: Well, there was a pretty well-defined Defense Department policy about where you should incarcerate certain categories of offenders. The serious ones would go to Leavenworth, which is basically a federal prison. Then we had some brigs pretty well spread around the Navy that could handle the situation pretty well. But there were a lot of places like Memphis, where they had a large sailor population in old World War II converted barracks.

Paul Stillwell: What other issues occur to you?

Admiral Lawrence: I think that's it. I think that's it. I think we pretty well covered everything. We covered women, that the only real issue I felt I had was, of course, was that pregnancy issue. But we were expanding women going into the non-traditional roles, including going on ships and flying planes. The other thing I guess I did when I was with them, I learned we had a policy where the women helicopter pilots who were doing the vertical-replenishment mission were allowed to go aboard ship only off the East Coast. For some reason somebody decided not to let women VertRep pilots go on ships that were deploying to the Mediterranean, Indian Ocean, and the Far East. I said, "Why is the Atlantic Coast any different?" So I made the decision to recommend to the CNO that we allow women helicopter pilots who go on service force ships or around the world without restriction, under the provision of the law that said women could go aboard ship up to 180 days as long as there's little likelihood of combat. So that was one major change.

The other change I made was regarding a pilot project in which women enlisted in one P-3C squadron on one coast and one P-3C squadron on the other coast, and this was done from pressure from DACOWITS.* And I could tell that everybody in the Navy was resisting this. They gave me a status report, and I could see there were really no problems that these women were causing. It just made sense to me to have enlisted women in every VP squadron, so I directed that we put women into every VP squadron. I didn't even ask the CNO or anybody. I just said, "Do it." Boy, everybody raised a hue and cry and said, "You're really going to destroy VP aviation," but it turned out to work extremely well.

Maybe I'd better shut off at this point.

Paul Stillwell: Well, I wonder if we have another session's worth to discuss.

---

* DACOWITS – Defense Department Advisory Committee on Women in the Services.

Admiral Lawrence: Yes, well I guess we are probably going to terminate this whole life's history at the end of the Chief of Naval Personnel. Why don't we just make it active duty?

Paul Stillwell: Well, I don't know. Why don't we do one more and finish the job?

Admiral Lawrence: Yes, I think I can probably wrap everything up in another hour.

Paul Stillwell: Okay, thank you.

Interview Number 22 with Vice Admiral William P. Lawrence, U.S. Navy (Retired)
Place: U.S. Naval Institute, Annapolis, Maryland
Date: Friday, 8 March 1991

Paul Stillwell: Admiral, we begin our last session today, and we've had quite a few of them. What do you have to put the finishing touches on the discussion of your time as Chief of Naval Personnel?

Admiral Lawrence: Well, just a couple of things. I made the point about the very poor communication between the Chief of Naval Operations and the Secretary of the Navy during my tenure of 1983 to '86 as Chief of Naval Personnel. People would be amazed at the minimal communication both Admiral Hayward and then Admiral Watkins had with Secretary John Lehman. I've given some previous examples. Uniform policy was another example of many that could be provided of how we did things very inefficiently and wasted a lot of money in that era.

After Secretary Lehman had been in office for a while, he got to feeling more powerful, and then he started getting into areas that had traditionally been the uniformed military area's purview. Admiral Hayward had made certain uniform decisions that were to take effect over the next several years. So we made out our resource allocation, budgets, and so forth, to accomplish that. One was to have the white dress uniform for officers be standardized on what they called a certified Navy twill uniform. This was a polyester-type uniform that was basically wrinkle free, and it really had a very nice appearance. Our Navy uniform laboratory up at Natick, Massachusetts, had developed this working with the clothing industry. But the early uniforms had some problems that they were working on to solve, like a tendency to pill and snag.

Paul Stillwell: And there was a concern about fire hazard too.

Admiral Lawrence: Yes, but the concept with regard to fire hazard was that people would not wear that uniform in which a fire risk existed. It was principally a liberty and dress-type uniform. We had working uniforms, like the khakis for officers and chiefs and the dungaree-type blue working uniform for the enlisted, that would give them adequate fire protection. But, anyway, we were basically committed to this full transition to certified Navy twill. We had millions of dollars allocated for this and for the phase-out of the poly-cotton uniform and the cotton uniform. For example, midshipmen over here were still wearing all-cotton uniforms.

In 1985, we were in full motion when Secretary of the Navy John Lehman suddenly said, "Stop, I don't like that uniform. We're not going to go to the certified Navy twill. We're going to keep these other uniforms." We had a big debate about this, but the Secretary of the Navy wouldn't talk to the CNO about this issue. It was basically being handled by the Vice Chief of Naval Operations. So the communication on the subject was very inhibited, because we couldn't really sit down and address all the points of this issue. Anyway, the Secretary made a decision to retain the cotton and the poly-cotton uniform in addition to certified Navy twill. So we had to commit millions of dollars to this plan. This wasteful action on our part bothered me, and it was just due to poor communications.

I strongly opposed another action that he took—and it was just purely to make points with the young inexperienced junior officers in aviation—to have brown shoes for naval aviators. So here we had an item of uniform that only naval aviators wore. So what's the problem? It's another pair of shoes that have to be produced and distributed in the system—additional pairs of shoes that aviators have to maintain.

But the bad thing about it was not only the expense, but it created resentment on the part of the rest of the Navy that aviators wore brown shoes and they wore black. This was after all the stress that we put over the years on naval aviators being naval officers first and aviators second. All that emphasis was just really impacted by the Secretary of the Navy's decision to do something for young, inexperienced aviators, who really don't understand. I talked to a lot of young aviators who said, "Gosh, we'd like to get rid of those brown shoes we have to wear with our khaki uniforms."

Paul Stillwell: They had the flight jacket issue also, didn't they?

Admiral Lawrence: Well, yes, of course, he made the decision, of course, to widely put the flight jacket in effect and allow young aviators to wear this to and from work. Of course, the flight jacket was already in the system, and it didn't really entail that much expenditure of money.

Another thing I heard about was that he went out one time to an Air Force base, and he saw that Air Force officers were going to the happy hour—social hour—wearing tailored blue flight suits like the Blue Angels wear. Then he just made a decision to have them distributed in the Navy system. I'm sure that cost millions of dollars to put a blue flight suit in, which pilots would never wear operationally, because can you imagine an aviator going down in the ocean with a blue flight suit? I mean, how easy he would be seen as compared to another color. So now the young aviators don't wear it, because they think it looks absurd to wear that with their green harness. The thing that bothered me about the Secretary of the Navy was that he would make these decisions without any real concern for the costs involved; it was purely for image purposes. The poor communications with the CNO on so many issues impacted the efficiency of the Navy.

The other area that I strongly disagreed with was his total focus on the Soviet threat, particularly the European environment. He advocated taking carriers up to the North Cape. I'd spent two years as a numbered fleet commander in the Pacific and every day, boy, I had observed what the Soviets were doing and told you about the two big exercises I conducted right on the periphery of the Soviet Union to see what their reaction would be, and it was minimal

So I came back in '83, and I said, "I don't think the Soviets are aggressive anymore. When I see what's happening down there in the Middle East with the problem we're having in Lebanon and the Iran-Iraq War, we've got to, I think, focus more on the Middle East and not build these sophisticated ships oriented toward the Soviet threat." That included the *Seawolf* submarines that cost enormously. But I was really muzzled for saying that the Soviet threat was diminishing.

Paul Stillwell: How muzzled?

Admiral Lawrence: I was just told to shut up.

Paul Stillwell: By whom?

Admiral Lawrence: It got sent back from Secretary Lehman's office through the Vice Chief of Naval Operations that we were not supposed to say that there was a reduced Soviet threat. The rationale was we'd never get the money in the budget.

Anyway, those were just two other issues that I wanted to mention.

Now I want to talk about the events that led to my retirement. In February of 1985, after I'd been in the office approaching two years, I went down and got my ex-POW physical in Pensacola. It's part of a research project, as well being as for our own benefit.

I really got high marks in my physical, and the psychologist always or the psychiatrist sometimes talks to us about how we're doing. And I felt really good, even though I had all these frustrations that any Chief of Naval Personnel has. But I really felt basically good that I was getting on top of the job. But then, about a month after I got back in March, I really started feeling bad.

Paul Stillwell: Physically?

Admiral Lawrence: Physically, yes. I just lost my energy and had difficulty concentrating, but I really couldn't put my finger on it. I guess my reaction was like it was when this happened often in the past. I just said, "Well, it's one of these things I'll get through." But it started getting progressively worse, and I really made a very big mistake in not taking the time to go and go back down to Pensacola with the doctor who had been following this for years, Captain Bob Mitchell, and talking it over. I just felt I could gut it out. Over the next several months I knew that I had some problem, but I couldn't put my finger on it. It was just a lack of energy, a lack of ability to concentrate. Then I started worrying about that—my efficiency being reduced. The problem was exacerbated by the fact that the CNO had told me many months before that I would be promoted to four stars and become the next Vice Chief of Naval Operations, and that I was his personal choice to succeed him as Chief of Naval Operations.

Paul Stillwell: How did that exacerbate the situation?

Admiral Lawrence: Well, it worried me that I was not going to be prepared to assume this role when he retired. When the flag changes were due to occur in the July-August time frame, it really concerned me because I knew that serving as Vice Chief of Naval Operations is a very immense responsibility. So I guess I let myself worry too much about my capability to handle that, and my condition didn't get better. But I really made the mistake, as I say, of not going and getting a real medical check.

Then in July, when I was already on the nomination list to be promoted to four stars, I just felt so bad that I had to go and turn myself in at Bethesda. They hospitalized me for two weeks and looked me over. They just had to come to the conclusion that I was in what they called a state of depression, and, as I say, I never could put my finger on any cause, nor could they. After that two weeks of hospitalization I came back, and, of course, the CNO told me that, regretfully, because of my medical problem they were going to have to remove me from the promotion list. That, of course, was a very devastating thing to me, and I think that exacerbated my mental attitude.

Then after, I guess, about another month when I was still acting as Chief of Naval Personnel, I had to go back into the hospital. I just really felt terrible; I just couldn't concentrate, couldn't function. That led to the decision to retire me under a disability retirement. Of course, the whole problem that I had at whatever cost, it was very much exacerbated by just the disappointment and embarrassment of not being able to do what the Navy had wanted me to do. I felt like I disappointed a lot of people that were really supporters of mine like Admiral Burke and Admiral Carney and Admiral Moorer.[*]

I guess the medical analysis was that what I was retired for on disability was what they called melancholia, but it's really what's commonly termed as a depression. But it took me about four years to really get back to battery. I figured for much of those four years I was working at about 50% efficiency. But when it was determined I was going to retire, Ross Perot, who's a very close friend of mine from midshipman days, contacted me. I think he knew from talking to the doctors that I had a medical problem from which

---

[*] Admiral Arleigh A. Burke, Admiral Robert B. Carney, and Admiral Thomas H. Moorer were all former Chiefs of Naval Operations.

I'd recuperate. So he offered me to take the Naval Academy leadership chair, which he would endow. I accepted because there was nothing else I wanted to do any more than that. But, of course, I wasn't capable.

I didn't start getting well until the summer of '89, after a lot of medical treatment. In fact, when Ross Perot saw I wasn't making progress, he insisted that I go up and spend a week at Mayo, and then he insisted that I go down to Menninger's, which is the top mental-health facility in the country. I spent several months at Menninger's. I just never could come up with a definition of the problem, so it's hard for me to explain what happened to me. After I finally got well, I was able to start thinking rationally about it. I think probably what happened to me was that I just got into a real burnout situation. Before I realized it, I was into it, and I just didn't take the action to extract myself from it. Then it just started snowballing on me.

In retrospect, I'd gone seven years in that Vietnam War without a day off. Every day in the POW camp was a battle. Then I came back, and the first thing I found out when I came back was that my wife had divorced me, and I had to immediately go on the fast track to start getting my kids squared away and make a lot of public appearances. The Navy gave us every opportunity to reestablish our careers, so I went into the National War College and master's program.

But in retrospect, going back from '85, when I got sick, to the early '60s, I'd had about 25 years with about a maximum of about a week's leave and all the demands of the Vietnam War. So my best theory is that I just burned out, but I didn't realize it till too late. My wife perceived that I was having problems but was reluctant to say anything. If I had just gone on about a two-months' stand-down, I may have averted the problem. Anyway, it was difficult to go through that, because it was a great disappointment that I hadn't realized my full potential in the Navy. When I finally started getting well in '89, I went through some interesting phases: one was being very bitter—that it happened to me. But finally I had to say to myself that that's just the way life is. You have adversities, and you handle them the best you can and get them behind you and try to benefit from the experience. But you should never be bitter about things that happen in your past, because if you are, it just degrades your performance in the present.

But it was a tough thing to go through. In some respects, those four years of what they called depression were more difficult than the POW experience. At least in the POW experience, you went through the exhilaration of winning battles against your captors. That's a lot different from having a medical problem.

Paul Stillwell: Were the doctors able to help?

Admiral Lawrence: Well, the bad thing about a situation like that is that when they can't really determine the origin, the doctors get frustrated, and they start experimentation with certain medications. They gave me a certain type of medication in the hope that it would be beneficial, but when you have something like depression or melancholia, often if they give you the wrong medication, it's worse than not having it. They got into a kind of an experimentation of medication that exacerbated the problem.

Paul Stillwell: Who functioned as Chief of Naval Personnel while you were going through this?

Admiral Lawrence: Well, when I went into the hospital, it lasted probably only about three months. For those three months, my deputy, Rear Admiral Larry Burkhardt, was basically running the operation. When I got out of the hospital the second time, then Admiral Dudley Carlson was brought in to be the next Chief of Naval Personnel.[*] Then I had about two months in limbo while we were waiting for the retirement action to be completed and the medical boards and all that.[†]

Paul Stillwell: I wonder if part of the situation was that you had set such high standards for yourself throughout your life that you had this concern about possibly not being able to measure up.

---

[*] Vice Admiral Dudley L. Carlson, USN, served as acting Chief of Naval Personnel in November-December 1985 and then officially from January 1986 to October 1987.
[†] Admiral Lawrence's official retirement date was 1 February 1986.

Admiral Lawrence: Well, I'm sure that was a factor, because I had tremendous frustrations with the problems that were principally caused by Secretary Lehman on handling the flag detailing and promotions. But, as I say, you always have frustrations in anything you do. I really felt good up until about 1 March, and then it was just like somebody had thrown a switch. But I'm sure that all of those frustrations and concerns contributed to what I call the burnout—that's the best explanation that I can give to it. I think through medical tests and everything—and I went through every conceivable medical test in the Navy and at Mayo, at Menninger, but—that we didn't come up with any organic cause.

So it just shows you the complexities of the mental health, even though they're learning more and more about depression as a medical phenomenon that's much more commonplace than people ever thought in the past. My whole problem was complicated because right in the middle of all of that, I got bacterial endocarditis, because I had this heart leakage—aortic insufficiency. I had a cyst cut off my tongue, and they didn't give me antibiotics as they should have done, and that pushed me into a bacterial endocarditis situation. So I had to go on five weeks of intravenous antibiotics in Bethesda Naval Hospital. That was very demoralizing as well.

So it was a rough go for about four years, and I was amazed, though, that I kept coming to work and teaching courses. But I was, as I say, about 50% efficiency, and I really felt badly. As I told Ross Perot, I didn't feel like I was pulling my oar. But he was very understanding. I owe a lot to him because of his concern. And he helped my wife greatly, because it was a tough time for her running her business during this whole thing.

But I'm very philosophical about it now. Everybody experiences adversity in life, and the big thing is to get it behind you and try to derive as much value as you can from having gone through the experience. I think in a lot of ways I came through it as a stronger person. I'm probably a lot more understanding about things and maybe somewhat less of a perfectionist now than maybe I was in the past. I don't know.

Paul Stillwell: Sounds, as you describe it, that it was a cumulative process, rather than being one overt thing that broke the camel's back.

Admiral Lawrence: Oh, I'm sure it was. When you get into a burnout situation like that, it has to be a cumulative thing. Probably I would have been smart at some point in there to have gone into an extended leave situation—sabbatical—because after seven years in that Vietnam War and coming back and immediately going on the fast track was probably a mistake. Most other POWs just decided not to really give it that max effort. They took themselves out of the running after a few years. But I kept hanging in there, I guess. But those are the things that happen in life.

One thing I can do now is help advise people how to conduct themselves so as not to get in a situation like that. Eventually, I'll write something on this, but I think one of the things is that leaders—particularly in the military, because we tend to be so dedicated and strong work ethic—have to really be watchful of people around them who can get themselves into this burnout situation. They must be perceptive enough to see the incipient phases of it. Diane feels very badly because she saw this coming on for at least two months, and she just chose not to say anything about it because she didn't want to upset me, but I knew for two or three months beforehand that I was really getting into a situation.

Anyway, once I finally got recovered back in '89, since that time, the last two years, I've really felt good and probably as productive as I've ever been in my life. I've really tried to apply my efforts in the most effective way to help the Navy first and then society. So I really have a very happy and fulfilled life right now. I guess the big lesson I would tell to other people is that you simply are not going to be a happy person in life unless you can handle adversity, because everybody's going to handle adversity of some form in their life—in a family situation or professionally. That's all part of it, but if you can handle it well, you can end up with a very happy, fulfilled person; but if you can't you probably will never be happy.

Paul Stillwell: Please talk about your work with the midshipmen since you've been here.

Admiral Lawrence: Well, it's been a very pleasant endeavor. Now we've kind of settled into a program where I teach a course every semester, which we call the Advanced Leadership Seminar. In any given course we'll have 20 to 30 midshipmen. We have the maximum number we've ever had right now, 31 midshipmen. Each class session is conducted in a lecture hall, where, in addition to the midshipmen enrolled in that course, anybody at the academy—including retired people—can come in and attend.

When I'm lecturing or when I have a guest lecturer in, we'll often have several other people who will sit in the lectures. As I say, it's a seminar course, which basically means that there's very strong class participation. So it's good, because we have a lot of good discussions with the midshipmen. I have a topic for each lecture, but I let the midshipmen determine the direction in which it's going. And, of course, I modify the lectures—like with the war on, I've given a lot of lectures on the war itself, because that's what the midshipmen are interested in, which I felt would be the most valuable thing.

But in addition to the course that I teach, I do a lot of lecturing to other midshipman groups. During the course of a midshipman's four years, I'll probably speak at least twice to his entire class. For example, last fall I spoke to all of the first class on the concepts of loyalty and loyal dissent. That was part of what they called the colloquium program, where they bring in distinguished speakers. Then I usually speak to the entire plebe class and give them a kind of a general leadership lecture, strongly emphasizing the importance of integrity and the honor concept. Also, I do a lot of speaking to midshipmen groups like at company mess nights. Then I try, in addition to that, to do a fair amount of writing, like for *Proceedings*. Any timely topic that I see that's worthy of my addressing, I write about that. I write often for the *Navy Times* and other newspapers.

Also, I'm doing a fair amount of speechmaking. In the last 15 months I've spoken to 13 Naval Academy alumni chapters and two Naval Academy parents' clubs, which we have around the country. I've spoken twice at West Point to various groups, and then twice out at the Air Force Academy. Next week I'm going up to talk to a Naval War College graduation. So most of my speaking is related to the Navy and the service academies. I'm not really seeking to get out in the private sector just to grab honoraria like a lot of people are, because I really want to speak to groups where I feel I can have some impact.

But I have been asked to speak to corporate groups on leadership. I went up last year and spoke to one classroom session of a Harvard Business School section. They have 18 sections in a Harvard Business School class, and one section has about 100 to 120 people. I gave them several topics, and the one they wanted me to speak on was the one they called "Our Foundation and Strength," which was keyed to the qualities and values that we had to have to get through the POW experience.

I do a fair amount of work in the academic world, like I've spoken to the Fletcher School at Tufts, and I speak out at the University of Kentucky at the Patterson School of Diplomacy, International Commerce. So it's a very diversified activity, mostly, as I say, scholarly in nature because that's what my interests are. Also, I've started helping the Association of Naval Aviation right now.

Paul Stillwell: Please tell me more about that.

Admiral Lawrence: Well, I started volunteering my time to the Association of Naval Aviation last year just because I have expertise in that area. I wanted to help, because I could see the immense challenges of that. I've been the vice president for personnel development for the last year, and he's really the guy who addresses the personnel issues. I've done a fair amount of writing and speaking on aviation personnel issues.

Admiral Holloway, who's the chairman of the board of ANA—and he was a previous president—and Admiral Moorer, who's the chairman of the board emeritus, have asked me to become the next national president of ANA to take over in April to succeed Admiral Wes McDonald.* He'll move up to be the chairman of the board, and Admiral Holloway and Admiral Moorer will be both the chairmen of the board emeritus. So I'm looking forward to that, and I'll spend maybe about three days a week over there and two days a week at the Naval Academy. I told them that I really felt a president of that organization should be in there about three years and then turn it over to a younger person who's got the energy and is more current on the issues, although I try to stay up on issues. I write a monthly column for the *Shipmate* called "Capitol Hill," because I want to study the issues. So I'll give my best shot to the Association of Naval Aviation

---

* In his last active duty billet, Admiral Wesley L. McDonald, USN, served as Supreme Allied Commander Atlantic, Commander in Chief Atlantic, and Commander in Chief Atlantic Fleet from 30 September 1982 to 27 November 1985.

for three years, but as things are going right now, I don't think we're going to have any airplanes after three years. [Laughter]

Paul Stillwell: How would you describe the role of that organization?

Admiral Lawrence: Well, I like to describe it as a professional fraternal society—professional in the sense that we try to educate people on the roles, capabilities, and missions of naval aviation. And fraternal in the sense that it, by having 39 chapters or squadrons around the country, we bring former naval aviators, naval aviators, and those interested in naval aviation together in a fraternal setting.

Some people will say we're a lobbying organization, and I say, "Look, we're not a lobbying organization in the sense of other Washington groups. We are a professional organization. We try to educate people on issues, and, of course, the key group you have to educate because of the nature of our government is Congress, so we do go over and talk to congressmen, send things over to Congress." But it's not lobbying; we're basically supporting the formally stated position of the Navy. We will not take a position contrary to that which Secretary of the Navy and Chief of Naval Operations have established. Though we will sometimes take a position different from the Secretary of Defense or the Congress. But nothing we do has not been approved in advance by the Assistant Chief of Naval Operations for Air Warfare. So it's a very broad effort.

One of our key things is four times a year we put out a magazine called the *Wings of Gold*. I'm doing a lot more writing for that now and trying to get that better focused, a more productive effort. I've seen some steady improvement in the last several issues. So I really enjoy that, because, as I say, I enjoy writing and speaking and scholarly activity and associating with young people. The job does put me in contact with a lot of young aviators. So doing that and working with the midshipmen is a very, very satisfying activity for me.

Paul Stillwell: What are the satisfactions? This is a much closer relationship to midshipmen than you had as superintendent.

Admiral Lawrence: Not really. No, it's not, because I used to probably interface more as superintendent with midshipmen than I do now because my activities are principally concentrated in leadership, classroom, and Luce Hall environment. As superintendent, I was more active in broad activities like athletics and academic and professional.

I am very much a proponent of what I call mentorship. I think that when a person gets to my point in life, you have a responsibility to serve as a mentor to help young people learn and to develop and not make the same mistakes that my generation made. I'm very happy at this point in my life to serve in that role. I've never had any aspiration to acquire any great wealth. I have more than adequate amount of money to live comfortably. To me wealth is not defined by money. It's defined by many other things.

Paul Stillwell: Just having the wife you have makes you a rich man.

Admiral Lawrence: Oh, sure, yes. I've always told the midshipmen that there are four components of happiness. The first one is a proud, close-knit family, second is good solid friendships, third is a good reputation—and you can only get a good reputation by doing things that are worthwhile in your life—and fourth is good health. And I say, "You'll notice in those four components of happiness that money is not included, because I can tell you right now that money does not make you happy. Certainly you have to have an adequate amount, but in my opinion, beyond a certain point it's not going to make you happy and probably will contribute to your being less happy."

But, anyway, that's my philosophy. I try to really impress midshipmen with that idea, and most midshipmen, of course, would not be here if they weren't service-oriented-type people. I tell them that anybody who sets out as the primary goal in life to make money, that is a formula for an unhappy life. But, anyway, what I'm doing right now, is very enjoyable. I feel good that I'm making a contribution.

Paul Stillwell: There was a report in a newspaper last year that you were going to go down to Tennessee. What was the story on that?

Admiral Lawrence: Well, I determined that I was going to formally terminate this chair of leadership on 1 January. Ross Perot and I talked this over, because I wanted to feel free to do other things. I really had a desire to spend more time down in my home state, because I'd left there at 17, and I really wanted to establish closer ties with family and friends who are still down there. So I offered my services to the governor, because he was going through a major educational upgrade program. So from time to time I go down there and make some speeches to schools and to civic clubs and things like that, espousing the importance of quality education for the program down there. I'm down in Tennessee, probably at least every other month making speeches and meeting people.

It looks like, because I got associated more actively in the Association of Naval Aviation, that I'll spend less time down in Tennessee, because at the time I made this plan to spend more time down there was before I'd been asked to become the president of ANA. But I'll still go down there about every other month. Of course, one of my incentives for going down there is that my daughter lives down there. She's a doctor at Vanderbilt Hospital, and my brother and all sorts of relatives live there. So it's a way of staying closer to my family down there.

So the nice thing about my life right now is that I'm doing a number of broad activities, all of them are interesting, and I can set my own agenda. When you're on active duty, you're basically a slave to the system. You do what the system asks you to do. Now I'm very selective about what I do, and it's all very enjoyable.

Paul Stillwell: What comments or observations do you have on the mess that the Naval Academy's been through in the last couple of years?

Admiral Lawrence: Well, it's unfortunate as to what has happened. I don't think it's indicative of any real malaise at the academy. I think the academy's still very sound and we're getting the right type of young person. I think there was just a combination of factors that occurred here, and with regard to the woman being chained to the commode incident, that was not a malicious, premeditated act by these young men, based on their anti-woman feelings. It was part of the pre-Army-Navy game nip-ups that just degenerated into a cruel prank. It was a spontaneous thing that got out of hand. But it still was indicative of a flawed attitude on the part of many male midshipmen here, a male chauvinistic attitude, and that's the way that was manifested in that particular action, because if that had not been a woman, it probably would never have happened. So as unfortunate and regrettable as that was, it did get the whole issue out on the table, and it forced the academy and the Navy to really take significant action to improve attitudes here at the academy. Unfortunately, it got blown into the national media, and then it just started going like a snowball.

At the very early stages of that incident, the academy made some fundamental errors, in my opinion. One was not realizing that it was a sensationalistic event and going to the local newspaper. I found out about the chaining incident about two months after the fact when a woman officer came in to see me to express her concerns with the acceptance of women here at the academy. In the course of talking this over, she brought out this chaining incident. I said, "Tell me that again. I'm amazed that I haven't heard about that." It was obvious to me that the academy was doing everything to keep that very quiet.

So I called up the public affairs officer here at the academy, and I said, "Look, I'll tell you, as a former superintendent, this is the type of event that you simply have to go out and talk to the local newspaper about, because if it gets leaked, they're really going to beat you to death. One thing I learned as superintendent is that when something happens that's very newsworthy, you just have to bite the bullet and go out and tell the press. Often they'll print the statement you give them, but if it leaks, they write their own article, and that's often not what you want to have written."

But the public affairs officer said, "No, the superintendent has made the decision not talk about this to the press."

So I called the Vice Chief of Naval Operations, Admiral Edney, whom I knew very well, and he'd been a commandant of midshipmen. I told him, "In my opinion, Bud, this is something that you'd better talk to the press about, because if it gets leaked, you're going to be beat to death."

He said, "Well, we defer to the superintendent. We don't tell him what to do."

So I went to the Chief of Naval Personnel, whom I knew very well, Admiral Boorda. I couldn't convince him that they should go to the media. And then, of course, two months later it got leaked to the Annapolis newspaper in big inch-high headlines, and the next thing you knew it was all over the national news.

Paul Stillwell: How did it get out?

Admiral Lawrence: It was getting to be such common knowledge, like the Defense Advisory Committee on Women in the Service, I was over giving them a presentation in April. All of the women on—and men too—who were on the DACOWITS knew about it. In fact, they chided me about this, how the academy had treated this as a boys-will-be-boys-type thing.

But I think the thing that was probably the real catalyst that got it into the media was that the father was very upset about this. I think he was talking to a lot of people about it.

Paul Stillwell: He's a Naval Academy graduate.

Admiral Lawrence: That's right, he was a Naval Academy graduate.[*]

This event occurred the week of the Army-Navy game, which was in December of 1989. Then because of the Army-Navy game was followed immediately by Christmas leave, the academy didn't have any direct interface with this woman's parents. Her father felt irritated that the academy didn't discuss this with him. And I'm not one to say, "Well, when I was superintendent, we did this," but . . .

Paul Stillwell: But you did do it much more sensitively when you were superintendent.

Admiral Lawrence: When I was superintendent I had a cardinal rule that any major disciplinary event, the first thing we did was to go immediately to the parents. The rationale behind that was that often the midshipmen would not give an accurate explanation to the parents. The other thing was that I didn't want the parents reading

---

[*] Midshipman Gwen Marie Dreyer, USN, was originally to be in the class of 1992. She resigned following the incident. Her father was Captain Gregory F. Dreyer, USNR.

about it for the first time in the media. So we always had the commandant or the deputy commandant call the parents, discuss it with them rationally, and try not to get them upset. Somehow that practice terminated here. I don't know whether Admiral Hill chose not to do that.* But the father got very upset, because over a month after the event no one had really talked to him, so he had to ask for an appointment. He came in, sat down and talked to the commandant about it. I think because he talked to people, that was a big factor in initially it getting in the media.

So it was a public relations failure probably more than any other failure here, because I don't think we had a serious anti-woman attitude here, although we certainly had one that needed to be addressed. It was unfortunate it took that dramatic event to make us take action.

But the other thing that happened here at the academy was in the very early days when we were introducing women while I was here, we had very extensive sexual harassment training, all sorts of informational programs for midshipmen. I used to have a consultant come in here, Edie Seashore, who was an expert in this area. She looked over everything we did. I told the director of professional development—I called him the "dean of women"—that his responsibility was to very carefully monitor every aspect of women at the academy. Over the years, as the women were here for a while, they stopped doing all those things. I think their rationale was, "Why should we make women a big deal? They've been here, we shouldn't single them out." There was a very important psychological reason I did that, because I wanted everybody to perceive that a Navy captain was riding herd on this program, as well as the superintendent and everybody else.

The other thing is all the sexual harassment training stopped. Then you had a superintendent and commandant who came in after never having women under their commands. One had been in submarines, where they didn't have women; and, of course, the other was a very operationally oriented aviator, where he never really served before with women. So I think that they didn't really understand all the nuances of the situation here and didn't really perceive that there was this very prevalent anti-woman attitude. So

---

* Rear Admiral Virgil L. Hill, Jr., USN, served as Superintendent of the Naval Academy from 18 August 1988 to 15 June 1991.

they got caught by surprise. That was unfortunate, but the good thing about it is that it made the academy take very dramatic action with regard to the acceptance of women, so I think they've taken a quantum step up.

The other situation here that very much upset me was the firing of the electrical engineering department chairman, because I knew that professor very well. Professor Santoro is one of the most distinguished electrical engineering professors in the country and had been a 25-year member of the faculty.* Nobody told me anything about that situation in advance, and, boy, when I read it in the paper, I was just aghast that the academy would do something like that. It just really sent a terrible signal to the faculty, and it was perceived so adversely.

Paul Stillwell: The background was that the grades were low, and the dean, I guess, directed that they be raised.

Admiral Lawrence: Yes. Then when the dean didn't get the response that he wanted, I guess he felt a little bit threatened or something. He felt he had to really, dramatically assert his authority, and then he replaced the departmental chairman. I'm amazed that the superintendent would have permitted that. If a dean had come to me and said he was going to fire a 25-year departmental chairman, I would never have let it happen. If you feel that somebody in that position is not doing the job you want, you don't remove him from the job in that manner; you do it in a much more graceful way. You basically make it appear as a due-course-type change of responsibility, as opposed to making it appear like it's a firing.

But, anyway, the dean was new at that time, and he wasn't completely sure of himself. In my opinion, the superintendent simply should not have let that happen. He should have had a broad enough cognizance of what was going on here. You have to delegate many things, but there are some things you don't delegate. As a result, the administration lost a lot of stock with the faculty, which they're still trying to regain. I

---

* In February 1990 the Naval Academy's academic dean, Dr. Robert H. Shapiro, removed Dr. Ralph P. Santoro, a civilian, from his post as chairman of the electrical engineering department. The action, taken in mid-semester, came when Santoro refused to raise the grades of midshipmen who were engineering majors.

think they are regaining that, but that was another incident that I thought was a very unfortunate, avoidable type of incident.

Paul Stillwell: Well, I can understand why Naval Academy people would be hesitant to read the newspaper, because there was so much bad news.

Admiral Lawrence: Yes, that was a bad period, but I think now things are back on the right track, and, hopefully, we'll stay out of the media. If the new superintendent comes in and asks my opinion, I'll tell him that you simply have to be very public relations-conscious here.[*] You have to be proactive. You just can't sit back and let things happen. Because of our proximity to Washington and Baltimore, anything that's sensationalistic that gets in the newspaper has every potential for going into the national news. So you simply have to control your relationship with that newspaper. As I say, it was my practice that whenever I knew something sensationalistic that happened here, we put the statement out to the Annapolis *Capital*. They didn't get their nose out of joint as a result of that, but on this chaining incident, they really got their nose out of joint, and they went on a kind of a vendetta against the academy. So you just can't ignore the press or feel resentment towards them; you have to live with them.

    I describe the press as kind of like your mother-in-law. You don't necessarily like her, but you don't want to get rid of her; you've got to get along with her. [Chuckle]

Paul Stillwell: Well, Admiral, do you have anything else to add?

Admiral Lawrence: No, I don't have anything, Paul. I've really enjoyed it.

Paul Stillwell: Well, I was going to ask you, do you have any summing up to do on this career we've discussed.

---

[*] Rear Admiral Thomas C. Lynch, USN, served as superintendent of the Naval Academy from 15 June 1991 to 1 August 1994.

Admiral Lawrence: No, but I want to thank you all for giving me the opportunity to do this, because it'll be useful to me when I write my book some time in the future.* I just hope the experiences that I have had will help some people in the future, and to learn the lessons of the past. So I hope it's a very useful, historical contribution.

Paul Stillwell: Well, I want to thank you on that regard for giving us the opportunity to record it, because it certainly is. I appreciate both the thoroughness with which you've covered it and the candor that you've made available. Both of those will enhance its usefulness for historians.

Admiral Lawrence: Well, thank you very much, Paul, and I look forward to reading it whenever the opportunity is available.

Paul Stillwell: Great. Thank you.

---

* The book is William P. Lawrence with Rosario Rausa, *Tennessee Patriot* (Annapolis: Naval Institute Press, 2006). Much of the material in the book was derived from this oral history.

Launched in 1969, the U.S. Naval Institute's award-winning oral history program is among the oldest in the country. Used in combination with documentary sources, oral histories offer a richer understanding of naval history through candid recollections and explanations rarely entered into contemporary records. In addition, they help depict the atmosphere of a particular event or era in a manner not available in official documents.

The nonprofit Naval Institute accomplishes its history projects solely through contributed funds and gratefully accepts tax-deductible gifts of all sizes for this purpose. This support allows the Institute to preserve the life experiences of today's service men and women so they may enlighten and inspire future generations.

For information about opportunities to underwrite Naval Institute oral history projects, please contact the Naval Institute Foundation at 291 Wood Road, Annapolis, Maryland 21402; by phone at (410) 295-1054; or by e-mail at foundation@usni.org.

Index to the Oral History of
Vice Admiral William P. Lawrence, U.S. Navy (Retired)

A-7 Corsair II
Role of Light Attack Wing Pacific Fleet in administering 23 squadrons of A-7s in the mid-1970s, 386-400

A-12 Avenger
Developmental Navy aircraft program killed in 1991 because of high cost, 402, 560-563

Adams, General Paul D., USA (USMA, 1928)
World War II service in the Army, 242-244
In the early 1960s served as the first commander in chief of the U.S. Strike Command and MEAFSA, 236-265
Personality and leadership style, 243-247, 251-257
Expressed concerns in 1964-65 that the Vietnam War would be long and difficult, 255-256, 263-265

Africa
U.S. military connections in the mid-1960s, 247-253

Air Force, U.S.
In the early 1960s provided air intercept radar training to naval flight officers who were going to be in the F4H/F-4 Phantom II, 187-188, 191-192
Sent airplanes to the Key West Naval Air Station during the Cuban Missile Crisis in late 1962, 209
U.S. Navy concern about Air Force criticism in the early 1960s for being over-flown by Soviet bombers, 224-226
Took part in a flyover for John F. Kennedy's funeral in 1963, 234-235
In the early 1960s some Air Force units became part of the new U.S. Strike Command, 236-241
Involvement in the Congo in the mid-1960s, 247-250, 252
Had a number of F-4 Phantoms at MacDill Air Force Base in the mid-1960s, 260
General Curtis LeMay as Chief of Staff, 1961-66, 260-261
Lawrence's observations comparing Air Force and Navy officers, 267
Air Force officers as prisoners in North Vietnam, 1967-73, 312, 318-319, 321, 324-325, 343, 349-351
Air Force planes carried released prisoners of war out of Vietnam and back to the United States in 1973, 355, 360
Reluctance to give operational billets to returned POWs from Vietnam, 386
Joint testing with the Navy in the mid-1970s on jamming techniques, 397-398
Competition in the mid-1970s of the Air Force F-15 and Navy F-14, 404-405
Cooperation in a joint North Pacific warfare exercise in 1983, 545-546

Air Force Academy, Colorado Springs, Colorado
Over the years has had a much more stringent honor code than that of the Naval Academy, 43-45, 462-463

Aitcheson, Rear Admiral George A. Jr., USN
In the late 1950s was a student at Test Pilot School, 156
In 1983 served as Commander Carrier Group Seven, 539

Alcohol
Lawrence's concern about underage midshipman drinking at the Naval Academy in the late 1970s-early 1980s, 475-477
Navy policy on alcohol abuse in the mid-1980s, 583-584

Aleutian Islands
Adak, Alaska, is an important patrol plane base for antisubmarine warfare, 517

Alvarez, Commander Everett, USN
In August 1964 became the first U.S. pilot to become a prisoner of war in Vietnam, 263, 318, 338-339

Anderson, Rear Admiral George W., Jr., USN (USNA, 1927)
In 1958-59 commanded Carrier Division Six, 157-160, 165, 172-174, 178
In the late 1970s complained to Lawrence about disciplining an intoxicated midshipman who was involved in a fatal accident, 475-477

Annapolis, Maryland, Naval Station
Role in the late 1970s-early 1980s in supporting the Naval Academy, 483-490

Antiair Warfare
North Vietnamese surface-to-air missiles and guns fired against U.S. aircraft in 1966-67, 273-274, 277, 300, 303-307
Mission in June 1967 in which Lawrence was shot down by gunnery and became a prisoner of war, 303-307

Antisubmarine Warfare
In the early 1980s the Third Fleet had ASW as one of its missions, 504, 518-520
In connection with the first Pacific deployment of the Trident submarine *Ohio* (SSBN-726) in the summer of 1982, 524-525
Use of *Los Angeles* (SSN-688)-class submarines in a North Pacific exercise in 1983, 541-544
Graded battle group ASW exercises at the Pacific Missile Range at Barking Sands, Hawaii, in the early 1980s, 547-548
Limited P-3 contact with Soviet submarines in the Pacific in the early 1980s, 548-549

Antonelli, Lieutenant Colonel John W., USMC (USNA, 1940)
    Served on the Naval Academy staff circa 1950, 55

Army, U.S.
    Service in World War II by General Paul D. Adams, 242-244
    Lawrence's brother Thomas served in the 82nd Airborne Division during the Vietnam War, 21
    In 1953 sent troops to visit the aircraft carrier *Oriskany* (CVA-34) off Korea, 100, 115-116
    In the early 1960s some Army units became part of the new U.S. Strike Command, 236-241
    In 1965 the U.S. Strike Command identified units capable of early deployment to Vietnam, 255, 263-265
    Army officer career patterns include a lot of schooling and staff work, 266-267

Association of Naval Aviation
    As a professional, fraternal organization in the 1990s, 413-414, 603-606
    Relationship in the 1990s to the Tailhook Association, 413-414

Astronauts
    Test pilots were chosen as the NASA program began in the late 1950s, 120, 130-131, 142-144, 154

Austin, Captain Frank H. Jr., Medical Corps, USN
    In the mid-1960s counseled Lawrence on his heart murmur, 268

Aviation Officers Candidate School (AOCS)
    Comparison in the early 1960s of officers from NROTC and other commissioning sources, 221-224

B-52 Stratofortress
    Bombing raids on North Vietnam in 1972, 345-348

Bailey, Lieutenant (junior grade) James W., USNR
    Shot down over North Vietnam in June 1967 while serving as rear-seat RIO in Lawrence's F-4, 306-307

Baldwin, Vice Admiral Robert B., USN (USNA, 1945)
    Commanded Naval Air Force Pacific Fleet, 1973-76, 394-396
    As Chief of Naval Personnel, 1978-80, 452

Barrow, General Robert H., USMC
    Did not respond to invitations from the Naval Academy during his tenure as Commandant, 1979-83, 456

Baseball
Naval Academy team in the late 1940s-early 1950s, 51, 60-61

Basketball
Naval Academy team in the late 1940s-early 1950s, 60-61, 69-70, 72-73, 80-81

Bear (Soviet Bomber)
U.S. Navy concern about being over-flown in the early 1960s by Soviet bombers, 224-226

Bell, Commander James F., USN (USNA, 1954)
Former prisoner of war who attended the Industrial College of the Armed Forces after his return to the United States in 1973, 382

Belzer, Midshipman Elizabeth Ann, USN (USNA, 1980)
Victim of pranks while in the first class of women at the Naval Academy, 440-441

Bennett, Captain Frederick G., USN (USNA, 1936)
Commanded the heavy cruiser *Newport News* (CA-148) in 1960-61, 193, 196-197

Billig, Commander Donal M., MC, USN
Navy surgeon convicted of involuntary manslaughter in 1986, 586-587

Bishop, Max F.
Coached baseball at the Naval Academy, 1938-62, 59-61

Bombs/Bombing
By F2H Banshees of Fighter Squadron 193 (VF-193) in the mid-1950s, 123-124
On North Vietnam by F-4 Phantoms of Fighter Squadron 143 (VF-143) in 1966, 270-287
On North Vietnam by F-4 Phantoms of Fighter Squadron 143 (VF-143) in 1967, 294-307
B-52 raids on North Vietnam in 1972, 345-348

Boorda, Vice Admiral Jeremy M., USN
Served in the early 1980s as executive assistant to the Chief of Naval Personnel and from 1988 to 1991 was CNP himself, 551-552, 565-567, 607-608

Born, Lieutenant Terry R., USNR
F-4 pilot who flew as Lawrence's wingman during Vietnam combat in 1966, then did a repeat tour in the war soon after, 285

Bowler, Commander Roland T. E., Jr., USN (Ret.) (USNA, 1945)
Director of the Naval Institute in the early 1980s, 445

Brown, Rear Admiral Thomas F. III, USN
Served as officer in tactical command when U.S. Third Fleet ships conducted an exercise in the North Pacific in the early 1980s, 511-512, 515-516

Brown, Midshipman Wesley A., USN (USNA, 1949)
Experiences as a black Naval Academy midshipman, late 1940s, 74-75

Buck, Commander Clarence Carlton Jr., USN
Commanded Fighter Squadron 14 (VF-14) in 1962-64, 212-213, 222

Budgetary Issues
In naval aviation in the mid- and late 1970s, 403, 410
Money for preservation and updating of the Naval Academy's physical plant in the late 1970s-early 1980s, 479-480
In the mid-1980s for Navy personnel costs, 565-569, 588

Bureau of Naval Personnel
Reassignment of Lawrence in 1964 to become executive assistant to Commander in Chief Strike Command, 236
Emphasis in the mid-1980s on contact between junior officers and detailers, 550-552
Flag officer detailing in the mid-1980s, 552-560
Functions in the 1980s vis-à-vis OP-01, 564-569
Challenges in the 1980s in detailing married couples, 585

Burkhardt, Rear Admiral Lawrence III, USN (USNA, 1954)
In the mid-1980s was Assistant DCNO (Manpower, Personnel and Training), 580, 599

Bush, President George H. W.
Played baseball at Yale in the late 1940s, 17
Spoke at the Naval Academy graduation in 1981, 499-500

Busik, Captain William S., USN (Ret.) (USNA, 1943)
Headed the Naval Academy Alumni Association, 1971-94, 491-492

C-141 Starlifter
Air Force transport that carried released prisoners of war out of Vietnam in 1973, 355, 360

Caldwell, Captain Henry Howard, USN (USNA, 1927)
Served 1949 to 1951 as Naval Academy athletic director, 65-66

Calvert, Vice Admiral James F., USN (USNA, 1943)
Naval Academy superintendent in the early 1970s, 435

Carl, Lieutenant Colonel Marion E, USMC
Commanded Marine Photo Squadron One in 1954-55, 117

Carnevale, Bernard L. "Ben"
Coached basketball at the Naval Academy, 1947-67, 59-60, 72-73

Carr, Commander Donald E Jr., USN (USNA, 1941)
In 1953-54 commanded Fighter Squadron 193 (VF-193), 95-96, 99-101

Carrier Division Six
Operations in the Atlantic and Mediterranean in 1959-60, 157-170

Carson, Midshipman Theo K., USN (USNA, 1951)
Played football for the Naval Academy in the late 1940s-early 1950s, 62-63

Carter, President James E., Jr. (USNA, 1947)
Lean defense budgets during the early years of his administration, 410
Emphasized energy conservation, 497-499

Cassidy, Rear Admiral Thomas J. Jr., USN
In 1985 was relieved as Commander Fighter, Airborne Early Wing Pacific Fleet over perceived irregularities in parts prices, 573-574

Catapults
Lawrence experienced a cold catapult shot on board the aircraft carrier *Oriskany* (CVA-34) in the mid-1950s, 112-113
Difficulties on board the aircraft carrier *Franklin D. Roosevelt* (CVA-42) in the early 1960s, 219-220

Cecil Field, Jacksonville, Florida
Operations in the early 1960s, 233-236

Chaplains
Value at the Naval Academy in the late 1970s-early 1980s in counseling midshipmen and keeping the superintendent informed, 423-424

Chew, Captain John L., USN (USNA, 1931)
Served in the early 1950s a deputy commandant of midshipman at the Naval Academy, 41, 45-46, 52, 86-87

Clark Air Force Base, Philippines
Stopover point for released POWs en route from North Vietnam to the United States in 1973, 356-360

Clark, Vice Admiral Glenwood Jr., USN (USNA, 1949)
In 1985 became the first Commander Space and Naval Warfare Systems Command, 578

Clark, Rear Admiral Thurston B., USN (USNA, 1927)
In the late 1950s commanded the Naval Air Test Center at Patuxent River, 153-154

Clark, W. Ramsey
Anti-war protester who visited North Vietnam, 317

Clarke, Captain Walter E., USN
Commanded the aircraft carrier *Franklin D. Roosevelt* (CVA-42), 1962-63, 226

Claytor, W. Graham Jr.
As Secretary of the Navy in 1978 overruled those who wanted a nuclear-trained flag officer as superintendent of the Naval Academy and approved Lawrence, 419
Involved in the dismissal of Naval Academy midshipman who used drugs, 493
View on the Navy's Navy policy on gays in the late 1970s, 585-586

Coast Guard, U.S.
Involvement in the controversial arrival of the first Trident missile submarine, USS *Ohio* (SSBN-726) at Seattle in August 1982, 523-524

Cockell, Rear Admiral William A. Jr., USN
Unable to get a suitable flag assignment in the 1980s, 555

Code of Conduct
Application to Vietnam prisoners of war in the 1960s-70s, 310-311, 341-342, 350-351

Collisions
In May 1960 the German freighter *Bernd Leonhardt* collided in the Atlantic with the aircraft carrier *Saratoga* (CVA-60), 169-172

Commercial Ships
In May 1960 the German freighter *Bernd Leonhardt* collided in the Atlantic with the aircraft carrier *Saratoga* (CVA-60), 169-172

Communications
Problems in the early 1960s with F3H Demons of Fighter Squadron 14 (VF-14), 213-214

Congo
U.S. military involvement in the mid-1960s, 247-250, 252

Congress, U.S.
    Role in getting Lawrence an appointment to the Naval Academy in 1947, 16-17
    Investigation of transportation to a Tailhook Association convention in the mid-1970s, 411-413
    In the 1980s expressed concern about Navy selection board results, 561, 576
    Involved in the mid-1980s in the Navy's budget requests for personnel, 569

Conrad, Lieutenant Charles Jr., USN
    Test pilot who was selected for the astronaut program in the early 1960s, 131, 141-144

***Constellation*, USS (CVA-64)**
    Deployment to the Western Pacific and bombing of North Vietnam in 1967, 291-307

Coppedge, Captain John O., USN (Ret.) (USNA, 1947)
    Served as the Naval Academy's athletic director, 1968-88, 435-436, 486-490

***Coral Sea*, USS (CVB-43)**
    Summer training cruise to the Mediterranean in 1948, 76-78
    In the mid-1970s the news media in San Francisco criticized the ship's ability to perform her mission, 395-397

Cornwell, Lieutenant Robert R., USN (USNA, 1951)
    In the late 1950s did postgraduate work at Princeton University, 141-142

Corpus Christi, Texas, Naval Air Station
    Site of Navy flight training in the early 1950s, 90

Craig, Captain Kenneth, USN (USNA, 1926)
    Former basketball player who headed the Naval Academy's aviation department circa 1950, 65-66

Cuba
    In 1963 Fighter Squadron 14 (VF-14) stood hot-pad duty at Key West to protect U.S. recon flights to Cuba, 230-232

Cuban Missile Crisis
    Loading up of Key West Naval Air Station in late 1962 to deal with contingencies, 209-210

Curry, Commander Matthew A., Chaplain Corps, USN (Ret.)
    Retired chaplain who was helpful to Lawrence and his family in the late 1960s-early 1970s, 371-372

Danang, South Vietnam
    Site of an airfield used by Navy planes in the mid-1960s, 286

Darby, Captain Jack N., USN
    Served 1978-79 as the Naval Academy's commandant of midshipmen, 427

Davidson, Dr. Bruce M.
    As academic dean at the Naval Academy in the late 1970s-early 1980s, 471-472

DeMars, Vice Admiral Bruce, USN (USNA, 1957)
    As president of an officer selection board in the mid-1980s, challenged Secretary of the Navy John Lehman, 561, 575

Denbigh, Ensign Robert S. Jr., USN (USNA, 1950)
    Served as officer of the deck in the aircraft carrier *Oriskany* (CVA-34) in the mid-1950s, 113

Denton, Commander Jeremiah A., Jr., USN (USNA, 1947)
    Strong leader as a Vietnam prisoner of war, 1965-73, 333, 345, 348-349, 356, 387

Desert Strike, Exercise
    Large armor exercise in the California desert in May 1964, 254, 261

***Des Moines*, USS (CA-134)**
    Served in 1959 as flagship for Commander Sixth Fleet, 173

Dobony, Midshipman Charles, USN (USNA, 1950)
    As president of the class of 1950 at the Naval Academy, helped end the "dope system" of passing test information, 40-41

Dominican Republic
    Site of U.S. intervention in 1965, 240-241

Donnell, Rear Admiral Joseph S., USN
    Delayed getting to a new billet in 1985 because of a hold-up in his orders, 557-558

Donovan, Vice Admiral Francis R., USN (USNA, 1959)
    As deputy commandant at the Naval Academy in the late 1970s-early 1980s, assisted the parents of a sexual assault victim, 427-429
    Head of professional development at the academy, 441

Dornin, Commander Robert E., USN (USNA, 1935)
    Served on the Naval Academy staff circa 1950, 53-55

Duke, Captain Irving T., USN (USNA, 1924)
    Commanded the battleship *Missouri* (BB-63) cautiously after her 1950 grounding, 81-82

Dreyer, Midshipman Gwen Marie, USN (USNA, 1992)
    In 1989 was chained to a urinal in the Naval Academy dormitory, 426, 606-609

Drugs
    As part of the Navy culture in the mid-1970s, 390
    At the Naval Academy in the late 1970s-early 1980s, 424-427
    CNO Thomas Hayward dealt with the Navy drug problem in the early 1980s, 426-427
    Evolving urinalysis detection facilitates discovering offenders, 582-583

EA-3 Skywarrior
    Electronic intelligence plane that accompanied carrier air strikes on North Vietnam in 1966, 279-280

Easterling, Vice Admiral Crawford A., USN
    Served 1982-85 as Commander Naval Air Force Pacific Fleet, 532, 540

Education
    Lawrence's experiences in school in Tennessee in the 1930s and 1940s, 7, 9, 12, 17, 19-20
    Academics at the Naval Academy in the late 1940s-early 1950s, 28, 30-32, 39-40, 52-53, 55-56, 67-69
    Academics at the Naval Academy in the late 1970s-early 1980s, 466-472
    Lawrence's view of contributors to success in schools circa 1990, 24-25

Ejection Seat
    Martin-Baker seat tested in 1957 in an F9F-8T trainer at Patuxent River Naval Air Station, 151-152

Elder, Captain Robert M., USN
    Did flight test evaluation of the F4H Phantom II in the late 1950s, 132-133

Electronic Warfare
    Limited capability in the U.S. Navy in the early 1960s, 205
    F-4 Phantoms had no ECM protection against North Vietnam surface-to-air missiles in 1966, 273
    Upgrades to the F-4s of Fighter Squadron 143 (VF-143) in 1966-67, 275, 290
    Joint testing with the Air Force in the mid-1970s on jamming techniques, 397-398

Ellis, Rear Admiral William E., USN (USNA, 1930)
    In 1961-62 commanded Carrier Division Two, 203-204

Engen, Vice Admiral Donald D., USN (Ret.)
    Served as a Navy test pilot in the late 1950s, later was head of the Federal Aviation Administration in the 1980s, 132, 148-150
    Member of the Carrier Aviation Hall of Fame, 151

Enlisted Personnel
 In Fighter Squadron 193 (VF-193) in the mid-1950s, 121-122
 On board the heavy cruiser *Newport News* (CA-148) in the early 1960s, 205-206
 On board the aircraft carrier *Ranger* (CVA-61) in 1966, 286-287
 On board the battleship *New Jersey* (BB-62) in 1983, 539-540
 Efforts in the 1980s to put the nuclear surface ship crews on par with submariners, 580-581

ced*Enterprise*, USS (CVAN-65)
 Operations in the early 1960s, 214-217
 Combat operations bombing North Vietnam in 1967, 293
 High refueling cost, 402
 Ran aground San Francisco in April 1983, 532-534

Erdelatz, Edward J.
 Naval Academy head football coach, 1950-59, 70-72

Errington, Ensign Harry R., USN
 In the early 1960s was a crackerjack maintenance control officer in Fighter Squadron 14 (VF-14), 227

***Essex*, USS (CVA-9)**
 As flagship circa 1960 for Commander Carrier Division Six, 161
 Operations circa 1960 in company with the aircraft carrier *Saratoga* (CVA-60), 172-174

***Essex* (CVA-9)-Class Aircraft Carriers**
 Limited capabilities by the early 1960s, 161, 217-218

Ethiopia
 Visited by U.S. CinC MEAFSA in 1964, 249

Everest, Colonel Frank K. Jr., USAF
 In the early 1960s commanded combat crew training at MacDill Air Force Base, 260

F2H Banshee
 Flown by Fighter Squadron 193 (VF-193) in the mid-1950s, 95-124
 Early work in night-flying operations, 93, 102-111, 114, 119-123
 Use of by VF-193 for bombing, 123-124

F3D Skyknight
 Used in the early 1960s to train naval flight officers as radar intercept officers for the F4H/F-4 Phantom II, 182-183, 186-187

F3H Demon
 The airplane was chronically underpowered, 211

Mediterranean deployment in 1962-63 in Fighter Squadron 14 (VF-14), 210-220
In 1963 Fighter Squadron 14 (VF-14) transitioned from the F3H Demon to the F-4 Phantom II, 195, 209-210, 226-229

F4H/F-4 Phantom II
Competitive flight-testing in the late 1950s against the Chance Vought F8U-3 Crusader III, 131-135, 147
Fleet introduction training in the early 1960s by VF-101 and VF-121, 181-192
In 1963 Fighter Squadron 14 (VF-14) transitioned from the F3H Demon to the F-4 Phantom II, 195, 209-210, 226-233
Two-man crew with pilot and radar intercept officer, 229-230
Operations in the early 1960s at Cecil Field in Jacksonville, 233-236
Took part in a flyover for John F. Kennedy's funeral in 1963, 234-235
Air Force version at MacDill Air Force Base in the mid-1960s, 260
Bombing attacks on North Vietnam in 1966 by Fighter Squadron 143 (VF-143) based on the aircraft carrier *Ranger* (CVA-61), 270-287
Electronic warfare upgrades to the F-4s of Fighter Squadron 143 (VF-143) in 1966-67, 275, 290
Bombing attacks on North Vietnam in 1966 by Fighter Squadron 143 (VF-143) based on the aircraft carrier *Constellation* (CVA-64), 294-307
Mission in June 1967 in which Lawrence was shot down and became a prisoner of war, 303-307

F5D Skylancer
Jet fighter that was tested in the late 1950s but did not go into production, 137

F6F Hellcat
Used for flight training in the early 1950s, 90-91, 94

F8F Bearcat
Used for flight training in the early 1950s, 90-91

F8U-1 Crusader
Set a transcontinental speed record in 1957, 155
Difficult plane to handle around aircraft carriers, 1950s-1960s, 146-147
Photo version was used in the Mediterranean in the late 1950s for saluting, 165
Not a good aircraft for night operations, 221

F8U-3 Crusader III
Competitive flight-testing in the late 1950s against the McDonnell F4H Phantom II, 131-139, 146, 153-154

F9F-6 Cougar
Test-flown and evaluated by Lawrence at Patuxent River in the mid-1950s, 127-128

F9F-8T Cougar
    Used for a 1957 ejection-seat test in 1957 at Patuxent River Naval Air Station, 151-152

F-14 Tomcat
    Resolution of various problems when it entered the fleet in the mid-1970s, 403-404
    Competition against the Air Force F-15, 404-405

F-15 Eagle
    Competition in the mid-1970s between the Air Force F-15 and Navy F-14, 404-405

F/A-18 Hornet
    Emerged in the 1970s as a lightweight Navy strike fighter, 401-402

FJ-4 Fury
    Jet aircraft used for crosswind carrier takeoff and landing tests and rocket power in the late 1950s, 135-136, 139-140, 148-150

Fallon, Nevada, Naval Air Station
    Site of weapons training in the mid-1950s for Fighter Squadron 193 (VF-193), 106

Falvey, Lieutenant (junior grade) Bernard James, USNR
    Naval flight officer who served in Fighter Squadron 143 (VF-143) in 1967, 297

Federal Aviation Administration
    Relationship with the Navy in the mid-1970s on airspace allocation, 408-409

Felt, Admiral Harry D., USN (USNA, 1923)
    As CinCPac in the early 1960s objected to the creation of the joint U.S. Strike Command, 238-241, 254

Fighter Squadron 14 (VF-14)
    Deployment to the Mediterranean in 1962-63 with F3H Demons, 211-226
    In 1963 transitioned from the F3H Demon to the F-4 Phantom II, 195, 209-210, 226-229
    Makeup of the squadron in the early 1960s from different commissioning sources, 221-224
    In 1963 stood hot-pad duty at Key West to protect U.S. recon flights to Cuba, 230-232
    Operations in the early 1960s at Cecil Field in Jacksonville, 233-236

Fighter Squadron 74 (VF-74)
    In the early 1960s became the first fleet operational squadron to transition to the F4H/F-4 Phantom II, 189-191

Fighter Squadron 101 (VF-101)
In the early 1960s the squadron's Detachment Alfa did fleet introduction training for the F4H/F-4 Phantom fighter, 181-191
Had to move training from Key West to Jacksonville in late 1962 because of the Cuban Missile Crisis, 209-210

Fighter Squadron 121 (VF-121)
In the early 1960s did fleet introduction training for the F4H/F-4 Phantom fighter, 182-190

Fighter Squadron 143 (VF-143)
Deployment to the Western Pacific and bombing of North Vietnam in 1966 on board the aircraft carrier *Ranger* (CVA-61), 270-287
Nickname "Pukin' Dogs," 276-277
Enlisted men on board in 1966, 286-287
Stand-down at Miramar between 1966 and 1967 Vietnam deployments, 281-283, 289-290
Deployment to the Western Pacific and bombing of North Vietnam in 1967 on board the aircraft carrier *Constellation* (CVA-64), 294-307
Loss of an F-4 and crew in a flat-hatting incident before the squadron's 1967 deployment, 291-292
Mission in June 1967 in which Lawrence was shot down and became a prisoner of war, 303-307

Fighter Squadron 193 (VF-193)
Gunnery training with the F2H Banshee in the early 1950s, 95-96
Four-man acrobatic team known as the "Mangy Angels," 96-97, 101
Deployment to the Western Pacific in 1953-54, 97-102, 111-112, 115-116
Early work in jet carrier night operations in the mid-1950s, 93, 102-111, 114, 119-123
Enlisted men in the squadron in the mid-1950s, 121-122
Use of the F2H Banshee for bombing in the mid-1950s, 123-124

First Air Cavalry Division, U.S. Army
Identified in the mid-1960s as one of the first units to be shipped to Vietnam, 251, 255, 264-265

First Infantry Division, U.S. Army
Identified in the mid-1960s as one of the first units to be shipped to Vietnam, 263-264

Fleming, Captain Allan F., USN (USNA, 1936)
Commanded the aircraft carrier *Saratoga* (CVA-60), 1959-60, 166, 169-172
In May 1960, while under Fleming's command, the *Saratoga* collided with a German merchant ship, 169-172

Flight Training
In Florida and Texas, 1951-53, 87-95

Flint, Commander Lawrence E. Jr., USN
Did flight test evaluation of the F8U-3 Crusader III in the late 1950s, 132-133

Flynn, Colonel John P., USAF
Strong leader as a Vietnam prisoner of war, 1967-73, 387-388

Fogarty, Captain William M., USN
Commanded the battleship *New Jersey* (BB-62) in 1982-83, 536-540

Foley, Admiral Sylvester R., Jr., USN (USNA, 1950)
Commanded the U.S. Pacific Fleet, 1982-85, 510, 520, 530, 541-542

Fonda, Jane
Antiwar protester who visited North Vietnam, 316-317

Football
Lawrence played in high school, 16
At the Naval Academy in the late 1940s-early 1950s, 56, 59-64, 70-77
At Pensacola Naval Air Station in the early 1950s, 87-88
Successful football teams at the Naval Academy in the late 1970s-early 1980s, 71-72, 433-435, 486-487
Scheduling of Army-Navy football games in the late 1970s-early 1980s, 463-464, 487-488

Forbes, Commander Bernard B., Jr., USN (USNA, 1945)
In the early 1960s was air officer in the crew of the aircraft carrier *Franklin D. Roosevelt* (CVA-42), 212, 216

Fort Riley, Kansas
Home of the Army's First Infantry Division, one of the first units to go to Vietnam, 264

***Fox*, USS CG-33)**
Cruiser visited by Lawrence as Commander Third Fleet in the early 1980s, 429

Foxgrover, Lieutenant Commander James H., USN
In the late 1950s did postgraduate work at Princeton University, 141-142
In the early 1960s served in Fighter Squadron 74 (VF-74), 191

France
World War II fighting by the U.S. 36th Infantry Division, 242-243

Franklin D. Roosevelt, USS (CVA-42)
    Deployment to the Mediterranean in early 1963, 211-227
    Based at Mayport, Florida, between deployments in the early 1960s, 234-236

Freeman, Dr. Douglas Southall
    Examples of military leadership qualities are demonstrated in his biographies of Robert E. Lee, George Washington, and Cadmus Wilcox, 33-34, 38

Fuller, Commander Robert Byron, USN (USNA, 1951)
    Vietnam prisoner of war, 1967-73, 319-310
    Post-POW sea duty, 380

Galvani, Commander Amedeo H., USN (USNA, 1943)
    In the early 1960s served as executive officer of the heavy cruiser *Newport News* (CA-148), 193

Gayler, Admiral Noel A. M., USN (USNA, 1935)
    As CinCPac, greeted released POWs when they reached the Philippines from North Vietnam in 1973, 356

Gilbert, Lieutenant Wilmer R., USN
    Pilot in Fighter Squadron 193 (VF-193) in the mid-1950s, 110

Glenn, Colonel John H. Jr., USMC (Ret.)
    Served as a test pilot at Patuxent River in the mid-1950s, 101, 154-155
    Service on the staff of the Bureau of Aeronautics in the late 1950s, 154
    Selected for the astronaut program in the late 1950s, 101, 130-131
    Served as a U.S. Senator from 1974 to 1999, 154-155

Godley, G. McMurtrie
    U.S. ambassador to the Congo, 1964-66, 249

Goldsborough, USS (DDG-20)
    Crew member killed by a freak wave in 1982 when heavy weather hit Hawaii, 529-531

Goodpaster, Lieutenant General Andrew J., USA (Ret.) (USMA, 1939)
    Served 1977-81 as superintendent of the Military Academy, 462-464, 487

Gordon, Lieutenant (junior grade) Richard F. Jr., USN
    Did flight test evaluation of the F4H Phantom II in the late 1950s, 132
    In the early 1960s, as part of Fighter Squadron 121 (VF-121), did fleet introduction training on the F4H/F-4 Phantom II, 184

Gray, General Alfred M., Jr., USMC
    Reluctant for Naval Academy graduates to serve in the Marine Corps, 457

Greene, General Wallace M. Jr., USMC (USNA, 1930)
Former Marine Commandant who was upset by James Webb's 1981 Naval Academy novel *A Sense of Honor*, 445

Griffin, Captain Charles Donald, USN (USNA, 1927)
Commanded the aircraft carrier *Oriskany* (CVA-34), 1953-54, 98, 112*

Grosvenor, Captain Alexander Graham Bell, USN (USNA, 1950)
Sailing enthusiast who commanded the Annapolis Naval Station in the late 1970s, 485-486

Gunnery-Naval
Aerial gunnery practice in Fighter Squadron 193 (VF-193) in the early 1950s, 95-96
By the heavy cruiser *Newport News* (CA-148) in the early 1960s, 198-199, 206-207

Haines, General Ralph E., USA
In the 1960s commanded the U.S. Third Army, 252

Halsey, Admiral William F., Jr., USN (USNA, 1904)
Third fleet commander in December 1944 during a typhoon that sank three ships, 528-529

Harlow, Rear Admiral David L., USN
Served in the mid-1980s as Commander Naval Military Personnel Command, 567-569

Harnish, Captain William Max, USN (USNA, 1943)
Commanded the aircraft carrier *Ranger* (CVA-61) in 1966, 283-284

Harris, Major General Richard Lee, USA (USMA, 1951)
In the mid-1960s had a short tour of duty as executive assistant to General Paul Adams, 251

Haskins, Captain Michael D., USN (USNA, 1966)
Commanded Patrol Squadron One (VP-1) in the early 1980s, 534-535

Hawaii
Pearl Harbor as Third Fleet headquarters and base in the early 1980s, 503-530
Controversy in the early 1980s over the use of Kahoolawe for Navy target practice, 525-527
A P-3 Orion crashed into a mountain on the island of Kauai in June 1983 and killed the entire crew, 534-535
Graded battle group ASW exercises at the Pacific Missile Range at Barking Sands, Hawaii, in the early 1980s, 547-548

Hawkins, Midshipman William F., USN (USNA, 1950)
Played baseball and football for the Naval Academy, late 1940s-early 1950s, 61

Hays, Admiral Ronald J., USN (USNA, 1950)
As CinCPac in 1987 recommended the relief of Admiral James Lyons as CinCPacFlt, 559

Hayward, Admiral Thomas B., USN (USNA, 1948)
As a test pilot, went through astronaut screening in the late 1950s, 130, 420
In 1978, as CNO, selected Lawrence to be superintendent of the Naval Academy, 418-420
Involvement in dealing with the Navy's drug problem while serving as CNO in the early 1980s, 426-427
In 1981, as CNO, selected Lawrence to be Commander Third Fleet, 502-503
In the early 1980s, at odds with Secretary of the Navy John Lehman, 517-518, 554, 571-572, 593

Hekman, Rear Admiral Peter M. Jr., USN (USNA, 1958)
In the early 1980s was Commander Cruiser-Destroyer Group One, 537

Hickey, Lieutenant (junior grade) Robert P., USN
In 1967 was a junior pilot in Fighter Squadron 143 (VF-143), 298-299

Hill, Vice Admiral Harry W., USN (USNA, 1911)
Served as superintendent of the Naval Academy from 1950 to 1952, 42, 45-52, 55

Hill, Rear Admiral Virgil L. Jr., USN (USNA, 1961)
Served as superintendent of the Naval Academy from 1988 to 1991, 457

Holcomb, Vice Admiral M. Staser, USN (USNA, 1953)
Served as Commander Seventh Fleet, 1981-83, 516-518
Was not promoted to a fourth star after John Lehman became Secretary of the Navy in 1981, 517-518
Retired from active duty in May 1985, sooner than expected, 570-571

Holloway, Rear Admiral James L., Jr., USN (USNA, 1919)
Served as superintendent of the Naval Academy from 1947 to 1950, 45-46

Holloway, Admiral James L. III, USN (Ret.) (USNA, 1943)
Commanded the aircraft carrier *Enterprise* (CVAN-65), 1965-67, 293
As CNO in the mid-1970s pushed the V/STOL concept, 411
Response to an investigation of a Tailhook Association in the mid-1970s, 413
Put the Naval Academy in his chain of command, 495

Holzapfel, Commander Jon D., USN USNA, 1967)
Commanded Patrol Squadron One (VP-1) in 1982-83, 534-535

Homosexuality
    Inconclusive investigation of the possibility of lesbians on the Naval Academy basketball team in the late 1970s, 473-475
    Navy policy on gays in the 1970s and 1980s, 585-586

Hong Kong, British Crown Colony
    Visited by the aircraft carrier *Oriskany* (CVA-34) in the mid-1950s, 118

Hooks, Benjamin L.
    As executive director of the NAACP, visited the Naval Academy around 1980, 14

Houser, Vice Admiral William D., USN (USNA, 1942)
    Served 1972-76 as Deputy CNO (Air Warfare), 401-409

Hudner, Lieutenant (junior grade) Thomas J. Jr., USN (USNA, 1947)
    Medal of Honor recipient who was a flight instructor in the early 1950s, 92-93

Hunter, Captain Charles B., USN (USNA, 1954)
    In 1979 was on the CinCUSNavEur staff when a Naval Academy yacht was caught in a storm in the British Isles, 437, 484-485

Hyland, Vice Admiral John J., USN (USNA, 1934)
    Commanded the aircraft carrier *Saratoga* (CVA-60), 1958-59, 166-167, 172
    Commander Seventh Fleet, 1965-67, 166

Instrument Flying
    Training and development of in the early 1950s, 89
    Pioneering jet operations by Fighter Squadron 193 (VF-193) in the early 1950s, 93, 102-111, 114, 119-123
    By the early 1960s aircraft carrier night operations were commonplace, 180, 221
    The F8U Crusader was not a good aircraft for night operations, 221
    By Fighter Squadron 143 (VF-143) off Vietnam in 1966-67, 285-285, 296

Intelligence
    Lawrence received extensive intelligence debriefings after being released from prison in North Vietnam in 1973, 362-363, 368-369

***Intrepid*, USS (CVA-11)**
    Carrier used in the late 1950s for crosswind takeoff and landing tests with the FJ-4 Fury, 135-136, 139, 148-150

Iraq
    U.S. logistics buildup in 1990-91 in Desert Shield, 259
    Desert Shield combat operations in early 1991, 506

Isaman, Captain Roy M., USN
Around 1960 served as staff operations officer for Carrier Division Six, 174

Istanbul, Turkey
Visited in 1959 by the aircraft carrier *Saratoga* (CVA-60), 166-167

Italy
Site of U.S. Army combat in 1944-45, 244
Visited in the early 1960s by the aircraft carrier *Franklin D. Roosevelt* (CVA-42), 218-219
Command headquarters for CinCSouth in the mid-1960s, 243

Jackson, Captain Gordon R., USMC (USNA, 1970)
Served as Lawrence's aide at the Naval Academy in the late 1970s, 455-456

Jacksonville, Florida, Naval Air Station
Operations in the early 1960s at Cecil Field in Jacksonville, 233-236

Japan
The aircraft carrier *Oriskany* (CVA-34) used the pinwheel maneuver at Yokosuka in the mid-1950s, 118-119

Japanese Maritime Self-Defense Force
In the early 1980s took part in RimPac exercises near Hawaii in conjunction with allied forces, 513-515

Johnson, President Lyndon B.
Directed bombing attacks against North Vietnam in the mid-1960s, 272, 282, 291, 303, 320

Joint Strategic Target Planning Staff (JSTPS)
The Navy sent several of its promising officers to the staff in the early 1960s, 215

KC-130
Tanker that Air Force Chief of Staff Curtis LeMay "flew" in the mid-1960s, 260-261

Kahoolawe, Hawaii
Controversy in the early 1980s over the island's use for Navy target practice, 525-527

Kean, Major Timothy J., USMC
Marine pilot who was killed while flight-testing the F8U-3 fighter in the late 1950s, 138-139

Keith, Captain Robert Taylor Scott Jr., USN (USNA, 1958)
In the early 1980s was chief of staff to Commander Third Fleet, 536, 544-545

Kelly, Admiral Robert J., USN (USNA, 1959)
Commanding officer when the aircraft carrier *Enterprise* (CVN-65) ran aground San Francisco in April 1983, 532-534

Kelso, Vice Admiral Frank B. II, USN (USNA, 1956)
In 1985 transferred from the SecNav staff to become Commander Sixth Fleet, 571-572

Kennedy, President John F.
Observed a naval exercise in the Atlantic in early 1962, 201-202
Assassination and funeral of in November 1963, 234-235

Key West, Florida, Naval Air Station
Loaded up with aircraft during the Cuban Missile Crisis in late 1962, 209-210
In 1963 Fighter Squadron 14 (VF-14) transitioned from the F3H Demon to the F-4 Phantom II, 195, 209-210, 226-229
In 1963 Fighter Squadron 14 (VF-14) stood hot-pad duty at Key West to protect U.S. recon flights to Cuba, 231-232

Kimmel, Captain Thomas K., USN (USNA, 1936)
Commanded the heavy cruiser *Newport News* (CA-148) in 1961-62, 193, 197-204

King, Fleet Admiral Ernest J., USN (USNA, 1901)
Leadership qualities of, 35, 39

King, Commander Jerome H. Jr., USN
Served 1959-60 as surface operations officer on the staff of Commander Carrier Division Six, 174-177

Kirk, Lieutenant Colonel Thomas H. Jr., USAF
Vietnam prisoner of war, 1967-73, 321, 330, 357

Korean War
In 1953, in the aftermath of the armistice, the aircraft carrier *Oriskany* (CVA-34) operated off Korea, 100, 115-116
Pilots recalled to active duty for the war were released after the armistice in 1953, 100

Lake, Commander Julian S., USN
In the early 1960s was commanding officer of the first fleet F4H/F-4 Phantom II squadron, Fighter Squadron 74 (VF-74), 191

Landing Signal Officers
Role in the mid-1950s during early jet night operations in straight-deck carriers, 107-111

Lawrence, Anne Williams
    Married William Lawrence in 1951 and was the mother of their three children, 53-54, 85, 87-90, 129, 181-184, 192, 194-195, 416-417, 500
    Divorced her husband while he was a prisoner of war and married another man in the early 1970s, 337, 354-358, 367-380

Lawrence, Diane Wilcox
    Physical therapy work, 383-384, 399-400, 458
    Courtship and marriage to William Lawrence, 1973-74, 381, 383-384, 387, 390-392, 413
    Role as a Navy wife, 392, 399-400, 605
    At the Naval Academy, 1978-81, 421-422, 431, 440-441, 447-449, 458, 500

Lawrence, Laurie M.
    Daughter of William and Anne Lawrence, 129, 357-358, 361, 366-367, 371, 375-378, 384-385, 499-500, 606

Lawrence, Lieutenant Commander Wendy B., USN (USNA, 1981)
    Daughter of William and Anne Lawrence, 129, 357-358, 361, 367, 374-380, 392, 400, 415-417
    As a Naval Academy midshipman, 1977-81, 415-417, 420-422, 430, 499-500

Lawrence, Vice Admiral William P., USN (USNA, 1951)
    Ancestors, 1-8, 18-19
    Parents, 3-12, 15-24, 27-28, 52, 85, 337-338, 354, 361, 366, 368-370, 373, 379, 381, 390
    Siblings, 11, 17, 20-21, 361-362
    Boyhood in Tennessee in the 1930s and 1940s, 3-29
    Naval Academy midshipman, 1947-51, 3, 7, 26, 29-86
    Brief stint as an ensign on the Naval Academy staff in 1951, 86-87
    Flight training in Florida and Texas, 1951-53, 87-95
    As a member of Fighter Squadron 193 (VF-193), 1952-55, 95-124
    From 1956 to 1959 served in various capacities at the Naval Air Test Center, 124-157
    In 1959-60 was aide to Commander Carrier Division Six, 157-181
    In 1960-61 was a pilot in Fighter Squadron 101 (VF-101), 181-190
    In 1961-62 was navigator of the heavy cruiser *Newport News* (CA-148), 183-184, 193-200
    Served 1962-64 in Fighter Squadron 14 (VF-14), 195, 209-236
    Served 1964-66 as executive assistant to Commander in Chief Strike Command, 236-269
    Flew with Fighter Squadron 143 from 1966 until he was shot down over North Vietnam in 1967, 269-307
    Held as a prisoner in North Vietnam from June 1967 until March 1973, 309-352
    As a POW composed what became the state poem of Tennessee, 329-330, 365-366

In 1973 was repatriated to the United States and dealt with a number of family issues, 353-381

In 1973-74 was a student at the National War College, 379-386

In 1974-75 commanded Light Attack Wings Pacific Fleet, 386-400

Served 1975-78 in the OP-05 organization in OpNav, 401-410

From 1978 to 1981 was superintendent of the Naval Academy, 11-12, 14, 418-501

Commanded the U.S. Third Fleet, 1981-83, 429, 502-549

Served 1983-85 as Chief of Naval Personnel, 363, 533, 538, 549-599

Nominated in 1985 to become Vice Chief of Naval Operations, 596-597

Plagued by depression from 1985 to 1989, 596-601

Post-retirement activities included writing, teaching, speaking, and work with the Association of Naval Aviation, 601-611

Lawrence, William P. Jr.
Son of William and Anne Lawrence, 129, 357-358, 361, 364, 367, 375, 377

Leave and Liberty
In the Far East during deployments in the mid-1950s by the aircraft carrier *Oriskany* (CVA-34), 118-119

In Italy in the early 1960s, 218-219

In Olongapo in the Philippines during the Vietnam War, 200-300

Lee, Captain Bobby C., USN
Served in the mid-1980s as Sixth Fleet chief of staff, 572

Lee, Vice Admiral Kent L., USN
Commanded Air Group Six on board the aircraft carrier *Enterprise* (CVAN-65) in 1962-63

Served 1973-76 as Commander Naval Air Systems Command, 406-407

Lehman, John F., Jr.
As Secretary of the Navy in the 1980s, tried to influence the Naval Academy's academic curriculum, 471

Limited contact in 1981 while Lawrence was still at the Naval Academy, 502-503

In the early 1980s, at odds with CNO Thomas Hayward, 517-518, 554, 571-572, 593

Active proponent of the battleship program in the 1980s, 538-540

Strong role in flag officer selection and slating in the 1980s, 554-561, 563-564, 570-576

Firing of various officers in the 1980s, 570-575

Role in hardware acquisition programs, 1980s, 560-563

Establishment of the material professional community for naval officers, 576-577

Reorganization of OpNav in 1985, including elimination of the Naval Material Command, 560, 577-579

Slow to commit to Navy policy on alcohol abuse in the mid-1980s, 583-584

Advocated an aggressive maritime strategy toward the Soviet Union in the 1980s, 595-596

LeMay, General Curtis E., USAF
Served 1961-65 as Chief of Staff of the Air Force, 241, 260-261

Lemoore, California, Naval Air Station
Headquarters for Commander Light Attack Wing Pacific Fleet in the mid-1970s, 388-390, 393, 399-400

Light Attack Wing Pacific Fleet
Role in administering 23 squadrons of A-7s in the mid-1970s, 386-400
Emphasis in the mid-1970s on aircraft maintenance and antiship warfare, 394-397

Long, Admiral Robert L. J., USN (USNA, 1944)
Served as Vice Chief of Naval Operations, 1977-79, 425, 454
Commander in Chief Pacific, 1979-83, 522

Los Angeles **(SSN-688)-Class Submarines**
Use of in a North Pacific exercise in 1983, 541-544

Loughlin, Rear Admiral C. Elliott, USN (Ret.) (USNA, 1933)
Served on the Naval Academy staff circa 1950, 55
In the 1970s and 1980s, ran the Naval Academy Foundation to support prep school education for potential midshipmen, 464-465

Luke, Lieutenant (junior grade) Preston, USN
Served in the early 1950s in Fighter Squadron 193 (VF-193), 96

Lyons, Admiral James A., Jr., USN (USNA, 1952)
Championed for four-star billets by Secretary of the Navy John Lehman in the mid-1980s, 557-559
Relieved as Commander in Chief Pacific Fleet in September 1987, 559

MacArthur, Brigadier General Douglas, USA (USMA, 1903)
As superintendent of the Military Academy established honor code in the 1920s, 43

MacDill Air Force Base, Tampa, Florida
In the 1960s housed the headquarters of U.S. Strike Command, 236, 252-253, 259-260, 268

Mandeville, Lieutenant Robert C. Jr., USNA, 1950)
In the late 1950s did postgraduate work at Princeton University, 141-142

Marine Corps, U.S.
Often-tenuous relationship between the Corps and the Naval Academy, 455-457

Martin, Vice Admiral Edward H., USN (USNA, 1954)
In 1985 transferred from Commander Sixth Fleet to become OP-05, 571-572

Martin-Baker Ejection Seat
Tested in 1957 in an F9F-8T trainer at Patuxent River Naval Air Station, 151-152

Massey, Rear Admiral Forsyth, USN (USNA, 1931)
In 1964 became chief of staff to General Paul Adams, Commander in Chief, U.S. Strike Command, 238-239, 258

Mastin, First Lieutenant Ronald L., USAF
Vietnam prisoner of war, 1967-73, 318

Mathis, Rear Admiral William W., USN
In the early 1980s did Tomahawk development work on the Third Fleet staff, 545

Mauz, Vice Admiral Henry H. Jr., USN (USNA, 1959)
Delayed getting to a new billet in 1985 because of a hold-up in his orders, 557-558

Mayport, Florida, Naval Station
Homeport circa 1960 for the aircraft carrier *Saratoga* (CVA-60), 169, 174-175

McCain, Commander John S. III, USN (USNA, 1958)
Vietnam prisoner of war, 1967-73, 330, 333, 345
In 1973 served as matchmaker for Lawrence and his second wife, 383-384

McCorkle, Captain Francis D., USN (USNA, 1926)
Headed the Naval Academy department of seamanship and navigation circa 1950, 65-67

McDaniel, Captain Eugene B., USN
Vietnam War prisoner from 1967 to 1973, believed not all POWs were returned when the war ended, 364-365

McDonald, Admiral David L., USN (USNA, 1928)
In the 1960s served as Commander Carrier Division Six, CinCUSNavEur, and CNO, 241-242

McDonnell, James S.
Headed the McDonnell Aircraft Corporation for many years, 132-133

McKee, Admiral Kinnaird R., USN (USNA, 1951)
Was superintendent of the Naval Academy when women first entered in 1976, 416-421
Changes to the Naval Academy curriculum, 466
Served 1978-79 as Commander Third Fleet, 420

In 1982 replaced Admiral Hyman Rickover as head of the nuclear power program, 580-582

McKeldin, Theodore R.
Around 1950 attended a Naval Academy pep rally with his wife, who was hit in the head with toilet paper, 50

McKellar, Captain Edwin D. Jr., USN
In the mid 1970s commanded Naval Air Station Alameda, 396

McKellar, Kenneth D.
U.S. Senator who got Lawrence an appointment to the Naval Academy in 1947, 17

McNamara, Robert S.
In the early 1960s established the U.S. Strike Command as a joint rapid-reaction conventional force, 236-238, 241, 245

McNitt, Rear Admiral Robert W., USN (Ret.) (USNA, 1938)
Naval Academy dean of admissions from 1972 to 1985, 464, 486

Medical Problems
Lawrence had appendicitis in his plebe year at the Naval Academy, 1947-48, 61-62
Lawrence's heart murmur showed up in astronaut screening in the late 1950s but did not prevent him from flying airplanes, 130-131, 144-146, 267-269
Lawrence caught a case of dysentery during a trip to Africa in 1964, 252-253
Problems discovered in Lawrence's health after he was released from prison in 1973, 358-359, 365, 368
Navy medical problems, including malpractice, in the mid-1980s, 586-590
Lawrence was plagued by depression from 1985 to 1989, 596-601

Memphis, Tennessee, Naval Hospital
Provided care to Lawrence after he was released as a prisoner of war in 1973, 361-365, 378-379

***Midway* (CV-41)-Class Aircraft Carriers**
Limitations in comparison with later classes, 76-78, 217-218, 221

Middle East, Africa South of the Sahara, and Southern Asia (MEAFSA)
Unified joint U.S. command created in the early 1960s, 238, 241-243
Involvement in the Congo in the mid-1960s, 247
The U.S. Middle East Force came under this command in the mid-1960s, 254
Took part in the Central Treaty Organization created in 1955, 259-260

Middle East Force, U.S.
In the mid-1960s came under the U.S. unified Middle East, Africa South of the Sahara, and Southern Asia (MEAFSA), 254

Military Academy, West Point, New York
Attempted to recruit Lawrence in the late 1940s, 16
Over the years has had a much more stringent honor code than that of the Naval Academy, 43-45, 462-463
Makeup of the faculty in the late 1970s-early 1980s, 467-468
Scheduling of Army-Navy football games in the late 1970s-early 1980s, 463-464, 487-488

Miller, Edgar E. "Rip"
As assistant athletic director and assistant football coach for the Naval Academy in the late 1940s, 16, 63-64, 490

Miller, Lieutenant Colonel Edison W., USMC
Vietnam prisoner of war, 1967-73, censured for collaboration, 323, 326, 340-341

Miller, Admiral Paul David, USN
Served 1981-86 as executive assistant to Secretary of the Navy John Lehman, 558-560, 575-576
Selection for flag rank in 1984 essentially directed by the Secretary of the Navy, 556
Success as a flag officer, 560

Miramar Naval Air Station, San Diego, California
In the early 1960s was the site of fleet introduction training for the F4H/F-4 Phantom II, 182-190
Fighter Squadron 143 (VF-143) stand-down at Miramar between 1966 and 1967 Vietnam deployments, 281-283, 289-290
In 1985 three top officials were fired over the high cost of spare parts, 573-574
Site of drug rehab facility, 582

Missiles
Sidewinder was used in the 1960s by the F4H/F-4 Phantom II, 187-188
North Vietnamese surface-to-air missiles fired against U.S. aircraft in 1966-67, 273-274, 277, 300
In the early 1980s the Third Fleet developed tactical doctrine for the use of the Tomahawk cruise missile, 504-509
Controversial arrival of the first Trident missile submarine, USS *Ohio* (SSBN-726) at Seattle in August 1982, 523-524

***Missouri*, USS (BB-63)**
Grounding near Norfolk in January 1950, 80-84
Midshipman summer training cruise in 1950 before being sent to Korea, 80-83

Mitchell, Lieutenant (junior grade) John Robert Cummings, USN (USNA, 1952)
Served in Fighter Squadron 193 (VF-193) in the mid-1950s, 96, 105, 109-110

Moffett Field Naval Air Station, Sunnyvale, California
Site of night jet development work in the mid 1950s by VC-3, 106
Base for Fighter Squadron 193 (VF-193) in the mid-1950s, 114-115

Moore, Lieutenant General William G. Jr., USAF
Greeted released POWs when they reached the Philippines from North Vietnam in 1973, 356

Moorer, Lieutenant Commander Joseph P., USN (USNA, 1945)
In the late 1950s was operations officer for the Test Pilot School at Patuxent River, 152-153, 157

Moorer, Admiral Thomas H., USN (Ret.) (USNA, 1933)
Personality and leadership qualities of, 35-36, 156, 160-161, 163-164, 168-170
Served 1959-60 as Commander Carrier Division Six, 153, 157-171, 175-176, 178, 181
Served 1965-67 as SACLant/CinCLant, 240-242, 254-256
In 1973 visited Tennessee to honor his former aide, Lawrence, 365
As Chairman of the Joint Chiefs in the early 1970s, facilitated returned prisoners of war getting back on career tracks, 377

Mountbatten, Admiral of the Fleet, Lord Louis, Royal Navy
Served 1959-65 as Britain's Chief of Defence Staff, 262

Mulloy, Rear Admiral Paul J., USN
Headed the Navy's anti-drug program in the mid-1980s, 582-583

Nance, Commander James W., USN (USNA, 1945)
In the early 1960s was air operations officer in the aircraft carrier *Franklin D. Roosevelt* (CVA-42), 221

Naples, Italy
Visited in the early 1960s by the aircraft carrier *Franklin D. Roosevelt* (CVA-42), 218-219
Command headquarters for CinCSouth in the mid-1960s, 243

National Aeronautics and Space Administration (NASA)
In the late 1950s selected the first group of astronauts from among test pilots, 101, 120, 130-131, 142-144

National War College, Washington, D.C.
Lawrence's study there in 1973-74 after his return from POW camp, 382-385

NATOPS (Naval Air Training and Operations Procedures System)
Value over the years in improving naval aviation safety, 96, 267

Naval Academy, Annapolis, Maryland
    Plebe year, 1947-48, 29
    Social life for midshipmen, 1947-51, 30, 62-63
    Academics, 1947-51, 28, 30-32, 39-40, 52-53, 55-56, 67-69
    End of the "dope system" and development of the honor concept and honor boards in the early 1950s, 39-48, 52, 86-87
    Midshipman privileges in the late 1940s-early 1950s, 45-46
    Athletics as part of the overall program in the late 1940s-early 1950s, 22-23, 51, 56-64, 69-77, 80-81
    Parades circa 1950, 51-52
    Role of the brigade staff in the late 1940s-early 1950s, 51, 57-58, 69
    Faculty members and Bancroft Hall staff, late 1940s-early 1950s, 53-55, 65-71
    Social life for midshipmen in the late 1940s-early 1950s, 56-57
    Black midshipmen, late 1940s-early 1950s, 74-75
    Summer training cruises, 1948-50, 75-84
    June Week, 1951, 85-86
    Comparison in the early 1960s of officers from the Naval Academy and other commissioning sources, 221-224
    Naval Academy graduates as strong leaders in North Vietnam prison camps, 333, 349
    Women as midshipmen in the late 1970s-early 1980s, 11-12, 415-417, 420-422, 427-433, 437-444, 459, 488-489
    Weekend dates accommodated in the superintendent's house, 431-432
    Sports in the late 1970s-early 1980s, 11-12, 71-72, 433-435. 484-490
    The Naval Academy sailing yacht *Alliance* was caught in a storm in the British Isles in 1979, 436-437
    Matured version of the honor concept by the late 1970s differed from the honor codes of the Military and Air Force Academies, 461-462
    Chapel services and chaplains in the late 1970s-early 1980s, 421-424
    Black midshipmen in the late 1970s-early 1980s self-segregated, 423, 459-460
    Successful football teams in the late 1970s-early 1980s, 433-435, 486-487
    James Webb's writings about the Naval Academy, 1979-81, 442-446
    Access to the superintendents' quarters, 447-449
    Reduction in midshipman and junior officer attrition, late 1970s-early 1980s, 449-451
    Controversy in 1980 concerning selection of midshipmen for the nuclear power program, 451-455
    Often-tenuous relationship between the Marine Corps and the Naval Academy, 455-457
    Admissions and appointment practices, late 1970s-early 1980s, 463-464
    Academics in the late 1970s-early 1980s, 466-472
    Disciplinary issues, late 1970s-early 1980s, 472-477
    Lawrence's concern about underage midshipman drinking at the Naval Academy in the late 1970s-early 1980s, 475-476
    Preservation and updating of the physical plant in the late 1970s-early 1980s, 479-483, 491

Razing of Isherwood Hall to make room for the brigade activities center, 481-483, 491
Sailing program, late 1970s-early 1980s, 484-486
Role of the Naval Academy Alumni Association, late 1970s-early 1980s, 490-492
Formal parades, late 1970s-early 1980s, 495-497
Energy-saving steps circa 1980, 497-498
Low-key observance of the academy's 135th anniversary in 1980, 500-501
Midshipman Gwen Dreyer chained to a urinal in 1989, 426, 606-609
Lawrence's interaction with midshipmen, late 1980s-early 1990s, 601-605
Electrical engineering department chairman fired in 1990 for not raising midshipman grades, 610-611

Naval Academy Preparatory School, Newport, Rhode Island
Provides additional educational background and training for potential midshipmen, 465

Naval Air Systems Command
Role in naval aviation in the mid-1970s, 404-407

Naval Air Test Center, Patuxent River, Maryland
Curriculum and procedures in Test Pilot School in 1956-57, 124-130
Flight test work in the late 1950s, principally competition between the F4H and the F8U-3 fighter planes, 131-147

Naval Flight Officers
The F3D Skyknight was used in the early 1960s to train naval flight officers as radar intercept officers for the F4H/F-4 Phantom II, 182-183, 186-187
In the early 1960s the F-4 went into service with a two-man crew, a pilot and a radar intercept officer, 229-230

Naval Investigative Service
Investigated drug use at the Naval Academy in the late 1970s-early 1980s, 424-426
Inconclusive investigation of the possibility of lesbians on the Naval Academy basketball team in the late 1970s, 473-475

Naval Military Personnel Command (NMPC)
Emphasis in the mid-1980s on contact between junior officers and detailers, 550-552
Flag officer detailing in the mid-1980s, 552-560
Functions in the 1980s vis-à-vis OP-01, 564-569
Challenges in the 1980s in detailing married couples, 585

Naval Material Command
Disestablished in 1985, 577-578

Naval Ordnance Test Station, Inyokern, California
Site of weapons training in the mid-1950s for Fighter Squadron 193 (VF-193), 106

Naval Reserve, U.S.
Pilots recalled to active duty for the Korean War were released after the armistice in 1953, 100
Administration of in the mid-1980s, 588

Naval Reserve Officers Training Corps (NROTC)
Comparison in the early 1960s of officers from NROTC and other commissioning sources, 221-224

Navigation
Grounding of the battleship *Missouri* (BB-63) near Norfolk in January 1950, 80-84
Problem on board the aircraft carrier *Saratoga* (CVA-60) circa 1960, 174-175
On board the heavy cruiser *Newport News* (CA-148) in the early 1960s, 84, 183-184, 193-194, 199-200, 203
Radar navigation by F-4 Phantoms in Vietnam in 1966, 280-281
Problems involving the battleship *New Jersey* (BB-62) in 1983, 536-537

***New Jersey*, USS (BB-62)**
Deployment in 1983-84 took her to the Pacific, Central America, and the Mediterranean, 536-540
Navigation problems in 1983, 536-537
Enlisted crew in 1983, 539-540

***Newport News*, USS (CA-148)**
Navigation of in the early 1960s, 84, 183-184, 193-194, 199-200, 203
Operations in the Atlantic in the early 1960s, 193-199, 201-202
Gunnery, 198-199, 206-207
Deployment to the Mediterranean in 1961, 194, 199-201, 203
Participation in a fleet exercise for President John Kennedy in early 1962, 201-202
As Second Fleet flagship in early 1962, 200-202, 206-207
Enlisted crewmen in the early 1960s, 205-206

News Media
In the mid-1970s the media in San Francisco criticized the ability of the aircraft carrier *Coral Sea* (CVA-43) to perform her mission, 395-397
Lawrence's policy of notifying the news media of unfavorable information about the Naval Academy when he was superintendent, 1978-81, 426, 428-433, 460-461, 477-478, 606-608, 611
In the early 1980s Japanese officials wanted Lawrence to present a distorted version of the truth in contacts with the media, 513-515
Coverage of the controversial arrival of the first Trident missile submarine, USS *Ohio* (SSBN-726) at Seattle in August 1982, 523-524
Honolulu coverage of the Kahoolawe controversy in the early 1980s, 526-527
Coverage of a 1989 incident in which a midshipman was chained to a urinal, 606-609

Night Flying
    Pioneering jet operations by Fighter Squadron 193 (VF-193) in the early 1950s, 93, 102-111, 114, 119-123
    By the early 1960s aircraft carrier night operations were commonplace, 180, 221
    The F8U Crusader was not a good aircraft for night operations, 221
    By Fighter Squadron 143 (VF-143) off Vietnam in 1966-67, 285-285, 296

Nimitz, Fleet Admiral Chester W., USN (USNA, 1905)
    Issued a noteworthy letter in 1945 after Third Fleet ships were lost in a typhoon, 528-529

Norfolk Naval Shipyard, Portsmouth, Virginia
    In early 1962 upgraded the flagship capability of the heavy cruiser *Newport News* (CA-148), 200

North Atlantic Treaty Organization (NATO)
    International members of the standing group military committee observed an exercise off North Carolina in 1959, 158-159
    North Atlantic naval exercise in 1960, 161-162, 165-166

Nuclear Power Program
    Controversy in 1980 concerning selection of Naval Academy midshipmen for the program, 451-455
    Efforts in the 1980s to put the nuclear surface ship crews on par with submariners, 580-581
    In 1982 Admiral Kinnaird McKee replaced Admiral Hyman Rickover as head of the program, 580-582

Nuclear Weapons
    Weapons delivery training in the mid-1950s by Fighter Squadron 193 (VF-193), 103-105
    Planning in the late 1950s for possible use, 167-168
    Sixth Fleet exercises in the Mediterranean in the early 1960s, 179. 214
    Controversial arrival of the first Trident missile submarine, USS *Ohio* (SSBN-726) at Seattle in August 1982, 523-524

Oceana Naval Air Station, Virginia Beach, Virginia
    In the early 1960s was the base for Fighter Squadron 101 (VF-101), 181-184, 233

O'Hara, Captain Jack F., USN
    Commanded the Lemoore Naval Air Station in the mid-1970s, 393-394

***Ohio*, USS (SSBN-726)**
    Controversial arrival of the first Trident submarine at Seattle in August 1982, 523-524
    Command arrangement during Pacific patrols, 531-532

Olongapo, Philippine Islands
  Liberty site for Navy men during the Vietnam War, 299-300

OP-05
  Management of various naval aviation programs in the mid-1970s, 401-415

***Oriskany*, USS (CVA-34)**
  Deployment to the Western Pacific in 1953-54, 97-102, 112-116
  Deployment to the Western Pacific in 1955, 116-117
  Early work in jet carrier operations in the mid-1950s, 93, 102-111, 114, 119-123

O'Rourke, Commander Gerald G., USN (USNA, 1945)
  In the early 1960s commanded Fighter Squadron 101 (VF-101) Detachment Alfa that did fleet introduction training for the F4H/F-4 Phantom, 182-183, 189-191
  In the early 1960s commanded Fighter Squadron 102 (VF-102) in the aircraft carrier *Enterprise* (CVAN-65)

Ortland, Henry Jr.
  Naval Academy swimming coach, 1919-50, 73-74

P-3 Orion
  Plane from Patrol Squadron One (VP-1) crashed into a mountain in Hawaii in June 1983 and killed the entire crew, 534-535
  Limited P-3 contact with Soviet submarines in the Pacific in the early 1980s, 548-549
  Addition of women to P-3 squadrons in the 1980s, 591

Paisley, Melvyn R.
  Role in hardware acquisition programs during his tenure in the 1980s as Assistant Secretary of the Navy, 560-562, 576

Palmer, Commander Frederick F., USN
  Commanded Carrier Air Wing 14 (CVW-14) in 1966 during bombing attacks against North Vietnam, 284

Palmer, Captain Leslie N., USN (USNA, 1959)
  Commanded the guided missile cruiser *Fox* (CG-33), 1980-82, 429

Patrol Squadron One (VP-1)
  A P-3 Orion crashed into a mountain in Hawaii in June 1983 and killed the entire crew, 534-535

Patuxent River, Maryland, Naval Air Station
  Flight test work in the late 1950s, principally competition between the F4H and the F8U-3 fighter planes, 131-147

Pearl Harbor, Hawaii
As Third Fleet headquarters and base in the early 1980s, 503-530

Pensacola, Florida, Naval Air Station
Site of flight training in the early 1950s, 87-90

Perot, H. Ross, USN (USNA, 1953)
As president of the Naval Academy class of 1953, had a role in the honor concept development, 43, 47
Believed not all U.S. POWs were returned when the Vietnam War ended in 1973, 364-365
Monetary donations to the Naval Academy in the late 1970s-early 1980s, 491-492
Provided support in the 1980s as Lawrence recovered from depression, 597-600

Persian Gulf War
U.S. logistics buildup in 1990-91 in Desert Shield, 259

Petersen, Vice Admiral Forrest S., USN (USNA, 1945)
Served in the 1970s as OP-05 and Commander Naval Air Systems Command, 409-410

Philippine Islands
Subic Bay was a support base during the U.S war in Vietnam in the mid-1960s, 292, 294-299-300
Clark Air Force Base was a stopover point for released POWs en route from North Vietnam to the United States in 1973, 356-360

Pirie, Captain Robert B., USN (USNA, 1926)
Served from 1949 to 1952 as the Naval Academy's commandant of midshipmen, 45-52, 86
Commander Second Fleet, 1957-58, 50

Princeton University, Princeton, New Jersey
In the late 1950s had naval officers as postgraduate students in aeronautical engineering, 141-142

Prisoners of War
U.S. servicemen held in North Vietnam, 1964-73, 263, 309-352
Application of the Code of Conduct to Vietnam prisoners, 310-311, 341-342, 350-351
Interrogation and torture of prisoners, 311-317, 325-328, 340
Communication among prisoners, 316-328, 332-334, 368-369
Naval Academy graduates as strong leaders in prison camp, 333, 349
Escape attempts, 342-343
Release of prisoners from North Vietnam in 1973 and their return to the United States, 353-370

In the early 1970s Navy leadership helped returned POWs get back on career tracks, 377

Profilet, Commander Leo T., USN
Commanded Attack Squadron 196 (VA-196) until he ejected from his A-6 Intruder when it was hit over North Vietnam on 21 August 1967, 292-293

Promotion of Officers
Secretary of the Navy John Lehman's impact on during the 1980s, 555-560

Proxmire, William
Senator who investigated Navy transportation to a Tailhook Association convention in the mid-1970s, 411-413

Public Relations
Lawrence did extensive speechmaking in the United States in 1973 after being released as a prisoner of war, 364-366, 369, 380-381
Lawrence's policy of notifying the news media of unfavorable information about the Naval Academy when he was superintendent, 1978-81, 426, 428-433, 460-461, 477-478, 606-608, 611
Naval Academy formal parades, late 1970s-early 1980s, 495-497
Lawrence was able to elicit favorable Honolulu newspaper coverage of the Kahoolawe controversy in the early 1980s, 526-527

Racial Issues
Bitterness between the black and white races over the years, 14-15
Black citizens in the South in the 1930s and 1940s, 10-13
Racial problems in the Navy in the early 1970s, 393-394
Black midshipmen at the Naval Academy in the late 1970s-early 1980s self-segregated, 423, 459-461

Radar
The F3D Skyknight was used in the early 1960s to train naval flight officers as radar intercept officers for the F4H/F-4 Phantom II, 182-183, 186-187
Use of by F-4 Phantoms in Vietnam in 1966, 280-281

Ramage, Commander James D., USN (USNA, 1939)
Commanded Carrier Air Group 19 in the early 1950s, 98-100

Ramsey, Henry C.
Foreign Service Officer who served in the mid-1960s as political advisor to Commander in Chief U.S. Strike Command, 246-247

Ranger, USS (CVA-61)
Deployment to the Western Pacific and bombing of North Vietnam in 1965-66, 270-287

Enlisted men on board in 1966, 286-287
Deployment to Central America in 1983, 538-539
Abuse of brig prisoners in the 1980s, 590

Reagan, President Ronald W.
Brought a different approach on national defense and other issues when he took office in 1981, 482

Rees, Vice Admiral William L., USN (USNA, 1921)
Served 1956-60 as Commander Naval Air Force Atlantic Fleet, 169-170

Religion
In the Lawrence family in Tennessee in the 1930s and 1940s, 18
For U.S. prisoners of war in Vietnam, 344-345
As factor in Lawrence's divorce and his first wife's remarriage, 371-376
Naval Academy chapel services in the late 1970s-early 1980s, 421-423

Renneman, Midshipman Robert A., USN (USNA, 1951)
Played football for the Naval Academy, circa 1950, 56-57, 71

Replenishment at Sea
Organization of in the Sixth Fleet circa 1960, 177-178
By the heavy cruiser *Newport News* (CA-148) in the early 1960s, 196-197

Repp, Lieutenant Frank J., USNR
Pilot in Fighter Squadron 193 (VF-193) in the mid-1950s, 110

Rhodes Scholarships
Lawrence emphasized Naval Academy midshipmen seeking scholarships when he was superintendent, 1978-81, 470-471

Rickover, Admiral Hyman G., USN (Ret.) (USNA, 1922)
Personality of, 17
Relationship with midshipmen in the 1970s-80s as accessions to the Navy nuclear power program, 419, 451-455, 470-471, 494
Replaced as head of the nuclear power program in 1982, 580-582

RimPac, Exercise
In the early 1980s allied navies conducted RimPac exercises, 513-515

Risner, Lieutenant Colonel James B., USAF
Strong leader as Vietnam prisoner of war, 1965-73, 344, 349

Rockets
In the late 1950s the FJ-4 Fury was tested with an add-on rocket engine, 135-136, 139, 148-150

Rodger, Lieutenant Thomas W., USN
Served in 1967 in Fighter Squadron 143 (VF-143), present when Lawrence was shot down, 305-307

Rogers, Captain Thomas S. Jr., USN (USNA, 1950)
Commanded the aircraft carrier *Coral Sea* (CVA-43), 1973-75, 396

Romano, Lieutenant John A., USNR
Flew an F2H-2P photo plane during an early 1950s Western Pacific deployment by the aircraft carrier *Oriskany* (CVA-34), 97

Rowden, Vice Admiral William H., USN (USNA, 1952)
Had difficulty getting a suitable flag assignment in the 1980s, 555

Royal Air Force
Demonstrated a Martin-Baker ejection seat in 1957 in an F9F-8T trainer at Patuxent River Naval Air Station, 151-152

Royal Navy
Participated in a NATO naval exercise circa 1960, 161-165

Rules of Engagement
In 1963 Fighter Squadron 14 (VF-14) stood hot-pad duty at Key West to protect U.S. recon flights to Cuba but had limited options, 231-232

Russell, Admiral James S., USN (USNA, 1926)
As CinCSouth in 1964 hosted a visit by General Paul D. Adams, 243

S-3 Viking
Fleet introduction in the mid-1970s, 405-406

SNJ Texan
Aircraft used for Navy flight training in the early 1950s, 88-90, 93-94

Safety
Naval aviation was unsafe in many ways in the 1950s, often because of poor pilot proficiency, 96-97, 151
Value of NATOPS, 96

Sagerholm, Midshipman James A., USN (USNA, 1952)
Role in the development of the Naval Academy honor concept in the early 1950s, 40-43, 47

Sailing
The Naval Academy sailing yacht *Alliance* was caught in a bad storm in the British Isles in 1979, 436-437, 484-485

Naval Academy sailing program, late 1970s-early 1980s, 484-486

San Francisco, California
The aircraft carrier *Enterprise* (CVAN-65) ran aground San Francisco in April 1983, 532-534

Santoro, Dr. Ralph P.
Naval Academy department chairman fired in 1990 for not raising midshipman grades, 610-611

***Saratoga*, USS (CVA-60)**
As flagship circa 1960 for Commander Carrier Division Six, 161, 165-175
Overhaul period in early 1960 at the New York Naval Shipyard, 161, 169
Collision in May 1960 with a German merchant ship, 169-172

Saudi Arabia
Primitive conditions in the country in 1964, 248

Sauer, George H.
Head football coach of the Naval Academy, 1948-49, 60, 71-72, 76

Sawyer, George
As Assistant Secretary of the Navy for Shipbuilding in the 1980s, 555, 562

Schacht, Commander Kenneth G., USN (USNA, 1935)
Served on the Naval Academy staff circa 1950, 53-54

Schoultz, Vice Admiral Robert F., USN
In 1985 transferred from OP-05 to Deputy CinCUSNavEur, 571, 574-575

Seashore, Edith Whitfield
Served as a consultant to the Naval Academy when women first entered as midshipmen in the 1970s, 438

Seattle, Washington
Controversial arrival of the first Trident missile submarine, USS *Ohio* (SSBN-726) at Seattle in August 1982, 523-524

***Seawolf* (SSN-21)-Class Submarines**
High cost for ships of the class, which entered the fleet in the late 1990s, 562

Second Fleet, U.S.
Heavy cruiser *Newport News* (CA-148) as fleet flagship in early 1962, 200-202, 206-207

Seiberlich, Rear Admiral Carl J., USN
    In the mid-1970s served as OP-05B, 411-412

Selassie, Haile
    Ethiopian Emperor visited by U.S. CinC MEAFSA in 1964, 249

Selection Boards
    Secretary of the Navy John Lehman's impact on during the 1980s, 555-560, 563-564, 575-576
    Congress passed a law in the mid-1980s to limit the ability of the Secretary of the Navy to intervene in selection boards, 576

Seventh Fleet, U.S.
    Deployment by the aircraft carrier *Ranger* (CVA-61) to the Western Pacific and bombing of North Vietnam in 1965-66, 270-287
    Detachment in Saigon approved news releases on fleet activities in the Vietnam War, 277
    Relationship with the U.S. Third Fleet in the early 1980s, 516-518

***Shangri-La*, USS (CVA-38)**
    As flagship circa 1960 for Commander Carrier Division Six, 166

Shapiro, Dr. Robert H.
    In 1990, as the Naval Academy's academic dean, fired a department chairman for not raising midshipmen's grades, 610-611

Shelton, Rear Admiral Doniphan B., USN (USNA, 1945)
    Greeted Lawrence in 1973 when he was in the Philippines after being released from prison in Vietnam, 359

Shepard, Commander Alan B., USN (USNA, 1945)
    Skill as an aviator, 80, 120
    As a member of Fighter Squadron 193 (VF-193) in the early 1950s, 93, 96, 99-101, 104-105, 111-113, 119-120
    Served as a test pilot in the mid- and late 1950s, 101, 124, 136-138
    Selected for the astronaut program in the late 1950s, 101, 130-131

Ship Handling
    In the aircraft carrier *Oriskany* (CVA-34) in the mid-1950s, 112-113, 118-119
    In the heavy cruiser *Newport News* (CA-148) in the early 1960s, 196-198

Shumaker, Lieutenant Commander Robert H., USN (USNA, 1956)
    Strong leader as Vietnam prisoner of war, 1965-73, 333, 349

Shuman, Captain Edwin Arthur III, USN (USNA, 1954)
    Sailing enthusiast who commanded the Annapolis Naval Station, 1978-82, 484-486

Sidewinder Missile
Used in the 1960s by the F4H/F-4 Phantom II, 187-188

Sieglaff, Rear Admiral William Bernard, USN (USNA, 1931)
In the early 1960s commanded Cruiser Division Two, 200

Sijan, First Lieutenant Lane P., USAF
Vietnam prisoner of war, 1967-68, awarded posthumous Medal of Honor, 324-325, 351

Sinclair, Midshipman Alexander M., USN (USN, 1951)
Played junior varsity football at the Naval Academy circa 1950, 66

Sixth Fleet, U.S.
The aircraft carrier *Coral Sea* CVB-43) made a summer training cruise to the Mediterranean in 1948, 76-78
Deployments in 1962-63 by the aircraft carriers *Franklin D. Roosevelt* (CVA-42) and *Enterprise* (CVAN-65), 211-227

Small, Admiral William N., USN (USNA, 1948)
Retired from active duty in August 1985, sooner than expected, 570-571

Smedberg, Vice Admiral William R. III, USN (USNA, 1926)
Served 1960 to 1964 as Chief of the Bureau of Naval Personnel, 236-239, 242

Smith, Lieutenant (junior grade) Gordon H., USN
Served as a flight instructor in the early 1950s, 92

Smith, Admiral Harold Page, USN (Ret.) (USNA, 1924)
Commanded the battleship *Missouri* (BB-63) briefly in 1950 after her grounding, 81
As SACLant/CinCLant in the early 1960s objected to the creation of the joint U.S. Strike Command, 238-241, 254

Smith, Captain John Victor, USN (USNA, 1934)
Commanded the heavy cruiser *Newport News* (CA-148), 1959-60, 197

Snyder, Augustus Kent "Doc"
Served as athletic trainer for the Naval Academy baseball and basketball teams, circa 1950, 61-62

Solomon, Commander Jerome E. Jr., USN (USNA, 1950)
Best man at Lawrence's second wedding, in 1974, 392

Son Tay, North Vietnam
Site of U.S. raid in 1970 in an attempt to rescue prisoners of war, 343-344

South, Captain Thomas W. II, USN (USNA, 1934)
   In 1958-59 commanded the aircraft carrier *Essex* (CVA-9) and then became chief of staff to Commander Carrier Division Six, 161

Soviet Navy
   Minimal naval presence in the Mediterranean in the early 1960s, 179, 205, 224-225
   U.S. Navy concern about being over-flown in the early 1960s by Soviet bombers, 224-227
   Limited reaction in 1982-83 when the Third Fleet conducted exercises in the Northern Pacific, 509-512, 519-520
   Response to the deployment of the first Trident submarine, USS *Ohio* (SSBN-726), in the Pacific in the summer of 1982, 523-525
   Limited P-3 contact with Soviet submarines in the Pacific in the early 1980s, 548-549
   Secretary of the Navy John Lehman advocated an aggressive maritime strategy toward the Soviet Union in the 1980s, 595-596

Soviet Union
   In 1982-83 the Third Fleet conducted exercises in the Northern Pacific, near the Soviet Union, 509-513, 519-520

Space and Naval Warfare Systems Command
   Established in 1985 without much planning, 577-579

Stahlman, Captain James G., USNR
   Nashville newspaper publisher who helped Lawrence get an appointment to the Naval Academy in 1947, 17

Stockdale, Captain James B., USN (USNA, 1947)
   Strong leader as a prisoner of war in North Vietnam, 1965-73, 314-315, 317-319, 322, 326-327, 333, 348-349, 387
   Released from captivity in 1973, 359
   Wrote a revealing memoir with his wife, 368-369

Storrs, Captain Aaron P. III, USN (USNA, 1923)
   Commanded the aircraft carrier *Coral Sea* (CVB-43) in 1947-48, 77

Strategy
   Secretary of the Navy John Lehman advocated an aggressive maritime strategy toward the Soviet Union in the 1980s, 595-596

Stratton, Captain Richard A., USN
   Former Vietnam War POW who served as the Naval Academy's director of operations, circa 1980, 436-437

Strike Command, U.S.
Established in the early 1960s by Secretary of Defense Robert McNamara as a joint rapid-reaction force, 236-241
Command relationship difficulties between the joint command and the Navy, 238-241, 253-254
Conducted exercises in the mid-1960s, 254-255

Subic Bay, Philippines
Support base during the U.S war in Vietnam in the mid-1960s, 292, 294-299-300

Submarine Warfare
Use of *Los Angeles* (SSN-688)-class submarines in a North Pacific exercise in 1983, 541-544

Survival, Evasion, Resistance, and Escape (SERE)
Training at Warner Springs, California, in 1966, 309-310

Swimming
At the Naval Academy in the late 1940s-early 1950s, 73-74

T-28 Trojan
Propeller-driven trainer that Lawrence flew on a trip from Patuxent to Princeton in 1959, 142-144

T-33 Shooting Star
Air Force trainer that Lawrence used for proficiency flying in the mid-1960s, 260

Tu-95 Bear (Soviet Bomber)
U.S. Navy concern about being over-flown in the early 1960s by Soviet bombers, 224-226

TV-1 Seastar
Used for jet training in the early 1950s, 91

Tachen Islands
The aircraft carrier *Oriskany* (CVA-34) provided support during the evacuation of these islands in early 1955, 117

Tailhook Association
Investigation of transportation to a convention in the mid-1970s, 411-413
Relationship in the 1990s to the Association of Naval Aviation, 413-414

Talley, Commander George C. Jr., USN (USNA, 1944)
In the early 1960s served on the Joint Strategic Target Planning Staff, 215-216
In the early 1960s commanded Carrier Air Group One on board the aircraft carriers *Enterprise* (CVAN-65) and *Franklin D. Roosevelt* (CVA-42), 212-215

Greeted Lawrence in Hawaii in 1973 after his release as a POW, 360

Tallman, Lieutenant General Kenneth L., USAF (USMA, 1946)
Served as superintendent of the Air Force Academy, 1977-81, 462-463

Taylor, Lieutenant (junior grade) Frank Lee, USN
Served in the early 1960s as avionics officer in Fighter Squadron 14 (VF-14), 213

Taylor, Vice Admiral John McNay, USN (USNA, 1926)
Commanded the U.S. Second Fleet, 1861-62, 202-203, 206-207

Taylor, General Maxwell D., USA (USMA, 1922)
Served in the 1960s as Chairman of the Joint Chiefs of Staff and ambassador to South Vietnam, 241, 245, 255, 261-262

Test Pilots
Curriculum and procedures in Test Pilot School in 1956-57, 124-130
Testing and evaluation of new aircraft in the late 1950s, 130-147

Test Pilot School
Curriculum and procedures in 1956-57, 124-130
Lawrence as an instructor in 1959, 152-156

Thach, Captain John S., USN (USNA, 1927)
Fighter pilot who developed the Thach Weave tactic, 94-95

Thayer, W. Paul
In 1983, as Deputy Secretary of Defense, spoke at the Third Fleet change of command, 549

Third Fleet, U.S.
Dealt with disastrous typhoons in 1944-45, 528
Lawrence's learning curve in 1981, prior to taking command, 503-504
In the early 1980s had antisubmarine warfare as one of its missions, 504, 518-519
In the early 1980s developed tactical doctrine for the use of the Tomahawk cruise missile, 504-509
In 1982-83 the Third Fleet conducted exercises in the Northern Pacific, near the Soviet Union, 509-512, 515-516, 519-520, 541-544
In the early 1980s conducted RimPac exercises near Hawaii in conjunction with allied forces, 513-515
Relationship with the U.S. Seventh Fleet in the early 1980s, 516-518
Social aspects of the fleet commander's role in the early 1980s, 520-522
Oversaw the arrival of the Trident submarine *Ohio* (SSBN-726) as Seattle in August 1982, 523-524
Hit by typhoon in November 1982, 528-531

Graded battle group ASW exercises at the Pacific Missile Range at Barking Sands, Hawaii, in the early 1980s, 547-548

Tissot, Commander Ernest Eugene Jr., USN
Commanded Carrier Air Wing 14 (CVW-14) in 1967-68, 292-293

Tomahawk Missile
In the early 1980s the Third Fleet developed tactical doctrine for the use of the Tomahawk cruise missile, 504-509
First combat use was in Desert Storm in 1991, 506

Townsend, Commander Marland W. Jr., USN
In 1966-67 commanded Fighter Squadron 143 (VF-143), 274-278, 294

Training
Naval Academy summer cruises, 1948-50, 75-84
Flight Training in Florida and Texas, 1951-53, 87-95
Survival, Evasion, Resistance, and Escape (SERE) training at Warner Springs, California, in 1966, 309-310

***Triton*, USS (SSRN-586)**
Rear Admiral Thomas Moorer, Commander Carrier Division Six, visited in 1960 165

Trower, Captain Ross H., CHC, USN
As Service Force chaplain in 1973, talked with returning POWs in 1973, 356-357

Turkey
Istanbul visited in 1959 by the aircraft carrier *Saratoga* (CVA-60), 166-167

Turner, Vice Admiral Frederick C., USN
Served 1976-79 as DCNO (Air Warfare), 409-410

Typhoons
U.S. Third Fleet ships ran into disastrous typhoons in 1944-45, 528-529
A large storm hit Oahu, Hawaii, in November 1982, 527-531

Uniforms-Naval
Full-dress uniform for Naval Academy midshipmen, circa 1950, 48-51
Released Vietnam War prisoners received new uniforms in 1973, 360
In 1980, for the 135th anniversary of the Naval Academy, some midshipmen wore 1850s-type uniforms, 500-501
Secretary of the Navy John Lehman's inputs on uniforms during his tenure in the 1980s, 593-595

VF-14
See: Fighter Squadron 14 (VF-14)

VF-74
    See: Fighter Squadron 74 (VF-74)

VF-101
    See: Fighter Squadron 101 (VF-101)

VF-121
    See: Fighter Squadron 121 (VF-121)

VF-143
    See: Fighter Squadron 143 (VF-143)

VF-193
    See: Fighter Squadron 193 (VF-193)

VP-1
    See: Patrol Squadron One (VP-1)

Vertical/Short Takeoff and Landing Aircraft (V/STOL)
    Concept explored for naval aviation in the 1970s, but it did not come to fruition, 411

Vietnam War
    In 1965 the U.S. Strike Command identified units capable of early deployment to Vietnam, 255, 263-265
    General Paul Adams's concerns in 1964-65 that the war would be long and difficult, 255-256, 263-265
    Lawrence's brother Thomas served in the Army's 82nd Airborne Division, 21
    Prisoners of war, 1964-73, 263, 309-334
    Bombing attacks on North Vietnam in 1966 by Fighter Squadron 143 (VF-143) based on the aircraft carrier *Ranger* (CVA-61), 270-287
    Bombing attacks on North Vietnam in 1967 by Fighter Squadron 143 (VF-143) based on the aircraft carrier *Constellation* (CVA-64), 294-307
    Antiwar protesters Jane Fonda and Ramsey Clark visited North Vietnam, 316-317
    Son Tay raid in 1970 in an attempt to rescue U.S. prisoners of war, 343-344
    Release of prisoners from North Vietnam in 1973 and their return to the United States, 353-360

Warner, John W.
    As Secretary of the Navy in 1973, censured some Vietnam prisoners of war for collaboration with the enemy, 340-341

Watkins, Admiral James D., USN (USNA, 1949)
    As Chief of Naval Personnel in 1978, wanted a nuclear-trained flag officer as superintendent of the Naval Academy, 419-420
    Vice Chief of Naval Operations, 279-281, 453, 493

As CNO, 1982-86, relationship with Secretary of the Navy John Lehman, 553-554, 557-560, 571, 593

Weather
U.S. Third Fleet ships ran into disastrous typhoons in 1944-45, 528-529
Damaging mistral storms in the Mediterranean circa 1960, 203-204
The Naval Academy sailing yacht *Alliance* was caught in a storm in the British Isles in 1979, 436-437
A typhoon hit Oahu, Hawaii, in November 1982, 527-531

Weaver, Rear Admiral John C., USN (USNA, 1955)
F/A-18 program manager who displeased Secretary of the Navy John Lehman in the 1980s, 554-555

Webb, James H. Jr. (USNA, 1968)
Views on the value of the Naval Academy, 31
Writings about the Naval Academy, 1979-81, 442-446

Weisner, Commander Maurice F., USN (USNA, 1941)
In the mid-1950s commanded Fighter Squadron 193 (VF-193), which was training in night operations and nuclear weapons delivery, 104-105, 111-114, 121
Service in the Bureau of Naval Personnel in the early 1960s, 236

Welsh, George T. (USNA, 1956)
Successful Naval Academy head football coach, 1973-81, 71-72, 433-435, 486-487

Wheeler, General Earle G., USA (USMA, 1932)
Served as Army Chief of Staff and Chairman of the Joint Chiefs of Staff in the 1960s, 245, 255-256, 262, 265

White, Admiral Steven A., USN
In the mid-1980s served as Chief of Naval Material, 555-556, 576-579

Wilber, Commander Walter Eugene, USN
Vietnam prisoner of war, 1967-73, censured for collaboration, 323, 340-341

Williams, Rear Admiral MacPherson B., USN (Ret.) (USNA, 1930)
Shot down in the Philippines in World War II, 192, 357
Father of Lawrence's first wife Anne, 53-54, 85, 87-88, 90, 192, 194-195, 357, 367-368, 374, 417

Wolkensdorfer, Rear Admiral Daniel J., USN
As Commander Patrol Wings Pacific Fleet, investigated a P-3 crash in 1983, 534-535

Wooldridge, Rear Admiral Edmund T. Jr., USN (USNA, 1950)
  In the early 1960s was involved in the fleet introduction of the F4H/F-4 Phantom II, 190, 217

Woolsey, R. James, Jr.
  As Under Secretary of the Navy, interest in the Naval Academy curriculum in the late 1970s, 467, 493-494

Women
  As Naval Academy midshipmen in the late 1970s-early 1980s, 11-12, 415-417, 420-422, 427-433, 437-444, 459, 488-489
  Sexual assault on a female midshipman in the late 1970s-early 1980s, 427-429
  Midshipman Gwen Dreyer was chained to a urinal at the Naval Academy in 1989, 426, 606-609
  Balance of career and family obligations, circa 1990, 26-27
  Concern about shipboard radiation effects on pregnant crew members, 584-585
  Increasing job opportunities for women in the Navy in the 1980s, 591
  Ending of sexual harassment training at the Naval Academy, 609-610

Wright, Anne St. Clair
  Annapolis preservationist who acquiesced in the Naval Academy's razing of Isherwood Hall in the early 1980s, 481

Yale University, New Haven, Connecticut
  Attempted to recruit Lawrence in the late 1940s, 16

Yates, Captain Earl P., USN
  In the mid-1960s headed a Seventh Fleet detachment in Saigon that approved news releases on fleet activities in the Vietnam War, 277

Yokosuka, Japan
  The aircraft carrier *Oriskany* (CVA-34) used the pinwheel maneuver in the port in the mid-1950s, 118-119

Zech, Vice Admiral Lando W., Jr., USN (USNA, 1945)
  As Chief of Naval Personnel, 1980-83, 554

Zimolzak, Colonel Frank, USMC
  Head of the English and history department at the Naval Academy in the late 1970s, 442-443

Zumwalt, Admiral Elmo R., Jr., USN (USNA, 1943)
  As Chief of Naval Operations in the early 1970s, facilitated returned prisoners of war getting back on career tracks, 377, 386
  Impact his Z-gram policy directives had on the Navy of the 1970s, 388, 392-393
  Touted high-low mix on hardware acquisition in the 1970s, 401-402

www.ingramcontent.com/pod-product-compliance
Lightning Source LLC
Chambersburg PA
CBHW082147070526
44585CB00020B/2122